Natural Language Processing

With a machine learning approach and less focus on linguistic details, this gentle introduction to natural language processing develops fundamental mathematical and deep learning models for NLP under a unified framework. NLP problems are systematically organised by their machine learning nature, including classification, sequence labelling, and sequence-to-sequence problems. Topics covered include statistical machine learning and deep learning models, text classification and structured prediction models, generative and discriminative models, supervised and unsupervised learning with latent variables, neural networks, and transition-based methods. Rich connections are drawn between concepts throughout the book, equipping students with the tools needed to establish a deep understanding of NLP solutions, adapt existing models, and confidently develop innovative models of their own. Featuring a host of examples, intuition, and end of chapter exercises, plus annotated sample code available as an online resource, this textbook is an invaluable tool for the upper undergraduate and graduate student.

Yue Zhang is an associate professor at Westlake University. Before joining Westlake, he worked as a research associate at the University of Cambridge and then a faculty member at Singapore University of Technology and Design. His research interests lie in fundamental algorithms for NLP, syntax, semantics, information extraction, text generation, and machine translation. He serves as an action editor for TACL, and as area chairs of ACL, EMNLP, COLING, and NAACL. He gave several tutorials at ACL, EMNLP and NAACL, and won a best paper award at COLING in 2018.

Zhiyang Teng is currently a postdoctoral research fellow in the natural language processing group of Westlake University, China. He obtained his Ph.D. from Singapore University of Technology and Design (SUTD) in 2018, and his Master's from the University of Chinese Academy of Science in 2014. He published conference papers for ACL/TACL, EMNLP, COLING, NAACL, and TKDE. His research interests include syntactic parsing, sentiment analysis, deep learning and variational inference.

Natural Language Processing
A Machine Learning Perspective

YUE ZHANG

Westlake University

ZHIYANG TENG

Westlake University

CAMBRIDGE
UNIVERSITY PRESS

University Printing House, Cambridge CB2 8BS, United Kingdom

One Liberty Plaza, 20th Floor, New York, NY 10006, USA

477 Williamstown Road, Port Melbourne, VIC 3207, Australia

314–321, 3rd Floor, Plot 3, Splendor Forum, Jasola District Centre,
New Delhi – 110025, India

79 Anson Road, #06–04/06, Singapore 079906

Cambridge University Press is part of the University of Cambridge.

It furthers the University's mission by disseminating knowledge in the pursuit of
education, learning, and research at the highest international levels of excellence.

www.cambridge.org
Information on this title: www.cambridge.org/9781108420211
DOI: 10.1017/9781108332873

© Yue Zhang and Zhiyang Teng 2021

First published 2021

Printed in the United Kingdom by TJ Books Limited, Padstow Cornwall

A catalogue record for this publication is available from the British Library.

ISBN 978-1-108-42021-1 Hardback

Additional resources for this publication at www.cambridge.org/zhangteng

Contents

Preface

In recent years, artificial intelligence has received increasing attention. Deep learning technology has enabled intelligent systems to perform tasks that are far more complex compared to what machines could do a decade ago. Investigating automatic understanding and generation of natural language texts, natural language processing has been a central topic of artificial intelligence since its dawn, and human language dialogue capabilities has been recognised as a major metric for evaluating artificial intelligence. Advances in the field allow intelligent systems to perform automatic speech to speech translation, question answering, essay scoring, automatic auditing and algorithm trading by news reading.

The field of natural language processing has evolved since the early days of computer science, going through three main stages, where rule-based methods, statistical methods and deep learning methods dominate the literature, respectively. Researchers and engineers have seen a shift from linguistic feature engineering to parameter tuning in their daily work as the state-of-the-art approaches shift from statistical learning to deep learning. Today, deep learning not only allows natural language processing systems to perform much better on existing tasks such as syntactic parsing and automatic machine translation, but also enables new tasks to be investigated.

This textbook aims to introduce the field of natural language processing from a machine learning perspective, laying out the mathematical and algorithmic foundations for the major technologies of this field. The **organisation** of chapters follows the order of increasing complexity, which is also largely consistent with the development history of NLP technologies. In particular, an overview of major NLP tasks is introduced in the first chapter, and the remaining chapters evolve around machine learning methods. We take a gentle approach in introducing mathematical concepts, based on a unified notation system. The underlying connections between concepts are drawn across chapters wherever useful.

Targeted readers include senior-year undergraduate students and graduate students majoring in computer science, artificial intelligence or a related interdisciplinary subject. The textbook can also serve as a theoretical reference for NLP engineers. **Prerequisites** include linear algebra, calculus, basic probability theory and algorithms. After reading this book, a student would be expected to have a comprehensive understanding of the NLP field in the mathematical aspect, and be comfortable in reading any top conference paper or journal article in the research literature. An engineer would be expected to know the underlying technologies behind NLP softwares and tools, be capable of adapting existing models to best fit a use scenario, and make necessary innovations by following new advances in the research field.

Uniqueness

One unique feature of this textbook, as compared to the other major NLP textbooks, is that the organisation is driven by fundamental approaches and algorithms such as conditional random fields and neural topic models, rather than specific NLP tasks such as sentiment classification, stance detection, part-of-speech tagging and semantic role labelling. There are two main reasons for the choice. First, the use of machine learning techniques, in particular deep learning methods, makes it common for the same fundamental algorithm to give the state-of-the-art results for a wide range of NLP problems, which can be much different in their linguistic nature. For example, both sentiment classification and news categorisation can be solved as classification problems, while both part-of-speech tagging and semantic role labelling can be solved as sequence labelling tasks. Thus we introduce the abstract problems of text classification and sequence labelling as the main topics, discussing their relevance to the specific NLP tasks where applicable.

Second, development of the research field has been closely related to the development of machine learning technologies, which gives us a convenient basis for developing the chapters. For example, statistical methods began to dominate the literature in the late 1980s, when features began to replace linguistic rules in solving NLP problems. Statistical models were first built for solving text classification tasks, and then applied to sequence labelling and more complex structured prediction tasks. In this process, the same machine learning principle was used in increasingly more NLP problems in the literature, with specific features being designed for different tasks. The same observations were made during the rise of deep learning in the 2010s, where the same representation learning method was investigated for an increasingly large number of NLP problems, reaching new state of the art for each task. For example, the recent advances in contextualised word representation pre-trained over large raw texts have led to new leader-board records for syntactic, semantic, text mining and a range of other NLP tasks.

Strong connections exist between more recent deep learning techniques and seminal statistical learning methods thanks to the fact that new technologies evolve upon the success of prior research. Concepts such as features, typical learning objectives, optimisation techniques and evaluation metrics have been inherited over time, and terminologies have been largely consistent in the literature over the past decades. This makes it convenient for the narrative order of the book to largely follow the chronological order of the research literature.

Content Coverage. We try to cover all that is essential for knowing the field but leave out what is not. This book covers the definition of the vast majority of NLP tasks, but without details such as specific corpus annotation guidelines. NLP tasks are introduced with respect to their nature from the machine learning perspective. We cover all major approaches for modelling NLP, ranging from statistical models to deep learning models, from generative models to discriminative models, from classification models to structured prediction models, from exact inference algorithms to approximate inference algorithms and from supervised models to unsupervised models. For each topic, we aim to choose the most salient concepts and algorithms, aiming to make the reading and teaching process smooth and comfortable, but leaving out details that are peculiar to certain tasks or models, which can be easily picked up by reading relevant literature after learning the content of the book.

Outline. There are 18 chapters in the book, which are organised into three parts.

- Part I (Basics; Chapters 1–6) discusses the most fundamental concepts of NLP modelling, introducing the basic ideas of representing natural language text, foundational models and training algorithms.
- Part II (Structures; Chapters 7–12) discusses how the basic techniques of Part 1 can be applied to structures, including sequence structures and tree structures, which are common in NLP.
- Part III (Deep Learning; Chapters 13–18) focuses on topics that are specific to deep learning. It starts by a transition from single-layer perceptron to multi-layer perceptron, and then discusses neural classification and structured prediction, before introducing more advanced neural models.

Each part above contains six chapters. In particular,

- Chapter 1 gives an overview of the NLP field and lays out the structure of this book;
- Chapter 2 introduces the basic idea of modelling, and discusses a basic form of generative probabilistic models for NLP;
- Chapter 3 introduces the concept of feature vectors, and discusses two discriminative linear text classifiers;
- Chapter 4 introduces log-linear models for text classification, and unifies various linear classification models into a generalised perceptron;
- Chapter 5 introduces the use of information theory in NLP;
- Chapter 6 discusses basic techniques for modelling hidden variables;
- Chapter 7 introduces generative probabilistic models for sequence labelling;
- Chapter 8 discusses discriminative models for sequence labelling;
- Chapter 9 discusses discriminative models for sequence segmentation;
- Chapter 10 discusses generative and discriminative models for predicting tree structures;
- Chapter 11 introduces a transition-based framework for structured prediction;
- Chapter 12 discusses Bayesian methods for NLP;
- Chapter 13 introduces neural network models, word embeddings and a basic convolutional network text classifier;
- Chapter 14 introduces representation learning, discussing recurrent network, self-attention network and the representation of trees and graphs;
- Chapter 15 discusses neural models for graph-based and transition-based structured prediction;
- Chapter 16 discusses deep end-to-end learning for sequence-to-sequence and text-matching tasks;
- Chapter 17 discusses the pre-training of neural representations;
- Chapter 18 discusses neural networks with hidden variables.

Readers are advised to read the chapters in their given order, since the content of a chapter can depend heavily on its preceding chapters. The material can be taught as a course in 36 to 72 hours, with 2 to 4 teaching hours for each chapter.

Supplementary materials. To accompany the book, we make available a set of supplementary materials at our Cambridge University Press website, which include a set of course slides and a manual for instructors.

Acknowledgements

We are grateful for the tremendous help from our colleagues. In particular, Guangsheng Bao, Stephen Clark, Chenhua Chen, Trevor Cohn, Leyang Cui, Hang Li, Zhenghua Li, Qingkai Min, Joakim Nivre, Barbara Plank, Bing Qin, Kai Song, Linfeng Song, Fangfang Su, Kewei Tu, Chaojun Wang, Houfeng Wang, Xiangpeng Wei, Meishan Zhang, Hao Zhou, Xiaoyan Zhu and Chengqing Zong gave valuable inputs and suggestions. Xuefeng Bai, Guangsheng Bao, Chenhua Chen, Yulong Chen, Leyang Cui, Wenyu Du, Qiankun Fu, Yuze Gao, Dandan Huang, Chen Jia, Jinhao Jiang, Shuailong Liang, Xiaobo Liang, Hanmeng Liu, Jian Liu, Qingkai Min, Zebin Ou, Xiuming Qiao, Libo Qin, Yuefeng Shi, Fangfang Su, Cunxiang Wang, Qiang Wang, Yile Wang, Sen Yang, Ye Yuan, Yu Yuan, Junchi Zhang and Yuan Zhang assisted with type-setting of the LaTeXsource, equations, figures, tables and slides. Without all these contributions it would have been impossible for us to finish the manuscript in time.

Notation

We use the following terminology and notation:

x: a variable x.

w, c, x denote a word from a vocabulary, a class label from a label set, or a specific value of a variable x, respectively.

$X_{1:n} = [x_1, x_2, \ldots, x_n]$: an array of n variables.

$X_{1:n} = x_1 x_2 \ldots x_n$: a sequence of words or tags. In particular, $W_{1:n} = w_1 w_2 \ldots w_n$ denotes a sentence of n words and $T_{1:n} = t_1 t_2 \ldots t_n$ denotes a sequence of n tags.

$X_{i:j} = x_i, x_{i+1}, \ldots, x_j (i \leq j)$ a subsequence from the ith element to the jth element.

$X = \{x_i\}|_{i=1}^{N}$ or $X = \{x_1, x_2, \ldots, x_N\}$: a set of N elements.

x_i: the ith element in an array. In particular, w_i indicates the ith word in a sentence.

x_i: a certain element labelled with i in a set. In particular, w_i indicates the ith word in the vocabulary.

$x \sim P(x)$: draw a sample from a probability distribution P.

$\vec{x} = \langle x_1, x_2, \ldots x_{|\vec{x}|} \rangle$ (Chapters 1–13) and $\mathbf{x}$ (Chapters 13–18): a vector x.

$\mathbf{X}$: a matrix X.

$P(x)$: the probability of a random variable x.

$\exp(x)$: the exponent of a variable x.

$\log(x)$: the logarithm of a variable x.

$\mathbb{E}_{x \sim P(x)} f(x)$: the mathematical expectation of a function $f(x)$ given a random variable distributed by $P(x)$.

$\sigma(x)$: the sigmoid activation ($\frac{1}{1+e^{-x}}$) of a variable x.

$\mathbf{x}[i]$: the ith element in vector $\mathbf{x}$.

$\mathbf{x}[\ell_i]$: the element in vector $\mathbf{x}$ corresponding to the label ℓ_i.

$\mathbf{X} = [\mathbf{x}_1; \mathbf{x}_2; \ldots; \mathbf{x}_n]$: juxtaposing $\mathbf{x}_1, \mathbf{x}_2, \ldots, \mathbf{x}_n$ ($\mathbf{x}_i \in \mathbb{R}^{m \times 1}, i \in [1, \ldots, n]$) resulting in $\mathbf{X} \in \mathbb{R}^{m \times n}$.

$\mathbf{y} = \mathbf{x}_1 \oplus \mathbf{x}_2 \oplus \ldots \oplus \mathbf{x}_n$: the concatenation of column vectors $\mathbf{x}_1, \mathbf{x}_2, \ldots, \mathbf{x}_n$. $\mathbf{x}_i \in \mathbb{R}^{m \times 1}$ ($i \in [1, \ldots, n]$) resulting in a vector $\mathbf{y} \in \mathbb{R}^{mn}$.

$\mathbf{y} = \mathbf{x}_1 \otimes \mathbf{x}_2$: the element-wise product of two vectors.

$\mathbf{x} = \text{ONEHOT}(k)$: $\mathbf{x}$ is the one-hot vector with the kth element being one and the other elements being zeros.

$\mathbf{W}[i; j]$ denotes the element of the ith row and jth column of $\mathbf{W}$.

$\mathbf{W}[i;]$ and $\mathbf{W}[; j]$ denote the ith row of $\mathbf{W}$ and jth column of $\mathbf{W}$, respectively.

$\mathbf{X}^\mathsf{T}$: the transpose of matrix $\mathbf{X}$.

$\frac{\partial x}{\partial y}$: the partial derivative of x with respect to y.

$\delta(x, y)$: the Kronecker delta function; equals 1 when $x = y$ and 0 otherwise.

$KL(P, Q)$: the KL-divergence between two probability distributions P and Q.

Part I

Basics

1   Introduction

Languages are a crucial part of human intelligence and important for human communication. Investigating automatic understanding and generation of human languages, **natural language processing** (NLP) has been a central subfield of artificial intelligence research. Since the 1950s, NLP technology has received continued research attention, and great advances have been achieved. Today, NLP technology is becoming an indispensable part of our business and daily lives. For example, search engines automatically process trillions of documents over the Internet, gaining knowledge from them and answering user queries based on understanding. Online retailers process millions of product descriptions and user comments, for recommending the most suitable product given a user search. Automatic dialogue systems and translation systems are being increasingly widely used to facilitate communication. In business, text analytics engines have been replacing manual labour in analysing huge amounts of documents for better decision making. Such progress has been largely driven by advances in machine learning techniques, which contribute to fundamental algorithms and foundational models of NLP. This book introduces these techniques, starting from the most elementary models based on counting relative frequencies, moving incrementally towards more advanced techniques such as discriminative structural models, probabilistic graph models and deep neural networks. In this chapter, we introduce NLP and NLP tasks, explaining why it is beneficial to learn NLP from a machine learning perspective.

1.1   What is NLP?

In the broadest sense, NLP refers to the study of automatically processing or synthesising human languages. This can range from simple string pattern matching algorithms using regular expressions to sophisticated intelligent systems using artificial neural networks to translate between different languages. NLP is an inter-disciplinary research area. Some work falls between linguistics and computer science, investigating computational methods to model languages and to address linguistic questions. Some work originates from an artificial intelligence perspective, aiming to equip intelligent systems with human language capabilities. Some work is more data-science oriented, considering the automatic processing of large-scale text data in order to extract useful structured knowledge. Some work is also related to psychology, cognitive science and neural science. We will see the spectrum of tasks investigated in NLP research in Section 1.2 and more details of representative tasks in relevant chapters.

    NLP research started in the 1950s, as a central part of artificial intelligence. Seminal methods relied heavily on linguistic rules, with machine translation being one of the tasks that received the most attention. Within a decade or so, however, people began to realise that it is challenging to develop a set of rules that can handle NLP in general. The main reason is the prevalence of **ambiguity** in languages. For example, words can have different meanings in different contexts. The sentence *"They can fish here"* can mean both that they are allowed to catch fish in this place and that they put fish into containers in this place. In the sentence *"This camera is a beast"*, the word *"beast"* means that the performance of the electronic device is outstanding. As a second example, the use of language can be highly flexible. It can be easy for a person to understand that *"She pillowed his head"* probably means that she threw a pillow at his head, although the word *"pillow"* is a noun by definition. In addition, misspelled words such as *"niiiiiiice!"* can be perfectly understandable in Tweets. Such flexibility makes it difficult for rules to cover open cases. Awareness of such challenges led to a significant cut of US funding of machine translation research in the late 1960s. At that time there was a well-quoted example, where the sentence *"The spirit is strong, but the flesh is weak"* is incorrectly translated into *"The vodka is delicious, but the meat tastes bad."*

From the late 1980s, statistical methods and machine learning gradually replaced rule-based methods in both the research literature and industry. The idea is for algorithms to learn the statistical distributions of linguistic patterns from data, and to use these to make decisions. For example, if a verb is followed by a noun more frequently than a verb in data, then we put higher probability on "noun" when seeing an unknown or ambiguous word after a verb. This method turned out to be far more effective for dealing with prevalent ambiguities in languages as compared with coining hard-coded rules. As a result, there was a resurgence of NLP research. In statistical NLP research, the job of linguists changes from designing rules to annotating datasets. They play increasingly less important roles as the field moves on. In NLP algorithms, the use of linguistic rules is transformed into the use of *features*, or linguistic patterns for which statistics are collected and used by machine learning models. We will see the foundations of machine learning, features and statistics for NLP in relevant chapters.

Since the late 2000s, deep learning has risen to surpass traditional statistical methods as the dominant approach. The idea is to train artificial neural networks of multiple stacked layers, which have the power of learning arbitrarily complex functions. Deep learning has empirically shown stronger results compared to traditional statistical methods for a wide range of NLP tasks. Such models can be almost free from linguistic features, relying fully on neural networks for learning underlying associations between inputs and outputs. This form of machine learning is also referred to as end-to-end learning. The research trend has further weakened the influence of linguistics in NLP research, but nurtured more investigation of comprehensive tasks and user applications. Despite the strong power of neural representations, lack of linguistic patterns can make the models less interpretable or visualisable.

Traditional discrete statistical methods and current deep learning approaches are deeply connected, with the same underlying machine learning principles and optimisation techniques. Yet each method offers unique advantages and limitations from both scientific and engineering perspectives. We will see more details in Section 1.3 and relevant chapters of this book. In particular, Parts I and II of the book lay the common underlying foundations for both methods, while introducing discrete features, and Part III concentrates on deep learning.

1.2 NLP Tasks

NLP is a rather broad area. There have been a wide range of tasks studied in NLP, which can be categorised according to different criteria. For example, there are *fundamental NLP tasks* that draw interest from the linguistic perspective, *information extraction tasks* that are more driven by the need in text mining applications, and *applications* such as document summarisation systems, open question answering systems and machine translation systems. We give an overview of NLP tasks in this section, which provides a background for discussing machine learning algorithms in the remaining chapters. Note that our introduction of linguistic and task-specific concepts is brief, as this is not the main goal of the book. Interested readers can refer to dedicated materials listed in the chapter notes at the end of the chapter for further reading.

1.2.1 Fundamental NLP Tasks

Fundamental NLP tasks extract linguistic information such as syntax and semantics from words, sentences and documents. While they can provide useful information for user-end applications such as machine translation and automatic dialogue systems, they are interesting on their own from a linguistic perspective. Consequently, these tasks are also referred to as **computational linguistics** tasks.

On the word level, **morphology** is a branch of linguistics that investigates the structure and formation of words. In NLP, the task of **morphological analysis** studies automatic prediction of morphological features of input words, such as morphemes. Here a *morpheme* is a minimum meaningful morphological unit, such as "*do*", "*ing*" and "*s*" (plural form) in English.

Table 1.1 Morphological analysis, tokenisation, word segmentation and part-of-speech tagging. "*wktAbnA*" : walking; "*Wochenarbeitszeit*" : weekly working hours; "其中" : among with; "国外" : forcign; "企业" : company; "中国" : China; "外企" : foreign company; "业务" : business; "はきもの" : shoes; "を" : case marker "脱ぐ" : take off; "きもの" : Kimono; "着る" : wear.

Task	Input	Output
Morphological Analysis	(English) *walking*	*walk + ing*
	(Arabic) *wktAbnA*	*w + ktAb + nA*
	(German) *Wochenarbeitszeit*	*Wochen + arbeits + zeit*
Tokenisation	*Mr. Smith visited*	*Mr. Smith visited*
	Wendy's new house.	*Wendy 's new house .*
Word segmentation	其中国外企业	其中 国外 企业
	中国外企业务	中国 外企 业务
	はきものを脱ぐ	はきものを 脱ぐ
	きものを着る	きものを 着る
POS Tagging	I can open this can	PRP MD VB DT NN

For many languages, words can be segmented directly into morphemes. Table 1.1 shows some morphological segmentation cases in English, Arabic and German. In the Arabic example, "*wktAbnA*", which means "*and our book*", contains the morphemes "*w*", "*ktAb*" and "*nA*", which mean "*and*", "*book*" and "*our*", respectively. In the German example, the word "*Wochenarbeit-szeit*" (working week) contains morphemes "*wochen*" (week), "*arbeit*" (work) and "*zeit*" (time). In some languages, morphemes that compose with each other can span over multiple words. In morpohology, a **lemma** is the canonical form or dictionary form of a word. For example, the lemma of "*walking*" is "*walk*". The NLP task of **lemmatisation** is to find the lemma of each word in a sentence.

For languages such as Chinese, Japanese and Thai, sentences are written as continuous sequences of characters without explicit space delimitations between words. As a result, **word segmentation** has become a necessary upstream task for many NLP problems. As shown in Table 1.1, given the sentence "其中国外企业 (among which foreign companies)" and "中国外企业务 (foreign business in China)", a word segmentor can yield the segmented word sequences "其中 (among which)", "国外 (foreign)", "企业 (companies)" and "中国 (China)", "外企 (foreign companies)", "业务 (business)", respectively.

For alphabetical languages, word segmentation can be unnecessary. However, ambiguity exists between words and punctuation. Intuitively, punctuation should be treated as specific tokens and separated from words. On the other hand, some punctuation, such as the abbreviation marker in "*Mr.*" and "*Ms.*", the possessive marker in "*'s*" and "*'*" after plural nouns ending with "*s*", and decimal point markers such as "*3.1*" should be regarded as integral parts of words. As a result, a necessary NLP task is **tokenisation**, which is to recognise standardised tokens in a given sentence written with flexible spacing. The output of this task is typically a sequence of space-separated tokens. For example, "*Mr. Smith visited Wendy's new house.*" can be tokenised into "*Mr. Smith visited Wendy 's new house .*", as shown in Table 1.1.

• **Syntactic Tasks** investigate the composition structures of languages, ranging from the word level to the sentence level.

Part-of-speech (POS) tagging has been taken as a common upstream task in NLP. Here a *part-of-speech* refers to a basic role that words play in a sentence, such as *the noun*, *the verb* and *the preposition*. There can be more than 30 POS categories for a language, and such lexical-syntactic roles can also be referred to as **lexical categories**. Table 1.2 shows a list of common POS for English.[1] The task of POS-tagging is to assign a POS-tag to each word in a given sentence, which represents its disambiguated POS in the given context. For example, given the sentence "*I can open this can*", a POS-tagger can give the output "*I/PRP can/MD open/VB this/DT can/NN*", as shown in Table 1.1, where the two occurrences of "*can*" take different POS in different contexts.

Beyond lexical categories, the syntactic structure of sentences can be analysed according to various grammar formalisms, and the tasks are known as **syntactic parsing**. A large number of grammar formalisms have been investigated for parsing, including *constituent grammars*,

---

[1] For more information about these labels, refer to the Penn Treebank at http://www.ling.upenn.edu/

Table 1.2 Common POS-tags for English.

Tag	Description	Tag	Description
CC	Coordinating conjunction	CD	Cardinal number
DT	Determiner	EX	Existential *there*
FW	Foreign word	IN	Preposition or subordinating conjunction
JJ	Adjective	JJR	Adjective, comparative
JJS	Adjective, superlative	LS	List item marker
MD	Modal	NN	Noun, singular or mass
NNS	Noun, plural	NNP	Proper noun, singular
NNPS	Proper noun, plural	PDT	Predeterminer
POS	Possessive ending	PRP	Personal pronoun
PRP$	Possessive pronoun	RB	Adverb
RBR	Adverb, comparative	RBS	Adverb, superlative
RP	Particle	SYM	Symbol
TO	*to*	UH	Interjection
VB	Verb, base form	VBD	Verb, past tense
VBG	Verb, gerund or present participle	VBN	Verb, past participle
VBP	Verb, non-3rd person singular present	VBZ	Verb, 3rd person singualr present
WDT	Wh-determiner	WP	Wh-pronoun
WP$	Possessive wh-pronoun	WRB	Wh-adverb

dependency grammars, *combinatory categorial grammars* (*CCG*), *tree adjoining grammars* (*TAG*), *lexical functional grammars* (*LFG*), *head-driven phrase structure grammars* (*HPSG*), *link grammars* and so on. Here we use the first three as examples to illustrate parsing problems.

As shown in Figure 1.1(a), **constituent parsers** analyse sentences in hierarchical phrase structures, assigning phrase labels to each constituent, such as "noun phrase" (*NP*), "verb phrase" (*VP*) and "prepositional phrase" (*PP*). For example, "*a book*" in the figure is a noun phrase and "*bought a book for Mary*" is a verb phrase. As a result, constituent grammars are also referred to as **phrase-structure grammars**. A list of common phrase labels are shown in Table 1.3.[1] In contrast, **dependency parsers** analyse a sentence in word-pair relations, which are represented as directed arcs between *head words* and *dependent words*. As shown in Figure 1.1 (b), dependency arcs are labelled and directed, pointing from head words to dependent words, with the arc label indicating the type of dependency relation. For example, an "nsubj" label indicates that the dependent is a nominal subject of the head, and an "obj" label indicates that the dependent is an object of the head. In this example, "*book*" is the object of "*bought*". Table 1.4 shows a list of common dependency arc labels.[2] Given a sentence, each word depends on exactly one head

---

[2] For more information about these labels, refer to the Universal Dependencies documentation http://universaldependencies.org/.

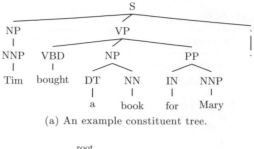

(a) An example constituent tree.

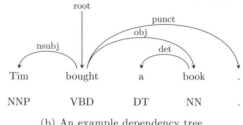

(b) An example dependency tree.

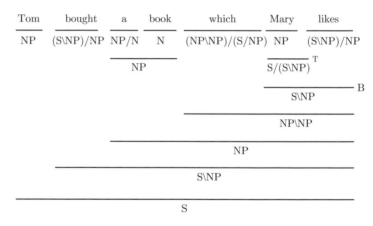

(c) An example CCG derivation.

Figure 1.1 Syntactic structures.

word, except for a *root word* of the sentence. As a result, dependency syntax structures form tree structures.

Combinatory Categorial Grammar (CCG) is a highly *lexicalised grammar*, with much syntactic information being represented by lexical categories on words. *CCG lexical categories* are more complex compared to POS. There are a few basic lexical categories, such as "the noun" (*N*), "the noun phrase" (*NP*) and "the preposition" (*P*). Complex lexical categories are composed by recursive combinations of basic categories using forward "/" and backward "\" slashes, which indicate compositional characteristics of the lexical categories. For example, intransitive verbs take the category *S\NP*, which indicates that they combine with a noun phrase (subject) on the left

Table 1.3 Common constituent phrase labels.

Phrase label	Description	Phrase label	Description
ADJP	Adjective phrase	ADVP	Adverb phrase
CONJP	Conjunction phrase	FRAG	Fragment
INTJ	Interjection	LST	List marker
VP	Verbal phrase	NP	Noun phrase
PP	Prepositional phrase	PRN	Parenthetical
PRT	Particle	QP	Quantifier phrase
WHPP	Wh-prepositional phrase	WHADJP	Wh-adjective phrase
WHAVP	Wh-adverb phrase	WHNP	Wh-noun phrase
NAC	Not a constituent	X	Unknown, uncertain

Table 1.4 Common dependency arc labels.

Arc label	Description	Arc label	Description
obj	Object	iobj	Indirect object
nsubj	Nominal subject	csubj	Clausal subject
xcomp	Open clausal complement	ccomp	Clausal complement
conj	Conjunct	cc	Coordinating conjunction
amod	Adjectival modifier	advmod	Adverbial modifier
det	Determiner	aux	Auxiliary
root	Root	mark	Marker
nmod	Nominal modifier	nummod	Numeric modifier
punct	Punctuation	acl	Clausal modifier of noun

(direction indicated by the backward slash "\"), resulting in a sentence (S) structure. Similarly, transitive verbs and di-transitive verbs take the lexical categories $(S\backslash NP)/NP$ and $((S\backslash NP)/NP)/NP$, respectively, where $/NP$ indicates the composition potential with a noun phrase (object) on the right. As a result, a transitive verb can potentially combine with one noun phrase on the right and one noun phrase on the left, while a di-transitive verb can potentially combine with two noun phrases on the right, and one noun phrase on the left.

Given the lexical category of each word, the structure of a sentence can be analysed by applying a set of *composition rules* recursively, merging smaller input spans into larger ones while combining their lexical categories into phrase-level syntactic categories. For example, when the phrase $\frac{bought}{(S\backslash NP)/NP}$ and $\frac{a\ book}{NP}$ are combined into a larger phrase "*bought a book*", the categories $(S\backslash NP)/NP$ and NP are combined into $S\backslash NP$, resulting in $\frac{bought\ a\ book}{S\backslash NP}$. These binary combination rules take the form $(X/Y)\ Y \Rightarrow X$ and $X\ (X\backslash Y) \Rightarrow Y$, where X and Y are basic lexical categories. In addition to the binary rules, there are also unary type-changing rules, which change the category of a span for facilitating further composition, such as $\frac{Mary}{NP} \Rightarrow \frac{Mary}{S/(S\backslash NP)}$. The final goal is to compose smaller phrases recursively bottom-up, until a sentence (S) category covers the whole

Tim	bought	a	book		Tim	bought	a	book
PRP	VBD	DT	NN		NP	(S\NP)/NP	NP/N	N

(a) POS-tagging   (b) CCG supertagging

Figure 1.2 Comparison between POS-tagging and CCG supertagging.

sentence. An example is shown in Figure 1.1(c), where the syntactic category *NP* (noun phrase) on "*Mary*" was changed to the category $S/(S\backslash NP)$ (which composites with an intransitive verb on the right to make a sentence) by a unary type-changing rule, so that the clause "*Mary likes*" can be correctly recognised.

Lexical categories in lexicalised grammars such as CCG contain rich syntactic information, knowledge of which can make syntactic parsing relatively easier. As a result, a sub-task in CCG parsing is **supertagging**, which is to assign lexical categories to each word in a given input sentence. Supertagging can be taken as a pre-processing step before parsing, or as an upstream task for problems that require syntactic information. It is similar to POS-tagging but significantly more difficult due to ambiguities that result from a large number of lexical categories. Figure 1.2 shows a contrast between POS-tagging and CCG supertagging. Since lexical categories contain rich syntactic information, supertagging is sometimes also referred to as "shallow parsing".

A shallow parsing task for constituent syntax is **syntactic chunking**, which is to identify basic syntactic phrases from a given sentence. For example, given the sentence "*He made a request for cutting down the operation budget.*", a syntactic chunker can yield the output "[*NP He*] [*VP made*] [*NP a request*] [*PP for*] [*VP cutting down*] [*NP the operation budget*]".

• **Semantic Tasks** investigate the meaning of texts.

On the word level, there are a number of NLP tasks related to **lexical semantics**. Formally, the meaning of a word is referred to as its **sense**. Word senses are defined on lemmas, and are associated with parts-of-speech. For example, the verb "*book*" can mean "to make a reservation", while the noun "*book*" can mean "a published written work". A word with a certain POS can also have multiple senses, which makes them **polysemous**. For example, the noun "*trunk*" can mean "the central part of a tree", or "the long nose of an elephant". The NLP task that disambiguates the sense of a word given a certain context, such as a sentence, is called **word sense disambiguation** (WSD). The usage of words can be **metaphoric**, where senses from typically more common domains are used to describe senses in a relatively less common domain. For example, in the sentence "*The machine ate my dollar.*", the "swallow food" sense of "*eat*" is used to describe a machine behaviour. **Metaphor detection** is an NLP task to discover metaphoric uses of words in texts.

A number of lexical semantics tasks study sense relations between multiple words. Example relations include **synonyms**, which are pairs of words with similar senses, **antonyms**, which are pairs of words with opposite relations, **hyponyms**, which are pairs of words in subtype–type relations and **meronyms**, which are pairs of words in part–whole relations. Some examples of word pairs in these relations are shown in Table 1.5, where "*quick – fast*" is a synonym, "*big – small*" is an antonym, "*car – vehicle*" is a hypernym and "*leaf – tree*" is a meronym. NLP tasks investigating these relationships include **word similarities**, which is to measure the degree of similarity between

Table 1.5 Four types of sense relations.

Type	Examples
synonym	quick – fast, bad – poor, big – large
antonym	big – small, positive – negative, easy – difficult
hypernym	car – vehicle, apple – fruit, cat – animal
meronym	leaf – tree, nose – face, roof – house

a pair of words, **hyponym mining**, which is to discover hyponyms from texts, and so on. There have also been tasks for detecting or mining word-pair similarities, or **analogy**. For example, the word–pair relation "*Beijing/China — London/UK*" is an analogy, as are the word pair relations "*King/Queen — Man/Woman*" and "*Piano/Play — Novel/Read*".

On the sentence level, the semantic relation between verbs and their syntactic subjects and objects belongs to **predicate–argument relations**, which denote meaning of events. For example, in "*Tim bought the book for $1*", the verb "*buy*" is a *predicate*, and the subject "*Tim*" is an *argument* to the predicate, which indicates the **semantic role** "agent". The object "*the book*" is another argument to the predicate, which indicates the "patient" role. In this event, "*$1*" also plays a semantic role, which indicates the price of the purchase. Because there are multiple ways to describe an event, the correlation between predicate-argument structures and syntactic structures can be one-to-many. For example, the same predicate–argument structure above can also be expressed by the sentence "*The book was bought by Tim for $1*", where the patient "*book*" is the subject in the sentence and the agent "*Tim*" is a prepositional object. Non-verbs can also serve as the predicate. For example, the same meaning above can also be expressed by "*Purchase of the book cost Tim $1*", where the predicate of the noun "*book*" is "*purchase*".

A typical NLP task on predicate-argument structures is **semantic role labelling** (SRL), which identifies the argument of a given predicate in a sentence. An example is shown in Figure 1.3(a), where the given predicate is "*bought*", the first argument (ARG0) is "*Tim*", the second argument (ARG1) is "*book*" and the third argument (ARG2) is "*$1*". Given a specific predicate, there is a specific set of possible arguments. In this example, ARG0 is the agent, ARG1 is the patient and ARG2 carries predicate-specific information, namely the price for purchases.

A lexical semantics task related to predicate–argument structures is **selectional preference**, which finds out which words are more likely to serve a certain semantic role given a verb predicate. For example, given the predicate "*buy*" the agent is typically a person, or organisation. Given the predicate "*eat*", the patient is typically something edible. The selectional preference task calculates a likelihood of candidates for a given predicate. For example, given the predicate "*eat*", the output of a selectional preference system can be "*meal*: 0.05; *lunch*: 0.03; *tyre*: 7×10^{-9}".

On the more abstract event level, a formal way to denote the meaning of events is to use semantic **frames**, which is a schematic representation of conceptual event structures. Semantic frames consist of **frame elements**, which are semantic roles. For example, the event of purchase belongs to the theme of "TRANSACTION", of which the semantic roles include the "BUYER", the "SELLER", the "MERCHANDISE", the "QUANTITY", the "PRICE",

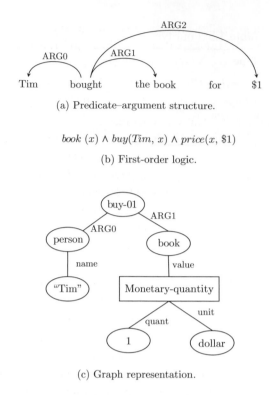

(a) Predicate–argument structure.

$$book\ (x) \land buy(Tim,\ x) \land price(x,\ \$1)$$

(b) First-order logic.

(c) Graph representation.

Figure 1.3 Semantic representations for *"Tim bought this book for $1"*.

the "TIME" and the "LOCATION". In contrast to the predicate–argument structures in Figure 1.3(a), **thematic roles** such as "BUYER" and "SELLER" are more specific compared with the **generalised roles** such as "AGENT" and "PATIENT". The same theme can be represented by different verbs. For example, both *"buy"* and *"sell"* represent the "TRANSACTION" theme, with the "AGENT" role being mapped to the "BUYER" and the "SELLER" role, respectively.

In addition to predicate–argument and frame structures, **logic** is another typical representation of semantics. In particular, *formal logic* refers to systems for evaluating the truth of arguments and reasoning. There are a range of formal logic systems, among which *predicate logic* is commonly used for representing natural language statements. It can be regarded as a symbolic system in which objects are represented by constants or variables, and statements are represented by predicates (which can be seen as functions that return "true"). Logic operators such as $\land$ (and), $\lor$ (or) and $\lnot$ (not) can be applied between predicates. *First-order logic* is a simple form of predicate logic. Figure 1.3(b) shows a *first-order logic* representation of the sentence *"Tim bought the book for $1."* In this representation, the agent *"Tim"* is a *constant*, the patient *"the book"* is a *variable*, and the price *"$1"* is a *constant*. In particular, we use x to denote *"the book"*, and a *predicate* *"book"* to state the fact that x is a book. In this example, the main predicate $buy(Tim, x)$ represents the event, and the predicate $price(x, \$1)$ represents the price of x.

Logic cannot express all the nuances that can be expressed by natural language sentences. The main advantage of using logic is that it facilitates **inference**. For example, given that "*Everyone who bought this book loves it*" and "*Tim bought this book*", we can infer that "*Tim loves this book*" by inferring $book(x) \land love(Tim, x)$ from $\forall y \big(book(x) \land buy(y, x) \Rightarrow love(y, x) \big)$ and $book(x) \land buy(Tim, x)$. In the example above, $\forall$ is a quantifier for the variable y, which makes y a bound variable that represents "for all y", rather than a free variable as x.

Yet another form of semantic representation is **semantic graphs**, which represent concepts as graph nodes and their relations as edges between nodes. Figure 1.3(c) shows a graph representation of the same sentence "*Tim bought this book for $1*", where both the predicate "*buy*" and the arguments "*Tim*" and "*book*" are represented by nodes. Semantic roles such as "ARG0" and "ARG1", together with attributes such as "name" and "price", are represented by edges.

Semantic representations can also be driven by end tasks. For example, for database driven question answering, the semantics of questions can be represented using database query languages such as SQL. Data tables can also be seen as semantic representations.

The task of **semantic parsing** is to derive the semantic representation of a given text. For example, semantic role labelling is a shallow semantic parsing task. The process of deriving the semantic frame given a sentence by identifying from the input sentence both the lexical unit that represents the frame and its frame elements (semantic roles) is called **frame semantic parsing**. In addition, the parsing of free text into other semantic forms, such as logic, semantic graphs and SQL, also belongs to semantic parsing. As a first sub-task, semantic parsers typically perform word sense disambiguation, since mapping word forms to senses is necessary for determining the semantic frame for the predicate for semantic role labelling, the constants and functions for logic representations and the nodes for semantic graphs.

Textual entailment is a directional semantic relation between *two* texts. Intuitively, if we can infer that a piece of text is true provided that another piece of text is true, then the latter text entails the former. The task of **textual entailment recognition** is to decide whether a hypothesis text is entailed by a given premise text. For example, given the premise "*Tim went to the Riverside for dinner*", the hypotheses "*The Riverside is an eating place*" and "*Tim had dinner*" are entailed, but the hypothesis "*Tim had lunch*" is not. A related task, **natural language inference** (NLI) is the task of determining whether a hypothesis is true, false or undetermined given a premise, which reflect entailment, contradiction and neutral relations between the two input texts, respectively. **Paraphrase detection** is another semantic task between two sentences, which is to decide whether they are paraphrases of each other.

• **Discourse Tasks** analyse text structures at the passage level. A **discourse** refers to a piece of text with multiple *sub-topics* and *coherence relations* between them, such as "explanation", "elaboration" and "contrast". A discourse typically contains more than one sentence. A dialogue is also a kind of discourse.

There are many different discourse structure formalisms. *Rhetoric structure theory* (RST) is a representative formalism which we use for discussion. Figure 1.4(b) shows the discourse structure of the text "*The movie is interesting and Tim wants to watch it. But he cannot do it this week*

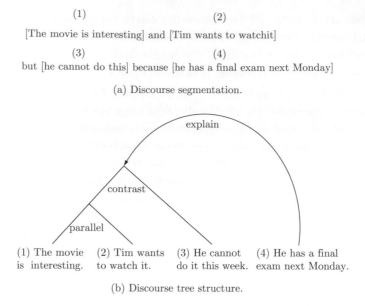

(1)   (2)
[The movie is interesting] and [Tim wants to watchit]
        (3)   (4)
but [he cannot do this] because [he has a final exam next Monday]

(a) Discourse segmentation.

(b) Discourse tree structure.

Figure 1.4 Discourse examples.

because he has a final exam next Monday." There are four sub-topics in this discourse: (1) *"The movie is interesting"*; (2) *"Tim wants to watch it"*; (3) *"He cannot do it this week"*; and (4) *"He has a final exam next Monday"*. The coherence relation between (1) and (2) is *parallel*, while the relation between (3) and (1;2) is *contrast*, for which (4) gives the *explanation*. In the relation between (1;2;3) and (4), (1;2;3) is a relatively central sub-topic, which is referred to as the **nucleus**; (4) is referred to as the **satellite** in this relation. For parallel and contrast relations, there are no central sub-topics, and hence no nucleuses and satellites.

A task of **discourse parsing** is to analyse the above coherence relations between sub-topics in a discourse. For RST, a typical first sub-task for discourse parsing is **discourse segmentation**, which is to segment a discourse into sub-topics. As shown by the example in Figure 1.4(a), discourse segments are not necessarily full sentences. They are typically sub-sentences separated by commas or discourse markers such as *"and"*, *"but"* and *"because"*. After discourse segmentation, discourse relations shown in Figure 1.4(b) can be detected. Discourse markers are useful for correctly identifying coherence relations. However, the majority of discourse relations are not explicitly indicated by discourse markers.

1.2.2 Information Extraction Tasks

Information extraction (IE) refers to obtaining structured information from unstructured texts. Here structured information can be regarded as knowledge in tabular forms, which can be stored in relational databases. IE is highly related to syntax and semantics, but is more application-driven. Common targets for IE include entities, relations, events and sentiments.

• **Entities**

Entities are a foundational element in IE. While common entity mentions such as *"the car"* and *"the red car"* can be relatively easy to extract from texts, others are relatively more difficult. Named entities are one example. They are an open set, and the way in which they are expressed (e.g., *"Apple Inc. is $200 per share"* can also be *"Apple is $200 per share"*) can be highly flexible. As a result, **named entity recognition** (NER) is a common task in IE, which is to identify all named entity mentions from a given piece of text. An example is shown in Table 1.6, where a category label is also assigned to each recognised named entity mention as a part of the output. Common named entity categories include person (e.g., *"Samir Rath"*), organisation (e.g., *"Google Inc."*), location (e.g., *"Himalaya"*) and geopolitical entity (e.g., *"Singapore"*). In addition to named entity recognition, there have also been investigations on *numerical entity extraction* and *temporal expression extraction*.

Given a text document, there can be multiple mentions of the same entity, with some being nouns while others are pronouns. For example, in *"Tim bought a book. He liked it."*, both the pronoun *"he"* and the proper noun *"Tim"* represent a person, while the pronoun *"it"* and the noun *"book"* represent the same object. A useful task in NLP is **anaphora resolution**, which identifies the entity that a pronoun refers to in a discourse. Sometimes pronouns can be dropped from a sentence. For example, in *"This book is interesting. Really like it."*, the pronoun *"I"* is implicit in the second sentence. **Zero-pronoun resolution** refers to the task of detecting and interpreting dropped pronouns. Anaphora resolution can be seen as a fundamental NLP task rather than a task in IE.

A document-level entity extraction task is **coreference resolution**, which is to find all expressions that refer to the same entities in a text document. An example is shown in Table 1.7. In the first example, there are two entities, namely *"Tim"* and *"eight Harry Potter movies"*, which are mentioned by the expressions {*"Tim"*, *"He"*} and {*"eight Harry Potter movies"*, *"the series"*}, respectively. In the second example, there are three entities and each has different mentions.

• **Relations**

Relations between entities represent knowledge. Common relations include PART–WHOLE (e.g., Bangkok–Thailand), TYPE–INSTANCE (e.g., Hilton–hotel), AFFILIATION (e.g., Bill Gates–Microsoft), PHYSICAL (e.g., Singapore–Malaysia, which are located near each other) and SOCIAL (e.g., family relations). Relations can be hierarchical. For example, AFFILIATION can be further

Table 1.6 Named Entities. PER – person; ORG – organisation; GPE – Geo-political entity; LOC – location.

Input	Output
Michael Jordan is a Professor at University of Berkeley, located near Silicon Valley, USA.	*[Michael Jordan]$_{PER}$ is a Professor at [University of Berkeley]$_{ORG}$, located near [silicon valley]$_{LOC}$, [USA]$_{GPE}$.*
Mary went to Chicago to meet her boyfriend John Smith.	*[Mary]$_{PER}$ went to [Chicago]$_{LOC}$ to meet her boyfriend [John Smith]$_{PER}$.*

Table 1.7 Coreference resolution.

Input	Output
Tim watched eight Harry Potter movies. He found the series fascinating.	*{Tim, he},* *{eight Harry Potter movies, the series}*
" I had a very bad dinner at The Oceanside.", said Jennifer, "It was too salty." She did not like the restaurant itself either, since it was very crowded.	*{I, Jennifer, She}* *{dinner, It}* *{The Oceanside, the restaurant, it}*

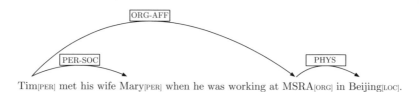

Figure 1.5 Relation extraction.

categorised into AFFILIATION–FOUNDER, AFFILIATION–MEMBER, AFFILIATION–EMPLOYEE, etc. They can also be highly domain-specific, such as DRUG–SIDE-EFFECT. The task of **relation extraction** is to identify relations between entity mentions given a sentence, under a set of pre-specified relation categories, as illustrated in Figure 1.5.

Large-scale entity and relation knowledge can be stored in a **knowledge graph** (KG), a type of database where entities form nodes and relations form edges. Named entity mentions from texts can be ambiguous, with the same entity having multiple names (e.g., "*US*" and "*the States*"), and the same name referring to different entities under different contexts (e.g., "*Jordan*"). As a result, a relevant task is **entity linking**, which determines the identity of entity mentions from texts. Such identities are typically specified by anchor nodes in knowledge graphs. Entity linking is also referred to as entity disambiguation, and is related to the task of *named entity normalisation*, which finds a canonical term for named entity mentions.

Knowledge graphs allow knowledge inference. For example, given that "*John is a singer*", "*John is from Rome*" and "*Rome is in Italy*", one can infer that "*John is from Italy*" and that "*Italy has a singer*". It is unnecessary and infeasible to store all these five relations in a single knowledge graph. Instead, inference is a common task when extracting knowledge. This task of predicting relation links that are not existent in a KG is also called *link prediction* or **knowledge graph completion**.

• **Events**

The task of **event extraction** is to identify mentions of events from texts. Here events can be defined as open-domain semantic frames, or a set of specific frames of concern in a certain domain, such as "*cooking*". Event mentions contain *trigger words*, which can be both verb phrases and noun phrases. The detection of event trigger words can be more challenging compared to detecting entity mentions since trigger words can take different parts of speech. For example, in the sentence "*Trump visited Tokyo.*", the verb "*visited*" represents an event. In the sentence "*Trump's Tokyo visit has finished.*", the noun "*visit*" represents the event. After trigger detection, one can perform *event type classification* given a set of predefined event classes in a domain such as "DIPLOMATIC VISIT", and *argument extraction*, such as "VISITOR=Trump".

Events have timing. While some events have happened, others are yet to happen or expected to happen. Several NLP tasks are related to event times. One example is **news event detection**, or *first story detection*, which is to detect events that have just emerged from news or social media texts. A second example is to predict the likelihood of event happenings. This task is called **event factuality prediction**. For example, in "*Trump's visit to Tokyo has finished.*", the likelihood of the event is 1. On the other hand, in "*Trump's visit to Tokyo is scheduled on June 1.*", the likelihood of the event can be 0.96. In "*Trump is likely to visit Tokyo in this Asia trip.*", the likelihood can be 0.7. A third example is *event time extraction*, which is to extract the time of events from text. One related task is *temporal ordering of events*, which is to find out temporal relations of events using textual clues, which are not necessarily in their narrative order. A last example is *causality detection*, which is to identify whether a given event is caused by a second event.

Events also have coreferences. For example, in the text "*I interviewed Mary yesterday. It went very smoothly.*", the word "*it*" refers to the interviewing event. *Event coreference resolution* is a useful task in event extraction. Similar to zero-pronouns, verb phrases in event mentions can sometimes also be omitted. For example, in "*Mary went to Russia to see the World Cup. Tom too.*", there is a *verb phrase ellipsis* in the second sentence, detection of which is useful for event extraction.

One more NLP task related to events is **script learning**. Here a *script* refers to a set of partially ordered events in a stereotypical scenario, together with their participant roles. For example, in the scenario "restaurant visit", typical events can include "customer to be seated", "customer to order food", "waiter to serve food", "customer to eat food", "customer to pay", etc. Script learning aims to extract such commonsense knowledge automatically from narrative texts, which can be useful for inferring contexts that are not explicitly mentioned in automatic text understanding.

• **Sentiment**

Sentiment analysis, or **opinion mining** is an NLP task that extracts sentiment signals from texts. There are numerous task variations. A simple task is **sentiment classification**, which is to predict the subjectivity and sentiment polarity of a given text, which can be a sentence or a full document. Examples are shown in Table 1.8(a). The output can be a binary *subjective/objective* class, or a ternary *positive/negative/neutral* class. More fine-grained output labels can be defined, such as a scale of $[-2, -1, 0, 1, 2]$, which corresponds to [very negative, negative, neutral, positive, very positive], respectively.

There are also tasks that offer more fine-grained details in sentiments. For example, **targeted sentiment** (Table 1.8(b)) investigates the sentiment of a text towards a certain target entity. For example, in the sentence "*I like Facebook more than Twitter.*", the sentiment towards "*Facebook*" is positive, while that towards "*Twitter*" is negative. A related task is **aspect-oriented sentiment** (Table 1.8(c)), which is typically defined in the product review domain. The goal is to extract

Table 1.8 Sentiment analysis.

	Task	Input	Output
(a)	Sentiment classification	*This is a film well worth seeing.* *It's too slowly paced to be a thriller.*	positive negative
(b)	Targeted sentiment	*[IOS]* is much better than *[Android]*. *Does [Amazon] support [Alipay]?*	{IOS: positive, Android: negative} {Amazon: neutral, Alipay: neutral}
(c)	Aspect-oriented sentiment	*The USB receiver is small and fits inside the mouse when not in use. Batteries are easy to install. It is shorter than a normal mouse, which is going to take some getting used to. I wish it were the same size as a normal mouse.*	{USB receiver: positive, Battery: positive, Size: negative}
(d)	More fine-grained sentiment classification	*Tim blamed Mary for not buying the watch.*	{*Opinion holder*: Tim *Opinion target*: Mary *Opinion expression*: not buying the watch *Sentiment polarity*: negative}

different aspects given a certain topic, together with the sentiment signals towards each aspect. For example, from a camera review post, different product features, such as "weight", "image quality" and "price" can be mentioned, each with a sentiment polarity. These features are regarded as individual aspects for sentiment classification.

More fine-grained sentiment analysis (Table 1.8(d)) extracts not only the opinion target, but also the opinion holder and the opinion expression. For example, in the sentence "*Mary believed that Tim made a big mistake.*", the opinion holder is "*Mary*", the opinion target is "*Tim*" and the opinion expression is "*made a big mistake*", with a negative sentiment polarity.

Other tasks related to sentiment analysis include **sarcasm detection**, which is to classify whether a text contains sarcasm or not, and **sentiment lexicon acquisition**, which is to acquire from texts a lexicon that contains sentiment-bearing words, together with their polarities and strengths from texts. The resulting lexicons are used for sentiment analysis. Sentiment analysis is also related to **stance detection**, which is to detect the stance of a text towards a certain subject (i.e., "for" or "against"), and also **emotion detection**, which is to extract the emotion of the narrator, such as "angry", "disappointed" and "excited".

1.2.3 Applications

There are many end tasks in NLP, some of which by themselves can be large research areas in the literature.

Information retrieval refers to the finding of unstructured data from large collections according to certain information needs. *Web search* is an example. Information retrieval (IR) and NLP are intersecting research fields, with IR considering tasks outside NLP, such as image and audio retrieval, and efficient document databases. IR-related topics under NLP include **text classification**, which is to assign a text into a set of specified categories, and **text clustering**, which is to group similar texts together without pre-specifying text categories. For example, news documents can be classified according to topics such as "finance" and "sports". *Language identification* classifies a piece of given text as being written in a specific language (e.g., French, English). *Spam detection* is also a classification task, where the input is typically a text document such as email. *Opinion spam detection* checks whether a given review contains deceptive false opinions. A related classification task is *rumour detection*, which is to find out whether a given text contains false statements. A last classification example is *humour detection*, which classifies a given text into whether it contains humour or not.

Machine translation is a practical application, which is one of the most important branches of the NLP research field, driving its growth since the beginning of NLP research. Machine translation is typically performed on the sentence level. On the other hand, document level machine translation can consider more coherence information. A related task is *computer aided human translation*, where algorithms are designed to help human translators to improve efficiency, such as by offering auto-completion.

Machine translation is a *text-to-text* task, where both the input and output are texts. A related task is **text summarisation**. According to the input, summarisation can be classified into *single-document summarisation* and *multi-document summarisation*. According to the output, tasks relevant to summarisation include *title generation* and *key phrase generation*. The latter refers to the task of generating a set of key phrases for representing the main topics. If all key phrases or keywords exist in the input text, the task is also referred to as **key phrase extraction** or **keyword extraction**. The task is commonly used for scientific documents. While summarisation is typically defined on the document level, there has also been work on **sentence compression**.

Grammar error correction can also be regarded as a text-to-text task, where the input is a sentence with grammar errors, and the output is a fluent sentence with the same meaning. A simpler task is *grammar error detection*, which does not offer corrections for identified errors. On the word level, a related task is *spelling checking*. One more related task is *disfluency detection*, which has been used to process speech texts. Disfluency detection and grammar error detection can also be used for *automatic essay scoring* or *automatic translation quality assessment*.

In addition to text-to-text tasks, there has been investigation on **data-to-text** generation, where the input is non-linguistic. For example, it can be useful to turn forms, football match statistics and stock charts to text descriptions. Image captioning aims to automatically add captions to images, and video captioning can be used to add commentary to football match videos. Since these tasks involve both NLP and other disciplines of AI such as computer vision, they are also called *multimodal* tasks. Text generation is also related to *computational creativity*, where work has been done on generating poems, humorous texts and lyrics for music.

Not an NLP application on its own but highly related to what we are discussing here, **text generation** has also been investigated as an abstract problem, which investigates the generation of natural language sentences, typically from a semantic or syntactic representation. When the input is an unordered syntactic tree, the text generation task is also called **tree linearisation**. When the input is an abstract semantic representation, text generation is also called **realisation**.

Question answering (QA) is a more comprehensive task, in the sense that it involves both the understanding of a question, and the finding of an answer from relevant knowledge sources. Depending on the source of information for answers, QA systems can be classified into knowledge base QA and QA from text. For the latter, there has been work on automating answers given *community* QA data, such as Yahoo! Answers[3] or Quora[4]. Simple forms of QA can be factual, where the answer is typically an entity. More complex QA involves reasoning and explanations. **Reading comprehension** or **machine reading** requires a system to understand given text passages so that it can answer questions in interpretive ways. Reading comprehension can require a system to perform evidence integration, commonsense reasoning or mathematical calculation. A comprehensive QA task that involves IR and machine reading is *open QA*, where given a question, the answer is derived by first retrieving a set of relevant documents, and then performing answer extraction.

Dialogue systems are a multi-turn text-to-text task. Research on dialogue systems can be classified into *chit-chat* dialogues and *task-oriented* dialogues, with the latter being designed for solving tasks such as hotel booking and navigation. Typical sub-tasks for task-oriented dialogue systems include natural language understanding, dialogue state tracking (DST), dialogue management and text generation.

NLP can also be used for building **recommendation systems**, which aims to predict how much a user will like a product, service or other types of items. For example, if two users tend to give similar ratings for most movies both have watched, then the rating of one user of a new movie can be useful for predicting the rating of the movie by the other user. NLP has been used to leverage text reviews for recommending movies, restaurants, services and jokes.

NLP is also related to **text mining** and **text analytics**, which is the process of deriving high-quality information from text. Here 'high quality' usually refers to a combination of relevance, novelty and interest. While typical IE and IR tasks can be regarded as belonging to text mining, more typical tasks include association analysis, visualisation and predictive analytics. One example is *stock market prediction*, which is to predict stock returns based on information from the Internet, such as news and sentiments. Similar tasks include *movie revenue prediction* based on movie reviews, and *presidential election results prediction* based on tweets. There has also been attempts to predict the number of citations of research papers automatically by reading their contents.

1.2.4 Summary

The above tasks give a broad representation of problems and applications of NLP. In practice, there can be far more specific task variations and custom applications. NLP is a dynamically evolving field, with new tasks being brought into attention and less challenging or useful tasks fading out of the active research field.

---

[3] For more information about these labels, refer to the Yahoo! Answers http://answers.yahoo.com/.

[4] For more information about these labels, refer to the Quora http://quora.com/.

1.3   NLP from a Machine Learning Perspective

Although there is a plethora of NLP tasks in the linguistic or application perspective, NLP tasks can be categorised into much fewer types when viewed from a machine learning perspective. For example, the tasks of POS-tagging, syntactic chunking, word segmentation, supertagging, named entity recognition, targeted sentiment classification can all be seen as the same task in machine learning, solved using the same principled method, which we detail in Chapters 7, 8 and 15. As a second example, although the CCG syntactic structure and the constituent tree of a sentence can be highly different linguistically, as shown in Figure 1.1, they can be structurally identical from the machine learning perspective, both being tree structures that can be modelled by the same algorithms (Chapters 10 and 11). As a third example, the same framework described in Chapters 11 and 15 can be used to solve all the above problems and additionally syntactic parsing, semantic parsing, relation extraction etc.

One of the main reasons behind the above fact is the nature of mathematical modelling (Chapter 2) – we cast NLP tasks into the mathematical domain when building machine models, and as a result, linguistic structures are mapped into mathematical structures such as probability graphs (Chapters 2, 6, 12 and 18), vectors in high-dimensional spaces (Chapters 3 and 13) or states in finite state transducers (Chapters 11 and 15). While it is highly interesting to consider clever ways of casting linguistic problems into mathematical forms, for most of the tasks discussed in Section 1.2 a small set of linguistic knowledge can be sufficient for building a competitive machine learning model. In fact, a computational linguist who does not speak Bahasa can build a state-of-the-art syntactic parser for the language! As we have seen in Section 1.1, the NLP field has been driven by the development of methods rather than tasks. In fact, a technical advance typically leads to improvements over a range of NLP tasks. Hence we center around methods for the remainder of this book, describing tasks of the same nature together.

How can we categorise NLP tasks according to their machine learning nature? There are different perspectives. According to the output, there are **classification** tasks (e.g., rumour detection), for which the output is a distinct label from a set, and **structured prediction** tasks (e.g., POS-tagging and dependency parsing), where the outputs are structures with inter-related sub structures. In some cases, the output is neither a class label nor a structure, but a real-valued number. For example, predicting stock prices can be cast as such a task, which is a **regression** problem. Automatic essay scoring can also be treated as a regression problem. Many NLP tasks are structured prediction tasks, ranging from word segmentation and syntactic parsing to semantic role labelling, relation extraction and machine translation. As a result, how to deal with structures is a highly important problem for NLP. We will see classification tasks in Chapters 2, 3, 4, 5, 6, 12, 13 and 14, and structured prediction tasks in Chapters 7, 8, 9, 10, 11, 12, 15, 16, 17 and 18.

NLP tasks can also be classified according to the nature of training data for machine learning. When the set of training data does not contain gold-standard outputs (i.e., manually labelled POS-tags for POS-tagging and manually labelled syntactic trees for parsing), the task setting is **unsupervised learning**. In contrast, when the set of training data consists of gold-standard outputs the task setting is **supervised learning**. In between the two settings, **semi-supervised learning** uses both data with gold-standard labels and data without annotation. Take POS tagging for example. In the supervised learning setting, the training data consist of sentences with each word being annotated with its gold-standard POS. The unsupervised learning POS-tagging task (i.e., POS induction), on the other hand, uses only raw text as training data. For semi-supervised learning, a relatively small set of data with human labels and a relatively large amount of raw text can be used simultaneously. We will see supervised learning tasks in most of the chapters, and unsupervised and semi-supervised tasks in Chapters 3, 4, 6, 7, 12, 16 and 18.

The remaining of the book is organised in three main parts, where Part I discusses the basis of mathematical modelling for NLP, Part II focuses on structures and Part III is dedicated to deep learning techniques. Similar patterns are repeated in our narrative order. For example, in each of the three parts, we discuss supervised learning before moving on to unsupervised learning. For both statistical models and deep learning methods, we discuss binary classification before moving on to multi-class classification and structured prediction. For all types of tasks and models, we introduce the intuition first, before moving on to the mathematical details and then further to more theory behind. Overall, the narrative order of the book is also aligned with the chronological order of technological development in the field. We take a unified approach to introduce all technologies, where the same mathematical framework and notations is used throughout the book. Since concepts are frequently correlated across chapters, we give cross-chapter references for strengthening the understanding.

Summary

In this chapter we have introduced:

- What is natural language processing (NLP)?
- A spectrum of NLP problems;
- Categorising NLP problems according to machine learning nature.

Chapter Notes

Jurafsky and Martin (2008) introduced NLP tasks with rich linguistic background. Eisenstein (2019) introduced NLP techniques with focuses on learning, search and meaning representation. Bender (2013) and Bender and Lascarides (2019) discussed linguistic fundamentals for NLP. Manning and Schütze (1999) discussed statistical NLP. Bird et al. (2009) gave a hands-on tutorial of NLP tasks using Python.

Among specific NLP tasks, Chomsky (1957) discussed formal grammars. Tesnière (1959) developed dependency grammar in the syntax of natural languages. Steedman (2000) introduced the theoretical system of combinatory categorical grammar. Kübler et al. (2009) introduced dependency parsing. Fillmore and Baker (2001) discussed frame semantics. Gildea and Jurafsky (2002) introduced semantic role labelling systems. Moens (2006) introduced information extraction. One can refer to Nadeau and Sekine (2007) on named entity recognition and Mintz et al. (2009) for relation extraction. Pang and Lee (2008) and Liu (2012) introduced sentiment anaysis. McKeown (1992) introduced text generation. Manning et al. (2008) discussed modern approaches to information retrieval. Aggarwal and Zhai (2012) introduced text mining. Koehn (2009) gave a comprehensive introduction of statistical machine translation and Koehn (2020) introduced neural machine translation.

Exercises

1.1 Perform manual tokenisation for the following sentences.
   (a) *"I'm a student."*
   (b) *"He didn't return Mr. Smith's book."*
   (c) *"We have no useful information on whether users are at risk, said James A. Talcott of Boston's Dana-Farber Cancer Institute."*

1.2 Assign POS tags to the sentence *"They can fish."* How many valid POS sequences can be assigned? Draw the dependency tree structure of each interpretation.

1.3 Draw the constituent tree structures of *"I saw the man with my telescope."* and *"I saw the man with my wallet."*, respectively. What are the main differences? Think about the main sources of information that can be used to resolve the ambiguities.

1.4 Assign CCG supertags to the sentence *"I saw her duck."* How many different sequences can be assigned? Draw the CCG derivation of each. (Note: the lexical category of di-transitive verbs is $(S\backslash NP)/NP/NP$, transitive verbs $(S\backslash NP)/NP$ and adjectives NP/NP.)

1.5 What are the similarities and differences between noun phrase (NP) chunking and named entity recognition?

1.6 Look up a dictionary for the senses of the words *"bank"* and *"saw"*, noting the correlation between senses and POS. The *citation form* of each word in a dictionary is called a **lemma**, which can be different from **word forms** in a sentence. How many lemmas can the word form *"saw"* have?

1.7 What contexts do antonyms commonly co-occur in? Can you define some simple regular expressions to mine out antonyms from large-scale text data?

1.8 Draw the predicate–argument structures of the sentence *"Mary went to Chicago, and visited John."* How many predicates are there in the sentence? Do the predicate-argument relations form a tree structure over the sentence? Discuss similarities and differences between predicate–argument structures and dependency tree structures.

1.9 Consider the logical form of Figure 1.3(b). If both *"Tim"* and *"book"* are treated as variables rather than functions, what is the logic form of the same sentence?

1.10 Draw the logical forms of *"Not all of Jason's classmates like Jason."* and *"None of Jason's classmates like Jason."*, respectively. What are the main differences? The semantic difference is related to **negation scope** ambiguities.

1.11 State the main differences between anaphora resolution and coreference resolution.

1.12 Which of the tasks below can benefit from knowledge of POS in an input sentence?

- named entity recognition
- discourse segmentation
- morphological analysis
- machine translation

1.13 Which of the tasks below can benefit from dependency syntax information of input sentences?

- POS tagging
- named entity recognition
- semantic role labelling
- relation extraction

1.14 *Open domain targeted sentiment analysis* is the task to monitor a stream of text, detecting named entity mentions and the sentiment polarities towards each mention. Hence it consists of two sub-tasks, namely NER and targeted sentiment classification. What other tasks can be performed jointly? Discuss the advantage of doing the two tasks jointly as compared to a pipeline method.

1.15 Text summarisation can be solved using *abstractive* and *extractive* methods. The former synthesises a summary using text generation techniques, while the latter makes a summary from excerpts of the original articles. Think of the relative advantages and challenges of each method.

1.16 Automatic essay scoring is useful for students. Automatic stock prediction is useful for traders. Can you think of downstream NLP applications that are useful in other areas, such as technology, sports and entertainment?

2   Counting Relative Frequencies

The term "model" is one of the most frequently mentioned terms in the NLP literature and in this book. Formally, a *model* is an imaginary, abstract and simplified version of a subject, in which exact mathematical calculation is feasible. The concept of modelling can be demonstrated by text-book examples in maths and physics. For example, consider the well-known problem of modelling the falling of a ball off a cliff. In order to calculate the time it takes for the ball to reach the ground, a typical solution is to model the ball as a mass point, thereby abstracting away its attributes such as colour and material, and also air resistance. This model considers only the initial velocity, the height of the cliff and gravity in deriving conclusions.

Modelling natural language texts is similar in spirit. Examples in this book will repeatedly show how specific tasks are simplified by abstracting away factors that are relatively less important to the solution, or cause troubles in computation by introducing significant complexities. As a start, this chapter discusses a conceptually simplest model — a probabilistic model by counting relative frequencies. We begin by using a simple coin-tossing example to review the most important concepts in probabilistic modelling, and then show how such concepts can be used to build NLP models. In particular, various language models and a text classification model by counting relative frequencies are introduced, through which the basic concepts in probability theory that are the most relevant to this book are also reviewed.

2.1   Probabilistic Modelling

To begin with, consider the problem of tossing a coin. We want to know whether it will land facing up or down. Apparently, this depends on numerous factors, such as the mass and mass distribution of the coin, its shape and relative position to the fingers and table, and the amount of friction, etc., which makes precise calculation infeasible. To this problem, a simple probabilistic model can serve as a handy rescue. The basic idea is to model the chance, or probability, of the coin facing up, thereby abstracting away all the intricacies in the physical tossing process. Here **probability** represents the intrinsic uncertainty of some *random event*, such as tossing a coin. In the empirical sense, it represents the relative frequency of certain outcomes in the long run.

A simplest probabilistic model for the coin tossing problem directly takes the probability of coin facing up (i.e., head) as a **parameter**, denoted as $P(head) = \theta$. Correspondingly, we have $P(tail) = 1 - \theta$. An intuitive way to **estimate** the value of θ is to toss the coin for a number of times, and calculate the relative frequencies of heads and tails. If k out of N tosses result in heads, then θ can be fixed to k/N.

This example illustrates the basic idea of a probabilistic model **trained** by counting relative frequencies, which is the main topic of this chapter. Here *training* refers to the process of parameter value estimation. In our coin tossing model, there is only one parameter, namely θ, which is estimated over a set of **training data** $D = \{y_1, y_2, \ldots, y_N\}$, where each **training example** $y_i \in \{head, tail\}$ represents a trial toss. Training is conducted by counting the relative frequency of heads. The resulting model with a trained θ value can then be used to predict the probability of *head* in **test** scenarios, which is a constant (i.e., θ) for this problem.

2.1.1 Maximum Likelihood Estimation (MLE)

Theoretically, our **training method** above by counting relative frequencies aligns with the principle of **maximum likelihood estimation** (MLE), which estimates the parameters of a model by finding a model that maximises the likelihood (i.e., overall probability as given by the model) of observed data. Intuitively, MLE assumes that the set of observed training data represents the most likely sample among all such data, and adjusts the model parameters to make the model probability conform to this assumption. In the coin tossing case, our training data consists of an experiment of N tosses, with k resulting in heads. MLE training finds the parameter values that maximise the probability of the training data among all experiments of N coin tosses.

To show how maximum likelihood estimation leads to counting relative frequencies, we first formally define the MLE training objective for our coin tossing model, and then find the model parameter value θ by maximising the objective function. In particular, we formalise the coin-tossing experiments as a controlled sampling process, where each training sample (i.e., toss) is obtained under exactly the same condition, and independently of the other samples. Such a set of random events are known as **independent and identically distributed**, or **i.i.d.** for short. Under the *i.i.d.* condition, the probability of the data $D = \{y_1, y_2, \ldots, y_N\}$ as a whole is equivalent to the product of individual sample probabilities $P(y_1), P(y_2), \ldots, P(y_N)$:

$$
\begin{aligned}
P(D) &= P(y_1, y_2, \ldots, y_N) \\
&= P(y_1)P(y_2)\ldots P(y_N) \\
&= P(head)^k P(tail)^{N-k} \\
&= \theta^k (1-\theta)^{N-k}.
\end{aligned}
\tag{2.1}
$$

Given Eq 2.1, the MLE **training objective** is to find a value of θ that maximises $P(D)$, namely the likelihood of D given θ:

$$
\hat{\theta} = \arg\max_{\theta} P(D),
$$

which is equivalent to $\arg\max_{\theta} \log P(D)$. Here $\arg\max_x f(x)$ denotes the value of the argument x that maximises the function $f(x)$.

At the maximum value, the derivative $\frac{\partial \log P(D)}{\partial \theta}$ of the convex function is zero. Hence the arg max value $\hat{\theta}$ can be found by solving

$$
\begin{aligned}
\frac{\partial \log P(D)}{\partial \theta} &= \frac{\partial \left(\log \theta^k (1-\theta)^{N-k} \right)}{\partial \theta} \\
&= \frac{\partial \left(k \log \theta + (N-k) \log(1-\theta) \right)}{\partial \theta} \\
&= \frac{k}{\theta} - \frac{N-k}{1-\theta} = 0 \\
&\Rightarrow \hat{\theta} = \frac{k}{N},
\end{aligned}
$$

which is the relative frequency of heads.

We thus obtain a nice analytical solution to the MLE training objective for the coin tossing problem. However, as we will see later, the likelihood functions of more complex probabilistic models may not have closed-form optima. Consequently, numerical solutions to MLE can be necessary. As a general principle for training a model, MLE is connected to a range of other machine learning principles, such as maximum entropy, minimum cross-entropy, minimum KL-divergence, maximum a posteriori and Bayesian learning, which we will see later in this book.

2.1.2 Modelling the Probability of Words

The coin tossing model describes the probabilities of two discrete outcomes using $(\theta, 1-\theta)$. When the number of outcomes rise beyond two, a similar random event can be probabilistically modelled using more parameters. Take casino dice casting for example. There are six possible outcomes, which correspond to the numbers $1, 2, \ldots, 6$ on a die. The probabilities of the six discrete outcomes can be parameterised as $\theta_1, \theta_2, \theta_3, \theta_4, \theta_5$ and θ_6, respectively, where $\sum_{i=1}^{6} \theta_i = 1$. This model consists of six parameters (essentially five parameters since $\theta_6 = 1 - \sum_{i=1}^{5} \theta_i$), the estimation of which can intuitively be performed by following exactly the same approach, namely doing trial experiments. In particular, given a data set $D = \{y_1, y_2, \ldots, y_N\}$, where the counts of the outcomes are $c_1, c_2, \ldots, c_6$, respectively ($\sum_{i=1}^{6} c_i = N$), the data likelihood is

$$
P(D) = \prod_{j=1}^{N} P(y_j) = \prod_{i=1}^{6} (\theta_i)^{c_i}. \tag{2.2}
$$

It can be shown that similar to coin tossing, MLE also leads to the training method of counting relative frequencies for the discussed problem. In particular, for casino dice casting, maximising $P(D)$ from Eq 2.2 leads to $\theta_i = c_i/N$. Exercise 2.1 discusses more details of the derivation.

Modelling random word drawing. Now consider the modelling of randomly drawing a word from text. How likely can the word "*thank*" be, and how likely can the word "*hyperbole*" be? Intuition tells us that the former is much more likely, which reflects an underlying probability of words from a **vocabulary**. Similar to dice casting, there are more than two possible outcomes for the random event, where the set of all possible outcomes is the vocabulary. Formally, denoting a vocabulary as $V = \{w_1, w_2, \ldots, w_{|V|}\}$, where $|V|$ denotes the number of words in V, we can build a model of words that gives $P(w)$ for $w \in V$.

In this book, we use the term **word** to indicate all tokens in a sentence, including punctuation. As a result, the vocabulary also consists of punctuation. Intuitively, number tokens such as 1, 15 and 0.23 make an open set, which can lead to $|V|$ being infinity if all number tokens are included. In practice, we do not face this problem due to two facts. First, a vocabulary is typically extracted over a set of text, which contains a finite number of distinct tokens. Second, it can be useful to replace all numbers with a special ⟨NUM⟩ token when working with numbers.

Training a word model. MLE tells us that our word model $P(w)$ can be estimated by counting relative frequencies. This can be done over a large collection of texts written by humans, which is commonly referred to as a **corpus**. For example, a large collection of newspaper articles or novels makes a corpus. Such a corpus can contain millions or billions of sentences.

Formally, given a training corpus D, under the assumption that each word is written independently (thus *i.i.d.*), MLE training has

$$P(w) = \frac{\#w \in D}{\sum_{w' \in V}(\#w' \in D)}.$$

Here $\#w$ represents the count of a vocabulary word w in a training corpus. For example, if the word "*hello*" occurs 100 times in a text corpus of 500,000 words, then its probability $P(hello) = 100/500,000 = 0.0002$.

2.1.3 Models and Probability Distributions

We have discussed two types of **random events** in the previous sections, namely the coin-tossing events and the dice-casting (i.e., word-drawing) events. We model each event using a **random variable**, for which each distinct value represents a distinct outcome of the random event. For example, for coin-tossing there are two possible values, namely *heads* and *tails*. For dice casting there are six possible values, namely 1, 2, …, 6. The goal of our modelling task is to compute the probabilities of a random variable. For example, for the coin-tossing problem, we need a model to compute both $P(y = heads)$ and $P(y = tails)$. The specification of a detailed equation to compute such probabilities involves the definition of model parameters, and we call this process a **parameterisation** process. Parameterisation is a very important step in modelling, through which we can make necessary abstractions and select useful sources of information. For our coin-tossing, dice-casting and word drawing problems, the parameterisation is simple because the target random variable is simple. For problems later in this book, we will model more complex random variables such as sentences, syntactic structures and translation, in which we shall see more complex parameterisation methods, including the use of linear functions and neural networks to calculate probabilities.

In statistics, the probabilities of all possible values of a discrete random variable is a **probability distribution**. A model that can compute the probabilities of a random variable should compute the probabilities of all its possible values, namely the full probability distribution. For the remainder of

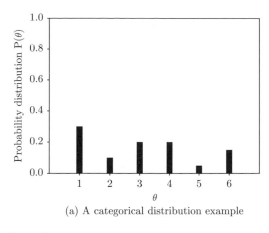

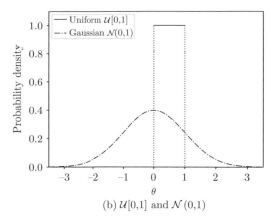

(a) A categorical distribution example   (b) $\mathcal{U}[0,1]$ and $\mathcal{N}(0,1)$

Figure 2.1 An example probability distribution for discrete categorical random variables (a) and two example probability density functions for continuous random variables (b).

this book, we use $P(y)$ to indicate a model of the distribution of a random variable y, and $P(y = v)$ to denote the probability of specific value v of the random variable y, as computed by the model.

The coin tossing problem follows a **Bernoulli distribution**, which represents the probability of two distinct outcomes. The dice-casting problem follows a **categorical distribution**, or **multinoulli distribution**, which can be regarded as an extension of the Bernoulli distribution for random events with more than two distinct outcomes. Figure 2.1(a) shows an example categorical distribution with six possible values of a random variable θ.

Bernoulli distributions are closely related to **binomial distribution**s, which we will encounter later in the book. A binomial distribution describes the results of n *i.i.d.* Bernoulli distributions. Still taking the coin-tossing problem as an example, a binomial distribution describes the number of heads and tails in n *i.i.d.* tosses. Denoting the probability distribution of each *i.i.d.* coin toss as $\langle P_{\text{BER}}(heads), P_{\text{BER}}(tails) \rangle$, the probability of n tosses with k heads is:

$$P_{\text{BIN}}(k,n) = \frac{n!}{k!(n-k)!}P_{\text{BER}}(heads)^k P_{\text{BER}}(tails)^{n-k}. \tag{2.3}$$

In Eq 2.3, $\frac{n!}{k!(n-k)!}$ is the number of distinct experiments in which k heads are observed in n trials. It is called the *binomial coefficient*.

Bernoulli distributions can be viewed as a special case of Binomial distributions, with only one sample. $P_{\text{BER}}(heads) = P_{\text{BIN}}(1,1)$ and $P_{\text{BER}}(tails) = P_{\text{BIN}}(0,1)$.

Given a set of observations $D = \{y_1, \ldots, y_N\}$, where the number of *heads* is k, the data likelihood function in Eq 2.1 differs from the binomial distribution $P_{\text{BIN}}(k,n)$ in Eq 2.3 only by the binomial coefficient. This is because D is one of the $\frac{n!}{k!(n-k)!}$ possible (n-toss) events with k heads. Interestingly, since both k and n are constants with regard to θ, maximising Eq 2.3 also leads to the same model. This intuitively means that maximising the likelihood of one experiment of n tosses with k heads (e.g., *heads, heads, tails, heads, heads, tails*) gives the same model as maximising the overall likelihood of all experiments of n tosses with k heads.

A **multinomial distribution** describes the outcome of n *i.i.d.* categorical random events. Formally, given a categorical distribution $P_{\text{CAT}}(y)$, where $y \in \{1, \ldots, K\}$ and K is the total number of categories, the probability of n *i.i.d.* samples with the count of each outcome being $c_1, c_2, \ldots, c_K$, respectively, is:

$$P_{\text{MUL}}(c_1, c_2, \ldots, c_K, n) = \frac{n!}{c_1! \cdots c_K!} P_{\text{CAT}}(1)^{c_1} \cdots P_{\text{CAT}}(K)^{c_K}. \qquad (2.4)$$

The correlation between a multinomial distribution and a categorical distribution is similar to that between a binomial distribution and a Bernoulli distribution. First, a categorical distribution can be regarded as a special case of a multinomial distribution with one sample. Second, the likelihood function in Eq 2.2 is proportional to the probability function of Eq 2.4 except for the coefficient term $\frac{n!}{c_1! \cdots c_K!}$. MLE over Eq 2.2 gives the same model as over Eq 2.4. We will encounter multinominal distributions many times in this chapter and later in this book. For the remainder of this section, we continue to discuss distributions that will be encountered in the book. However, they are not directly useful for this chapter, and you can choose to skip to the next section.

Continuous random variables. The three problems that we have discussed model the probabilities of **discrete random variables**, which take integer values. For the remainder of this book we will discuss **continuous random variables** also, which take real values. Still take the coin-tossing problem for instance. If we consider the probability distribution of $\theta = P(head)$ itself, we work with a continuous random variable since θ can potentially take any value in $[0, 1]$. We will see in Chapter 12 the reason why we want to consider the probability distribution of θ itself. Here briefly speaking, this probability reflects a belief, or prior knowledge, about the coin, which can influence our final parameter estimation given training data. For instance, if we believe that the coin being tossed is fair, then we should have $P(\theta)$ being distributed towards 0.5. This can lead to a final estimation of θ value that is closer to 0.5 even if relative frequencies say that it is 0.2.

Intuitively, for a continuous random variable y, it is more reasonable to describe the probability of $y \in [a, b]$ than the pointwise probability of $y = a$, where a and b are real values and $a < b$, because the latter is strictly zero. As a result, the distribution of y is described as a continuous function $f(y)$, which is called the **probability density function** (p.d.f.). The probability of $y \in [a, b]$ can be calculated by $\int_a^b f(y)dy$.

Figure 2.1(b) shows the p.d.f.s of two typical distributions, namely a **uniform distribution** and a **Gaussian distribution** (or **normal distribution**). The former describes a continuous random variable in $[L, H]$ ($-\infty < L < H < \infty$) and the latter describes a continous random variable in $(-\infty, \infty)$. Formally, a uniform distribution in $[L, H]$ can be denoted as $\mathcal{U}[L, H]$. It describes a random variable for which all possible values are equally probable. Given that the total probability $\int_L^H f(y)dy = 1$, we have

$$f(y) = \frac{1}{H - L} \text{ for } y \in [L, H].$$

A Gaussian distribution describes a random variable for which the value is most likely close to a mean value μ, but can range in $(-\infty, \infty)$. The probability of a value is increasingly less when the value is increasingly different from μ. As shown in Figure 2.1, the p.d.f. of a Gaussian distribution follows a bell shape, which is symmetric for values greater than μ and less than μ. The shape is controlled by a variance parameter σ^2, with a large value of σ^2 describing less sharp distribution. Formally, a Gaussian distribution can be denoted as $\mathcal{N}(\mu, \sigma^2)$, where $f(y) = \frac{1}{\sqrt{2\pi}\sigma} \exp(-\frac{(y-\mu)^2}{2\sigma^2})$ and $\exp(x)$ denotes the exponential function e^x.

Random vectors. In addition to scalar random variables, we will also see **vector random variables** in this book, and in particular random vectors for which each element takes a continuous value. They can be seen as extensions of continuous random variables into multiple dimensions, which follow **multivariate distributions**. Random vectors can help us model a set of correlated variables such as a phrase of multiple words. Throughout this book, random vectors contain *i.i.d.* elements, and as a result, the computation is conceptually relatively simple. Here let us use uniform distributions and Gaussian distributions to illustrate the concepts.

Formally, given n continuous scalar random variables $x_1, x_2, \ldots, x_n$, a multivariate uniform distribution describes an n-dimensional random vector $\vec{X} = \langle x_1, x_2, \ldots, x_n \rangle$. The value range of each element can be denoted using two vectors $\vec{L} = \langle l_1, l_2, \ldots, l_n \rangle$ and $\vec{H} = \langle h_1, h_2, \ldots, h_n \rangle$, where $\vec{L}$ is the lower bound and $\vec{H}$ is the upper bound, $-\infty < l_i < h_i < \infty$ for $1 \leq i \leq n$. We have $l_i \leq x_i \leq h_i$. The p.d.f. of a multivariate situation can be written as

$$f(x_1, x_2, \ldots, x_n) = \frac{1}{\prod_{i=1}^{n}(H_i - L_i)}, \text{ for } L_i \leq x_i \leq H_i, 1 \leq i \leq n$$

where the denominator $\prod_i (H_i - L_i)$ denotes the volume of the bounded space. It can be seen as the product of individual p.d.f.s for each element.

The probability of $a_1 \leq x_1 \leq b_1, a_2 \leq x_2 \leq b_2, \ldots, a_n \leq x_n \leq b_n$ ($l_1 \leq a_1 < b_1 \leq h_1, l_2 \leq a_2 < b_2 \leq h_2, \ldots, l_n \leq a_n < b_n \leq h_n$) can be calculated by:

$$P(a_1 \leq x_1 \leq b_1, a_2 \leq x_2 \leq b_2, \ldots, a_n \leq x_n \leq b_n)$$
$$= \int_{a_1}^{b_1} \int_{a_2}^{b_2} \cdots \int_{a_n}^{b_n} f(x_1, x_2, \ldots, x_n) dx_1 dx_2 \ldots dx_n. \tag{2.5}$$

We use $\mathcal{U}[\vec{L}, \vec{H}]$ to denote multivariate uniform distributions.

The multivariate Gaussian distribution is the most widely used multidimensional probability distribution. Given $\vec{X} = \langle x_1, x_2, \ldots, x_n \rangle$, the p.d.f. of a multivariate Gaussian distribution is

$$f(x_1, \ldots, x_n) = f(\vec{X}) = \frac{1}{(2\pi)^{n/2}|\Sigma|^{1/2}} \exp\left(-\frac{1}{2}(\vec{X} - \vec{\mu})^T \Sigma^{-1} (\vec{X} - \vec{\mu})\right). \tag{2.6}$$

Compared to the univariate case, the single random vector y and the single mean μ are replaced by a vector random variable $\vec{X}$ and a mean vector $\vec{\mu}$, respectively. The single variance σ^2 is replace by an $n \times n$ covariance matrix Σ, where $\sum[i;j] = Cov(x_i, x_j)$. For this book we are concerned only with multivariate Gaussians that have diagonal co-variance matrices. Therefore, you can understand a multivariate Gaussian as a vector of individual scalar Gaussian variables.

2.2 *n*-gram Language Models

Equipped with the basic knowledge of modelling, we are ready to embark on modelling more complex structures, where parameterisation is more challenging. In this section, we extend our word-drawing problem to the modelling of sentences. A **language model** (LM) measures the probability of natural language sentences, giving higher scores to those sentences that are more probable, which are more common, fluent and grammatical. An easy way to differentiate probable and non-probable sentences is simply to look at the words. For example, the word "*thanks*" is much more probable than the word "*hyperbole*". This intuition forms the basis of *unigram language models*, which model a sentence with bold abstractions by disregarding all connections between words in the sentence, thus treating sentences as bags of words. More complicated language models take word relations into consideration, such as phrases and syntactic structures. This section discusses *n-gram language models*, where an **n-gram** refers to a sequence of *n* consecutive words. 1-grams, 2-grams and 3-grams are also named **unigram**s, **bigram**s and **trigram**s, respectively.

2.2.1 Unigram Language Models

Unigram models take a sentence as a set of words, abstracting away the order between words. Such models are often referred to as **bag-of-word** models. A unigram language model can tell that the sentence "*thanks very much*" is more probable compared to the sentence "*hidden Markov model*" based on the fact that the words "*thanks*", "*very*" and "*much*" are more probable compared to the words "*hidden*", "*Markov*" and "*model*".

Formally, a unigram language model makes an *i.i.d.* assumption between words in a sentence. Consequently, a unigram language model effectively regards a sentence as being generated by a sequence of *i.i.d.* casting of a die, which has many faces, each with a unique word. Given a sentence $s = w_1 w_2 \ldots w_n$, the probability $P(s)$ is calculated as

$$P(s) = P(w_1)P(w_2)\ldots P(w_n) = \prod_i P(w_i). \tag{2.7}$$

Thus our unigram LM is parameterised by word probabilities, which we already know how to estimate. Formally, a unigram LM consists of only one **parameter type**, which is the probability of a word. On the other hand, it contains $|V|$ **parameter instances**, corresponding to the probability of each word in a vocabulary $|V|$. Thus the size of a unigram language model can be tens of thousands in the number of parameter values. For training, MLE is used over a corpus. For testing, given a sentence $s = w_1 w_2 \ldots w_n$, it calculates $P(s) = P(w_1)P(w_2)\ldots P(w_n)$.

Given a training corpus, we can obtain a vocabulary by extracting all unique words that are found in it. Here two typical approaches can be taken. The first approach turns all words in the corpus to lower case before extracting the vocabulary and training the language model, which results in a *lower-case language model*. The second approach leaves all words in their original casing, resulting in a *true-case language model*. A lower case language model contains a smaller vocabulary, and is more robust for flexible letter cases in unseen test data. In contrast, a true case language model can learn more about the use of casing in the sentence structures, and hence can be more accurate. When the training corpus is large, true-case language models are more useful.

Dealing with unknown words. No training data can contain all words that might be seen in test data, and a test word that does not exist in the training vocabulary is called an **out-of-vocabulary** (OOV) word. There are two reasons for the existence of OOV words. First, language is dynamic and there are constantly new words being coined. Second, there can be typos and informal spellings (e.g., "*tmrw*" for "*tomorrow*").

OOV words can cause a problem for our language models. For example, consider the following two sentences:

1. "⟨*OOV*⟩ *said hello*"
2. "⟨*OOV*⟩ *taught calculus*"

According to a word model, the probability of the two sentences above are

$$P(\langle OOV \rangle)P(said)P(hello)$$

and

$$P(\langle OOV \rangle)P(taught)P(calculus),$$

respectively, which, unfortunately, are both 0 since $P(\langle OOV \rangle) = 0$ according to MLE due to 0 occurrence of ⟨*OOV*⟩ in training data.

To address this issue, a common approach is to use a special token ⟨UNK⟩ to represent all OOV words in a test set. In order to assign a probability to this token, we tweak the probability distribution in Figure 2.2(a) slightly, redistributing some probability mass from in-vocabulary words to ⟨UNK⟩. A possible resulting distribution after tweaking Figure 2.2(a) is shown in Figure 2.2(b). Compared to Figure 2.2(a), Figure 2.2(b) is less spiky and more smooth. Hence the transformation is also called **smoothing**.

One simple smoothing technique is called **add-one smoothing**, which adds one to the count of all words, including OOV words that occur in the test data:

$$P(w) = \frac{(\#w \in D) + 1}{\sum_{w' \in V}((\#w' \in D) + 1)} = \frac{(\#w \in D) + 1}{|V| + \sum_{w' \in V}(\#w' \in D)}.$$

With add-one smoothing, the probabilities of OOV words in the test data are non-zeros, and thus our word model is able to tell that example 1 is more probable compared to example 2 above based on $P(said)$, $P(hello)$, $P(taught)$ and $P(calculus)$.

More sophisticated smoothing techniques have been studied in the NLP literature, aiming to better estimate the probability of OOV words. More examples will be introduced in subsequent sections.

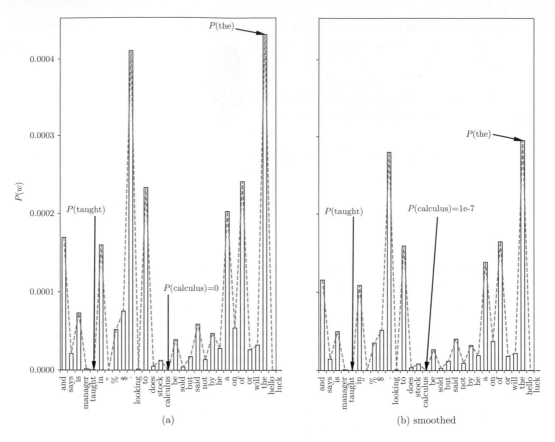

Figure 2.2 Unigram distributions. Add-10 smoothing is used in (b).

2.2.2　Bigram Language Models

Unigram language models can be used to differentiate "*hello*" from "*hyperbole*", but face challenge in comparing "*he ate pizza*" and "*he drank pizza*", which requires knowledge on verb–object relations. Apparently, while the unigrams "*ate*" and "*drank*" can be equally probable, the bigram "*ate pizza*" is common but the bigram "*drank pizza*" is rare. Bigram language models consider bigrams $w_1 w_2$ when calculating sentence probabilities, by computing **conditional probabilities** $P(w_2 | w_1)$, which are interpreted as the probabilities of a word w_2 given its previous word w_1. For example, for the bigram "*ate pizza*", the probability $P(pizza | eat)$ represents the probability of the word "*pizza*" given that the previous word is "*eat*".

Conditional probabilities can take very different values compared to unconditional probabilities of random events. Consider, for example, the words "*big*" and "*bigger*". Intuitively, the unconditional probability of the adjective "*big*" should be higher than its comparative "*bigger*" based on relative frequencies in their usage. However, given that the previous word is "*much*", the conditional probability $P(big | much)$ should be much smaller than the conditional probability $P(bigger | much)$.

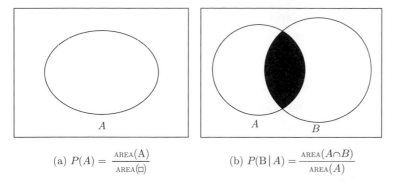

(a) $P(A) = \frac{\text{AREA}(A)}{\text{AREA}(\square)}$ (b) $P(B|A) = \frac{\text{AREA}(A \cap B)}{\text{AREA}(A)}$

Figure 2.3 Venn diagrams for (a) unconditional probabilities and (b) conditional probabilities.

Training bigram language models. How do we calculate a conditional probability by counting relative frequencies? A convenient tool for gaining such intuition is *Venn diagrams*. Figure 2.3 gives a brief review of Venn diagrams for unconditional and conditional probabilities. In Figure 2.3(a), the rectangle represents a set of all random events, and the shape A represents the set of random events A. The probability $P(A)$ is the area of A divided by the area of the rectangle. In Figure 2.3(b), A and B represent two different random events, with their unconditional probabilities being their sizes relative to the rectangle area, respectively. Now when calculating the conditional probability of B given A, we should use the ratio between the intersected area $A \cap B$ and the area of A. This is intuitively because given a condition such as A, we should count events only if A also happens. Thus the range for counting B changes from the whole rectangle area to the area A.

According to the intuition above, MLE for the conditional probabilities $P(w_2|w_1)$ can be carried out as follows, given a corpus D:

$$P(w_2|w_1) = \frac{(\#w_1 w_2 \in D)}{\sum_{w \in V}(\#w_1 w \in D)}$$

Here $w_1 w_2$ and $w_1 w$ represent bigrams such as "*much bigger*", where $w_1 =$"*much*" and $w/w_2 =$"*bigger*". This equation can be understood as counting the relative frequency of w_2 among all words, under the constraint that the previous word must be w_1. For example, if the word "*much*" is seen 500 times in a corpus, in which it is followed by "*bigger*" 30 times, then $P(bigger|much) = \frac{30}{500} = 0.06$. Intuitively, the number of bigrams $w_1 w_2$ in a corpus can be much smaller compared to the number of w_2 in the same corpus, given a specific w_1. In addition, the chance of the number of $w_1 w_2$ being 0 can be much higher compared to the chance that the word w_2 does not exist in the corpus. This situation is formally called **sparsity** or **sparseness**, which makes smoothing necessary. A bigram language model is more sparse than a unigram language model.

Back-off and hyper-parameters. A commonly used technique to reduce sparsity in bigram language models is **back-off**. The basic idea is to use unigram probabilities to approximate unseen bigram probabilities. Formally, when a bigram $w_1 w_2$ is sparse, the probability $P(w_2|w_1)$ can be replaced with its back-off version, namely the probability $P(w_2)$. In addition, to simultaneously consider sparse and non-sparse cases, $P(w_2|w_1)$ can be calculated by using a linear interpolation of $P(w_2|w_1)$ and $P(w_2)$:

$$P_{\text{backoff}}(w_2|w_1) = \lambda P(w_2|w_1) + (1 - \lambda)P(w_2).$$

Here λ is a weight to adjust the back-off ratio, which ranges in $[0, 1]$. When $\lambda = 1$, $P_{\text{backoff}}(w_2|w_1) = P(w_2|w_1)$. As λ decreases, an increasing portion of $P_{\text{backoff}}(w_2|w_1)$ is approximated by $P(w_2)$. This makes the estimation of the bigram probability less accurate according to MLE. On the other hand, when the bigram w_1w_2 is absent from the training corpus, but the unigram w_2 is not, the probability $P_{\text{backoff}}(w_2|w_1)$ remains non-zero.

To balance accuracy and robustness, λ can typically take a value that is close to 1, such as 0.9. λ is a part of the model. However, its value is not trained during the training process of the model, but rather fixed in advance. This type of model parameter is called a **hyper-parameter**. Its value can be set empirically – by trying out a range of different values, and choosing one that leads to the best model.

Add-α smoothing. By introducing a hyper-parameter, we can make add-one smoothing more flexible by generalising it into **add-α smoothing**, where the additional count α is a hyper-parameter. For unigram language models, we have

$$P(w) = \frac{(\#w \in D) + \alpha}{\sum_{w' \in V}((\#w' \in D) + \alpha)}.$$

The values of the hyper-parameter α can be **tuned**, or selected, empirically (see Section 2.3.2), and they can be larger than 1, or even between 0 and 1, so that a more accurate model can be derived compared with add-one smoothing. More theoretical background for add-α smoothing is discussed in Chapter 12.

Calculating the probability of a sentence. Similar to unigram language models, bigram language models calculate the probabilities of *sentences*. Given conditional probabilities $P(w_i|w_{i-1})$, the probability of a sentence $s = w_1w_2 \ldots w_n$ according to a bigram language model is

$$
\begin{aligned}
P(s) &= P(w_1w_2 \ldots w_n \langle /s \rangle | \langle s \rangle) \\
&= P(w_1|\langle s \rangle)P(w_2|w_1) \ldots P(w_n|w_{n-1})P(\langle /s \rangle|w_n).
\end{aligned}
\tag{2.8}
$$

Here a pseudo-word "$\langle s \rangle$" is added to the vocabulary for denoting the beginning of a sentence, and "$\langle /s \rangle$" for denoting the end of a sentence. With these two pseudo-words, a bigram language model can capture the probability of words starting a sentence by $P(w_1|\langle s \rangle)$ and words ending a sentence by $P(\langle /s \rangle|w_n)$.

We can show the correctness of Eq 2.8 by deriving it as follows. First, given two random events A and B, we have

$$P(B|A) = \frac{P(A, B)}{P(A)}. \tag{2.9}$$

Here $P(A, B)$ is the **joint probability** of A and B, which is the relative frequency random events that satisfy both A and B (e.g., both being after "*much*" and being "*bigger*" itself). Again we resort to Venn diagrams for reviewing the intuition. $P(A, B)$ is the area $A \cap B$ divided by the rectangle area in Figure 2.3(b). Equation 2.9 can be intuitively explained by Figure 2.3(b), where

$$P(B|A) = \frac{\text{AREA}(A \cap B)}{\text{AREA}(A)} = \frac{\frac{\text{AREA}(A \cap B)}{\text{AREA}(\square)}}{\frac{\text{AREA}(A)}{\text{AREA}(\square)}} = \frac{P(A, B)}{P(A)}.$$

Equation 2.9 can also be written as

$$P(A, B) = P(B|A)P(A). \tag{2.10}$$

According to Eq 2.10, the probability of our sentence can be written as

$$P(w_1 w_2 \ldots w_n \langle /s \rangle | \langle s \rangle) = P(w_1 | \langle s \rangle) P(w_2 \ldots w_n \langle /s \rangle | \langle s \rangle w_1)$$

by regarding w_1 as A and the joint event $w_2 \ldots w_n \langle /s \rangle$ as B, with "$\langle s \rangle$" as a condition.

The same can be repeated for isolating $w_2, \ldots w_n$ and $\langle /s \rangle$, resulting in

$$\begin{aligned} P(s) &= P(w_1 w_2 \ldots w_n \langle /s \rangle | \langle s \rangle) \\ &= P(w_1 | \langle s \rangle) P(w_2 | \langle s \rangle w_1) \ldots P(\langle /s \rangle | \langle s \rangle w_1 w_2 \ldots w_n). \end{aligned} \tag{2.11}$$

Equation 2.11 is called the **chain rule** of joint probabilities. *n*-gram language models can be derived from this rule by further making **independence assumptions**. For example, a bigram language model assumes that a word is dependent only on its previous word, thereby abstracting away word relations beyond two consecutive words:

$$P(w_i | \langle s \rangle w_1 \ldots w_{i-1}) = P(w_i | w_{i-1}).$$

Accordingly, Eq 2.11 can be simplified to

$$P(s) = P(\langle s \rangle) P(w_1 | \langle s \rangle) P(w_2 | w_1) \ldots P(\langle /s \rangle | w_n).$$

Independence assumptions remove the conditions $\langle s \rangle w_1 \cdots w_{i-2}$ from the probability $P(w_i | \langle s \rangle w_1 \cdots w_{i-1})$. In Figure 2.3, independence of B to A means that $P(B) = P(B|A)$, which can be intuitively understood as the fact that $\frac{\text{AREA}(B)}{\text{AREA}(\square)} = \frac{\text{AREA}(A \cap B)}{\text{AREA}(A)}$. If such probabilistic independence happens with a third event C as a condition, where we have $P(B|C) = P(B|A, C)$, we can also say that B is *conditionally independent* of A. Note that *conditional independence* here is the same as the concept of *independence* in the *i.i.d.* conditions in Eq 2.1 and Eq 2.7.

2.2.3 Trigram Language Models and Beyond

The chain rule and independence assumptions can be used to derive higher-order *n*-gram language models. For example, trigram language models are based on conditional probabilities of trigrams $P(w_i|w_{i-2}w_{i-1})$. Given a sentence $s = w_1w_2\ldots w_n$, its probability can be derived as follows

$$
\begin{aligned}
P(s) &= P(w_1w_2\ldots w_n\langle/s\rangle|\langle s\rangle\langle s\rangle) \\
&= P(w_1|\langle s\rangle\langle s\rangle)P(w_2|\langle s\rangle w_1)\ldots P(w_n|w_1w_2\ldots w_{n-1}) \\
&\quad P(\langle/s\rangle|w_1w_2\ldots w_{n-1}w_n) \quad \text{(chain rule)} \\
&= P(w_1|\langle s\rangle\langle s\rangle)P(w_2|\langle s\rangle w_1)\ldots P(w_n|w_{n-2}w_{n-1})P(\langle/s\rangle|w_{n-1}w_n).
\end{aligned}
\tag{2.12}
$$

(independence assumptions)

For a trigram model, we insert two $\langle s \rangle$ symbols at the beginning of the sentence to make the probability of the sentence beginning $P(w_1|\langle s\rangle\langle s\rangle)$ formally a trigram probability.

Parameter estimation can be done using MLE, where given D:

$$
P(w_3|w_1w_2) = \frac{(\#w_1w_2w_3 \in D)}{\sum_{w\in V}(\#w_1w_2w \in D)}.
$$

Smoothing techniques such as add-α smoothing and back-off can be used to reduce sparsity. Below we introduce two more smoothing techniques, namely Good–Turing smoothing and Kneser–Ney smoothing, which are among the most practically used smoothing techniques for n-gram language models.

Good–Turing smoothing aims to make a rational guess of the count of OOV words if a larger corpus were given containing them. Such a guess is based on observing relations between the numbers of words that occurred once, twice, three times and so on in the existing corpus. Intuitively, if the corpus shrunk, then a number of words that occur once would disappear, while a number of words that occur twice would occur only once, or disappear. Based on the observations, Good–Turing smoothing recalculates the count of each word in a projected larger corpus, so that OOV words receive non-zero counts.

Formally, denoting the number of distinct n-grams that occur r times in a corpus as N_r, the smoothed count c_r corresponding to the observed count r is calculated as

$$
c_r = (r+1)\frac{N_{r+1}}{N_r}.
$$

$(r+1)N_{r+1}$ is the total count of the n-grams that occur $(r+1)$ times in the corpus (i.e., N_{r+1} distinct n-grams, each occurring $r+1$ times), which is used to estimate the smoothed count of the n-grams that occur r times.

In particular, the counts of the unseen n-grams c_0 is estimated by reading the counts of the n-grams that only appear once. Formally, $c_0 = \frac{N_1}{N_0}$, where N_0 is the total number of unknown n-grams (i.e., possible n-grams unseen in the training corpus).

Let us take trigrams for example. Suppose that the vocabulary size is 10,000. The total number of possible trigrams are $10,000^3 = 10^{12}$. Given a corpus D that contains a million (10^6) trigrams, including 750,000 trigrams that occur once. In this case, $N_0 = 10^{12} - 10^6$, and $N_1 = 7.5 \times 10^5$. Consequently, the re-estimated count of unseen trigrams is

$$
c_0 = (0+1)\frac{7.5 \times 10^5}{10^{12} - 10^6} \approx 7.5 \times 10^{-7}.
$$

In addition, suppose that the number of trigrams that occur twice and three times in D are 2×10^5 and 9×10^4, respectively. We can similarly calculate the smoothed counts

$$c_1 = (1+1)\frac{2 \times 10^5}{7.5 \times 10^5} \approx 0.53$$

$$c_2 = (2+1)\frac{9 \times 10^4}{2 \times 10^5} \approx 1.35.$$

As can be seen, the N_0 unseen trigrams receive non-zero counts by Good–Turing smoothing, while seen trigrams in D receive discounted counts: those N_1 with count 1 in D now have smoothed counts of 0.53 instead, while those with a count of 2 in D have a smoothed count of 1.35.

Intuitively, Good-Turing smoothing gives the estimated counts of n-grams that occur r times in a corpus by reweighing a count of $r+1$ using a "count of counts" ratio (i.e., $\frac{N_{r+1}}{N_r}$). Good–Turing smoothing can be theoretically derived by modelling each *n*-gram as independently distributed (where the number of occurrences of each *n*-gram follows a binomial distribution), and calculating the expectation of *n*-gram counts conditioned on observed (i.e., empirical) counts in a corpus. A formal proof requires more details, which we leave out of our discussion.

Kneser–Ney smoothing is designed to work with back-off, which relies on the probabilities of lower-order *n*-grams for estimating those of high-order *n*-grams. For example, unigram probabilities are used in a back-off version of bigram probabilities. Kneser–Ney smoothing fixes one issue of lower-order *n*-gram probabilities as calculated by naïve relative frequency estimation, by considering the history context. Take unigrams for example. The word "*conditioning*" may not be a rare word as compared with the word "*fencing*". However, it can exist in relatively much fewer bigrams in a corpus, with "*air conditioning*" being a dominant one. In this case, we want to assign a lower unigram probability to "*conditioning*" as compared with "*fencing*".

Given a corpus D, Kneser–Ney smoothing replaces the naïve count of a unigram w, namely $\#(w \in D)$ with a new count $c_{\text{KN}}(w) = \#(\{w'' : w''w \in D\})$. The unigram probability is consequently:

$$P_{\text{KN}}(w) = \frac{c_{\text{KN}}(w)}{\sum_{w'} c_{\text{KN}}(w')}.$$

Given $P_{\text{KN}}(w), w \in V$, we can define *n*-gram probabilities $P_{\text{KN}}(w|u)$ by combining it with back-off estimation:

$$P_{\text{KN}}(w|u) = \begin{cases} P_{\text{AD}}(w|u), \text{ if } \#(u, w \in D) > 0 \\ \lambda_u \times P_{\text{KN}}(w), \text{ otherwise} \end{cases},$$

where u denotes a history context (e.g., word context for bigram probabilities and bigram context for trigram probabilities), $P_{\text{AD}}(w|u)$ denotes a relative-frequency estimation of *n*-gram probability with absolute discount, used in place of naïve relative frequency estimation, which we discuss below, and λ_u is a coefficient that ensures that $\sum_w P_{\text{KN}}(w|u) = 1$.

An empirical observation finds that the difference between the frequency count r and the smoothed frequency count c_r for seen words in Good–Turing smoothing is around 0.75. **Absolute discount smoothing** formulates this observation by subtracting a fixed discount δ ($0 < \delta < 1$) from the non-zero counts. In addition, it interpolates a lower order model similar to the back-off model. Formally, for a bigram model, the probability distribution estimated by absolute discount smoothing is given by

$$P_{AD}(w|w') = \frac{\max(\#(w'w) - \delta, 0)}{\sum_w \#(w'w)} + \lambda_w P(w), \tag{2.13}$$

where $P(w)$ is the unigram model and λ_w is a hyper-parameter to ensure that $\sum_{w''} P_{AD}(w''|w') = 1$.

Working with log probabilities. In practice, calculating $P(s)$ by a product of probabilities can cause arithmetic underflow problems in computers, since the product can be small. Instead, we can work in the *log* space, calculating $\log P(s)$. In this way, multiplications are transformed into additions. Taking the trigram language model for example, $\log P(s) = \log \left(\prod_{i=1}^{n+1} P(w_i|w_{i-2}w_{i-1}) \right) = \sum_{i=1}^{n+1} \log P(w_i|w_{i-2}w_{i-1})$. In this way, the results are more numerically stable.

High-order n-gram language models. From unigram language models to trigram language models, we make increasingly less independence assumptions, resulting in increasingly more complex models with larger numbers of parameter instances. Compared with unigram language models, trigram language models offer a more precise description of natural language sentences. On the other hand, they are more sparse and typically require more training data to reach satisfactory performance. In practice, 4-gram and 5-gram language models have been deployed in complex NLP systems such as statistical machine translation platforms. However, n-gram language models of further higher orders have been rarely used, largely due to the issue of sparsity. The sheer number of parameter instances in the scale of $|V|^n$ also makes n-gram language models with higher n larger and slower. In contrast, neural language models, as introduced in Chapter 17, offer a nice solution to the sparsity issue, and are thus able to model infinitely long sentences without making independence assumptions.

2.2.4 Generative Models

Now let us take another look at the probability chain rule. It treats a sentence as being generated from left to right, as a sequence of random events, each depending on its predecessors. The generative process can be depicted in Figure 2.4(a), in which each circle represents a random word-drawing event, and the directed arc represents conditional dependence. In the figure, the drawing of w_1 is dependent only on $\langle s \rangle$, the drawing of w_2 depends on $\langle s \rangle$ and w_1, etc. This generative process is also called a generative story, and a probabilistic model of such a process is called a **generative model**.

n-gram language models are generative models under different independence assumptions. Unigram language models, shown in Figure 2.4(b), assume that each word is drawn independently, thereby containing a set of isolated events. They can also be compactly depicted in a *nested plate notation*, as shown in Figure 2.4(c). Bigram language models assume conditional dependence only on the previous word, which corresponds to Figure 2.4(d). Trigram language models assume that each word depends only on its two immediate predecessors, and hence correspond to Figure 2.4(e). In probability theory, independence assumptions in bigram and trigram language models are referred to as **Markov assumptions**, which assume that random events in a

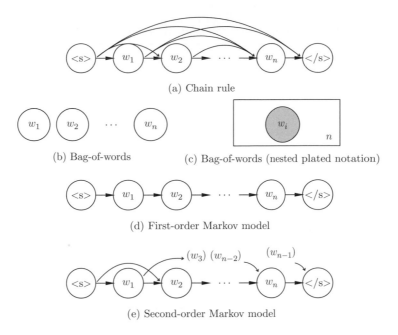

Figure 2.4 Generative models and Markov assumptions.

chain are conditionally dependent only on a finite number of predecessors. Depending on the number of conditionally dependent predecessors, bigram language models take the form of **first-order Markov chains**, and trigram language models take the form of **second-order Markov chains**.

Table 2.1 gives an intuitive contrast between unigram, bigram and trigram language models by showing some sample outputs when using them to generate scripts of Shakespeare plays, respectively. In the table, all the three language models are trained using MLE without smoothing on a collection of Shakespeare plays.[1] Sentences are generated using each language model, by simulating the generative process in Figure 2.4. At each step, a word is drawn randomly according to the corresponding n-gram probability distribution. As can be seen from the table, the outputs are closer to real Shakespeare plays as the order of the n-gram language model grows higher. In some cases, it can be difficult for the authors to tell the trigram language outputs from real Shakespeare plays! While such comparisons are only qualitative, Chapter 5 gives a quantitative method for **evaluating language models** (Section 5.2.1).

2.3   A Probabilistic Model for Text Classification

In addition to language modelling, probabilistic models based on counting relative frequencies have been applied to many other NLP tasks. This section describes a case of text classification, which includes topic classification, spam detection, sentiment classification, etc. The

---

[1] http://cs.stanford.edu/people/karpathy/char-rnn/shakespeare_input.txt

Table 2.1 Sentences generated using different n-gram language models.

Model	Samples
Unigram	*out this like there Against me you, made?* *he Cupid to thou too thee My he tricks that heart one thing* *face as not fear she on face Athens. let Good and and,* *kiss affection a PRINCE ?*
Bigram	*All my sometime like himself, –What's master.* *As much good news? tell you foolish thought.* *Can it like a man whom there but it is eaten up Lancaster* *and it, sir? Away! why* *Where is the lady of the house of York.*
Trigram	*My servant, Ariel, thy blood and made to understand you,* *hear me speak a word, Mortimer! We should have had* *such faults; makes him to this woman to bear him home.* *Those that betray them do it secretly, alone,* *and I will believe thou hast done!*

input is a piece of text, which can be as short as a sentence, or as long as a full news article. The output is a class label out of a fixed set of labels. Depending on the number of possible output class labels, text classification tasks can be further classified into **binary classification** problems, which have two possible outputs, and **multi-class classification** problems, which have three possible classes or more. An example binary classification task is tweet sarcasm detection, for which the input is a tweet, and the output includes two classes, representing whether the tweet contains sarcasm or not, respectively. An example of multi-class classification is news topic classification, for which the input is a news article and the outputs include topic classes such as "politics", "business", "world", "technology", "sports" and so forth.

2.3.1 Naïve Bayes Text Classification

Let us consider a simple model for text classification by trying to apply the probabilistic modelling techniques in the previous sections. Formally, the input of this task is a text document $d = w_1 w_2 \ldots w_n$, and the output is a class $c \in C$, where w denotes a word, n is the number of words in the text document and C is the set of all possible output calls labels. Here d can consist of one sentence or multiple sentences, and tokenisation is performed as for language models. Intuitively, a probabilistic model should be able to estimate $P(c|d)$ for all classes c given an input d, and then select the most probable class $\hat{c} = \arg\max_{c \in C} P(c|d)$ as the output. For training, one needs a corpus of documents that are manually assigned their **gold-standard** class labels $D = \{(d_i, c_i)\}|_{i=1}^{N}$, from which parameters of the probabilistic model can be estimated.

Apparently, modelling text classification as a coin-tossing problem by parameterising $P(c|d)$ directly does not work, due to sparsity of documents. We cannot estimate such conditional probabilities by counting relative frequencies. In particular, if $P(c|d)$ are directly taken as model parameters, MLE of their values has the form

$$P(c|d) = \frac{\#(d, c) \in D}{\#d \in D},$$

where $\#(d, c)$ represents the number of times the document d is assigned the gold-standard class label c in the training corpus, and $\#d$ is the number of times d occurs in the corpus. This form of estimation will result in 0s for almost all test documents d, since documents are so sparse that the chance for a given test document d to exist in a set of training data is very tiny. Parameterising $P(c|d)$ directly is essentially to ask the model to recite the set of training data, which cannot generalise to unseen documents, just as it is difficult for a language model that recites a set of known sentences to generalise to unseen sentences. Some structure is needed to allow more fine-grained parametrisation, so that the sparsity of model parameters can be significantly lower than d, and the model becomes computationally manageable.

In language modelling, we have seen a tool to this end, which is a generative story by using the *probability chain rule* and making *independence assumptions*. It can be used to break the probability of a word sequence into the product of n-gram probabilities, which are less sparse and can be parametrised directly. For our classification task, we want to break the structure of $d = w_1 w_2 \ldots w_n$ into elementary units. This, however, cannot be done directly on $P(c|d)$, which is equal to $P(c|w_1 w_2 \ldots w_n)$, because d is in the condition, rather than being the random event, which makes it difficult to apply the probability chain rule directly.

The Bayes rule. A useful tool to solve the issue is the **Bayes rule**, which states that

$$P(A|B) = \frac{P(B|A)P(A)}{P(B)}$$

for two random events A and B.

The Bayes rule can be derived from Eq 2.9 of conditional probabilities, which states that

$$P(B|A) = \frac{P(A, B)}{P(A)}.$$

From this equation, we have

$$P(A, B) = P(B|A)P(A)$$

and similarly

$$P(A, B) = P(A|B)P(B).$$

Hence $P(A, B) = P(A|B)P(B) = P(B|A)P(A)$, and therefore

$$P(A|B) = \frac{P(B|A)P(A)}{P(B)}. \tag{2.14}$$

The Bayes rule has traditionally been referred to as a **source–channel model** in NLP due to its application in signal processing, where the task is to model a source signal A, which is distorted by transmission over a noisy channel, resulting in a noisy signal B. We use a probabilistic model $P(A|B)$ to investigate the probability of the original signal A given the observation B. According to the Bayes rule, $P(A|B) = P(A)P(B|A)/P(B)$, where $P(A)$ corresponds to some prior knowledge about the source signal A, and $P(B|A)$ corresponds to a model of the noisy channel from A to B. $P(B)$ does not play a crucial role in the model since the signal B is the readily observed signal.

Defining the Naïve Bayes model for text classification. In our text-classification setting, given a document d and a candidate class c, we have

$$P(c|d) = \frac{P(d|c)P(c)}{P(d)} \tag{2.15}$$

according to the Bayes rule, where $P(c)$ represents prior knowledge about the class c, and $P(d|c)$ represents the probability of a document d given a class label c. $P(d)$ is not important in this equation, since the document d is already given, and hence the most likely class label

$$\hat{c} = \arg\max_{c \in C} \frac{P(d|c)P(c)}{P(d)} = \arg\max_{c \in C} P(d|c)P(c).$$

For a precise calculation of $P(c|d)$, we can make use of the fact that $P(c|d)$ is a probability distribution, and therefore $\sum_{c' \in C} P(c'|d) = 1$. Based on this fact, and the fact that $P(c|d) \propto P(d|c)P(c)$, we can calculate the exact value of $P(c|d)$ by normalising $P(d|c)P(c)$ over all $c' \in C$:

$$P(c|d) = \frac{P(d|c)P(c)}{\sum_{c' \in C} P(d|c')P(c')}. \tag{2.16}$$

For parameterising $P(d|c)$, the sparse document d is now a random event, which can be broken down using the probability chain rule:

$$P(d|c) = P(w_1 w_2 \ldots w_n|c) = P(w_1|c)P(w_2|w_1, c) \ldots P(w_n|w_1 \ldots w_{n-1}, c).$$

The Naïve Bayes model further assumes that the words in d are conditionally independent given the class label c, thereby resulting in

$$P(d|c) = P(w_1|c)P(w_2|c) \ldots P(w_n|c).$$

The final form of a **Naïve Bayes text classifer** is

$$P(c|d) \propto P(d|c)P(c) \approx \prod_i P(w_i|c)P(c) \tag{2.17}$$

where "naïve" refers to the strong "bag-of-words" independence assumption, and "Bayes" refers to the use of Bayes rule. The Naïve Bayes model has two parameter types, namely $P(w|c)$ and $P(c)$, respectively.

Training a Naïve Bayes classifier. Given $D = \{(d_i, c_i)\}|_{i=1}^N$, the probability $P(c)$ is typically not sparse and can be estimated using MLE:

$$P(c) = \frac{\#c \in D}{\sum_{c'} (\#c' \in D)} = \frac{\#c \in D}{|D|},$$

where $\#c \in D$ is the number of times the class label c is assigned to a document in D, and $\sum_{c'} \#c' \in D$ is equivalent to the total number of documents in the training corpus.

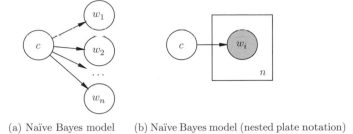

(a) Naïve Bayes model   (b) Naïve Bayes model (nested plate notation)

Figure 2.5 Generative story of Naïve Bayes models.

The values of $P(w|c)$ for each w and c pair can also be estimated using MLE:

$$P(w|c) = \frac{\#(w,c) \in D}{\sum_{w'} (\#(w',c) \in D)},$$

where $\#(w,c)$ denotes the number of times w is seen in documents with the label c in the training corpus. Similar to n-gram language models, the parameter $P(w|c)$ can be sparse for text classification, and smoothing techniques such as add-α smoothing can be used to address this issue.

A generative story for Naïve Bayes classifiers. According to Eq 2.15, a Naïve Bayes text classifier computes $P(d|c)P(c)$, which equals $P(d,c)$ (Eq 2.10). The joint probability is broken down to

$$P(d,c) = \sum_{i=1}^{n} P(w_i|c)P(c).$$

This model can be regarded as a generative model, which generates a document and its class label jointly, by first generating its class label according to $P(c)$, and then generating a bag of words for the document according to $P(w_i|c)$. This generative story can be visualised as Figure 2.5(a), and Figure 2.5(b) in nested plate notation.

Similar to language models, the values of $P(c|d)$ can be very small. As a result, it is a common practice to work with the logarithm space in Naïve Bayes text classification, calculating $\log P(c)$ and $\log P(w|c)$ as model parameters and $\log P(c|d)$ to score candidate class labels.

2.3.2 Evaluating Text Classifiers

Naïve Bayes classifiers are conceptually simple baselines for text classification. In subsequent chapters, a range of other text classification models will be introduced, which have been shown to give better performances. Now how do we know the performance of text classification models and make comparisons between them? A common approach is to split a manually annotated corpus, using a small portion as a **test set**, and the remaining as the training set. A model is trained on the training set and then used to predict the label of each document in the test set. The predicted labels are then compared with the gold-standard labels, and the ratio between correctly labelled documents and all test documents is used as a metric to evaluate the performance of the classification model. This ratio is called the **accuracy**, which is a basic **evaluation metric** for classification tasks.

When there are hyper-parameters such as α in add-α smoothing, a **development set** should be further separated from the training set for deciding their optimal values. In particular, models can be trained using different hyper-parameter values, and tested on the development set. The model that gives the best accuracies is chosen as the final model. Note that the values of hyper-parameters cannot be tuned on the test set, which is used to estimate the performance of a final model on *unseen* data. Hence a test set should be used only once as a final measure of accuracies, as if it were unseen data. In other words, the development set is used for model selection, and the test set is used only for model assessment.

2.3.3 Calculating Marginal Probabilities

Marginal probabilities are another important concept that we use frequently in this book, and which we review in this section. A comparison between Eq 2.15 and Eq 2.16 suggests that

$$P(d) = \sum_{c' \in C} P(d|c')P(c') = \sum_{c' \in C} P(d, c'), \tag{2.18}$$

which represents the relationship between a joint probability $P(d, c')$ and a **marginal probability** $P(d)$. Here a marginal probability represents the probability of a subset of a random event in a joint probability distribution. With respect to the distribution $P(d, c')$, for example, both $P(d)$ and $P(c')$ are marginal probabilities.

The equation $P(d) = \sum_{c' \in C} P(d, c')$ can be interpreted as follows: given a joint probability distribution $P(d, c')$, the marginal probability $P(d)$ can be calculated by summing up the probability $P(d, c')$ for all possible outcomes of the random event $c' \in C$. Such summation is also referred to as **marginalisation**, where the random event $c' \in C$ is marginalised out. Venn diagrams provide intuition on marginalisation also. Consider again Figure 2.3(b) for example, where two random variables A and B are illustrated, each having two possible values. Here we can view the rectangle area as consisting of both possible outcomes of a random event A, with the area A representing A happening and the remaining area $\bar{A}$ representing A not happening. According to this split, the area B can be divided into a sub area $A \cap B$ and a sub area $\bar{A} \cap B$, where

$$\text{AREA}(B) = \text{AREA}(A \cap B) + \text{AREA}(\bar{A} \cap B),$$

which corresponds to the fact that

$$P(B) = P(A, B) + P(\bar{A}, B).$$

2.3.4 Features

As mentioned earlier, a Naïve Bayes text classifier consists of two types of parameters, one being the prior probability of classes $P(c)$ and the other being the conditional probability of a word w given a class c, $P(w|c)$. The number of parameter instances can be large, in the scale of $|C| + |V| \times |C|$, where $|V|$ is the vocabulary size and $|C|$ denotes the number of classes.

In NLP, the patterns that are used to parameterise a model, such as a word, a word bigram and a word–class pair, are typically referred to as **features**. Our unigram language model, bigram language model and trigram language model each has only one type of feature (i.e., $P(w)$, $P(w_2|w_1)$ and $P(w_3|w_1 w_2)$, respectively), and the Naïve Bayes classifier has two types of features (i.e., $P(c)$ and $P(w|c)$). Intuitively, the more features we have, the better we can potentially model an NLP task, since we can obtain more evidence for making a correct prediction. On the other hand, all the models above achieve parameterisation by making a generative story through the use of the probability chain rule, independence assumptions and the Bayes rule, which can limit the use of features. As shown in Figure 2.5, one characteristic of such generative models is that each feature is generated only once in the process, and therefore no **overlapping features** can be defined. Here overlapping features refer to those features that involve the same variables. For example, given a sentence $W_{1:n} = w_1 w_2 \ldots w_n$, unigrams $P(w_i)$, bigrams $P(w_i|w_{i-1})$ and trigrams $P(w_i|w_{i-2} w_{i-1})$ arc overlapping features for each word w_i ($i \in [1, \ldots, n]$). We cannot in principle define a generative story that accommodates both bigram and trigram features,[2] since each word can only be generated once. The following chapters describe methods that avoid this issue.

Summary

In this chapter we have learned:

- probabilistic modelling and parametrisation techniques;
- maximum likelihood estimation;
- n-gram language models;
- Naïve Bayes models for text classification.

Chapter Notes

The concepts of n-grams and the derivation of their probabilities using Markov assumptions were proposed by Markov (1913). The use of n-grams to model English sentences was popularised by Shannon (1948). Gale and Church (1994) gave a survey of add-one smoothing algorithms. Church and Gale (1991) applied Good–Turing smoothing to language modelling, and Chen and Goodman (1996) proposed a widely used version of Kneser–Ney smoothing algorithm for language modelling. Back-off was used for reducing sparsity in language models by Katz (1987).

Maron and Kuhns (1960) introduced Naïve Bayes. Yang and Liu (1999) and Sahami (1996) investigated text classification based on Naïve Bayes. Domingos and Pazzani (1997) and Ng and Jordan (2002) discussed the characteristics of Naïve Bayes.

---

[2] This can be achieved by back-off, though, which is mainly a way to better estimate a sparse probability value. It thus can be regarded as an **engineering trick** outside a main generative model.

Exercises

2.1 Derive a maximum likelihood estimator for casting a dice.

2.2 Explain the difference between parameter types and parameter instances.

2.3 Which of the following are n-grams from the sentence *"Tim bought a book for $1."*?

- Tim bought
- bought a
- a book for
- for $1.

- Tim a for
- Tim
- Tim bought book
- book a

2.4 Given three sentences *"all models are wrong"*, *"a model is wrong"* and *"some models are useful"*, and a vocabulary $V = \{\langle s \rangle, \langle /s \rangle, a, all, are, model, models, some, useful, wrong\}$.

(a) Calculate the probabilities of all bigrams without smoothing.
(b) Calculate the probabilities of all bigrams and the unseen bigram *"a models"* with add-one smoothing.
(c) Calculate the probabilities of all bigrams and the unseen bigram *"a models"* with add-α smoothing. Try $\alpha = 0.05$ and $\alpha = 0.15$.
(d) Calculate the probabilities of all bigrams and the unseen bigram *"a models"* with back-off. Try $\lambda = 0.95$ and $\lambda = 0.75$.

2.5 As shown in Section 2.2.3, Good–Turing smoothing reallocates the probability mass of the rich n-grams to the poor n-grams.

(a) Given a corpus D, suppose that we treat all the unknown unigrams as $\langle \text{UNK} \rangle$, thus the vocabulary is $\{w : w \in D\} \cup \{\langle \text{UNK} \rangle\}$ and $N_0 = 1$. Calculate r, N_r for all the unigrams in Exercise 2.4.
(b) For $r < 3$, calculate c_r and the probabilities of all the unigrams.
(c) For the maximum r value, $N_{r+1} = 0$. In this case, the probability $P(w : \#w = r)$ can still be estimated by MLE. Calculate the probability of unigrams in Exercise 2.4 which appear the most frequently, i.e., $r = 3$.
(d) Show that the sum of the probabilities of all the unigrams given in (b) and (c) is not 1. Try to normalise the probabilities.
(e) In a large corpus, N_r can be zeros for large r values. This can be problematic, leading the estimation values c_{r-1} to be zeros. One way to solve this problem is to use a smoothed line to approximately fit the known N_r value distribution. Suppose that we change the second example sentence in Exercise 2.4 to be *"a model is wrong wrong wrong wrong"* so that $N_4 = 0$ but $N_5 = 1$. Guess a good smoothed value of N_4. Use the approximated value of N_4 and the original N_r value of the other frequency counts to calculate the probabilities of all the unigrams.

2.6 Recall Kneser–Ney smoothing discussed in Section 2.2.3.

(a) Derive the formula of λ_u for absolute discount smoothing and Kneser–Ney smoothing.
(b) Give absolute discounting values of all the bigrams in Exercise 2.4 and the unseen bigram "*a models*" when $\delta = 0.75$.
(c) Give Kneser–Ney smoothed values of all the bigrams in Exercise 2.4 and the unseen bigram "*a models*" when $\delta = 0.75$.

2.7 True or False

(a) If B is independent of A, then A is also independent of B. (If $P(B) = P(B|A)$ then $P(A) = P(A|B)$).
(b) If B is independent of A, then B is also conditionally independent of A. (If $P(B|A) = P(B)$ then $P(B|A, C) = P(B|C)$).
(c) $P(B|A)P(A) = P(A|B)P(B)$.
(d) $P(A, B, C) = P(A|B, C)P(B|A, C)P(C|A, B)$.
(e) $P(A, B, C) = P(A)P(B)P(C)$ under *i.i.d.* assumption.

2.8 What are the differences between hyper-parameters and parameters?

2.9 Hyper-parameters are tuned over_____.
(a) training data (b) development data (c) test data.

2.10 The term "Naïve" in Naïve Bayes classification refers to the *i.i.d.* assumption. Extend the Naïve Bayes classifier using the concept of bigram language modelling. The new model loses the "Naïve" attribute. Can you integrate bag-of-word features into this model by leveraging smoothing techniques?

2.11 Which of the following feature sets contain overlapping features?

(a) Bag-of-words and bag-of-bigrams for document modelling.
(b) Full word, prefix and suffix for word modelling.
(c) A class label and a bag of words for document modelling.
(d) The first letter of a word, and a binary feature indicating whether the word is capitalised.
(e) Number of words in a document, and bag of words.
(f) Word–class pairs and bag of words for document classification.

3 Feature Vectors

The Naïve Bayes model is a simple yet highly effective text classifier. It works by using the probability of text classes $P(c)$ and the probability of individual words given a class $P(w|c)$ as the only feature types. Intuitively, words themselves can tell much about text classes. For example, the words "*goal*", "*club*", "*fans*" and "*tournament*" strongly indicate sports topics, while the words "*stock*", "*earning*", "*CEO*" and "*loan*" suggest financial topics. Hence each word can serve as a unique scale, against which a document is weighted with respect to a unique aspect of meaning. Each document is understood from many different viewpoints, each corresponding to a specific word.

The observation leads to a **vector space model** of texts, which maps documents into points in a high-dimensional **feature vector** space, with each coordinate representing the importance of a specific word to the document. Using the resulting vector space representation of documents, we can intuitively tell the similarity between documents by measuring their distances in the vector space. In addition, classification can be performed in a vector space by finding hyperplanes that separate points representing different classes of documents. Further, the coordinates of such vector spaces can be generalised from bag-of-words to arbitrary features, which do not necessarily obey probability independence. Hence, feature vector models are remarkable in NLP in that they map *unstructured texts* into *structures* in the mathematical domain, over which statistical computation is feasible.

3.1 Modelling Documents in Vector Spaces

Let us consider the representation of a document in a vector space, where each coordinate represents a word. Suppose that the vocabulary is $V = \{w_1, w_2, \ldots, w_{|V|}\}$, where each vocabulary word has a unique index. For example, we can have $w_1 = $ "*a*", $w_{1001} = $ "*book*" and $w_{2017} = $ "*bought*". The ordering of vocabulary words is not important as long as there is a one-to-one mapping between vocabulary words and indices. We are interested in mapping text documents into points in a $|V|$-dimensional vector space, where each dimension corresponds to a word w_i in the vocabulary.

Given a document d, its vector representation takes the form

$$\vec{v}(d) = \langle f_1, f_2, \ldots, f_{|V|} \rangle, \tag{3.1}$$

where f_i shows the importance of the vocabulary word w_i to the document. A simplest way to define f_i is to use the count of the vocabulary word w_i in the document, since intuitively more important words are mentioned more frequently. Hence $f_i = \#w_i$ and $\vec{v}(d) = \langle \#w_1, \#w_2, \ldots, \#w_{|V|} \rangle$.

Table 3.1 Vector representations of documents.

Features	d_1	d_2	d_3	d_4	d_1	d_2	d_3	d_4
$w_1 =$ "a"	1	1	0	2	0.415	0.415	0	0.83
$w_2 =$ "ah"	0	0	1	0	0	0	2.0	0
			...					
$w_{1001} =$ "$book$"	1	1	0	1	0.415	0.415	0	0.415
$w_{2017} =$ "$bought$"	1	0	0	0	2.0	0	0	0
$w_{2100} =$ "boy"	0	0	0	1	0	0	0	2.0
$w_{3400} =$ "I"	0	0	1	1	0	0	1.0	1.0
$w_{4400} =$ "is"	0	1	0	0	0	2.0	0	0
			...					
$w_{5002} =$ "$know$"	0	0	1	0	0	0	2.0	0
$w_{6013} =$ "$reading$"	0	1	0	1	0	1.0	0	1.0
$w_{7034} =$ "saw"	0	0	0	1	0	0	0	2.0
$w_{8400} =$ "Tim"	1	1	1	0	0.415	0.415	0.415	0
			...					
$w_{13200} =$ ","	0	0	1	0	0	0	2.0	0
$w_{13201} =$ "."	1	0	1	0	1.0	0	1.0	0
			...					
(a) count-based vectors				(b) TF-IDF vectors (loga-rithms are to the base 2)				

Table 3.2 Common stop words in English.

a	the	on	of	with	about	and	in	at	to	"	,	?	oh	.

Using this method, the vector representation of the sentence "*Tim bought a book.*" can be $\langle f_1 = 1, 0, 0, \ldots, 0, 0, f_{1001} = 1, 0, \ldots, 0, f_{2017} = 1, 0, 0, \ldots, 0, f_{8400} = 1, 0, \ldots, f_{13201} = 1, \ldots, 0 \rangle$, which is $|V|$-dimensional with the only non-zero elements appearing in the indices for "*Tim*", "*bought*", "*a*", "*book*" and ".", respectively, as shown in column d_1 of Table 3.1(a). Similarly, the vector representations of "*Tim is reading a book*", "*ah, I know Tim.*" and "*I saw a boy reading a book*" are shown in d_2, d_3 and d_4 in Table 3.1(a), respectively. Words not shown in the table have 0 values in all the three examples. Since $|V|$ can be very large, such vector representations can be high-dimensional sparse vectors, with most elements being zeros.

Intuitively, using the above vector representation, documents on different topics will reside in different locations in the vector space, with sports documents having relatively larger values on the "*goal*", "*tournament*" and "*player*" coordinates, and finance documents having relatively larger values on the "*earning*", "*CEO*" and "*stock*" coordinates. On the other hand, some high-frequency words such as "*a*", "*on*" and punctuation can occur in most documents, and therefore do not characterise any document. It is therefore unnecessary or even harmful to use them as features when representing documents. Such words are referred to as **stop words**. A list of common stop words are shown in Table 3.2. Stop words can be removed from the vocabulary when mapping documents to vectors.

TF-IDF vectors. A potential limitation of stop words is that there is no universal standard which words are stop words. In addition, for different tasks, stop words can differ. While removing stop words can be regarded as a set of *hard rules* to filter uninformative words, there is a *soft* alternative to this end, which addresses the above issues. The idea is to reduce the importance value of words that occur frequently in most documents, even if they occur frequently in the document of concern. Formally, given a set of documents D, we use **document frequency** (DF) to denote the percentage of documents that contain a certain word w_i:

$$DF(w_i) = \frac{\#\{d|d \in D, w_i \in d\}}{|D|}. \tag{3.2}$$

In d_1, d_2, d_3 and d_4 above, $DF(``a") = \frac{3}{4}$ and $DF(``saw") = \frac{1}{4}$. The larger the document frequency is, the more likely it is that a word is an uninformative high-frequency word.

In addition, we formally denote the count of a word w_i in a document d_j as its **term frequency** (TF):

$$TF(w_i, d_j) = \#w_i \in d.$$

The count-based vector representation above uses only term frequencies of vocabulary words to represent a document:

$$\vec{v}_{count}(d_j) = \langle TF(w_1, d_j), TF(w_2, d_j), \ldots, TF(w_{|V|}, d_j) \rangle,$$

where $f_i = \#w_i = TF(w_i, d_j)$ in Eq 3.1.

In contrast, document frequencies can be added to reduce the importance values of uninformative words:

$$\vec{v}_{tf\text{-}idf}(d_j) = \langle \frac{TF(w_1, d_j)}{DF(w_1)}, \frac{TF(w_2, d_j)}{DF(w_2)}, \ldots, \frac{TF(w_{|V|}, d_j)}{DF(w_{|V|})} \rangle, \tag{3.3}$$

with $f_i = \frac{TF(w_i, d_j)}{DF(w_i)}$. For example, for $d_1, f_1 = \frac{TF(w_1, d_1)}{DF(w_1)} = \frac{4}{3}$.

The term $\frac{1}{DF(w_i)}$ is commonly referred to as the **inverse document frequency** (IDF) of w_i, and Eq 3.3 is thus commonly referred to as the **TF-IDF** representation of text documents. Equation 3.3 can be rewritten in terms of TF and IDF

$$\vec{v}_{tf\text{-}idf}(d_i) = \langle TF(w_1, d_i)IDF(w_1), TF(w_2, d_i)IDF(w_2), \ldots, TF(w_n, d_i)IDF(w_n) \rangle.$$

When $|D|$ is large, the *IDF* terms can outweigh *TF* terms significantly. In order to balance the influences of *TF* and *IDF*, the *IDF* term of w_i can be defined as the logarithm of w_i's inverted document frequency

$$IDF(w_i) = \log \frac{|D|}{\#\{d|d \in D, w_i \in d\}}$$

for the same *TF-IDF* vector representation of documents.

Table 3.1(b) shows the TF-IDF vectors for the same examples as shown in Table 3.1(a).

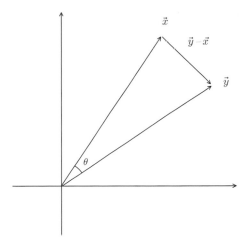

Figure 3.1 Euclidean distance and cosine similarity.

3.1.1 Clustering

The representations $\vec{v}_{count}(d)$ and $\vec{v}_{tf\text{-}idf}(d)$ can be seen as **feature vector** representations of a document d, where bag-of-word features are used. Compared to count-based vectors $\vec{v}_{count}(d)$, which contain **discrete** features, *TF-IDF* vectors $\vec{v}_{tf-idf}(d)$ consist of **real-valued** features. The process of transforming a document d into its feature vector representation $\vec{v}(d)$ is referred to as **feature extraction**. Feature vectors serve as a basis of a wide range of statistical NLP models, mapping unstructured texts and NLP structures into a vector form in the mathematical domain, which is ready for computation. This section discusses a simple example: clustering.

Vector space distances. Vector representations of documents can be used to calculate their semantic similarities, which are represented by their distances in the vector space. There are multiple ways to measure vector distances. As shown in Figure 3.1, the **Euclidean distance** between two points $\vec{x} = \langle x_1, x_2, \ldots, x_n \rangle$ and $\vec{y} = \langle y_1, y_2, \ldots, y_n \rangle$ in a vector space is defined as:

$$\text{dis}^{eu}(\vec{x}, \vec{y}) = ||\vec{y} - \vec{x}|| = \sqrt{(x_1 - y_1)^2 + (x_2 - y_2)^2 + \cdots + (x_n - y_n)^2}.$$

We can alternatively use the **cosine similarity** between two documents to measure their similarity, which is defined as

$$\cos(\vec{x}, \vec{y}) = \frac{\vec{x} \cdot \vec{y}}{|\vec{x}||\vec{y}|}$$

$$= \frac{x_1 y_1 + x_2 y_2 + \cdots + x_n y_n}{\sqrt{x_1^2 + x_2^2 + \cdots + x_n^2}\sqrt{y_1^2 + y_2^2 + \cdots + y_n^2}}.$$

The **cosine distance** between two documents is defined using cosine similarity:

$$\text{dis}^{\cos}(\vec{x}, \vec{y}) = 1 - \cos(\vec{x}, \vec{y}).$$

As shown in Figure 3.1, intuitively, given two vectors $\vec{x}$ and $\vec{y}$, the Euclidean distance measures the length of their difference $|\vec{y} - \vec{x}|$, and the cosine distance measures the size of the angle θ

between them, without considering their lengths. Intuitively, vector similarity can be measured by the **inner product** (i.e., dot product) $\vec{x}{\cdot}\vec{y} = \sum_i x_i y_i = |\vec{x}||\vec{y}|\cos(\vec{x}, \vec{y})$. When $\vec{x}$ and $\vec{y}$ are **orthogonal**, $\cos(\vec{x}, \vec{y}) = 0$ and thus $\vec{x} \cdot \vec{y} = 0$. The cosine distance measure normalises $\vec{x} \cdot \vec{y}$ using the sizes ($|\vec{x}|$ and $|\vec{y}|$) of the vectors $\vec{x}$ and $\vec{y}$. Therefore, if d_2 contains two duplicates of d_1, the cosine similarity between d_2 and d_1 is 1, the same as $\cos(d_1, d_1)$.

The choice between distance measures is typically empirical given a vector space and task. For the remainder of this chapter, we use the Euclidean distance as the metric. A measure of distance in vector space allows **clustering**, which is to find groups of vectors that are relatively close to each other.

3.1.2 k-Means Clustering

There are many different clustering algorithms, which vary in their prerequisites, output assumptions, grouping criteria and time complexities. A simple example is **k-means**, which iteratively assigns points to clusters based on their distances to the cluster centroids.

Pseudocode of k-means is shown in Algorithm 3.1. The input is a set of points $\vec{v}_1, \vec{v}_2, \ldots, \vec{v}_M$ in a vector space. For the output, the number of clusters k must be pre-specified. The algorithm begins by randomly selecting k points from the input as cluster centroids. At each iteration, it assigns each input point to the cluster whose centroid is the closest to the point among all cluster centroids. After all points have been assigned a cluster, the set of cluster centroids are calculated again from scratch, by averaging all the points in each cluster. With the new centroids, cluster assignments

---

Algorithm 3.1. k-means.

Inputs: $\vec{V} = \{\vec{v}_1, \vec{v}_2, \ldots, \vec{v}_M\}, K$;
Initialization: $clusters = [], centroids = []$
for $j \in [1, \ldots, K]$ **do**
    $clusters.\text{APPEND}([])$;
    $n \leftarrow \text{RANDOM}(i \in [1, \ldots, M] \text{ and } \vec{v}_i \notin centroids)]$;
    $centroids.\text{APPEND}(\vec{v}_n)$;
repeat
    $clusters\_old \leftarrow clusters$;
    ▷ assign points to clusters
    for $i \in [1, \ldots, M]$ **do**
        $j' \leftarrow \arg\min_j \text{DIST}(\vec{v}_i, centroids[j])$;
        $clusters[j'].\text{APPEND}(\vec{v}_i)$;
    ▷ calculate centroids
    for $j \in [1, \ldots, K]$ **do**
        $centroids[j] \leftarrow \text{AVERAGE}(clusters[j])$;
until $clusters = clusters\_old$;
Outputs: $clusters$;

---

can be done afresh in a subsequent iteration. The same process repeats until the cluster contents stabilise, and the final clusters are returned as outputs.

Intuitively, if we know the correct cluster centroids, we can assign points to a cluster by measuring their distances to all the centroids. In the reverse direction, if we know all the cluster contents, we can easily calculate their centroids. However, neither condition is known initially. k-means works by randomly selecting some centroids, and then relying only on the iterative process for converging to a reasonable set of cluster contents. The initial condition can have an influence on the resulting cluster contents. Chapter 6 gives more theoretical background behind such iterative algorithms.

Given the TF-IDF vectors d_1, d_2, d_3 and d_4 in Table 3.1 (b), 2-means clustering groups three sentences "*Tim bought a book.*", "*Tim is reading a book*" and "*I saw a boy reading a book*" as a cluster and the sentence "*ah, I know Tim.*" itself as another cluster. The first cluster mainly talks about "*book reading*" while the second cluster mentions acquaintance of "*Tim*". Similarly, 3-means clustering generates three clusters, with the sentences "*Tim bought a book.*" and "*Tim is reading a book*" being the first cluster, the sentence "*ah, I know Tim.*" being the second cluster and the sentence "*I saw a boy reading a book*" being the third cluster. The first cluster includes information about "*Tim*" and "*book*", the second cluster describes the relationship between "*I*" and "*Tim*" and the third cluster is related to "*a boy*".

3.1.3 Classification

Document clustering methods are **unsupervised learning** approaches in the sense that they do not require manually labelled gold-standard training data. In contrast, the Naïve Bayes classifier is a **supervised** method, which requires training data with gold-standard class labels. Compared with supervised learning methods, unsupervised methods are less costly by saving manual labour. However, they can be limited by fully relying on patterns from the data.

Let us take the contrast between clustering and classification as an example. Suppose that someone's emails consist of two major topics, one being work-related and the other being leisure. Within each category, there are some emails related to travelling. It is difficult to tell whether a 2-means clustering algorithm will automatically cluster the emails into work/leisure, travel/non-travel or neither of the two, since we do not know the most salient distribution of the document vectors given all their words. Intuitively, different features play different roles for different classification problems. If we want to classify the emails into travel and non-travel, then the words "*booking*", "*reservation*" and "*flight*" might have high importance. Likewise, if we want to classify the emails into work/leisure, then specific words that occur only in work and leisure emails becomes important instead. In this case, if common destinations of business travel include Amsterdam, London and Singapore, while common destinations for leisure include Bali, Bangkok and Auckland, a classifier might learn that the words "*Amsterdam*", "*London*" and "*Singapore*" indicate work, while the words "*Bali*", "*Bangkok*" and "*Auckland*" indicate leisure.

It is difficult for a document clustering algorithm to make the fine-grained distinctions above, because the only information sources available come from the training documents themselves. All words have equal importance in a document vector. In contrast, supervised learning methods such

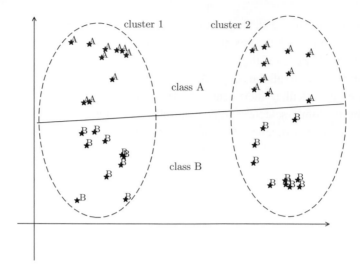

Figure 3.2 Clustering vs classification.

as Naïve Bayes are able to pick up the important words for a specific classification task, thanks to the availability of gold-standard class labels. In the above example, the model can tell the difference between city names in different document types. In particular, Naïve Bayes can weight the same words for different classes using $P(w|c)$. Hence, relative frequencies are calculated beyond general counts and *TF-IDF* values, with counting being performed based on each individual class label.

Such a contrast between clustering and classification can be demonstrated by Figure 3.2. In this example, the points are generally located in two big clusters. In each cluster, there are some points that belong to class A, with the rest belonging to class B. A clustering algorithm can find a separation between the two main clusters. However, it is difficult for a clustering algorithm to separate class-A and class-B points based solely on vector space distances. In contrast, if the points are manually labelled A or B, we can build a model to cut the vector space into two subspaces, with one containing only class A points and the other containing only class B points. This is the basic setting for training a classifier given gold-standard data, with the space separation being defined by the model parameters. For testing, if an unseen input point resides in the class A subspace, it is assigned the class label A; otherwise it is assigned the class label B.

Given a document vector space and a set of labelled points, if a **hyperplane** separation boundary can be found, these training examples are **linearly separable**. Here a hyperplane is a linear shape in high-dimensional vector spaces, generalised from *lines* in two-dimensional spaces and *planes* in three-dimensional spaces. A linear classification model learns to separate training examples using hyperplanes. Linear models have been the most common models in discrete statistical NLP, with a desirable balance between accuracy and complexity. This section introduces two commonly used linear models, namely support vector machines and the perceptron algorithm.

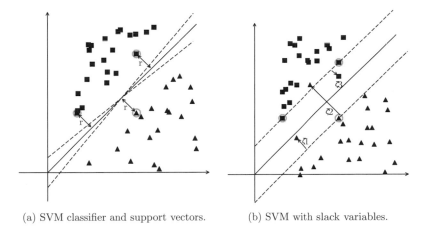

(a) SVM classifier and support vectors.   (b) SVM with slack variables.

Figure 3.3 Support vector machine. (■: class + ▲: class −)

3.1.4 Support Vector Machine

A **support vector machine** (SVM) is a linear model for binary classification, given input representations in a vector space. As shown in Figure 3.3(a), given a set of training examples with two class labels + and −, respectively, an SVM finds a hyperplane that best separates the two classes of training examples, by maximising the distance between the hyperplane and the training examples that are the closest to it. The points that are the closest to the separating hyperplane are called the **support vectors**, and their distances to the hyperplane reflect **margins** of separation. As a result, SVMs are **maximum margin** models by maximising the separation margin. Intuitively, there are an infinite number of separating hyperplanes if the training examples are linearly separable. Choosing the max-margin separation allows the thc largest degree of generalisability to unseen test data in vector spaces.

Formally, denote the set of training examples as $\{(x_i, y_i)\}|_{i=1}^{N}$, where $i \in [1, \ldots, N]$, x_i is an input such as a text document, and y_i is a gold-standard class label in $\{+1, -1\}$, where $+1$ corresponds to class label + and -1 to class label −. For notational convenience, an input x_i with $y_i = +1$ is also denoted with x_i^+. Similarly, an input x_i with $y_i = -1$ is denoted as x_i^-. Each x_i is mapped into the vector space by calculating a feature vector representation $\vec{v}(x_i)$, such as the count-based representation $\vec{v}_{count}$ and the *TF-IDF* representation $\vec{v}_{tf\text{-}idf}$ discussed earlier.

Defining the hyperplane. The model parameters of SVMs represent hyperplanes, which are mathematically described by $\vec{\omega}^T \vec{v} + b = 0$. Here $\vec{\omega}$ is a *normal vector* of the hyperplane $\vec{\omega}^T \vec{v} + b = 0$ in vector space, which is perpendicular to the hyperplane. $\vec{v}$ represents a vector variable. The model parameters are the pair $(\vec{\omega}, b)$. We want x_i^+ to be on the positive side of the hyperplane, with $\vec{\omega}^T \vec{v}(x_i^+) + b > 0$, and x_i^- to be on the negative side of the hyperplance with $\vec{\omega}^T \vec{v}(x_i^-) + b < 0$.

Note that there is an infinite number of $(\vec{\omega}, b)$ pairs that describe the same hyperplane, since given any $(\vec{\omega}, b)$ such that $\vec{\omega}^T \vec{v} + b = 0$ for all points v in a hyperplane, we have $(\alpha \vec{\omega}, \alpha b)$ that satisfies $\alpha \vec{\omega}^T \vec{v} + \alpha b = 0$ for all $\alpha \neq 0$. As a result, it is necessary to choose one unique pair $(\vec{\omega}, b)$

as the set of model parameters. SVM chooses the scale according to a given set of training data, requiring that $|\vec{\omega}^T \vec{v}(x_s) + b| = 1$ for all support vectors $\vec{v}(x_s)$, which makes the training objective easier to optimise.

Now given a training example $\vec{v}(x_i)$, its distance to the separating hyperplane is (see Exercise 3.5 for a proof)

$$r = \frac{|\vec{\omega}^T \vec{v}(x_i) + b|}{||\vec{\omega}||}.$$

Further, given our requirement earlier that for all support vectors $\vec{v}(x_s)$, $|\vec{\omega}^T \vec{v}(x_s) + b| = 1$, the distance between $\vec{v}(x_s)$ and the separating hyperplane is:

$$r = \frac{1}{||\vec{\omega}||}.$$

Finding the hyperplane. As the hyperplane changes, this distance r will change accordingly. The goal of SVM training is to find among all separating hyperplanes the one that has the maximum margin, where the **margin** is formally defined as $2r$, considering both x_s^+ and x_s^-. This translates to finding a hyperplane $\vec{\omega}^T \vec{v} + b = 0$ that maximises $2r = \frac{2}{||\vec{\omega}||}$ for the support vectors $\vec{v}(x_s)$, which is equivalent to minimising $\frac{1}{2}||\vec{\omega}||^2$, under the condition that x^+ and x^- reside on different sides of the hyperplane (i.e., a *separation* hyperplane). In addition, since for all x, $r(x) = \frac{|\vec{\omega}^T \vec{v}(x) + b|}{||\vec{\omega}||} \geq r(x_s) = \frac{|\vec{\omega}^T \vec{v}(x_s) + b|}{||\vec{\omega}||} = \frac{1}{||\vec{\omega}||}$, we have $|\vec{\omega}^T \vec{v}(x) + b| \geq 1$ for all x if the hyperplane separates x^+ and x^-. Thus we can assume that $\vec{\omega}^T \vec{v}(x^+) + b \geq 1$ and $\vec{\omega}^T \vec{v}(x^-) + b \leq -1$ for all separating hyperplanes. These two cases can be generalised to $y(\vec{\omega}^T \vec{v}(x) + b) \geq 1$.

As a result, the full training objective is a constrained optimisation task, which is to find a hyperplane $(\hat{\vec{\omega}}, \hat{b})$ that maximises $2r$:

$$(\hat{\vec{\omega}}, \hat{b}) = \underset{(\vec{\omega}, b)}{\arg\min} \frac{1}{2}||\vec{\omega}||^2,$$

$$\text{such that } y_i \left(\vec{\omega}^T \vec{v}(x_i) + b \right) \geq 1, \text{ for all } (x_i, y_i) \in D. \tag{3.4}$$

The above training objective is a constrained convex quadratic programming task, and can be solved using numerical methods. We will introduce a general optimisation framework in Chapter 4, which is used to train SVM and most other models of this book.[1]

Test scenario. At test time, classification is performed by checking which side of the separating hyperplane the vector representation of an input x is. If $\vec{\omega}^T \vec{v}(x) + b > 0$, then x is on the side of x^+, and hence should be assigned the class label $+1$; otherwise it is assigned the class label -1.

---

[1] A traditional solution for SVM training is called sequential minimal optimisation (SMO), which is a *coordinate descent* method for numerical optimisation (see Section 6.3 for a specific example of coordinate descent).

Algorithm 3.2. The perceptron training algorithm.

Input: $D = \{(x_l, y_l)\}|_{i=1}^N, y_i \in \{-1, +1\}$

Initialization: $\vec{\omega} \leftarrow \vec{0}; b \leftarrow 0; t \leftarrow 0$

repeat

    for $i \in [1, \ldots, N]$ **do**

        $z_i \leftarrow \text{SIGN}(\vec{\omega}^T \vec{v}(x_i) + b);$

        if $z_i \neq y_i$ **then**

            $\vec{\omega} \leftarrow \vec{\omega} + \vec{v}(x_i) \times y_i;$

            $b \leftarrow b + y_i;$

    $t \leftarrow t + 1;$

until $t = T;$

3.1.5 Perceptron

The **perceptron** is another linear model for classification. Its test scenarios are the same as those of SVMs: given a set of inputs x and a feature mapping function $\vec{v}(x)$, a set of model parameters $(\vec{\omega}, b)$ is used to classify x into $+1$ or -1 according to whether $\vec{\omega}^T \vec{v}(x) + b$ is positive or negative, respectively. For brevity, denote the output class label $z = \text{SIGN}(\vec{\omega}^T \vec{v}(x) + b)$, where $z \in \{-1, +1\}$ and SIGN returns the sign of a number.

Given a set of training examples $\{(x_i, y_i)\}$, where $i \in [1, \ldots, n], y_i \in \{-1, +1\}$, the perceptron algorithm learns the model parameters $(\vec{\omega}, b)$ incrementally, by initialising $\vec{\omega}$ and b to all zeros and iterating over the set of training examples multiple times, using the current model parameters to predict the class label of each input x_i. The model parameters are corrected at each iteration according to z_i and y_i, if the output z_i is different from the gold-standard label y_i.

Pseudocode of the algorithm is shown in Algorithm 3.2, where t represents the current iteration number, i represents the index of the current training example and T represents the total **number of training iterations**. At each iteration, the model output z_i is compared to the gold-standard label y_i. If the output is correct, the algorithm moves on to the next training example without updating the model. However, if the output z_i is incorrect, the model parameters are updated according to the gold-standard class label y_i. If $y_i = +1$, the model parameter $\vec{\omega}$ is updated by adding the feature vector $\vec{v}(x_i^+)$ to its current value, and the model parameter b is updated by adding 1 to its current value; if $y_i = -1$, the model parameter w is updated by subtracting the feature vector $\vec{v}(x_i^-)$ from its current value, and b is updated by subtracting 1 from its current value.

Intuitively, the perceptron update adjusts the model parameters $(\vec{\omega}, b)$ in the direction of correcting its own prediction errors. The vector space interpretation can be shown in Figure 3.4. Suppose that the correct training example $\vec{v}(x_i^+)$ falls on the wrong side of the hyperplane $\vec{\omega}^T \vec{v}(x) + b = 0$, scoring $\vec{\omega}^T \vec{v}(x_i^+) + b < 0$. The perceptron update changes the normal vector $\vec{\omega}$ of the hyperplane towards $\vec{v}(x_i^+)$, thereby tilting the hyperplane towards below $\vec{v}(x_i^+)$. It also changes b by 1, moving the hyperplane towards $-\infty$ on both coordinates. The resulting hyperplane thus likely has $\vec{v}(x_i^+)$ on the correct side. The update can also be understood

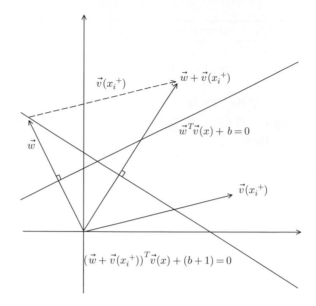

Figure 3.4 Perceptron update.

numerically. Suppose that given a model $(\vec{\omega}, b)$, the current instance x_i^+ has $\vec{\omega}^T x_i^+ + b < 0$. The new model becomes $(\vec{\omega} + \vec{v}^T x_i^+, b + 1)$ after the update, and the new value of z_i is the SIGN: $(\vec{\omega} + \vec{v}(x_i^+))^T \vec{v}(x_i^+) + b + 1 = (\vec{\omega}^T \vec{v}(x_i^+) + b) + (\vec{v}(x_i^+))^2 + 1$, which is strictly larger than the old value $\vec{\omega}^T v(x_i^+) + b$. Thus x_i^+ will be more likely on the positive side of the new hyperplane.

The number of training iterations T for the perceptron algorithm is a hyper-parameter, which can be adjusted over a set of development test data. For example, we can train a perceptron algorithm for a large number of training iterations (e.g., 100), using the resulting model after each training iteration to label a set of development test data, measuring the classification accuracies. Among all these models, the one that gives the highest development test accuracy is selected as the final model.

Similar to SVMs, the perceptron algorithm can also be seen as a linear max-margin model, which learns a separating hyperplane between two classes of training examples. It can be proved theoretically that the perceptron algorithm can find a value for $(\vec{\omega}, b)$ such that $y_i = $ SIGN$\left(\vec{\omega}^T \vec{v}(x_i) + b \right)$ for all training examples (x_i, y_i), if the training data are linearly separable. In other words, the perceptron algorithm can find a separating hyperplane that differentiates x^+ and x^- with 100% accuracy. We will see more connections between the perceptron model and SVM in the next chapter.

Online learning and batch learning. SVM is called **batch learning**, optimising a training objective over a full set of training dataset D. In constrast, the perceptron updates its parameters incrementally for each training example. This style of training is called **online learning**.

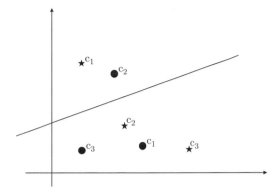

Figure 3.5 Multi-class classification. ($\star$ and $\bullet$ are two documents, c_1, c_2 and c_3 are three class labels. The gold label for $\star$ is c_1 and the gold label for $\bullet$ is c_2).

3.2   Multi-Class Classification

The previous section focuses on binary classification tasks, for which one single hyperplane is sufficient for separating different documents in vector space. For multi-class classification with more than two output classes, however, more than one hyperplane is needed to divide a vector space. To this end, one naïve solution is **one-vs-rest**, which is to train n two-way classifiers for n-way classification, each one serving as a hyperplane to separate out a particular class of documents from the rest. Containing multiple sub-models, this method is not theoretically elegant since it is difficult to guarantee agreement between different sub-models given a test input.

A more principled solution should find a proper way to define the vector space, so that a single hyperplane can perform multi-class classification. This seemingly challenging task is feasible by working with vector spaces of *output* representations rather than *input* representations. In particular, if each point in the vector space represents an input–output pair $\vec{v}(x, c)$ rather than an input $\vec{v}(x)$, multi-class classification can be modelled as the task of separating *correct* outputs (x_i, c_i) from *incorrect* outputs (x_i, c), $(c \neq c_i)$, given a set of training examples $\{(x_i, c_i)\}$, $i \in [1, \dots, N]$. A hyperplane is sufficient to this end since there are now two main types of points again. The vector space is illustrated in Figure 3.5, where each input document now corresponds to $|C|$ vectors rather than one, where C denotes the set of class labels. For each input document, there is only one correct class label among the $|C|$ labels, and the corresponding feature vector should be on the positive side of the separating hyperplane of the model. The remaining $|C| - 1$ feature vectors are on the negative side.

3.2.1   Defining Output-Based Features

A common way to extend an input-based feature vector $\vec{v}(x)$ to an output-based feature vector $\vec{v}(x, c)$ is to make a Cartesian product between $\vec{v}(x)$ and c. Take count-based $\vec{v}(d)$ for example, the resulting output-based $\vec{v}(d, c)$ has the form:

$$\vec{v}(d,c) = \langle \#w_1c_1, \#w_2c_1, \ldots, \#w_{|V|}c_1,$$
$$\#w_1c_2, \#w_2c_2, \ldots, \#w_{|V|}c_2,$$
$$\ldots \tag{3.5}$$
$$\#w_1c_{|C|}, \#w_2c_{|C|}, \ldots, \#w_{|V|}c_{|C|} \rangle,$$

where $\#wc$ represents the number of times w occurs in d, which has a class label c.

$\vec{v}(x,c)$ can be regarded as duplicating $\vec{v}(x)$ by $|C|$ times, each for a specific value of c. Correspondingly, the dimensionality of the vector space is raised by a factor of $|C|$, so that different class labels do not directly compete for the same $\vec{v}(x)$ when finding a separating hyperplane. Given a document d and a class label c, the only non-zero values in $\vec{v}(d,c)$ are on the row that corresponds to c in Eq 3.5 and only for words $w \in d$. Suppose that the input document is "*Tim went to Amsterdam to meet Jason*", with a document class label "Work", $\vec{v}(d,c)$ has six non-zero values, including "*Tim*|Work", "*went*|Work", "*to*|Work", "*Amsterdam*|Work", "*meet*|Work" and "*Jason*|Work", with counts 1, 1, 2, 1, 1 and 1, respectively.

3.2.2 Multi-Class SVM

Given a set of training examples $D = \{(x_i, c_i)\}|_{i=1}^{N}$, we can follow the binary classifier case for defining a multi-class SVM. In particular, we take all $\vec{v}(x_i, c_i)$ as *positive examples*, and all $\vec{v}(x_i, c)$ where $c \neq c_i$, as *negative examples*, finding a hyperplane that best separates the two types of examples. The binary classification SVM formulation can be applied directly, resulting in the following training objective:

$$\hat{\omega}, \hat{b} = \arg\min_{\vec{\omega}, b} \frac{1}{2}||\vec{\omega}||^2,$$

$$\text{such that for all } i, x_i \in D \begin{cases} \vec{\omega}^T \vec{v}(x_i, c_i) + b \geq 1 \\ \text{for all } c \neq c_i, \vec{\omega}^T \vec{v}(x_i, c) + b \leq -1. \end{cases} \tag{3.6}$$

In this equation, the positive examples $\vec{v}(x_i, c_i)$ correspond to the class $+1$ documents $\vec{v}(x^+)$ in Eq 3.4, and the negative examples $\vec{v}(x_i, c)$, $c \neq c_i$ correspond to the class -1 documents $\vec{v}(x^-)$ in Eq 3.4. In the multi-class case, the ratio between the numbers of positive and negative examples is constantly $(1 : |C| - 1)$.

At test time a trained model should assign a class label out of the label set C given each input x. According to Figure 3.5, we should choose the one class c that has $\vec{\omega}^T \vec{v}(x, c) + b > 1$ from all the classes. However, a potential issue is that there may be multiple class labels on the positive side of the hyperplane, since there is no theoretic guarantee of the feature vector distributions of test samples. One way we can solve the problem is to choose the class that is the farthest from the hyperplane, namely the one with the largest $\frac{\vec{\omega}^T \vec{v}(x,c)+b}{||\vec{\omega}||}$, that is the one with the largest $\vec{\omega}^T \vec{v}(x, c) + b$ value.

Understanding linear models as scoring functions. Equation 3.6 can be understood in a scoring perspective, in addition to the vector space geometry perspective introduced in

Section 3.1. In particular, the score of (x, c) is calculated based on the dot product of $\vec{\omega}$ and $\vec{v}(x, c)$

$$score(x, c) = \vec{\omega}^T \vec{v}(x, c) + b$$

given our linear model parameters $\vec{\omega}$ and b. Here each element in $\vec{\omega}$ gives a weight for a specific feature in $\vec{v}(x, c)$, such as "*Amsterdam* Work" in the example above. Intuitively, more indicative features should receive higher weights. Given a test input x, the model finds the class label $\hat{c}$ with the highest score as the output:

$$\hat{c} = \arg\max_{c \in C} score(x, c) = \arg\max_{c \in C} \vec{\omega}^T \vec{v}(x, c) + b.$$

A final form of multi-class SVM training objective. The training goal of Eq 3.6 is to enforce that the scores are at least 1 for all positive examples and at most -1 for all negative examples. However, we have a test scenario now where the output is simply the highest-scored class label. Accordingly, the training goal can be relaxed slightly, requesting that for all $x_i \in D$,

$$\left(\vec{\omega}^T \vec{v}(x_i, c_i) + b \right) - \left(\vec{\omega}^T \vec{v}(x_i, c) + b \right) \geq 2 \text{ for all } c \neq c_i$$

namely

$$\vec{\omega}^T \vec{v}(x_i, c_i) - \vec{\omega}^T \vec{v}(x_i, c) \geq 2 \text{ for all } c \neq c_i. \tag{3.7}$$

Intuitively, if Eq 3.6 holds, then Eq 3.7 also holds. However, the reverse is not true. Equation 3.7 is less strict compared to Eq 3.6 in requiring only that the scores of all gold-standard outputs are higher than the scores of their corresponding incorrect outputs by 2, without forcing the former to be no less than 1 and the latter to be no more than -1. Such constraints are easier to achieve, yet also sufficient for disambiguating different class labels – given a test input x, we predict its class label as $\hat{c} = \arg\max_{c'} \vec{\omega}^T \vec{v}(x, c')$ without worrying whether $\vec{\omega}^T \vec{v}(x, \hat{c})$ is greater than 0.

In practice, the score margin 2 in Eq 3.7 is commonly set to 1, resulting in a final form of **multi-class SVM**, which is to find

$$\hat{\vec{\omega}} = \arg\min_{\vec{\omega}} \frac{1}{2} ||\vec{\omega}||^2,$$
$$\text{such that } \vec{\omega}^T \vec{v}(x_i, c_i) - \vec{\omega}^T \vec{v}(x_i, c) \geq 1 \text{ for all } c \neq c_i. \tag{3.8}$$

The bias term b no longer exists in the new set of parameters, since we are only concerned about the score differences between positive and negative examples, rather than the absolute scores of input–output pairs themselves. b is necessary for binary-classification SVMs because the absolute scores of inputs decide the outputs by their signs.

A final remark is that multi-class SVMs are not used as frequently as binary SVMs or multi-class perceptrons discussed in the next section. However, they provide a theoretical basis for

---

Algorithm 3.3. Multi-class perceptron.

Input: $D = \{(x_i, c_i)\}|_{i=1}^{N}$, $c_i \in C$
Initialization: $\vec{\omega} \leftarrow \vec{0}$; $t \leftarrow 0$;
repeat
    for $i \in [1, \ldots, N]$ **do**
        $z_i \leftarrow \arg\max_{\mathfrak{z}} \vec{\omega}^T \vec{v}(x_i, \mathfrak{z})$;
        if $z_i \neq c_i$ **then**
            $\vec{\omega} \leftarrow \vec{\omega} + \vec{v}(x_i, c_i) - \vec{v}(x_i, z_i)$;
    $t \leftarrow t + 1$;
until $t = T$;

---

structural SVMs and more importantly, share common thinking with multi-class perceptrons and other multi-class classifiers in Chapters 4 and 13.

3.2.3 Multi-class perceptron

The same thinking as above can be applied to extend our binary classification perceptron algorithm into a multi-class perceptron, where a vector space is separated into correct output and incorrect output subspaces, by using output-based feature vectors $\vec{v}(x, c)$. Pseudocode of this algorithm is shown in Algorithm 3.3. Given a set of training examples $D = \{(x_i, c_i)\}|_{i=1}^{N}$, the algorithm initialises a parameter vector $\vec{\omega}$ to all zeros. $\vec{\omega}$ has the same dimension size as output-based document vectors $\vec{v}(x, c)$. The online training algorithm goes through D for multiple iterations, using the current $\vec{\omega}$ to predict the class label $z_i = \arg\max_{\mathfrak{z}} \vec{\omega}^T \vec{v}(x_i, \mathfrak{z})$ for each training input x_i; $\mathfrak{z}$ denotes any possible output class. If x_i equals c_i, the algorithm passes the current training examples without modifications to the model; otherwise the model parameter vector $\vec{\omega}$ is updated by adding the feature vector of the correct output $\vec{v}(x_i, c_i)$ and subtracting the feature vector of the incorrect prediction $\vec{v}(x_i, z_i)$. After T training iterations, the final value of $\vec{\omega}$ is used as the model parameter. Similar to multi-class SVMs, the multi-class perceptron does not use a bias b parameter.

Intuitively, the multi-class perceptron algorithm works by correcting its own prediction errors, in a similar way that the binary classification perceptron works. Let us understand the intuition from the scoring perspective this time. In particular, when the current model $\vec{\omega}$ makes a mistake on the training input x_i, we must have $\vec{\omega}^T \vec{v}(x_i, z_i) > \vec{\omega}^T \vec{v}(x_i, c_i)$. In other words, $score(x_i, c_i) - score(x_i, z_i) = \vec{\omega}^T \left(\vec{v}(x_i, c_i) - \vec{v}(x_i, z_i) \right) < 0$. After parameter update, $\vec{\omega}$ becomes $\vec{\omega} + \vec{v}(x_i, c_i) - \vec{v}(x_i, z_i)$, and therefore the new score difference is $\left(\vec{\omega} + \left(\vec{v}(x_i, c_i) - \vec{v}(x_i, z_i) \right) \right) \cdot \left(\vec{v}(x_i, c_i) - \vec{v}(x_i, z_i) \right) = \vec{\omega}^T \left(\vec{v}(x_i, c_i) - \vec{v}(x_i, z_i) \right) + ||\vec{v}(x_i, c_i) - \vec{v}(x_i, z_i)||^2 > \vec{\omega}^T \left(\vec{v}(x_i, c_i) - \vec{v}(x_i, z_i) \right)$, which is the old score difference. In other words, after the parameter update, the score difference between the correct output c_i and the incorrect output z_i for the input will increase. If the new score difference is greater than 0, then the model will no longer choose z_i as its output.

3.3   Discriminative Linear Models

We have thus far discussed three models for classification, namely Naïve Bayes classifiers, SVMs and and perceptrons. The three models can use the same sources of information, namely class distributions and word–class relations. In particular, the parameter vector $\vec{\omega}$ of SVM and perceptron models takes a similar role to $P(w|c)$ in Naïve Bayes, with the weight for the feature $\#w_i c$ indicating the strength of association between w_i and class label c. To add class distribution information to SVMs and perceptrons, one can extend $\vec{v}(x,c)$ by adding a new feature type $\#c$, in addition to the feature type $\#wc$ in Eq 3.5, resulting in a $|V||C| + |C|$ dimensional feature vector,

$$\begin{aligned}
\vec{v}(d,c) = \langle &\#c_1, \#c_2, \ldots, \#c_{|C|}, \\
&\#w_1c_1, \#w_2c_1, \ldots, \#w_{|V|}c_1, \\
&\#w_1c_2, \#w_2c_2, \ldots, \#w_{|V|}c_2, \\
&\ldots, \\
&\#w_1c_{|C|}, \#w_2c_{|C|}, \ldots, \#w_{|V|}c_{|C|}\rangle,
\end{aligned} \tag{3.9}$$

the elements of which include an enumeration of all class labels. For each document d with class label c, only the element that corresponds to c is non-zero in the first row of Eq 3.9, with the value being 1. The corresponding weight in $\vec{\omega}$ serves a similar role as $P(c)$ in Naïve Bayes models indicating a class bias. On the other hand, different from Naïve Bayes, which has strong independence assumptions between features, SVMs and perceptrons are free from such constraints.

3.3.1   Disciminative Models and Features

Unlike Naïve Bayes models, SVMs and perceptron models do not classify input texts by defining a generative story. Given an input x and an output class c, they directly calculate their **model score** from a feature representation $\vec{v}(x,c)$. As a result, they are called **discriminative models**. The biggest advance of discriminative models over generative models is that they can use overlapping features, such as word and bigram features.

Overlapping features for text classification. *Bigram features* are useful for text classification because they offer more specific information about text classes. For example, the words "*world*" and "*cup*" may not be strong indicators of document classes. However, the bigram "*world cup*" is a strong indicator of the "sports" class. Similarly, "*abnormal return*" indicates "finance", although "*abnormal*" and "*return*" do not have strong indications of document classes.

Bigram features can be defined on top of bag-of-words features for discriminative models, in which case a document vector becomes $\vec{v}(d) = \langle w_1, w_2, \ldots, w_{|V|}, bi_1, bi_2, \ldots, bi_{|BI|}\rangle$, where bi_i represents a unique bigram and *BI* represents the set of all distinct bigram features. For example, with bigram features, the feature vector for the sentence "*Tim bought a book.*" in Table 3.1 is $\langle f_1 = w_1 = 1, f_2 = w_2 = 0, \ldots, f_{1001} = w_{1000} = 1, \ldots, f_{2017} = w_{2017} = 1, \ldots, f_{8400} = w_{8400} = 1, \ldots, f_{13201} = w_{13201} = 1, \ldots, f_{|V|+1} = bi_1 = 0, \ldots, f_{|V|+108} = bi_{108} = 1, \ldots, f_{|V|+3650} = bi_{3650} = 1, \ldots, f_{|V|+4950} = bi_{4950} = 1, \ldots, f_{|V|+113525} = bi_{113525} = 1, \ldots \rangle$ where $w_1, w_{1001}, w_{2017},$

w_{8400} and w_{13201} correspond to the words "*a*", "*book*", "*bought*", "*Tim*" and ".", respectively, and bi_{108}, bi_{3650}, bi_{4950} and bi_{113525} correspond to the bigrams "*a book*", "*book .*", "*bought a*" and "*Tom bought*", respectively. Since bigrams are more sparse compared to words, $|BI|$ can be much larger than $|V|$, and therefore making the feature vector much longer and more sparse.

The corresponding output-based feature types can consist of $\#c$, $\#wc$ and $\#bi \cdot c$, and a feature vector can take the form:

$$
\begin{aligned}
\vec{v}(x, c) = \langle & \#c_1, \#c_2, \dots, c_{|C|}, \\
& \#w_1c_1, \#w_2c_1, \dots, \#w_{|V|}c_1, \\
& \#w_1c_2, \#w_2c_2, \dots, \#w_{|V|}c_2, \\
& \dots \\
& \#w_1c_{|C|}, \#w_2c_{|C|}, \dots, \#w_{|V|}c_{|C|}, \\
& \#bi_1c_1, \#bi_2c_1, \dots, \#bi_{|BI|}c_1, \\
& \#bi_1c_2, \#bi_2c_2, \dots, \#bi_{|BI|}c_2, \\
& \dots \\
& \#bi_1c_{|C|}, \#bi_2c_{|C|}, \dots, \#bi_{|BI|}c_{|C|} \rangle.
\end{aligned}
\tag{3.10}
$$

Feature templates. The feature extraction process can be regarded as a process of matching **feature templates** to output structures, **instantiating** them into feature instances. Here a feature template defines the form of feature instances, and a feature vector contains the *count* of each feature instance. In our classifier above, there are three feature templates, namely c, wc and $bi \cdot c = w_1w_2c$. Conventionally, we say that a feature *fires* if its value is non-zero during feature instantiation. For more sophisticated tasks, there can be tens of feature templates and billions of feature instances. Nevertheless, for a given output, only a few fire.

Note that for count-based features, $\#$ does not need to be specified in the feature templates (e.g., wc above). The corresponding values in a feature vector are counts of feature instances by default, which are discrete. Real-value features such as the *TF-IDF* feature representation of documents must be specified explicitly in the definition of feature templates.

3.3.2   Dot-Product Form of Linear Models

Conventionally, a feature vector is denoted as $\vec{\phi}(x, c)$ and the set of model parameters $\vec{\theta}$. Using the new notation, given an input x, its score is computed by

$$
score(x, c) = \vec{\theta} \cdot \vec{\phi}(x, c),
\tag{3.11}
$$

where $\vec{\phi}(x, c)$ is a **feature vector** of x and the output class c and $\vec{\theta}$ is the model **parameter vector**, or weight vector. Equation 3.11 is a general form of a **linear model**, which can be trained using SVM, the perceptron, or other methods that will be introduced later in Chapter 4.

3.4   Vector Spaces and Model Training

Intuitively, more features reflect richer information, and therefore can improve model performances. Theoretically, the definition of features directly determines the structure of vector spaces, since each feature corresponds to one unique coordinate. The more features there are, the higher the dimensionality of vector spaces. This can influence the linear separability of datasets. Better-designed feature vectors allow better linear separability. The process of defining a useful set of features is referred to as **feature engineering**, which can be a costly process. In this section we discuss vector spaces and model training.

3.4.1   Separability and Generalisability

Separability. Thus far we have been discussing training data that are **linearly separable**. It can be shown theoretically that SVMs and perceptrons converge to 100% accuracy for linearly separable training data. In practice, however, it is difficult to find datasets with 100% linear separability, regardless how document vectors are defined. This is mainly because of ambiguity in natural languages, which makes it extremely difficult to design a set of features that can separate different output classes perfectly, when the data size is sufficiently large. Nonetheless, typical data sets can be largely linearly separable given proper feature definitions. The degree of linear separability of training data can be found by measuring the classification accuracy of linear models on training data.

The capability of correctly separating training instances is referred to as the **fitting power** of a model. This is different from separability, which reflects the nature of training data. A model with strong fitting power can correctly separate training data that are difficult to separate. Linear models have fitting power that is restricted to a hyperplane. In Chapter 13 we will learn about models that separate vectors using arbitrary surface shapes, which have stronger fitting power.

Generalisability. The separability issue is also related to the issue of **generalisability** to test data. In the extreme situation, one can define a very specific feature vector, which effectively memorises the training data, thereby making it 100% accurate in separating training examples. However, such document vectors are likely to be too specific to generalise to unseen test data, relying on peculiarities in the training data that do not apply to unseen data. Such phenomenon is called **overfitting**. In the opposite case, features can be so simple that they cannot capture necessary patterns to separate training data points, leaving the accuracy of classifying training data using the model rather low. This phenomenon is called **underfitting**. A useful model should neither overfit nor underfit the training data, balancing between separability and generalisability. A useful way to test the generalisability of a model is to measure its accuracy on a set of development data.

3.4.2   Dealing with Non-Linearly Separable Data

When the training data are not linearly separable, our assumption of finding a separating hyperplane (e.g., Eq 3.4) no longer holds. We examine SVMs and perceptrons again when the training data are largely linearly separable.

Binary SVM. Assuming that the training data are not linearly separable, there is no possible value of $(\vec{\omega}, b)$ that satisfies the constraints in Eq 3.4 for separating training examples. To address this issue, we can modify the *hard* constraints $y\left(\vec{\omega}^T\vec{v}(x) + b\right) \geq 1$ slightly into *soft* constraints $y\left(\vec{\omega}^T\vec{v}(x) + b\right) = 1 - \xi$ for all (x_i, y_i), where ξ_i ($i \in [1, ..., |D|]$) are called **slack variables**, which take non-negative values and are minimised. An illustration of slack variables for SVM is shown in Figure 3.3(b), which contains vectors with non-zero ξ values. All such vectors violate the separation constraints by being too close to the separating hyperplane or residing on the wrong side. A negative value of ξ does not make sense since it implies a correctly located vector.

Apparently, we want to limit the value of $\sum_{i=1}^{|D|} \xi_i$ because we want to ensure that the training accuracy is as high as possible. This can be done by adding $\sum_{i=1}^{|D|} \xi_i$ to the training objective, resulting in

$$(\vec{\omega}, b) = \underset{(\vec{\omega},b)}{\arg\min} C\sum_i \xi_i + \frac{1}{2}||\vec{\omega}||^2,$$

$$\text{such that for all } i, y_i\left(\vec{\omega}^T\vec{v}(x_i) + b\right) = 1 - \xi_i, \xi_i \geq 0. \tag{3.12}$$

When $y_i\left(\vec{\omega}^T\vec{v}(x_i)+b\right) \geq 1, \xi_i = 0$ since there is no violation of separability. When $y_i\left(\vec{\omega}^T\vec{v}(x_i)+b\right) < 1, \xi_i = 1 - y_i\left(\vec{\omega}^T\vec{v}(x_i) + b\right)$. Accordingly, the above training objective can be turned into a form of unconstrained minimisation:

$$(\vec{\omega}, b) = \underset{(\vec{\omega},b)}{\arg\min} C\sum_i \max\left(0, 1 - y_i(\vec{\omega}^T\vec{v}(x_i) + b)\right) + \frac{1}{2}||\vec{\omega}||^2, \tag{3.13}$$

where $\max\left(0, 1 - y_i(\vec{\omega}^T\vec{v}(x_i) + b)\right)$ represents the values of ξ_i, which are non-negative and represent the degree of violation of linear separability.

Multi-class SVM. For multi-class SVMs, slack variables are useful as in the binary classification case, the introduction of which results in the following final form of training goal, under the $\vec{\theta}, \vec{\phi}$ notation:

$$\hat{\vec{\theta}} = \underset{\vec{\theta}}{\arg\min} \frac{1}{2}||\vec{\theta}||^2 + C\left(\sum_{i=1}^N \xi_i\right) \tag{3.14}$$

$$\text{such that for all } (x_i, c_i) \in D: \vec{\theta} \cdot \vec{\phi}(x_i, c_i) = \vec{\theta} \cdot \vec{\phi}(x_i, c) + 1 - \xi_i, c \neq c_i, \xi_i \geq 0$$

Similar to Eq 3.13, the violations $0 \leq \xi_i = 1 - \vec{\theta} \cdot \vec{\phi}(x_i, c_i) + \vec{\theta} \cdot \vec{\phi}(x_i, c)$ can be directly written into the training objective, resulting in an unconstrained form:

$$\hat{\vec{\theta}} = \underset{\vec{\theta}}{\arg\min} \frac{1}{2}||\vec{\theta}||^2 + C\left(\sum_{i=1}^N \max\left(0, 1 - \vec{\theta} \cdot \vec{\phi}(x_i, c_i) + \max_{c\neq c_i}\left(\vec{\theta} \cdot \vec{\phi}(x_i, c)\right)\right)\right). \tag{3.15}$$

In Eq 3.15, $\max\left(0, 1 - \vec{\theta} \cdot \vec{\phi}(x_i, c_i) + \max_{c\neq c_i}\left(\vec{\theta} \cdot \vec{\phi}(x_i, c)\right)\right)$ is 0 if $1 - \vec{\theta} \cdot \vec{\phi}(x_i, c_i) + \vec{\theta} \cdot \vec{\phi}(x_i, c) < 0$ for all $c \neq c_i$, and $\max_{c\neq c_i}\left(1 - \vec{\theta} \cdot \vec{\phi}(x_i, c_i) + \vec{\theta} \cdot \vec{\phi}(x_i, c)\right)$ otherwise. Here the most violated constraint is used for representing all constraints.

Perceptron. As an online learning algorithm without a global objective function, the perceptron works by correcting model prediction errors regardless of whether the training data are separable or not. It can be proved theoretically that in the case where the training data are not linearly separable, the perceptron can still converge to a model that gives reasonably small numbers of training errors. Thus there is no need to change the algorithm for such cases.

Summary

In this chapter we have introduced:

- vector representations of documents;
- support vector machine and perceptron algorithms for binary text classification;
- feature representations of input–output pairs;
- multi-class SVMs and perceptrons;
- discriminative models vs generative models;
- The importance of features to the separability of training data and generalisation to test data.

Chapter Notes

Salton et al. (1975) introduced vector space models for representing text documents. Luhn (1957) introduced term weighting by using term frequency (TF). Spärck (1972) introduced inverse document frequency (IDF) to measure term specificity. Salton and McGill (1983) used TF-IDF to represent documents for similarity computation. The k-means clustering algorithm was introduced and first used for classification by MacQueen et al. (1967). Support vector machine (SVM) was proposed for binary classification problems by Cortes and Vapnik (1995), and then extended to multi-class SVM (Weston et al., 1999; Crammer and Singer, 2001). Rosenblatt (1958) proposed the original perceptron; Novikoff (1962) and Minsky and Papert (1969) reported a series of theoretical studies on the model. Jebara (2004) discussed learning in discriminative models and generative models theoretically. Medin and Schwanenflugel (1981) analysed linear separability in classification learning.

Exercises

3.1 Suppose that the vocabulary is {*cat, dog, car, bus, ran, fast, the, and, sat*}. There are two document classes, namely *animal* and *vehicle*. The training dataset of a text classification model consists of only three sentences, which include "*the dog ran fast*", "*the cat sat*" and "*the car and the bus ran fast*". The first two sentences are labelled *animal* and the last sentence is labelled *vehicle*.

(a) Draw count-based vector representations of all three sentences using bag-of-word features.
(b) Manually cluster the training examples using 2-means.
(c) Manually calculate the values of all parameters for a Naïve Bayes classifier, using them to predict the class label of each training example, and the class label of the unseen test example "*the dog sat*".
(d) Manually calculate the feature vectors for multi-class SVM for all the training example above, and the feature vector of the unseen example "*the dog sat*" if the output is *vehicle*.

3.2 Verify the 2-means and 3-means clustering results for the examples in Table 3.1(b), discussed at the end of Section 3.1.2.

3.3 Feature vectors are arrays mathematically. On the other hand, they are indexed by sparse discrete features. Discuss the possibility of using hash tables to store feature vectors. Compare the time complexity of calculating model scores of SVMs and perceptrons using array data structures and hash table data structures to implement feature vectors and parameter vectors.

3.4 k-nearest-neighbour (kNN) is a **non-parametric** text classifier, which uses no fixed set of model parameters, but takes *instance-based learning*. Given a set of inputs, it records the feature representation of each input, and their corresponding output labels. For testing, given an unseen input, kNN uses the k nearest neighbours of the input in the feature vector space to determine the output class label. In particular, Euclidean distance can be used to measure vector space distance, and simple voting of training data class labels can be used to determine the class label of the test input.

(a) Compare kNN with Naïve Bayes for their training speed and testing speed theoretically.
(b) Does kNN require linearly separable training data?
(c) Does the value of k affect the decision of kNN? Give examples to demonstrate your conclusion.

3.5 Prove that the distance between a vector $\vec{v}_0$ and a hyperplane $\vec{\omega}^T \vec{v} + b = 0$ is

$$r = \frac{|\vec{\omega}^T \vec{v}_0 + b|}{||\vec{\omega}||}.$$

(Hint: find a vector $\vec{v}_1$ on the hyperplane, such that $\vec{v}_1 - \vec{v}_0$ is perpendicular to the hyperplane. You have $\vec{\omega}^T \vec{v}_1 + b = 0$ ($\vec{v}_1$ on hyperplane) and $\vec{v}_1 - \vec{v}_0 = \alpha \vec{\omega}$ (perpendicular to hyperplane). Solve the equations for $\vec{v}_1$. The distance is then $|\vec{v}_1 - \vec{v}_0|$.)

3.6 Suppose that we have defined three feature templates for document classification, including c, wc and $bi \cdot c$, where c represents a document class, w represents a vocabulary word and bi represents a bigram.

(a) How large is the size of a feature vector for representing any labelled document?
(b) The size of such a feature vector can be intolerably large due to the number of bigrams that theoretically exist, which is $|V|^2$, where $|V|$ is the vocabulary size. In practice, one can

define elements in a feature vector using only feature instances that exist in a set of training data. As a result, OOV words will not exist in feature vectors. How can this method reduce the number of possible feature instances for the feature templates c, wc and $bi \cdot c$, respectively?

(c) If feature vectors are defined using the method (b) above, what happens if a feature instance in an unseen test sample is not an element in the feature vector defined using the training data? For this test instance, will a perceptron model trained using the feature vector in (b) give a different class label compared to one trained using the feature vector in (a)?

(d) When training SVMs and perceptrons, we consider not only gold-standard training instances, but also *violated constraints*, namely incorrectly labelled training inputs that receive high model scores. These incorrectly labelled samples are referred to as *negative examples*, in contrast to the *positive examples* in the gold-standard training data. Intuitively, there can be feature instances from negative examples that do not exist in the feature vectors defined in (b). For example, the feature instance $\langle w =$"*football*", $c =$"*food*"$\rangle$ from a negative example is highly unlikely to exist in a set of gold-standard training data. We call such feature instances **negative features**. It has been shown empirically that using negative features to augment the feature vector defined in (b) can lead to better results by SVMs and perceptrons. Discuss why negative features can be useful.

(e) Extract feature instances for the document "*A cat sat on the mat.*" with the class label "*hobby*". (Note that tokenisation is a necessary pre-processing step.)

(f) Extract feature instances for the document "*The cat sat on the mat.*" with the class label "*sports*". If the instance in (e) is a gold-standard example, then the instance here is a negative example. Extract feature instances for this sample. Which feature instances are likely negative features?

3.7 Recall the WSD task introduced in Chapter 1. Given a word (e.g., "*bank*") and a context window in a sentence, which typically consists of k words to the left and k words to the right of the target word, the goal is to predict the sense of the target word in the sentence (e.g., "*financial bank*").

Given a training corpus $D = \{(x_i, y_i)\}|_{i=1}^{N}$, where $x_i = (w_i, c_i)$, with c_i denoting the context window of w_i, WSD can be modelled as a supervised classification task. It turns out that two classes of features are highly useful. One is bag-of-word features, with template $w \in c_i$, and the other is *collocational features*, with $2k$ different feature templates $w_j^c \in c_i, j \in [-k, -k + 1, \ldots, -1, 1, 2, \ldots, k]$. Here j denotes the relative position of the context word w_j^c with respect to the target word. The feature template w_j^c can also be denoted as $w\text{POSITION}(w)$, which combines a word and its relative position index. For example, given a context window with $k = 3$ "*went to a **bank** to withdraw some*", the feature template w_{-3}^c is instantiated once with "*went*", and the feature template w_2^c is instantiated once with the word "*withdraw*".

(a) If only bag-of-word features are used, derive a Naïve Bayes classifier for the WSD task.

(b) The model above can be extended by integrating collocational features also, resulting in a "bag-of-features" Naïve Bayes model, where each feature instance is generated conditionally

independently given a word sense. While more features can empirically improve the accuracies, do you find this model theoretically flawless? Why?

(c) If both bag-of-word and collocational features are used for discriminative WSD, and the
vocabulary size is $|V|$, how large is a feature vector for $|C|$ word senses? (Hint: there are
$2k + 1$ combined feature templates in total.)

(d) Further, if position-sensitive part-of-speech (POS) labels in the context window are also used
as features, and there are in total $|L|$ different POS labels, how large is a feature vector?

3.8 Recall the multi-class SVM definition in Eq 3.6, in which we have a bias term b, which can
be regarded as a prior for the positive class. One alternative way to define Eq 3.6 is to have a bias
b_c for each individual class c, resulting in

$$\hat{\vec{w}} = \arg\min_{\vec{w}} \frac{1}{2}||\vec{w}||^2,$$

$$\text{such that for all } i, x_i \in D \begin{cases} \vec{w}^T\vec{v}(x_i, c_i) + b_{c_i} \geq 1 \\ \text{for all } c \neq c_i, \vec{w}^T\vec{v}(x_i, c) + b_c \leq -1. \end{cases}$$

Now follow the same simplification process of Eq 3.7 and Eq 3.8, deriving a definition of multi-
class SVM with multiple bias terms. Which features in the Naïve Bayes model do these bias terms
correspond to?

4   Discriminative Linear Classifiers

We have thus far learned two types of discriminative linear models for text classification, namely SVMs and perceptron models, both of which score a given input–output pair (x, y) using $score(x, y) = \vec{\theta} \cdot \vec{\phi}(x, y)$, where $\vec{\phi}(x, y)$ is a feature vector representation of (x, y) and $\vec{\theta}$ is the model (i.e., parameter vector). Compared to generative models such as the Naïve Bayes model, the discriminative models can be more accurate thanks to flexibility in feature definition and a direct training goal of minimising prediction errors. Using the discriminative models, we assume that a higher-scored output is a more correct output. However, score values from perceptrons and SVMs are numbers without a direct interpretation. This is unlike the Naïve Bayes model, for which a model score represents the joint probability of generating an input–output pair, which can be a useful source of information.

Log-linear models are a type of discriminative linear model that give probabilistically interpretable scores to outputs. In particular, they directly calculate $P(y|x)$ given a pair of input and output (x, y). This chapter introduces log-linear models, and then shows that SVMs, perceptrons and log-linear models can be seen as different instances of a general linear discriminative model. At the end of the chapter, we discuss how to make use of multiple models simultaneously for better performances.

4.1   Log-Linear Models

Our goal is to define a *probabilistic* linear *discriminative* model. The inspiration can come from an observation of the Naïve Bayes classifier, which calculates

$$P(c|d) \propto \prod_{i=1}^{n} P(w_i|c)P(c).$$

The log form of $P(c|d)$ is a linear model:

$$\log P(c|d) \propto \sum_{i=1}^{n} \log P(w_i|c) + \log P(c). \tag{4.1}$$

Equation 4.1 is similar to a discriminative linear model for document classification using bag-of-word features wc, and a feature template c. Here the values $\log P(w_i|c)$ and $\log P(c)$ serve as the parameter vector $\vec{\theta}$ in a linear model, which uses the features in Eq 3.9.

Log-linear model for multi-class classification. Inspired by Eq 4.1, we make a **log-linear** probabilistic discriminative model, by making $P(y|x)$ proportional to $e^{\vec{\theta} \cdot \vec{\phi}(x, y)}$, so that the *loga-*

rithm of $P(y|x)$ is a linear model $\log P(y|x) \propto \vec{\theta} \cdot \vec{\phi}(x, y)$. In addition, since $P(y|x) \in [0, 1]$ and $\sum_{y \in C} P(y|x) = 1$, we can derive $P(y|x)$ of log-linear models by normalisation over C:

$$P(y|x) = \frac{e^{\vec{\theta} \cdot \vec{\phi}(x,y)}}{\sum_{y' \in C} e^{\vec{\theta} \cdot \vec{\phi}(x,y')}}, \tag{4.2}$$

where C specifies the set of all possible outputs. Equation 4.2 can also be described as:

$$P(y|x) = softmax_C\left(\vec{\theta} \cdot \vec{\phi}(x, y)\right),$$

where *softmax* is an exponential function that maps an input in $[-\infty, \infty]$ to $[0, 1]$.

Log-linear model for binary classification. While Eq 4.2 is suitable for multi-class classification, there is a specific form of log-linear models for binary classification. In particular, the *sigmoid* function is an exponential function that maps a number in $[-\infty, \infty]$ to $[0, 1]$:

$$sigmoid(x) = \frac{e^x}{1 + e^x}.$$

Using the *sigmoid* function, a binary classifier $score(y = +1) = \vec{\theta} \cdot \vec{\phi}(x) \in [-\infty, +\infty]$ can be mapped into a probabilistic classifier:

$$P(y = +1|x) = sigmoid\left(\vec{\theta} \cdot \vec{\phi}(x)\right)$$
$$P(y = -1|x) = 1 - sigmoid\left(\vec{\theta} \cdot \vec{\phi}(x)\right). \tag{4.3}$$

A log-linear model for binary classification is also referred to as a **logistic regression** model.

Training log-linear models. Given the definitions of log-linear models above, we want to train the parameters $\vec{\theta}$ so that the scores $P(\cdot)$ in Eqs 4.2 and 4.3 truly represent probabilities. To this end, we can use maximum likelihood estimation (MLE) to train a log-linear model.

Formally, given a set of training examples $D = \{(x_i, y_i)\}|_{i=1}^N$, the training objective is:

$$P(Y|X) = \prod_i P(y_i|x_i). \tag{4.4}$$

Equation 4.4 is different from Eq 2.1 in Chapter 2 for MLE in that the objective contains *conditional* probabilities $P(y|x)$ rather than *joint* probabilities $P(x, y)$. This reflects a difference between *discriminative* probabilistic models and *generative* probabilistic models – while the former focuses on differentiating output candidates given an input, the latter models a probabilistic process to generate both the input and the output. As a result, the training objective in Eq 4.4 can also be referred to as maximising the *conditional likelihood* of training data.

4.1.1 Training Binary Log-Linear Models

Given $P(y = +1|x) = \frac{e^{\vec{\theta} \cdot \vec{\phi}(x)}}{1 + e^{\vec{\theta} \cdot \vec{\phi}(x)}}$, our MLE training objective is to maximise over D:

$$P(Y|X) = \prod_i P(y_i|x_i) = \prod_{i+} P(y = +1|x_i) \prod_{i-} \left(1 - P(y = +1|x_i)\right),$$

where i^+ indicates all i such that $y_i = +1$, and i^- indicates all i such that $y_i = -1$. $P(Y|X)$ denotes the conditional likelihood of D. Maximising $P(Y|X)$ can be achieved by maximising:

$$
\begin{aligned}
\log P(Y|X) &= \sum_i \log P(y_i|x_i) \\
&= \sum_{i^+} \log P(y = +1|x_i) + \sum_{i^-} \log \left(1 - P(y = +1|x_i)\right) \\
&= \sum_{i^+} \log \frac{e^{\vec{\theta}\cdot\vec{\phi}(x_i)}}{1 + e^{\vec{\theta}\cdot\vec{\phi}(x_i)}} + \sum_{i^-} \log \frac{1}{1 + e^{\vec{\theta}\cdot\vec{\phi}(x_i)}} \\
&= \sum_{i^+} \left(\vec{\theta}\cdot\vec{\phi}(x_i) - \log \left(1 + e^{\vec{\theta}\cdot\vec{\phi}(x_i)}\right)\right) - \sum_{i^-} \log \left(1 + e^{\vec{\theta}\cdot\vec{\phi}(x_i)}\right).
\end{aligned}
\tag{4.5}
$$

In Chapter 2, we derived a closed-form solution for MLE for the problem of tossing a coin — which is to count relative frequencies – by finding zero values of the likelihood gradient. For our log-linear model, the gradient of the objective is:

$$
\begin{aligned}
\vec{g} &= \frac{\partial \log P(Y|X)}{\vec{\theta}} \\
&= \sum_{i^+} \left(\vec{\phi}(x_i) - \frac{e^{\vec{\theta}\cdot\vec{\phi}(x_i)}}{1 + e^{\vec{\theta}\cdot\vec{\phi}(x_i)}}\vec{\phi}(x_i)\right) - \sum_{i^-} \left(\frac{e^{\vec{\theta}\cdot\vec{\phi}(x_i)}}{1 + e^{\vec{\theta}\cdot\vec{\phi}(x_i)}}\vec{\phi}(x_i)\right) \\
&= \sum_{i^+} \left(1 - \frac{e^{\vec{\theta}\cdot\vec{\phi}(x_i)}}{1 + e^{\vec{\theta}\cdot\vec{\phi}(x_i)}}\right)\vec{\phi}(x_i) - \sum_{i^-} \left(\frac{e^{\vec{\theta}\cdot\vec{\phi}(x_i)}}{1 + e^{\vec{\theta}\cdot\vec{\phi}(x_i)}}\right)\vec{\phi}(x_i) \\
&= \sum_{i^+} \left(1 - P(y = +1|x_i)\right)\vec{\phi}(x_i) - \sum_{i^-} P(y = +1|x_i)\vec{\phi}(x_i).
\end{aligned}
\tag{4.6}
$$

Unlike the case of coin tossing, Eq 4.6 does not have a general analytical solution for $\vec{g} = \vec{0}$. As a result, we have to resort to numerical methods to find approximate solutions. Below we introduce a simple solution, namely stochastic gradient descent (SGD), which is relevant to all our discriminative models, and further to the neural network models in Part III of this book.

Gradient descent. SGD is a variant of gradient descent, which we discuss first. Gradient descent is a simple numerical solution to the minimisation of convex functions, the idea of which is to climb down the valley shape of a function in a high-dimensional space incrementally, by repeatedly taking a step in the steepest direction. Here the steepest direction downslope is given by the gradient of the objective function. Intuitively, for maximising a training objective function, *gradient ascent* should be used instead, which climbs up a slope shape. However, we can use gradient descent on the negation of the objective to achieve the same goal. Thus we stick to gradient descent and SGD in the book.

A formal definition of gradient descent is shown in Algorithm 4.1. Given a certain objective function $F(\vec{\theta})$ and a random starting point $\vec{\theta}_0$, the algorithm works incrementally, each time finding the gradient $\vec{g} = \frac{\partial F(\vec{\theta})}{\partial \vec{\theta}}$, and updating $\vec{\theta}$ to $\vec{\theta} - \alpha\vec{g}$, where $\alpha \in (0, 1]$ is called the **learning rate**. The model converges when the values of $\vec{\theta}$ at step t and the previous step $t - 1$ are sufficiently close (e.g., less than a small hyper-parameter ϵ).

Algorithm 4.1. Gradient descent.

Inputs: An objective function F;

Initialisation: $\vec{\theta}_0 \leftarrow random(), t \leftarrow 0, \alpha \leftarrow \alpha_0$;

repeat

$\quad\quad g_t \leftarrow \frac{\partial F(\vec{\theta}_t)}{\partial \vec{\theta}_t}$;

$\quad\quad \vec{\theta}_{t+1} \leftarrow \vec{\theta}_t - \alpha \vec{g}_t$;

$\quad\quad t \leftarrow t + 1$;

until $||\vec{\theta}_t - \vec{\theta}_{t-1}|| < \epsilon$;

Outputs: $\vec{\theta}_t$

Algorithm 4.2. Gradient descent for training log-linear models for binary classification.

Inputs: $D = \{(x_i, y_i)\}|_{i=1}^{N}$;

Initialisation: $\vec{\theta}_0 \leftarrow random(), \alpha \leftarrow \alpha_0, t \leftarrow 0$;

repeat

$\quad\quad \vec{g}_t \leftarrow \vec{0}$;

$\quad\quad$ **for** $i \in [1, \ldots, N]$ **do**

$\quad\quad\quad\quad P(y = +1 | x_i) \leftarrow \frac{e^{\vec{\theta}_t \cdot \vec{\phi}(x_i)}}{1 + e^{\vec{\theta}_t \cdot \vec{\phi}(x_i)}}$;

$\quad\quad\quad\quad$ **if** $y_i = +1$ **then**

$\quad\quad\quad\quad\quad\quad \vec{g}_t \leftarrow \vec{g}_t + \big(P(y = +1 | x_i) - 1\big)\vec{\phi}(x_i)$;

$\quad\quad\quad\quad$ **else**

$\quad\quad\quad\quad\quad\quad \vec{g}_t \leftarrow \vec{g}_t + P(y = +1 | x_i)\vec{\phi}(x_i)$;

$\quad\quad \vec{\theta}_{t+1} \leftarrow \vec{\theta}_t - \alpha \vec{g}_t$;

$\quad\quad t \leftarrow t + 1$;

until $||\vec{\theta}_t - \vec{\theta}_{t-1}|| < \epsilon$;

Outputs: $\vec{\theta}_t$

The learning rate α is a hyper-parameter. Intuitively, it influences both the accuracy and the efficiency of gradient descent. If α is too large, the algorithm might not be able to converge to the optimal value, stepping over the bottom of the valley shape back and forth. On the other hand, if α is too small, it can take too much time to descend to the optimal value. As a result, the value of α is typically selected on development data sets.

Gradient descent can be used to minimise the negative log-likelihood of log-linear models. At each iteration, the value of gradient $\vec{g}_t$ is the derivative of the negative log-likelihood function $-\log P(Y|X)$ with respect to $\vec{\theta}$, which is $\sum_{i-} P(y = +1|x_i)\vec{\phi}(x_i) + \sum_{i+} \big(P(y = +1|x_i) - 1\big)\vec{\phi}(x_i)$ according to Eq 4.6. Algorithm 4.2 shows pseudocode of using gradient descent to train our log-linear model.

Algorithm 4.3. Stochastic gradient descent.

Inputs: An objective function $F(x, y, \vec{\theta})$ to minimise, and $D = \{(x_i, y_i)\}|_{i=1}^N$;

Initialisation: $\vec{\theta}_0 \leftarrow random()$, $\alpha \leftarrow \alpha_0$, $t \leftarrow 0$;

repeat

$\quad$ $\vec{\theta}_{t+1} \leftarrow \vec{\theta}_t$;

$\quad$ **for** $i \in [1, \ldots, N]$ **do**

$\quad\quad$ $\vec{g}_{t,i} \leftarrow \dfrac{\partial F(x_i, y_i, \vec{\theta}_{t+1})}{\partial \vec{\theta}_{t+1}}$;

$\quad\quad$ $\vec{\theta}_{t+1} \leftarrow \vec{\theta}_{t+1} - \alpha \vec{g}_{t,i}$;

$\quad$ $t \leftarrow t + 1$;

until $t = T$;

Outputs: $\vec{\theta}_t$

Stochastic gradient descent. For convex objective functions, gradient descent can converge to the optimal value of the function. For non-convex objective functions, gradient descent can converge to a local optimal point, which can be the global optimal point, depending on the random initial value $\vec{\theta}_0$. In practice, gradient descent can be computationally inefficient. Taking Eq 4.6 for example. To train a log-linear model, finding $\vec{g}$ at each iteration requires going through the whole training set D, summing up the gradient of each $P(y_i|x_i)$. It can thus be intolerably slow to train on a large set of examples using gradient descent.

One solution to this issue is **stochastic gradient descent** (SGD), which works by iterating through a given set of training examples, calculating a **local train objective** for each training example, and updating model parameters locally. As a result, parameters are updated much more frequently compared with gradient descent. SGD is called an *online* optimisation algorithm. In contrast, gradient descent is a *batch* optimisation technique. Pseudocode of SGD is shown in Algorithm 4.3. Given a local training objective $F(x, y, \vec{\theta})$ on individual training examples, the algorithm works by taking T iterations over a training set D, where T is a hyper-parameter. For each training example $(x_i, y_i) \in D$, SGD calculates the gradient of $F(x_i, y_i, \vec{\theta})$, and uses the value for updating the parameter vector. Intuitively, the algorithm trains a model $\vec{\theta}$ by starting with a random initialisation, and then iteratively adjusting its value over training examples in the direction of optimising local training objectives. Under the general SGD method, most of the supervised learning models in this book can be trained.

Pseudocode of SGD training of our log-linear model is shown in Algorithm 4.4, where the total number of training iterations T can be chosen empirically over a set of development data. Compared with the batch gradient descent version in Algorithm 4.2, the update of model parameters is in the inner loop, rather than the outer loop, which makes parameter updates occur more frequently (i.e., after each training example is processed). Similar to gradient descent, the initial model parameter value can be a random vector. However, we can also initialise $\vec{\theta}$ to a vector of all zeros, which can make the results more reproducible. For SGD training algorithms in this chapter we adopt the latter strategy.

Algorithm 4.4. SGD for training log-linear models binary classification.

Inputs: $D = \{(x_i, y_i)\}|_{i=1}^{N}$;

Initialisation: $\vec{\theta} \leftarrow \vec{0}, \alpha \leftarrow \alpha_0, t \leftarrow 0$;

repeat

    for $i \in [1, \ldots, N]$ **do**

        $P(y = +1|x_i) \leftarrow \frac{e^{\vec{\theta} \cdot \vec{\phi}(x_i)}}{1 + e^{\vec{\theta} \cdot \vec{\phi}(x_i)}}$;

        if $y_i = +1$ **then**

            $\vec{\theta} \leftarrow \vec{\theta} - \alpha\Big(P(y = +1|x_i) - 1\Big)\vec{\phi}(x_i)$;

        else

            $\vec{\theta} \leftarrow \vec{\theta} - \alpha P(y = +1|x_i)\vec{\phi}(x_i)$;

    $t \leftarrow t + 1$;

until $t = T$;

Outputs: $\vec{\theta}$

Compared to gradient descent, SGD has been shown to converge much faster. On the other hand, since the direction of local parameter updates are not always towards minimising the global objective function, SGD does not always converge to the same optimal point as gradient descent. It has be shown theoretically that SGD can be optimal under certain conditions. Empirically, SGD has been shown to perform competitively for a wide range of NLP tasks compared to batch gradient descent.

Comparison with perceptrons. The SGD version of the log-linear model training algorithm in Algorithm 4.4 is highly similar in structure to the perceptron algorithm in Algorithm 3.2 of Chapter 3, except for the parameter update details. In particular, given a training example x_i^+, the perceptron updates the parameters by $\phi(x_i^+)$ if $\vec{\theta} \cdot \phi(x_i^+) < 0$, and 0 otherwise. In contrast, Algorithm 4.4 updates parameters by $\phi(x_i^+)\big(1 - P(y = +1|x_i^+)\big)$. Intuitively, the smaller $P(y = +1|x_i^+)$ is, the more aggressive the update is. When $P(y = +1|x_i^+) = 0$, the log-linear model update is identical to the perceptron update. When $P(y = +1|x_i^+) = 1$, the log-linear model does not change the value of $\vec{\theta}$, which is also the same as the perceptron. However, when $0 < P(y = +1|x_i^+) < 1$, the log-linear model updates $\vec{\theta}$ by weighting $\phi(x_i^+)$ according to $1 - P(y = +1|x_i^+)$, which is more fine-grained compared to the 0/1 update of the perceptron. Here $1 - P(y = +1|x_i^+)$ reflects the degree of model incorrectness. A similar comparison can be made for x_i^-. This results in a probabilistically interpretable model score $\vec{\theta} \cdot \vec{\phi}(x)$.

Mini-batch SGD. A compromise between gradient descent and SGD training is **mini-batch SGD**. The idea is to split the set of training examples D into several equal-sized subsets $D_1, D_2, \ldots, D_M$, each containing N/M training examples. A local training objective is calculated for each mini-batch, and model parameters are updated by using gradients of each local training objective, rather than the global training objective. In the extreme case, when $M = N$, mini-batch SGD falls back to SGD. In the other extreme case when $M = 1$, mini-batch SGD becomes gradient descent. Hence the mini-batch size N/M controls the trade-off between efficiency and accuracy of

---

Algorithm 4.5. Mini-batch gradient descent for training log-linear models for binary classification.

Inputs: $D = \{(x_i, y_i)\}|_{i=1}^{N}$;

Initialisation: $\vec{\theta} \leftarrow random()$, $\alpha \leftarrow \alpha_0$, $t \leftarrow 0$;

for $i \in [1, \ldots, M]$ **do**

$\quad D_i \leftarrow \{(x_j, y_j)\}|_{j=1+\lfloor(i-1)*\frac{N}{M}\rfloor}^{\lfloor i*\frac{N}{M}\rfloor}$;

repeat

$\quad$ **for** $i \in [1, \ldots, M]$ **do**

$\quad\quad \vec{g} \leftarrow \vec{0}$;

$\quad\quad$ **for** $j \in [1, \ldots, |D_i|]$ **do**

$\quad\quad\quad P(y = +1|x_j^i) \leftarrow \dfrac{e^{\vec{\theta}_t \cdot \vec{\phi}(x_j^i)}}{1 + e^{\vec{\theta}_t \cdot \vec{\phi}(x_j^i)}}$;

$\quad\quad\quad$ **if** $y_i = +1$ **then**

$\quad\quad\quad\quad \vec{g} \leftarrow \vec{g} + \left(P(y = +1|x_i^j) - 1\right)\vec{\phi}(x_i^j)$;

$\quad\quad\quad$ **else**

$\quad\quad\quad\quad \vec{g} \leftarrow \vec{g} + P(y = +1|x_i^j)\vec{\phi}(x_i^j)$;

$\quad\quad \vec{\theta} \leftarrow \vec{\theta} - \alpha\vec{g}$;

$\quad t \leftarrow t + 1$;

until $t = T$;

Outputs: $\vec{\theta}$

---

approximation. It is a hyper-parameter, which can be set according to development experiments, since the best trade-off is an empirical question. Pseudocode of using mini-batch SGD to train our log-linear model is shown in Algorithm 4.5, where $\left(x_i^j, y_i^j\right)$ denotes the i-th training example in D_j.

Shuffling data. For both SGD and mini-batch gradient descent, we can make a **random shuffle** to the training set before each training iteration, so that the order in which local updates are made are different at each iteration. This has been shown to empirically improve the accuracies for some NLP tasks and datasets.

4.1.2 Training Multi-Class Log-Linear Models

For multi-class classification, our dataset consists of training pairs (x_i, y_i), where $y_i \in C$ and $|C| \geq 2$. Using output-based feature vectors $\vec{\phi}(x_i, y_i)$ to represent (x_i, y_i), the probability of $y_i = c$ ($c \in C$) is:

$$P(y_i = c|x_i) = \frac{e^{\vec{\theta} \cdot \vec{\phi}(x_i, c)}}{\sum_{c' \in C} e^{\vec{\theta} \cdot \vec{\phi}(x_i, c')}},$$

as given in Eq 4.2.

Algorithm 4.6. SGD training for multi-class log-linear models.

Inputs: $D = \{(x_i, y_i)\}|_{i=1}^{N}$;

Initialisation $\vec{\theta} \leftarrow \vec{0}$, $\alpha \leftarrow \alpha_0$, $t \leftarrow 0$;

repeat

    for $i \in [1, \ldots, N]$ **do**

        $\vec{g} \leftarrow \vec{0}$;

        for $c \in C$ **do**

$$P(y = c | x_i) \leftarrow \frac{e^{\vec{\theta} \cdot \vec{\phi}(x_i, c)}}{\sum_{c'} e^{\vec{\theta} \cdot \vec{\phi}(x_i, c')}};$$

$$\vec{g} \leftarrow \vec{g} + \left(\vec{\phi}(x_i, c) - \vec{\phi}(x_i, y_i) \right) P(y = c | x_i);$$

        $\vec{\theta} \leftarrow \vec{\theta} - \alpha \vec{g}$;

    $t \leftarrow t + 1$;

until $t = T$;

Outputs: $\vec{\theta}$

The conditional likelihood of D is

$$P(Y|X) = \prod_i P(y_i | x_i) = \prod_i \frac{e^{\vec{\theta} \cdot \vec{\phi}(x_i, y_i)}}{\sum_{c \in C} e^{\vec{\theta} \cdot \vec{\phi}(x_i, c)}}$$

and the log-likelihood of D is

$$\log P(Y|X) = \sum_i \log P(y_i | x_i) = \sum_i \left(\vec{\theta} \cdot \vec{\phi}(x_i, y_i) - \log \Big(\sum_{c \in C} e^{\vec{\theta} \cdot \vec{\phi}(x_i, c)} \Big) \right).$$

Similar to the binary classification case, gradient descent, SGD and mini-batch gradient descent can be used to train this model. Below we discuss the training details using SGD.

For each training example (x_i, y_i), the log-likelihood is

$$\vec{\theta} \cdot \vec{\phi}(x_i, y_i) - \log \Big(\sum_{c \in C} e^{\vec{\theta} \cdot \vec{\phi}(x_i, c)} \Big)$$

and the local gradient is

$$
\begin{aligned}
\vec{g} = \frac{\partial \log P(y_i | x_i)}{\partial \vec{\theta}} &= \vec{\phi}(x_i, y_i) - \frac{\sum_{c \in C} e^{\vec{\theta} \cdot \vec{\phi}(x_i, c)} \cdot \vec{\phi}(x_i, c)}{\sum_{c' \in C} e^{\vec{\theta} \cdot \vec{\phi}(x_i, c')}} \\
&= \sum_{c \in C} \left(\vec{\phi}(x_i, y_i) - \vec{\phi}(x_i, c) \right) \frac{e^{\vec{\theta} \cdot \vec{\phi}(x_i, c)}}{\sum_{c' \in C} e^{\vec{\theta} \cdot \vec{\phi}(x_i, c')}} \\
&= \sum_{c \in C} \left(\vec{\phi}(x_i, y_i) - \vec{\phi}(x_i, c) \right) P(y = c | x_i).
\end{aligned}
\tag{4.7}
$$

Pseudocode of the SGD training algorithm is shown in Algorithm 4.6.

Comparison with perceptron models. Algorithm 4.6 is structurally highly similar to Algorithm 3.3 in Chapter 3 for training multi-class perceptrons, both updating model parameters $\vec{\theta}$

by using feature vector differences $\vec{\phi}(x_i, y_i) - \vec{\phi}(x_i, c)$ between the gold output y_i and a class label c, where $c \neq y_i$. There are two main differences. First, the log-linear model updates $\vec{\theta}$ using all class labels $c \neq y_i$, while the perceptron uses only the most violated constraint $z_i = \arg\max_c \vec{\theta} \cdot \vec{\phi}(x_i, c)$. Second, the log-linear model additionally weighs the difference vector $\vec{\phi}(x_i, y_i) - \vec{\phi}(x_i, c)$ by a factor $P(y = c|x_i)$. Intuitively, the more probability that the model assigns to an incorrect output c, the more aggressive the update should be. In the extreme case when $P(c|x_i) = 1$, our log-linear model update becomes a perceptron update. The use of $P(c|x_i)$ and all incorrect output classes allow the log-linear model to receive more fine-grained parameter updates, leading to a probabilistically interpretable model score $\vec{\theta} \cdot \vec{\phi}(x_i, y_i)$.

4.1.3 Using Log-Linear Models for Classification

During testing, given an input x, a log-linear model makes a prediction by finding $\hat{y} = \arg\max_{y \in C} P(y|x)$, which is equal to $\arg\max_{y \in C} \vec{\theta} \cdot \vec{\phi}(x, y)$. Hence the test scenario of log-linear models is identical to that of SVMs and perceptron models.

4.2 SGD Training of SVMs

Chapter 3 introduced SVMs without discussing their training. As a general tool for optimisation, SGD can be used to train SVMs. This section shows SGD training for SVM for binary classification and multi-class classification, respectively. It turns out the SGD training of SVM has underlying connections to perceptron training. In this light, we demonstrate the objective function that perceptron training algorithms optimise.

4.2.1 Training SVMs for Binary Classification

As discussed in Chapter 3, the training objective of binary classification SVM with slack variables is to minimise $\frac{1}{2}||\vec{\omega}||^2 + C\sum_i \max\left(0, 1 - y_i(\vec{\omega} \cdot \vec{\phi}(x_i) + b)\right)$ given $D = \{(x_i, y_i)\}|_{i=1}^N$. For notational convenience, we ignore b,[1] and denote $score(x_i) = \vec{\theta} \cdot \vec{\phi}(x_i)$. The training objective becomes to minimise $\frac{1}{2}||\vec{\theta}||^2 + C\sum_i \max\left(0, 1 - y_i(\vec{\theta} \cdot \vec{\phi}(x_i))\right)$. This objective is equivalent to minimising

$$\sum_i \max\left(0, 1 - y_i(\vec{\theta} \cdot \vec{\phi}(x_i))\right) + \frac{1}{2}\lambda||\vec{\theta}||^2, \tag{4.8}$$

where λ is a hyper-parameter of the model, serving the role of C.

---

[1] This has been shown not to empirically hurt the performance when the feature vector $\phi(x)$ is expressive. In addition, in case a bias term is necessary, we can achieve the original scoring function by adding a constant 1 as one additional feature instance to $\vec{\phi}(x)$, so that the corresponding weight in $\vec{\theta}$ plays the role of b.

Algorithm 4.7. SGD training for binary classification SVM.

Inputs: $D = \{(x_i, y_i)\}|_{i=1}^{N}$;
Initialisation: $\vec{\theta} \leftarrow \vec{0}, \alpha \leftarrow \alpha_0, t \leftarrow 0$;
repeat
    for $i \in [1, \ldots, N]$ **do**
        if $y_i \vec{\theta} \cdot \vec{\phi}(x_i) < 1$ **then**
            $\vec{\theta} \leftarrow \vec{\theta} - \alpha\left(\lambda\vec{\theta} - y_i\vec{\phi}(x_i)\right)$;
        else
            $\vec{\theta} \leftarrow \vec{\theta} - \alpha\lambda\vec{\theta}$;
    $t \leftarrow t + 1$;
until $t = T$;
Outputs: $\vec{\theta}$

Equation 4.8 is not differentiable due to the max function. To address this, we can use sub-gradients instead. In particular, for each training example, the derivative of the local training objective $\max\left(0, 1 - y_i(\vec{\theta} \cdot \vec{\phi}(x_i))\right) + \frac{1}{2}\lambda||\vec{\theta}||^2$ is:

$$\begin{cases} \lambda\vec{\theta} & \text{if } 1 - y_i\left(\vec{\theta} \cdot \vec{\phi}(x_i)\right) \leq 0 \\ \lambda\vec{\theta} - y_i\vec{\phi}(x_i) & \text{otherwise} \end{cases}.$$

Consequently, Eq 4.8 can be optimised using sub-gradient descent, as shown in Algorithm 4.7.

Comparison with perceptron models. Algorithm 4.7 is highly similar to the perceptron algorithm in Chapter 3, both adding $\vec{\phi}(x_i^+)$ to $\vec{\theta}$ or subtracting $\vec{\phi}(x_i^-)$ from $\vec{\theta}$ under necessary conditions in order to adjust model parameters. There are three main differences. First, the perceptron checks whether $y_i\left(\vec{\theta} \cdot \vec{\phi}(x_i)\right) < 0$ as the condition for parameter updates, while SVM checks whether $y_i\left(\vec{\theta} \cdot \vec{\phi}(x_i)\right) \leq 1$ instead. Second, SVM additionally subtracts $\lambda\vec{\theta}$ from the model parameters at each training example while the perceptron does not. We will discuss this later in Section 4.3.3. Third, SVM uses a **learning rate** α to weight the parameter update, while the perceptron model we have discussed has a learning rate of 1 implicitly.

4.2.2 Training SVM for Multi-Class Classification

As shown in Chapter 3, the training objective of multi-class SVM is to minimise

$$\frac{1}{2}||\vec{\theta}||^2 + C\sum_i \max\left(0, 1 - \vec{\theta} \cdot \vec{\phi}(x_i, y_i) + \max_{c \neq y_i} \vec{\theta} \cdot \vec{\phi}(x_i, c)\right), \tag{4.9}$$

Algorithm 4.8. SGD training for multi-class SVM.

Inputs: $D = \{(x_i, y_i)\}|_{i=1}^{N}, y_i \in C$;

Initialisation $\vec{\theta} \leftarrow 0, t \leftarrow 0$;

repeat
    for $i \in [1, \ldots, N]$ **do**
        $\vec{g} \leftarrow \vec{0}$;
        $z_i \leftarrow \arg\max_{c \neq y_i} \vec{\theta} \cdot \vec{\phi}(x_i, c)$;
        if $\vec{\theta} \cdot \vec{\phi}(x_i, y_i) - \vec{\theta} \cdot \vec{\phi}(x_i, z_i) < 1$ **then**
            $\vec{g} \leftarrow \vec{g} - (\vec{\phi}(x_i, y_i) - \vec{\phi}(x_i, z_i))$;
        $\vec{\theta} \leftarrow \vec{\theta} - \alpha(\vec{g} + \lambda\vec{\theta})$;
        $t \leftarrow t + 1$;
until $t = T$;

Outputs: $\vec{\theta}$;

---

which is equivalent to minimising

$$\sum_i \max\left(0, 1 - \vec{\theta} \cdot \vec{\phi}(x_i, y_i) + \max_{c \neq y_i} \vec{\theta} \cdot \vec{\phi}(x_i, c)\right) + \frac{1}{2}\lambda||\vec{\theta}||^2, \qquad (4.10)$$

where $(x_i, y_i) \in D, \lambda = \frac{1}{C}$.

For optimising the objective, the local derivative for each training example (x_i, y_i) is:

$$\begin{cases} \lambda\vec{\theta} & \text{if } 1 - \vec{\theta} \cdot \vec{\phi}(x_i, y_i) + \vec{\theta} \cdot \vec{\phi}(x_i, z_i) \leq 0 \\ \lambda\vec{\theta} - (\vec{\phi}(x_i, y_i) - \vec{\phi}(x_i, z_i)) & \text{otherwise}, \end{cases} \qquad (4.11)$$

where $z_i = \arg\max_{c \neq y_i} \vec{\theta} \cdot \vec{\phi}(x_i, c)$.[2]

Accordingly, pseudocode of SGD training is shown in Algorithm 4.8.

Comparison with perceptron models. Algorithm 4.8 is similar to the perceptron algorithm in Chapter 3 in that the model parameter $\vec{\theta}$ is adjusted by adding $\vec{\phi}(x_i, y_i) - \vec{\phi}(x_i, z_i)$ when necessary. It is different in three main aspects. First, the condition for parameter update is $\vec{\theta} \cdot \vec{\phi}(x_i, y_i) - \vec{\theta} \cdot \vec{\phi}(x_i, z_i) \leqslant 1$, rather than $\vec{\theta} \cdot \vec{\phi}(x_i, y_i) - \vec{\theta} \cdot \vec{\phi}(x_i, z_i) < 0$ for perceptron training. Second, $-\lambda\vec{\theta}$ is included in the parameter update. Third, a learning rate α is used to weigh the update value.

4.2.3 A Perceptron Training Objective Function

The online learning versions of both SVMs and log-linear models have been derived by using SGD over a global objective function. Both share similarities with perceptron training algorithms. This leads to a question whether perceptron updates can also be viewed as SGD training of a

---

[2] In the very rare case that two outputs have identical maximum score, we randomly choose one as z_i. The same strategy can be used for making predictions in test scenarios.

Algorithm 4.9. Online learning for a generalised linear model.

Inputs: $D = \{(x_i, y_i)\}|_{i=1}^{N}$;
Initialisation: $\vec{\theta} \leftarrow random(), t \leftarrow 0$;
repeat
    for $i \in [1, \ldots, N]$ **do**
        $\vec{g}_i^t \leftarrow \text{LOCALUPDATE}(x_i, y_i, \vec{\theta})$;
        $\vec{\theta} \leftarrow \vec{\theta} + \vec{g}_i^t$;
    $t \leftarrow t + 1$;
until $t = T$;
Outputs: $\vec{\theta}$;

---

certain objective function. The answer is yes. Drawing from the similarities between SVM and perceptron parameter updates, the perceptron update for binary classification can be regarded as sub-gradients of minimising the following training objective:

$$\max\left(0, -y_i\big(\vec{\theta} \cdot \vec{\phi}(x_i)\big)\right).$$

The corresponding global training objective is hence to minimise

$$\sum_{i=1}^{N} \max\left(0, -y_i\big(\vec{\theta} \cdot \vec{\phi}(x_i)\big)\right).$$

For multi-class classification, the global training objective can be derived similarly:

$$\sum_{i=1}^{N} \max\left(0, -\vec{\theta} \cdot \vec{\phi}(x_i, y_i) + \max_c \vec{\theta} \cdot \vec{\phi}(x_i, c)\right).$$

4.3   A Generalised Linear Model

A closer examination of SVMs, perceptrons and log-linear models shows that they can be regarded as instances of a single generalised linear classification model, which consists of a parameter vector $\vec{\theta}$ of the same dimension size as a feature vector $\vec{\phi}$. Given any test input x, it decides the class label y using the dot product $\vec{\theta} \cdot \vec{\phi}$. For binary classification, $y = \text{SIGN}(\vec{\theta} \cdot \vec{\phi}(x))$; for multi-class classification, $y = \arg\max_c \vec{\theta} \cdot \vec{\phi}(x, c)$.

Our generalised linear classifier can be illustrated by Figure 4.1. It takes a number of input signals, which correspond to features, and yields one (for the binary case) or many (for the multi-class case) output scores. Given an input feature vector $\vec{\phi}$, the output score values are calculated first via a dot product $\vec{\theta} \cdot \vec{\phi}$. For log-linear models, *sigmoid* and *softmax* functions are further applied to $\vec{\theta} \cdot \vec{\phi}$ to derive probabilistic outputs. Such functions can be regarded as **activation functions**, mapping $\vec{\theta} \cdot \vec{\phi}$ to $f(\vec{\theta} \cdot \vec{\phi})$. For perceptrons and SVMs, the effective activation function is an identity

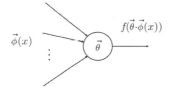

Figure 4.1 Generalised linear classification model.

activation function $f(x) = x$, which is linear. In contrast, both *sigmoid* and *softmax* activation functions are non-linear. Note that non-linear activation functions do not make the classifiers here non-linear, because they are applied on the score value only. They do not affect the decision of test outputs, but influence training only. Chapter 13 discusses non-linear models for classification. The generalised linear model can also be referred to as a generalised perceptron model, which is the term used in Chapter 13.

Given a set of training data, gold-standard outputs are used to estimate the model parameters $\vec{\theta}$. SVMs, perceptrons and log-linear models differ mainly in training. Below we show a training algorithm for the generalised linear model, discussing the correlations between specific models.

4.3.1 Unified Online Training

The online learning algorithms for the perceptron models (Algorithm 3.2 and Algorithm 3.3 in Chapter 3), log-linear models (Algorithm 4.4 and Algorithm 4.6) and SVMs (Algorithm 4.7 and Algorithm 4.8) can be summarised in Algorithm 4.9. Given a set of training data $D = \{(x_i, y_i)\}|_{i=1}^{N}$, the algorithm goes over D for T iterations, processing each training example (x_i, y_i), calculating a local update vector $\vec{g}_i^t$ according to the current model parameters $\vec{\theta}$ (i.e., LOCALUPDATE$(x_i, y_i, \vec{\theta})$). As we saw earlier, the local update vector is essentially the gradient of a training objective function calculated on the instance (x_i, y_i) with respect to $\vec{\theta}$. For SVM and log-linear models, a learning rate factor α is further added. After calculating $\vec{g}_i^t$, the model parameters are updated on the training instance (x_i, y_i) by adding $\vec{g}_i^t$ to the old value. The total iteration number T is a hyper-parameter and can be decided empirically on a set of development data.

Table 4.1 summarises the details of LOCALUPDATE$(x_i, y_i, \vec{\theta})$ for the three specific linear model instances under binary and multiple-class classification, respectively. Their differences result from different training objective functions, which we discuss further in the next two sub-sections.

4.3.2 Loss Functions

The training objectives for SVMs, perceptron models and log-linear models under the binary and multi-class settings are summarised in Table 4.2. These training objectives can be regarded as attempts to minimise different **loss functions** of a model over a training set, which reflects the difference between a desired score value on a set of training instances and the score value as given by the model. In particular, disregarding the term $\frac{1}{2}\lambda||\vec{\theta}||^2$ (which we discuss in Section 4.3.3), the loss functions of SVMs and perceptrons are similar, with the value being 0 when $\vec{\theta} \cdot \vec{\phi}$ is

Table 4.1 LOCALUPDATE $(x_i, y_i, \vec{\theta})$ for SVMs, perceptrons and log-linear models.

Feature	Model	Update rule
Binary classification	Perceptron	$y_i\vec{\phi}(x_i)$ **if** $y_i\left(\vec{\theta}\cdot\vec{\phi}(x_i)\right) < 0$
	SVM	$\begin{cases} \alpha y_i\vec{\phi}(x_i) - \alpha\lambda\vec{\theta} \text{ } \textbf{if } y_i\left(\vec{\theta}\cdot\vec{\phi}(x_i)\right) \leqslant 1 \\ -\alpha\lambda\vec{\theta} \quad \text{otherwise} \end{cases}$
	Log-linear models	$\begin{cases} \alpha\left(1 - P(y=+1\|x_i)\right)\vec{\phi}(x_i) \textbf{ if } y_i = +1 \\ \alpha\left(-P(y=+1\|x_i)\right)\vec{\phi}(x_i) \text{ otherwise} \end{cases}$
Multi-class classification	Perceptron	$\vec{\phi}(x_i, y_i) - \vec{\phi}(x_i, z_i) \textbf{ if } z_i \neq y_i$ $z_i = \arg\max_c \vec{\theta}\cdot\vec{\phi}(x_i, c)$
	SVM	$\begin{cases} \alpha\left(\vec{\phi}(x_i, y_i) - \vec{\phi}(x_i, c)\right) - \alpha\lambda\vec{\theta} \\ \quad \textbf{if } \vec{\theta}\cdot\vec{\phi}(x_i, y_i) - \vec{\theta}\cdot\vec{\phi}(x_i, z_i) \leqslant 1 \\ -\alpha\lambda\vec{\theta} \quad\quad \text{otherwise} \end{cases}$ $z_i = \arg\max_{c\neq y_i} \vec{\theta}\cdot\vec{\phi}(x_i, c)$
	Log-linear models	$\alpha\sum_c \left(\vec{\phi}(x_i, y_i) - \vec{\phi}(x_i, c)\right)P(y=c\|x_i)$

sufficiently large for a gold-standard positive instance, but increases linearly as $\vec{\theta}\cdot\vec{\phi}$ decreases beyond a threshold. We call such loss functions **hinge loss**. In contrast, the loss function for log-linear models are called **log-likelihood loss**, which never reaches absolute 0.

A contrast between different loss functions in the binary classification setting is shown in Figure 4.2, where the x-axis shows the value of $y_i\left(\vec{\theta}\cdot\vec{\phi}(x_i)\right)$ and the y-axis shows the loss value. The loss values of all the models tend to 0 when the model gives large positive scores to x^+ and negative scores with large absolute values to x^-. In contrast, the loss increases when the score of x^+ is low and the score of x^- is high. This shows that all the models are trained to give high scores to x^+ and low scores to x^-. However, the loss function shapes differ across models. Intuitively, the perceptron training objective is "satisfied" as long as positive examples have positive scores and negative examples have negative scores, in which case it gives a 0 loss value. However, if a positive example receives a negative score, then the perceptron loss is proportional to the absolute score value. The SVM objective is more stringent in that it is "satisfied" only when the score of positive examples are greater than 1. In contrast, the log-likelihood loss is never 0 – it tends to 0 as the score of positive examples tends to infinity. While both perceptrons and SVMs have sharp

Table 4.2 Loss functions of SVMs, perceptrons and log-linear models.

Feature	Model	Loss function
Binary classification	Perceptron	$\sum_{i=1}^{N} \max\left(0, -y_i\vec{\theta} \cdot \vec{\phi}(x_i)\right)$
	SVM	$\sum_{i=1}^{N} \max\left(0, 1 - y_i\vec{\theta} \cdot \vec{\phi}(x_i)\right) + \frac{1}{2}\lambda\|\vec{\theta}\|^2$
	Log-linear models	$\sum_{i=1}^{N} \log(1 + e^{-y_i\vec{\theta} \cdot \vec{\phi}(x_i)})$
Multi-class classification	Perceptron	$\sum_{i=1}^{N} \max\left(0, -\vec{\theta} \cdot \vec{\phi}(x_i, y_i) + \max_{c} \vec{\theta} \cdot \vec{\phi}(x_i, c)\right)$
	SVM	$\sum_{i=1}^{N} \max\left(0, 1 - \vec{\theta} \cdot \vec{\phi}(x_i, y_i) + \max_{c \neq y_i} \vec{\theta} \cdot \vec{\phi}(x_i, c)\right) + \frac{1}{2}\lambda\|\vec{\theta}\|^2$
	Log-linear models	$\sum_{i=1}^{N} \left(\log\left(\sum_{c} e^{\vec{\theta} \cdot \vec{\phi}(x_i, c)}\right) - \vec{\theta} \cdot \vec{\phi}(x_i, y_i)\right)$

turning points, the curves for log-linear models are more smooth. We will see another perspective on log-likelihood losses in Chapter 5.

The differences in loss functions reflect fundamental differences in the training strategy for linear classification models. In theory, loss measures the price paid by incorrect classification. A natural way to define loss functions for classifiers is **0/1 loss**, where the loss is 1 for an incorrect output, and 0 for a correct output. Such a loss function, however, is non-convex and non-smooth, making optimisation highly difficult. Compared with 0/1 loss, hinge loss and log-likelihood loss are easier to optimise, and sensitive to the model score. Although Figure 4.2 illustrates only binary classification losses, multi-class classification losses can be understood similarly considering correct outputs as positive examples and incorrect outputs as negative examples.

Risks. The loss functions in Table 4.2 can be viewed as approximations of underlying **risks** of models. In particular, let us consider a random instance which we may or may not see in the training data. We want to give high scores to a positive instance and low scores to a negative instance. If the scores are sufficient for making a correct prediction, then we are safe. Otherwise we risk making a mistake. The lower the score we assign to a positive instance, the higher the risk. The instance-level loss should reflect this risk, which belongs to the inherent characteristics of a model. Theoretically, our training objective should correspondingly be to minimise the **expected risk** over arbitrary instances. Formally, for a linear model with a parameter vector $\vec{\theta}$ the expected risk can be formulated as

$$risk(\vec{\theta}) = \sum_{x,y} loss\left(\vec{\theta} \cdot \vec{\phi}(x, y)\right) P(x, y),$$

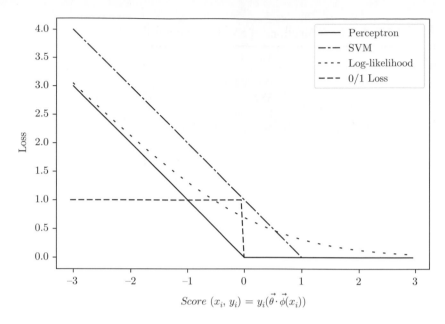

Figure 4.2 Loss functions.

where (x, y) denotes a random input–output pair, and *loss* here represents the instance-level risk of making the score assignment $\vec{\theta} \cdot \vec{\phi}(x, y)$. This true expected risk cannot be practically calculated because it can be difficult to enumerate (x, y) from open sets. As a result, classification models use **empirical risk** as a proxy instead, where the empirical probability of a training instance $\tilde{P}(x_i, y_i) = 1/N$ $(i \in [1, \ldots, N])$ and

$$\widetilde{risk}(\vec{\theta}) = \frac{1}{N} \sum_{i=1}^{N} loss\left(\vec{\theta} \cdot \vec{\phi}(x_i, y_i)\right), \ (x_i, y_i) \in D.$$

4.3.3 Regularisation

As discussed earlier, a difference between SVMs and perceptrons is the $\frac{1}{2}\lambda||\vec{\theta}||^2$ term in SVM loss, which can be intuitively interpreted as minimising the size of the parameter vector. In practice, such a term can be regarded as a **regularisation** term for the training objective, which can be used for perceptron and log-linear models also. While different regularisation terms can be used to enrich loss functions for different purposes, we discuss regularisation terms that directly minimise a polynomial of $\vec{\theta}$. In particular, the term $\frac{1}{2}\lambda||\vec{\theta}||^2$ is commonly referred to as **L2 regularisation**. Correspondingly, a term $\lambda||\vec{\theta}||_1$ is called **L1 regularisation**. Both L1 and L2 regularisation are useful for reducing the size of the parameter vector. While L2 regularisation typically reduces the absolute values of weights in $\vec{\theta}$, L1 regularisation can result in sparser $\vec{\theta}$, with more 0 weights.

L1 and L2 regularisation can empirically help reduce overfitting of models on given training data. An intuition from SVMs is that L2 regularisation allows the model to select a "safe" separating hyperplane, one that is far away from support vectors from both sides. From another perspective, a large element in the parameter vector implies heavy reliance on its corresponding feature. L2 and L1 regularisation prevent a model from leaning towards certain features too much unnecessarily, which can lead to overfitting on peculiarities of the training data.

4.4 Choosing and Combining Models

Given a set of training data D, we can obtain different discriminative linear model instances according to different training objectives (e.g., large margin or log-likelihood), different feature definitions, different hyper-parameters (e.g., number of training iterations; learning rate) and so on. Given different models for the same task, two natural questions can arise. First, how can one decide which model is the best choice? Second, can one leverage multiple models to obtain better performances than using a single model? Sections 4.4.1 and 4.4.2 discuss these issues, respectively.

4.4.1 Comparing Model Performances

There are some rules of thumb to compare different models. For example, in general, discriminative models with rich features can outperform simple generative models with basic features. On the other hand, it can be difficult to theoretically show that one model is superior compared to another on certain tasks and datasets. For example, it is difficult to tell whether the log-linear model training objective is a better choice compared to the SVM objective under certain settings. The answer depends on the characteristics of a specific set of training data, as well as the test samples. As a result, a useful way to make a choice between alternative models is to make *empirical comparisons*, where different models can be trained on the same set of data, with their hyper-parameters being tuned on the same development data, and then evaluated on the same test data. The model that gives the highest accuracies is likely a better choice for unseen test cases.

Significance tests. Given a specific set of test data, we can compare different models, finding the top performer. However, we cannot tell for sure that the top performer will be the top performer on new test samples, because we do not know the characteristics of unseen samples. Take text classification for example: if model A gives an accuracy of 93.1% on a test set and model B gives an accuracy of 93.3%, we may not be able to confidently say that model B is superior to model A in general. To address this issue, there is a method for using the *empirical errors* on a given test set to estimate the *generalisation errors* on unseen test samples.

In particular, assuming that the generalisation error of two models are the same, we can calculate the probability of obtaining the observed test results by both models. The smaller the probability, the less likely the two models are the same, and therefore the more likely that the empirically better model is generally better. We take small values of such a probability as *significance levels*, and the evaluation of the probability value a **significance test**. A commonly used significance test is the *pairwise t-test*. Using significance levels, we can measure the degree of generalisability. For example, we can say that model B's 93.3% is better than model A's 93.1% significantly, at

$p = 10^{-3}$ using t-test. This indicates that there is only a 10^{-3} probability that the two models are the same. By convention, a significance level of less than 0.05 indicates statistical significance.

4.4.2 Ensemble Models

Intuitively, different models make different empirical errors, and thus complement each other. It is hence *possible* that a combination of multiple models gives better performance compared to the use of a single model. This strategy is the **ensemble approach**. Below we discuss two different methods to this end, namely voting and stacking, using text classification as the task.

Voting. A simple ensemble method to combine different models is **voting**. Formally, given a set of models $M = \{m_1, m_2, \ldots, m_{|M|}\}$ and output classes $C = \{c_1, c_2, \ldots, c_{|C|}\}$, the output class y for a given input x can be decided by counting the vote for each class $v_1, v_2, \ldots, v_{|C|}$, where

$$v_i = \sum_{j=1}^{|M|} \mathbf{1}\Big(y(m_j), c_i\Big).$$

Here $y(m_j)$ denotes the output class label of m_j and $\mathbf{1}\Big(\circ, \circ\Big)$ is the indicator function.

There are two common strategies for making a decision. The first is *majority voting*, which chooses the class label that receives more than half of the total votes (i.e., $|M|/2$ votes). A disadvantage of this strategy is that the voting results will be rejected if no class label receives the majority of votes. The second strategy is *plurality voting*, which chooses the class label with the most votes. If there is more than one class label that receives the most votes, a choice can be made randomly.

Instead of counting *hard* 0/1 votes, *soft* voting can be performed using the scores assigned by each model to each class label instead, which reflect the confidence levels of each model. This more fine-grained voting method calculates v_i using

$$v_i = \sum_{j=1}^{|M|} score(c_i, m_j),$$

where $score(c_i, m_j)$ denotes the score m_j assigns to label c_i.

Soft voting assumes that the scores given by each model is on the same scale. As a result, models trained using different learning algorithms (e.g., SVM and perceptron) are not suitable for this method, since the score differences interpreted by each model are not compatible. As a result, soft voting is commonly used for models trained with the same training algorithm but having different features or hyper-parameters.

A weight α_j can be given to each model m_j in the voting process, which results in the linear interpolation of scores

$$v_i = \sum_{j=1}^{|M|} \alpha_j score(c_i, m_j)$$

Table 4.3 A stacking example for combining two classifiers on the document *"Ronaldo donated* 600, 000 *to charity"*. The document label should be "sports" or "finance", the output label of the classifier B is "sports" and the corresponding probability distribution is *sports* = 0.7, *finance* = 0.3. Classifier A can use classifier B's output class label y_B or the probability $P(y)_B$ as input features.

Model	Feature Type	Features
B	Bag-of-words	w_1 =Ronaldo, w_2 =donated, w_3 =€, w_4 =600,000, w_5 =to, w_6 =charity
A	Bag-of-words + B's output label	w_1 =Ronaldo, w_2 =donated, w_3 =€, w_4 =600,000, w_5 =to, w_6 =charity, y_B =sports
A	Bag-of-words + B's probability outputs	w_1 =Ronaldo, w_2 =donated, w_3 =€, w_4 =600,000, w_5 =to, w_6 =charity, $P(y_B = sports) \in [0.6, 0.7]$, $P(y_B = finance) \in [0.2, 0.3]$

where $\alpha_j > 0$ and $\sum_{j=1}^{|M|} \alpha_j = 1$. The motivation is that some models can be more accurate compared to others, and therefore can be trusted relatively more. The values of α_i can be tuned on a set of development data.

With more hyper-parameters, weighted voting is more flexible compared with simple average voting. However, its performance is tuned on a certain set of development data, and hence can suffer from overfitting. If the test domain is unknown, simple average voting can be a default choice.

Stacking. A second way to integrate different models is **stacking**, which uses the outputs of one model as features to inform another model. Formally, given a test input x, a model B is first used to predict its output y_B. Both x and y_B are then used as inputs to a model A for predicting the final output y_A. Table 4.3 shows a stacking example, where different features from B's output are integrated to A's feature set.

Assume that both A and B are trained on the same D. Unlike the voting method, which trains each model independently using D, the stacking method trains A after B is trained. Similar to the test scenario, B's predictions on the training data D are used as features in A. However, the performance of model B is expected to be significantly higher on the training data D compared with a test input, which has not been seen before. As a result, the training scenario for model A is easier compared to the test scenario, with more near-gold-standard output features from y_B. This inconsistency can lead to model A being less accurate in the test scenario, where the features from model B outputs y_B are less accurate.

Table 4.4 k-fold jackknifing.

Training set	Model	Test set
$D_2, \ldots, D_k$	B_1	D_1
$D_1, D_3, \ldots, D_k$	B_2	D_2
$\ldots$	$\ldots$	$\ldots$
$D_1, D_2, \ldots, D_{k-1}$	B_k	D_k

To address the issue above, a common strategy is **k-fold jackknifing**, which simulates test-scenario features from y_B for the training of model A. The basic idea is to make model B output accuracies on the training data as close to the test scenario as possible. To achieve this, the method splits the training data D into k equal sections, $D_1, D_2, \ldots, D_k$ for training k versions of model B, denoted as $B_1, B_2, \ldots, B_k$, respectively. Each B_i is trained using $\{D_1, \ldots, D_{i-1}, D_{i+1}, \ldots, D_k\}$, as shown in Table 4.4. After training, each B_i is used to predict the output y_{B_i} for the respective D_i. Since D_i is excluded from the training set for B_i, the stacking features from B_i on D_i resemble those on unseen test data. Common k values include 5 and 10.

Making training and testing settings consistent. k-Fold jackknifing is a general strategy with many other applications. For example, for syntactic parsing tasks, POS-tagging can be taken as a pipelined pre-processing task. Training data for syntactic parsers typically contain gold-standard POS tags. However, for training a parser it can be undesirable to use gold POS-tagging as inputs, since during testing POS-tags are predicted by a POS-tagger, which can have mistakes. A parser trained using gold POS-tag inputs does not know how to handle POS-tagging errors. To address this issue, k-fold jackknifing can be performed on the training data for assigning automatic POS-tags for parser input. In addition to k-fold jackknifing, we will see later in the book other strategies for making the training and testing settings similar, which allows a model to learn from real data distributions for better testing performance.

4.4.3 Semi-Supervised Learning

In addition to ensemble modelling, a different way of leveraging multiple models is *data augmentation*, which makes use of unlabelled data to enlarge the training set D. The basic idea is to use different models trained on D to predict the labels on a set of unlabelled data U, augmenting D with the outputs that most models agree on. Since both annotated and unannotated data are used, such methods belong to *semi-supervised learning*.

Co-training uses two models A and B to label raw text data. Pseudocode is shown in Algorithm 4.10. Given D and U as defined above, the method trains A and B using D, and then uses them to predict the output label of each sample x'_i in U. If both A and B are confident on a certain output z'_i, then (x'_i, z'_i) is added to D. The confidence value threshold is a hyper-parameter. The same process can repeat for several iterations, each time incrementally enlarging D. Assuming that A and B are sufficiently different (e.g., they have different features), co-training makes use of complementary information for better performance.

Algorithm 4.10. Co-training.

Inputs: $D = \{(x_i, y_i)\}|_{i=1}^{N}$, $U = \{x_i'\}|_{i=1}^{M}$, models A and B;

Initialisation: t ← 0;

repeat

    t ← t+1;

    TRAIN(A, D);

    TRAIN(B, D);

    for $x_i' \in U$ **do**

        $z_A' \leftarrow$ PREDICT(A, x_i');

        $z_B' \leftarrow$ PREDICT(B, x_i');

        if $z_A' = z_B' = z_i'$ **and** CONFIDENT(A, x_i', z_i') **and** CONFIDENT(B, x_i', z_i') **then**

            ADD($D, (x_i', z_i')$);

            REMOVE(U, x_i');

until $t = T$;

Algorithm 4.11. Self-training.

Inputs: $D = \{(x_i, y_i)\}|_{i=1}^{N}$, $U = \{x_i'\}|_{i=1}^{M}$, model A;

Initialisation: t ← 0;

repeat

    t ← t+1;

    TRAIN(A, D);

    for $x_i' \in U$ **do**

        $z_i' \leftarrow$ PREDICT(A, x_i');

        if CONFIDENT(A, x_i', z_i') **then**

            ADD($D, (x_i', z_i')$);

            REMOVE(U, x_i');

until $t = T$;

A related algorithm is **self-training**, which augments D using outputs of a single model A on U according to model confidence. The motivation is that more confident outputs are more likely to be correct, and hence useful for enlarging a training set. Pseudocode of this algorithm is shown in Algorithm 4.11. The framework is similar to the co-training method, except that only one model A is used to label each sample x_i' in U.

The effectiveness of co-training and self-training is largely empirical, although there has been some study on the conditions when these methods will outperform a baseline model A trained on D. In general, the more accurate the baseline models are on U, the more likely that the new data from U can be correct and useful.

Summary

In this chapter we have introduced:

- log-linear models for binary and multi-class classification;
- stochastic gradient descent (SGD) training of log-linear models and SVMs;
- a generalised linear discriminative model for text classification;
- significance testing;
- ensemble methods.

Chapter Notes

Log-linear models (Gujarati and Porter, 2009) are also referred to as logistic regressions models (Cox and Snell, 1989) for classification, and maximum-entropy models (Berger et al., 1996) in NLP. They were used for text classification (Nigam et al., 1999), but more for structured prediction tasks (Ratnaparkhi, 1996) in NLP, which will be discussed in Part II of the book. Stochastic gradient descent (SGD) was developed by Robbins and Monro (1951). Bottou (1998) gave a detailed introduction for SGD training in neural networks.

Minibatch SGD was introduced by Cotter et al. (2011) and Li et al. (2014). Tsuruoka et al. (2009) discussed SGD training for L1-regularised log-linear models. Shalev-Shwartz et al. (2011) investigated SGD optimization of SVMs. The concept of loss function was discussed in statistics by Wald (1950). Poggio et al. (1985) discussed the use of regularisation. Co-training (Blum and Mitchell, 1998) has been shown useful for parsing (Steedman et al., 2003) and word sense disambiguation (Mihalcea, 2004). Self-training was first used for word sense disambiguation (Yarowsky, 1995; Abney, 2002), and subsequently for parsing (Charniak, 1997) and other tasks.

Exercises

4.1 What is the relationship between SVM updates and log-linear models updates using SGD? The SVM counterpart for the weights $P(y = +1|x_i) - 1$ and $P(y = +1|x_i)$ for log-linear models in Algorithm 4.3 and Algorithm 4.4 is a condition that parameters are updated only if $\vec{\theta} \cdot \left(\vec{\phi}(x_i, y_i) - \vec{\phi}(x_i, c) \right) < 1$, which can be viewed as a *hard condition* alternative to the *soft* weights of log-linear models for controlling parameter updates according to violations.

4.2 One alternative loss function for multi-class SVM is the *indicator loss function*, which considers all violations $L = \sum_{i=1}^{N} \sum_{c} \max \left(0, 1 - \vec{\theta} \cdot \vec{\phi}(x_i, y_i) + \vec{\theta} \cdot \vec{\phi}(x_i, c) \right) + \frac{1}{2}\lambda||\vec{\theta}||^2$ instead of a single most-violated constraint.

(a) Calculate the derivative $\frac{\partial L}{\partial \vec{\theta}}$.

(b) Based on $\frac{\partial L}{\partial \theta}$, give the SGD training algorithm, comparing its update rules with log-linear models and perceptrons.

4.3 Define a log-linear model training objective with $L2$ regularisation. What is the parameter update formula for this training objective in SGD training?

4.4 Some researchers say that regularised perceptron is as good as SVM. Can you give some theoretical justification for this claim?

4.5 The generalised linear model allows flexible loss functions to be defined. With SGD training, define the parameter updates for the models below. Can each be regarded as a log-linear model, SVM or perceptron?

(a) a discriminative linear model with a large-margin objective and $L1$-regularisation, where the loss function is:

$$loss(\vec{\theta}) = \frac{1}{N} \sum_{i=1}^{N} \ell\left(x_i, y_i, \vec{\theta}\right) + \lambda||\vec{\theta}||$$

and

$$\ell(x_i, y_i, \vec{\theta}) = \max_{y \neq y_i} \left(\vec{\theta} \cdot \vec{\phi}(x_i, y) + 1\right) - \vec{\theta} \cdot \vec{\phi}(x_i, y_i).$$

(b) a discriminative linear model with a maximum log-likelihood objective and L2 regularisation, where the loss function is:

$$loss(\vec{\theta}) = -\sum_{i=1}^{N} \log P(y_i|x_i) + \frac{\lambda}{2}||\vec{\theta}||^2.$$

4.6 For text classification tasks, the output classes can be **unbalanced**, with one text class being much more frequent compared with other classes. Take spam filtering for example, the number of spam emails can be much larger than that of non-spam emails. If the training data are highly unbalanced, a classifier may decide to predict the majority class label for every test input. For example, if the class $+1$ is 9 times the class -1, then a fixed guess of $+1$ for all test samples can give a 90% accuracy. One way to address this issue is to **under sample** training instances, so that the number of training samples for all classes are balanced. This method has been shown to be effective empirically. However, this *data-level* method can fail to make use of all gold-standard training samples. Let us consider some *algorithm-level methods* instead. For simplicity, only binary classification is discussed.

(a) For probabilistic models (e.g., log-linear models), one method to alleviate our prediction of the majority class is to adjust the *decision threshold*. In particular, we have assumed that $P(y = +1|x) = 0.5$ is the threshold so that instances with $P(y = +1|x) \geqslant 0.5$ is assigned class $+1$, and others class -1. If the datasets are unbalanced, discuss how the threshold 0.5 can be adjusted.

(b) For large-margin models (e.g SVMs and perceptrons), the score $\vec{\theta} \cdot \phi(x)$ cannot be interpreted directly. However, we can adjust the training objective so that the minority class has a better chance of being considered. One example is **cost-sensitive training**, where the training objective becomes to minimise

$$\frac{1}{2}||\vec{w}||^2 + C^+ \sum_{i+} \xi_i + C^- \sum_{i-} \xi_i$$

such that

$$y_i \times \left(\vec{w}^T \vec{v}(x_i) + b\right) = 1 - \xi_i, \qquad \xi_i \geqslant 0.$$

This can translate to

$$(\vec{w}, b) = \underset{(\vec{w},b)}{\arg\min} \left(C^+ \sum_{i+} \max \left(0, 1 - \left(\vec{w}^T \vec{v}(x_i) + b\right)\right) \right.$$
$$\left. + C^- \sum_{i-} \max \left(0, 1 + \left(\vec{w}^T \vec{v}(x_i) + b\right)\right) + \frac{1}{2}||\vec{w}||^2 \right).$$

Discuss how to set the costs C^+ and C^-.

4.7 Consider SGD training for log-linear models and SVM.

(a) Consider adding L1 regularisation to log-linear models. The regularisation term is not differentiable. Specify a sub-gradient for the weight update, following examples from SVM training.

(b) Unlike feature vectors, which are highly sparse, with only a few non-zero elements for each training instance, (sub-)gradients for L1 and L2 regularisation can have non-zero values for most elements in $\vec{\theta}$. As a result, SGD training can be significantly slower at each iterative step. One way to expedite training is **lazy update**. The main idea is not to update a weight value if the corresponding feature is not used in the current training instance. Instead, a record can be used to remember the last iteration at which the weight is updated. For most weight values, there is a constant incremental change through a large number of iterations. When a weight value is used or updated, the constant incremental value per iteration can be cumulatively added to the weight, by multiplication with the number of iterations from the last update to the current iteration. Use the lazy update strategy to optimise log-linear models with L1 and L2 regularisation, writing pseudocode.

4.8 Consider again Algorithm 4.10 for co-training. **Tri-training** uses three different models for labelling U. Given a set of annotated training examples D and a set of raw input data U, the algorithm starts by training three different models A, B and C using D. The three models are then used to predict the output of each sample x_i' in U. If two models agree on a certain output z_i', (x_i', z_i') is added to D. After U has been exhausted, a new training set D is obtained. The same process can repeat for several iterations, each time with D being enlarged. Write pseudocode for tri-training following Algorithms 4.10 and 4.11.

4.9 Generalise self-training, co-training and tri-training into one unified semi-supervised algorithm, and write its pseudocode.

4.10 Bagging. Given a model A and a set of training examples D, the bagging method randomly extracts k different subsets of D, denoted as $D_1, D_2, \ldots, D_k$, respectively. k different models are trained, using each subset, which are denoted as $A_1, A_2, \ldots, A_k$, respectively. Voting is then performed between A_i given a test case. Bagging has been shown to outperform a single model A trained on D empirically for many tasks. Discuss the correlation between bagging and ensemble.

5   A Perspective from Information Theory

In the previous chapter, we used the *sigmoid* and *softmax* functions to define log-linear models, which constrain the score $\vec{\theta} \cdot \vec{\phi} \in [-\infty, \infty]$ of a linear model to $f(\vec{\theta} \cdot \vec{\phi}) \in [0, 1]$. Given the fact that there are many alternative functions that map a score in $[-\infty, \infty]$ to a score in $[0, 1]$, a question is why *sigmoid* and *softmax* are chosen for log-linear models. It turns out that there is a deeper information theoretic motivation, namely the **maximum entropy** principle. For building a probabilistic model, the maximum entropy principle indicates that a model should maximise the entropy, or uncertainty of the output distribution, given knowledge conveyed by a set of training data. It can be intuitively understood as: the best way to model something unknown is to make the least assumptions about it. We will show in this chapter that this principle leads to the log-linear model formulation.

Investigating the characteristics of random variables, information theory is closely related to probabilistic modelling. In addition to describing the characteristics of a single probability distribution, it can also be used for quantifying the correlation between two distributions of the same variable. This is useful for measuring how well a model distribution fits a data distribution. For example, *cross-entropy* and *Kullback–Leibler divergence* have been used for defining training objectives. A related concept, *perplexity*, has been taken as the main evaluation metric of language models. In addition to the above, *mutual information* measures the relatedness of two random variables. It has been used to define both features and learning objectives of NLP models. In this chapter, we discuss these concepts and their uses in the field.

5.1   The Maximum Entropy Principle

Entropy is a concept in **information theory**, which investigates the mathematics of encoding and transmitting data. Here **information** is used as knowledge to resolve *uncertainty* about random events. Information is measured in *bits*, based on the assumption that data are represented using binary numbers. For example, one bit of information is sufficient for resolving the uncertainty of an unknown event with two equally possible outcomes, such as coin tossing. In particular, for informing a receiver the outcome of a coin toss, one can use "0" to encode "heads", and "1" to encode "tails". Similarly, two bits of information is sufficient for resolving the uncertainty of four equally possible outcomes, such as the suit of a randomly drawn card from a 52-card deck for bridge. In particular, "spade", "heart", "diamond" and "club" can be encoded using "00", "01", "10" and "11", respectively.

In general, to learn the outcome of a random event with n equally possible results, $\lceil \log_2 n \rceil$ bits of information is necessary. The amount of information can also be measured for partially resolving uncertainty. For example, if we know that a randomly drawn card is heart or diamond, then only 1 bit of information is further necessary for learning the suit (e.g., 0 for heart and 1 for diamond). In this case, our prior knowledge contains 1 bit of information. As a second example, for learning the outcome of a fair die, $\log_2 6$ bits of information is necessary. However, knowledge that the outcome is big (i.e., 4, 5 or 6) results in $\log_2 3$ bits of remaining uncertainty, hence reducing the uncertainty by $\log_2 6 - \log_2 3 = 1$ bits. Similarly, knowing that the outcome is 1 or 6 reduces the uncertainty by $\log_2 6 - \log_2 2 = \log_2 3$ bits.

In the above examples, all the outcomes of a random event are equally likely. On the other hand, in a non-uniform distribution, the probability distribution of different outcomes affects the amount of information in each outcome. The more likely an outcome is, the less information we gain by learning the outcome. For example, consider the event of drawing a ball from a box, which can be either red or green. Without prior knowledge, we assume that there is an equal number of red and green balls in the box, and hence knowing the colour of a drawn ball reduces the uncertainty by a half, which equals $\log_2 k - \log_2 \frac{k}{2} = 1$ bit of information, where k is the total number of balls. On the other hand, if we know that there are m red balls and n green balls in the box, knowledge of the drawn ball being red reduces the uncertainty from $\log_2 (m + n)$ bits to $\log_2 m$ bits, thus equalling $\log_2 \frac{m+n}{m}$ bits, or $-\log_2 \widetilde{P}(red)$, where $\widetilde{P}(red) = \frac{m}{m+n}$ is the *empirical probability* of a ball being red. This observation can be generalised: supposing that there are M outcomes of a random event $z_1, z_2, \ldots, z_M$, and the probability of a certain outcome z_i is $P(z_i)$, the information received by learning this outcome is $-\log_2 P(z_i)$.

According to the above, we can calculate the amount of information contained in each outcome z_i of a random event e, if the probability distribution of all the outcomes are known. We can further derive a single number to denote the *expected* number of bits to encode *any* outcome of the variable, for conveniently knowing its overall uncertainty. **Entropy** serves this purpose. Formally, denoting the probability of z_i as $P(z_i)$, the entropy of the distribution P is

$$H(P) = -\sum_{i=1}^{n} P(z_i) \log_2 P(z_i)$$

$$= \sum_{i=1}^{n} P(z_i) \log_2 \frac{1}{P(z_i)} \qquad (5.1)$$

$$= E(\log_2 \frac{1}{P(z_i)}).$$

Equation 5.1 can be interpreted as using $\log_2 \frac{1}{P(z_i)}$ bits to encode the outcome z_i, which is exactly the amount of information the outcome z_i conveys. E denotes a probability-weighted average, namely the **mathematical expectation** of the number of bits for encoding one arbitrary outcome. In contrast to *information*, which analyses individual outcomes, entropy analyses overall events with all possible outcomes.

Events with uniform output distributions have the largest entropy. The more uneven the distribution is, the smaller the entropy is. Consider again the dice throwing example. For a fair dice, $-\log_2 \frac{1}{6} \approx 3$ bits are necessary to encode one arbitrary outcome. For example, one can encode the outcomes 1, 2, 3, 4, 5 and 6 using "000", "001", "010", "011", "100" and "101", respectively. As a result, 300 bits of information is needed to inform a receiver of the outcomes of 100 throws. On the other hand, if we know that the die is unfair, with a 50% chance that the outcome is 1, and a 10% chance that the outcome is 2, 3, 4, 5 and 6, respectively, we can reduce the *average* number of bits for encoding the outcome, by using less bits to encode the most probable outcome. In particular, we can use $-\log_2 \frac{50}{100} = 1$ bit to encode the most likely outcome and $-\log_2 \frac{10}{100} \approx 4$ bits to encode every other outcome. For example, we can use "0" to encode the outcome 1, and "1000", "1001", "1010", "1011" and "1100" to encode the outcomes 2, 3, 4, 5 and 6, respectively. To transmit the outcome of 100 throws, we now need on average $1 \times 50 + (4 \times 10) \times 5 = 250$ bits, which is smaller compared to 300 bits for a uniform distribution.

As mentioned in Chapter 2, for text classification and other tasks in NLP, a discrete output (e.g. a class label) can be viewed as a random event, or *random variable*. A probabilistic model gives a distribution of its possible *values*, typically conditioned on a given input. We call this distribution a *model distribution*. In this section we show how the maximum entropy principle can be applied for deriving probabilistic models.

5.1.1 A Naïve Maximum Entropy Model

To begin with, let us consider the derivation of a probabilistic model for categorical distributions without any training data. As discussed in Chapter 2, the random event of casino dice casting, or drawing a word from a random text, both belong to categorical distributions. We parameterise the model by taking the probability of each value directly as a parameter. When building a probabilistic model for a random event e with M possible outcomes $z_1, z_2, \ldots, z_M$, the **maximum entropy** principle finds a model with the probability distribution that maximises the entropy $H(P)$ of e

$$\hat{P} = \arg\max_P H(P) = \arg\max_P \left(-\sum_{i=1}^{M} P(z_i) \log_2 P(z_i) \right).$$

The intuition is to find a model that does not make any assumptions about the distribution (without prior knowledge). The maximum entropy principle coincides with *Occam's razor*, a principle attributed to the fourteenth-century English Franciscan friar William of Ockham, which states that "*entities should not be multiplied beyond necessity*".

Now our objective is to find

$$
\begin{aligned}
\hat{P}(e) &= \arg\max_P H(e) \\
&= \arg\min_P (-H(e)) \\
&= \arg\min_P \sum_{i=1}^{M} P(z_i) \log_2 P(z_i)
\end{aligned}
\tag{5.2}
$$

under the constraint that

$$\sum_{i=1}^{M} P(z_i) = 1. \tag{5.3}$$

Regarding each $P(z_i)$ as a separate variable, this is a standard constrained optimisation problem, which can be solved using Lagrange multipliers. The Lagrangian equation for Eq 5.2 under the constraint of Eq 5.3 is

$$\Lambda\Big(P(z_1), P(z_2), \ldots, P(z_M), \lambda\Big) = \sum_{i=1}^{M} P(z_i) \log_2 P(z_i) + \lambda\Big(1 - \sum_{i=1}^{M} P(z_i)\Big),$$

where λ is a Lagrangian multiplier.

A necessary condition for optimality in the constrained problem is that $\frac{\partial \Lambda}{\partial P(z_i)} = 0$ for $i \in [1, \ldots, M]$. Taking the partial derivative of Λ with respect to $P(z_1), P(z_2), \ldots, P(z_M)$, respectively, we arrive at

$$\begin{cases} 1 + \log_2 P(z_1) - \lambda = 0 \\ 1 + \log_2 P(z_2) - \lambda = 0 \\ \cdots \\ 1 + \log_2 P(z_M) - \lambda = 0 \end{cases},$$

respectively, which suggests that

$$P(z_1) = P(z_2) = \cdots = P(z_M).$$

Further because $\sum_{i=1}^{M} P(z_i) = 1$, we have $P(z_1) = P(z_2) = \cdots = P(z_M) = 1/M$, which leads to a single candidate optimal value $\hat{P}(e) = -\log_2 M$. This conclusion can be intuitively understood as the fact that the uniform distribution contains the most uncertainty, which conforms to our observation at the beginning of Section 5.1.

Below we show how the maximum entropy principle can be used for deriving probabilistic models given a set of training data, and with feature-based parameterisation.

5.1.2 Conditional Entropy

For a conditional probability distribution $P(y|x)$, the uncertainty is measured by a **conditional entropy** value $H(y|x)$, where

$$\begin{aligned} H(y|x) &= -\sum_{x} \sum_{y} P(x, y) \log_2 P(y|x) \\ &= -\sum_{x} \sum_{y} P(x)P(y|x) \log_2 P(y|x) \end{aligned} \tag{5.4}$$

where x denotes a possible value of x and y denotes a possible value of y.

The above definition can be intuitively understood as follows. Suppose that the random variable x is known, the minimum number of bits to encode the random variable y can be calculated according to the standard entropy definition, which is

$$H(Y|X = x) = -\sum_{y} P(y|x) \log_2 P(y|x).$$

Now given that x follows a probability distribution $P(x)$, $H(y|x)$ should be the average number of bits to encode each y given each distinct value of x, namely the mathematical expectation of $H(y|x = x)$ for all possible x. Therefore

$$H(y|x) = \sum_x P(x)H(y|x = x)$$

$$= -\sum_x P(x) \sum_y P(y|x) \log_2 P(y|x)$$

$$= -\sum_x \sum_y P(x)P(y|x) \log_2 P(y|x).$$

The connection between the conditional entropy $H(y|x)$ and the unconditional entropy $H(y)$ can be written as follows

$$H(y|x) = -\sum_x \sum_y P(x,y) \log_2 P(y|x)$$

$$= -\sum_x \sum_y P(x,y) \log_2 \frac{P(x,y)}{P(x)}$$

$$= -\sum_x \sum_y P(x,y) \left(\log_2 P(y) + \log_2 \frac{P(x,y)}{P(x)P(y)} \right)$$

$$= -\sum_x \sum_y P(x,y) \log_2 P(y) - \sum_x \sum_y P(x,y) \log_2 \frac{P(x,y)}{P(x)P(y)}$$

$$= -\sum_y P(y) \log_2 P(y) - \sum_x \sum_y P(x,y) \log_2 \frac{P(x,y)}{P(x)P(y)}$$

$$= H(y) - \sum_x \sum_y P(x,y) \log_2 \frac{P(x,y)}{P(x)P(y)}.$$

(5.5)

It can be shown that $\sum_x \sum_y P(x,y) \log_2 \frac{P(x,y)}{P(x)P(y)} \geq 0$ (Exercise 5.5), hence $H(y|x) \leq H(y)$. Intuitively, if x and y are conditionally dependent, knowledge of x reduces uncertainty of y. Only when $P(x,y) = P(x)P(y)$, namely when x is conditionally independent of y, we have the fact that $H(y|x) = H(y)$.

5.1.3 Maximum Entropy Model and Training Data

It is not difficult to show that without any prior knowledge, the maximum entropy model for a conditional event is a uniform conditional distribution over all y, which is similar to the unconditioned case in Section 5.1.1. On the other hand, given a set of training examples, we gain knowledge of $P(y|x)$, which makes it non-uniform. The degree of deviation from a uniform distribution depends on the amount and nature of the training data. In this section, we derive a maximum entropy model for feature-based discriminative classification.

Formally, denote the set of training data as $D = \{(x_j, y_j)\}|_{j=1}^N$. Each input–output pair is represented by a feature vector of m dimensions, according to m feature templates $f_1, f_2, \ldots, f_m$. As discussed in Chapter 3, the features are count-based, with the value of each feature instance being the number of matches between a feature template f_i and a pair of input and output (x, y), denoted as $f_i(x, y)$. For example, if f_{1038} is the word "*bank*" under document class "*finance*", then $f_{1038}(x, y)$ will be the count of the word "*bank*" in x if $y =$"*finance*", and 0 otherwise.

The conditional entropy to maximise is

$$H(y|x) = -\sum_x \sum_y P(x)P(y|x) \log_2 P(y|x),$$

where $P(y|x)$ is the model to build, and $P(x)$ is a prior distribution of the input data. It can be impossible to enumerate all possible values of x in practice since the input to many tasks can be an open set. Therefore, we use the *empirical distribution*

$$\tilde{P}(x) = \frac{\#x}{\sum_{x' \in D} \#x'} = \frac{\#x}{|D|} \qquad \text{(which is typically } \frac{1}{|D|}\text{)}$$

to represent $P(x)$ for each seen input, resulting in

$$H(y|x) = -\sum_x \sum_y \tilde{P}(x)P(y|x) \log_2 P(y|x). \tag{5.6}$$

Equation 5.6 contains only one variable, namely the model probability $P(y|x)$.

For our feature-based discriminative classifier, each pair (x_i, y_i) is represented by a feature vector. Consequently, knowledge in D can be represented in terms of feature instances f_i. In particular, for every feature f_i, we can count the *expected* number of times that it occurs in a gold-standard pair of input and output (x, y)

$$\begin{aligned} E(f_i) &= \sum_x \sum_y P(x, y)f_i(x, y) \\ &= \sum_x \sum_y P(x)P(y|x)f_i(x, y). \end{aligned} \tag{5.7}$$

Again $P(y|x)$ is our model in Eq 5.7, and we can use the empirical distribution $\tilde{P}(x)$ to replace $P(x)$,

$$\begin{aligned} E(f_i) &= \sum_x \sum_y \tilde{P}(x)P(y|x)f_i(x, y) \\ &= \sum_{j=1}^{|D|} \tilde{P}(x_j)P(y|x_j)f_i(x_j, y). \end{aligned} \tag{5.8}$$

Equation 5.8 can be regarded as the mathematical expectation of $f_i(x, y)$ in the set of gold-standard data, *according to our model*. On the other hand, we can also calculate the *empirical* expectation of f_i in the set of gold-standard data D as

$$\tilde{E}(f_i) = \sum_{j=1}^{|D|} \tilde{P}(x_j, y_j)f_i(x_j, y_j) \quad \left((x_j, y_j) \in D\right),$$

where

$$\tilde{P}(x_j, y_j) = \frac{\#(x_j, y_j)}{|D|} \qquad \text{(which is typically } \frac{1}{|D|} \text{)}.$$

We thus represent prior knowledge in D by assuming that $E(f_i) = \tilde{E}(f_i)$ for all features, namely assuming that the model is consistent with the data distribution with regard to f_i. As a result, the maximum entropy principle suggests a model $\hat{P}(y|x)$ that satisfies:

$$\hat{P}(y|x) = \arg\max_P - \sum_x \sum_y \tilde{P}(x)P(y|x) \log_2 P(y|x)$$

$$\text{such that} \begin{cases} \text{for all } i, E(f_i) = \tilde{E}(f_i) \\ \sum_y P(y|x) = 1 \end{cases}$$

which is equivalent to

$$\hat{P}(y|x) = \arg\min_P \sum_x \sum_y \tilde{P}(x)P(y|x) \log_2 P(y|x)$$

$$\text{such that} \begin{cases} \text{for all } i, E(f_i) = \tilde{E}(f_i) \\ \sum_y P(y|x) = 1 \end{cases}.$$

Following the process in Section 5.1.1, we solve the above constrained minimisation task using Lagrange multipliers. The Lagrangian equation is

$$\Lambda(P, \vec{\lambda}) = -H(y|x) + \sum_{i=1}^m \lambda_i \left(\tilde{E}(f_i) - E(f_i) \right) + \sum_x \lambda_{m+1}^x \left(1 - \sum_y P(y|x) \right),$$

where λ_{m+1}^x is a Lagrange multiplier for a particular input x.

A necessary condition for the constrained minimum value of $-H(y|x)$ is that the partial derivative of $\Lambda(P, \vec{\lambda})$ equals 0 with respect to all x and y, resulting in

$$\frac{\partial \Lambda}{\partial P} = \tilde{P}(x)(\log_2 e + \log_2 P) - \sum_i \tilde{P}(x)\lambda_i f_i(x, y) - \lambda_{m+1}^x = 0 \text{ for all } (x, y).$$

Solving these equations, we find that for all x, y

$$P = C^x \exp \left(\sum_{i=1}^m \lambda_i f_i(x, y) \right),$$

where C^x is a constant for each x. Further because for each x $\sum_y P(y|x) = 1$, we have

$$P(y|x) = \frac{\exp \left(\sum_{i=1}^m \lambda_i f_i(x, y) \right)}{\sum_{y'} \exp \left(\sum_{i=1}^m \lambda_i f_i(x, y') \right)}. \qquad (5.9)$$

Equation 5.9 holds for all values x and y and therefore is a general form of $P(y|x)$. It is exactly the log-linear model that we have discussed in Chapter 4. In other words, we have arrived at a log-linear form of $P(y|x)$ using the maximum entropy principle. This model form is a necessary condition for the constraint minimum for $\Lambda(P, \vec{\lambda})$. Unlike in Section 5.1.1, there is now more than one candidate optimal value, with varying $\dot{\lambda}$. In order to find the minimum value of $\Lambda(P, \vec{\lambda})$ from all λ that satisfy Eq 5.9, we need to solve for $\min_{\vec{\lambda}} \Lambda(P, \vec{\lambda})$, which is

$$
\begin{aligned}
\vec{\lambda} &= \arg\min_{\vec{\lambda}} \Lambda(P, \vec{\lambda}) \\
&= \arg\min_{\vec{\lambda}} -H(y|x) + 0 + 0 \quad \text{(conditional minimum)} \\
&= \arg\min_{\vec{\lambda}} -\frac{1}{|D|} \sum_x \sum_y P(y|x) \log_2 P(y|x) \\
&= \arg\min_{\vec{\lambda}} -\sum_x \sum_y \left(P(y|x) \left(\sum_i \lambda_i f_i(x, y) - \log_2 \sum_{y'} e^{\sum_i \lambda_i f_i(x, y')} \right) \right) \\
&= \arg\min_{\vec{\lambda}} -\sum_i \lambda_i \left(\sum_x \sum_y P(y|x) f_i(x, y) \right) + \\
&\qquad\qquad \sum_x \left(\sum_y P(y|x) \log_2 \sum_{y'} e^{\sum_i \lambda_i f_i(x, y')} \right) \\
&= \arg\min_{\vec{\lambda}} -\sum_i \lambda_i \left(\sum_{j=1}^{|D|} f_i(x_j, y_j) \right) + \\
&\qquad\qquad \sum_x \left(\left(\sum_y P(y|x) \right) \log_2 \sum_{y'} e^{\sum_i \lambda_i f_i(x, y')} \right) \\
&\qquad\qquad \left(E(f_i) = \tilde{E}(f_i) \right) \\
&= \arg\min_{\vec{\lambda}} -\sum_j \sum_i \lambda_i f_i(x_j, y_j) + \sum_j \log_2 \sum_{y'} e^{\sum_i \lambda_i f_i(x_j, y')} \\
&= \arg\min_{\vec{\lambda}} -\sum_j \left(\sum_i \lambda_i f_i(x_j, y_j) - \log_2 \sum_{y'} e^{\sum_i \lambda_i f_i(x_j, y')} \right).
\end{aligned}
$$

$$(5.10)$$

Equation 5.10 is exactly the training objective for minimising negative log-likelihood of D, the training task of finding the model parameters $\vec{\theta} = \langle \lambda_1, \lambda_2, \ldots, \lambda_m \rangle$ for log-linear models in Chapter 3. We have used SGD to minimise its value. As a result, log-linear models can sometimes be referred to as **maximum entropy models** in the NLP literature.

5.2 KL-Divergence and Cross-Entropy

In Chapter 4 we have identified a general training objective function for a linear model, which is to minimise the empirical risk of a model with a parameter vector $\vec{\theta}$ given a set of data $D = \{d_i\}|_{i=1}^N$:

$$
\tilde{risk}(\vec{\theta}) = \frac{1}{N} \sum_{i=1}^N loss\left(\vec{\theta} \cdot \vec{\phi}(d_i) \right)
$$

where $\vec{\phi}$ denotes a global feature vector of a data instance.

For a probabilistic model in general, we have an empirical probability of each instance $\tilde{P}(d_i)$, which can be obtained by counting relative frequencies, and a model probability of each instance $Q(d_i)$. A natural way to define a general training objective function is to modify the risk function above, replacing the score-based *loss* function with a difference measure based on the two distributions:

$$\tilde{risk}(\vec{\theta}) = \frac{1}{N} \sum_{i=1}^{N} diff\Big(\tilde{P}(d_i), Q(d_i)\Big).$$

One way to define the *diff* function is to take the difference between $\log_2 \tilde{P}(d_i)$ and $\log_2 Q(d_i)$ for each d_i, which results in

$$\tilde{risk}(\vec{\theta}) = \frac{1}{N} \sum_{i=1}^{N} \Big(\log_2 \tilde{P}(d_i) - \log_2 Q(d_i)\Big).$$

Intuitively, the risk above measures the difference between the empirical log probability and the model log probability of each training instance. Minimising this risk thus synchronises the model distribution with the empirical distribution. Now let us take a closer look at the whole loss function. In particular, noticing that the relative frequency of each data instance, $\tilde{P}(d_i)$, is $1/N$, the above equation can also be written as:

$$\tilde{risk}(\vec{\theta}) = \sum_{i=1}^{N} \tilde{P}(d_i) \Big(\log_2 \tilde{P}(d_i) - \log_2 Q(d_i)\Big) = \sum_{i=1}^{N} \tilde{P}(d_i) \log_2 \frac{\tilde{P}(d_i)}{Q(d_i)}, \qquad (5.11)$$

which is the expected value of $\log_2 \tilde{P}(d_i) - \log_2 Q(d_i)$ under the distribution $\tilde{P}(d_i)$. The term $\sum_{i=1}^{N} \tilde{P}(d_i) \log_2 \frac{\tilde{P}(d_i)}{Q(d_i)}$ is a general measure of the difference between two probability distributions, namely the **Kullback–Leibler divergence**, or **KL-divergence**. Formally, given a random variable e with M possible values $z_1, z_2, \ldots, z_M$, KL-divergence between two distributions $P(e)$ and $Q(e)$ is defined as

$$KL(P, Q) = \sum_{i=1}^{M} P(z_i) \log_2 \frac{P(z_i)}{Q(z_i)} = E_{e \sim P(e)} \log_2 \frac{P(e)}{Q(e)}.$$

KL measures how different two distributions of the same random variable are. For example, suppose that P and Q represent word distributions in two text documents. $P(w)$ represents the relative frequency of a word w in the first document. In this case, $KL(P, Q)$ represents how different the word distributions are in the two documents. As a second example, suppose that e denotes a topic label such as *sports* and *finance*, and P and Q represent two sets of labelled documents. In this case, $KL(P, Q)$ represents how different the two sets of documents are in terms of topic distribution. KL is non-symmetric because the expectation is calculated using $P(e)$. Thus $P(e)$ takes a more central role compared with $Q(e)$ in $KL(P, Q)$, and $KL(P, Q)$ can be interpreted as "how different is the distribution Q from the distribution P of e".

The general training objective in Eq 5.11 can be viewed as minimising the KL-divergence between the model distribution with respect to the empirical distribution over D.

5.2.1 KL-Divergence and MLE

What do we obtain by minimising KL-divergence in Eq 5.11? The loss function can be rewritten as:

$$KL(P,Q) = \sum_{i=1}^{N} \tilde{P}(d_i) \left(\log_2 \tilde{P}(d_i) - \log_2 Q(d_i) \right)$$

$$= \sum_{i=1}^{N} \tilde{P}(d_i) \log_2 \tilde{P}(d_i) - \sum_{i=1}^{N} \tilde{P}(d_i) \log_2 Q(d_i). \qquad (5.12)$$

There are two terms in the loss function, namely $\sum_{i=1}^{N} \tilde{P}(d_i) \log_2 \tilde{P}(d_i)$ and $-\sum_{i=1}^{N} \tilde{P}(d_i) \log_2 Q(d_i)$. Because the model calculates $Q(d_i)$, all the model parameters are in the second term. Thus minimising $KL(P,Q)$ is equivalent to maximising

$$\sum_{i=1}^{N} \tilde{P}(d_i) \log_2 Q(d_i) = \frac{1}{N} \sum_{i=1}^{N} \log_2 Q(d_i). \qquad (5.13)$$

Equation 5.13 is exactly the log-likelihood of the dataset D. As a result, minimising KL-divergence gives the same model as maximising the log-likelihood, namely MLE.

Now let us consider Eq 5.12 again. The first term $\sum_{i=1}^{N} \tilde{P}(d_i) \log_2 \tilde{P}(d_i)$ is the negative entropy of the data $-H(D)$ according to the definition. The second term $-\sum_{i=1}^{N} \tilde{P}(d_i) \log_2 Q(d_i)$ is similar in form, but with $Q(d_i)$ in the place of $\tilde{P}(d_i)$. Intuitively, this value denotes the expected number of bits to encode each d_i using the encoding scheme Q instead of $\tilde{P}$, despite that d_i is distributed under $\tilde{P}$. It also measures the difference between two distributions Q and $\tilde{P}$. Due to its similarity with entropy, the term is referred to as **cross-entropy**.

Formally, given a random variable e with possible values $\{z_1, z_2, \ldots, z_M\}$ and two distributions P and Q, the cross-entropy $H(P,Q)$ is defined as

$$H(P,Q) = -\sum_{i=1}^{M} P(r_i) \log_2 Q(r_i) = E_{e \sim P} \log_2 \frac{1}{Q(e)}.$$

Given this definition, Eq 5.12 can be rewritten as

$$KL(P,Q) = \sum_{i=1}^{N} \tilde{P}(d_i) \log_2 \tilde{P}(d_i) - \sum_{i=1}^{N} \tilde{P}(d_i) \log_2 Q(d_i) = H(P,Q) - H(P),$$

which is the difference between the cross-entropy between P and Q and the entropy P. As a result, KL-divergence is also called **relative entropy**.

It has been shown that entropy represents the length of the theoretically most efficient (i.e., the smallest) encoding. As a result, for a random variable e distributed under $P(e)$, using $-\log_2 \frac{1}{P(z_i)}$ to encode each possible value z_i gives a lower expected encoding size compared with using any other scheme. For example, suppose that e has four possible values, distributed under $P(z_i) = 1/2, 1/4, 1/4$ and $1/8$ for $i = 1, 2, 3$ and 4, respectively. In addition, suppose that a different distribution $Q(z_i) = 1/4$ for $i = 1, 2, 3$ and 4, respectively. Under the encoding scheme P, the encoding size of the four values are 1, 2, 2, and 3 bits, respectively, and the expected size of encoding one value is $0.5 + 0.25 \times 2 + 0.25 \times 2 + 0.125 \times 3 = 1.875$ bits. In contrast, under the encoding scheme Q, the encoding size of the four values are all 2, and the expected size of encoding one value is $0.5 \times 2 + 0.25 \times 2 + 0.25 \times 2 + 0.125 \times 2 = 2.25$, which is larger than 1.875. Thus we know that $H(P, Q) \geq H(P)$, where the equal sign holds only when $Q = P$. Correspondingly we have $KL(P, Q) \geq 0$, and the equal sign holds only when $Q = P$.

Cross-entropy loss. By the definition of cross-entropy above, given a training set $D = \{d_i\}|_{i=1}^{N}$ and a model $Q(d_i)$, the cross-entropy between the model distribution and the data distribution is:

$$H(\tilde{P}, Q) = -\sum_{i=1}^{N} \tilde{P}(d_i) \log_2 Q(d_i) = -\frac{1}{N} \sum_{i=1}^{N} \log_2 Q(d_i),$$

which is the negative data log-likelihood. Thus maximising the log-likelihood of data is equivalent to minimising the cross-entropy between a model distribution and the data distribution. Consequently, log-likelihood loss is also referred to as cross-entropy loss.

5.2.2 Model Perplexity

Perplexity is a concept in information theory closely related to entropy. Formally, given a random event e with a set of outcomes $\{z_i\}$, $i \in [1, \ldots, M]$, the perplexity of e under the distribution P is defined as

$$\Upsilon(P) = 2^{H(P)} = 2^{-\sum_i P(z_i) \log_2 P(z_i)},$$

where $H(P)$ is the entropy of the distribution P.

Intuitively, $H(P)$ represents the *expected* number of bits necessary for encoding each outcome r_i. As a result, the perplexity $\Upsilon(P) = 2^{H(P)}$ represents the *expected* number of outcomes of the event e. If the outcomes of e take a uniform distribution, perplexity represents exactly the total number of outcomes. For example, for a fair coin, the entropy is $-(0.5 \times \log_2 0.5 + 0.5 \times \log_2 0.5) = 1$, and perplexity is $2^1 = 2$. For a fair die, the entropy is $-6 \times (\frac{1}{6} \times \log_2 \frac{1}{6}) = -\log_2 \frac{1}{6} = \log_2 6$, and the perplexity is $2^{\log_2 6} = 6$. In general, for a fair k-sided die, the entropy is $\log_2 k$ and the perplexity is k. Non-uniform distributions have perplexities smaller than k.

Perplexity and cross-entropy. Cross-entropy can also be used as the power term for calculating perplexity. Such perplexity can be used for model evaluation. In particular, the perplexity of a set of test data as measured using a model distribution is called **model perplexity**, which can be used to evaluate how well a model fits the test data. Formally, given a set of data $D = \{d_i\}|_{i=1}^{N}$ and a probabilistic model Q, the perplexity of the model Q as evaluated on D is:

$$\Upsilon(Q, D) = 2^{H(\tilde{P}(d), Q)} = 2^{-\sum_{i=1}^{N} \tilde{P}(d_i) \log_2 Q(d_i)} = 2^{-\frac{1}{N} \sum_{i=1}^{N} \log_2 Q(d_i)}. \tag{5.14}$$

Intuitively, the power term $-\frac{1}{N} \sum_{i=1}^{N} Q(d_i)$ can be understood as the average number of bits necessary to encode each data sample d_i, according to the encoding scheme of Q. Correspondingly, the perplexity $\Upsilon(Q, D)$ reflects the effective number of distinct values in D as encoded by Q. It represents the degree of "surprise" seeing the data D according to the model Q. Apparently, the less the perplexity is, the better the model fits the data.

Evaluating language models. We have discussed evaluation of classification models in Chapter 3, but not yet of language models in Chapter 2. For a typical document classification task, there is a fixed gold-standard class label for each input document. As a result, *accuracy* is a suitable evaluation metric. In contrast, for language modelling, there is no single absolute answer for what is a "correct" next word given a partial sentence, since there are multiple ways to complete a sentence. The differences between different answers are subtle, depending on both grammaticality and semantic plausibility. As a result, *perplexity* is a better evaluation metric. The basic idea is to test how "surprised" a language model Q is when seeing a set of human-written sentences D.

According to Eq 5.14, given a set of test data $D = \{s_i\}|_{i=1}^N$, where s_i is a human-written sentence, the perplexity of a language model Q can be calculated as

$$2^{-\frac{1}{N} \sum_{i=1}^N \log_2 Q(s_i)}.$$

Under this evaluation, the perplexity of the n-gram language models introduced in Chapter 2 on newswire data can be 2^{190}, which intuitively means that there are effectively 2^{190} sentences in the language. This number can intuitively be understood as the number of faces that a fair sentence die has.

Because sentences are sparse, sentence-level perplexity takes very large numbers. A more commonly used evaluation metric is **per-word perplexity**. Assuming that the language model under evaluation can give the probability of each word according to their sentential context, we regard the test data as a set of words $D = \{w_i\}|_{i=1}^{|D|}$ in their sentential contexts, calculating the perplexity of the language model using

$$2^{-\frac{1}{|D|} \sum_{i=1}^{|D|} \log Q(w_i)}.$$

Per-word perplexity of n-gram language models can be around 250 for newswire English, which means that the model is as confused on D as if it had to choose uniformly among 250 different words when writing every word. The effective number of bits to encode each word is thus $\log_2 250 \approx 8$ bits. Today, the best language models on English reduces this number to 30 and even lower.

5.3   Mutual Information

KL-divergence and cross-entropy measure the relatedness of *two* distributions for encoding the *same* random variable, and therefore are useful for training or evaluating a probabilistic model on gold-standard data. In this section, we return to the encoding of two *different* random variables.

It has been mentioned in Section 5.1.2 that the conditional entropy $H(y|x)$ between two random variables y and x measures the expected number of bits needed for encoding each outcome of the random variable y when the outcome of x is known. Further, we have $H(y|x) \leq H(y)$ since knowledge of x can contain information about y. The only case when $H(y|x) = H(y)$ is when x and y are conditionally independent, which can be seen in Eq 5.5.

In the equation, the difference $H(y|x) - H(y)$ is $\sum_{x,y} P(x,y) \log_2 \frac{P(x,y)}{P(x)P(y)}$, which is 0 when $P(x,y) = P(x)P(y)$, namely when x and y are independent. This difference increases as the random variable y is more dependent on x. In general, the difference between $H(y)$ and $H(y|x)$ measures the number of bits we can save for encoding each outcome of y if x is known, in mathematical expectation. We name this difference the **mutual information** between x and y, denoted as $I(x, y)$.

Mutual information is symmetric between x and y – the number of bits we can save for encoding y if x is know is equivalent to the number of bits we can save for encoding x if y is known. This can be proved as follows:

$$H(x) - H(x|y)$$

$$= \sum_{x,y} P(x, y) \log_2 P(x|y) - \sum_x P(x) \log_2 P(x)$$

$$= \sum_{x,y} P(x, y) \log_2 P(x|y) - \sum_x \left(\sum_y P(x, y) \right) \log_2 P(x) \quad \text{(marginal probability)}$$

$$= \sum_{x,y} P(x, y) \log_2 P(x|y) - \sum_{x,y} P(x, y) \log_2 P(x) \tag{5.15}$$

$$= \sum_{x,y} P(x, y) \log_2 \frac{P(x|y)}{P(x)}$$

$$= \sum_{x,y} P(x, y) \log_2 \frac{P(x, y)}{P(x)P(y)},$$

which is equal to $H(y) - H(y|x)$ in Eq 5.5.

5.3.1 Pointwise Mutual Information

Given two random variables x and y, their mutual information can be viewed as the expectation of $\log_2 \frac{P(x,y)}{P(x)P(y)}$ over all possible values x, y:

$$I(x, y) = \sum_{x,y} P(x, y) \log_2 \frac{P(x, y)}{P(x)P(y)} = E_{x,y} \left(\log_2 \frac{P(x, y)}{P(x)P(y)} \right).$$

For each outcome pair (x, y), $\log_2 \frac{P(x,y)}{P(x)P(y)}$ is called **Pointwise Mutual Information** (PMI) between x and y. In particular,

$$\log_2 \frac{P(x, y)}{P(x)P(y)} = \log_2 P(x, y) - \log_2 P(x) - \log_2 P(y). \tag{5.16}$$

Here $-\log_2 P(x)$ is the number of bits necessary for encoding the specific value x of x and $-\log_2 P(y)$ is the number of bits necessary for encoding the specific value y of y. They measure the uncertainty in x and y respectively, as shown in Eq 5.1. For a contrast with PMI, they are also referred to as **self-information**. $-\log_2 P(x, y)$ is self information of the joint value that both x and y happens. As a result, the intuitive interpretation of PMI is the number of bits necessary to encode x and y individually, minus the number of bits to encode the joint value (x, y).

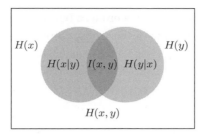

Figure 5.1 $H(x)$, $H(y)$, $H(x|y)$, $H(y|x)$, $H(x,y)$ and $I(x,y)$.

In Eq 5.16, the denominator represents the joint probability $P(x,y) = P(x)P(y)$ when x and y are independent, while the numerator is $P(x,y)$. Hence their ratio reflects the probabilistic dependence between the two variables. When $P(x,y) > P(x)P(y)$, the two values tend to co-occur; when $P(x,y) < P(x)P(y)$ the two values tend to *not* co-occur, which is also a form of conditional dependence. When $P(x,y) = P(x)P(y)$, $PMI(x,y) = 0$ and x and y are independent. When $PMI(x,y) > 0$, we say that x and y are *positively dependent*, and when $PMI(x,y) < 0$, we say that x and y are *negatively dependent*. *PMI* between x and y ranges from $-\infty$ to ∞.

The entropy of the joint value (x,y) is also referred to as the *joint entropy* of x and y, where

$$H(x,y) = -\sum_{x,y} P(x,y) \log_2 P(x,y).$$

Given this definition, mutual information can also be written in terms of $H(x,y)$:

$$
\begin{aligned}
I(x,y) &= \sum_{x,y} P(x,y) \log_2 \frac{P(x,y)}{P(x)P(y)} \\
&= \sum_{x,y} P(x,y) \log_2 P(x,y) - \sum_{x,y} P(x,y) \log_2 P(x) - \sum_{x,y} P(x,y) \log_2 P(y) \\
&= -H(x,y) - \sum_x P(x) \log_2 P(x) - \sum_y P(y) \log_2 P(y) \\
&= H(x) + H(y) - H(x,y),
\end{aligned}
\tag{5.17}
$$

which can be interpreted as the expected number of bits to encode x and y individually, minus the expected number of bits to encode the joint variable (x,y).

The correlation between $H(x)$, $H(y)$, $H(x|y)$, $H(y|x)$, $H(x,y)$ and $I(x,y)$ can be demonstrated in the Venn diagram of Figure 5.1.

5.3.2 Using PMI to Mine Knowledge from Texts

PMI represents statistical correlation between two random variables, and therefore can be leveraged for mining useful information from text. Below we give two examples.

Learning sentiment lexicons. A rule-based method of performing sentiment analysis is to use a **sentiment lexicon**, which contains information about the polarity (i.e., positive or negative) and strength of sentiment words. For a word w, a typical sentiment lexicon contains a value $\text{LEX}(w)$ in $[-\alpha, \alpha]$, where the sign represents the sentiment polarity and the absolute value $\alpha > 0$ represents the strength.

Given a document $d = w_1 w_2 \ldots w_n$, we can calculate its sentiment polarity and strength using the average of all sentiment words in it:

$$\text{SENTI}(d) = \frac{\sum_i \text{LEX}(w_i)}{|\{w_i | \text{LEX}(w_i) \neq 0\}|}, \ i \in [1, \ldots, n],$$

assuming that $\text{LEX}(w_i)=0$ for all w_i out of the sentiment lexicon. The denominator in the equation represents the number of sentiment words in d. This simple method does not consider semantic operations such as negation and intensification, yet works surprisingly well as a strong baseline.

There are two general ways to obtain a sentiment lexicon, namely by doing manual annotation and by mining from data, respectively. Compared to the latter, the former is more costly. One way to automatically learn the sentiment value of a word is to calculate the correlation between the word and certain seed sentiment words, for example "*good*" as a positive seed word and "*bad*" as a negative seed word. PMI can be leveraged to this end. In particular, given a corpus D, the PMI between a word w and a *seed* word

$$PMI(w, seed) = \log_2 \frac{P(w, seed)}{P(w)p(seed)},$$

where $P(w)$ is calculated empirically as the relatively frequency of the word w in D

$$P(w) = \frac{\#w \in D}{|D|}.$$

Here $|D|$ denotes the total number of words in D.

$P(w_1, w_2)$ can be calculated empirically as

$$P(w_1, w_2) = \frac{\#\left(\text{COOCCUR}(w_1, w_2) \in D\right)}{|D|^2},$$

where $\text{COOCCUR}(w_1, w_2)$ can be defined as the number of times that w_1 and w_2 co-occur in a certain context, such as a 10-word window.

Finally, after obtaining $PMI(w, \text{"}good\text{"})$ and $PMI(w, \text{"}bad\text{"})$, respectively, the sentiment value of the word w can be defined as

$$\text{LEX}(w) = PMI(w, \text{"}good\text{"}) - PMI(w, \text{"}bad\text{"}).$$

For Twitter sentiment analysis, a pair of seed positive and negative words can be ":)" and ":(", respectively, which are common emoticons to denote sentiments. Since tweets are restricted to a 140-character-limit, COOCCUR can be defined as the number of times that two words exist in the same tweet.

Note that PMI is a better metric compared to simple co-occurrence counts for measuring the correlation between two words, since two words can co-occur frequently together, but on the other hand be frequent words and therefore co-occur also frequently with other words, in which case the co-occurrence value does not reflect their inherent correlation.

Collocation extraction. *Collocation* refers to words that are conventionally used together for certain meaning. For example, *"Mr President"* is a collocation but *"Mr Executive"* is not a typical collocation. Similarly, *"high temperature"* is a typical collocation but *"big temperature"* is not. PMI can be used to automatically extract collocations from texts. In particular, given two particular words w_1 and w_2, and a corpus D, their association can be calculated using

$$PMI(w_1, w_2) = \log_2 \frac{P(w_1 w_2)}{P(w_1)P(w_2)},$$

where $P(w_1 w_2)$ denotes the probability of the bigram $w_1 w_2$ in D,

$$P(w_1 w_2) = \frac{\#(w_1 w_2 \in D)}{\sum_{w'' w'} w'' w' \in D} = \frac{\#(w_1 w_2 \in D)}{|D|};$$

$P(w_1)$ and $P(w_2)$ denote the relative frequencies of w_1 and w_2 in D, respectively; and $w'' w'$ denotes a bigram in D.

Intuitively, the PMI value above measures the relative frequency of the bigram $w_1 w_2$ with respect to the frequencies of w_1 and w_2. As a result, it can serve as a strong indicator of collocation. Such a measure can further serve as a basis for extracting multi-word expressions. For character-based languages such as Chinese, collocation between characters can also be strong indicators of words.

5.3.3 Using PMI to Select Features

As shown in Chapter 3, there can be millions of feature instances in a discriminative text classification. Intuitively, some features are relatively less important compared to others. For example, using the feature template wc, where w denotes a word in the document and c denotes the document class label, the words *"goal"*, *"statement"* and *"president"* are apparently more useful compared to the words *"a"*, *"in"* and *"does"*. As a result, there is a motivation to reduce the size of the feature vector by removing feature instances that are less useful. This can lead to smaller models, faster runtime speeds and possibly improved accuracy.

A commonly used metric for feature selection is PMI. In particular, PMI between the input component (e.g., w in wc) and the output component (e.g., c in wc) of a feature instance is measured, and used as an indicator of its usefulness. Take the feature *"goal/sport"* under the template wc as an example, $PMI(\text{"goal"}, \text{"sport"})$ can be calculated for each feature instance, serving as the usefulness indicator value. Intuitively, the more frequently a certain pair of w and c co-occur relative to the individual occurrences of w and c, the more likely w is a strong indicator of c.

There are other commonly used methods for feature selection, including *information gain* and χ^2, which we leave as an exercise (see Exercise 5.8).

5.3.4 PMI and Vector Representations of Words

In Chapter 3, we have discussed a type of vector representation of documents based on their words; such representations include count-based and TF-IDF vectors. Representing documents as vectors provides a basis for further mathematical modelling and computation such as document clustering and text classification. The same principle applies to words also – vector representations of words provides a mathematical foundation for the modelling of word clustering, classification and other word-level tasks.

One simple approach to vector representation of words is to apply the count-based document representation, treating each word as a "document". The resulting word vector is a vocabulary-size feature representation, with the element that corresponds to the given word being 1, and the remaining elements being 0. This type of **word representation** is called **one-hot vectors**, in reflection of the above characteristics. One-hot word representation is conceptually very simple, and can be used as input to NLP models or as a basis for computing more complex word representations (Chapter 13 has one example). However, one-hot vectors do not contain any further information about a word except for its identity. As a result, we cannot perform tasks such as word similarity calculation by directly using one-hot vectors.

One way to address this limitation is to make use of **distributional hypothesis** on the meaning of words, which states that words with similar meanings tend to co-occur in documents, or in plain words, "You shall know a word by the company it keeps!". Here the company of a word typically refers to its neighbours in a context window. Table 5.1 shows some example k-word windows ($k \in \{2, 5, 7\}$), where the context includes k words on the left and k words on the right. $\langle /s \rangle$ denotes the end of the sentence. Intuitively, the words "*bank*" and "*river*" both co-occur frequently with neighbour words "*water*", "*rock*" and "*island*", while the words "*equation*" and "*algorithm*" do not. The company a word keeps tells us much information about its attributes.

According to this observation, we can define a **count-based word representation**. In particular, for a certain word w, we can count the frequency of each vocabulary word $w_i \in V$ being its neighbour in a corpus D, resulting in a vector $\langle \#w_1, \#w_2, \ldots, \#w_{|V|} \rangle$. This vector has the same form as the document vector representation in Table 3.1. Table 5.2 shows examples

Table 5.1 k-word windows for the word "*bank*". s_1 denotes the sentence "*There happened to be a rock sticking out of the water halfway between the* bank *and the island.*" s_2 denotes the sentence "*The checks that have been written but are not included with the* bank *statement are called outstanding checks.*"

Sentence	k	Context
s_1	2	{*between, the, and, the* }
	5	{*the, water, halfway, between, the, and, the, island, ., $\langle /s \rangle$*}
	7	{*out, of, the, water, halfway, between, the, and, the, island, ., $\langle /s \rangle$, $\langle /s \rangle$, $\langle /s \rangle$*}
s_2	2	{*with, the, statement, are*}
	5	{*are, not, included, with, the, statement, are, called, outstanding, checks*}
	7	{*written but, are, not, included, with, the, statement, are, called, outstanding, checks, ., $\langle /s \rangle$*}

Table 5.2 Various representations of the words "*cat*" and "*dog*". w_{121} = "*cat*", w_{35} = "*leg*", w_1 = "*a*" and w_{500} = "*dog*".

Word	Representation	Feature vector
cat	One-hot	$\langle f_1 = 0, \ldots, f_{121} = 1, \ldots, f_{500} = 0, \ldots, f_{10000} = 0 \rangle$
	Context	$\langle f_1 = 1280, f_2 = 0, \ldots, f_{35} = 332, \ldots, f_{10000} = 0 \rangle$
	PPMI	$\langle f_1 = 0.3, f_2 = 0, \ldots, f_{35} = 2.32, \ldots, f_{10000} = 0 \rangle$
dog	One-hot	$\langle f_1 = 0, \ldots, f_{121} = 0, \ldots, f_{500} = 1, \ldots, f_{10000} = 0 \rangle$
	Context	$\langle f_1 = 1190, f_2 = 19, \ldots, f_{35} = 271, \ldots, f_{10000} = 0 \rangle$
	PPMI	$\langle f_1 = 0.44, \ldots, f_{12} = 0.05, \ldots, f_{35} = 5.56, \ldots, f_{10000} = 0 \rangle$

for the words "*cat*" and "*dog*", making a comparison between one-hot vectors and count-based vectors. For example, using one-hot features in Table 5.2, the cosine similarity between "*cat*" and "*dog*" is 0, which is non-intuitive since both words describe animals. Introducing context information can alleviate the feature sparsity problem to some extent. For the "context" rows, a word is identified by its surrounding contexts and its vector consists of the number of occurrences of each vocabulary word in its context. For example, in Table 5.2, f_{35} denotes the context word "*leg*", the values of which are 332 and 271 in the context representation vectors for both "*cat*" and "*dog*", respectively. This contributes to a non-zero vector similarity between the two words.

One limitation of this count-based vector form, as in the document representation case, is that it contains many elements that co-occur frequently with most words, which are not differentiating. For example, it is difficult to tell anything about a word if we know its frequent neighbours include the words "*the*", "*it*" and "*not*". In addition, the counts are not normalised, and can vary across different training data D.

PMI can serve as a more effective measure of association between words, compared to counts. The resulting vector representation of a word w_i is

$$\overrightarrow{Vec(w)} = \langle PMI(w, w_1), PMI(w, w_2), \ldots, PMI(w, w_{|v|}) \rangle.$$

For calculating PMI(u, v) of two words u and v given a corpus D, we need to calculate $P(u, v)$, $P(u)$ and $P(v)$. In particular, we can define

$$P(u, v) = \frac{\#(u \text{ and } v \text{ in each other's context window})}{\#(\text{any two words in each other's context window})}$$

$$= \frac{\#(u \text{ and } v \text{ in each other's context window})}{2k|D|^2}.$$

$P(u)$ and $P(v)$ can be defined as their empirical probabilities, or relative frequencies, in D.

PPMI. Since (u, v) can be sparse and infrequent, negative PMI with $P(u, v) < P(u)P(v)$ can be non-informative. As a result, researchers use only positive PMI (PPMI) instead, where

$$PPMI(u, v) = \max(PMI(u, v), 0).$$

Using PPMI, uninformative words will have a small contribution to the distributional word representation, since their own probabilities are relatively high. This serves a similar role as the IDF term in TF-IDF representations of documents. Thus TF-IDF values can be regarded as motivated by information theory. In fact, if each context window for a word w in a D can be treated as a "document", the vector form of w can be calculated using TF-IDF vectors also. Another effective distributional vector representation of words is based on t-test introduced in Chapter 4, which we leave for exercise (see Exercise 5.6).

Summary

In this chapter we have introduced:

- the maximum entropy principle for defining probabilistic models, and its application in deriving log-linear model forms;
- KL-divergence, cross-entropy and model perplexity for measuring the consistency between model distributions and data distributions;
- mutual information and pointwise mutual information (PMI) for measuring the statistical correlation between different random variables;
- word representation.

Chapter Notes

Information theory was founded by Shannon (1948), where the concepts of entropy were defined. The maximum entropy principle was originally proposed by Jaynes (1957). KL-Divergence was discussed by Kullback and Leibler (1951). Nigam et al. (1999) built a maximum entropy model for text classification. Brown et al. (1992) presented an estimate of an upper bound of 1.75 bits for the entropy of characters in printed English. Berger et al. (1996) discussed the correlation between maximum entropy training and log-linear models.

PMI was used in NLP models for drawing feature correlations (Church and Hanks, 1990; Turney, 2002; Peng et al., 2005). The distributional hypothesis was first proposed by Harris (1954), which influenced research on both word and document representation.

Exercises

5.1 In a game of guessing a randomly drawn word from a dictionary

(a) What is the amount of information obtained for knowing the answer?
(b) Compare the amounts of information learning that the answer is "*the*" and "*zoo*".
(c) Compare the amounts of information learning that the answer begins with '*t*' and '*z*'.

(d) What is the entropy of the word guess event?

(e) If a word is drawn from a corpus rather than a dictionary, compare the amounts of information again for learning that the answer is "*the*" and "*zoo*".

5.2 Multiple choices

(A) self-information

(B) mutual information

(C) PMI

(D) entropy

(E) perplexity

(F) cross-entropy

(G) model perplexity

(H) KL-divergence

(a) Which of the above measures concern individual outcomes of random events?

(b) Which of the above measures are event-level measures?

(c) Which of the above measures study a single distribution?

(d) Which of the above measures study two different distributions?

(e) Entropy and _____ represent the same knowledge in different forms.

(f) Cross-entropy and _____ represent the same knowledge in different forms.

5.3 State the correlation between log-linear model and entropy/cross-entropy.

5.4 Given a training corpus for document classification, can you use PMI between words and class labels to find out which words are the most representative for each class? Compare this with the weights on feature instances for log-linear classification for the same words.

5.5 Prove in Eq 5.5 that $\sum_x \sum_y P(x,y) \log_2 \frac{P(x,y)}{P(x)P(y)} \geq 0$. (Hint: $\log_2 a \leq (a-1)\log_2 e$, which indicates $\log_2 \frac{P(x,y)}{P(x)P(y)} \geq (1 - \frac{P(x)P(y)}{P(x,y)}) \log_2 e$.)

5.6 Use t-test as introduced in Chapter 4 to define distributional vector representations of words of a document.

5.7 Consider again the classification task with unbalanced data. Suppose that we have manually labelled a set of training data $D = \{(x_i, c_i)\}|_{i=1}^N$, the main training objective can be to maximise the likelihood $\sum_{i=1}^N \log P(c_i|x_i)$. Now suppose that we have balanced samples of each C_i in D, but the distribution of class labels on unseen data is very imbalanced, with $P(c_i) = \gamma_i$, $i \in [1\ldots|C|]$. Here γ_i are prior knowledge. We can integrate this knowledge of class label distribution into our training objective, by measuring the KL divergence of our model-given class distribution and the prior knowledge class distribution $P(c_i)$. In particular, the model-given class distribution can be estimated by using a current model to label a large set of raw inputs $R = \{x_i'\}|_{i=1}^{N'}$, and then counting the relative frequencies of class labels $Q(c_i)$ on the outputs. The final training objective, after integrating this knowledge, is $\sum_{i=1}^N \log P(c_i|x_i) - \lambda KL\Big(P(c_i), Q(c_i)\Big)$, where λ is a hyper-parameter to control the importance of the regularisation term.

(a) How can the value of λ be determined?

(b) Can $Q(c_i)$ be calculated using relative frequencies of c_i over the model output on R? Why? (Hint: should the regularisation term be a constant or a function of model parameters?)

(c) A reasonable way to calculate $Q(c_i)$ is to use the *mathematical expectation* $\sum_{x'_j \in R} \left(P(c_i|x'_j) \cdot Q(x'_j, c_i) \right)$ as $Q(c_i)$. Now define $Q(x'_j, c_i)$ in order to use the model score $P(c|x)$ as the only term to denote $Q(c_i)$. (This method is named **expectation regularisation**.)

(d) Denoting the feature vector of a pair (x, c) as $\vec{\phi}(x, c)$, calculate the derivative of the training objective with respect to a model parameter $\vec{\theta}$.

(e) Derive a SGD training algorithm for the training objective above.

5.8 *Information gain* and χ^2 *statistic* have been used as the criteria for feature selection. Consider a text classifier with bag-of-word features. Given a set of labelled training documents here, the *information gain* of a word w is defined as:

$$IG(w) = -\sum_{i=1}^{n} \tilde{P}(c_i) \log \tilde{P}(c_i)$$
$$+ \left(\tilde{P}(w) \sum_{i=1}^{n} \tilde{P}(c_i|w) \log \tilde{P}(c_i|w) \right) \tag{5.18}$$
$$+ \tilde{P}(\overline{w}) \sum_{i=1}^{n} \tilde{P}(c_i|\overline{w}) \log \tilde{P}(c_i|\overline{w}) \Big),$$

where $C = \{c_1, \ldots, c_n\}$ is the set of class labels and $\overline{w}$ denotes a word which is not in the training set for (w, c_i). $\tilde{P}$ denotes empirical distribution.

The χ^2 statistic is defined as

$$\chi^2(w, c_i) = \frac{N \times (AD - CB)^2}{(A + C) \times (B + D) \times (A + B) \times (C + D)}, \tag{5.19}$$

where A is the number of times w and c_i co-occur in a training document, B is the number of times w occurs without c_i, C is the number of times c_i occurs without w and D is the number of times neither c_i nor w occurs in a training document. A word feature w can be selected using

$$\chi^2_{avg}(w) = \sum_{i=1}^{n} \tilde{P}(c_i)\chi^2(w, c_i) \tag{5.20}$$

or

$$\chi^2_{max}(w) = max_{i=1}^{n}\chi^2(w, c_i). \tag{5.21}$$

As discussed in Section 5.3.3, using pointwise mutual information

$$PMI(w, c_i) = \log_2 \frac{\tilde{P}(w, c_i)}{\tilde{P}(w)\tilde{P}(c_i)} = \frac{A \times N}{(A + B) \times (A + C)}, \tag{5.22}$$

w can be selected using

$$PMI_{avg}(w) = \sum_{i=1}^{n} \tilde{P}(c_i) \times PMI(w, c_i).\qquad(5.23)$$

or

$$PMI_{max}(w) = max_{i=1}^{n} PMI(w, c_i).\qquad(5.24)$$

Discuss the correlation between $TF(w) \cdot IDF(w)$, $IG(w)$, $\chi^2(w)$ and $PMI(w)$ for feature selection. What are the similarities? What can be their relative strengths?

6   Hidden Variables

We have thus far learned several probabilistic models including Naïve Bayes models and log-linear models. When these models are trained, both the inputs and the outputs are **observed variables** since they are labelled in a corpus. MLE can be used to estimate model parameters by counting relative frequencies. In practice, there are also situations where some variables in a model are not observable in training data. For example, manually labelled corpora can be scarce for low-resource languages and domains. As a second example, for machine translation modelling, it is relatively easy to find bi-lingual sentence pairs that are translations of each other, but labelling the alignment between word pairs in a sentence pair can be extremely costly. In such cases, those unlabelled variables are **hidden variables**, which adds to the training difficulty because it is infeasible to count the relative frequencies of hidden variables directly from data.

    Expectation maximisation (EM) is an iterative training algorithm that can deal with hidden variables. Given a randomly initialised model, EM contains two iterative steps, namely the expectation step and the maximisation step. The expectation step uses the current model parameters to derive the probability distribution of the counts of hidden variables over a training set. The maximisation step uses the resulting count distributions as a basis for updating the model parameters. This chapter introduces the EM algorithm, and three applications of EM in NLP, including the unsupervised Naïve Bayes model, IBM model 1 for machine translation and the probabilistic latent semantic analysis (PLSA) model. Towards the end of the chapter, theoretical justifications of EM are given.

6.1   Expectation Maximisation

EM is a general algorithm to train models with hidden variables. Formally, suppose that we have a set of observed variables O, a set of hidden variables H and a set of model parameters Θ. The model calculates $P(O, H | \Theta)$, namely the joint probability of observed and hidden variables. Given a specific problem, the techniques that we discussed in Chapter 2, such as the probability chain rule and independence assumptions can be used to parameterise the joint probability distribution.

    Due to the existence of H, our notations are different from those of the previous chapters, where the data consists of inputs X and outputs Y, both being observed. There is no fixed mapping between (O, H) and (X, Y). For example, we will see cases where O consists of the inputs and H consists of the outputs, and also cases where O consists of both the inputs and the outputs, and H consists of only intermediate variables that help to better model O. We will discuss EM using the (O, H) setting for notational convenience.

It is worth noting that the above notation reflects the *training setting* with latent variables, but not the *model structure* or parameterisation. In fact, the same model can be trained using both supervised MLE and EM, depending on whether there are unobserved variables in the training data. Such examples include the Naïve Bayes text classifier in this chapter and the Hidden Markov Model in the next chapter. In addition to the (O, H) notation, we will include Θ in conditional probabilities in order to differentiate their values when different versions of the same parameters exist in an equation.

Hidden variables and relative frequency counting. The existence of hidden variables H makes counting relative frequencies infeasible. In particular, given a dataset $D = \{o_i\}|_{i=1}^{N}$ the joint likelihood is

$$L(\Theta) = \sum_{i=1}^{N} \log P(o_i, h_i | \Theta) = \log P(O, H | \Theta), \tag{6.1}$$

which is unspecified and thus cannot be maximised directly, because H is unobserved in D. Let us take Naïve Bayes text classification as an example. Given a document $d = W_{1:n} = w_1 w_2 \ldots w_n$ with a class label c, the model calculates $P(d, c) = P(c) \prod_{j=1}^{n} P(w_j | c)$. Given a dataset $D = \{(d_i, c_i)\}|_{i=1}^{N}$, the data likelihood can be specified as

$$P(D) = \prod_{i=1}^{N} P(d_i, c_i) = \prod_{i=1}^{N} \left(P(c_i) \prod_{j=1}^{|d_i|} P(w_j^i | c_i) \right)$$

$$= \left(\prod_{c \in C} P(c)^{N_c} \right) \cdot \left(\prod_{w \in V} \prod_{c \in C} P(w|c)^{N_{w,c}} \right),$$

where w_j^i denotes the jth word in d_i, C denotes the set of class labels, V denotes the vocabulary, N_c denotes the number of documents under the class c in D and $N_{w,c}$ denotes the number of occurrences of word w in documents with class c. The parameter set is $\Theta = \{P(c), P(w|c)\}$ for $w \in V$ and $c \in C$.

In the above likelihood, the terms $\prod_{c \in C} P(c)^{N_c}$ and $\prod_{w \in V} \prod_{c \in C} P(w|c)^{N_{w,c}}$ can be seen as two independent distributions, each representing the probability of a set of *i.i.d.* samples according to a categorial distribution (i.e., $P(c)$ and $P(w|c)$, respectively). As discussed in Chapter 2, by maximising $P(D)$ we can derive the values of $P(c)$ $(c \in C)$ and $P(w|c)$ $(w \in V, c \in C)$ by counting relative frequencies (i.e., N_c and $N_{w,c}$). Now given a set of unlabelled documents $D = \{d_i\}|_{i=1}^{N}$, we cannot obtain the counts N_c or $N_{w,c}$. As a result, the data likelihood is not specified, and direct MLE training is infeasible.

One way to solve the problem is to use an iterative approach. In particular, suppose that we have a model that calculates $P(h_i | o_i)$ in Eq 6.1, we can calculate estimated *counts* of the hidden variables given observed varibles. For example, in the Naïve Bayes case, this can be achieved using at least three methods, including (1) by calculating the most likely values of the hidden variables given the observed variables, (2) by simply calculating a distribution $P(c|d)$, where the probabilities serve as pseudo counts, and (3) by sampling a set of (d, c) pairs according to the generative story of Naïve Bayes. In case (1) above, each hidden variable instance receives a fixed value. We determine a fixed class label for each document in D. In contrast, in cases (2) and (3) above, each hidden variable can have different values. For example, for method (2), each document distributes its class label counts to each possible class c according to $P(c|d)$, and for method (3) we are likely to sample different class labels for each document at different sampling rounds. We will discuss methods (1) and (2) in this chapter, and method (3) in Chapter 12 for Bayesian learning.

With the estimated counts of hidden variables, we can re-estimate the model using MLE. Then with this re-estimated model, we can have better estimations of hidden variable counts again. Thus the iterative approach can alternate the estimation of model parameters and hidden variable counts. According to this observation, EM works by randomly initialising Θ, and then iteratively executing count estimation steps and model optimisation steps. The former finds the expected counts of H according to the current model Θ using method (2), while the latter updates Θ by maximising the joint likelihood of O and H with the expected counts of H.

EM and k-means clustering. We have seen one iterative algorithm in this book, namely k-means clustering. The algorithm groups a given set of feature vectors into k clusters in the vector space according to their relative distances, by randomly initialising a set of cluster centroids, and then iteratively performing cluster assignment and centroid calculation. It turns out that this algorithm is connected to EM. In particular, if the cluster centroids are taken as model parameters and the cluster assignment taken as hidden variables, k-means can be regarded as belonging to a simplified EM version by replacing method (2) above with method (1), which is conceptually simpler. We therefore introduce EM by first revisiting k-means, discussing the simplified EM version before introducing the full EM algorithm.

6.1.1   k-Means Revisited

Let us describe k-means in light of the aforementioned EM framework by first writing it down as a model with hidden variables, and then specifying its parameterisation in terms of $P(O, H|\Theta)$. Formally, given a set of observed variables (i.e., input vectors) $O = \{\vec{v}_i\}|_{i=1}^{N}$, the learning objective of k-means can be defined as minimising

$$L(\Theta) = \sum_{i=1}^{N} \sum_{k=1}^{K} h_{ik} ||\vec{v}_i - \vec{c}_k||^2, \tag{6.2}$$

where $\vec{c}_k$ is the centroid of the cluster k, and h_{ik} is an indicator variable:

$$h_{ik} = \begin{cases} 1 & \text{if } \vec{v}_i \in \text{ cluster } k \\ 0 & \text{otherwise.} \end{cases}$$

In this model, $H = \{h_{ik}\}|_{i=1,k=1}^{N,K}$ are hidden variables and $\Theta = \{\vec{c}_k\}|_{k=1}^{K}$ are model parameters. h_{ik} represents the assignment of input vectors to output clusters. For every $\vec{v}_i$, only one h_{ik} can be 1 among all $k \in [1, \ldots, K]$.

k-means uses an iterative approach to minimise Eq 6.2. It randomly initialises each $\vec{c}_k$ to $\vec{c}_k^0$, and then determines the values of hidden variables H^t at the tth iteration by fixing the model parameters

$\vec{c}_k = \vec{c}_k^t$ and allocating every input $\vec{v}_i$ to the closest cluster centroid:

$$H^t \leftarrow \arg\min_H \sum_{i=1}^{N} \sum_{k=1}^{K} h_{ik} ||\vec{v}_i - \vec{c}_k^t||^2.$$

In this way, we obtain

$$h_{ik}^t = \begin{cases} 1 & \text{if } k = \arg\min_{k'} ||\vec{v}_i - \vec{c}_{k'}^t||^2 \\ 0 & \text{otherwise} \end{cases}. \tag{6.3}$$

The above step serves as one expectation step, based on which k-means takes a maximisation step to re-estimate the model parameters $\vec{c}_k$ ($k \in [1, \ldots, K]$):

$$\Theta^{t+1} \leftarrow \arg\min_{\vec{c}_1, \vec{c}_2, \ldots, \vec{c}_K} \sum_{i=1}^{N} \sum_{k=1}^{K} h_{ik}^t ||\vec{v}_i - \vec{c}_k||^2.$$

Taking the derivatives of $\sum_{i=1}^{N} \sum_{k=1}^{K} h_{ik}^t ||\vec{v}_i - \vec{c}_k||^2$ with respect to every $\vec{c}_k$, and setting the derivative values to zeros, we obtain the optimal values of the model parameters for the next iteration:

$$\vec{c}_k^{t+1} = \frac{\sum_{i=1}^{N} h_{ik}^t \vec{v}_i}{\sum_{i=1}^{N} h_{ik}^t}, \tag{6.4}$$

which is the average of all vectors in the cluster k.

The iterative process above continues until the algorithm converges.

k-means as a probabilistic algorithm. We can turn the distance measure for k-means into a probability distribution. In particular, rewrite Eq 6.2 as follows:

$$
\begin{aligned}
\min L(\Theta) &= \min \sum_{i=1}^{N} \sum_{k=1}^{K} h_{ik} ||\vec{v}_i - \vec{c}_k||^2 && \text{(minimising loss)} \\
&= \max \sum_{i=1}^{N} \sum_{k=1}^{K} -h_{ik} ||\vec{v}_i - \vec{c}_k||^2 && \text{(maximising negative loss)} \\
&= \max \sum_{i=1}^{N} \log e^{-\sum_{k=1}^{K} h_{ik} ||\vec{v}_i - \vec{c}_k||^2} && (x = \log e^x) \\
&= \max \sum_{i=1}^{N} \log \frac{e^{-\sum_{k=1}^{K} h_{ik} ||\vec{v}_i - \vec{c}_k||^2}}{Z} && (Z \text{ is a constant}) \\
&= \max \sum_{i=1}^{N} \log P(\vec{v}_i, h_i | \Theta),
\end{aligned}
\tag{6.5}
$$

where $P(\vec{v}_i, h_i | \Theta)$ is a probability distribution using h_i to denote $h_{i1}, h_{i2}, \ldots, h_{ik}$, and Z is a normalising constant, where $Z = \sum_{h'} \exp(-\sum_{k=1}^{K} h_{ik}' ||\vec{v}_i - \vec{c}_k||^2)$. Here h' is a valid cluster assignment,

---

Algorithm 6.1. k-means as a "hard" EM algorithm.

Inputs: observed data $O = \{\vec{v}_i\}|_{i=1}^{N}$;
Hidden Variables: $H = \{h_i\}|_{i=1}^{N}$;
Initialisation: model $\Theta^0 \leftarrow$ RandomModel$()$, $t \leftarrow 0$;
repeat
    | **Expectation step:**
    | $H^t \leftarrow \arg\max_H \log P(O, H|\Theta^t)$;   ▷ Eq 6.3;
    | **Maximisation step:**
    | $\Theta^{t+1} \leftarrow \arg\max_\Theta \log P(O, H^t|\Theta)$;   ▷ Eq 6.4;
    | $t \leftarrow t + 1$;
until Converge(H, Θ);

---

with only one h'_{ik} ($k \in [1, \ldots, K]$) being 1, and the others being 0. Therefore,

$$
\begin{aligned}
P(\vec{v}_i, h_i|\Theta) &= P(\vec{v}_i, h_{i1}, h_{i2}, \ldots, h_{iK}|\Theta) \\
&= \frac{e^{-\sum_{k=1}^{K} h_{ik}||\vec{v}_i - \vec{c}_k||^2}}{Z} \\
&= \mathcal{N}(\sum_{k=1}^{K} h_{ik}\vec{v}_i, I)
\end{aligned}
\tag{6.6}
$$

is a multivariate Gaussian distribution (Chapter 2), where I is an identity matrix.

Similarly, the finding of cluster centroids can be written as

$$
\arg\min_H \sum_{i=1}^{N} \sum_{k=1}^{K} h_{ik}||\vec{v}_i - \vec{c}_k||^2 = \arg\min_H \sum_{i=1}^{N} P(\vec{v}_i, h_i|\Theta).
$$

k-Means and EM. Given the probabilistic interpretation of each step in k-means, we can draw correlation between k-means and Eq 6.1. Formally, k-means optimises in alternation

$$
\begin{aligned}
\mathcal{H} &= \arg\max_{\mathcal{H}'} P(O, H = \mathcal{H}'|\Theta) = \arg\max_{\mathcal{H}'} \sum_{i=1}^{N} P(\vec{v}_i, h_i = \hbar'_i|\Theta), \\
\Theta &= \arg\max_\Theta P(O, H = \mathcal{H}|\Theta) = \arg\max_\Theta \sum_{i=1}^{N} P(\vec{v}_i, h_i = \hbar_i|\Theta).
\end{aligned}
\tag{6.7}
$$

The second step in Eq 6.7 corresponds to the optimisation for Θ by maximising Eq 6.1. The iterative optimisation process for Θ is shown in Algorithm 6.1. The model parameters Θ are randomly initialised to Θ^0. At the tth iteration, Θ^t is fixed first and H^t is predicted. Then, H^t is kept unchanged and acts as training labels at the maximisation step to find Θ^{t+1} for the next iteration. This algorithm can be viewed as a "hard" EM algorithm, differing from the EM algorithm in the calculation of expectation. The next section discusses EM by making a change to this algorithm.

6.1.2 Expectation Maximisation

Different from k-means (or hard EM), which uses the most likely values of hidden variables as the expectations of the variables, the expectation maximisation (EM) algorithm calculates the hidden variable distributions by considering all possible values of hidden variables. This applies to both the expectation (E) step and the maximisation (M) step.

E-step. Rather than predicting only one expected value of H, the expectation step of EM produces a distribution of H. Denote this distribution as P_C, where $P_C(H = \mathcal{H})$ (or $P_C(\mathcal{H})$ in brief) is the probability of a specific value $\mathcal{H}$ from the set of all possible values for the hidden variables H. In particular, the distribution $P_C(H)$ is defined as $P(H|O, \Theta)$, which is the posterior distribution of H given observations O and the model parameters Θ (we will see the reason in Section 6.3). For example, under the k-means task setting, the E-step would calculate $P(h_i|\vec{v}_i, \Theta)$ for all the K possible cluster assignments h_i given each vector $\vec{v}_i$, which can be $\frac{\|\vec{v}_i - \vec{c}_k\|^2}{2}$ for $h_i = \text{ONEHOT}(k)$ ($k \in [1, \dots, K]$). We will see more examples in Section 6.2.

M-step. The maximisation step optimises Θ by maximising the expected log-likelihood $\log P(O, H|\Theta)$ given the distribution $P(H|O, \Theta)$,

$$
\begin{aligned}
\hat{\Theta} &= \arg\max_{\Theta} E_{H \sim P(H|O,\Theta)} \log P(O, H|\Theta) \\
&= \arg\max_{\Theta} \sum_{\mathcal{H}} P(H = \mathcal{H}|O, \Theta) \log P(O, \mathcal{H}|\Theta).
\end{aligned}
\tag{6.8}
$$

In Eq 6.8, $P(H = \mathcal{H}|O, \Theta)$ are the values of $P_C(\mathcal{H})$ for each possible hidden variable $\mathcal{H}$, as calculated in the E-step. As a result, they are fixed in finding $\arg\max_{\Theta}$. In this equation, the parameter Θ to adjust exists only in $P(O, \mathcal{H}|\Theta)$. The M-step is typically a constrained optimisation process, for which the Lagrange multiplier method can be used, as we have discussed in Chapter 5. We will see detailed examples in Section 6.2.

Algorithm 6.2 shows pseudocode of the EM algorithm over a dataset $O = \{o_i\}|_{i=1}^{N}$, where each o_i is associated with a set of hidden variables h_i. The algorithm starts from a randomly initialised model, repeatedly performing expectation and maximisation steps until convergence. Here CON-VERGE can be defined as returning true when the Θ values between two iterations become similar by a certain measure, and false otherwise. The iteration number is denoted as a variable t. Variable values determined in a certain iteration t are denoted with t as a superscript and taken as constants. Free variables are denoted without t. In particular, in the maximisation step to find Θ^{t+1}, Θ^t in the objective function $Q(\Theta, \Theta^t)$ is regarded as a constant while Θ in $Q(\Theta, \Theta^t)$ is a variable to optimise. Exercise 6.2 discusses a version of k-means using EM instead of hard EM.

Given a random start, it has been shown that EM can always reach a local optimum of the model training objective. However, local optima can be highly different from the global optimum. As a result, the initial value Θ^0 has a large influence on the final model.

Q function and EM. In Algorithm 6.2, the objective function $Q(\Theta, \Theta^t)$ for the M-step is:

$$
Q(\Theta, \Theta^t) = \sum_{\mathcal{H}} P(H = \mathcal{H}|O, \Theta^t) \log P(O, H = \mathcal{H}|\Theta),
\tag{6.9}
$$

Algorithm 6.2. Expectation maximisation.

Inputs: data $O = \{o_i\}|_{i=1}^{N}$;
Hidden Variables: $H = \{h_i\}|_{i=1}^{N}$;
Initialisation: model $\Theta^0 \leftarrow \text{RANDOMMODEL}(), t \leftarrow 0$;
repeat
   | **Expectation step:**
   | Compute $P(H = \mathcal{H}|O, \Theta^t)$ for each possible $\mathcal{H}$ (i.e.,
   | $P(h_i = \hbar|o_i, \Theta^t)$ for each value $\hbar$ of h_i ($i \in [1, \dots, N]$));
   | **Maximisation step:**
   | $Q(\Theta, \Theta^t) \leftarrow \sum_{\mathcal{H}} P(H = \mathcal{H}|O, \Theta^t) \log P(O, H = \mathcal{H}|\Theta)$ (i.e.,
   | $\sum_{i=1}^{N} \sum_{\hbar} P(\hbar|o_i, \Theta^t) \log P(o_i, \hbar|\Theta)$);
   | $\Theta^{t+1} \leftarrow \arg\max_{\Theta} Q(\Theta, \Theta^t)$;
   | $t \leftarrow t + 1$;
until CONVERGE (H, Θ);

---

which is called a **Q-function**. This function is central to EM. We can view EM as iteratively optimising this function. As mentioned earlier, this training objective is the expectation of the joint likelihood to optimise, and therefore can also be called the *expectation function*.

The Q-function can be regarded as a weighted version of Eq 6.1

$$\hat{\Theta} = \arg\max_{\Theta} \sum_{\mathcal{H}} w_{\mathcal{H}} \log P(O, H = \mathcal{H}|\Theta),$$

where $w_{\mathcal{H}}$ is the corresponding weight for the specific hidden variable assignment $\mathcal{H}$. In particular, $w_{\mathcal{H}} = P(H = \mathcal{H}|O, \Theta)$ is a constant value found in the E-step. Now if in the training data, each o_i is manually given a gold-standard label y_i, we can define

$$P(h_i|o_i, \Theta^t) = \begin{cases} 1 & \text{if } h_i = y_i \\ 0 & \text{otherwise,} \end{cases} \tag{6.10}$$

in which case the Q-function in Eq 6.9 becomes:

$$Q(\Theta, \Theta^t) = \sum_{i=1}^{N} \sum_{\hbar} P(\hbar|o_i, \Theta^t) \log P(o_i, \hbar|\Theta)$$

$$= \sum_{i=1}^{N} \log P(o_i, y_i|\Theta),$$

which is exactly the maximum log-likelihood training objective.

This also shows the importance of $P(h|o, \Theta)$ to the success of EM training. With complete knowledge of $P(H|O, \Theta)$ such as Eq 6.10, EM becomes equivalent to fully supervised training. The parameterisation of $P(H|O, \Theta)$ can convey prior knowledge about the problem to solve, which guides the learning of H through the optimisation of O. For example, in the k-means algorithm, we draw connections between O and H by knowing the correlation between cluster centroids and cluster assignments. In this light, the initial values of Θ also play a crucial role in the success of EM.

Using the Q-function as a training objective, every possible value of the hidden variables can make a contribution to the parameter update. In Section 6.3, we will give theoretical justifications of Algorithm 6.2, showing that this algorithm is guaranteed to converge.

6.2 Using EM for Training Models with Hidden Variables

We discuss three examples of EM training, namely the unsupervised Naïve Bayes model, IBM model 1 for machine translation and probabilistic latent semantic analysis (PLSA). For each task, we follow Algorithm 6.2 to: (1) parameterise the complete data likelihood $P(O, H|\Theta)$, (2) compute $P(H|O, \Theta)$, (3) maximise $Q(\Theta, \Theta^t)$, where (2) and (3) are executed iteratively.

6.2.1 Unsupervised Naïve Bayes Model

Let us return to Naïve Bayes models for text classifications. In Chapter 2, we discussed supervised settings. Given a set of documents and their corresponding labels $D = \{(d_i, c_i)\}|_{i=1}^{N}$, where $c_i \in C$, $d_i = \{w_1^i, w_2^i, \ldots, w_{|d_i|}^i\}$, and $w_j^i \in V$ denotes the jth word in document d_i, MLE is used to estimate the model parameter by counting relative frequencies. In particular, we have:

$$
\begin{aligned}
P(c) &= \frac{\sum_{i=1}^{N} \delta(c_i, c)}{N} \\
P(w|c) &= \frac{\sum_{i=1}^{N} \left(\delta(c_i, c) \cdot \sum_{j=1}^{|d_i|} \delta(w_j^i, w) \right)}{\sum_{i=1}^{N} \delta(c_i, c)|d_i|}
\end{aligned}
\tag{6.11}
$$

for each $w \in V$ and $c \in C$. $\delta(c_i, c)$ tests whether c_i equals c.

Now let us consider unsupervised settings, where the output classes are not available. In this case, the inputs are still documents d but the outputs are hidden class labels h. Similar to k-means, let us suppose that there are K document classes. Since we do not have control over the meaning of each class, we can denote the set of class labels as $C = \{1, 2, \ldots, K\}$. Now given a set of documents $D = \{d_i\}|_{i=1}^{N}$, for each document d_i, the data likelihood with each possible class $h \in C$ is:

$$
P(d_i, h|\Theta) = P(h|\Theta)P(d_i|h, \Theta) = P(h|\Theta) \prod_{j=1}^{|d_i|} P(w_j^i|h, \Theta).
\tag{6.12}
$$

In Eq 6.12, $P(d_i, h|\Theta)$ is the main model, where the parameters Θ consist of $P(h)$ and $P(w|h)$ for all $w \in V$ and $h \in C$. Following Naïve Bayes, we assume that each word is conditionally independent given h and Θ. As a result, the model is a bag-of-words model and hence the name unsupervised Naïve Bayes model.

We use EM as shown in Algorithm 6.2 to train this model, which iteratively calculates $P(h|d)$ for all $h \in C$ and maximises $\sum_{i=1}^{N} \sum_{h} P(h|d_i) \log P(d_i, h)$. Similar to Section 6.1.2, Θ is included in the conditional probability in order to denote parameter and hidden variable values at the same time. In particular, $P(\hbar|d_i)$ becomes $P(\hbar|d_i, \Theta)$ and $P(d_i, \hbar)$ becomes $P(d_i, \hbar|\Theta)$. Θ^0 are randomly initialised, and at iteration t, one E-step is first taken, where $P(\hbar|d_i, \Theta^t)$ is calculated by

$$P(\hbar|d_i, \Theta^t) = \frac{P(d_i, \hbar|\Theta^t)}{\sum_{\hbar \in C} P(d_i, \hbar|\Theta^t)} = \frac{P(\hbar|\Theta^t) \prod_{i=1}^{|d_i|} P(w_i|\hbar, \Theta^t)}{\sum_{\hbar \in C} P(\hbar|\Theta^t) \prod_{i=1}^{|d_i|} P(w_i|\hbar, \Theta^t)}. \tag{6.13}$$

We then take one M-step to maximise $Q(\Theta, \Theta^t)$, namely:

$$Q(\Theta, \Theta^t) = \sum_{i=1}^{N} \sum_{\hbar \in C} P(\hbar|d_i, \Theta^t) \log P(d_i, \hbar|\Theta).$$

As discussed in Section 6.1.2, in order to find $\arg\max_\Theta Q(\Theta, \Theta^t)$ such that $\sum_{\hbar \in C} P(\hbar|\Theta) = 1$ and $\sum_{w \in V} P(w|\hbar, \Theta) = 1$, we use Lagrangian optimisation, where the Lagrangian function with the constraints is

$$\Lambda(\Theta, \lambda) = Q(\Theta, \Theta^t) - \lambda_0 \left(\sum_{\hbar \in C} P(\hbar|\Theta) - 1 \right) - \sum_{\hbar \in C} \lambda_\hbar \left(\sum_{w \in V} P(w|\hbar, \Theta) - 1 \right)$$

$$= \sum_{i=1}^{N} \sum_{\hbar \in C} P(\hbar|d_i, \Theta^t) \log P(d_i, \hbar|\Theta) - \lambda_0 \left(\sum_{\hbar \in C} P(\hbar|\Theta) - 1 \right)$$

$$- \sum_{\hbar \in C} \lambda_\hbar \left(\sum_{w \in V} P(w|\hbar, \Theta) - 1 \right)$$

$$= \sum_{i=1}^{N} \sum_{\hbar \in C} P(\hbar|d_i, \Theta^t) \left(\log P(\hbar|\Theta) + \sum_{j=1}^{|d_i|} \log P(w_j|\hbar, \Theta) \right)$$

$$- \lambda_0 \left(\sum_{\hbar \in C} P(\hbar|\Theta) - 1 \right) - \sum_{\hbar \in C} \lambda_\hbar \left(\sum_{w \in V} P(w|\hbar, \Theta) - 1 \right),$$

where $\lambda = \lambda_0, \lambda_1, \ldots, \lambda_K$ are Lagrangian multipliers. Taking partial derivatives of $\Lambda(\Theta, \lambda)$ with respect to $P(\hbar|\Theta)$ gives

$$\frac{\partial \Lambda(\Theta, \lambda)}{\partial P(\hbar|\Theta)} = \frac{\sum_{i=1}^{N} P(\hbar|d_i, \Theta^t)}{P(\hbar|\Theta)} - \lambda_0.$$

Letting $\frac{\partial \Lambda(\Theta, \lambda)}{\partial P(\hbar|\Theta)} = 0$, we have

$$P(\hbar|\Theta) = \frac{\sum_{i=1}^{N} P(\hbar|d_i, \Theta^t)}{\lambda_0}.$$

Under the constraint that $\sum_{\hbar \in C} P(\hbar|\Theta) = 1$, we have

$$\sum_{\hbar \in C} P(\hbar|\Theta) = \sum_{\hbar \in C} \frac{\sum_{i=1}^{N} P(\hbar|d_i, \Theta^t)}{\lambda_0}$$

and thus

$$\lambda_0 = \sum_{\hbar \in C} \sum_{i=1}^{N} P(\hbar|d_i, \Theta^t) = \sum_{i=1}^{N} \sum_{\hbar \in C} P(\hbar|d_i, \Theta^t) = N.$$

Therefore, we have

$$P(\hbar|\Theta) = \frac{\sum_{i=1}^{N} P(\hbar|d_i, \Theta^t)}{N}, \tag{6.14}$$

which is taken as the value of $P(\hbar|\Theta^{t+1})$ for the next iteration. Similarly,

$$\frac{\partial \Lambda(\Theta, \lambda)}{\partial P(w|\hbar, \Theta)} = \frac{\sum_{i=1}^{N} P(\hbar|d_i, \Theta^t) \sum_{j=1}^{|d_i|} \delta(w_j, w)}{P(w|\hbar, \Theta)} - \lambda_\hbar,$$

where the delta function $\delta(w_j, w)$ connects $w_j \in d_i$ with $w \in V$.

Given $\frac{\partial \Lambda(\Theta, \lambda)}{\partial P(w|\hbar, \Theta)} = 0$ and $\sum_{w \in V} P(w|\hbar, \Theta) = 1$, we have

$$\lambda_\hbar = \sum_{w \in V} \sum_{i=1}^{N} P(\hbar|d_i, \Theta^t) \sum_{j=1}^{|d_i|} \delta(w_j, w) = \sum_{i=1}^{N} P(\hbar|d_i, \Theta^t)|d_i|$$

$$P(w|\hbar, \Theta) = \frac{\sum_{i=1}^{N} P(\hbar|d_i, \Theta^t) \sum_{j=1}^{|d_i|} \delta(w_j, w)}{\lambda_\hbar} = \frac{\sum_{i=1}^{N} P(\hbar|d_i, \Theta^t) \sum_{j=1}^{|d_i|} \delta(w_j, w)}{\sum_{i=1}^{N} P(\hbar|d_i, \Theta^t)|d_i|}, \tag{6.15}$$

which is taken as the value of $P(w|\hbar, \Theta^{t+1})$ for the next iteration.

The above process as shown in Algorithm 6.3, is executed iteratively, taking the expectation step using Eq 6.13 and the maximisation step using Eq 6.14 and Eq 6.15 until the differences between $P(\hbar|\Theta^{t+1})$ and $P(\hbar|\Theta^t)$ and between $P(w|\hbar, \Theta^{t+1})$ and $P(w|\hbar, \Theta^t)$ are below a threshold. After convergence, $P(\hbar|\Theta)$ and $P(w|\hbar, \Theta)$ are taken as the final model.

Unsupervised Naïve Bayes vs Naïve Bayes. Comparing Eq 6.14 and Eq 6.15 with Eq 6.11, it is easy to find that the terms $P(c)$ vs $P(\hbar|\Theta)$ and $P(w|c)$ vs $P(w|\hbar, \Theta)$ are quite similar. In particular, for the ith example, setting $P(c|d_i, \Theta^t) = \delta(c_i, c)$ makes Eq 6.14 and Eq 6.15 identical to Eq 6.11. This is very intuitive. In supervised settings, $\sum_{i=1}^{N} \delta(c_i, c)$ in Eq 6.11 is the total actual count for the label c, while $\sum_{i=1}^{N} P(\hbar|d_i, \Theta^t)$ denotes the expected count for label $\hbar$ in unsupervised settings. Similarly, underlying connections can be made between $\sum_{i=1}^{N} \left(\delta(c_i, c) \cdot \sum_{j=1}^{|d_i|} \delta(w_j^i, w) \right)$ in Eq 6.11 and $\sum_{i=1}^{N} P(\hbar|d_i, \Theta^t) \sum_{j=1}^{|d_i|} \delta(w_j, w)$ in Eq 6.15.

Unsupervised Naïve Bayes vs k-means. Unsupervised Naïve Bayes is a clustering model for documents. Compared with the k-means clustering algorithm in Chapter 2, there are two main differences. First, k-means is based on vector space geometry, finding a partition of vector space based on vector points and Euclidean distances. In contrast, Naïve Bayes is a direct probability model of documents and words. Second, an unsupervised Naïve Bayes model is optimised with EM, while k-means is a hard variant of EM. Note that similar to k-means clustering, there is no direct interpretation of each class label by unsupervised classification. The automatically induced classes do not necessarily correspond to a specific set of class labels such as {Word, Leisure} or {Travel, Non-Travel}. Manual inspection of documents in each class is typically necessary for understanding each class label.

Algorithm 6.3. EM algorithm for unsupervised Naïve Bayes model.

Input: D = $\{d_i\}|_{i=1}^{N}$;
Variables: $count(w|h)$; $count(h)$; $doc\text{-}total(h)$;
Initialisation: $P(w|h) \leftarrow$ RANDOMDISTRIBUTION() **for** $h \in [1, \dots, K]$,
$P(h) \leftarrow$ RANDOMDISTRIBUTION();
repeat
 $count(w|h) \leftarrow 0$;
 $count(h) \leftarrow 0$;
 for $d_i \in D$ **do**
  Calculate $P(h|d_i)$ according to Eq 6.13 using $P(w|h)$ and $P(h)$;
  for $h \in [1, \dots, K]$ **do**
   $count(h) \leftarrow count(h) + P(h|d_i)$;
   $doc\text{-}total(h) \leftarrow P(h|d_i) \times |d_i|$;
   for $j \in [1, \dots, |d_i|]$ **do**
    $w \leftarrow w_j$;
    $count(w|h) \leftarrow count(w|h) + P(h|d_i)$;
 for $h \in [1, \dots, K]$ **do**
  $P(h) \leftarrow \frac{count(h)}{N}$;
  for $w \in V$ **do**
   $P(w|h) \leftarrow \frac{count(w|h)}{doc-total(h)}$;
until CONVERGE($P(w|h)$) and CONVERGE($P(h)$);
Output: $P(w|h)$ and $P(h)$.

6.2.2 IBM Model 1

Given a *source* sentence X, the task of *machine translation* (MT) is to find a corresponding *target* language translation Y. Here $X = x_1 x_2 \dots x_{|X|}$, where x_i ($i \in [1, \dots, |X|]$) is a source word, and $Y = y_1 y_2 \dots y_{|Y|}$, where y_j ($j \in [1, \dots, |Y|]$) is a target word. A simple probabilistic model for machine translation calculates $P(Y|X)$, namely the probability of a candidate target translation Y given a source sentence X. Since both X and Y are sentences, which are highly sparse, we parameterise the model by defining a generative story using the techniques in Chapter 2.

A probabilistic model for MT. According to the Bayes rule, we have

$$P(Y|X) = \frac{P(X|Y)P(Y)}{P(X)} \propto P(X|Y)P(Y). \tag{6.16}$$

In Eq 6.16, $P(Y)$ is the probability of the candidate target sentence, and therefore serves as a *language model* to ensure fluency. $P(X|Y)$ is the probability of X given Y, which serves as a *translation model* to ensure adequacy. The above generative story yields a sentence pair (X, Y) by first yielding Y, and then yielding X given Y. This design offers modularity by introducing a fluency component $P(Y)$, compared to a model for $P(Y|X)$ directly without using the Bayes rule.

Table 6.1 Word alignment examples.

ID	Source	Target	Alignment
1 (*French*)	J'$_1$(I) aime$_2$(like) lire$_3$(reading)	I$_1$ like$_2$ reading$_3$	$\{1\rightarrow1, 2\rightarrow2, 3\rightarrow3\}$
2 (*German*)	Ich$_1$(I) lese$_2$(read) hier$_3$(here) ein$_4$(a) Buch$_5$(book)	I$_1$ read$_2$ a$_3$ book$_4$ here$_5$	$\{1\rightarrow1, 2\rightarrow2, 3\rightarrow5, 4\rightarrow3, 5\rightarrow4 \}$
3 (*Chinese*)	我$_1$ (I) 在$_2$ (at) 这里$_3$ (here) 读$_4$ (read) 一$_5$ (a) 本$_6$ (this) 书$_7$ (book)	I$_1$ read$_2$ a$_3$ book$_4$ here$_5$	$\{1\rightarrow1, 2\rightarrow5, 3\rightarrow5, 4\rightarrow 2, 5\rightarrow3, 6\rightarrow$NULL$, 7\rightarrow4\}$
4 (*Japanese*)	私は$_1$(I) 家で$_2$(at home) 本を$_3$(a book) 読む$_4$(read)	I$_1$ read$_2$ a$_3$ book$_4$ at$_5$ home$_6$	$\{1\rightarrow1, 2\rightarrow\{5, 6\}, 3\rightarrow\{3, 4\}, 4\rightarrow2\}$

Next we simplify $P(X|Y)$, deriving model parameters by using the probability chain rule and making independence assumptions. According to the chain rule, we have

$$\begin{aligned}P(X|Y) &=P(x_1x_2\ldots x_{|X|}|y_1y_2\ldots y_{|Y|})\\&=P(x_1|y_1y_2\ldots y_{|Y|})P(x_2|x_1y_1\ldots y_{|Y|})\cdots\\&\quad P(x_{|X|}|x_1\ldots x_{|X|-1}, y_1\ldots y_{|Y|}).\end{aligned}$$

Further assuming that each source word x_i is conditionally dependent to only one target word y_{a_i}, we have

$$\begin{aligned}P(X|Y) &=P(x_1|y_1y_2\ldots y_{|Y|})P(x_2|x_1y_1\ldots y_{|Y|})\cdots\\&\quad P(x_{|X|}|x_1\ldots x_{|X|-1}, y_1\ldots y_{|Y|})\\&=P(x_1|y_{a_1})P(x_2|y_{a_2})\ldots P(x_{|X|}|y_{a_{|X|}}).\end{aligned}$$

Here a_i denotes the index of the target word that the ith source word translates to. Given two sentences X and Y, the set $A = \{a_i\}|_{i=1}^{|X|}$ is referred to as their **word alignment**. There are several types of word alignments between sentence translation pairs, as shown in Table 6.1. In particular, the alignment in example 1 is *monotonic*, with $a_i = i$. The alignment in example 2, however, is *non-monotonic*, with $a_1 = 1, a_2 = 2, a_3 = 5, a_4 = 3$ and $a_5 = 4$. Example 3 contains *many-to-one* alignments (i.e., $a_2 = a_3 = 5$) and *null* alignments (i.e., $a_6 = $ NULL). Example 4 contains *one-to-many* alignments, with $a_2 = \{5, 6\}$ and $a_3 = \{3, 4\}$. To simplify our model, we treat one-to-many alignments as illegal, considering a as a function mapping from a source index to a unique target index or NULL.

The final model $P(Y|X)$ therefore consists of two main parameter types, namely word translation probabilities $P(x|y)$ for $P(X|Y)$ and language model parameters (e.g., a trigram LM) for $P(Y)$. $P(x|y)$ denotes the probability of a source *vocabulary* word $x \in V_x$ given a target *vocabulary* word $y \in V_y$, which is similar to a dictionary with probability values. Below we focus on $P(X|Y)$ since language models have been discussed in Chapter 2.

EM training. Datasets that consist of sentence translation pairs $D = \{(X_i, Y_i)\}|_{i=1}^N$ are relatively easy to obtain. On the other hand, gold-standard word alignments are extremely costly to obtain. As a result, given a sentence translation pair (X_i, Y_i), the word alignment A_i between them has to be treated as a hidden variable. In this case, the observed variables are $O = (X_i, Y_i)$ and the hidden variables are $H = \{A_i\}$.

If A_i are known, the training of our translation model can be achieved using standard MLE by counting relative frequencies, where

$$P(x|y) = \frac{\#(x \text{ aligned to } y \text{ in } D)}{\#(y \text{ in } D)}.$$

In the reverse direction, if the model $P(x|y)$ is given, one can calculate the expected values of A_i. Consequently, EM can be used to derive our model, with Θ being $P(x|y)$, H being A_i, the E-step being the process of deriving a model distribution of A_i using $P(x|y)$, and the M-step being the estimation of $P(x|y)$ using the distribution of A_i.

For notational convenience, let us use one specific training instance to illustrate the EM process, denoting the sentence pair as $O = (X, Y)$ and the alignment as $H = A$. According to Algorithm 6.2, at each iteration t, the expectation step calculates $P(H|O, \Theta^t)$ and the maximisation step maximises $\sum_H P(H|O, \Theta^t) \log P(O, H|\Theta) = \sum_A P(A|X, Y, \Theta^t) \log P(X, A|Y, \Theta)$. We now need to denote $P(A|X, Y)$ and $P(X, A|Y)$ in terms of $P(x|y)$, our translation model parameters. In particular,

$$P(A|X, Y) = \frac{P(A, X|Y)}{P(X|Y)} \text{ (Eq 2.9; conditioned on } Y).$$

$P(A, X|Y)$ (i.e., $P(X, A|Y)$) can be further decomposed into

$$P(A, X|Y) = P(A|Y)P(X|A, Y). \tag{6.17}$$

Thus for calculating the joint distribution $P(A, X|Y)$, we can calculate $P(A|Y)$ first, which are the probabilities of generating A given Y, and then $P(X|A, Y)$, which are the probabilities of generating X given Y and A.

For a simplest model, assume that given a target sentence, the alignment of a source word to each target word in the sentence is equally probable. Further since we assume that each x_i is aligned to exactly one y_j or NULL,

$$P(A|Y) = (\frac{1}{|Y| + 1})^{|X|} = \frac{1}{(|Y| + 1)^{|X|}}, \tag{6.18}$$

where 1 accounts for NULL in $(|Y| + 1)$.

$P(X|A, Y)$ is straightforward to calculate when the alignment A and the target Y are both known. Assuming that each x_i is generated independently of all the other $x_{i'}$ $(i' \neq i)$, x_i depends only on the word y_{a_i}, we have

$$P(X|A, Y) = \prod_{i=1}^{|X|} P(x_i|y_{a_i}), \tag{6.19}$$

and therefore substituting Eq 6.18 and Eq 6.19 into Eq 6.17 we have

$$\begin{aligned} P(A, X|Y) &= P(A|Y)P(X|A, Y) \\ &= \frac{\prod_{i=1}^{|X|} P(x_i|y_{a_i})}{(|Y| + 1)^{|X|}}. \end{aligned}$$

We further calculate $P(X|Y)$ by marginalising out A

$$\begin{aligned} P(X|Y) &= \sum_A P(A, X|Y) \\ &= \sum_A \frac{\prod_{i=1}^{|X|} P(x_i|y_{a_i})}{(|Y| + 1)^{|X|}} \\ &= \sum_{a_1=0}^{|Y|} \sum_{a_2=0}^{|Y|} \cdots \sum_{a_{|X|}=0}^{|Y|} \frac{\prod_{i=1}^{|X|} P(x_i|y_{a_i})}{(|Y| + 1)^{|X|}} \\ &= \frac{1}{(|Y| + 1)^{|X|}} \sum_{a_1=0}^{|Y|} \sum_{a_2=0}^{|Y|} \cdots \sum_{a_{|X|}=0}^{|Y|} \prod_{i=1}^{|X|} P(x_i|y_{a_i}) \\ &= \frac{1}{(|Y| + 1)^{|X|}} \prod_{i=1}^{|X|} \sum_{j=0}^{|Y|} P(x_i|y_j), \quad \text{(distributivity)} \end{aligned} \tag{6.20}$$

where $a_i = 0$ denotes that the ith source word is aligned to NULL (i.e., we have a special target word y_0=NULL). The last step above uses the law of distributivity to transform a sum of products to a product of sums, the proof of which is left for Exercise 6.6. With this change, an exponential number of products are reduced to a linear number of sums, which is computationally tractable.

The alignment probability $P(A|X, Y)$ is given by

$$\begin{aligned} P(A|X, Y) &= \frac{P(A, X|Y)}{P(X|Y)} \\ &= \frac{\prod_{i=1}^{|X|} P(x_i|y_{a_i})}{\prod_{i=1}^{|X|} \sum_{j=0}^{|Y|} P(x_i|y_j)} \\ &= \prod_{i=1}^{|X|} \frac{P(x_i|y_{a_i})}{\sum_{j=0}^{|Y|} P(x_i|y_j)}. \end{aligned}$$

We have now obtained the form of $P(A|X, Y)$ and $P(A, X|Y)$ in terms of our model parameter $P(x|y)$, which can serve as a basis for the E-step. Further, for a time step t, the M-step optimises

Θ by maximising:

$$Q(\Theta, \Theta^t) = \sum_A P(A|X, Y, \Theta^t) \log P(A, X|Y, \Theta)$$

$$= \sum_A P(A|X, Y, \Theta^t) \log \frac{\prod_{i=1}^{|X|} P(x_i|y_{a_i}, \Theta)}{(|Y| + 1)^{|X|}}.$$

(6.21)

Here we introduce Θ to the probabilities in Eq 6.17, so that we can explicitly use Θ and Θ^t to denote adjusted and fixed model parameters, respectively. Given the probability constraint $\sum_x P(x|y) = 1$ for every y, we can define a Lagrangian function

$$\Lambda(\Theta, \lambda) = Q(\Theta, \Theta^t) - \sum_y \lambda_y \left(\sum_x P(x|y, \Theta) - 1 \right)$$

$$= \sum_A P(A|X, Y, \Theta^t) \log \frac{\prod_{i=1}^{|X|} P(x_i|y_{a_i}, \Theta)}{(|Y| + 1)^{|X|}} - \sum_y \lambda_y \left(\sum_x P(x|y, \Theta) - 1 \right)$$

$$= \sum_A P(A|X, Y, \Theta^t) \left(\sum_{i=1}^{|X|} \log P(x_i|y_{a_i}, \Theta) - |X| \log(|Y| + 1) \right)$$

$$- \sum_y \lambda_y \left(\sum_x P(x|y, \Theta) - 1 \right).$$

Taking derivatives of $\Lambda(\Theta, \lambda)$ with respect to $P(x|y, \Theta)$, we have

$$\frac{\partial \Lambda(\Theta, \lambda)}{\partial P(x|y, \Theta)} = \frac{\sum_A P(A|X, Y, \Theta^t) \sum_{k=1}^{|X|} \delta(x, x_k)\delta(y, y_{a_k})}{P(x|y, \Theta)} - \lambda_y.$$

Setting $\frac{\partial \Lambda(\Theta, \lambda)}{\partial P(x|y, \Theta)} = 0$ gives

$$P(x|y, \Theta) = \frac{\sum_A P(A|X, Y, \Theta^t) \sum_{k=1}^{|X|} \delta(x, x_k)\delta(y, y_{a_k})}{\lambda_y}$$

$$\propto \sum_A P(A|X, Y, \Theta^t) \sum_{k=1}^{|X|} \delta(x, x_k)\delta(y, y_{a_k})$$

which can serve as $P(x|y, \Theta^{t+1})$ in the next iteration for EM.

So far we have only considered a single sentence pair. Moving back to the whole corpus, the summation should be calculated over all sentence pairs:

$$P(x|y, \Theta) \propto \sum_{(X_i, Y_i) \in D} \sum_{A_i} P(A_i|X_i, Y_i, \Theta^t) \sum_{k=1}^{|X|} \delta(x, x_k^i)\delta(y, y_{a_k}^i).$$

To derive pseudocode for the above process, let us define

$$\text{EXPECTEDALIGN}(x, y, X, Y) = \sum_A P(A|X, Y) \cdot \sum_{k=1}^{|X|} \delta(x, x_k)\delta(y, y_{a_k})$$

$$= E_{A \sim P(A|X,Y)}\left(\sum_{k=1}^{|X|} \delta(x, x_k)\delta(y, y_{a_k})\right),$$

which is the *expected* alignment between a word pair of source and target vocabulary words x and y in a sentence translation pair (X, Y) given a model $P(x|y)$. To calculate its value, we have

$$\text{EXPECTEDALIGN}(x, y, X, Y) = \sum_A P(A|X, Y) \cdot \sum_{k=1}^{|X|} \delta(x, x_k)\delta(y, y_{a_k})$$

$$= \sum_A \prod_{i=1}^{|X|} \frac{P(x_i|y_{a_i})}{\sum_{j=0}^{|Y|} P(x_i|y_j)} \cdot \sum_{k=1}^{|X|} \delta(x, x_k)\delta(y, y_{a_k}) \quad (6.22)$$

$$= \frac{P(x|y)}{\sum_{j=0}^{|Y|} P(x|y_j)} \sum_{i=1}^{|X|} \delta(x, x_i) \sum_{j=0}^{|Y|} \delta(y, y_j).$$

The last step of Eq 6.22 can be derived using similar tricks as Eq 6.20, which we leave for Exercise 6.7. Intuitively, $\sum_{i=1}^{|X|} \delta(x, x_i) \sum_{j=0}^{|Y|} \delta(y, y_j)$ is the total alignment count of the word x and the word y in the sentence X and the sentence Y, and $\frac{P(x|y)}{\sum_{j=0}^{|Y|} P(x|y_j)}$ is a weight probability score. In this respect, $\text{EXPECTEDALIGN}(x, y, X, Y)$ represents a soft count.

For the maximisation step, we take this expected count as a real count and perform MLE to obtain the Θ^{t+1} value that maximises $Q(\Theta, \Theta^t)$. In particular, for a source vocabulary word x and a target vocabulary word y,

$$P(x|y) = \frac{\sum_{(X_i, Y_i) \in D} \text{EXPECTEDALIGN}(x, y; X_i, Y_i)}{\sum_{(X_i, Y_i) \in D} \left(\sum_{x'} \text{EXPECTEDALIGN}(x', y; X_i, Y_i)\right)}.$$

The equation above can be implemented using Algorithm 6.4, where $\text{CONVERGE}(P(x|y))$ can be calculated based on the perplexity (mentioned in Chapter 5) of the model over the corpus D. In particular, the perplexity of a translation model can be defined as

$$\Upsilon(P) = 2^{-\sum_{i=1}^N \log_2 P(X_i|Y_i)},$$

where (X_i, Y_i) is a sentence pair in the bilingual corpus D. During training $\Upsilon(P)$ decreases. When $\Upsilon(P)$ becomes stable, the algorithm can stop.

The model above was named *IBM model 1*, which is the simplest among five probabilistic models for statistical machine translation developed at IBM in the early 1990s. IBM models are *word-based* machine translation models, performing translation word by word. It has been discovered in the 2000s that translating a source sentence phrase-by-phrase gives significantly better translation quality. As a result, *phrase-based* translation systems replaced word-based translation systems as the state of the art at that time. The dominant approach was further overtaken by neural machine translation (NMT) in the 2010s, which will be discussed in Chapter 16.

Algorithm 6.4. Word alignment.

Input: $D = \{(X_i, Y_i)\}|_{i=1}^{N}$;
Variables: $count(x|y)$; $count(y)$; $sent\text{-}total(x)$;
Initialisation $P(x|y) \leftarrow$ UNIFORMDISTRIBUTION();
repeat
    $count(x|y) \leftarrow 0$;
    $count(y) \leftarrow 0$;
    for $(X, Y) \in D$ **do**
        for $x_i \in X$ **do**
            $sent\text{-}total(x_i) \leftarrow 0$;
            for $y_j \in Y_i$ **do**
                $sent\text{-}total(x_i) \leftarrow sent\text{-}total(x_i) + P(x_i|y_j)$;
        for $x_i \in X$ **do**
            for $y_j \in Y$ **do**
                $count(x_i|y_j) \leftarrow count(x_i|y_j) + \frac{P(x_i|y_j)}{sent\text{-}total(x_i)}$;
                $count(y_j) \leftarrow count(y_j) + \frac{P(x_i|y_j)}{sent\text{-}total(x_i)}$;
    for $x \in$ SOURCEVOCAB$(D), y \in$ TARGETVOCAB$(D), y \in D$ **do**
        $P(x|y) = \frac{count(x|y)}{count(y)}$;
until CONVERGE$(P(x|y))$;

6.2.3 Probabilistic Latent Semantic Analysis

We have seen several methods for representing a document into the vector space, such as count-based vectors and TF-IDF vectors. They are high-dimensional vectors. **Latent semantic allocation** is a different method for representing documents, using lower-dimensional vectors, each element of which represents a semantic attribute of the document. To this end, **probabilistic latent semantic analysis** (PLSA) is a generative model, which represents a document by its topic distribution. Given a set of documents $D = \{d_i\}|_{i=1}^{N}$, where d_i consists of $w_1^i, w_2^i, \ldots, w_{|d_i|}^i$, PLSA assumes that each document d_i contains a mixture of **topics**, where each topic refers to a semantic class such as "politics" or "sports". Following our discussion of k-means and unsupervised Naïve Bayes, let us define the set of topics as $T = \{1, \ldots, K\}$. The goal of PLSA is to calculate a multinomial document–topic distribution $P(\hbar|d_i)$ as a dense vector in R^K to represent every document d_i, where each element is the probability of a specific topic value $\hbar \in T$.

Given the document–topic correlation, we assume that w_j^i in d_i are generated from a topic–word distribution $P(w|\hbar)$. For each topic $\hbar$, $P(w|\hbar)$ decides the probabilities of vocabulary words under $\hbar$, which reflects the meaning of the topic $\hbar$. For example, if $\hbar$ is highly correlated with words such as "*policy*", "*election*", "*president*", "*tax*", "*economic*" and "*healthcare*", then $\hbar$ is likely a politics-related topic. In contrast, $\hbar$ tends to be a finance-related topic if $P(w|\hbar)$ is dominated by words such as "*stock*", "*IPO*", "*share*", "*trade*", "*market*" and "*investment*".

Given D, topics are hidden variables. They serve as a link in a generative story that helps to better represent a document. In particular, PLSA treats each document as being generated by

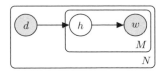

Figure 6.1 PLSA in plate notation.

generating a bag of words, where each word is generated according to a topic. A plate notation for this generative process is shown in Figure 6.1. For a document d_i, the generative story of $w_1^i, w_2^i, \ldots, w_{|d_i|}^i$ can be considered as: for every word location index j, (1) generate a topic h_j according to $P(h|d)$; (2) generate the word w_j according to $P(w|h)$. One thing to note here is that d_i in $P(h|d)$ in this generative process is not directly regarded as a sequence of words. Instead, it is rather symbolic serving as a more abstract representation of each $d_i \in D$, as a start for generating the word sequence, as shown in the plate notation. The purpose is to learn the distribution of topics for each d_i, namely $P(h|d_i)$. As a result, both d_i ($i \in [1, \ldots, N]$) and w_j^i ($j \in [1, \ldots, |d_i|]$) are observed variables, and the topics in T are hidden variables.

According to the above generation process, the complete data likelihood of a word–topic pair $\langle w, h \rangle$ under a certain document d is

$$P(w, h|d) = P(h|d)P(w|h).$$

$P(w, h|d)$ is thus the target joint probability of the PLSA model, with $P(h|d)$ and $P(w|h)$ being its parameter types. We train this model using EM over D. $P(h|d, \Theta^0)$ and $P(w|h, \Theta^0)$ can be randomly initialised. At iteration t, the E-step calculates $P(H|O, \Theta^t)$ for every combination of H and O, namely $P(h|d_i, w, \Theta^t)$ for every document $d_i \in D$ and word $w \in V$, which can be used to define the Q-function. In particular,

$$
\begin{aligned}
P(h|d_i, w, \Theta^t) &= \frac{P(h, w|d_i, \Theta^t)}{P(w|d_i, \Theta^t)} \\
&= \frac{P(h|d_i, \Theta^t)P(w|h, \Theta^t)}{\sum_{h'} P(h', w|d_i, \Theta^t)} \\
&= \frac{P(h|d_i, \Theta^t)P(w|h, \Theta^t)}{\sum_{h'} P(h'|d_i, \Theta^t)P(w|h', \Theta^t)}.
\end{aligned}
\tag{6.23}
$$

Correspondingly, $Q(\Theta, \Theta^t)$ is

$$
\begin{aligned}
Q(\Theta, \Theta^t) &= \sum_{i=1}^{N} \sum_{w_j^i \in d_i} \sum_{h} P(h|d_i, w_j^i, \Theta^t) \log P(h, d_i, w_j^i|\Theta) \\
&= \sum_{i=1}^{N} \sum_{w_j^i \in d_i} \sum_{h} P(h|d_i, w_j^i, \Theta^t) \Big(\log P(h|d_i, \Theta) + \log P(w_j^i|h, \Theta) \Big) \\
&= \sum_{i=1}^{N} \sum_{w \in V} C(w, d_i) \sum_{h} P(h|d_i, w, \Theta^t) \Big(\log P(h|d_i, \Theta) + \log P(w|h, \Theta) \Big),
\end{aligned}
\tag{6.24}
$$

where $C(w, d_i)$ denotes the count of w in document d_i.

The M-step optimises $Q(\Theta, \Theta^t)$. Given that $\sum_\hbar P(\hbar|d_i, \Theta) = 1$ and $\sum_w P(w|\hbar, \Theta) = 1$, we can define a Lagrangian function

$$\Lambda(\Theta, \lambda) = Q(\Theta, \Theta^t) - \sum_i \lambda_{d_i} \left(\sum_\hbar P(\hbar|d_i, \Theta) - 1 \right) - \sum_\hbar \lambda_\hbar \left(\sum_w P(w|\hbar, \Theta) - 1 \right). \quad (6.25)$$

Taking derivatives of $\Lambda(\Theta, \lambda)$ with respect to $P(\hbar|d_i, \Theta)$, we have

$$\frac{\partial \Lambda(\Theta, \lambda)}{\partial P(\hbar|d_i, \Theta)} = \frac{\sum_{w \in V} C(w, d_i) P(\hbar|d_i, w, \Theta^t)}{P(\hbar|d_i, \Theta)} - \lambda_{d_i}. \quad (6.26)$$

Considering $\frac{\partial \Lambda(\Theta, \lambda)}{\partial P(\hbar|d_i, \Theta)} = 0$ and $\sum_\hbar P(\hbar|d_i, \Theta) - 1 = 0$ gives

$$\lambda_{d_i} = \sum_{\hbar \in T} \sum_{w \in V} C(w, d_i) P(\hbar|d_i, w, \Theta^t) = \sum_{w \in V} C(w, d_i)$$

$$P(\hbar|d_i, \Theta) = \frac{\sum_{w \in V} C(w, d_i) P(\hbar|d_i, w, \Theta^t)}{\lambda_{d_i}} = \frac{\sum_{w \in V} C(w, d_i) P(\hbar|d_i, w, \Theta^t)}{\sum_{w \in V} C(w, d_i)}, \quad (6.27)$$

which serves as $P(\hbar|d_i, \Theta^{t+1})$ for the next EM training iteration.

Intuitively, $\sum_{w \in V} C(w, d_i) P(\hbar|d_i, w, \Theta^t)$ is the expected counts of a latent topic $\hbar$ in document d_i, and $\sum_{w \in V} C(w, d_i)$ is the document length. Similarly, we can obtain

$$P(w|\hbar, \Theta) = \frac{\sum_{i=1}^N C(w, d_i) P(\hbar|d_i, w, \Theta^t)}{\sum_{i=1}^N \sum_{w \in V} C(w, d_i) P(\hbar|d_i, w, \Theta^t)}, \quad (6.28)$$

which serves as $P(w|\hbar, \Theta^{t+1})$ for the next EM training iteration.

PLSA Applications. PLSA is useful for NLP applications by providing a semantic vector representation of texts via topic distributions, which can be less sparse compared to word count vectors. For information retrieval, for example, PLSA can be used to better evaluate the similarities between queries and documents compared to token matching. When a new query q comes in, the topic of q can be inferred according to a topic–word distribution $P(w|\hbar, \Theta)$ shared between q and d. Once we know the latent topic distribution $P(\hbar|q, \Theta)$ of the query q, we can calculate the distance between the query q and a document d using cosine similarity between the two topic distributions $P(\hbar|q, \Theta)$ and $P(\hbar|d, \Theta)$, and the documents with higher similarity scores can be returned as retrieval targets. It is intuitively better to measure similarity in the latent semantic space instead of the original word-based feature space since the words appearing in the query and documents might be different, but in the latent space, their topics might be the same. For example, "*bank*" and "*ATM*" are different, but their topics might be all about "money". On the other hand, the topic of the same word in different documents might be different. For example, the topics of "*bank*" in "*the bank of the River Ganges*" and "*the commercial bank manager*" are different.

6.2.4 The Relative Advantages of Generative Models

The models we discussed in this section are generative models, which make generative stories in parameterisation, rather than directly scoring output candidates using rich overlapping features.

They model a joint probability distribution $P(X, Y)$ of the input X and output Y rather than $P(Y|X)$. Compared to discriminative models such as SVMs and log-linear models, the relative advantages of generative models is their interpretability. They can be used to explain the production process of X with the help of hidden variables. As exemplified by Figure 6.1, parameters in a generative model explain why a set of data is observed, by explaining their origin from a set of inter-related factors, such as topics. In addition, generative models can be used to synthesise data, by sampling random variables according to model probabilities, as shown in the example of using language models to generate sentences in Chapter 2.

6.3   Theory behind EM

In this section, we show why EM works by demonstrating that it optimises a maximum likelihood objective. Formally, given a dataset $O = \{o_i\}|_{i=1}^N$, the model that we train calculates $P(O, H|\Theta)$. Since we do not know the full data likelihood, the model can be trained indirectly by maximising only the log-likelihood of the observed data O given Θ:

$$
\begin{aligned}
L(\Theta) &= \log P(O|\Theta) \\
&= \log \sum_H P(O, H|\Theta).
\end{aligned}
\tag{6.29}
$$

In Eq 6.29, $\sum_H$ enumerates all possible values of H. Thus we effectively learn Θ in the $P(O, H|\Theta)$ parameter setting, by marginalising out H to obtain $P(O|\Theta)$.

Unfortunately, optimising log of sums is intractable. Therefore, it is difficult to directly optimise Eq 6.29. EM optimises a lower bound of Eq 6.29 using *Jensen inequality*. In particular, regarding the concave function $\log(\cdot)$, Jensen inequality states that if X is a random variable under distribution $P(X)$, then $\log\left(E_{X\sim P(X)} f(X)\right) \geq E_{X\sim P(X)}\left(\log(f(X))\right)$ for a real-valued function f. Let $P_C(H)$ be a certain probability distribution of H, where $\sum_H P_C(H) = 1$. Using Jensen inequality, we have

$$
\begin{aligned}
L(\Theta) &= \log \sum_H P(O, H|\Theta) \\
&= \log \sum_H P_C(H) \frac{P(O, H|\Theta)}{P_C(H)} \\
&= \log E_{H\sim P_C(H)} \frac{P(O, H|\Theta)}{P_C(H)} \\
&\geq E_{H\sim P_C(H)} \log \frac{P(O, H|\Theta)}{P_C(H)} \quad \text{(Jensen inequality)} \\
&= \sum_H P_C(H) \log \frac{P(O, H|\Theta)}{P_C(H)}.
\end{aligned}
\tag{6.30}
$$

Denote $F(\Theta, P_C) = \sum_H P_C(H) \log \frac{P(O, H|\Theta)}{P_C(H)}$. We have $L(\Theta) \geq F(\Theta, P_C)$ in Eq 6.30, which means that $F(\Theta, P_C)$ is a lower bound of $L(\Theta)$. Below we derive two different methods for optimising $F(\Theta, P_C)$, both of which lead to Algorithm 6.2.

6.3.1 EM and KL-Divergence

$F(\Theta, P_C)$ can be rewritten as

$$
\begin{aligned}
F(\Theta, P_C) &= \sum_H P_C(H) \log \frac{P(O, H|\Theta)}{P_C(H)} \\
&= \sum_H P_C(H) \log \frac{P(O|\Theta)P(H|O, \Theta)}{P_C(H)} \\
&= \sum_H P_C(H) \log P(O|\Theta) + \sum_H P_C(H) \log \frac{P(H|O, \Theta)}{P_C(H)} \\
&= \log P(O|\Theta) - \left(-\sum_H P_C(H) \log \frac{P(H|O, \Theta)}{P_C(H)} \right) \\
&= L(\Theta) - KL\Big(P_C(H), P(H|O, \Theta)\Big).
\end{aligned}
\tag{6.31}
$$

In Chapter 5 we learned that KL-divergence is always non-negative. In addition, $KL(P, Q)$ is zero if and only if $P = Q$. According to Eq 6.31, the difference between $F(\Theta, P_C)$ and $L(\Theta)$ is $KL\Big(P_C(H), P(H|O, \Theta)\Big)$. In order to make the bound as tight as possible, $KL\Big(P_C(H), P(H|O, \Theta)\Big)$ should be as small as possible. Since $KL\Big(P_C(H), P(H|O, \Theta)\Big) \geq 0$, letting $KL\Big(P_C(H), P(H|O, \Theta)\Big) = 0$ gives the best estimate of $P_C(H)$. Therefore, $P_C(H) = P(H|O, \Theta)$, which is the reason behind the choice in Section 6.1.2.

If the model parameters Θ are already known, $P_C(H) = P(H|O, \Theta)$ is the distribution of the hidden variable H given the observed data O according to the model. $P_C(H)$ can thus be regarded as the soft count of each hidden variable value H. In this scenario, finding the distribution $P_C(H)$ corresponds to the E-step in Algorithm 6.2.

We can now take the M-step to optimise $F(\Theta, P_C)$ by using the $P(H|O, \Theta)$ values we have obtained. To distinguish the fixed parameters (i.e., those in the value in $P(H|O, \Theta)$) and variables being adjusted (e.g., Θ in $P(O, H|\Theta)$), we again explicitly include the iteration number as superscripts, where $P_C^{t+1}(H) = P(H|O, \Theta^t)$ is fixed when finding Θ^{t+1}.

Substituting $P(H|O, \Theta^t)$ back into Eq 6.31, we have

$$
F(\Theta, P_C^{t+1}) = \sum_H P(H|O, \Theta^t) \log \frac{P(O, H|\Theta)}{P(H|O, \Theta^t)}.
\tag{6.32}
$$

Θ^{t+1} is given by

$$
\begin{aligned}
\Theta^{t+1} &= \arg\max_\Theta F(\Theta, P_C^{t+1}) \\
&= \arg\max_\Theta \sum_H P(H|O, \Theta^t) \log \frac{P(O, H|\Theta)}{P(H|O, \Theta^t)} \\
&= \arg\max_\Theta \sum_H P(H|O, \Theta^t) \log P(O, H|\Theta) \\
&= \arg\max_\Theta Q(\Theta, \Theta^t),
\end{aligned}
\tag{6.33}
$$

where $Q(\Theta, \Theta^t)$ is the same as Algorithm 6.2 and Eq 6.9.

6.3.2 EM Derivation Using Numerical Optimisation

As mentioned earlier, $F(\Theta, P_C)$ is a lower bound of $L(\Theta)$ to optimise. $F(\Theta, P_C)$ contains two variables, and as a result can be optimised via **coordinate ascent**. Different from gradient ascent, at each iteration, coordinate ascent chooses one coordinate in a multi-variate vector space (or a variable) to optimise, while keeping the others fixed. The gradient direction of coordinate ascent is along the current coordinate. For our problem, first, assuming that Θ^t is already known, we find $P_C^{t+1} = \arg\max_{P_C} F(\Theta^t, P_C)$. Then using P_C^{t+1}, we find $\Theta^{t+1} = \arg\max_\Theta F(\Theta, P_C^{t+1})$. The first step is the E-step and the second step is the M-step.

Expectation step. The E-step finds an optimum distribution $P_C(H)$ that maximises $F(\Theta^t, P_C)$:

$$
\begin{aligned}
P_C^{t+1} &= \arg\max_{P_C} F(\Theta^t, P_C) \\
&= \arg\max_{P_C} \sum_H P_C(H) \log \frac{P(O, H|\Theta^t)}{P_C(H)} \\
&= \arg\max_{P_C} \sum_H \Big(P_C(H) \log P(O, H|\Theta^t) - P_C(H) \log P_C(H) \Big).
\end{aligned}
\tag{6.34}
$$

This is a constrained optimisation problem. We can use Lagrange multipliers to incorporate the constraint $\sum_H P_C(H) = 1$. The corresponding Lagrange function is

$$
F_\lambda(\Theta^t, P_C) = \sum_H \Big(P_C(H) \log P(O, H|\Theta^t) - P_C(H) \log P_C(H) \Big) - \lambda \Big(\sum_H P_C(H) - 1 \Big),
$$

where $\lambda \in \mathbb{R}$. Taking partial derivatives of $F_\lambda(\Theta^t, P_C)$ with respect to $P_C(H)$, we have for all H

$$
\frac{\partial F_\lambda(\Theta^t, P_C)}{\partial P_C(H)} = \log P(O, H|\Theta^t) - \log P_C(H) - 1 - \lambda.
$$

Letting $\frac{\partial F_\lambda(\Theta^t, C)}{\partial P_C(H)} = 0$, we obtain

$$
P_C(H) = \frac{P(O, H|\Theta^t)}{e^{1+\lambda}} \text{ (for all possible } H).
$$

Further, given the fact that $\sum_H P_C(H) = 1$, we have

$$
e^{1+\lambda} = \sum_H P(O, H|\Theta^t) = P(O|\Theta^t)
$$

$$
P_C^{t+1}(H) = \frac{P(O, H|\Theta^t)}{P(O|\Theta^t)}
\tag{6.35}
$$

$$
= P(H|O, \Theta^t).
$$

Maximisation step. The M-step finds the optimal Θ^{t+1} for $F(\Theta, P_C^{t+1})$ using P_C^{t+1}. This step is the same as Section 6.3.1.

After setting the distribution $P_C^{t+1}(H) = P(H|O, \Theta^t)$, according to Eq 6.31, we know that

$$
L(\Theta^t) = F(\Theta^t, P_C^{t+1}).
\tag{6.36}
$$

Therefore, any Θ that can increase $F(\Theta, P_C^{t+1})$ can improve $L(\Theta)$.

Convergence. After one iteration of E-step and M-step, we can show that $L(\Theta^{t+1}) - L(\Theta^t) \geq 0$. In particular, we have

$$L(\Theta^t) = F(\Theta^t, P_C^{t+1}) \text{ (Eq 6.36)}$$
$$\leq F(\Theta^{t+1}, P_C^{t+1}) \; (\Theta^{t+1} = \arg\max_{\Theta} F(\Theta, P_C^{t+1}))$$
$$\leq F(\Theta^{t+1}, P_C^{t+2}) \; (P_C^{t+2} = \arg\max_{P_C} F(\Theta^{t+1}, P_C))$$
$$= L(\Theta^{t+1}) \text{ (Eq 6.36)}.$$

Therefore, $L(\Theta^t)$ is a monotonically increasing function with respect to t, where $L(\Theta^0) \leq L(\Theta^1) \leq L(\Theta^2) \cdots \leq L(\Theta^n)$. It can be proved that EM is guaranteed to converge to local optima. The initial values Θ^0 significantly affect the resulting models. In practice, it is useful to try multiple random starting points, selecting a best model on a set of development data.

Summary

In this chapter we have introduced:

- the concept of hidden variables;
- the expectation maximisation (EM) algorithm;
- EM for unsupervised text classification;
- IBM model 1 for statistical machine translation;
- probabilistic latent semantic allocation.

Chapter Notes

Hartley (1958) first proposed the EM algorithm. Dempster et al. (1977) and Wu (1983) discussed its convergence. Schafer (1997) analysed EM for learning from incomplete data. McLachlan and Krishnan (2007) gave detailed introduction to EM and its applications. Neal and Hinton (1998) and Minka (1998) proposed insightful explanations of EM in terms of lowerbound maximisation.

Brown et al. (1993) proposed IBM Models for machine translation, in which word alignments were obtained via EM algorithms. Hofmann (1999) proposed probabilistic latent semantic analysis (PLSA) for document representation.

Exercises

6.1 In Eq 6.9, which variables are fixed and which can be adjusted?

6.2 EM and k-means clustering

Table 6.2 A collection of documents for clustering.

Document	Document
Apple released iPod .	*Tom bought one iPod .*
Apple released iPhone .	*Tom bought one iPhone .*
Apple released iPad .	*Tom bought one iPad .*

(a) Section 6.1.2 mentions a hidden variable assignment $\mathcal{H}$. Give a specific example of hidden variable assignment in the case of k-means clustering.

(b) Eq 6.8 gives a corpus-level training objective for the M-step of EM. Change the equation to the instance-level supposing that $O = \{\vec{v}_i\}|_{i=1}^{N}$ and $H = \{h_i\}|_{i=1}^{N}$.

(c) Specify a version of k-means clustering using EM.

6.3 Given a collection of six documents as shown in Table 6.2, use the unsupervised Naïve Bayes model to cluster the documents into: (a) two classes (b) three classes. Initialise the model parameter $P(\hbar|\Theta)$ with $\frac{1}{K}$ for every class $\hbar$, where K is the total number of classes. For every class $\hbar$, initialise the model parameter $P(w|\hbar, \Theta)$ with $\frac{1}{|V|}$, where $|V|$ is the vocabulary size. Estimate the model parameters $P(\hbar|\Theta)$ and $P(w|\hbar, \Theta)$ according to Eq 6.14 and Eq 6.15, respectively. Compare the the 2-class clustering results with the 3-class results.

6.4 Consider a semi-supervised setting for the Naïve Bayes model, where a set of labelled documents $D = \{(d_i, c_i)\}|_{i=1}^{N}$ and a set of unlabelled documents $U = \{d_i\}|_{N+1}^{N+M}$ are available. The training objective is to maximise

$$L(\Theta) = \sum_{i=1}^{N} \log P(d_i, c_i|\Theta) + \sum_{j=N+1}^{N+M} \log P(d_j|\Theta). \qquad (6.37)$$

(a) Describe how to train the model parameters Θ using an algorithm similar to Algorithm 6.2.

(b) What is the role of the unlabelled data in this training objective? If we add a hyper-parameter λ to indicate how much attention we should pay to the unlabelled data, the training objective becomes

$$L(\Theta) = \sum_{i=1}^{N} \log P(d_i, c_i|\Theta) + \lambda \sum_{j=N+1}^{N+M} \log P(d_j|\Theta).$$

Compare the second term $\lambda \sum_{j=N+1}^{N+M} \log P(d_j|\Theta)$ with the L2-regulariser introduced in Chapter 3.

6.5 Given a parallel corpus as shown in Table 6.3, (a) execute IBM model 1 for one iteration and show the model parameters; (b) suppose that we already have a location dictionary, indicating that "กรุงเทพ" in Thai and "*Bangkok*" in English should always be connected, which means $P(\text{กรุงเทพ}|Bangkok) = 1$, run IBM model 1 from scratch again and show the model parameters.

Table 6.3 A parallel corpus.

ID	Source	Target
1	เขา(he) อาศัย(live) อยู่ใน(in) กรุงเทพ(Bangkok)	*He is living in Bangkok*
2	เขา(he) ชอบ(like) กรุงเทพ(Bangkok)	*He likes Bangkok*
3	เขา(he) ชอบ(like) อาศัย(live) อยู่ใน(in) กรุงเทพ(Bangkok)	*He likes living in Bangkok*

Table 6.4 A collection of documents for latent topic analysis.

ID	Document	ID	Document
1	*World Cup, Russia, host*	2	*World Cup, boost, Russia, economy*
3	*Russia, bid, World Cup*	4	*Russia, economy, growing, oil*
5	*Russia, economy, recover, continue*	6	*Russia, oil, dependence*

6.6 Prove the last step of Eq 6.20.

(Hint: Calculate $\sum_{a_{|X|}=0}^{|Y|} \prod_{i=1}^{|X|} P(x_i|y_{a_i}) = \left(\prod_{i=1}^{|X|-1} P(x_i|y_{a_i=0}) \right) \sum_{j=0}^{|Y|} P(x_{|X|}|y_j)$ first, and then $\sum_{a_{|X|-1}=0}^{|Y|} \sum_{a_{|X|}=0}^{|Y|} \prod_{i=1}^{|X|} P(x_i|y_{a_i}) = \prod_{i=1}^{|X|-2} P(x_i|y_{a_i=0}) \sum_{j=0}^{|Y|} P(x_{|X|-1}|y_j) \sum_{j=0}^{|Y|} P(x_{|X|}|y_j)$ before deriving $\sum_{a_1=0}^{|Y|} \sum_{a_2=0}^{|Y|} \cdots \sum_{a_{|X|}=0}^{|Y|} \prod_{i=1}^{|X|} P(x_i|y_{a_i}) \prod_{i=1}^{|X|} \sum_{j=0}^{|Y|} P(x_i|y_j)$.

6.7 Prove the last step of Eq 6.22.

6.8 Given a document collection as shown in Table 6.4, suppose that there are two latent topics, one is about "World Cup" and the other is about "Russia's economy". (a) Use PLSA to estimate the document–topic and topic–word probabilities; (b) compare the similarities of document pairs $\langle d_1, d_3 \rangle$, $\langle d_4, d_5 \rangle$ and $\langle d_2, d_5 \rangle$ using the document–topic distribution.

6.9 Self-training in Chapter 4 and hard EM are to some extent similar. They both predict labels for unlabelled instances and make use of automatically generated labels for iterative training. Show the similarities and differences between self-training and hard EM.

Part II

Structures

7 Generative Sequence Labelling

As shown in Chapter 1, structures are prevalent in NLP. Part-of-speech sequences, syntactic trees, entity relations and answers to questions are all structures in nature, in the sense that they contain interdependent components, rather than being a single class label. **Structured prediction** refers to tasks with structured outputs. It is more challenging compared with classification in two main aspects. First, features that represent structures are more challenging to define as compared to those representing class labels. Second, given an input, there can be an exponential or even factorial number of possible output structures, as compared to a constant number of class labels, which imposes challenges on searching for the highest-scored output for a given input in tractable time.

Despite the above differences, structured prediction models such as log-linear models share many underlying principles with their counterparts for classification. In this part of the book, we introduce how generative and discriminative models can be designed for structured prediction. In particular, we start with sequences in this chapter and the next chapter, before moving to more structures in subsequent chapters.

7.1 Sequence Labelling

Consider the problem of part-of-speech tagging (Section 1.2.1), where the input is a sentence $s = W_{1:n} = w_1 w_2 \ldots w_n$ and the output is a sequence of POS tags $T_{1:n} = t_1 t_2 \ldots t_n$, each corresponding to a word. An example is shown in Table 7.1. The task is a typical **sequence labelling** problem, which is to assign a class label to each item in an input sequence. Many NLP tasks can be addressed using sequence labelling, with different sets of output labels. For example, CCG supertagging is another sequence labelling task, where the set of labels is CCG lexical categories rather than POS tags. In addition to tagging, chunking tasks such as word segmentation and named entity recognition, can also be cast into sequence labelling problems (Chapter 9). Here we use POS-tagging as an example to introduce sequence labelling without losing generality.

Local vs structured modelling. A naïve solution for POS tagging is to treat the assignment of each POS tag t_i as a separate classification task, for which the input is the sentence s and the index of the current word i, and the output is t_i. Features can be extracted from a *five-word window* $[w_{i-2}, w_{i-1}, w_i, w_{i+1}, w_{i+2}]$, and classification models such as Naïve Bayes and discriminative classifiers can be used. Such a model is a **local** model.

A potential issue of local models is that they ignore dependencies between different output POS tags, which can be highly useful for making tagging decisions. For example, a determiner is more likely to precede a noun (*NN*) or adjective (*JJ*) compared with a verb (*VB*), and an adverb

Table 7.1 POS tagging examples.

Sentence	POS tag sequence
Jamie went to the shop yesterday .	*NNP VBD TO DT NN AD .*
What would you like to eat ?	*WP MD PRP VB TO VB .*
Tim is talking with Mary .	*NNP VBZ VBG IN NNP .*
I really appreciate it .	*PRP RB VBP PRP .*
John is a famous athlete .	*NNP VBZ DT JJ NN .*

(*AD*) is more likely to follow a verb (*VB*) compared with a possessive pronoun (*PRP$*). In order to capture such correlation, we can treat the output tag sequence $T_{1:n}$ *as a whole*, calculating its conditional probability $P(T_{1:n}|W_{1:n})$, or more generally a score $score(T_{1:n}, W_{1:n})$, so that features can be defined to include internal tag dependencies in $T_{1:n}$ when parameterising the POS-tagging model. Such a model is a **structured model**, in contrast to a local model (Exercise 7.1).

In general, for building generative and discriminative structured models, the same principled techniques for building text classification models can be applied. For example, as discussed in Part I of the book, for building a generative model, we need to apply the Bayes rule, the probability chain rule and make independence assumptions for breaking a sparse joint probability into model parameter terms. For building a discriminative model, we need to define expressive feature vector representations of the input–output pair. However, the number of structured outputs for a given input can be exponentially large or even larger, which makes structured modelling more challenging in several aspects. We will discuss complexity issues and tractable algorithms that deal with such issues for sequence labelling in this chapter and the next chapter. In particular, generative models will be discussed in this chapter, and discriminative models in the next chapter.

7.2   Hidden Markov Models

A generative model for calculating $P(T_{1:n}|W_{1:n})$ can be built using the techniques in Chapter 2 for parameterisation. In particular, the Bayes rule can be first used to factorise $P(T_{1:n}|W_{1:n})$ into two components:

$$P(T_{1:n}|W_{1:n}) = \frac{P(W_{1:n}|T_{1:n})P(T_{1:n})}{P(W_{1:n})}$$

$$\propto P(W_{1:n}|T_{1:n})P(T_{1:n}) \ (P(W_{1:n}) \text{ is constant for all } T_{1:n}).$$

(7.1)

$P(W_{1:n}|T_{1:n}) \cdot P(T_{1:n})$ is the joint word-tag-sequence probability $P(W_{1:n}, T_{1:n})$. Therefore, Eq 7.1 can be understood as a generative model that generates $(W_{1:n}, T_{1:n})$ by first generating the POS label sequence $T_{1:n}$, before generating its corresponding word sequence $W_{1:n}$. This process can intuitively be understood as first generating a sentence structure such as "*NNP* (proper noun) *VBZ* (verb third-person singular) *NN* (noun)", before filling in the details such as "*Jim reads thrillers*". Now that both $W_{1:n}$ and $T_{1:n}$ are highly sparse, $P(W_{1:n}|T_{1:n})$ and $P(T_{1:n})$ can be further parameterised using the probability chain rule and making independence assumptions. In particular,

$$P(W_{1:n}|T_{1:n}) = P(w_1|T_{1:n})P(w_2|w_1 T_{1:n})\ldots P(w_n|w_1 \ldots w_{n-1} T_{1:n}) \text{ (chain rule)}$$
$$\approx P(w_1|t_1)P(w_2|t_2)\ldots P(w_n|t_n) \text{ (independence assumption)}. \tag{7.2}$$

Equation 7.2 makes the assumption that each word is generated according to its corresponding POS alone.

The parameterisation of $P(T_{1:n})$ is analogous to calculating the probability of a sentence $P(s = W_{1:n})$, for which n-gram language models can be used, as shown in Chapter 2. Applying the chain rule to $P(T_{1:n})$, we have

$$P(T_{1:n}) = P(t_1)P(t_2|t_1)P(t_3|t_1 t_2)\ldots P(t_{n-1}|t_1 \ldots t_{n-2})P(t_n|t_1 \ldots t_{n-1}). \tag{7.3}$$

Making first-order Markov assumptions on the tag sequence, we obtain

$$P(T_{1:n}) \approx P(t_1)P(t_2|t_1)\ldots P(t_n|t_{n-1}). \tag{7.4}$$

Instead, making second-order Markov assumptions, we obtain

$$P(T_{1:n}) \approx P(t_1)P(t_2|t_1)P(t_3|t_1 t_2)\ldots P(t_{n-1}|t_{n-3}t_{n-2})P(t_n|t_{n-2}t_{n-1}). \tag{7.5}$$

Following our strategy for n-gram language models, where a special word $\langle s \rangle$ is defined to represent the beginning of a sentence, we can make a special POS-tag $\langle B \rangle$ to denote the beginning POS of a sentence so that Eq 7.4 and Eq 7.5 consist of only one parameter type. In particular, with $\langle B \rangle$, the equations become $P(T_{1:n}) \approx \prod_{i=1}^{n} P(t_i|t_{i-1})$ and $P(T_{1:n}) \approx \prod_{t=1}^{n} P(t_i|t_{i-2}t_{i-1})$, respectively, assuming that $t_{-1} = \langle B \rangle$ and $t_0 = \langle B \rangle$.

Integrating the above into Eq 7.1, we obtain a first-order model

$$P(T_{1:n}|W_{1:n}) \propto P(W_{1:n}, T_{1:n}) \approx \prod_{i=1}^{n} P(t_i|t_{i-1}) \cdot \prod_{i=1}^{n} P(w_i|t_i)$$

and a second-order model

$$P(T_{1:n}|W_{1:n}) \propto P(W_{1:n}, T_{1:n}) \approx \prod_{i=1}^{n} P(t_i|t_{i-2})t_{i-1} \cdot \prod_{i=1}^{n} P(w_i|t_i).$$

The full generative story of our first-order and second-order models are shown in Figure 7.1 (a) and (b), respectively. There are two types of parameters. The first is $P(w_i|t_i)$, which is referred to as the **emission probability** of a word given its POS, and the second is $P(t_i|t_{i-1} \ldots t_{i-k})$, which is referred to as the **transition probability** between consecutive POS tags. Here k is the order of Markov assumptions. The transition probabilities serve as features to model inter-dependence between sub structures in the output sequence, thereby differentiating our generative models from local models that label each word independently.

Given a sentence $W_{1:n}$, its POS sequence $T_{1:n}$ is not explicitly written. As a result, the sequence $T_{1:n}$ can be regarded as a hidden variable. With the hidden sequence being generated using Markov chains, and the observed sequence being generated from their corresponding hidden variables, our generative models are **Hidden Markov Models** (HMM). EM can be used to train HMMs given a set of observed word sequences, which we discuss in Section 7.4. For now let us start with a supervised learning setting.

7.2.1 Training Hidden Markov Models

Given a corpus with manually labelled POS-tag sequences, MLE can be used for supervised learning, estimating the values of both emissions and transition probabilities of an HMM. Take first-order HMM for example, given a set of training examples $D = \{(W_k, T_k)\}|_{k=1}^{N}$, where $W_k = w_1^k w_2^k \ldots w_{n_k}^k$ and $T_k = t_1^k t_2^k \ldots t_{n_k}^k$, the training objective is to maximise the likelihood:

$$P(D) = \prod_{k=1}^{N} P(W_k, T_k) \approx \prod_{k=1}^{N} \left(\prod_{i=1}^{n_k} P(t_i^k | t_{i-1}^k) \cdot \prod_{i=1}^{n_k} P(w_i^k | t_i^k) \right).$$

As we have shown in Chapter 2, the optimisation problem has a closed-form solution. In particular, the emission probabilities can be estimated as

$$P(w|t) = \frac{\#(w|t)}{\sum_{w'} \#(w'|t)}, \tag{7.6}$$

where w is a vocabulary word and $w|t$ denotes a w being labelled with a POS-tag $t \in L$ in D. An English tagset can be found in Table 1.2 in Chapter 1.

Similarly, the transition probabilities can be estimated as

$$P(t_2|t_1) = \frac{\#(t_1 t_2)}{\sum_t \#(t_1 t)}, \tag{7.7}$$

where $t_1 \in L$, $t_2 \in L$ and $t \in L$ denote three POS-tags in D; $t_1 t_2$ and $t_1 t$ denote two consecutive POS-tags, or a POS-tag bigram. L denotes the set of POS-tags.

For second-order HMM, we have

$$P(t_3|t_1 t_2) = \frac{\#(t_1 t_2 t_3)}{\sum_t \#(t_1 t_2 t)},$$

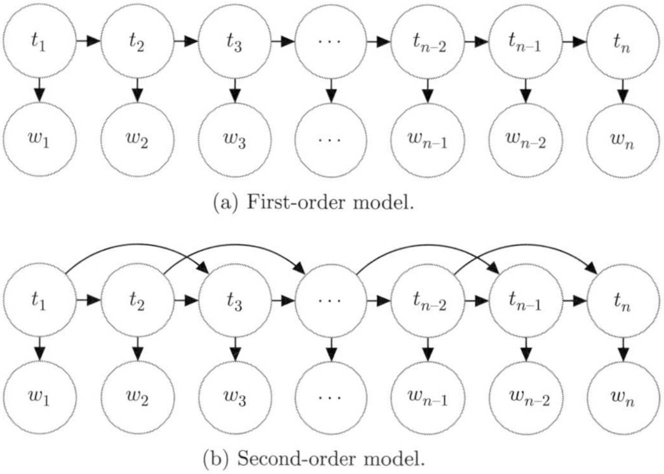

(a) First-order model.

(b) Second-order model.

Figure 7.1 HMM models.

where $t_1 \in L$, $t_2 \in L$, $t_3 \in L$ and $t \in L$ denote POS-tags in D; $t_1 t_2 t_3$ and $t_1 t_2 t$ denote POS-tag trigrams. Smoothing techniques discussed in Chapter 2 can be used to reduce sparsity of both emission and transmission probabilities.

7.2.2 Decoding

Decoding refers to the process of finding the highest-scored output given an input. For classification tasks, this process is trivial, as it is efficient to enumerate all possible class labels, comparing their model scores. For structured prediction, however, decoding is important in the design of a model. Take POS-tagging for example, given an input sentence $W_{1:n}$, the total number of POS-tag sequences is $|L|^n$, where L is the set of all possible POS tags. Exhaustive search has exponential computational complexity, which is intractable. Fortunately, HMMs make Markov assumptions on the POS sequence, enabling the score $P(W_{1:n}, T_{1:n})$ to be calculated incrementally. This makes dynamic programming possible for the decoding task.

First-order HMM decoding. For first-order HMM, the joint probability $P(W_{1:n}, T_{1:n})$ is calculated by $P(W_{1:n}, T_{1:n}) = \prod_{i=1}^{n} P(t_i|t_{i-1})P(w_i|t_i)$. The calculation can be performed recurrently, where

$$P(W_{1:i}, T_{1:i}) = P(W_{1:i-1}, T_{1:i-1}) \cdot \left(P(t_i|t_{i-1})P(w_i|t_i) \right) \tag{7.8}$$

for $i \in [2, \ldots, n]$, and

$$P(W_{1:1}, T_{1:1}) = P(t_1|t_0)P(w_1|t_1).$$

Let us consider how we can make use of this incremental process for dynamic programming. We want to find *optimal sub problem* structures, where a highest-scored tag sequence contains certain highest-scored tag subsequences, so that we can find the highest scored output by incrementally computing highest-scored subsequences, thereby avoiding exponential enumeration. In particular, at each step, $P(W_{1:i}, T_{1:i})$ differs from $P(W_{1:i-1}, T_{1:i-1})$ by a factor of $P(t_i|t_{i-1})P(w_i|t_i)$, which is local to a tag bigram $t_{i-1}t_i$. Now denote the highest-scored sequence among all $T_{1:i}$ as $\hat{T}_{1:i} = \hat{t}_1 \hat{t}_2 \ldots \hat{t}_{i-1} \hat{t}_i$, in which the last two tags are $\hat{t}_{i-1}$ and $\hat{t}_i$. It is easy to show that the sub sequence $\hat{T}_{1:i-1}$ must be the highest scored among all tag sequences $T_{1:i-1}$ that end with $\hat{t}_{i-1}$, denoted as $T_{1:i-1}(t_{i-1} = \hat{t}_{i-1})$. We leave the proof to Exercise 7.2.

Now let us consider all sequences $T_{1:i} = t_1 t_2 \ldots t_i$ with the last tag $t_i = t$, denoted as $T_{1:i}(t_i = t)$. Denote the highest-scored tag sequence among $T_{1:i}(t_i = t)$ as $\hat{T}_{1:i}(t_i = t)$; it serves as the optimal sub problem structure for dynamic programming. Given the recurrent scoring process in Eq 7.8, we can incrementally calculate $\hat{T}_{1:i}(t_i = t)$ for all t with increasing i. In particular, at step i, suppose that we have obtained $\hat{T}_{1:i-1}(t_{i-1} = t')$ for all $t' \in L$, $\hat{T}_{1:i}(t_i = t)$ for all t can be obtained by enumerating the $|L|$ subsequences $\hat{T}_{1:i-1}(t_{i-1} = t')$, each with a different t'. Formally, $\hat{T}_{1:i}(t_i = t)$ can be calculated by

$$\hat{T}_{1:i}(t_i = t) = \underset{\hat{T}_{1:i-1}(t_{i-1}=t'),\ t' \in L}{\arg\max} P\left(W_{1:i-1}, \hat{T}_{1:i-1}(t_{i-1} = t') \right) \left(P(t|t')P(w_i|t) \right),$$

Algorithm 7.1. Viterbi decoding for first-order HMM.

Input: $s = W_{1:n}$, first-order HMM model with $P(t|t')$ for $t, t' \in L$, and $P(w|t)$ for $w \in V, t \in L$;

Variables: tb, bp;

Initialisation:

  $tb[\langle B \rangle][0] \leftarrow 1$;

  $tb[t][i] \leftarrow 0, bp[t][i] \leftarrow$ NULL for $t \in L, i \in [1, \ldots, n]$;

for $t \in L$ **do**

  | $tb[t][1] \leftarrow tb[\langle B \rangle][0] \times P(t|\langle B \rangle) \times P(w_i|t)$

for $i \in [2, \ldots, n]$ **do**

  | **for** $t \in L$ **do**

  | | **for** $t' \in L$ **do**

  | | | **if** $tb[t][i] < tb[t'][i-1] \times P(t|t') \times P(w_i|t)$ **then**

  | | | | $tb[t][i] \leftarrow tb[t'][i-1] \times P(t|t') \times P(w_i|t)$;

  | | | | $bp[t][i] \leftarrow t'$;

$y_n \leftarrow \arg\max_t tb[t][n]$;

for $i \in [n, \ldots, 2]$ **do**

  | $y_{i-1} \leftarrow bp[y_i][i]$;

Output: $y_1, \ldots, y_n$;

Table 7.2 Example first-order HMM, where $L = \{\ell_1, \ell_2\}$ and the sentence is $W_{1:3} = w_1 w_2 w_3$.

$P(\ell_1|\langle B \rangle) = 0.8$	$P(\ell_1|\ell_1) = 0.3$	$P(\ell_1|\ell_2) = 0.6$
$P(\ell_2|\langle B \rangle) = 0.2$	$P(\ell_2|\ell_1) = 0.7$	$P(\ell_2|\ell_2) = 0.4$

(a) transition probabilities.

$P(w_1|\ell_1) = 0.5$	$P(w_2|\ell_1) = 0.4$	$P(w_3|\ell_1) = 0.1$
$P(w_1|\ell_2) = 0.2$	$P(w_2|\ell_2) = 0.2$	$P(w_3|\ell_2) = 0.6$

(b) emission probabilities.

	$i=0$	$i=1$	$i=2$	$i=3$
$\langle B \rangle$	$\hat{T}_{0:1}(\langle B \rangle) = 1$	–	–	–
ℓ_1	–	$\hat{T}_{0:2}(\ell_1)=0.4$	$\hat{T}_{0:3}(\ell_1)=0.048$	$\hat{T}_{0:4}(\ell_1)=0.00336$
ℓ_2	–	$\hat{T}_{0:2}(\ell_2)=0.04$	$\hat{T}_{0:3}(\ell_2)=0.056$	$\hat{T}_{0:4}(\ell_2)=0.02016$

(c) Viterbi chart for the model given $W_{1:3}$.

which takes $O(|L|)$ time. As a result, the calculation of $\hat{T}_{1:i}(t_i = t)$ can be executed with increasing $i \in [1, \ldots, n]$, which takes $O(n|L|)$ time. Finally, after obtaining $\hat{T}_{1:n}(t_n = t)$ for all $t \in L$, the highest scored output $\hat{T}_{1:n}$ can be found by finding $\arg\max_{\hat{T}_{1:n}(t_n=t), t \in L} P(W_{1:n}, \hat{T}_{1:n}(t_n = t))$.

Pseudocode of the decoding algorithm is shown in Algorithm 7.1. Given an input $W_{1:n}$, it builds a table tb with $|L|$ rows and n columns (disregarding $\langle B \rangle$), where $tb[t][i]$ records

$P(W_{1:i}, \hat{T}_{1:i}(t_i = t))$. In addition, a separate table bp is used to store back pointers for each cell $tb([t][i])$, recording $\arg\max_{t' \in L} P\Big(W_{1\cdot i-1}, \hat{T}_{1:i-1}(t_{i-1} - t')\Big)\Big(P(t|t')P(w_i|t)\Big)$; tb and bp are initialised as empty, and filled incrementally, column by column, according to the incremental step above, where $tb[t][i] = P(w_i|t) \max_{t' \in L} tb[t'][i-1]P(t|t')$.

Example. Table 7.2 shows an example first-order HMM model on a sentence of three words, where we assume that there are only two POS-tags ℓ_1 and ℓ_2. The relevant transition and emission probabilities are shown in Tables 7.2(a) and 7.2(b), respectively. Now when we execute Algorithm 7.1, the structure of tb is shown in Table 7.2(c). In particular, the table is built left-to-right, top-down. For example, when the cell $tb[\ell_1][2]$ was constructed, the values of $tb[\ell_1][1] \times P(\ell_1|\ell_1) \times P(w_2|\ell_1) = 0.4 \times 0.3 \times 0.4$ and $tb[\ell_2][1] \times P(\ell_1|\ell_2) \times P(w_2|\ell_1) = 0.04 \times 0.6 \times 0.4$ are compared, with the larger one (i.e., 0.048) being chosen. The table bp is correspondingly filled ($bp[\ell_1][2] = \ell_1$), which we do not show in Table 7.2.

Working with log probabilities. Considering numerical stability, $tb([t][i])$ can record $\log P(W_{1:i}, \hat{T}_{1:i}(t_i = t))$, in which case

$$tb[t][i] = \log P(w_i|t) + \max_{t' \in L} \Big(tb[t'][i-1] + \log P(t|t')\Big).$$

Viterbi decoding for second-order HMM. The same thinking can be used to build a dynamic programming decoder for second-order HMMs. In this case the incremental step is

$$P(W_{1:i}, T_{1:i}) = P(W_{1:i-1}, T_{1:i-1})\Big(P(t_i|t_{i-2}t_{i-1})P(w_i|t_i)\Big).$$

Correspondingly, the highest scored sub sequence $\hat{T}_{1:i}$ must contain the highest scored subsequence $\hat{T}_{1:i-1}(t_{i-2}t_{i-1} = \hat{t}_{i-2}\hat{t}_{i-1})$ among all subsequences $T_{1:i-1}$ that end with POS-tag bigram $\hat{t}_{i-2}\hat{t}_{i-1}$. As a result, a dynamic program can be built to find $\hat{T}_{1:i}(t_{i-1}t_i = t't)$ for all $i \in [1, \ldots, n]$, $t \in L$ and $t' \in L$ incrementally, where

$$\hat{T}_{1:i}(t_{i-1}t_i = t't) = \max_{t''} P(W_{1:i-1}, \hat{T}_{1:i-1}(t_{i-2}t_{i-1} = t''t'))\Big(P(t|t''t')P(w_i|t)\Big).$$

Pseudocode of this dynamic programming decoder is shown in Algorithm 7.2, which has a similar structure to Algorithm 7.1. The main difference is the structure of tb and bp, which are now three-dimensional, with $tb[t'][t][i]$ recording $P(W_{1:i}, \hat{T}_{1:i}(t_{i-1}t_i = t't))$, and $bp[t'][t][i]$ recording $\arg\max_{t''} P\Big(W_{1:i-1}, \hat{T}_{1:i-1}(t_{i-2}t_{i-1} = t''t')\Big)\Big(P(t|t''t')P(w_i|t)\Big)$. Note that $\hat{T}_{1:i}(t_{i-1}t_i = t't)$ and $\hat{T}_{1:i-1}(t_{i-2}t_{i-1} = t''t')$ share $t_{i-1} = t'$, and therefore the POS tag t_{i-1} needs to be enumerated only once for both $\hat{T}_{1:i}(t_{i-1}t_i = t't)$ and $\hat{T}_{1:i-1}(t_{i-2}t_{i-1} = t''t')$.

The asymptotic complexity of Algorithm 7.2 is $O(n|L|^3)$, which is larger compared with $O(n|L|^2)$ of the first-order case in Algorithm 7.1, due to the additional loop over $t_{i-2} = t''$ for every word w_i. The main reason is the use of $P(t|t''t')$ as a feature, which models a larger context and thus changes the complexity of the incremental step. In general, the runtime complexity of a dynamic programming decoder is determined by the range of features. The more **non-local** the features are, the more complex the incremental step in dynamic programming is, and thus the larger the asymptotic complexity is. For local models, in contrast, decoding is trivial since the probability of a sequence is not explicitly modelled, with each word being labelled separately.

Algorithm 7.2. Viterbi decoding for second-order HMM.

Input: $s = W_{1:n}$, second-order HMM model $P(t|t't'')$ for $t, t', t'' \in L$, and $P(w|t)$ where $w \in V, t \in L$;

Variables: tb, bp;

Initialisation:

    $tb[\langle B \rangle][\langle B \rangle][0] \leftarrow 1$;

    $tb[t'][t][i] \leftarrow 0, bp[t'][t][i] \leftarrow$ NULL **for** $t, t' \in L, i \in [1, \ldots, n]$;

for $t \in L$ **do**

    $|$ $tb[\langle B \rangle][t][1] = tb[\langle B \rangle][\langle B \rangle][0] \times P(t|\langle B \rangle \langle B \rangle) \times P(w_i|t)$

for $t \in L$ **do**

    for $t' \in L$ **do**

        $|$ $tb[t'][t][2] = tb[\langle B \rangle][t'][1] \times P(t|\langle B \rangle t') \times P(w_i|t)$

for $i \in [3, \ldots, n]$ **do**

    for $t \in L$ **do**

        for $t' \in L$ **do**

            for $t'' \in L$ **do**

                if $tb[t'][t][i] < tb[t''][t'][i-1] \times P(t|t''t') \times P(w_i|t)$ **then**

                    $tb[t'][t][i] \leftarrow tb[t''][t'][i-1] \times P(t|t''t') \times P(w_i|t)$;

                    $bp[t'][t][i] \leftarrow t''$;

            $tb[t'][t][i] \leftarrow tb[t'][t][i] \times P(w_i|t)$;

$y_{n-1}y_n \leftarrow \arg\max_{t't} tb[t'][t][n]$;

for $i \in [n, \ldots, 3]$ **do**

    $|$ $y_{i-2} \leftarrow bp[y_{i-1}][y_i][i]$;

Output: $y_1 y_2 \ldots y_n$;

Both Algorithm 7.1 and Algorithm 7.2 are named the **Viterbi algorithm**, after the American electrical engineer Andrew Viterbi.

7.3   Finding Marginal Probabilities

Structured models score an output sequence as a unit, considering interdependencies between sub structures. However, there is sometimes a need to isolate out a sub structure in order to study its own characteristics. For the POS-tagging task, a typical problem is to find the probability of a certain label assignment $P(t_i = t|W_{1:n})$. Because our structured model gives the probabilities of full tag sequences $P(W_{1:n}, T_{1:n})$, $P(t_i|W_{1:n})$ can be calculated as a marginal probability, by summing up the probabilities of all $t_{i'}, i' \neq i$:

$$
\begin{aligned}
P(t_i = t|W_{1:n}) &= \sum_{t_1 \in L} \sum_{t_2 \in L} \cdots \sum_{t_{i-1} \in L} \sum_{t_{i+1} \in L} \cdots \sum_{t_n \in L} P\big(T_{1:n}(t_i = t)|W_{1:n}\big) \\
&\propto \sum_{t_1 \in L} \sum_{t_2 \in L} \cdots \sum_{t_{i-1} \in L} \sum_{t_{i+1} \in L} \cdots \sum_{t_n \in L} P\big(W_{1:n}, T_{1:n}(t_i = t)\big).
\end{aligned}
\tag{7.9}
$$

A naïve solution to calculating the value of Eq 7.9 consists of $|L|^{n-1}$ summation terms, and therefore is intractable. For HMM models, however, thanks to the locality of features, dynamic programming is feasible. The idea is similar to the Viterbi algorithm, which is to find sub problems incrementally, leveraging locality of features.

Since the location of t_i can be in the middle of a sentence, we first use Bayes rule to break $P(t_i = t|W_{1:n})$ into two components, one consisting of $W_{1:i}$ and the other consisting of $W_{i+1:n}$, so that each component can be calculated incrementally using dynamic programming. In particular,

$$
\begin{aligned}
P(t_i = t|W_{1:n}) &= \frac{P(t_i = t, W_{1:n})}{P(W_{1:n})} \qquad \text{(Bayes rule conditioned on } W_{1:i}) \\
&= \frac{P(t_i = t, W_{1:i}, W_{i+1:n})}{P(W_{1:n})} \\
&= \frac{P(W_{1:i}, t_i = t)P(W_{i+1:n}|t_i = t, W_{1:i})}{P(W_{1:n})} \\
&= \frac{P(W_{1:i}, t_i = t)P(W_{i+1:n}|t_i = t)}{P(W_{1:n})} \\
&\qquad (W_{i+1:n} \text{ is conditionally independent of } W_{1:i} \text{ given } t_i) \\
&\propto P(W_{1:i}, t_i = t)P(W_{i+1:n}|t_i = t) \\
&\qquad\qquad (P(W_{1:n}) \text{ is constant for all } t).
\end{aligned}
\tag{7.10}
$$

Equation 7.10 suggests a three-step method to calculate $P(t_i = t|W_{1:n})$:

- (1) Calculate

$$
\alpha(t_i = t) = P(W_{1:i}, t_i = t) = \sum_{t_1 \in L}\sum_{t_2 \in L}\cdots\sum_{t_{i-1} \in L} P\big(W_{1:i}, T_{1:i}(t_i = t)\big).
$$

- (2) Calculate

$$
\beta(t_i = t) = P(W_{i+1:n}|t_i = t) = \sum_{t_{i+1} \in L}\sum_{t_{i+2} \in L}\cdots\sum_{t_n \in L} P(W_{i+1:n}, T_{i+1:n}|t_i = t).
$$

- (3) Normalise $\alpha(t_i = t)\beta(t_i = t)$ so that $\sum_{t \in L} P(t_i = t|W_{1:n}) = 1$.

Sections 7.3.1, 7.3.2 and 7.3.3 discuss the steps (1) (2) (3) for first-order HMMs, respectively.

7.3.1 The Forward Algorithm

Step (1) above involves an exponential number of summations. For HMM, the **forward algorithm** can be used to find the values of α in linear time. Let us start with the first-order case, where

$$
P(W_{1:i}, T_{1:i}) = \prod_{j=1}^{i} P(t_j|t_{j-1})P(w_j|t_j),
$$

assuming that $t_0 = \langle B \rangle$.

Algorithm 7.3. Forward algorithm for first-order HMM.

Inputs: $s = W_{1:n}$, first-order HMM model with $P(t|t')$ for $t, t' \in L$, and $P(w|t)$ where $w \in V, t \in L$;

Variables: α;

Initialisation: $\alpha[\langle B \rangle][0] \leftarrow 1$, $\alpha[t][i] \leftarrow 0$ for $i \in [1, \ldots, n], t \in L$;

for $t \in L$ **do**

$\quad$ | $\quad \alpha[t][1] \leftarrow \alpha[\langle B \rangle][0] \times P(t|\langle B \rangle) \times P(w_1|t)$

for $i \in [2, \ldots, n]$ **do**

$\quad$ | **for** $t \in L$ **do**

$\quad\quad$ | **for** $t' \in L$ **do**

$\quad\quad\quad$ | $\quad \alpha[t][i] \leftarrow \alpha[t][i] + \alpha[t'][i-1] \times P(t|t') \times P(w_i|t)$;

Output: α;

Since $P(W_{1:i-1}, T_{1:i-1}) = \prod_{j=1}^{i-1} (P(t_j|t_{j-1})P(w_j|t_j))$, we have

$$P(W_{1:i}, T_{1:i}) = P(W_{1:i-1}, T_{1:i-1})\Big(P(t_i|t_{i-1})P(w_i|t_i)\Big). \tag{7.11}$$

According to Eq 7.11, if we know that

$$\alpha(t_{i-1} = t') = \sum_{t_1 \in L}\sum_{t_2 \in L}\cdots\sum_{t_{i-2} \in L} P(W_{1:i-1}, T_{1:i-1}(t_{i-1} = t')),$$

and then we have

$$\sum_{t_1 \in L}\sum_{t_2 \in L}\cdots\sum_{t_{i-2} \in L} P\big(W_{1:i}, T_{1:i}(t_{i-1}t_i = t't)\big)$$

$$= \sum_{t_1 \in L}\sum_{t_2 \in L}\cdots\sum_{t_{i-2} \in L} \Big(P\big(W_{1:i}, T_{1:i-1}(t_{i-1} = t')\big)\big(P(t|t')P(w_i|t)\big)\Big)$$

$$= \alpha(t_{i-1} = t')P(t|t')P(w_i|t),$$

namely $\alpha(t_i = t) = \sum_{t' \in L} \alpha(t_{i-1} = t')P(t|t')P(w_i|t)$.

We have thus arrived at an incremental step to calculate $\alpha(t_i = t)$ from $\alpha(t_{i-1} = t')$, which can serve as a basis for finding all values of α incrementally with increasing values of i. Algorithm 7.3 shows pseudocode of this algorithm, which builds a $|L| \times n$ table α, with $\alpha[t][i]$ storing $\alpha(t_i = t) = \sum_{t_1 \in L}\sum_{t_2 \in L}\cdots\sum_{t_{i-1} \in L} P\big(W_{1:i}, T_{1:i}(t_i = t)\big)$.

7.3.2 The Backward Algorithm

Similar to step (1) for calculating Eq 7.10, step (2) in finding the marginal probability $P(t_i = t|W_{1:n})$ also involves an exponential number of summations. Similar to step (1), a dynamic program can be derived for HMM leveraging locality of features. This time we need to move backwards, from the end of the sentence, for summation over $W_{i+1:n}$. As a result, the algorithm is named the **backward algorithm** in contrast to the forward algorithm.

Algorithm 7.4. Backward algorithm for first-order HMM.

Inputs: $s - W_{1:n}$, first-order HMM model with $P(t|t')$ for $t, t' \in L$, and $P(w|t)$ where $w \in V, t \in L$;

Variables: β;

Initialisation: $\beta[t][n] \leftarrow 1$ **for** $t \in L$, $\beta[t][i] \leftarrow 0$ **for** $i \in [1, \ldots, n-1], t \in L$;

for $i \in [n-1, \ldots, 1]$ **do**

   for $t' \in L$ **do**

      for $t \in L$ **do**

         $\beta[t'][i] \leftarrow \beta[t'][i] + \beta[t][i+1] \times P(t|t') \times P(w_{i+1}|t)$;

Output: β;

Again beginning with the first-order case, in order to find out the correlation between $\beta(t_i = t')$ and $\beta(t_{i+1} = t)$, we examine the correlation between $P(W_{i+1:n}, T_{i+1:n}|t_i)$ and $P(W_{i+2:n}, T_{i+2:n}|t_{i+1})$, where

$$P(W_{i+1:n}, T_{i+1:n}|t_i) = P(w_{i+1}, t_{i+1}, W_{i+2:n}, T_{i+2:n}|t_i)$$
$$= P(t_{i+1}|t_i)P(w_{i+1}|t_it_{i+1})P(W_{i+2:n}, T_{i+2:n}|w_{i+1}, t_it_{i+1}) \text{ (probability chain rule)}$$
$$= P(t_{i+1}|t_i)P(w_{i+1}|t_{i+1})P(W_{i+2:n}, T_{i+2:n}|w_{i+1}, t_it_{i+1})$$
$$(w_{i+1} \text{ conditionally independent of } t_i)$$
$$= P(t_{i+1}|t_i)P(w_{i+1}|t_{i+1})P(W_{i+2:n}, T_{i+2:n}|t_{i+1})$$
$$(T_{i+2:n} \text{ conditionally independent of } t_i \text{ given } t_{i+1}).$$

Consequently, we have

$$\beta(t_i = t') = \sum_{t_{i+1} \in L} \sum_{t_{i+2} \in L} \cdots \sum_{t_n \in L} P(W_{i+1:n}, T_{i+1:n}|t_i = t')$$
$$= \sum_{t_{i+1} \in L} \sum_{t_{i+2} \in L} \cdots \sum_{t_n \in L} P(t_{i+1}|t_i = t')P(w_{i+1}|t_{i+1})P(W_{i+2:n}, T_{i+2:n}|t_{i+1})$$
$$= \sum_{t_{i+1} \in L} P(t_{i+1}|t_i = t')P(w_{i+1}|t_{i+1}) \sum_{t_{i+2} \in L} \cdots \sum_{t_n \in L} P(W_{i+2:n}, T_{i+2:n}|t_{i+1})$$
$$= \sum_{t \in L} P(t|t')P(w_{i+1}|t)\beta(t_{i+1} = t).$$

When $i = n$, we have $\beta(t_{n-1} = t') = \sum_t P(w_n, t_n = t|t_{n-1} = t') = \sum_t P(t|t')P(w_n|t) \times 1$. Hence we set $\beta(t_n = t) = 1$.

A dynamic program can be used to build a table β of $|L|$ rows and n columns, where $\beta[t][i]$ records $\beta(t_i = t)$. The index i decreases from n to 1. Pseudocode is shown in Algorithm 7.4.

7.3.3 The Forward–Backward Algorithm

Equation 7.10 indicates that $P(t_i = t|W_{1:n}) \propto \alpha(t_i = t)\beta(t_i = t)$. Given the fact that $\sum_t P(t_i = t|W_{1:n}) = 1$, we can normalise $\alpha(t_i = t)\beta(t_i = t)$, such that $P(t_i = t|W_{1:n}) = \frac{\alpha(t_i=t)\beta(t_i=t)}{\sum_{t' \in L} \alpha(t_i=t')\beta(t_i=t')}$.

Algorithm 7.5. Forward–backward algorithm for first-order HMM.

Inputs: $s = W_{1:n}$, first-order HMM model with $P(t|t')$ for $t, t' \in L$, and $P(w|t)$ where $w \in V, t \in L$;
Variables: tb, α, β;
$\alpha \leftarrow \text{FORWARD}(W_{1:n}, model)$;
$\beta \leftarrow \text{BACKWARD}(W_{1:n}, model)$;
for $i \in [1, \ldots, n]$ **do**
    $total \leftarrow 0$;
    for $t \in L$ **do**
        $total \leftarrow total + \alpha[t][i] \times \beta[t][i]$
    for $t \in L$ **do**
        $tb[t][i] \leftarrow \frac{\alpha[t][i] \times \beta[t][i]}{total}$;
Output: tb;

Algorithm 7.5 shows pseudocode of the **forward–backward algorithm**. It fills a table tb of $|L|$ rows and n columns, where $tb[t][i]$ records $P(t_i = t|W_{1:n})$.

7.3.4 Forward–Backward Algorithm for Second-Order HMM

Similar to the case of Viterbi decoding, a second-order HMM leads to slower forward and backward algorithms due to fewer independence assumptions. Below we discuss these two algorithms, respectively.

Forward algorithm. In the second order case, the incremental step changes due to the use of a more non-local feature $P(t|t''t')$. Hence,

$$P(W_{1:i}, T_{1:i}) = P(W_{1:i-1}, T_{1:i-1})\Big(P(t_i|t_{i-2}t_{i-1})P(w_i|t_i)\Big).$$

Denoting $\alpha(t_{i-1}t_i = t't) = \sum_{t_1 \in L} \sum_{t_2 \in L} \cdots \sum_{t_{i-2} \in L} P\big(W_{1:i}, T_{1:i}(t_{i-1}t_i = t't)\big)$, we have

$$\sum_{t_1 \in L} \sum_{t_2 \in L} \cdots \sum_{t_{i-3} \in L} P\big(W_{1:i}, T_{1:i}(t_{i-2}t_{i-1}t_i = t''t't)\big)$$

$$= \sum_{t_1 \in L} \sum_{t_2 \in L} \cdots \sum_{t_{i-3} \in L} P\big(W_{1:i-1}, T_{1:i-1}(t_{i-2}t_{i-1} = t''t')\big)P(t|t''t')P(w_i|t)$$

$$= \alpha(t_{i-2}t_{i-1} = t''t')P(t|t''t')P(w_i|t).$$

Similarly, $\alpha(t_{i-1}t_i = t't)$ can be calculated incrementally:

$$\alpha(t_{i-1}t_i = t't) = \sum_{t''} \alpha(t_{i-2}t_{i-1} = t''t')P(t|t''t')P(w_i|t).$$

Algorithm 7.6 shows pseudocode of the forward algorithm for second-order HMM, which builds a $|L| \times |L| \times n$ table α, where $\alpha[t'][t][i]$ stores $\alpha(t_{i-1}t_i = t't) = \sum_{t_1 \in L} \sum_{t_2 \in L} \cdots \sum_{t_{i-2} \in L} P\big(W_{1:i}, T_{1:i}(t_{i-1}t_i = t't)\big)$.

Backward algorithm. In the second-order case, a connection can be built between $\beta(t_{i-1}t_i = t''t')$ and $\beta(t_it_{i+1} = t't)$, similar to the correlation between $\beta(t_i = t')$ and $\beta(t_{i+1} = t)$ for first-order HMM. We have

$$P(W_{i+1:n}, T_{i+1:n}|t_{i-1}t_i) = P(w_{i+1}, t_{i+1}, W_{i+2:n}, T_{i+2:n}|t_{i-1}t_i)$$

$$= P(t_{i+1}|t_{i-1}t_i)P(w_{i+1}|t_{i-1}t_it_{i+1})P(W_{i+2:n}, T_{i+2:n}|w_{i+1}, t_{i+1}, t_{i-1}, t_i)$$

$$\text{(probability chain rule)}$$

$$= P(t_{i+1}|t_{i-1}t_i)P(w_{i+1}|t_{i+1})P(W_{i+2:n}, T_{i+2:n}|w_{i+1}, t_{i+1}, t_{i-1}, t_i)$$

$$(w_{i+1} \text{ conditionally independent of } t_{i-1}, t_i)$$

$$= P(t_{i+1}|t_{i-1}, t_i)P(w_{i+1}|t_{i+1})P(W_{i+2:n}, T_{i+2:n}|t_i, t_{i+1})$$

$$(T_{i+2:n} \text{ conditionally independent of } t_{i-1} \text{ given } t_i, t_{i+1}).$$

Correspondingly, we have

$$\beta(t_{i-1}t_i = t''t')$$

$$= \sum_{t_{i+1}\in L}\sum_{t_{i+2}\in L}\cdots\sum_{t_n\in L} P(W_{i+1:n}, T_{i+1:n}|t_{i-1}t_i = t''t')$$

$$= \sum_{t_{i+1}\in L}\sum_{t_{i+2}\in L}\cdots\sum_{t_n\in L} P(t_{i+1}|t_{i-1}t_i = t''t')P(w_{i+1}|t_{i+1})P(W_{i+2:n}, T_{i+2:n}|t_i = t', t_{i+1})$$

$$= \sum_{t_{i+1}\in L} P(t_{i+1}|t_{i-1}t_i = t''t')P(w_{i+1}|t_{i+1})\sum_{t_{i+2}\in L}\cdots\sum_{t_n\in L} P(W_{i+2:n}, T_{i+2:n}|t_i = t', t_{i+1})$$

$$= \sum_{t\in L} P(t|t''t')P(w_{i+1}|t)\beta(t_it_{i+1} = t't).$$

Similar to the first-order case, the boundary value $\beta[t'][t][n] = 1$. Algorithm 7.7 shows a dynamic program to calculate $\beta[t'][t][i]$. The algorithm maintains a table β of size $|L| \times |L| \times n$, where the element $\beta[t''][t'][i]$ stores $\sum_{t_{i+1}\in L}\sum_{t_{i+2}\in L}\cdots\sum_{t_n\in L} P(W_{i+1:n}, T_{i+1:n}|t_{i-1}t_i = t''t')$.

7.4   EM for Unsupervised HMM Training

When gold-standard training examples $(W_{1:n}, T_{1:n})$ are unavailable, we can use the EM algorithm discussed in Chapter 6 to do unsupervised estimation of model parameters for HMM. As discussed earlier in Chapter 6, EM is a general algorithm for training probabilistic models with hidden variables. EM for unsupervised HMM training is also called the **Baum–Welch algorithm**. It is reminiscent of EM for unsupervised Naïve Bayes in Chapter 6.

Suppose that we are given a raw text corpus $D = \{W_i\}|_{i=1}^N$. In this case, the hidden variable is the POS sequence, the observation is the word sequence for each sentence. The goal is to find a model parameter Θ which maximises $\log P(D|\Theta)$. Now for each sentence, $\log P(W_{1:n}|\Theta)$ can be computed as

$$\log P(W_{1:n}|\Theta) = \log \sum_{\mathcal{T}_{1:n}} P(W_{1:n}, \mathcal{T}_{1:n}|\Theta), \qquad (7.12)$$

Algorithm 7.6. Forward algorithm for second-order HMM.

Inputs: $s = W_{1:n}$, second-order HMM model with $P(t|t''t')$ for $t, t', t'' \in L$, and $P(w|t)$ where $w \in V, t \in L$;

Variables: α;

Initialisation: $\alpha[\langle B \rangle][\langle B \rangle][0] \leftarrow 1$, $\alpha[t'][t][i] \leftarrow 0$ for $i \in [1, \ldots, n], t', t \in L$;

for $t \in L$ **do**
$\quad | \quad \alpha[\langle B \rangle][t][1] \leftarrow \alpha[\langle B \rangle][\langle B \rangle][0] \times P(t|\langle B \rangle\langle B \rangle) \times P(w_1|t)$

for $t \in L$ **do**
$\quad$ **for** $t' \in L$ **do**
$\quad\quad | \quad \alpha[t'][t][2] \leftarrow \alpha[\langle B \rangle][t'][1] \times P(t|\langle B \rangle t') \times P(w_2|t)$

for $i \in [3, \ldots, n]$ **do**
$\quad$ **for** $t \in L$ **do**
$\quad\quad$ **for** $t' \in L$ **do**
$\quad\quad\quad$ **for** $t'' \in L$ **do**
$\quad\quad\quad\quad | \quad \alpha[t'][t][i] \leftarrow \alpha[t'][t][i] + \alpha[t''][t'][i-1] \times P(t|t''t') \times P(w_i|t)$;

Output: α;

Algorithm 7.7. Backward algorithm for second-order HMM.

Inputs: $s = W_{1:n}$, second-order HMM model with $P(t|t''t')$ for $t, t', t'' \in L$, and $P(w|t)$ where $w \in V, t \in L$;

Variables: β;

Initialisation: $\beta[t'][t][n] = 1$ for $t', t \in L$, $\beta[t'][t][i] = 0$ for $i \in [1, \ldots, n-1], t', t \in L$;

for $i \in [n-1, \ldots, 2]$ **do**
$\quad$ **for** $t'' \in L$ **do**
$\quad\quad$ **for** $t' \in L$ **do**
$\quad\quad\quad$ **for** $t \in L$ **do**
$\quad\quad\quad\quad | \quad \beta[t''][t'][i] \leftarrow \beta[t''][t'][i] + \beta[t'][t][i+1] \times P(t|t''t') \times P(w_{i+1}|t)$;

for $t' \in L$ **do**
$\quad$ **for** $t \in L$ **do**
$\quad\quad | \quad \beta[\langle B \rangle][t'][1] \leftarrow \beta[\langle B \rangle][t'][1] + \beta[t'][t][2] \times P(t|\langle B \rangle t') \times P(w_2|t)$;

for $t \in L$ **do**
$\quad | \quad \beta[\langle B \rangle][\langle B \rangle][0] \leftarrow \beta[\langle B \rangle][\langle B \rangle][0] + \beta[\langle B \rangle][t][1] \times P(t|\langle B \rangle\langle B \rangle) \times P(w_1|t)$;

Output: β;

---

where $\mathcal{T}_{1:n} = t_1 t_2 \ldots t_n$ denotes an arbitrary POS sequence, in contrast to $T_{1:n}$ in the supervised case, which represents the gold-standard POS sequence for $W_{1:n}$.

As discussed in Chapter 6, EM is an iterative algorithm, using alternation of expectation (E) steps and maximisation (M) steps to approximately optimise Eq 7.12. In particular, the expectation step defines a Q-function (i.e., the expectation function) for representing the data likelihood according to the current model, and the maximisation step updates the current model by maximising the Q function. For HMMs, the E-step calculates the expected counts of transition events and emission events using the current model, and the M-step takes the expected counts as inputs to update the model according to Eqs 7.6 and 7.7.

7.4.1 EM for First-Order HMM

For first-order HMM, the transition events are tag bigrams $t't$ and the emission events are word–tag pairs $(t \rightarrow w)$. The model parameters are $\Theta = \{P(w|t), P(t|t')\}$, where $w \in V$ and $t \in L$. Following Chapter 6, let us specify the EM algorithm by defining the E-step and M-step, respectively.

Expectation. Formally, the expectation function $Q(\Theta, \Theta')$ is

$$Q(\Theta, \Theta') = \sum_{\mathcal{T}_{1:n}} P(\mathcal{T}_{1:n}|W_{1:n}, \Theta') \log P(W_{1:n}, \mathcal{T}_{1:n}|\Theta), \qquad (7.13)$$

where Θ' is the current estimation and Θ is the next round estimation to optimise in iterative EM.

We discussed the motivation of a Q-function in general in Chapter 6. Here let us briefly discuss it for HMM specifically. Intuitively, if a hidden tag sequence $\mathcal{T}_{1:n}$ for $W_{1:n}$ were known, the complete log-likelihood of this tag sequence is $P(W_{1:n}, \mathcal{T}_{1:n}|\Theta)$, parameterised by an HMM model. In this case, we could use MLE to maximise this log-likelihood function, where a new estimation of Θ can be derived by counting relative frequencies. However, for our unsupervised learning case, the specific path $\mathcal{T}_{1:n}$ is not available in advance, and we solve this problem by using a model with existing Θ' values to estimate $P(\mathcal{T}_{1:n}|W_{1:n}, \Theta')$, considering all the possible hidden path assignments by calculating an expectation function (Eq 7.13). The distribution $P(\mathcal{T}_{1:n}|W_{1:n}, \Theta')$ can be regarded as a probability weight score of the tag sequence $\mathcal{T}_{1:n}$. A tag sequence with a larger $P(\mathcal{T}_{1:n}|W_{1:n}, \Theta')$ contributes more log-likelihood $\log P(W_{1:n}, \mathcal{T}_{1:n}|\Theta)$ in the overall optimisation objective.

In particular, for first-order HMM, the expectation function is

$$Q(\Theta, \Theta') = \sum_{\mathcal{T}_{1:n}} P(\mathcal{T}_{1:n}|W_{1:n}, \Theta') \log P(W_{1:n}, \mathcal{T}_{1:n}|\Theta)$$

$$= \sum_{\mathcal{T}_{1:n}} P(\mathcal{T}_{1:n}|W_{1:n}, \Theta') \log \left(\prod_{i=1}^{n} P(t_i|t_{i-1})P(w_i|t_i) \right)$$

$$= \sum_{\mathcal{T}_{1:n}} P(\mathcal{T}_{1:n}|W_{1:n}, \Theta') \sum_{i=1}^{n} \left(\log P(w_i|t_i) + \log P(t_i|t_{i-1}) \right) \qquad (7.14)$$

$$= \sum_{i=1}^{n} \left(\sum_{w} \sum_{t} \log P(w|t) \sum_{\mathcal{T}_{1:n}} P(\mathcal{T}_{1:n}|W_{1:n}, \Theta') \delta(t_i, t) \delta(w_i, w) \right)$$

$$+ \sum_{i=1}^{n} \left(\sum_{t'} \sum_{t} \log P(t|t') \sum_{\mathcal{T}_{1:n}} P(\mathcal{T}_{1:n}|W_{1:n}, \Theta') \delta(t_{i-1}, t') \delta(t_i, t) \right),$$

where $w \in V$ denotes each word from the vocabulary V, $t \in L$ denotes each tag from the tagset L, and δ tests whether two values are the same.

$Q(\Theta, \Theta')$ looks complex, involving sums over whole tag sequences. Thanks to feature locality, the forward–backward algorithm can be used to simplify the calculation. In particular, let $\gamma_i(t) = \sum_{\mathcal{T}_{1:n}} P(\mathcal{T}_{1:n}|W_{1:n}, \Theta')\delta(t_i, t)$ and $\xi_i(t', t) = \sum_{\mathcal{T}_{1:n}} P(\mathcal{T}_{1:n}|W_{1:n}, \Theta')\delta(t_{i-1}, t')\delta(t_i, t)$, both of which can be computed efficiently. With these, Eq 7.14 can be rewritten as

$$Q(\Theta, \Theta') = \sum_{i=1}^{n} \left(\sum_{w \in V} \sum_{t \in L} \log P(w|t)\delta(w_i, w)\gamma_i(t) \right)$$
$$+ \sum_{i=1}^{n} \left(\sum_{t' \in L} \sum_{t \in L} \log P(t|t')\xi_i(t', t) \right). \tag{7.15}$$

Now let us look at the definitions of $\gamma_i(t)$ and $\xi_i(t', t)$. First,

$$\gamma_i(t) = \sum_{\mathcal{T}_{1:n}} P(\mathcal{T}_{1:n}|W_{1:n}, \Theta')\delta(t_i, t) = P(t_i = t|W_{1:n}, \Theta'), \tag{7.16}$$

which is exactly the marginal probability of $t_i = t$ defined by Eq 7.9. According to Eq 7.10, we have

$$\gamma_i(t) = \frac{\alpha(t_i = t)\beta(t_i = t)}{\sum_{t' \in L} \alpha(t_i = t')\beta(t_i = t')}, \tag{7.17}$$

where α and β are the forward variables (Section 7.3.1) and backward variables (Section 7.3.2), respectively.

Similarly, we have

$$\xi_i(t', t) = \sum_{\mathcal{T}_{1:n}} P(\mathcal{T}_{1:n}|W_{1:n}, \Theta')\delta(t_{i-1}, t')\delta(t_i, t)$$
$$= P(t_{i-1} = t', t_i = t|W_{1:n}, \Theta'), \tag{7.18}$$

which is the marginal probability of the tag bigram $t_{i-1}t_i = t't$. Using similar techniques as Eq 7.10, $\xi_i(t', t)$ can be rewritten as

$$\begin{aligned}
\xi_i(t', t) &= P(t_{i-1} = t', t_i = t|W_{1:n}, \Theta') \\
&\propto P(t_{i-1} = t', t_i = t, W_{1:n}|\Theta') \\
&= P(W_{i+1:n}, w_i, t_i = t, W_{1:i-1}, t_{i-1} = t'|\Theta') \\
&= P(W_{1:i-1}, t_{i-1} = t'|\Theta')P(t_i = t|W_{1:i-1}, t_{i-1} = t', \Theta') \\
&\quad P(w_i|t_i = t, W_{1:i-1}, t_{i-1} = t', \Theta')P(W_{i+1:n}|w_i, t_i = t, W_{1:i-1}, t_{i-1} = t', \Theta') \\
&\qquad\qquad\qquad \text{(chain rule)} \\
&= P(W_{1:i-1}, t_{i-1} = t'|\Theta')P(t_i = t|t_{i-1} = t', \Theta') \\
&\quad P(w_i|t_i = t, \Theta')P(W_{i+1:n}|t_i = t, \Theta') \\
&\qquad\qquad\qquad \text{(independence assumptions)} \\
&= \alpha(t_{i-1} = t')P(t|t', \Theta')P(w_i|t, \Theta')\beta(t_i = t).
\end{aligned} \tag{7.19}$$

$\xi_i(t', t)$ contains four factors, namely the forward probability $\alpha(t_{i-1} = t')$, the transition probability $P(t|t', \Theta')$, the emission probability $P(w_i|t, \Theta')$ and the backward probability $\beta(t_i = t)$. Since $\sum_{t'} \sum_t \xi_i(t', t) = 1$, we have

$$\xi_i(t', t) = \frac{\alpha(t_{i-1} = t')P(t|t', \Theta')P(w_i|t, \Theta')\beta(t_i = t)}{\sum_{u'} \sum_u \alpha(t_{i-1} = u')P(u|u', \Theta')P(w_i|u, \Theta')\beta(t_i = u)}, \qquad (7.20)$$

where $u' \in L$ and $u \in L$ denote the arbitrary tags.

Noticing that

$$\begin{aligned}
&\sum_{u'} \sum_u \alpha(t_{i-1} = u')P(u|u', \Theta')P(w_i|u, \Theta')\beta(t_i = u) \\
&= \sum_u \left(\sum_{u'} \alpha(t_{i-1} = u')P(u|u', \Theta')P(w_i|u, \Theta') \right)\beta(t_i - u) \\
&= \sum_u \alpha(t_i = u)\beta(t_i = u),
\end{aligned} \qquad (7.21)$$

where the last step holds according to our derivation of incremental calculation of $\alpha(t_i)$ at the end of Section 7.3.1. Equation 7.20 can be rewritten as

$$\xi_i(t', t) = \frac{\alpha(t_{i-1} = t')P(t|t', \Theta')P(w_i|t, \Theta')\beta(t_i = t)}{\sum_{u \in L} \alpha(t_i = u)\beta(t_i = u)}. \qquad (7.22)$$

Now that we can obtain tables of γ_i and ξ_i ($i \in [1, \ldots, n]$), the expectation function $Q(\Theta, \Theta')$ containing $\gamma_i(t)$ and $\xi_i(t', t)$ can be written as

$$\begin{aligned}
Q(\Theta, \Theta') &= \sum_{i=1}^n \sum_w \sum_t \log P(w|t)\delta(w_i, w)\gamma_i(t) \\
&+ \sum_{i=1}^n \sum_{t'} \sum_t \log P(t|t')\xi_i(t', t) \\
&= \sum_w \sum_t \log P(w|t) \sum_{i=1}^n \delta(w_i, w)\gamma_i(t) \\
&+ \sum_{t'} \sum_t \log P(t|t') \sum_{i=1}^n \xi_i(t', t).
\end{aligned} \qquad (7.23)$$

Here $P(w|t)$ and $P(t|t')$ are the emission and transition parameters we need to estimate. $\sum_{i=1}^n \delta(w_i, w)\gamma_i(t)$ can be regarded as the expected number of emssions from t to w over the sentence $W_{1:n}$. $\sum_{i=1}^n \xi_i(t', t)$ can be viewed as the expected number of transitions from t' to t over the sentence $W_{1:n}$.

Maximisation. Now considering $Q(\Theta, \Theta')$ and the normalisation constraints $\sum_w P(w|t) = 1$ and $\sum_t P(t|t') = 1$, we use Lagrange multipliers to find the optimal model parameters $\Theta =$

$\{P(w|t), P(t|t')\}$ for each $w \in V$, $t \in L$ and $t' \in L$. Define the Lagrange function:

$$
\begin{aligned}
\pi(\Theta, \Lambda) = &\sum_{w} \sum_{t} \log P(w|t) \sum_{i=1}^{n} \delta(w_i, w)\gamma_i(t) \\
&+ \sum_{t'} \sum_{t} \log P(t|t') \sum_{i=1}^{n} \xi_i(t', t) \\
&+ \sum_{t} \lambda_t^1 \left(1 - \sum_{w} P(w|t)\right) + \sum_{t'} \lambda_{t'}^2 \left(1 - \sum_{t} P(t|t')\right).
\end{aligned}
\tag{7.24}
$$

The partial derivative of $\pi(\Theta, \Lambda)$ with respect to $P(w|t)$ is

$$
\frac{\partial \pi(\Theta, \Lambda)}{\partial P(w|t)} = \frac{\sum_{i=1}^{n} \delta(w_i, w)\gamma_i(t)}{P(w|t)} - \lambda_t^1.
$$

We want to solve $\frac{\partial \pi(\Theta,\Lambda)}{\partial P(w|t)} = 0$ to find $P(w|t)$. In particular, $P(w|t)\lambda_t^1 = \sum_{i=1}^{n} \delta(w_i, w)\gamma_i(t)$. Given that $\sum_{w \in V} P(w|t) = 1$, we have

$$
\begin{aligned}
\lambda_t^1 &= \sum_{w} P(w|t)\lambda_t^1 = \sum_{w} \sum_{i=1}^{n} \delta(w_i, w)\gamma_i(t) \\
&= \sum_{i=1}^{n} \sum_{w} \delta(w_i, w)\gamma_i(t) = \sum_{i=1}^{n} \gamma_i(t) \sum_{w} \delta(w_i, w) = \sum_{i=1}^{n} \gamma_i(t)
\end{aligned}
$$

and

$$
P(w|t) = \frac{\sum_{i=1}^{n} \delta(w_i, w)\gamma_i(t)}{\lambda_t^1} = \frac{\sum_{i=1}^{n} \delta(w_i, w)\gamma_i(t)}{\sum_{i=1}^{n} \gamma_i(t)}.
\tag{7.25}
$$

Intuitively, the numerator denotes the expected counts of the event that the tag is t and the emission word of t is w, and the denominator represents the expected counts of tag t. Equation 7.25 can thus be understood as estimation by counting relative *expected* frequencies, which is a characteristic of EM as compared with MLE.

Similarly, we can obtain the estimated value for $P(t|t')$

$$
P(t|t') = \frac{\sum_{i=1}^{n} \xi_i(t', t)}{\sum_{u} \sum_{i=1}^{n} \xi_i(t', u)} = \frac{\sum_{i=1}^{n} \xi_i(t', t)}{\sum_{i=1}^{n} \sum_{u} \xi_i(t', u)} = \frac{\sum_{i=1}^{n} \xi_i(t', t)}{\sum_{i=1}^{n} \gamma_i(t')}.
\tag{7.26}
$$

The numerator $\sum_{i=1}^{n} \xi_i(t', t)$ is the expected transmission counts from tag t' to tag t, and the denominator is the expected counts of the tag t.

Now considering a corpus of N observation sequences $D = \{W_k\}|_{k=1}^{N}$, where $W_k = w_1^k w_2^k \ldots w_{n_k}^k$, we have overall

$$
\begin{aligned}
Q(\Theta, \Theta') = &\sum_{w} \sum_{t} \log P(w|t) \sum_{k=1}^{N} \sum_{i=1}^{n_k} \delta(w_i^k, w)\gamma_i^k(t) \\
&+ \sum_{t'} \sum_{t} \log P(t|t') \sum_{k=1}^{N} \sum_{i=1}^{n_k} \xi_i^k(t', t),
\end{aligned}
\tag{7.27}
$$

Algorithm 7.8. The EM algorithm for first-order HMM.

Inputs: $D = \{W_k\}|_{k=1}^{N}$;

Initialisations: randomly initialise a first-order HMM model with $P(t|t')$ for $t, t' \in L$, and $P(w|t)$ where $w \in V$, $t \in L$;

Variables: $\alpha, \beta, \gamma, \xi$;

while not CONVERGE($P(t|t'), P(w|t)$) **do**

    for $k \in [1, \ldots, N]$ **do**

        $\alpha \leftarrow$ FORWARD($W_k, model$);

        $\beta \leftarrow$ BACKWARD($W_k, model$);

        for $i \in [1, \ldots, |W_k|]$ **do**

            $total \leftarrow 0$;

            for $t \in L$ **do**

                $total \leftarrow total + \alpha[t][i] \times \beta[t][i]$;

            for $t \in L$ **do**

                $\gamma[k][t][i] \leftarrow \frac{\alpha[t][i] \times \beta[t][i]}{total}$;

                for $t' \in L$ **do**

                    $\xi[k][t][t'][i] \leftarrow \frac{\alpha[t'][i-1]P(t|t')P(w_i|t)\beta[t][i]}{total}$;

    for $t \in L$ **do**

        $total_t \leftarrow 0$;

        for $w \in V$ **do**

            $count[w] \leftarrow 0$;

        for $k \in [1, \ldots, N]$ **do**

            for $i \in [1, \ldots, |W_k|]$ **do**

                $total_t \leftarrow total_t + \gamma[k][t][i]$;

                $count[w_i] \leftarrow count[w_i] + \gamma[k][t][i]$;

        for $w \in V$ **do**

            $P(w|t) \leftarrow \frac{count[w]}{total_t}$;

    for $t' \in L$ **do**

        $total_{t'} \leftarrow 0$;

        for $t \in L$ **do**

            $count[t] \leftarrow 0$;

        for $k \in [1, \ldots, N]$ **do**

            for $i \in [1, \ldots, |W_k|]$ **do**

                $total_{t'} \leftarrow total_{t'} + \gamma[k][t'][i]$;

                for $t \in L$ **do**

                    $count[t] \leftarrow count[t] + \xi[k][t][t'][i]$;

        for $t \in L$ **do**

            $P(t|t') \leftarrow \frac{count[t]}{total_{t'}}$;

Output: the first-order HMM model $\{P(w|t), P(t|t')\}$ **for** $w \in V$ and $t, t' \in L$;

where $\delta(w_i^k, w)$ tests whether the ith word in W_k is w. $\gamma_i^k(t')$ and $\xi_i^k(t', t)$ denote the $\gamma_i(t')$ and $\xi_i(t', t)$ values of the kth instance, respectively. The values of $\gamma_i^k(t')$ and $\xi_i^k(t', t)$ are defined by using Eq 7.16 and Eq 7.18 on W_k, respectively.

With N observations, we need to correspondingly accumulate the counts from every observation sequence for the denominator and the numerator:

$$
\begin{aligned}
P(w|t) &= \frac{\sum_{k=1}^{N} \sum_{i=1}^{n_k} \delta(w_i^k, w) \gamma_i^k(t)}{\sum_{k=1}^{N} \sum_{i=1}^{n_k} \gamma_i^k(t)} \\
P(t|t') &= \frac{\sum_{k=1}^{N} \sum_{i=1}^{n_k} \xi_i^k(t', t)}{\sum_{k=1}^{N} \sum_{i=1}^{n_k} \gamma_i^k(t')}.
\end{aligned}
\tag{7.28}
$$

Algorithm 7.8 shows pseudocode for the EM algorithm for first-order HMM where Forward and Backward are defined in Algorithm 7.3 and 7.4, respectively. It first randomly initialises the target HMM model parameters. Then the algorithm calculates the expected counts $\gamma_i(t)$ and $\xi_i(t', t)$. Finally, it normalises the expectation counts and generates the distributions $P(w|t)$ and $P(t|t')$. The above process repeats until a converging criterion is satisfied. The converging condition can depend on the likelihood of the learning objective or the KL divergence of the distribution of $P(w|t)$ and $P(t|t')$ between two adjacent iterations. As for EM in general, Algorithm 7.8 can converge to a local optimum, which depends on the initialisation. Using multiple runs helps to find a more robust model.

We leave EM for second-order HMM to Exercise 7.9.

Summary

In this chapter we have introduced:

- Hidden Markov models (HMM);
- Viterbi decoding for HMMs;
- Forward–backward algorithms for HMMs;
- EM algorithms for HMMs.

Chapter Notes

Rabiner and Juang (1986), Jelinek (1997) and Eddy (1998) presented theory of HMMs in detail. The mathematics behind the HMMs was developed by Baum and Petrie (1966). The Viterbi algorithm (Viterbi, 1967) saw its early use in speech recognition (Vintsyuk, 1968). Baum (1972) adapted the forward and backward recursions described by Stratonovich (1965) to compute the marginal probabilities in HMM. Bilmes et al. (1998) described the application of EM to parameter estimation for HMMs.

One of the early applications of HMMs was speech recognition (Baker, 1975; Jelinek et al., 1975). Church (1989), Kupiec (1992) and Weischedel et al. (1993) applied the HMMs to POS tagging. Thede and Harper (1999) used a second-order HMM for POS tagging. Brants (2000) discussed the implementation of a state-of-the-art HMM POS tagger.

Exercises

7.1 Consider a local model for solving the POS tagging problem, using features from $[w_{i-2}, w_{i-1}, w_i, w_{i+1}, w_{i+2}]$ to predict $t_i \in L$ given an input sentence $s = W_{1:n}$, where L is the set of all possible POS labels.

(a) Build a Naïve Bayes classifier by treating $[w_{i-2}, w_{i-1}, w_i, w_{i+1}, w_{i+2}]$ as a document, and t_i as its class label. What are the parameter types and parameter instances? Draw a figure to tell the generative story of the model.

(b) Since the size of the input is fixed, can you relax the *i.i.d.* assumption between words, modelling w_{i-2}, w_{i-1}, w_i, w_{i+1} and w_{i+2} differently, sensitive to the position? What are the parameter types and parameter instances now? Compare the size of the model with the model in question (a) with regard to the number of parameter instances.

(c) Consider a discriminative linear model using the same parameter types as (b). What are the feature templates? What is the form of a feature vector? Can you use additional features?

7.2 Consider POS-tagging for $W_{1:n} = w_1 w_2 \ldots w_n$. Denote the highest-scored sequence among all $T_{1:i}$ as $\hat{T}_{1:i}$ ($i \in [1, \ldots, n]$), in which the last two tags are $\hat{t}_{i-1}$ and $\hat{t}_i$. Prove that the sub sequence $\hat{T}_{1:i-1}$ must be the highest scored among all tag sequences $T_{1:i-1}$ that ends with $\hat{t}_{i-1}$. (Hint: a proof can be made by contradiction.)

7.3 For the decoding algorithm of the second-order HMM, prove that the sub sequence $\hat{T}_{1:i-1}$ of the highest-scored tag sequence $\hat{T}_{1:i}$ must be the highest scored among all tag sequences $T_{1:i-1}$ that ends with the bigram $\hat{t}_{i-2}\hat{t}_{i-1}$.

7.4 Following the example in Section 7.2.2 for first-order HMM decoding, specify the Viterbi table structure for second-order HMM decoding using the model and input sentence in Table 7.4.

7.5 The Viterbi algorithm and the forward algorithm for first-order HMM are highly similar in structure, with the Viterbi algorithm using the *max* function for building the table, and the forward algorithm using the *sum* function for building the table. Can you think of a generic algorithm that can be instantiated into the Viterbi algorithm and the forward algorithm, respectively, with different operator and other necessary parameters?

7.6 Compute $P(t_2|W_{1:3})$ given Table 7.2 and $P(t_2|W_{1:6})$ given Table 7.4, respectively. Show the table structures of the forward and backward algorithms for both Table 7.2 and Table 7.4.

7.7 Compare a first-order HMM and a second-order HMM for POS tagging. A 0th-order HMM makes independence assumptions between output POS tags. Define a 0th-order HMM. Compare

Table 7.3 Example sentences.

Sentence	Frequency
John loves the cat	10
John loves Mary	10
Mary loves the cat	20

Table 7.4 Example second-order HMM, where $L = \{\ell_1, \ell_2, \ell_3\}$ and the sentence is $W_{1:6} = w_1 w_2 w_3 w_3 w_2 w_1$

$P(\ell_1|\langle B\rangle\langle B\rangle) = 0.6$	$P(\ell_1|\langle B\rangle\ell_1) = 0.1$	$P(\ell_1|\langle B\rangle\ell_2) = 0.3$	$P(\ell_1|\langle B\rangle\ell_3) = 0.25$
$P(\ell_2|\langle B\rangle\langle B\rangle) = 0.2$	$P(\ell_2|\langle B\rangle\ell_1) = 0.5$	$P(\ell_2|\langle B\rangle\ell_2) = 0.2$	$P(\ell_2|\langle B\rangle\ell_3) = 0.5$
$P(\ell_3|\langle B\rangle\langle B\rangle) = 0.2$	$P(\ell_3|\langle B\rangle\ell_1) = 0.4$	$P(\ell_3|\langle B\rangle\ell_2) = 0.5$	$P(\ell_3|\langle B\rangle\ell_3) = 0.25$
$P(\ell_1|\ell_1\,\ell_1) = 0.2$	$P(\ell_1|\ell_1\,\ell_2) = 0.2$	$P(\ell_1|\ell_1\,\ell_3) = 0.8$	$P(\ell_1|\ell_2\,\ell_1) = 0.3$
$P(\ell_2|\ell_1\,\ell_1) = 0.6$	$P(\ell_2|\ell_1\,\ell_2) = 0.1$	$P(\ell_2|\ell_1\,\ell_3) = 0.1$	$P(\ell_2|\ell_2\,\ell_1) = 0.3$
$P(\ell_3|\ell_1\,\ell_1) = 0.2$	$P(\ell_3|\ell_1\,\ell_2) = 0.7$	$P(\ell_3|\ell_1\,\ell_3) = 0.1$	$P(\ell_3|\ell_2\,\ell_1) = 0.4$
$P(\ell_1|\ell_2\,\ell_2) = 0.05$	$P(\ell_1|\ell_2\,\ell_3) = 0.5$	$P(\ell_1|\ell_3\,\ell_1) = 0.2$	$P(\ell_1|\ell_3\,\ell_2) = 0.4$
$P(\ell_2|\ell_2\,\ell_2) = 0.9$	$P(\ell_2|\ell_2\,\ell_3) = 0.3$	$P(\ell_2|\ell_3\,\ell_1) = 0.2$	$P(\ell_2|\ell_3\,\ell_2) = 0.25$
$P(\ell_3|\ell_2\,\ell_2) = 0.05$	$P(\ell_3|\ell_2\,\ell_3) = 0.2$	$P(\ell_3|\ell_3\,\ell_1) = 0.6$	$P(\ell_3|\ell_3\,\ell_2) = 0.35$
$P(\ell_1|\ell_3\,\ell_3) = 0.4$	$P(\ell_2|\ell_3\,\ell_3) = 0.1$	$P(\ell_3|\ell_3\,\ell_3) = 0.5$	

(a) transition probabilities.

$P(w_1|\ell_3) = 0.8$	$P(w_2|\ell_3) = 0.1$	$P(w_3|\ell_3) = 0.1$	
$P(w_1|\ell_1) = 0.5$	$P(w_2|\ell_1) = 0.4$		$P(w_3|\ell_1) = 0.1$
$P(w_1|\ell_2) = 0.2$	$P(w_2|\ell_2) = 0.2$		$P(w_3|\ell_2) = 0.6$

(b) emission probabilities.

it with first- and second-order HMMs, and with the models in Exercise 7.1 (a) and (b). What are the differences in model structures? What can be the impact on the performances?

7.8 Given the three sentences and their frequency counts in Table 7.3, and supposing there are three possible hidden states $\{N, V, D\}$, complete the following exercises.

(a) Estimate the parameters for a first-order HMM using EM.

(b) Suppose that the hidden tag sequences are partially observable, how would you change the standard EM algorithms for parameter estimation? More specifically, when the word "*the*" is always associated with the tag "D", what are the estimation results? Compare the estimation results with that of (a).

(c) As introduced before, we use $P(t_1|\langle B\rangle)$ to describe the first tag being t_1. This makes the estimation of the tag starting probability the same as that of the transition probabilities. Suppose now we do not use $\langle B\rangle$ in the beginning of the tagging sequence any more, and there is a parameter $\pi(t)$, which describes the probability of the first tag beginning t. Derive the estimation equations of EM algorithms for π.

7.9 Write out pseudocode of EM for a second-order HMM.

8   Discriminative Sequence Labelling

Both Hidden Markov Models and Naïve Bayes models are generative models, the structures of which can be drawn as probability graphs in Figure 7.1 and Figure 2.5(b), respectively. Both models estimate joint probabilities of inputs and outputs, which include all nodes in a probability graph. Compared with Naïve Bayes, which has only one output node in a graph, Hidden Markov Models have multiple output nodes constituting a structure. The contrast demonstrates the difference between classification and structured prediction models.

For classification tasks, discriminative models such as SVMs and log-linear models have the advantage of enabling rich features, as compared with generative models. A natural question that arises is how to build a discriminative model for sequence labelling tasks. In addition to feature constraints, one more potential limitation of HMMs is that the probabilities of each label in a sequence are trained separately and locally according to each tag's own context. However, for a given sentence, the output needs to be a highest-scored *sequence* of labels, which is a *global* search task. The inconsistency between local training and global testing can cause accuracy loss. One solution is to set a global training objective, directly modelling the probability of whole sequences of labels. Conditional random fields (CRFs) are a log-linear model to this end, which we introduce in this chapter. In the same spirit, we show how perceptrons and SVMs can be adapted for structured prediction tasks.

8.1   Locally Trained Models for Discriminative Sequence Labelling

Again our task is sequence labelling: given a word sequence $W_{1:n}$, the goal is to find a most probable tag sequence $\hat{T}_{1:n}$. Different from the previous chapter, however, this time we try to build a discriminative model which calculates $P(T_{1:n}|W_{1:n})$ directly, instead of $P(W_{1:n}, T_{1:n})$. According to the probability chain rule, the sequence-level probability can be factorised into

$$P(T_{1:n}|W_{1:n}) = \prod_{i=1}^{n} P(t_i|T_{1:i-1}, W_{1:n}).$$

Similar to the case of HMMs, Markov assumptions can be made over tag sequences. In particular, under the kth order Markov assumption, the value of a label t_i in a label sequence $T_{1:n}$ is conditionally dependent on only $T_{i-k:i-1}$, making $P(t_i|T_{1:i-1}, W_{1:n}) = P(t_i|T_{i-k:i-1}, W_{1:n})$.

Model. Let us consider a factorised discriminative sequence labelling model. In particular, given an input sentence $W_{1:n}$ and a corresponding label sequence $T_{1:n}$, the tag probability

$P(t_i|T_{i-k:i-1}, W_{1:n})$ can be estimated using a classification model, where the input includes a sequence of history tags $T_{i-k:i-1} = t_{i-k}, \ldots, t_{i-1}$ and the word sequence $W_{1:n} = w_1, w_2, \ldots, w_n$, and the output is the output label t_i on word w_i. The discriminative classification models discussed in Chapters 3 and 4 can be applied directly, by mapping an input–output pair $\left((T_{i-k:i-1}, W_{1:n}), t_i\right)$ into a feature vector $\vec{\phi}(t_i, T_{i-k:i-1}, W_{1:n})$ before calculating the probability $P(t_i|T_{i-k:i-1}, W_{1:n})$. For example, the log-linear model can be used, which scores each possible $t_i = t$ using

$$P(t_i = t|T_{i-k:i-1}, W_{1:n}) = \frac{\exp\left(\vec{\theta} \cdot \vec{\phi}(t_i = t, T_{i-k:i-1}, W_{1:n})\right)}{\sum_{t' \in L} \exp\left(\vec{\theta} \cdot \vec{\phi}(t_i = t', T_{i-k:i-1}, W_{1:n})\right)}, \qquad (8.1)$$

where L denotes the set of all possible labels and $\vec{\theta}$ denotes the parameter vector of the model. The discriminative model is also referred to as **maximum entropy Markov model** (MEMM), due to the association between maximum entropy models and log-linear models discussed in Chapter 5.

Training. $\vec{\theta}$ can be trained using manually labelled $(W_{1:n}, T_{1:n})$ pairs, broken down into a set of individual $\left((T_{i-k:i-1}, W_{1:n}), t_i\right)$ pairs as gold-standard examples. The standard SGD algorithm introduced in Chapter 4 can be used for optimisation of a log-likelihood training objective.

Features. Without making independence assumptions, $\vec{\phi}(t_i, T_{i-k:i-1}, W_{1:n})$ can be defined with rich overlapping features. An example set of feature templates for POS-tagging under the first-order Markov assumption (i.e., $k = 1$) is shown in Table 8.1, where $t_{i-1}t_i$ denotes tag bigrams, t_i denotes the current tag, $w_i t_i$ denotes word/tag pairs, and $w_{i-1}t_i/w_{i+1}t_i$ denote contextual word features. The fifth feature template denotes morphological features, where prefixes and suffixes can include all 1–4 character sub strings. The sixth feature template represents additional word shape features. The hyphen features indicate whether a word contain hyphens or not. Hyphenated compound words usually can be adjective words such as "*well-known*","*five-year-old*" and "*state-of-the-art*", or nouns such as "*sister-in-law*" and "*editor-in-chief*", or number words such as "*fifty-seven*". The case features detect whether the word is in upper case or not. For example, if a word is all upper case, then it is likely a proper noun, such as "*U.S.*" or "*NASA*". If a word is capitalised, it might be a person name, such as "*John*" and "*Mary*".

Given the sentence "*The man went to the park.*", the corresponding feature vector for labelling the word "*park*" with "*NN*" is $\{t_{i-1}t_i = $ DT|NN, $t_i = $ NN, $w_i t_i = $ park|NN, $w_{i-1}t_i = $ the|NN, $w_{i+1}t_i = $.|NN, $w_{i-2}t_i = $ to|NN, $w_{i+2}t_i = $ </S>|NN, $\textsc{Prefix}_1(w_i)t_i = $ "*p*"|NN, $\textsc{Prefix}_2(w_i)t_i = $ "*pa*"|NN, $\textsc{Prefix}_3(w_i)|t_i = $ "*par*"|NN, $\textsc{Prefix}_4(w_i)|t_i = $ "*park*"|NN, $\textsc{Suffix}_1(w_i)t_i = $ "*k*"|NN, $\textsc{Suffix}_2(w_i)t_i = $ "*rk*"|NN, $\textsc{Suffix}_3(w_i)t_i = $ "*ark*"|NN, $\textsc{Suffix}_4(w_i)t_i = $ "*park*"|NN, $\textsc{Hyphen}(w_i)t_i = $ 0|NN, $\textsc{Case}(w_i)t_i = $ 0|NN$\}$.

Table 8.1 Example set of feature templates for first-order POS tagging models.

ID	Feature Template
1	$t_{i-1}t_i$
2	t_i
3	$w_i t_i$
4	$w_{i-1}t_i, w_{i+1}t_i, w_{i-2}t_i, w_{i+2}t_i$
5	$\text{PREFIX}(w_i) \cdot t_i, \text{SUFFIX}(w_i) \cdot t_i$
6	$\text{HYPHEN}(w_i) \cdot t_i, \text{CASE}(w_i) \cdot t_i$

Decoding. For testing, given a model $\vec{\theta}$ and an input sequence $W_{1:n}$, the output is

$$
\begin{aligned}
\hat{T}_{1:n} &= \arg\max_{T_{1:n}} P(T_{1:n}|W_{1:n}) \\
&= \arg\max_{T_{1:n}} \prod_{i=1}^{n} P(t_i|T_{i-k:i-1}, W_{1:n}) \\
&= \arg\max_{T_{1:n}} \prod_{i=1}^{n} \frac{\exp\left(\vec{\theta} \cdot \vec{\phi}(t_i, T_{i-k:i-1}, W_{1:n})\right)}{\sum_{t \in L} \exp\left(\vec{\theta} \cdot \vec{\phi}(t, T_{i-k:i-1}, W_{1:n})\right)} \\
&= \arg\max_{T_{1:n}} \prod_{i=1}^{n} \exp\left(\vec{\theta} \cdot \vec{\phi}(t_i, T_{i-k:i-1}, W_{1:n})\right) \\
&= \arg\max_{T_{1:n}} \exp\left(\sum_{i=1}^{n} \vec{\theta} \cdot \vec{\phi}(t_i, T_{i-k:i-1}, W_{1:n})\right) \\
&= \arg\max_{T_{1:n}} \sum_{i=1}^{n} \vec{\theta} \cdot \vec{\phi}(t_i, T_{i-k:i-1}, W_{1:n}).
\end{aligned}
\tag{8.2}
$$

The goal of decoding is to find $\hat{T}_{1:n}$ given $W_{1:n}$. Disregarding the differences in feature definitions, this decoding goal is the same as the output goals of the discriminative linear classifiers in Chapters 3 and 4, which is to find the highest scored output using a linear model, except that now we have an exponential number of candidate output sequences, rather than a fixed number of candidate output labels.

Similar to the case of HMMs, the number of candidate outputs $T_{1:n}$ is exponential to the size of the input n, equaling $|L|^n$, where L is the set of all labels. As a result, brute-force enumeration of all possible label sequences is computationally intractable for finding $\hat{T}_{1:n}$. Fortunately, Markov assumptions on the label sequence $T_{1:n}$ make it feasible to use dynamic programming to this end. For simplicity, let us still take the first-order Markov case, where features are confined to a tag bigram $t_{i-1}t_i = t't$. This enables $\hat{T}_{1:n}$ to be found incrementally, with $\hat{T}_{1:i}(t_i = t)$ being $\arg\max_{t'} score(\hat{T}_{1:i-1}(t_{i-1} = t')) + \vec{\theta} \cdot \vec{\phi}(t_i = t, t_{i-1} = t', W_{1:n})$. As a result, Eq 8.2 can be efficiently solved by using the Viterbi algorithm, which is shown in Algorithm 8.1. The idea is similar to the Viterbi algorithm for HMMs, where a table tb is built incrementally. $tb[t][i]$ records the best

---

Algorithm 8.1. Viterbi decoding for first-order MEMM.

Input: $s = W_{1:n}$, first-order POS tagging model with feature vector $\vec{\phi}(t_i, t_{i-1}, W_{1:n})$ and feature weight vector $\vec{\theta}$;
Variables: tb, bp;
Initialization: $tb\,[t][i] \leftarrow -\infty$; $bp[t][i] \leftarrow$ NULL for $t \in L \cup \{\langle B \rangle\}, i \in [0, \ldots, n]$,
$tb[\langle B \rangle][0] \leftarrow 0$;
for $i \in [1, \ldots, n]$ **do**
$\quad$ **for** $t \in L$ **do**
$\quad\quad$ **for** $t' \in L \cup \{\langle B \rangle\}$ **do**
$\quad\quad\quad$ $score \leftarrow \vec{\theta} \cdot \vec{\phi}(t_i = t, t_{i-1} = t', W_{1:n})$;
$\quad\quad\quad$ **if** $tb[t'][i-1] + score > tb[t][i]$ **then**
$\quad\quad\quad\quad$ $tb[t][i] \leftarrow tb[t'][i-1] + score$;
$\quad\quad\quad\quad$ $bp[t][i] \leftarrow t'$;
$y_n \leftarrow \arg\max_t tb[t][n]$;
for $i \in [n, \ldots, 2]$ **do**
$\quad$ $y_{i-1} \leftarrow bp[y_i][i]$;
Output: $y_1 \ldots y_n$;

---

score $\hat{T}_{1:i}(t_i = t)$ at the ith position when $t_i = t$. For calculating $tb[t][i]$, the algorithm enumerates all possible t' for $tb[t'][i-1]$ at the $(i-1)$th position. A local score is calculated by $\vec{\theta} \cdot \vec{\phi}(t_i = t, t_{i-1} = t', W_{1:n})$, and $tb[t][i]$ is obtained by $\arg\max_{t'} \left(tb[t'][i-1] + \vec{\theta} \cdot \vec{\phi}(t_i = t, t_{i-1} = t', W_{1:n}) \right)$. In addition, a table bp is built for backtracing the optimal tag sequence.

Higher-order MEMMs can be derived using similar methods as first-order MEMMs (Exercise 8.1).

8.2   The Label Bias Problem

MEMMs break training label sequences into individual tag probabilities $P(t_i | T_{i-k:i-1}, W_{1:n})$ using the probability chain rule. While this facilitates the development of classification models $P(t_i | T_{i-k:i-1}, W_{1:n})$ with local training, there is a potential disadvantage by overlooking the distribution of full sequences of labels in the training data. Ultimately, we want to calculate the probability of label sequences $P(T_{1:n} | W_{1:n})$ globally during testing. However, our training procedure above only considers individual tag contexts locally when estimating $P(t_i | T_{i-k:i-1}, W_{1:n})$, disregarding the full tag sequence $T_{1:n}$. This inconsistency can lead to incorrect estimations of label sequence accuracies.

To give a specific example of this problem, let us temporarily ignore the input sequence, considering only output label sequences. Suppose that our label set contains only four labels: $L = \{\langle B \rangle, \ell_1, \ell_2, \ell_3\}$, where $\langle B \rangle$ indicates the beginning of a sentence. We want to train a first-order model, which estimates $P(t_1 t_2 t_3) = P(t_1 | \langle B \rangle) P(t_2 | t_1) P(t_3 | t_2)$. Given a training set $D = \{d_i\}|_{i=1}^6$

Table 8.2 Example training set.

ID	Tag Sequence	ID	Tag Sequence
d_1	$\ell_3\ell_3\ell_3$	d_4	$\ell_1\ell_3\ell_1$
d_2	$\ell_1\ell_1\ell_2$	d_5	$\ell_1\ell_3\ell_1$
d_3	$\ell_1\ell_1$	d_6	$\ell_1\ell_2\ell_2$

Table 8.3 Example maximum likelihood estimation of a first-order Markov POS tagging model.

Item	Probability	Item	Probability
$P(\ell_1\|\langle B\rangle)$	$\frac{5}{6}$	$P(\ell_1\|\ell_2)$	0
$P(\ell_2\|\langle B\rangle)$	0	$P(\ell_2\|\ell_2)$	1
$P(\ell_3\|\langle B\rangle)$	$\frac{1}{6}$	$P(\ell_3\|\ell_2)$	0
$P(\ell_1\|\ell_1)$	$\frac{1}{3}$	$P(\ell_1\|\ell_3)$	$\frac{1}{2}$
$P(\ell_2\|\ell_1)$	$\frac{1}{3}$	$P(\ell_2\|\ell_3)$	0
$P(\ell_3\|\ell_1)$	$\frac{1}{3}$	$P(\ell_3\|\ell_3)$	$\frac{1}{2}$

shown in Table 8.2, we can use maximum likelihood estimation to calculate $P(t_i|t_{i-1})$. The results are shown in Table 8.3.

Now according to these model parameter values, we have

$$P(d_4) = P(\ell_1\ell_3\ell_1) = P(\ell_1|\langle B\rangle)P(\ell_3|\ell_1)P(\ell_1|\ell_3) = \frac{5}{6} \times \frac{1}{3} \times \frac{1}{2} = \frac{5}{36} \qquad (8.3)$$

and

$$P(d_6) = P(\ell_1\ell_2\ell_2) = P(\ell_1|\langle B\rangle)P(\ell_2|\ell_1)P(\ell_2|\ell_2) = \frac{5}{6} \times \frac{1}{3} \times 1 = \frac{5}{18}. \qquad (8.4)$$

According to this local model, $P(d_6) > P(d_4)$. However, this contradicts the intuition by examining the dataset D, where $d_4 = d_5$ occurs twice yet d_6 occurs only once. By directly calculating $P(\langle B\rangle t_1 t_2 t_3)$ using maximum likelihood estimation over D,

$$P(d_4) = \frac{1}{3} > P(d_6) = \frac{1}{6}. \qquad (8.5)$$

The incorrect sequence probability of the locally trained model results from the fact of overlooking label sequence distributions. In particular, $P(\ell_2|\ell_2) = 1$ because ℓ_2 is succeeded only by ℓ_2 in our dataset. On the other hand, the label transition $\ell_2 \rightarrow \ell_2$ exists only once in the dataset. In contrast, the local probability $P(\ell_1|\ell_3) = \frac{1}{2}$ because the label ℓ_3 is succeeded by the label ℓ_1 only half of the time. On the other hand, the label transition $\ell_3 \rightarrow \ell_1$ occurs twice in our dataset, which is more frequent compared to $\ell_2 \rightarrow \ell_2$. Our local model overlooks this fact by normalising the condition $P(\cdot|\ell_2)$ locally, causing a bias towards selecting label sequences that contain $\ell_2 \rightarrow \ell_2$. This problem is called the **label bias** problem.

One solution to the label bias problem is to train a discriminative model that takes full sequences of labels as single units, calculating statistics (e.g., counting features) over full sequences of inputs and outputs before doing model normalisation. Sections 8.3, 8.4 and 8.5 discuss how this can be achieved using log-linear models, perceptrons and SVMs, respectively.

8.3   Conditional Random Fields

Conditional random fields (CRF) are log-linear models for sequence labelling, which take $P(T_{1:n}|W_{1:n})$ as a single unit. Formally, given an input sequence $W_{1:n}$, the probability of a candidate output sequence $T_{1:n}$ is directly modelled as:

$$P(T_{1:n}|W_{1:n}) = \frac{\exp\left(\vec{\theta} \cdot \vec{\phi}(T_{1:n}, W_{1:n})\right)}{\sum_{T'_{1:n}} \exp\left(\vec{\theta} \cdot \vec{\phi}(T'_{1:n}, W_{1:n})\right)}, \tag{8.6}$$

where $\vec{\phi}(T_{1:n}, W_{1:n})$ is a *global feature vector* that represents the input–output pair $(W_{1:n}, T_{1:n})$. $T'_{1:n}$ represents any possible label sequence. Disregarding the differences between feature vectors ϕ for sequence labelling and classification, Eq 8.6 is identical to the log-linear model for multi-class classification in Eq 4.2. Thus similar to MEMM, CRF is a log-linear model. The main difference between CRF and MEMM resembles the difference between Eq 8.5 and Eqs 8.3, 8.4. In particular, the former calculates the probability of a whole label sequence by normalising over all label sequences, thereby doing global training; in contrast, the latter breaks down the probability of a label sequence into the product of individual label probabilities, doing local normalisation. As a result, CRFs do not suffer from label bias, as MEMMs do.

8.3.1   Global Feature Vectors

With CRFs being discriminative models, the same rich features of MEMMs can be used. In particular, still making a kth order Markov assumption, we can define $\vec{\phi}(T_{1:n}, W_{1:n})$ by aggregating $\vec{\phi}(t_i, T_{i-k:i-1}, W_{1:n})$ over the input sequence $1 \leq i \leq n$. For the rest of this section, let us take the first-order Markov chain (i.e., $k = 1$) for example, where

$$\vec{\phi}(T_{1:n}, W_{1:n}) = \sum_{i=1}^{n} \vec{\phi}(t_i, t_{i-1}, W_{1:n}).$$

For instance, given the sentence "*The*/DT *man*/NN *went*/VBD *to*/TO *the*/DT *park*/NN *.*/." We have

$$\vec{\phi}(t_1, t_0, W_{1:7}) = <0, 0, \cdots, f_{47}(t_i = \text{DT}) = 1, 0, \cdots 0, f_{201}$$
$$(t_{i-1}t_i = \langle \text{B} \rangle \text{DT}) = 1, 0 \cdots 0, f_{501} \, (w_i = the, t_i = \text{DT})$$
$$= 1, 0, \cdots, 0>,$$
$$\vec{\phi}(t_2, t_1, W_{1:7}) = < \cdots, f_{59} = (t_i = \text{NN}), \cdots, f_{472} = (t_{i-1}t_i = \text{DT NN}),$$

$$\cdots, f_{748} = (w_i = man, t_i = NN)>,$$

$$\cdots$$

$$\vec{\phi}(t_6, t_5, W_{1:7}) = <\cdots, f_{59} = (t_i = NN), \cdots, f_{472} = (t_{i-1}t_i = DT\ NN),$$

$$\cdots, f_{932} = (w_i = park, t_i = NN), \cdots>$$

$$\vec{\phi}(t_7, t_6, W_{1:7}) = <\cdots, f_{80} = (t_i = .), \cdots, f_{516} = (t_{i-1}t_i = NN.),$$

$$\cdots, f_{1063} = (w_i = ., t_i = .) \cdots>$$

and

$$\vec{\phi}(T_{1:7}, W_{1:7}) = <0, \cdots, f_{47} = 1, \cdots, f_{59} = 2, 0, \cdots, f_{201} = 1, \cdots, f_{472} = 2, \cdots,$$

$$f_{501} = 1, 0, \cdots 0, f_{748} = 1, 0, \cdots 0, f_{932} = 1, \cdots, f_{1063} = 1, 0, \cdots 0>.$$

Note that f_{472} in $\vec{\phi}(T_{1:7}, W_{1:7})$, which corresponds to the feature instance $t_i = DT$ and $t_{i-1} = NN$, has a value of 2. This is because the corresponding tag bigram for both "*The man*" and "*the park*" are "DT NN". Vector addition results in summation of non-zero element values.

Cliques and clique potentials. Feature locality allows Eq 8.6 to be decomposed. In particular, each local feature context $T_{i-k:i-1}$ is called a **clique**. We have

$$
\begin{aligned}
P(T_{1:n}|W_{1:n}) &= \frac{1}{Z} \exp\left(\vec{\theta} \cdot \vec{\phi}(T_{1:n}, W_{1:n})\right) \\
&= \frac{1}{Z} \exp\left(\sum_{i=1}^{n} \vec{\theta} \cdot \vec{\phi}(t_i, T_{i-k:i-1}, W_{1:n})\right) \\
&= \frac{1}{Z} \prod_{i=1}^{n} \exp\left(\vec{\theta} \cdot \vec{\phi}(t_i, T_{i-k:i-1}, W_{1:n})\right) \\
&= \frac{1}{Z} \prod_{i=1}^{n} \psi(t_i, T_{i-k:i-1}, W_{1:n}),
\end{aligned}
\tag{8.7}
$$

where Z is the partition function. $\psi(t_i, T_{i-k:i-1}, W_{1:n})$ is referred to as a **clique potential**.

8.3.2 Decoding

Suppose that a model has been trained. Given a word sequence $W_{1:n}$, our goal is to find $\hat{T}_{1:n} = \arg\max_{T_{1:n}} P(T_{1:n}|W_{1:n}) = \arg\max_{T_{1:n}} \exp\left(\vec{\theta} \cdot \vec{\phi}(T_{1:n}, W_{1:n})\right)$, which is equal to $\arg\max_{T_{1:n}} \vec{\theta} \cdot \vec{\phi}(T_{1:n}, W_{1:n})$. Here $\vec{\phi}(T_{1:n}, W_{1:n})$ is a global feature vector that represents the input–output pair. Each element in $\vec{\theta}$ weighs a corresponding feature instance in $\vec{\phi}(T_{1:n}, W_{1:n})$.

Similar to the cases of HMM and MEMM, we leverage Markov properties over tag sequences to find $\hat{T}_{1:n}$ from an exponential number of $T_{1:n}$ efficiently. In particular, similar to Eq 8.7,

$$
\begin{aligned}
\vec{\theta} \cdot \vec{\phi}(T_{1:n}, W_{1:n}) &= \vec{\theta} \cdot \left(\sum_i \vec{\phi}(t_i, t_{i-1}, W_{1:n})\right) \\
&= \sum_i \left(\vec{\theta} \cdot \vec{\phi}(t_i, t_{i-1}, W_{1:n})\right).
\end{aligned}
\tag{8.8}
$$

Intuitively, Eq 8.8 means that the global score $\vec{\theta} \cdot \vec{\phi}(T_{1:n}, W_{1:n})$ can be computed incrementally from left to right, summing up local score components $\vec{\theta} \cdot \vec{\phi}(t_i, t_{i-1}, W_{1:n})$ step by step, with increasing i from 1 to n.

In Eq 8.8, each incremental component $\vec{\theta} \cdot \vec{\phi}(t_i, t_{i-1}, W_{1:n})$ is formally identical to the incremental score of MEMM decoding in Eq 8.1. As a result, the Viterbi decoder in Algorithm 8.1 for MEMM can be used for CRF decoding without change. Thus, both being discriminative linear models, MEMMs and CRFs are identical in their decoding goal $\hat{T}_{1:n} = \arg\max_{T_{1:n}} \vec{\theta} \cdot \vec{\phi}(t_i, t_{i-1}, W_{1:n})$ and decoding algorithms. The only difference lies in the training goal, with MEMM learning $P(t_i | t_{i-1}, W_{1:n})$ locally and CRFs learning $P(T_{1:n} | W_{1:n})$ globally. As seen in Section 8.2, global training eliminates the label bias issue.

8.3.3 Calculating Marginal Probabilities

Similar to the case of HMM, given a model $\vec{\theta}$ and an input–output pair $(W_{1:n}, T_{1:n})$, we sometimes need to calculate $P(t_i = t | W_{1:n})$. We introduce the calculation of marginal probability for CRF before introducing CRF training, because the latter requires the former as a step. Since a CRF model captures the label sequence probability $P(T_{1:n} | W_{1:n})$, the marginal probability can be calculated by summing up sequence probabilities with all possible $t_j (j \neq i)$:

$$P(t_i = t | W_{1:n}) = \sum_{t_1 \in L} \sum_{t_2 \in L} \cdots \sum_{t_{i-1} \in L} \sum_{t_{i+1} \in L} \cdots \sum_{t_n \in L} P(T_{1:n}(t_i = t) | W_{1:n}). \quad (8.9)$$

Equation 8.9 includes $O(|L|^{n-1})$ summations, the naïve implementation of which is intractable. Fortunately, the Markov properties in our feature defined in Section 8.3.1 allows a dynamic program that calculates the sum in polynomial time. In particular, according to Eq 8.7,

$$P(T_{1:n} | W_{1:n}) = \frac{\prod_i \exp\left(\vec{\theta} \cdot \vec{\phi}(t_1, t_{i-1}, W_{1:n})\right)}{Z},$$

where the partition function $Z = \sum_{T'_{1:n}} \exp\left(\vec{\theta} \cdot \vec{\phi}(T'_{1:n}, W_{1:n})\right)$. As a result, we have

$$P(t_i = t | W_{1:n}) = \sum_{t_1 \in L} \cdots \sum_{t_{i-1} \in L} \sum_{t_{i+1} \in L} \cdots \sum_{t_n \in L} \frac{1}{Z} \prod_{j=1}^{n} \exp\left(\vec{\theta} \cdot \vec{\phi}(t_j, t_{j-1}, W_{1:n})\right), t_i = t$$

$$= \frac{1}{Z} \left(\sum_{t_1 \in L} \cdots \sum_{t_{i-1} \in L} \prod_{j=1}^{i} \exp\left(\vec{\theta} \cdot \vec{\phi}(t_j, t_{j-1}, W_{1:n})\right) \right) \cdot$$

$$\left(\sum_{t_{i+1} \in L} \cdots \sum_{t_n \in L} \prod_{j=i+1}^{n} \exp\left(\vec{\theta} \cdot \vec{\phi}(t_j, t_{j-1}, W_{1:n})\right) \right), \quad (8.10)$$

where $t_i = t$ (distributivity).

Forward algorithm. Equation 8.10 cuts the full summation equation into the product of two terms, with the splitting point at i. Dynamic programs can be used to calculate each term efficiently. In particular, the first term and the second term of Eq 8.10 can be denoted as α and β, respectively, which involve output labels from the beginning of the sentence to the label t_i and from t_i to the end of sentence, respectively. First,

$$\alpha(j, t) = \sum_{t_1 \in L} \cdots \sum_{t_{j-1} \in L} \prod_{k=1}^{j} \exp\left(\vec{\theta} \cdot \vec{\phi}(t_k, t_{k-1}, W_{1:n})\right), \text{where } t_j = t.$$

We can calculate $\alpha(j, t)$ by summing up $\alpha(j - 1, t')$ for $t' \in L$,

$$\alpha(j, t) = \sum_{t' \in L} \left(\alpha(j - 1, t') \cdot \exp\left(\vec{\theta} \cdot \vec{\phi}(t_j = t, t_{j-1} = t', W_{1:n})\right) \right) \tag{8.11}$$

thanks to the fact that

$$\prod_{k=1}^{j} \exp\left(\vec{\theta} \cdot \vec{\phi}(t_k, t_{k-1}, W_{1:n})\right) = \left(\prod_{k=1}^{j-1} \exp\left(\vec{\theta} \cdot \vec{\phi}(t_k, t_{k-1}, W_{1:n})\right) \right) \cdot \exp\left(\vec{\theta} \cdot \vec{\phi}(t_j, t_{j-1}, W_{1:n})\right).$$

Setting $\alpha(0, \langle B \rangle) = 1$, Algorithm 8.2 can be used to calculate the values of $\alpha(j, t)$ with $j \in [1, \ldots, i], t \in L$.

Backward algorithm. Similarly,

$$\beta(j, t) = \sum_{t_{j+1} \in L} \cdots \sum_{t_n \in L} \prod_{k=j+1}^{n} \exp\left(\vec{\theta} \cdot \vec{\phi}(t_k, t_{k-1}, W_{1:n})\right), t_j = t.$$

We can calculate $\beta(j, t)$ by enumerating $\beta(j + 1, t')$ for all values of t', where

$$\beta(j, t) = \sum_{t' \in L} \left(\beta(j + 1, t') \cdot \exp\left(\vec{\theta} \cdot \vec{\phi}(t_{j+1} = t', t_j = t, W_{1:n})\right) \right). \tag{8.12}$$

Algorithm 8.2. Forward algorithm for first-order CRF.

Inputs: $s = W_{1:n}$, first-order CRF model for POS tagging with feature vector $\vec{\phi}(t_i, t_{i-1}, W_{1:n})$ and feature weight vector $\vec{\theta}$;

Variables: α;

Initialization: $\alpha[0][\langle B \rangle] \leftarrow 1, \alpha[i][t] \leftarrow 0$ for $i \in [1, \ldots, n], t \in L$;

for $t \in L$ **do**

    $\alpha[1][t] \leftarrow \alpha[0][\langle B \rangle] \cdot \exp\left(\vec{\theta} \cdot \vec{\phi}(t_1 = t, t_0 = \langle B \rangle, W_{1:n})\right)$

for $i \in [2, \ldots, n]$ **do**

    for $t \in L$ **do**

        for $t' \in L$ **do**

            $\alpha[i][t] \leftarrow \alpha[i][t] + \alpha[i-1][t'] \cdot \exp\left(\vec{\theta} \cdot \vec{\phi}(t_i = t, t_{i-1} = t', W_{1:n})\right);$

Output: α;

Algorithm 8.3. Backward algorithm for first-order CRF.

Inputs: $s = W_{1:n}$, first-order CRF model for POS tagging with feature vector
$\vec{\phi}(t_i, t_{i-1}, W_{1:n})$ and feature weight vector $\vec{\theta}$;
Variables: β;
Initialization: $\beta[i][t] \leftarrow 0$, $\beta[n+1][\langle \mathrm{B} \rangle] \leftarrow 1$ **for** $t \in L$, **for** $i \in [1, \ldots, n], t \in L$;
for $t \in L$ **do**
$\quad \mid \quad \beta[n][t] \leftarrow \beta[n+1][\langle \mathrm{B} \rangle] \cdot \exp \left(\vec{\theta} \cdot \vec{\phi}(t_{n+1} = \langle \mathrm{B} \rangle, t_n = t, W_{1:n}) \right);$
for $i \in [n-1, \ldots, 1]$ **do**
$\quad \mid \quad$ **for** $t' \in L$ **do**
$\quad \mid \quad \quad \mid \quad$ **for** $t \in L$ **do**
$\quad \mid \quad \quad \mid \quad \quad \mid \quad \beta[i][t'] \leftarrow \beta[i][t'] + \beta[i+1][t] \cdot \exp \left(\vec{\theta} \cdot \vec{\phi}(t_{i+1} = t, t_i = t', W_{1:n}) \right);$
Output: β;

Algorithm 8.3 can be used to calculate $\beta(j, t)$ for $j \in [n, \ldots, i], t \in L$. Due to their resemblance to Algorithms 7.3 and 7.4 for HMMs, respectively, Algorithms 8.2 and 8.3 are named the **forward algorithm** and the **backward algorithm**, respectively.

Similar to the case for HMMs, according to Eq 8.10, the final value of sum $P(t_i = t W_{1:n})$ can be calculated as $\frac{1}{Z} \alpha(i, t) \beta(i, t)$. Note that Z does not need to be calculated, since the values of $P(t_i = t | W_{1:n})$ for all $t \in L$ sum to 1.

Implementation trick: logsumexp. Since Eq 8.11 and Eq 8.12 contain multiplications of exponentials, it is possible that the result exceeds the numeric upper bound for certain hardware system architectures. In order to improve numerical stability, the *logsumexp trick* can be used here, which calculates the logarithm of the sum of exponentials,

$$logsumexp(x_1, x_2, \ldots, x_n) = \log \left(\exp(x_1) + \exp(x_2) + \cdots + \exp(x_n) \right)$$

$$= x_{max} + \log \left(\exp(x_1 - x_{max}) + \exp(x_2 - x_{max}) \right.$$

$$\left. + \cdots + \exp(x_n - x_{max}) \right),$$

where $x_{max} = \max(x_1, x_2, \ldots, x_n)$. Since $x_j \leq x_{max}$, $\exp(x_j - x_{max}) \leq 1$, and the numerical stability can be ensured. Using this trick, Eq 8.11 can be calculated as

$$\alpha(j, t) = \sum_{t' \in L} \left(\alpha(j-1, t') \cdot \exp \left(\vec{\theta} \cdot \vec{\phi}(t_j = t, t_{j-1} = t', W_{1:n}) \right) \right)$$

$$= \sum_{t' \in L} \left(\exp \left(\log \alpha(j-1, t') \right) \cdot \exp \left(\vec{\theta} \cdot \vec{\phi}(t_j = t, t_{j-1} = t', W_{1:n}) \right) \right)$$

$$= \sum_{l' \in L} \left(\exp \left(\log \alpha(j-1, t') + \vec{\theta} \cdot \vec{\phi}(t_j = t, t_{j-1} = t', W_{1:n}) \right) \right)$$

$$= \exp \left(logsumexp \left(\log \alpha(j-1, \ell_1) + \vec{\theta} \cdot \vec{\phi}(t_j = t, t_{j-1} = \ell_1, W_{1:n}), \right. \right.$$

$$\log \alpha(j-1, \ell_2) + \vec{\theta} \cdot \vec{\phi}(t_j = t, t_{j-1} = \ell_2, W_{1:n}), \tag{8.13}$$

$$\vdots \qquad\qquad \vdots$$

$$\left. \left. \log \alpha(j-1, \ell_{|L|}) + \vec{\theta} \cdot \vec{\phi}(t_j = t, t_{j-1} = \ell_{|L|}, W_{1:n}) \right) \right),$$

where $\{\ell_i = l\}$.

8.3.4 Training

Given a set of training data $D = \{(W_i, T_i)\}|_{i=1}^{N}$, where W_i is a sentence and T_i is a sequence of gold-standard output labels, the CRF training objective is to maximise the log-likelihood of D:

$$\vec{\theta} = \arg\max_{\vec{\theta}} \log P(D)$$

$$= \arg\max_{\vec{\theta}} \log \prod_i P(T_i|W_i) \quad (i.i.d.)$$

$$= \arg\max_{\vec{\theta}} \sum_i \log P(T_i|W_i)$$

$$= \arg\max_{\vec{\theta}} \sum_i \log \frac{\exp\left(\vec{\theta} \cdot \vec{\phi}(T_i, W_i)\right)}{\sum_{T'} \exp\left(\vec{\theta} \cdot \vec{\phi}(T', W_i)\right)} \tag{8.14}$$

$$= \arg\max_{\vec{\theta}} \sum_i \left(\log \exp\left(\vec{\theta} \cdot \vec{\phi}(T_i, W_i)\right) - \log \sum_{T'} \exp\left(\vec{\theta} \cdot \vec{\phi}(T', W_i)\right) \right)$$

$$= \arg\max_{\vec{\theta}} \sum_i \left(\vec{\theta} \cdot \vec{\phi}(T_i, W_i) - \log \sum_{T'} \exp\left(\vec{\theta} \cdot \vec{\phi}(T', W_i)\right) \right).$$

Similar to the cases in Chapter 4, SGD can be used for optimisation. The local training objective for each training example is to maximise

$$\vec{\theta} \cdot \vec{\phi}(T_i, W_i) - \log \left(\sum_{T'} \exp\left(\vec{\theta} \cdot \vec{\phi}(T', W_i)\right) \right).$$

Accordingly, the local gradient is

$$\frac{\partial \log P(T_i|W_i)}{\partial \vec{\theta}} = \vec{\phi}(T_i, W_i) - \frac{\sum_{T'} \exp\left(\vec{\theta} \cdot \vec{\phi}(T', W_i)\right) \cdot \vec{\phi}(T', W_i)}{\sum_{T''} \exp\left(\vec{\theta} \cdot \vec{\phi}(T'', W_i)\right)}$$

$$= \vec{\phi}(T_i, W_i) - \sum_{T'} \frac{\exp\left(\vec{\theta} \cdot \vec{\phi}(T', W_i)\right)}{\sum_{T''} \left(\vec{\theta} \cdot \vec{\phi}(T'', W_i)\right)} \cdot \vec{\phi}(T', W_i) \qquad (8.15)$$

$$= \vec{\phi}(T_i, W_i) - \sum_{T'} P(T'|W_i)\vec{\phi}(T', W_i) \quad \text{(definition of } P(T'|W_i)\text{)}.$$

Disregarding the structural nature of T_i and T', which affects $\vec{\phi}(T', W_i)$, Eq 8.15 is identical to Eq 4.7 in Chapter 4 for log-linear classifiers. In fact, by regarding T_i as a single unit, the log-linear formulation of discriminative sequence labellers is formally identical to log-linear classifiers. On the other hand, similar to the case for decoding, a major challenge arises from the fact that there is an exponential number of candidate outputs T' given an input W_i, which makes the calculation of $\sum_{T'} P(T'|W_i)\vec{\phi}(T', W_i)$ (i.e., the expected global feature vector over all possible output label sequences) computationally intractable.

Again we resort to feature locality to find a solution. In particular, denoting $T' = T'_{1:n_i} = t'_1 t'_2 \ldots t'_{n_i}$, where n_i is the length of W_i, we have

$$\vec{\phi}(T', W_i) = \sum_{j=1}^{n_i} \vec{\phi}(t'_j, t'_{j-1}, W_i).$$

As a result,

$$\sum_{T'} P(T'|W_i)\vec{\phi}(T', W_i) = \sum_{T'} P(T'|W_i)\left(\sum_j \vec{\phi}(t'_j, t'_{j-1}, W_i)\right)$$

$$= \sum_{T'} \sum_j P(T'|W_i)\vec{\phi}(t'_j, t'_{j-1}, W_i)$$

$$= \sum_j \left(\sum_{T'} P(T'|W_i)\vec{\phi}(t'_j, t'_{j-1}, W_i)\right) \qquad (8.16)$$

$$= \sum_j E_{T' \sim P(T'|W_i)}\vec{\phi}(t'_j, t'_{j-1}, W_i).$$

Equation 8.16 indicates that the expectation of the global feature vector $\vec{\phi}(T', W_i)$ over all T' is equal to the sum of expectations of each local feature vector $\vec{\phi}(t'_j, t'_{j-1}, W_i)$ over all possible T'.

Further, since a local feature $\vec{\phi}(t'_j, t'_{j-1}, W_i)$ is constrained to a *clique* that consists of only t'_j and t'_{j-1} (disregarding W_i since it is a static input sequence that does not need to be enumerated in the summation), we have

$$\sum_j E_{T' \sim P(T'|W_i)} \vec{\phi}(t'_j, t'_{j-1}, W_i)$$

$$= \sum_j E_{t'_{j-1}t'_j \sim P(t'_{j-1}t'_j|W_i)} \vec{\phi}(t'_j, t'_{j-1}, W_i) \tag{8.17}$$

$$= \sum_j \left(\sum_{t'_j \in L, t'_{j-1} \in L} P(t'_{j-1}t'_j|W_i) \vec{\phi}(t'_j, t'_{j-1}, W_i) \right).$$

Thus, if we can calculate the marginal probabilities $P(t'_{j-1}t'_j|W_i)$ efficiently, then the expectation of $\vec{\phi}(t'_j, t'_{j-1}, W_i)$ over all possible T' is equivalent to the expectation over all possible cliques $t'_{j-1}t'_j$, which takes $O(n_i|L|^2)$ time to enumerate, rather than $O(|L|^{n_i})$.

Similar to Section 8.3.3, the marginal probability can be calculated leveraging feature locality. In particular,

$$P(t'_{j-1}t'_j|W_i) = \sum_{t'_1 \in L} \cdots \sum_{t'_{j-2} \in L} \sum_{t'_{j+1} \in L} \cdots \sum_{t'_{n_i} \in L} P(T'_{1:n_i}|W_i)$$

$$= \sum_{t'_1 \in L} \cdots \sum_{t'_{j-2} \in L} \sum_{t'_{j+1} \in L} \cdots \sum_{t'_{n_i} \in L} \left(\frac{1}{Z} \prod_{k=1}^{n_i} \exp\left(\vec{\theta} \cdot \vec{\phi}(t'_k, t'_{k-1}, W_i) \right) \right)$$

$$= \frac{1}{Z} \left(\sum_{t'_1 \in L} \cdots \sum_{t'_{j-2} \in L} \prod_{k=1}^{j-1} \exp\left(\vec{\theta} \cdot \vec{\phi}(t'_k, t'_{k-1}, W_i) \right) \right) \tag{8.18}$$

$$\exp\left(\vec{\theta} \cdot \vec{\phi}(t'_j, t'_{j-1}, W_i) \right)$$

$$\left(\sum_{t'_{j+1} \in L} \cdots \sum_{t'_{n_i} \in L} \prod_{k=j+1}^{n_i} \exp\left(\vec{\theta} \cdot \vec{\phi}(t'_k, t'_{k-1}, W_i) \right) \right) \quad \text{(distributivity)}$$

Similar to calculating the marginal $P(t_j|W_{1:n})$, we can define

$$\alpha(k, t) = \sum_{t'_1 \in L} \cdots \sum_{t'_{k-1} \in L} \prod_{m=1}^{k} \exp\left(\vec{\theta} \cdot \vec{\phi}(t'_m, t'_{m-1}, W_i) \right), t'_k = t$$

and

$$\beta(k, t) = \sum_{t'_{k+1} \in L} \cdots \sum_{t'_{n_i} \in L} \prod_{m=k}^{n_i} \exp\left(\vec{\theta} \cdot \vec{\phi}(t'_{m+1}, t'_m, W_i) \right), t'_k = t$$

These definitions are the same as the definitions of $\alpha(j, t)$ and $\beta(j, t)$ in Eqs 8.11 and 8.12, respectively. Therefore, the forward–backward algorithm in Algorithm 8.4 can be used to build a table of $n_i \times |L|$ for α and β, respectively.

After obtaining the values of $\alpha(k, t)$ and $\beta(k, t)$ for all $k \in [1, \ldots, n_i]$ and $t \in L$, the value of $P(t'_{j-1}t'_j|W_i)$ can be calculated as

$$P(t'_{j-1}t'_j|W_i) \propto \alpha(j-1, t'_{j-1})\beta(j, t'_j) \exp\left(\vec{\theta} \cdot \vec{\phi}(t'_j, t'_{j-1}, W_i) \right)$$

according to Eq 8.18. Taking this value back to Eqs 8.16 and 8.15, we achieve efficient training of CRFs in polynomial time. Compared with the training of log-linear classifiers, CRF training involves a dynamic program for dealing with exponential summation.

Algorithm 8.4. Forward–backward algorithm for training first-order CRF.

Inputs: $s = W_{1:n}$, first-order CRF model for POS tagging with feature vector $\vec{\phi}(t_i, t_{i-1}, W_{1:n})$ and feature weight vector $\vec{\theta}$;

Variables: $table$, α, β;

$\alpha \leftarrow \text{FORWARD}(W_{1:n}, \vec{\phi}, \vec{\theta})$ using Algorithm 8.2;

$\beta \leftarrow \text{BACKWARD}(W_{1:n}, \vec{\phi}, \vec{\theta})$ using Algorithm 8.3;

for $j \in [1, \ldots, n]$ **do**

    $total \leftarrow 0$;

    for $t \in L$ **do**

        for $t' \in L$ **do**

            $table[t'][t][j] \leftarrow \alpha[t'][j-1] \cdot \beta[t][j] \cdot \exp\left(\vec{\theta} \cdot \vec{\phi}(t, t', W_{1:n})\right)$;

            $total \leftarrow total + table[t'][t][j]$;

    for $t \in L$ **do**

        for $t' \in L$ **do**

            $table[t'][t][j] \leftarrow \frac{table[t'][t][j]}{total}$;

Output: $table$;

8.4 Structured Perceptron

In Part I of this book, we have seen two types of discriminative models, including margin-based models (Chapter 3) and log-linear models (Chapter 4). The previous sections have shown CRFs as log-linear models for structured prediction. Similar to log-linear models, large-margin discriminative linear models such as the perceptron and SVMs can be adapted from classification to sequence labelling. We discuss perceptron in this section and SVM in the next section.

Following the idea in Section 8.3, we treat a whole label sequence structure as a single unit, mapping it, together with the input sequence, to a global feature vector, so that the same discriminative model can be used to score the sequence. The main challenge for sequence labelling tasks results from the fact that there is an exponential number of possible label sequences given an input sequence, which leads to difficulties in both training and decoding.

Model definition. Formally, given a pair of input and output sequences $(W_{1:n}, T_{1:n})$, the perceptron calculates

$$score(T_{1:n}, W_{1:n}) = \vec{\theta} \cdot \vec{\phi}(T_{1:n}, W_{1:n}), \tag{8.19}$$

which is consistent with linear discriminative classifiers and CRFs.

In Eq 8.19, $\vec{\phi}(T_{1:n}, W_{1:n})$ denotes a global feature vector, which represents the characteristics of $T_{1:n}$ in a vector space. The definition of $\vec{\phi}(T_{1:n}, W_{1:n})$ can be the same as log-linear models, such as Table 8.1 for POS tagging. $\vec{\theta}$ is the model parameter vector, which assigns a weight to each element in $\vec{\phi}(T_{1:n}, W_{1:n})$.

Decoding. Given an input sequence $W_{1:n}$, the task of decoding is to find $\hat{T}_{1:n} = \arg\max_{T_{1:n}} score(T_{1:n}, W_{1:n})$. Similar to the case of CRF, the Viterbi algorithm can be used to enumerate $|L|^n$ candidate label sequences in linear time to the sentence length n, thanks to the fact that $\vec{\phi}(T_{1:n}, W_{1:n}) = \sum_{i=1}^{n} \vec{\phi}(t_i, t_{i-1}, W_{1:n})$. Using the same feature templates, Algorithm 8.1 can be applied directly. In fact, similar to the case of classification, the model scoring function and decoding process of discriminative linear sequence labellers, including perceptrons, SVMs and CRFs, are the same.

Training. The objective of perceptron training is to find a separating hyperplane in the vector space that differentiates positive and negative training examples. For structured prediction, this objective can be the same as the objective for multi-class classification, where a positive example represents a gold-standard label sequence, and a negative example represents an incorrect label sequence. In fact, working with feature vectors $\vec{\phi}$ directly, the perceptron does not need to know the nature of the original output structure (i.e., class or sequence).

As a result, Algorithm 3.3 of Chapter 3 can be directly adapted here, with x being replaced with $W_{1:n}$, c being replaced by $T_{1:n}$ and $\vec{v}(x, c)$ being replaced by $\vec{\phi}(T_{1:n}, W_{1:n})$. The only complication is line 5, which calculates $Z_{1:n} = \arg\max_{Z'_{1:n}} score(Z'_{1:n}, W_{1:n})$. Finding the most violated margin constraints coincides with the decoder objective. Since the number of possible output sequences are exponential, the Viterbi algorithm should be used instead of brute force enumeration, which is used for classification.

Similar to the case of multi-class classification, given $D = \{W_i, T_i\}|_{i=1}^{N}$, the perceptron algorithm can be seen as minimising the following training objective:

$$\sum_{i=1}^{N} \left(\max_{Z'_i} \vec{\theta} \cdot \vec{\phi}(W_i, Z'_i) - \vec{\theta} \cdot \vec{\phi}(W_i, T_i) \right). \tag{8.20}$$

In summary, compared with training of multi-class perceptrons, structured perceptron training is more complex because of the need of a dynamic program for finding the most violated constraint from exponential output candidates.

8.4.1 Averaged Perceptron

There is a variation of the standard perceptron algorithm that is commonly used for structured prediction tasks, which is called the **averaged perceptron**. The basic idea is to record the values of $\vec{\theta}$ after each training example has been processed, taking their average value as the final model, instead of the last updated value of $\vec{\theta}$.

Formally, denoting the value of $\vec{\theta}$ after the ith training example has been processed in the tth training iteration as $\vec{\theta}^{i,t}$, each $\vec{\theta}^{i,t}$ can be regarded as a unique perceptron model. Their average is

$$\vec{\gamma} = \frac{1}{NT} \sum_{i \in [1...N], t \in [1...T]} \vec{\theta}^{i,t},$$

where N is the number of training examples and T is the number of training iterations. Given a pair of input and output (x, y), where y can be either a class label or a label sequence, the score

---

Algorithm 8.5. Averaged perceptron

Inputs: $D = \{(W_i, T_i)\}|_{i=1}^N$
Initialization: $\vec{\theta} \leftarrow \vec{0}; \vec{\sigma} \leftarrow \vec{0}; t \leftarrow 0;$
repeat
    for $i \in [1, \ldots, N]$ **do**
        $Z_i \leftarrow \arg\max_{\mathfrak{z}} \vec{\theta} \cdot \vec{\phi}(W_i, \mathfrak{z});$
        if $Z_i \neq T_i$ **then**
            $\vec{\theta} \leftarrow \vec{\theta} + \vec{\phi}(W_i, T_i) - \vec{\phi}(W_i, Z_i);$
        $\vec{\sigma} \leftarrow \vec{\sigma} + \vec{\theta};$
    $t \leftarrow t + 1;$
until $t = T;$
$\vec{\sigma} \leftarrow \frac{\vec{\sigma}}{NT};$

---

given by the averaged parameter vector is

$$\overline{score}(x, y) = \left(\frac{1}{NT} \sum_{i,t} \vec{\theta}^{i,t}\right) \cdot \vec{\phi}(x, y)$$

$$= \frac{1}{NT} \sum_{i,t} \left(\vec{\theta}^{i,t} \cdot \vec{\phi}(x, y)\right) \tag{8.21}$$

$$= \frac{1}{NT} \sum_{i,t} score^{i,t}(x, y),$$

where $score^{i,t}(x, y)$ denotes the score of (x, y) given by the parameter vector $\vec{\theta}^{i,t}$. Equation 8.21 indicates that the score of (x, y) given by the averaged parameter vector $\vec{\gamma}$ is equivalent to the averaged score of (x, y) given by each $\vec{\theta}^{i,t}$. As a result, the averaged perceptron is effectively a voting strategy (see Chapter 4), which can avoid overfitting. It has been shown empirically useful for a wide range of tasks and datasets.

Pseudocode of the algorithm is shown in Algorithm 8.5. In addition to the parameter $\vec{\theta}$, a sum vector $\vec{\sigma}$ is defined. $\vec{\sigma}$ is initialised as $\vec{0}$, and updated by adding $\vec{\theta}^{i,t}$ after the training example (x_i, y_i) has been processed at the tth iteration. After T training iterations, the average $\vec{\gamma} = \vec{\sigma}/NT$ is used as the final parameter vector.

Implementation trick: lazy update for computational efficiency. The averaged perceptron requires maintaining a whole set of parameters for every time step. With a large number of features, calculating the total parameter vector $\vec{\sigma}$ after each training example is expensive. Since the number of changed dimensions in the parameter vector $\vec{\theta}^{i,t}$ after each training example is a small proportion of the total vector, we can use a lazy update optimisation for the training process. In particular, define an update vector $\vec{\tau}$ to record the last time when each dimension of the averaged parameter vector was last updated. For each dimension of the model parameter, the corresponding dimension in $\vec{\tau}$ is a pair (i, t), which stores the training sentence index i and training iteration t for its last update. After each training sentence is processed, we update only the dimensions of the parameter vector that corresponds to the features in the training sentence.

Denote the sth dimension in each vector before processing the ith example in the tth iteration as $\vec{\theta}_s^{i-1,t}$, $\vec{\sigma}_s^{i1,t}$ and $\tau_s^{i-1,t} = (i_{\tau,s}, t_{\tau,s})$. Suppose that the decoder output Z_i is different from the training example T_i. Now $\vec{\theta}_s^{i,t}$, $\vec{\sigma}_s^{i,t}$, $\tau_s^{i,t}$ can be updated in the following way for each non-zero element s in either the feature vector $\vec{\phi}(W_i, T_i)$ or the feature vector $\vec{\phi}(W_i, Z_i)$:

$$\vec{\sigma}_s^{i,t} = \vec{\sigma}_s^{i-1,t} + \vec{\theta}_s^{i-1,t} \times \left(N(t - t_{\tau,s}) + (i - i_{\tau,s}) \right)$$

$$\vec{\theta}_s^{i,t} = \vec{\theta}_s^{i-1,t} + \vec{\phi}_s(W_i, T_i) - \vec{\phi}_s(W_i, Z_i)$$

$$\vec{\sigma}_s^{i,t} = \vec{\sigma}_s^{i,t} + \vec{\phi}_s(W_i, T_i) - \vec{\phi}_s(W_i, Z_i)$$

$$\tau_s^{i,t} = (i, t)$$

In the equation above, for each updated element s, the sum vector $\vec{\sigma}_s^{i,t}$ is updated by adding the old $\vec{\theta}$ value for all the training instances since its last update, before adding the new $\vec{\theta}$ value.

8.5 Structured SVM

The adaptation of SVM from multi-class classification tasks to structured prediction tasks can follow the same thinking as that for log-linear models and perceptron algorithms. Since the model form and decoding are the same as perceptrons, here we only discuss the training.

Training. The SVM training objective is to find a large-margin separation hyperplane in the vector space of training data. Similar to the case of the perceptron algorithm, once $\vec{\phi}(x, y)$ is given for a pair of input and output (x, y), the nature of the original output y (e.g., class label or sequence) is not directly important to this objective. As a result, the training objective in Eq 3.14 in Chapter 3 can be directly adapted for structured SVM, with x being replaced with $W_{1:n}$, c being replaced with $T_{1:n}$ and $\vec{\phi}(x, c)$ being replaced with $\vec{\phi}(W_{1:n}, T_{1:n})$. Given $D = \{(W_i, T_i)\}|_{i=1}^N$, the training objective for structured SVM is:

$$\min_{\vec{\theta}} \frac{1}{2}||\vec{\theta}||^2 + C\left(\sum_{i=1}^N \max\left(0, 1 - \vec{\theta} \cdot \vec{\phi}(W_i, T_i) + \max_{T' \neq T_i}\left(\vec{\theta} \cdot \vec{\phi}(W_i, T') \right) \right) \right), \qquad (8.22)$$

where C is a weight hyper-parameter. Algorithm 4.8 in Chapter 4 can be adapted directly to optimise this training objective. Similar to the case of perceptrons, finding $\arg\max_{T'} score(T', W_i)$ is intractable by brute-force search but the Viterbi algorithm can be used. Because the perceptron and SVM fix only the most violated constraint during training, it is unnecessary to consider efficient calculation of expectations of features over all possible outputs, as for CRFs.

8.5.1 Cost-Sensitive Training

Unlike classification tasks, a nature of structured prediction tasks is that all incorrect structures are not equally incorrect. For example, given a sequence of five words, a candidate POS tag sequence can contain only one incorrect POS tag, while another can contain four. For structured SVMs, now that each POS tag sequence is regarded as a single unit, represented by a single feature vector, different incorrect structures can be equally located in the negative sub feature space, regardless of their degree of incorrectness. On the other hand, if the model has to make a mistake, we would rather see the output with one incorrect POS tag than the one with four.

Formally, use $\Delta(T'_{1:n}, T_{1:n})$ to denote the **cost** of mistakenly predicting $T'_{1:n}$ when the gold-standard output is $T_{1:n}$. The cost function that measures the number of incorrectly labelled words in a word sequence, is also known as the *Hamming distance*. We want a **cost-sensitive** model, which is expected to assign not only a higher score to a correct output compared to an incorrect output, but also a higher score to a less costly incorrect output compared to a more costly one.

Cost-sensitive training objective. The above goal can be achieved by rescaling the score margin with the actual cost: for a more costly incorrect output, we can ask its vector representation to be relatively further away from the correct output vectors. This translates to a larger score margin between relatively more incorrect outputs and correct outputs, rather than a constant score margin of 1 (Eq 8.22).

Formally, given a set of training examples $D = \{(W_i, T_i)\}|_{i=1}^N$, the cost-sensitive structured SVM training objective is:

$$\min_{\vec{\theta}} \frac{1}{2}||\vec{\theta}||^2 + C\left(\sum_{i=1}^N \max\left(0, \Delta(\hat{T}'_i, T_i) - \vec{\theta} \cdot \vec{\phi}(W_i, T_i) + \vec{\theta} \cdot \vec{\phi}(W_i, \hat{T}'_i)\right)\right), \qquad (8.23)$$

where $\hat{T}'_i = \max_{T' \neq T_i}\left(\Delta(T', T_i) + \vec{\theta} \cdot \vec{\phi}(W_i, T')\right)$.

Cost-augmented decoding. In Eq 8.23, the margin violation is $\Delta(T', T_i) - \vec{\theta} \cdot \vec{\phi}(T_i, W_i) + \vec{\theta} \cdot \vec{\phi}(W_i, T')$, which scales with $\Delta(T', T_i)$. As a result, the most violated margin constraint $\max_{T'}\left(0, \Delta(T', T_i) - \vec{\theta} \cdot \vec{\phi}(T_i, W_i) + \vec{\theta} \cdot \vec{\phi}(T', W_i)\right)$ does not necessarily coincide with the highest-scored output $\arg\max_{T'} \vec{\theta} \cdot \vec{\phi}(T', W_i)$. Consequently, the Viterbi decoder in Algorithm 8.1 cannot be directly used for finding the most violated constraint. In addition, similar to the decoding task, brute force enumeration of candidate output structures T' is intractable.

Fortunately, just as our global feature vector $\vec{\phi}(T_{1:n}, W_{1:n})$, the Hamming distance cost $\Delta(T'_{1:n}, T_{1:n})$ can be decomposed into local components. In particular,

$$\Delta(T'_{1:n}, T_{1:n}) = \sum_{i=1}^n \delta(t'_i, t_i),$$

where $\delta(t'_i, t_i) = 1$ if and only if $t'_i = t_i$.

As a result, denoting $\Delta(T'_{1:i}, T_{1:i}) = \sum_{j=1}^i \delta(t'_j, t_j)$, we know that $\hat{T}'_{1:i} = \arg\max_{T'_{1:i}}$ $\left(\vec{\theta} \cdot \left(\sum_{j=1}^i \phi(t'_j, t'_{j-1}, W_{1:n})\right) + \Delta(T'_{1:i}, T_{1:i})\right)$ must contain $\hat{T}'_{1:i-1} = \arg\max_{T'_{1:i-1}}$ $\left(\vec{\theta} \cdot \left(\sum_{j=1}^{i-1} \phi(t'_j, t'_{j-1}, W_{1:n})\right) + \Delta(T'_{1:i-1}, T_{1:i-1})\right)$. More specifically,

---

Algorithm 8.6. Cost-augmented decoding for first-order POS tagging.

Input: Input word sequence $s = W_{1:n}$, gold-standard tag sequence $t_1^g t_2^g \dots t_n^g$, first-order POS tagging model with feature vector $\vec{\phi}(t_i, t_{i-1}, W_{1:n})$ for $t, t' \in L$, and feature weight vector $\vec{\theta}$;

Variables: tb, bp;

Initialization: $tb[t][i] \leftarrow -\infty$; $bp[t][i] \leftarrow$ NULL for $t \in L, i \in [1 \dots n]$;

for $i \in [1, \dots, n]$ do

    for $t \in L$ do

        for $t' \in L$ do

            $score \leftarrow \vec{\theta} \cdot \vec{\phi}(t_i = t, t_{i-1} = t', W_{1:n}) + \delta(t, t_i^g)$;

            if $tb[t'][i-1] + score > tb[t][i]$ then

                $tb[t][i] \leftarrow tb[t'][i-1] + score$;

                $bp[t][i] \leftarrow t'$;

$y_n \leftarrow \arg\max_t tb[t][n]$;

for $i \in [n, \dots, 2]$ do

    $y_{i-1} \leftarrow bp[y_i][i]$;

Output: $y_1 \dots y_n$;

$$
\hat{T}'_{1:i}(t'_i = t) = \underset{T'_{1:i-1}(t'_{i-1}=t')}{\arg\max} \left(\left(\vec{\theta} \cdot \left(\sum_{j=1}^{i-1} \vec{\phi}(t'_j, t'_{j-1}, W_{1:n}) \right) + \Delta(T'_{1:j-1}, T_{1:j-1}) \right) \right.
$$
$$
\left. + \left(\vec{\theta} \cdot \vec{\phi}(t'_i = t, t'_{i-1} = t', W_{1:n}) + \delta(t, t_i) \right) \right).
$$

(8.24)

Given the observation above, Algorithm 8.1 can be adjusted slightly, adding $\delta(t'_i, t_i)$ into the decoding process. Pseudocode of this algorithm is shown in Algorithm 8.6. This algorithm is also referred to as **cost-augmented decoding**, due to the consideration of the cost function in searching for the most violated constraints. Despite the name, it is used only in the training process, for the purpose of learning a cost-sensitive model. During testing, the decoding algorithm remains the same as Algorithm 8.1 regardless whether our linear model is cost-sensitive or not.

Summary

In this chapter we have introduced

- Maximum entropy Markov models (MEMM) and the label bias problem;
- Conditional random fields (CRF);
- Structured perceptron and averaged perceptron;
- Structured SVM and cost-sensitive training.

Chapter Notes

Ratnaparkhi (1996) introduced MEMM for POS-tagging. MEMMs were used by McCallum et al. (2000) for information extraction and segmentation. Toutanova et al. (2003) built a MEMM-style model with rich features. Lafferty et al. (2001) proposed CRFs for sequence labelling. Sutton et al. (2012) gave a detailed introduction to CRFs. CRF is widely used in NLP for sequence labelling. (Sha and Pereira, 2003; McCallum and Li, 2003). Collins (2002) first used perceptron algorithms to train sequence labelling models. Tsochantaridis et al. (2004) proposed structured SVM. Elkan (2001) discussed cost-sensitive training.

Exercises

8.1 Define a second-order MEMM by specifying $P(T_{1:n}|W_{1:n})$, the features used and the Viterbi decoder.

8.2 Which of the following features are local, allowing the Viterbi algorithm to be used to find $\hat{T}_{1:n} = \arg\max_{T_{1:n}} \vec{\theta} \cdot \vec{\phi}(T_{1:n}, W_{1:n})$ given a $W_{1:n}$?

(a) $t_{i-3}t_i$

(b) $\textsc{Len}(W_{1:n})t_i$

(c) $t_1 t_{i-1}$

(d) $t_i t_n$

(e) $t_1 t_n$

(f) $\textsc{Suffix}(t_i)\textsc{Prefix}(t_{i-2})$

8.3 Consider the features for POS tagging in Table 8.1.

(a) Can the feature vector be written as $\phi(t_i, t_{i-1}, w_{i-1}, w_i, w_{i+1})$?

(b) Why is t_i involved in each feature template?

(c) If w_1 and w_n are also used for some additional templates, will efficient training or decoding of CRF models be affected?

(d) If t_1 and t_n are used for additional feature templates, will efficient training or decoding of CRF be affected?

(e) Are the feature instances sensitive to the value of i? (For example, if both $w_1 t_1$ and $w_3 t_3$ are "the|DT", will they instantiate to two different feature instances or one feature instance two times?) Consider the case for both MEMMs and CRFs.

(f) Are Markov assumptions necessary for perceptrons and SVMs for sequence labelling tasks, as they are for CRFs?

(g) Derive a forward–backward algorithm that calculates $P(t_i, t_{i+1}|W_{1:n})$ given a first-order CRF model $\vec{\theta}$.

8.4 Derive the forward and backward algorithms for calculating $P(t_i = t|W_{1:n})$ given a second-order CRF model.

Table 8.4 Correlation between different models.

Task	Model		
	Log-linear model	Perception	SVM
Classification	Logistic regression		
Sequence labelling			

8.5 Consider the task of semantic role labelling (SRL) discussed in Chapter 1. If a predicate is given, cast the problem into sequence labelling. Table 8.1 defines a set of features for POS tagging. Can these features be useful for SRL? Are there other useful features for SRL? If a syntax tree is given for the input sentence, what features can be useful for SRL? Do they affect decoding efficiency?

8.6 Generative sequence labelling models such as HMM turn out not to be extremely useful for supervised word segmentation, giving significantly lower results compared with CRF. What is the main reason for their lower accuracies?

8.7 Complete Table 8.4 by using (a)–(e).

(a) CRF   (d) Naïve Bayes
(b) Standard Perceptron   (e) HMM
(c) Standard SVM

8.8 Compare CRFs and structured perceptrons for sequence labelling. What are their relative advantages, in terms of output scores, training speed, decoding speed and freedom in defining rich features?

9   Sequence Segmentation

We have seen generative models and discriminative models for sequence labelling. The task is different from classification in that labels in a sequence can be inherently correlated with each other, forming a structure. Structured prediction is different from classification due to exponential search spaces – we need to consider both training, which is to learn a model that assigns higher scores to more correct candidate outputs, and decoding, which is to find the highest-scored output candidate given an input. In this chapter and the next chapter, we will see how training and decoding are handled for more structures. In particular, we start with sequence segmentation in this chapter, which breaks a sequence into segments. Examples include word segmentation, noun phrase chunking and named entity recognition.

Sequence segmentation is closely related to sequence labelling in the sense that segmentation information can be represented by segmentation labels such as "separate" and "attach" on each input unit. As a result, sequence labelling methods can be applied to solve sequence segmentation tasks. One drawback of such solutions, however, is that Markov assumptions over label sequences make it difficult to make use of explicit segment-level features. For example, in addition to features over k consecutive words, information about full phrases with more than k words can be useful for noun phrase chunking. To allow segment-level features, we discuss specific training and decoding algorithms using dynamic programming. In addition, as a useful alternative choice to exact inference, we discuss perceptron and a beam-search framework for structured prediction, which allows even richer features without locality constraints.

9.1   Segmentation by Sequence Labelling

Sequence segmentation tasks take an input sequence and output *segment* sequences, where each segment is a sub sequence in the input. As shown in Table 9.1, example sequence segmentation tasks in NLP include *word segmentation*, *syntactic chunking* and *named entity recognition* (NER). In particular, for word segmentation, the input is a character sequence and the output is a word sequence. For syntactic chunking, the input is a word sequence and the output is a sequence of syntactic phrases. For named entity recognition, the input is a word sequence and the output can include both named entity chunks and words that do not belong to entities.

Sequence segmentation tasks can be mapped into sequence labelling tasks by representing segmentation information using segmentation labels. Take word segmentation for example, each input character is either separated from or attached to its predecessor in the output word sequence. As a result, two segmentation labels S (separate) and A (attach) can be assigned to each input

Table 9.1 Examples of sequence segmentation tasks.

Word segmentation	Input	那几年，南京市里面和米很贵
	Output	那 (Those) 几 (few) 年 (years) , 南京市 (Nanjing City) 里 (in) 面 (flour) 和 (and) 米 (rice) 很 (very) 贵 (expensive)
	Labels	S S S S B I E S S S S S S
Syntactic chunking	Input	*Mary went to Chicago to meet her boyfriend John Smith*
	Output	[*Mary*]$_{\text{NP}}$ [*went*]$_{\text{VP}}$ [*to*]$_{\text{PP}}$ [*Chicago*]$_{\text{NP}}$ [*to*]$_{\text{PP}}$ [*meet*]$_{\text{VP}}$ [*her boyfriend John Smith*]$_{\text{NP}}$.
	Labels	B-NP B-VP B-PP B-NP B-PP B-VP B-NP I-NP I-NP I-NP
Named entity recognition	Input	*Mary went to Chicago to meet her boyfriend John Smith*
	Output	[*Mary*]$_{\text{PER}}$ went to [*Chicago*]$_{\text{LOC}}$ to meet her boyfriend [*John Smith*]$_{\text{PER}}$
	Labels	B-PER O O B-LOC O O O O B-PER I-PER

character, representing that the character is separated from or attached to its preceding character, respectively. In practice, a more expressive label set is typically used, which consists of the
labels *B, I, E* and *S*, indicating the *b*eginning, *i*nternal and *e*nding of a multi-character word, and a
*s*ingle-character word, respectively. One example is shown in Table 9.1. This richer label set can
lead to more expressive features compared to the simple 2-label set, resulting in higher empirical
performance.

For syntactic chunking, a $\{B, I\}$ segmentation label set is typically adopted, which indicate
the *b*eginning and *i*nternal (non-beginning) of a syntactic phrase, respectively. A salient difference between chunking and word segmentation, as shown in Table 9.1, is that syntactic categories
are typically assigned to phrases in chunking tasks. As a result, for representing labelled segment sequences, a combination of segmentation labels and syntactic category labels is necessary,
resulting in labels such as *B-VP* or *I-NP*.

For NER, a $\{B, I, O\}$ label set is typically adopted, where the tags indicate the *b*eginning and
*i*nternal (non-beginning) of a named entity chunk, and a non-named-entity word, respectively.
Similar to the case of syntactic chunking, named entities can take category labels, such as PER
(person), LOC (location) and ORG (organisation). Hence a combination of segmentation and category labels can be used, as shown in Table 9.1. The label set $\{B, I, E, S\}$ for segmentation can
also be used for the NER task, resulting in a set $\{B\text{-}X, I, E, S\text{-}X, O\}$, where X indicates the type
of entity. This richer set of segmentation labels has been shown to outperform the *BIO* label set
empirically on several benchmarks.

Task characteristics. Discriminative sequence labellers such as CRFs and structured perceptrons can be used for all the tasks above. One thing to note is that given a segmentation label set,
some label transitions are illegal. Take the *BIES* tagset for example. When the previous label is *B*,
the current label cannot be *B* or *S*, since we cannot begin a second segment without finishing the

first segment. Similarly, when the previous label is E, the current label cannot be I and E. Such constraints can be added to the sequence labeller as hard constraints, so that the search space is not artificially enlarged with meaningless tag sequences. A salient difference when building models for different tasks is the definition of feature templates, which reflects the sources of information that are the most specific and empirically the most useful for each task. We discuss commonly used features in the next sections.

9.1.1 Sequence Labelling Features for Word Segmentation

Table 9.2 shows a set of typical feature templates for Chinese word segmentation using character-sequence labelling. Here c_i represents the ith character in the input sequence, PUNC returns whether a character is a punctuation or not, and TYPE returns the category of a character among four predefined character classes, such as numbers, date time indicators ("年" (year), "月" (month), "日" (day) "时" (hour) "分" (minute) and "秒" (second)), English letters and other types of characters. Given the sentence in Table 9.1, the feature template 4 ($c_{i-1}c_ic_{i+1}$) corresponds to the character trigram "那几年" when $i = 2$.

Each feature template in the table is paired with a set of tag feature templates during instantiation, which can include tag unigrams t_i, tag bigrams $t_{i-1}t_i$ and tag trigrams $t_{i-2}t_{i-1}t_i$. For example, the feature template 4 is expanded into $c_{i-1}c_ic_{i+1}t_i$, $c_{i-1}c_ic_{i+1}t_{i-1}t_i$ and $c_{i-1}c_ic_{i+1}t_{i-1}t_{i-1}t_i$ during instantiation, resulting in three feature instances "$c_{i-1}c_ic_{i+1} = $ 那几年, $t_i = S$", "$c_{i-1}c_ic_{i+1} = $ 那几年, $t_{i-1} = S, t_i = S$" and "$c_{i-1}c_ic_{i+1} = $ 那几年, $t_{i-2} = \langle B \rangle, t_{i-1} = S, t_i = S$" when $i = 2$, respectively, for the sentence in Table 9.1. In addition, the tag n-gram features t_i, $t_{i-1}t_i$ and $t_{i-2}t_{i-1}t_i$ can also be used alone, without being combined with the templates in Table 9.2.

In summary, there are 6×3 (Table 9.2 + tag) $+3$ (tag alone) $= 21$ feature templates. Intuitively, they provide complementary sources of information for segmentation disambiguation. For example, character bigram features give more specific information compared with character unigram features. The feature instance "$c_{i-1}c_i = $ 里面($inside$), $t_i = E$" can be a highly indicative source of information for the word "里面" (inside). The character trigram features $c_{i-1}c_ic_{i+1}$ are more specific but more sparse, and the feature template $c_{i-1}c_{i+1}$ can be seen as a back-off version of the trigram feature. In this light, punctuation and character type features can be viewed as less sparse alternatives to character information that are highly relevant to word segmentation.

Formally, given an input $C_{1:n} = c_1c_2 \ldots c_n$ with an output label sequence $T_{1:n} = t_1, t_2 \ldots t_n$, the global feature vector $\vec{\phi}(C_{1:n}, T_{1:n})$ for the input–output pair is obtained as the sum of local feature vectors $\vec{\phi}(C_{1:n}, T_{1:n}, i)$ over all $i \in [1, \ldots, n]$:

$$\vec{\phi}(C_{1:n}, T_{1:n}) = \sum_{i=1}^{n} \vec{\phi}(C_{1:n}, T_{1:n}, i), \tag{9.1}$$

where $\vec{\phi}(C_{1:n}, T_{1:n}, i)$ is defined by instantiating the 21 word-tag mixed feature templates for the ith tag.

In practice, feature engineering is necessary to find the most useful feature templates empirically for a given dataset. For the best performance, some features in Table 9.2 may not be included,

Table 9.2 Features for character-tagging-based Chinese word segmentation.

ID	Feature template	ID	Feature template
1	c_{i-1}, c_i, c_{i+1}	4	$c_{i-1}c_ic_{i+1}$
2	$c_{i-1}c_i, c_ic_{i+1}$	5	$\text{PUNC}(c_i)$
3	$c_{i-1}c_{i+1}$	6	$\text{TYPE}(c_{i-1})\text{TYPE}(c_i)\text{TYPE}(c_{i+1})$

Table 9.3 Features for sequence-labelling-based chunking.

ID	Feature template	ID	Feature template
1	$w_{i-2}, w_{i-1}, w_i, w_{i+1}, w_{i+2}$	4	$p_{i-1}p_i, p_ip_{i+1}, p_{i-1}p_{i+1}$
2	$p_{i-2}, p_{i-1}, p_i, p_{i+1}, p_{i+2}$	5	$w_{i-1}p_{i-1}, w_ip_i, w_{i+1}p_{i+1}$
3	$w_{i-1}w_i, w_iw_{i+1}, w_{i-1}w_{i+1}$		

and additional feature templates may be defined. For example, tone features (there are four pronunciation tones in Chinese), repetition features (whether $c_{i-1} = c_i$) and radical features (e.g., "火" (fire) for "烧" (heat); "扌" (hand) for "打" (beat)) can be added to the feature table. Note that such features can be challenging for generative sequence labelling models such as HMM, since they contain overlapping information with character features. Therefore, discriminative models are the dominant approach for Chinese word segmentation.

9.1.2 Sequence Labelling Features for Syntactic Chunking

Most work on syntactic chunking assumes that POS-tagging is performed as a pre-processing task, because POS-tag features are useful for chunking disambiguation. Table 9.3 shows a typical set of feature templates for syntactic chunking. Here w_i indicates the ith input word, p_i indicates the POS-tag of the ith word, and t_i indicates the ith output segmentation label. The feature templates consist of word and POS-tag features in the 5-word window and word bigram features in the 3-word window. Similar to segmentation, output tag features t_i and tag-tag transition features $t_{i-1}t_i$ are combined with each feature template in Table 9.3 and also used alone. For example, when the previous chunking label is I-VP, the probability of the next label being I-VP or B-NP can be relatively higher.

9.1.3 Sequence Labelling Features for NER

NER also takes POS-tagging as a pre-processing task, so that POS features can be used. A set of useful feature templates for NER is shown in Table 9.4, where each feature template can be combined with output label n-grams such as t_i, $t_{i-1}t_i$ and $t_{i-1}t_{i-1}t_i$. The feature templates consist of words in a context window, their POS, as well as their morphological features such as prefixes, suffixes, cases and hyphens. We have seen similar features for POS-tagging in Chapter 8 and syntactic chunking in the previous section. For NER, two types of features that are worth mentioning include *word shape* features and *gazetteer* features.

Table 9.4 Features for sequence-labelling-based NER.

ID	Feature template
1	$w_{i-2}, w_{i-1}, w_i, w_{i+1}, w_{i+2}$
2	$p_{i-2}, p_{i-1}, p_i, p_{i+1}, p_{i+2}$
3	PREFIX(w_i), SUFFIX(w_i)
4	CASE(w_i)
5	HYPHEN(w_i)
6	SHAPE(w_{i-2}), SHAPE(w_{i-1}), SHAPE(w_i), SHAPE(w_{i+1}), SHAPE(w_{i+2})
7	SHORTSHAPE(w_{i-2}), SHORTSHAPE(w_{i-1}), SHORTSHAPE(w_i), SHORTSHAPE(w_{i+1}), SHORTSHAPE(w_{i+1})
8	GAZETTEER(w_i)

Word shape. Hyphen features indicate whether a word contains a hyphen or not. A hyphen can sometimes be a useful clue of composite entities such as "*Semi-CRF*", "*ACL-2009*" and "*GM-CSF promoter*". Upper case, lower case and symbol combination also play a crucial role in NER. Relevant shape features can be obtained by replacing upper case letters in word forms with 'X', lower case letters with 'x' and numerical digits with 'd', leaving all punctuations (such as '-') unchanged. They offer a less sparse representation of word forms. For example, SHAPE(w_i = "*ELMo*") = "XXXx". A short shape further compresses consecutive occurrences of the same letter type into a single one, thereby further reducing sparsity. Word shape features play a similar role to character type features for word segmentation.

Gazetteer features indicate whether the current word exists in a certain gazetteer. Here, a gazetteer refers to a list of known person names, geolocation names, organisation names etc. Such features are particularly useful for named entity recognition, especially for restricted domains. In Table 9.4 GAZETTEER(w_i) can represent the index of a particular gazetteer that w_i exists in, if gazetteers of different named entity types are used.

9.1.4 Evaluating Sequence Segmentation Outputs

The output of sequence segmentation can be formulated as a set of tuples $\{(b_i, e_i, l_i)\}$, where b_i, e_i and l_i represent the beginning index, end index and label (if applicable) of a segment, respectively. For example, the gold NER output for the sentence "*John visited Las Vegas*" can be $\{(1, 1, PER), (3, 4, LOC)\}$, where $(1, 1, PER)$ represents "*John*" and $(3, 4, LOC)$ represents "*Las Vegas*". For word segmentation, labels can be ignored.

Given a gold output S_g and a system output S, we can find a common subset of segments $S_m = S_g \cap S$. If the system output is incorrect, there may be segments in S_g that are not in S_m, and also segments in S that are not in S_m. We use **precision** to denote the percentage of segments in S that are correct:

$$P = \frac{S_m}{S}$$

and **recall** to denote the percentage of gold segments that are predicted:

$$R = \frac{S_m}{S_g}.$$

The **F-score** can be used for evaluating segmentation, which combines information on precision and recall:

$$F = \frac{2PR}{P + R}.$$

Intuitively, when the precision and recall are both 1, $F = 1$, which indicates a correct output. On the other hand, when either the precision or the recall is low, the F value decreases. Our F-score gives a balanced combination of precision and recall scores, without biasing towards either. It is also denoted as $F1$ in the literature.

9.2 Discriminative Models for Sequence Segmentation

As we have seen in Chapter 8, sequence labelling models make Markov assumptions over output label sequences for efficient decoding and training. Take Chinese word segmentation for example. A second-order Markov model allows features to be defined over three consecutive segmentation labels. However, such features cannot represent full words with more than three characters. As a result, useful features such as

$$\text{``} w_{i-1} = 萧规曹随 \text{ (to follow convention)}, t_i = B\text{''}$$

cannot be directly included. Similarly, for chunking and NER tasks, full segment features can be useful, which cannot be directly used by Markov-chain sequence labelling models.

To address this issue, we can model sequence segmentation by working with its output structure directly, building discriminative structured predictors that make use of segment-level features. Such models can be regarded as alternatives to discriminative sequence labellers with different output structures. As a result, structured prediction techniques discussed in Chapters 7 and 8 can be applied, but with different structural features and correspondingly different decoding and training algorithms. In particular, dynamic programs can be developed for finding the highest-scored outputs and for training log-linear models when the feature context is constrained to a fixed number of k consecutive segments.

This section discusses discriminative linear models for sequence segmentation using Chinese word segmentation as a running example. We start with feature definitions over segmented output structures, before moving to the model scoring function and decoding. Then we introduce different training algorithms for the discriminative model, including log-linear model training and large-margin training. The log-linear model is referred to as **semi-Markov CRF** (semi-CRF), due to its correlation with CRF models.

For word segmentation, the input units are characters and the output units are words. As a result, we use $C_{1:n} = c_1 c_2 \ldots c_n$ to represent the input and $W_{1:|W|} = w_1 w_2 \ldots w_{|W|}$ to represent the output throughout this section, without losing generality. For the next section, we switch to notation with word inputs and chunk outputs.

9.2.1 Word-Level Features for Word Segmentation

To model output structures directly, we want to extract features in the word level for segmentation. In particular, suppose that features are defined within two consecutive words, or a word bigram, over a segmented output. Given an input sentence $C_{1:n}$ and a segmented output $W_{1:|W|}$, we denote $w_j = c_{b(j)}c_{b(j)+1}\dots c_{e(j)}$, where $b(j)$ and $e(j)$ denote the character indices for the first and last characters in the word w_j, respectively. For example, given the sentence $C_{1:7}$="以前天下雨为例" (take the rain on the day before yesterday for example), there are seven input characters, with c_1 ="以" (take), c_2 ="前" (before) and c_7 ="例" (example). The correct output segmentation is the word sequence "以 (take) 前天 (the day before yesterday) 下雨 (rain) 为例 (for example)". There are four words in the output, where w_1 ="以" (take), w_2 ="前天" (the day before yesterday), w_3 ="下雨" (rain) and w_4 ="为例" (for example). Here $b(1) = 1$, $e(1) = 1$, $b(3) = 4$ and $e(3) = 5$. One incorrect segmentation is "以前 (before) 天下 (world) 雨 (rain) 为例 (for example)". There are four words in the output, where w_1 ="以前" (before), w_2 ="天下" (world), w_3 ="雨" (rain) and w_4 ="为例" (for example). Here $b(1) = 1$, $e(1) = 2$, $b(3) = 5$ and $e(3) = 5$.

For the input and output pair $(C_{1:n}, W_{1:|W|})$, a global feature vector $\vec{\phi}(W_{1:|W|})$ can be extracted by accumulating local features $\vec{\phi}(w_{j-1}, w_j)$ over all word bigrams $w_{j-1}w_j$:

$$\vec{\phi}(W_{1:|W|}) = \sum_{j=2}^{|W|} \vec{\phi}(w_{j-1}, w_j).$$

The same local feature vector $\vec{\phi}(w_{j-1}, w_j)$ can also be denoted using character indices as $\vec{\phi}_c(C_{1:n}, b(j-1), e(j-1), e(j))$. For example, in the output sentence "以 前天 下雨 为例" above, the local feature vector over "前天 下雨" can be denoted as $\vec{\phi}$("前天", "下雨") directly, or $\vec{\phi}_c$("以前天下雨为例", 2, 3, 5) using character indices over the input.

To better model the beginning and end of a sentence, we can additionally set $w_0 = \langle s \rangle$, thereby allowing special feature instances to be extracted for $\vec{\phi}(w_0, w_1)$ at the beginning.

Given the above notation, Table 9.5 shows a set of word-based feature templates for the local context above. Here $\text{LEN}(w_j)$ represents the number of characters in w_j, and $b(j)$ and $e(j)$ follow their meaning as mentioned before. This set of feature templates can be seen as a combination of the word bigram $w_{i-1}w_i$ and its various back-off forms. For example, the first character of a word and the length of a word can both be viewed as a less sparse representation of the word itself. A contrast between Table 9.5 and Table 9.2 earlier suggests that word-based features can be substantially different from character sequence labelling features for word segmentation, taking different sources of information.

As mentioned earlier, different from word segmentation, for chunking tasks and NER, output segments can have category labels. In addition, POS information can be taken as an additional source of features. Exercise 9.3 discusses possible feature templates for these tasks.

Table 9.5 Feature templates for word-based Chinese word segmentation.

ID	Feature template	ID	Feature template
1	word w_j	8	$c_{b(j)}c_{e(j)}$
2	word bigram $w_{j-1}w_j$	9	$w_j c_{e(j)+1}$
3	whether w_j is a single-character word, $\textsc{single}(w_j)$	10	$w_j c_{e(j-1)}$
4	$c_{b(j)}\textsc{len}(w_j)$	11	$c_{b(j-1)}c_{b(j)}$
5	$c_{e(j)}\textsc{len}(w_j)$	12	$c_{e(j-1)}c_{e(j)}$
6	space-separated characters, $c_{e(j-1)}c_{b(j)}$	13	$w_j\textsc{len}(w_{j-1})$
7	character bigram in w_j	14	$w_{j-1}\textsc{len}(w_j)$

9.2.2 Exact Search Decoding Using Dynamic Program

Model. Similar to the previous chapters, we use a discriminative linear model to score different segmentation outputs $W_{1:|W|}$ given an input $C_{1:n}$, according to the feature representation $\vec{\phi}(W)$. Denoting the model parameter vector as $\vec{\theta}$, we have

$$score(W) = \vec{\theta} \cdot \vec{\phi}(W).$$

For both log-linear models and large-margin models, the goal of decoding is the same, namely to find the highest-scored output $\hat{W}$ according to a given model $\vec{\theta}$:

$$\hat{W} = \arg\max_{W} \vec{\theta} \cdot \vec{\phi}(W).$$

Still assuming that features are extracted from word bigram context windows, the discriminative model score of a given output $W_{1:|W|}$ can be calculated incrementally, where

$$
\begin{aligned}
\vec{\theta} \cdot \vec{\phi}(W_{1:|W|}) &= \vec{\theta} \cdot \left(\sum_{j=2}^{|W|} \vec{\phi}(w_{j-1}, w_j) \right) \\
&= \sum_{j=2}^{|W|} \vec{\theta} \cdot \vec{\phi}(w_{j-1}, w_j) \\
&= \sum_{j=2}^{|W|} \vec{\theta} \cdot \vec{\phi}_c(C_{1:n}, b(j-1), e(j-1), e(j)).
\end{aligned}
\tag{9.2}
$$

Using $W(b, e)$ to denote an output sequence with the last word being $C_{b:e} = c_b c_{b+1} \ldots c_e$ ($b \leq e$), we have the following score correlation between two subsequences $W(b, e)$ and $W(b', b - 1)$ ($b' < b \leq e$) that differ by one word $C_{b:e}$:

$$score(W(b, e)) = score\big(W(b', b - 1)\big) + \vec{\theta} \cdot \vec{\phi}_c(C_{1:n}, b', b - 1, e).$$

The incremental nature of the score calculation above results in the availability of optimal sub problems. In particular, use $\hat{W}(b, e)$ to denote the highest-scored partial output with the last word being $C_{b:e}$. Further denote the second last word in $\hat{W}(b, e)$ as $C_{\hat{b}':b-1}$. We have that the subsequence

---

Algorithm 9.1. Dynamic programming decoder for sequence segmentation.

Input: Sequence $C_{1:n} = c_1 c_2 \ldots c_n$, model parameters $\vec{\theta}$;
Initialisation:
for $e \in [1, \ldots, n]$ **do**
$\quad$ **for** $b \in [1, \ldots, e]$ **do**
$\quad\quad$ $table[b, e] \leftarrow -\infty$;
$\quad\quad$ $bp[b, e] \leftarrow -1$;
$\quad$ $table[1, e] \leftarrow \vec{\theta} \cdot \vec{\phi}_c(C_{1:n}, 0, 0, e)$;
Algorithm:
for $e \in [2, \ldots, n]$ **do**
$\quad$ **for** $b \in [2, \ldots, e]$ **do**
$\quad\quad$ **for** $b' \in [1, \ldots, b-1]$ **do**
$\quad\quad\quad$ **if** $table[b', b-1] + \vec{\theta} \cdot \vec{\phi}_c(C_{1:n}, b', b-1, e) > table[b, e]$ **then**
$\quad\quad\quad\quad$ $table[b, e] \leftarrow table[b', b-1] + \vec{\theta} \cdot \vec{\phi}_c(C_{1:n}, b', b-1, e)$;
$\quad\quad\quad\quad$ $bp[b, e] \leftarrow b'$;
$max\_score \leftarrow \max_{b' \in [1, \ldots, n]} table[b', n]$; $W_{1:|W|} \leftarrow$ backtrace with bp;
Output: Segmented sequence $W_{1:|W|} = w_1 w_2 \ldots w_{|W|}$;

$\hat{W}(\hat{b}', b-1)$ in $\hat{W}(b, e)$ has the highest score among all possible output subsequences that ends with $C_{\hat{b}':b-1}$, denoted as $W(\hat{b}', b-1)$. A proof is straightforward by contradiction.

According to the equation, we can incrementally build a table that stores the scores of $\hat{W}(b, e)$ for all valid b and e

$$score(\hat{W}(b, e)) = \underset{1 \leq b' \leq b-1}{\arg\max} \left(score(\hat{W}(b', b-1)) + \vec{\theta} \cdot \vec{\phi}_c(C_{1:n}, b', b-1, e) \right). \qquad (9.3)$$

The final highest-scored output is then

$$\hat{W} = \underset{b \in [1, \ldots, n]}{\arg\max} \, score(\hat{W}(b, n)).$$

Pseudocode of this algorithm is shown in Algorithm 9.1. Two table structures are used, where $table[b, e]$ is used to hold $score(\hat{W}(b, e))$, and $bp[b, e]$ is used to hold the backtracing pointer

$$\underset{b' \in [1, \ldots, b-1]}{\arg\max} \, score(\hat{W}(b', b-1)) + \vec{\theta} \cdot \vec{\phi}_c(C_{1:n}, b', b-1, e).$$

The algorithm initiates $table[1, e]$ ($e \in [1, \ldots, n]$) with boundary features $\vec{\phi}_c(C_{1:n}, 0, 0, e)$, where $c_0 = \langle s \rangle$, and then incrementally builds the table by enumerating b and e from 2 to n. Finally, the highest output score is found by enumerating $b \in [1, \ldots, n]$ and finding the highest scored $table[b, n]$. The segmented sequence $W_{1:|W|}$ with the highest score can then be found by backtracking using bp (Exercise 9.4).

The complexity of Algorithm 9.1 is $O(n^3)$, due to the enumeration of e, b and b'. This decoder is significantly slower compared with the Viterbi decoding algorithm for sequence labelling in

Algorithm 8.1 in Chapter 8, which is linear to the input size. One way to reduce the complexity is to force a maximum word size M, which can be decided empirically according to a set of training data (Exercise 9.4). It gives linear time complexity to a modified version of Algorithm 9.1. On the other hand, it also imposes a hard limitation in that the algorithm cannot predict words that are longer than M characters, which can exist there in unseen test sentences.

The next two sections discuss training methods for the model. Following sequence labelling in the previous chapter, we consider both log-likelihood (Section 9.2.3) and large-margin (Section 9.2.4) training objectives for the discriminative linear model.

9.2.3 Semi-Markov Conditional Random Fields

This section discusses semi-CRF, a log-linear model for sequence segmentation. Similar to log-linear models for classification tasks and sequence labelling, semi-CRF scores output structures using their conditional probabilities. In particular, given a pair of input and output $(C_{1:n}, W_{1:|W|})$, the conditional probability $P(W|C)$ is calculated as

$$P(W|C) = \frac{\exp\left(\vec{\theta} \cdot \vec{\phi}(W)\right)}{\sum_{W' \in \text{GEN}(C)} \exp\left(\vec{\theta} \cdot \vec{\phi}(W')\right)},$$

where $\text{GEN}(C)$ denotes the set of all possible segmented outputs for C. This form of conditional probability computation is identical to log-linear classifiers discussed in Chapter 4 and CRFs discussed in Chapter 8. However, due to difference in the nature of output structures and consequently feature context ranges, specific dynamic programs should be designed. We begin with the computation of marginal probabilities for segments, which is useful for the training process.

Calculating marginal probabilities. Calculating the probability of a certain segment in sequence segmentation is analogous to the calculation of marginal label probabilities in sequence labelling. Still using word segmentation as an example, given an input $C_{1:n}$, denote the probability of $C_{b:e} = c_b c_{b+1} \ldots c_e$ being a word as $P(\text{IsWORD}(C_{b:e})|C_{1:n})$, where $\text{IsWORD}(C_{b:e})$ indicates that $C_{b:e}$ is a word in the output.

This marginal probability can be calculated by summing up segment sequence probabilities $P(W_{1:|W|}|C_{1:n})$. Formally, denote all possible segmentations of a character sequence $C_{1:n}$ as $\text{GEN}(C_{1:n})$. The marginal probability $P(\text{IsWORD}(C_{b:e})|C_{1:n})$ can be calculated as

$$P(\text{IsWORD}(C_{b:e})|C_{1:n}) = \sum_{W \in \text{GEN}(C_{1:n}) \text{ such that } C_{b:e} \in W} P(W|C_{1:n}) \tag{9.4}$$

Here $\left(W \in \text{GEN}(C_{1:n}) \text{ such that } C_{b:e} \in W\right)$ denotes all possible segmentations of $C_{1:n}$ that contain the word $C_{b:e}$.

Equation 9.4 contains an exponential number of summations, the naïve implementation of which is intractable. However, under our previous assumption that features are local to word bigrams, we can calculate the sum in polynomial time by exploiting dynamic programming. In particular, given a semi-CRF model $\vec{\theta}$, we have:

$$
\begin{aligned}
P(W|C_{1:n}) &= \frac{\exp\left(\vec{\theta} \cdot \vec{\phi}(W)\right)}{Z} \\
&= \frac{\exp\left(\vec{\theta} \cdot \left(\sum_j \vec{\phi}(w_{j-1}, w_j)\right)\right)}{Z} \\
&= \frac{\prod_j \exp\left(\vec{\theta} \cdot \vec{\phi}(w_{j-1}, w_j)\right)}{Z},
\end{aligned}
\tag{9.5}
$$

where Z is the partition function $\sum_W \exp\left(\vec{\theta} \cdot \vec{\phi}(W)\right)$.

According to Eq 9.4 and Eq 9.5, we have

$$
\begin{aligned}
P(\text{IsWord}(C_{b:e})|C_{1:n}) &= \sum_{W \in \text{Gen}(C_{1:n}) \text{ such that } C_{b:e} \in W} \left(\frac{1}{Z} \prod_{j=1}^{|W|} \exp\left(\vec{\theta} \cdot \vec{\phi}(w_{j-1}, w_j)\right)\right) \\
&= \frac{1}{Z}\left(\sum_{W^l \in \text{Gen}(C_{1:e}) \text{ such that } C_{b:e} \in W^l} \prod_{j=1}^{|W^l|} \exp\left(\vec{\theta} \cdot \vec{\phi}(w^l_{j-1}, w^l_j)\right)\right) \\
&\qquad \left(\sum_{W^r \in \text{Gen}(C_{b:n}) \text{ such that } C_{b:e} \in W^r} \prod_{j=1}^{|W^r|-1} \exp\left(\vec{\theta} \cdot \vec{\phi}(w^r_j, w^r_{j+1})\right)\right),
\end{aligned}
\tag{9.6}
$$

where $\text{Gen}(C_{b:n})$ represents all possible segmentations of the sub sequence $C1 : e = c1...ce$, and $\text{Gen}(C_{b:n})$ represents all possible segmentations to the sub sequence $c_b...c_n$. Thus $W^l = w^l_1 ... w^l_{|W^l|}$ and $W^r = w^r_1 ... w^r_{|W^r|}$ represent all possible sub sequences up to c_e and from c_b onwards, respectively. We have $w^l_{|W_l|} = w^r_1 = C_{b:e}$.

Equation 9.6 cuts the full summation into the product of two components, with the splitting point at $C_{b:e}$, which is shared by the two components. Similar to the case of CRFs, we denote them as the forward component α and the backward component β, respectively. Dynamic programming can be used to calculate the value of each component efficiently. In particular, for the forward component, denote

$$
\alpha(b', e') = \sum_{W^l \in \text{Gen}(C_{1:e'}) \text{ such that } C_{b':e'} \in W^l} \prod_{j=1}^{|W^l|} \exp\left(\vec{\theta} \cdot \vec{\phi}(w^l_{j-1}, w^l_j)\right).
\tag{9.7}
$$

$\alpha(b', e')$ can be calculated incrementally by summing up relevant values regarding $\alpha(b'', b'-1)$ for all valid b'':

$$
\alpha(b', e') = \sum_{b'' \in [1, \dots, b'-1]} \left(\alpha(b'', b'-1) \cdot \exp\left(\vec{\theta} \cdot \vec{\phi}_c(C_{1:e}, b'', b'-1, e')\right)\right),
$$

where $b' \in [1, \dots, e]$ and $e' \in [b', \dots, e]$.

Algorithm 9.2. Forward algorithm for semi-CRF model.

Inputs: $s = C_{1:e}$, semi-CRF model with feature weight vector $\vec{\theta}$;
Variables: α;
Initialisation:
for $e' \in [1, \ldots, e]$ **do**
$\quad \mid \quad \alpha[1, e'] \leftarrow \vec{\theta} \cdot \vec{\phi}_c(C_{1:e}, 0, 0, e')$;
Algorithm:
for $b' \in [2, \ldots, e]$ **do**
$\quad \mid \quad$ **for** $e \in [b', \ldots, e]$ **do**
$\quad \mid \quad \quad \mid \quad \alpha[b', e'] \leftarrow 0$;
$\quad \mid \quad \quad \mid \quad$ **for** $b'' \in [1, \ldots, b' - 1]$ **do**
$\quad \mid \quad \quad \mid \quad \quad \mid \quad \alpha[b', e'] \leftarrow \alpha[b', e'] + \alpha[b'', b' - 1] \cdot \exp\left(\vec{\theta} \cdot \vec{\phi}_c(C_{1:n}, b'', b' - 1, e')\right)$;
Output: α;

Starting from boundary values $\alpha(1, e') = \exp\left(\vec{\theta} \cdot \vec{\phi}_c(C_{1:e}, 0, 0, e')\right)$ for $e' \in [1, \ldots, e]$, Algorithm 9.2 builds a table for all $\alpha(b', e')$ where $b' \in [1, \ldots, e]$ and $e' \in [b', \ldots, e]$.

For calculating the second component in Eq 9.6, denote

$$\beta(b', e') = \sum_{W^r \in \text{GEN}(C_{b':n}) \text{ such that } C_{b':e'} \in W^r} \prod_{j=1}^{|W^r|-1} \exp\left(\vec{\theta} \cdot \vec{\phi}(w_j^r, w_{j+1}^r)\right). \tag{9.8}$$

$\beta(b', e')$ can be calculated incrementally by summing up relevant values from all $\beta(e' + 1, e'')$, where $e'' \in [e' + 1, \ldots, n]$:

$$\beta(b', e') = \sum_{e'' \in [e'+1, \ldots, n]} \left(\beta(e' + 1, e'') \cdot \exp\left(\vec{\theta} \cdot \vec{\phi}_c(C_{b:n}, b', e', e'')\right)\right),$$

where $b' \in [b, \ldots, n]$ and $e' \in [e + 1, \ldots, n]$.

Starting from boundary values $\beta(b', n) = 1$, Algorithm 9.3 draws a table from the end of the sentence backwards to calculate all $\beta(b', e')$, where $e' \in [b', \ldots, n]$ and $b' \in [b, \ldots, n]$.

After obtaining the values of $\alpha(b, e)$ and $\beta(b, e)$, $P(\text{ISWORD}(C_{b:e}|C_{1:n}))$ can be calculated as

$$\frac{1}{Z}\alpha(b, e)\beta(b, e).$$

In the above equation, $\alpha(b, e)$ corresponds to the first term and $\beta(b, e)$ corresponds to the second term in Eq 9.6. The partition function Z is the same as Eqs 9.5 and 9.6. It can be calculated using Algorithm 9.4, which is an adaptation of the decoding algorithm in Algorithm 9.1, where the maximum operator is changed to a summation operator. In the algorithm, $table[b, e]$ records $\sum_{W(b,e)} \exp\left(\vec{\theta}, \vec{\phi}(W(b, e))\right)$. Therefore, we have $table[b, e] = \sum_{b'} \left(table[b', b - 1] \cdot \exp\left(\vec{\theta} \cdot \vec{\phi}_c(C_{1:n}, b', b - 1, e)\right)\right)$. Similar to the case of CRF in Chapter 8, the logsumexp trick can be

---

Algorithm 9.3. Backward algorithm for semi-CRF model.

Inputs: $s = C_{b:n}$, semi-CRF model with feature weight vector $\vec{\theta}$;
Variables: β;
Initialisation:
for $b' \in [n, n-1, \ldots, b]$ **do**
  | $\beta[b', n] \leftarrow 1$;
Algorithm:
for $e' \in [n-1, n-2, \ldots, b]$ **do**
  | **for** $b' \in [e', e'-1, \ldots, b]$ **do**
  | | $\beta[b', e'] \leftarrow 0$;
  | | **for** $e'' \in [e'+1, \ldots, n]$ **do**
  | | | $\beta[b', e'] \leftarrow \beta[b', e'] + \beta[e'+1, e''] \cdot \exp\left(\vec{\theta} \cdot \vec{\phi}_c(C_{b:n}, b', e', e'')\right)$;
Output: β;

Algorithm 9.4. Partition function for semi-CRF model.

Inputs: $s = C_{1:n}$, semi-CRF model model and feature weight vector $\vec{\theta}$;
Initialisation:
for $e \in [1, \ldots, n]$ **do**
  | $table[1, e] \leftarrow \vec{\theta} \cdot \vec{\phi}_c(C_{1:n}, 0, 0, e)$;
Algorithm:
for $e \in [2, \ldots, n]$ **do**
  | **for** $b \in [2, \ldots, e]$ **do**
  | | $scores \leftarrow []$;
  | | **for** $b' \in [1, \ldots, b-1]$ **do**
  | | | APPEND$\left(scores, table[b', b-1] + \vec{\theta} \cdot \vec{\phi}_c(C_{1:n}, b', b-1, e)\right)$;
  | | $table[b, e] \leftarrow logsumexp(scores)$;
$Z \leftarrow \sum_{b \in [1, \ldots, n]} \exp(table[b, n])$;
Output: Z;

---

used to avoid numeric overflow, where we store $\log\left(\sum_{W(b,e)} \exp\left(\vec{\theta} \cdot \vec{\phi}(W(b,e))\right)\right)$ in $table[b, e]$ instead.

Training. Given a set of training data $D = \{(C_i, W_i)\}|_{i=1}^{N}$, where C_i is a sentence and W_i is its corresponding gold-standard segmentation, the semi-CRF training objective is to maximise the log-likelihood of D:

$$\vec{\theta} = \arg\max_{\vec{\theta}} \log P(D)$$

$$= \arg\max_{\vec{\theta}} \sum_i \log P(W_i|C_i)$$

$$= \arg\max_{\vec{\theta}} \sum_i \log \frac{\exp\left(\vec{\theta} \cdot \vec{\phi}(W_i)\right)}{\sum_{W' \in \text{GEN}(C_i)} \exp\left(\vec{\theta} \cdot \vec{\phi}(W')\right)} \tag{9.9}$$

$$= \arg\max_{\vec{\theta}} \sum_i \left(\vec{\theta} \cdot \vec{\phi}(W_i) - \log \left(\sum_{W' \in \text{GEN}(C_i)} \exp\left(\vec{\theta} \cdot \vec{\phi}(W')\right) \right) \right).$$

Similar to the training of CRF, SGD can be used for optimisation. The local training objective for each training example is to maximise

$$\vec{\theta} \cdot \vec{\phi}(W_i) - \log \left(\sum_{W' \in \text{GEN}(C_i)} \exp\left(\vec{\theta} \cdot \vec{\phi}(W')\right) \right).$$

Accordingly the local gradient over $\vec{\theta}$ is

$$\vec{\phi}(W_i) - \frac{\sum_{W' \in \text{GEN}(C_i)} \exp\left(\vec{\theta} \cdot \vec{\phi}(W')\right) \cdot \vec{\phi}(W')}{\sum_{W'' \in \text{GEN}(C_i)} \exp\left(\vec{\theta} \cdot \vec{\phi}(W'')\right)} \tag{9.10}$$

$$= \vec{\phi}(W_i) - \sum_{W' \in \text{GEN}(C_i)} P(W'|C_i)\vec{\phi}(W'), \text{ (definition of } P(W'|C_i)).$$

Equation 9.10 is structurally identical to Eq 8.10 in Chapter 8 for sequence labelling, except that the output structure is now a sequence of segments W rather than a label sequence T. Similar to sequence labelling, the major challenge in calculating Eq 9.10 lies in the second term, which involves a summation of exponential possible outputs.

Again we resort to feature locality to find a solution. The goal is to calculate $\sum_{W'} P(W'|C_i)\vec{\phi}(W')$ given a training example C_i in $D = \{(C_i, W_i)\}|_{i=1}^N$. Assuming that features are local to word bigrams, we have

$$\sum_{W'} P(W'|C_i)\vec{\phi}(W') = \sum_{W' \in \text{GEN}(C_i)} P(W'|C_i)\left(\sum_{j=1}^{|W'|} \vec{\phi}(w_{j-1}, w_j) \right)$$

$$= E_{W' \sim P(W'|C_i)}\left(\sum_{j=1}^{|W'|} \vec{\phi}(w_{j-1}, w_j) \right). \tag{9.11}$$

Equation 9.11 calculates feature expectations by enumerating all possible segmentations of C_i and then each word bigram in a given segmentation, weighing local feature vectors using the probabilities of the segmented outputs. With regard to each arbitrary possible word bigram $C_{b':b-1}C_{b:e}$, where $b' \in [1, \dots, |C_i| - 1]$, $b \in [b' + 1, \dots, |C_i|]$, $e \in [b, \dots, |C_i|]$, its local feature vector value

$\vec{\phi}_c(C_i, b', b-1, e)$ is accumulated over all possible segmentations of C_i that contain it, weighted by the segmentation probabilities:

$$E_{W' \sim P(W'|C_i)} \left(\sum_{j=1}^{|W'|} \vec{\phi}(w_{j-1}, w_j) \right)$$

$$= E_{W' \sim P(W'|C_i)} \left(\sum_{C_{b':b-1} \in W', C_{b:e} \in W'} \vec{\phi}_c(C_i, b', b-1, e) \right) \tag{9.12}$$

$$= \sum_{b', b, e} E_{C_{b':b-1} C_{b:e} \sim P(\text{IsBigram}(b', b-1, e)|C_i)} \vec{\phi}_c(C_i, b', b-1, e),$$

where $C_{b':b-1} C_{b:e}$ represents one arbitrary bigram in all possible segmentations of C_i. Equation 9.12 calculates the sum of the feature vectors $\vec{\phi}_c(C_i, b', b-1, e)$ weighted by the marginal bigram probability $P(\text{IsBigram}(b', b-1, e)|C_i)$. Here $\text{IsBigram}(b', b-1, e) = \text{IsWord}(b', b-1)$ and $\text{IsWord}(b, e)$ returns a Boolean value whether $C_{b':b-1} C_{b:e}$ is a word bigram.

Thus the task boils down to the calculation of the marginal probabilities $P(\text{IsBigram}(b', b-1, e)|C_i)$ efficiently for all valid values of b', b and e, after which the summation in Eq 9.12 can be achieved by enumerating over all bigrams, which takes $O(|C_i|^3)$ or $O(M^2|C_i|)$ if the maximum word size is restricted to M characters.

Similar to earlier in this section, the marginal probability can be calculated leveraging feature locality. In particular, according to the definition of $P(W|C_{1:n})$ in Eq 9.5, we have

$$P(\text{IsBigram}(b', b-1, e)|C_i)$$

$$= \sum_{W \in \text{Gen}(C_i),\ \text{such that } C_{b':b-1} \in W, C_{b:e} \in W} \frac{1}{Z} \prod_{j=1}^{|W|} \exp\left(\vec{\theta} \cdot \vec{\phi}(w_{j-1}, w_j) \right)$$

$$= \frac{1}{Z} \left(\sum_{W^l \in \text{Gen}(C_{1:b-1}),\ \text{such that } C_{b':b-1} \in W^l} \prod_{j=1}^{|W^l|} \exp\left(\vec{\theta} \cdot \vec{\phi}(w^l_{j-1}, w^l_j) \right) \right) \tag{9.13}$$

$$\left(\sum_{W^r \in \text{Gen}(C_{b:n}),\ \text{such that } C_{b:e} \in W^r} \prod_{j=1}^{|W^r|-1} \exp\left(\vec{\theta} \cdot \vec{\phi}(w^r_j, w^r_{j+1}) \right) \right),$$

where Z is the partition function as defined in Eq 9.5, which can be estimated efficiently using Algorithm 9.4.

Equation 9.13 can be computed efficiently using the same technique as Eq 9.6, with $\alpha(b', e')$ being defined exactly the same as in Eq 9.7 and $\beta(b', e')$ being defined exactly the same as in Eq 9.8. The same forward and backward algorithms in Algorithm 9.2 and Algorithm 9.3 can be used to find all values of $\alpha(b', e')$ and $\beta(b', e')$, respectively. After obtaining their values, the values of $P(\text{IsBigram}(b', b-1, e)|C_i)$ can be calculated as

$$P(\text{IsBigram}(b', b-1, e)|C_i) = \frac{\alpha(b', b-1)\beta(b, e) \exp\left(\vec{\theta} \cdot \vec{\phi}_c(C_i, b', b-1, e) \right)}{Z}.$$

Algorithm 9.5 shows pseudocode of the algorithm.

Algorithm 9.5. Forward backward algorithm for training semi-CRF.

Inputs: $s = C_{1:n}$, semi-CRF model with feature weight vector $\vec{\theta}$;
Variables: $table, \alpha, \beta$;
$\alpha \leftarrow \text{FORWARD}(C_{1:n}, \vec{\phi}, \vec{\theta})$ using Algorithm 9.2;
$\beta \leftarrow \text{BACKWARD}(C_{1:n}, \vec{\phi}, \vec{\theta})$ using Algorithm 9.3;
$Z \leftarrow \text{PARTITION}(C_{1:n}, \vec{\phi}, \vec{\theta})$ using Algorithm 9.4;
for $b \in [1, \ldots, n]$ **do**
    for $e \in [b, \ldots, n]$ **do**
        for $b' \in [1, \ldots, b-1]$ **do**
            $table[b'][b-1][e] \leftarrow \alpha[b'][b-1] \cdot \beta[b][e] \cdot \exp\left(\vec{\theta} \cdot \vec{\phi}_c(C_{1:n}, b', b-1, e)\right)/Z$;
Output: $table$;

9.2.4 Large-Margin Models

Large-margin discriminative models for sequence segmentation work largely the same as those for sequence labelling. Given an input $C_{1:n}$, structured perceptrons and structured SVMs map different $W \in \text{GEN}(C)$ in the feature space $\vec{\phi}(W)$, scoring each W with

$$score(W) = \vec{\theta} \cdot \vec{\phi}(W).$$

For both structured models, the training goal is to ensure a score margin between gold-standard training examples and non-gold outputs, given a set of training data $D = \{(C_i, W_i)\}|_{i=1}^{N}$. For structured perceptron, the training objective is to minimise

$$\sum_{i=1}^{N} \max\left(0, \max_{W'}\left(\vec{\theta} \cdot \vec{\phi}(W')\right) - \vec{\theta} \cdot \vec{\phi}(W_i)\right). \tag{9.14}$$

For structured SVM, the training objective is to minimise

$$\frac{1}{2}||\vec{\theta}||^2 + C\left(\sum_{i=1}^{N} \max\left(0, 1 - \vec{\theta} \cdot \vec{\phi}(W_i) + \max_{W' \neq W_i}\left(\vec{\theta} \cdot \vec{\phi}(W')\right)\right)\right). \tag{9.15}$$

In both Eq 9.14 and Eq 9.15 above, calculating $\max_{W'}\left(\vec{\theta} \cdot \vec{\phi}(W')\right)$ requires the decoding process for finding the most violated score constraints. Similar to sequence labelling, such decoding processes for perceptrons and SVM models are the same as for log-linear models, as shown in Algorithm 9.1. Compared with Eq 8.20 and Eq 8.22 for sequence labelling, respectively, the only difference in Eq 9.14 and Eq 9.15 above is in the mapping between input–output structures to feature vectors. In particular, the feature context for sequence segmentation differs from that for sequence labelling due to the inherent structural differences in the tasks. Because of such differences, the decoding algorithms for obtaining the most violated constraints $\arg\max_{s'} score(W')$ also differ from those for sequence labelling tasks (e.g., Algorithm 8.1 is different from Algorithm 9.1).

9.3   Structured Perceptron and Beam Search

Segment-level features are useful for sequence segmentation because they offer a wider context range and a direct source of information about the output structures. On the other hand, they also bring two potential issues to our structured models. The first issue is feature sparsity. For syntactic chunking, a possible noun phrase can span over tens of words, making the number of possible spans an open set, which can be extremely large. As a result, segment-level features can be highly sparse for some tasks and datasets. Therefore, care must be taken when defining chunk level features, and their effectiveness must be verified empirically given a specific task and dataset. This **feature engineering** process can be costly. We will discuss a more principled solution to the sparsity issue in Part III of this book.

The second potential issue with a larger feature context is decoding inefficiency. As discussed earlier, without constraints on the segment size, decoding with segment bigram feature context can take $O(n^3)$ time complexity with dynamic programming. If the feature context increases to segment trigrams, this complexity can increase to $O(n^4)$. Compared with Viterbi decoders introduced in Chapter 8, which have linear complexity concerning n, such complexity can bring down the decoding speed by orders of magnitudes in practice.

To address this intrinsic trade-off between feature context and decoding efficiency, one possible solution is *inexact search*, which frees the decoder from optimal sub problem constraints, thereby decoupling the feature context size from decoding efficiency. In particular, we discuss beam-search decoding, which incrementally processes the input sequence from left to right, building the output structure in linear time. A drawback of inexact search is that the candidate output structure with the highest model score is not guaranteed to be found by the decoder. Therefore, we risk losing accuracies. On the other hand, no model is perfect, in the sense that the highest model score does not always guarantee the most correct output for any input. This problem is intrinsic to all machine learning models due to inevitable empirical errors. It turns out that we can address model errors and search errors as a single problem, by casting modelling and decoding as a single task. This is achieved by setting the training objective as the minimisation of search errors. We discuss an adaptation of perceptron training to this end.

9.3.1   Relaxing Feature Locality Constraints

Notation-wise, we switch from character sequence segmentation in Section 9.2 to word sequence segmentation in this section, where the input is a sequence of words $W_{1:n} = w_1 \ldots w_n$ and the output is a sequence of segments $S_{1:|S|} = s_1 \ldots s_{|S|}$. Formally, given an input sequence $W_{1:n}$, we consider an algorithm that builds the output structure from left to right, incrementally handling each input word. At each step, we score partial outputs from the beginning of the sentence until the current word being processed. As mentioned earlier, we adopt beam search, in order to enable non-local feature vectors over whole partial outputs. Because there is no longer feature locality constraints, it does not matter whether sequence segmentation outputs are represented directly or indirectly using segmentation labels. Our decoder does not make Markov assumptions over segmentation label sequences. As a result, we adopt a sequence labelling representation for uniformly representing sequence labelling and sequence segmentation tasks.

Now for the input sequence $W_{1:n}$, the output is a label sequence $T_{1:n} = t_1 t_2 \ldots t_n$, where each t_i is a **partial output label** concerning the input w_i. For sequence labelling, t_i is the local tag on w_i. For sequence segmentation, t_i can be the segmentation label such as $t_i \in \{B, I, O\}$. For labelled sequence segmentation tasks such as NER, t_i also contains the label of the segment starting from w_i.

A beam-search decoder constructs $T_{1:n}$ from left to right. At the ith step, the feature vector for the partial output $T_{1:i}$ is built incrementally from the previous step, where

$$\vec{\phi}(W_{1:n}, T_{1:i}) = \vec{\phi}(W_{1:n}, T_{1:i-1}) + \vec{\phi}_\Delta(W_{1:n}, T_{1:i-1}, t_i)$$

where $\vec{\phi}_\Delta(W_{1:n}, T_{1:i-1}, t_i)$ indicates the incremental feature vector that consists of the partial structures concerning t_i, as described above.

$\vec{\phi}_\Delta(W_{1:n}, T_{1:i-1}, t_i)$ looks similar to the local feature for sequence labelling $\vec{\phi}(W_{1:n}, T_{i-k:i-1}, t_i)$ discussed in Chapter 8. However, there are two salient differences. First, there is no Markov restriction on the label context, and therefore t_i can be dependent on distant labels such as t_1. A feature instance in this spirit can be "the current tag is a verb and the beginning of the sentence is a wh-pronoun". Second, for sequence segmentation, features may not be extracted on segmentation labels, but can be defined directly on segmented sequences. For example, we can have a feature such as "the previous two words are '*the movie*', the current segment is '*New York*' and the current named entity type is a MISC type". In short, the incremental feature vector $\vec{\phi}_\Delta(W_{1:n}, T_{1:i-1}, t_i)$ is free from all forms of restrictions, and can be defined on arbitrary patterns concerning the current label t_i.

9.3.2 Beam Search Decoding

Algorithm 9.6 shows pseudocode of a beam search decoding algorithm that accommodates non-local features. Given an input sentence $W_{1:n}$, the algorithm builds partial output candidates $T_{1:n}$ incrementally from left to right, using an agenda to maintain the k highest scored partial output $T_{1:i}$ at each step. Starting from an initial agenda with an empty sequence, the decoder expands all the items in the agenda at each step, by enumerating all possible labels concerning the current word for each item. With a new label being appended to the partial output label sequence, scores are updated for each new candidate. The newly generated candidate outputs are then put back to the agenda, and the k highest scored ones are kept for the next step. The same process repeats until the end of the sentence, and the highest scored structure in the final agenda is taken for output.

In Algorithm 9.6, the data structure for *agenda* is a list of tuples, each consisting of a partial tag sequence $T_{1:i}$ and a corresponding score for the sequence. $\vec{\phi}_\Delta(W_{1:n}, T_{1:i-1}, t)$ extracts the incremental features $\vec{\phi}_\Delta(W_{1:n}, T_{1:i-1}, t_i = t)$. EXPAND$(T_{1:i-1}, t)$ appends t to the end of the tag sequence $T_{1:i-1}$. APPEND appends an element to the end of a list. TOP-K$(agenda, k)$ returns the k highest-scored elements in *agenda*.

Algorithm 9.6. Beam search decoding algorithm.

Inputs: $\vec{\theta}$ – discriminative linear model parameters;
$W_{1:n}$ – input sequence;
k – beam size;
Initialisation: $agenda \leftarrow [([], 0)]$;
Algorithm:
for $i \in [1, \ldots, n]$ **do**
  $candidates \leftarrow agenda$;
  $agenda \leftarrow []$;
  for $candidate \in candidates$ **do**
    $T_{1:i-1} \leftarrow candidate[0]$;
    $score \leftarrow candidate[1]$;
    for $t \in L$ **do**
      $T_{1:i} \leftarrow \text{EXPAND}(T_{1:i-1}, t)$;
      $new\_score \leftarrow score + \vec{\theta} \cdot \vec{\phi}_\Delta(W_{1:n}, T_{1:i-1}, t)$;
      $\text{APPEND}(agenda, (T_{1:i}, new\_score))$;
  $agenda \leftarrow \text{TOP-K}(agenda, k)$;
Output: $\text{TOP-K}(agenda, 1)[0]$;

Training. Now we develop a perceptron training algorithm to guide the above beam-search process, as discussed earlier. Pseudocode is shown in Algorithm 9.7. Given a set of training data D, each training instance can be denoted as $(W_{1:n}, G_{1:n})$, where $G_{1:n}$ represents the gold-standard word-level label sequence for $W_{1:n}$. The training algorithm works by initialising $\vec{\theta}$ to all zeros, and then repeatedly using the current model parameter $\vec{\theta}$ for decoding training instances. For each training instance, beam-search is applied as the decoding algorithm in Algorithm 9.6, while the algorithm monitors the score rank of the gold decision sequence $G_{1:i}$ at each step i.

If, at a certain step i, the gold local structure sequence $G_{1:i}$ falls out of *agenda*, it means that the model makes a mistake that cannot be recovered by subsequent steps. The algorithm thus stops the decoding process for the current input $W_{1:n}$, and updates the model parameters $\vec{\theta}$ using the standard perceptron algorithm, by taking $G_{1:i}$ as a positive example, and the corresponding highest-scored local structure $\hat{T}_{1:i}$ in the agenda as a negative example so that next time the same training instance is processed, the model will assign a higher score to the gold sequence $G_{1:i}$, thereby avoiding the same mistake. It can be seen that the training goal here is to fix search errors by adjusting model parameters.

If the decoding algorithm does not mistakenly prune away gold local structures throughout the incremental process, a standard perceptron update is applied in the end. In particular, the highest-scored output $\hat{T}_{1:n}$ is compared with the gold-standard output $G_{1:n}$. If $\hat{T}_{1:n}$ has a higher score compared with $G_{1:n}$, a perceptron update is executed by taking $G_{1:n}$ as a positive example and $\hat{T}_{1:n}$ as a negative example.

The algorithm can iterate through the set of training data D for M iterations, and the final value of $\vec{\theta}$ is taken as the model parameters. The averaged perceptron model in Chapter 8 can also be

---

Algorithm 9.7. Beam search training algorithm.

Inputs: D — gold standard training set; M — total number of training instances;
k — beam size;
Initialisation: $\vec{\theta} \leftarrow \vec{0}$;
Algorithm:
for $m \in [1, \ldots, M]$ **do**
    for $(W_{1:n}, G_{1:n}) \in D$ **do**
        $agenda \leftarrow [([], 0)]$
        for $i \in [1, \ldots, n]$ **do**
            $candidates \leftarrow agenda$;
            $agenda \leftarrow []$;
            for $candidate \in candidates$ **do**
                $T_{1:i-1} \leftarrow candidate[0]$;
                $score \leftarrow candidate[1]$;
                for $t \in L$ **do**
                    $T_{1:i} \leftarrow$ EXPAND$(T_{1:i-1}, t)$;
                    $new\_score \leftarrow score + \vec{\theta} \cdot \vec{\phi}_\Delta(W_{1:n}, T_{1:i-1}, t)$;
                    APPEND$(agenda, (T_{1:i}, new\_score))$;
            $agenda \leftarrow$ TOP-K$(agenda, k)$;
            if not CONTAIN$(G_{1:i}, agenda)$ **then**
                $pos \leftarrow G_{1:i}$;
                $neg \leftarrow$ TOP-K$(agenda, 1)[0]$;
                $\vec{\theta} \leftarrow \vec{\theta} + \vec{\phi}(pos) - \vec{\phi}(neg)$;
                return;
        if $G_{1:n} \neq$ TOP-K$(agenda, 1)[0]$ **then**
            $\vec{\theta} \leftarrow \vec{\theta} + \vec{\phi}(G_{1:n}) - \vec{\phi}(\text{TOP-K}(agenda, 1)[0])$;
Output: $\vec{\theta}$;

---

applied here for avoiding overfitting. Because the parameter update (i.e., $\vec{\theta} \leftarrow \vec{\theta} + \vec{\phi}(pos) - \vec{\phi}(neg)$) in the middle of the beam-search decoding process interrupts decoding for fixing search errors, the update is also referred to as **early-update** or **early-stop**.

Summary

In this chapter we have introduced:

- sequence segmentation using sequence labelling methods;
- discriminative models for sequence segmentation;
- semi-Markov conditional random fields (semi-CRF);
- a beam-search framework using perceptron training for sequence labelling.

Chapter Notes

Sequence labelling methods have been widely used for sequence segmentation (Xue and Shen, 2003; Peng et al., 2004; McCallum et al., 2000; Sha and Pereira, 2003; Pinto et al., 2003). Word-level features are considered for both word segmentation (Nakagawa, 2004; Zhang and Clark, 2007) and NER (Ratinov and Roth, 2009; Tkachenko and Simanovsky, 2012). Sarawagi and Cohen (2005) proposed the semi-CRFs model for sequence segmentation. Collins and Roark (2004) first proposed beam-search perceptron with early-update.

Exercises

9.1 Consider a sequence labelling model to solve the NER task. Suppose that the types of entities include person (PER), organisation (ORG), location (LOC) and geopolitical entities (GPE). Given a certain input $W_{1:n} = w_1 w_2 \ldots w_n$, how can the marginal probability of $w_j \ldots w_k$ $(j \leq k)$ being a PER entity be calculated?

9.2 Consider word-level features for Chinese segmentation.

(a) According to the feature templates in Table 9.5, what is the feature vector $\vec{\phi}(W_{1:4})$ for the segmentation "以 (take) 前天 (the day before yesterday) 下雨 (rain) 为例 (for example)"? Specify only the non-zero feature instances and their counts.

(b) If $w_0 = \langle s \rangle$ is additionally used, which feature templates in Table 9.5 can be applied to obtain $\vec{\phi}(w_0, w_1)$?

9.3 Discuss possible chunk-level features for (a) syntactic chunking and (b) NER. Compare them with features for word segmentation tasks. What are the salient differences? What are the similarities? Compare the feature templates to Table 9.3 and Table 9.4 for sequence labelling solutions to syntactic chunking and NER, respectively.

9.4 Consider Algorithm 9.1.

(a) How can the highest scored word sequence be recovered from the table bp? Give pseudocode here.

(b) Where can Algorithm 9.1 be adjusted if the maximum word size is constrained to M characters? Calculate the asymptotic complexity of the new algorithm.

(c) When the feature context is enlarged from word bigrams to word trigrams for character sequence segmentation, how should the decoding algorithm be adjusted?

9.5 We have learned in this chapter various discriminative models for sequence segmentation, which correspond to the sequence labelling methods in the previous chapter. In particular, semi-CRF can be regarded as a variant of CRF. However, we did not discuss generative models for sequence segmentation, which correspond to HMMs in Chapter 7. A hidden semi-Markov models

(HSMM) is such a model. Formally, an HSMM consists of a sequence of hidden variables $T_{1:m}$ and a set of observed variables $W_{1:n}$. The latter can be an input sentence and the former can be a sequence of chunk labels, for example. $T_{1:m}$ follows Markov assumptions. Each t_i corresponds to a chunk in the input $W_{b(i):e(i)}$. There are two types of probabilities in the model, namely a transition probability $P(t_i|T_{i-k:i-1})$ (kth order Markov model) and an emission probability $P(W_{b(i):e(i)}|t_i)$. The latter can itself be cast as a Markov model so that each word in $W_{b(i):e(i)}$ can be generated according to t_i and its preceding words.

(a) Fully specify the HSMM above. Compare the model with the HMM model we discussed. What are the similarities and what are the differences?
(b) Given a set of labelled training data, how can the HSMM model be trained?
(c) Given a set of unlabelled text, derive an EM estimator for HSMM by extending the EM algorithm for HMM.

9.6 The semi-CRF we discussed in this chapter can be viewed as a first-order semi-CRF. Consider a 0th order semi-CRF now, for which feature contexts are restricted to only one output segment.

(a) What is the implication for the decoding process?
(b) What is the implication for the process of calculating marginal probabilities of segments?
(c) What is the implication on the training process?
(d) Now consider labelled cases, where each output segment is assigned a label from L. Specify the decoding and training algorithms for 0th order semi-CRF.
(e) For labelled sequence segmentation, if the feature context is restricted to $\vec{\phi}(l(s_{j-1}), b(s_j), e(s_j), l(s_j))$, where $l(s)$ represents the label of a segment s, specify the decoding and training algorithms again.

9.7 Consider labelled sequence segmentation for first-order semi-CRF. How can Algorithm 9.1 for decoding and Algorithm 9.2, Algorithm 9.3 and Algorithm 9.4 for marginal probability calculation be adapted for accommodating label features?

9.8 In Algorithm 9.7, which lines perform early update? Which line ensures that the algorithm does not proceed with the current training instance after the update is executed? Which lines perform the final update as in the standard structured perceptron? Compare the feature vectors that participate in the early update and final update steps. What are the main differences?

9.9 Intuitively, different segmentation outputs can have varying numbers of incorrect segments given a certain input. Consider integrating such cost values into a large-margin sequence segmentor, similar to Section 8.5. Define the new training objectives by modifying Eqs 9.14 and 9.15. How can such a cost value be decomposable? How can cost-augmented decoding be achieved?

10 Predicting Tree Structures

Trees are another common structure in NLP. For example, the syntactic structures of natural language sentences can be represented as trees according to many grammar formalisms. Taking constituent parsing as a main example, this chapter demonstrates how generative and discriminative structured prediction models can be designed for tree-structured outputs. Concerning dynamic programming based training and decoding algorithms, the tradeoff between feature context size and runtime efficiency is a salient issue for trees as it is for sequences. We discuss one particular strategy to deal with this issue, namely reranking.

10.1 Generative Constituent Parsing

As discussed in Chapter 1, the task of constituent parsing is to predict the phrase-structure syntax for a given sentence. An example is shown in Figure 10.1(a), where the input is "*Here are the net contributions of the experts.*" and the output is a hierarchical constituent tree structure. There is one clause-level constituent S, which corresponds to the whole sentence, six phrase-level constituents, including *ADVP* ("*Here*"), *VP* ("*are*"), *NP* ("*the net contributions of the experts*"), *NP* ("*the net contributions*"), *PP*("*of the experts*") and *NP* ("*the experts*"), and nine word-level constituents, which correspond to the input words (including ".") with their POS tags. Since the constituent spans can be nested, the constituent tree can be represented using a *bracketed structure*:

> (S
>> (ADVP (RB "Here"))
>> (VP (VBP "are"))
>> (NP
>>> (NP (DT "the") (JJ "net") (NNS "contributions")))
>>> (PP (IN "of")(NP (DT "the") (NNS "experts"))))
>> (. "."))

Depending on the number of subnodes, tree nodes in a constituent tree can be classified into unary nodes, binary nodes, ternary nodes, etc. In general, n-ary nodes contains n subnodes. For example, the *ADVP* node in Figure 10.1(a) is a unary node, while the S node is a 4-ary node. n here is also called the *branching factor* or *arity*.

Constituent tree binarisation. While the branching factor of a constituent tree can be arbitrarily large, we focus on models and algorithms for binary-branching trees, which consist of only unary and binary nodes. There are multiple ways to convert arbitrary constituent trees into binary-branching trees without losing information. In paticular, the binarisation of a constituent

212

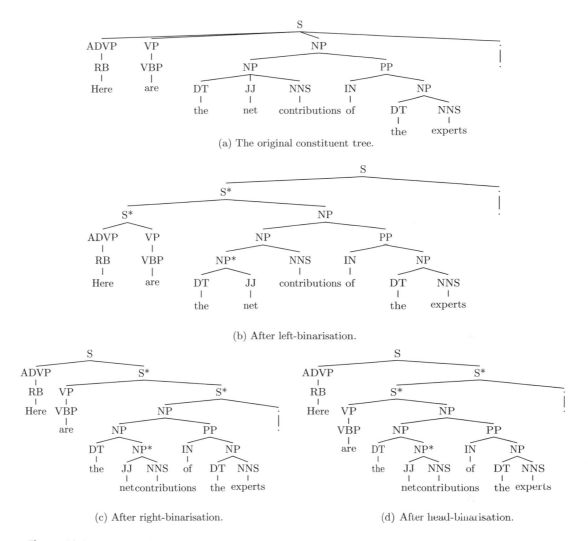

(a) The original constituent tree.

(b) After left-binarisation.

(c) After right-binarisation.

(d) After head-binarisation.

Figure 10.1 Binarisation methods for constituent trees.

tree involves the binarisation of its *n*-ary branching nodes, where $n > 2$. There are two naïve strategies to this end, namely **left-binarisation** and **right-binarisation**, respectively. As shown in Figure 10.1(b), the former transforms each flat *n*-ary branching non-terminal node into a binary-branching subtree that grows down to the left. In contrast, shown in Figure 10.1(c), the latter transforms each *n*-ary branching node by growing down a binary subtree to the right. In each case, temporary nodes that are constructed in the binarisation process are marked with *, so that the original tree can be reconstructed from the binarised version.

Left-binarisation and right-binarisation ignore the linguistic nature of constituent trees. For each constituent, there exists a dominating word, which is called the **head word**. For example, for the sentence-level constituent "*Tim loves Mary*", the main predicate verb "*loves*" is the head word; for the noun phrase "*a cat in the corner*", the noun "*cat*" is the head word. As shown in Figure 10.1(d), a more linguistically motivated, **head-binarisation** method grows a binary tree by keeping the head word in the trunk, branching out its left modifiers first, before its right modifiers in the inward direction. Take the constituent *S* in Figure 10.1(a) for example. It has four subnodes, namely *ADVP*, *VP*, *NP* and .. The head word of the constituent resides in the *VP* subnode. As a result, we take *VP* as the trunk, branching out modifier constituents. The head-binarisation result is shown in Figure 10.1(d). First, *ADVP* on the left is taken out, resulting in a binarised node *S* that consists of two subnodes *ADVP* and *S**, with the latter being a new temporary node effectively representing the three subnodes *VP*, *NP* and . for the original *S* constituent. Next we branch out modifiers on the right of the *VP* subnode, namely *NP* and .. The outmost node . is taken out first, resulting in a binarised node *S** that consists of two subnodes *S** and ., with the *S** subnode being a new temporary node consisting of the two subnodes *VP* and *NP*. At this stage, the constituent *S* is fully binarised.

With the above methods for binarisation, the constituent parsing task can be defined as finding a binarised constituent tree structure given an input sentence. Similar to sequence labelling and sequence segmentation, this parsing task is a structured prediction task because sub structures in a tree can be correlated with each other. However, tree structures are different in nature compared with sequence structures. For our tree-structured prediction task, there are two types of ambiguities to resolve. One is structural, where we need to find the constituent spans over the sentence. The other is label ambiguities, where we need to assign a constituent label to each span. We show how the generative and discriminative modelling techniques for structured prediction discussed in the previous chapters can be extended for modelling constituent parsing.

10.1.1 Probabilistic Context Free Grammar

Our goal is to find a generative model for constituent parsing, which models the probability of generating a natural language sentence together with its constituent tree given a start symbol *S*. Similar to the case of sequence labelling, such a model requires the overall probability of a tree to be factored into smaller parameters. For this purpose, constituent trees can be represented by **context free grammars (CFG)**.

Formally, a CFG is a 4-tuple $\langle N, \Sigma, R, S \rangle$, where N is the set of non-terminals (i.e., constituent labels including PoS tags such as *S*, *NP* and *VP*), Σ is the set of terminals (i.e., tokens in a sentence), R is the set of **production rules** and S is the *start symbol*. It is a convention in the literature to use lower letters (i.e., $a, b, c, \dots$) to represent terminal symbols, upper letters (i.e., $A, B, C, \dots$) to represent non-terminals and Greek symbols (i.e., $\alpha, \beta, \gamma, \dots$) to represent a string of zero or more terminals and non-terminals. Rules in CFG can be represented by $A \to \alpha$. For binarised trees, the set of rule schema $A \to BC, A \to B$ and $A \to a$ are sufficient to generate all constituent trees. The three types of rules can be written in a general form $A \to \gamma$.

A constituent tree can be generated from the start symbol *S* by repeated application of production rules. Given a string $\alpha A \beta$, the application of the grammar rule $A \to \gamma$ yields $\alpha \gamma \beta$:

$$\alpha A \beta \overset{A \to \gamma}{\Longrightarrow} \alpha \gamma \beta.$$

A sequence of rule applications that transforms a non-terminal node into a string is called a **derivation**. For example, $S \stackrel{*}{\Longrightarrow} w_1 w_2 \ldots w_n$ denotes a multi-step (represented by $*$) derivation that gives the constituent structure of a sentence $w_1 w_2 \ldots w_n$. In Figure 10.1(d), the derivation of the sentence "*Here are the net contributions of the experts* ." consists of the grammar rules $S \rightarrow ADVP\ S^*$, $ADVP \rightarrow RB$, $S^* \rightarrow S^*\ .$, $S^* \rightarrow VP\ NP$, $VP \rightarrow VBP$, $NP \rightarrow NP\ PP$, $NP \rightarrow DT\ NP^*$, $NP^* \rightarrow JJ\ NNS$, $PP \rightarrow IN\ NP$, $NP \rightarrow DT\ NNS$, $RB \rightarrow Here$, $VBP \rightarrow are$, $DT \rightarrow the$, $JJ \rightarrow net$, $NNS \rightarrow contributions$, $IN \rightarrow of$, $DT \rightarrow the$ and $NNS \rightarrow experts$.

Probabilistic CFG. A probabilistic context free grammar (PCFG) is a CFG augmented with rule probabilities. In particular, denote the probability of a grammar rule $A \rightarrow \gamma$ as $P(A \rightarrow \gamma)$. The probability of a one-step derivation is

$$P(\alpha \stackrel{A \rightarrow \gamma}{\Longrightarrow} \beta) = P(A \rightarrow \gamma).$$

In order to define the probability of a constituent tree, the probability of a multi-step derivation can be defined as

$$P(\alpha \stackrel{A_1 \rightarrow \gamma_1}{\Longrightarrow} \beta_1 \stackrel{A_2 \rightarrow \gamma_2}{\Longrightarrow} \beta_2 \Longrightarrow \ldots \stackrel{A_k \rightarrow \gamma_k}{\Longrightarrow} \beta_k) = \prod_{i=1}^{k} P(A_i \rightarrow \gamma_i).$$

The above equation regards the probability of a sequence of rule applications as the product of individual rule application probabilities, which can be regarded as using the probability chain rule and independence assumptions (i.e., the applications of each rule is independent of its predecessors). In particular, each $P(A_i \rightarrow \gamma_i) = P(\gamma_i | A_i)$.

Now given the constituent tree in Figure 10.1(d), the probability of the derivation $S \Rightarrow Here$ *are the net contributions of the experts* . can be calculated as $P(S \rightarrow ADVP\ S^*)P(ADVP \rightarrow RB)P(S^* \rightarrow S^*\ .)P(S^* \rightarrow VP\ NP)P(VP \rightarrow VBP)P(NP \rightarrow NP\ PP)P(NP \rightarrow DT\ NP^*)P(NP^* \rightarrow JJ\ NNS)P(PP \rightarrow IN\ NP)P(NP \rightarrow DT\ NNS)P(RB \rightarrow Here)P(VBP \rightarrow are)P(DT \rightarrow the)P(JJ \rightarrow net)P(NNS \rightarrow contributions)P(IN \rightarrow of)P(DT \rightarrow the)P(NNS \rightarrow experts)$.

Note that there can be different orders when applying rules to transform a string with more than one non-terminal symbol. One typical order is *leftmost derivation*, which substitutes for the leftmost non-terminal symbol first in each step. In this order, the sequence of constituents that are expanded (i.e., replaced by applying a grammar rule) is S, $ADVP$, RB, S^*, S^*, VP, VBP, NP, NP, DT, NP^*, JJ, NNS, PP, IN, NP, DT, NNS, .. This order of rule application is a natural choice when a derivation is viewed as an incremental string replacement process. Alternatively, we can view the derivation process as a *top-down* tree growing process. Consider the top-down growing of Figure 10.1(d), for example, where the sequence of expanded nodes is S, $ADVP$, S^*, RB, S^*, ., VP, NP, VBP, NP, PP, DT, NP^*, IN, NP, JJ, NNS, DT, NNS. Regardless of the order, we can observe that the probability of deriving a constituent span (e.g., " *of the experts*") from its dominating constituent node (e.g., PP) is the product of the probabilities of all the rules *within* the subtree dominated by the node (e.g., $P(PP \rightarrow IN\ NP)P(IN \rightarrow of)P(NP \rightarrow DT\ NNS)P(DT \rightarrow the)P(NNS \rightarrow experts)$). Formally, denote a constituent span and its dominating constituent node as (b, e, c), where b and e represent the start index and end index of the span in the sentence (e.g., 6 and 8 for "*of the experts*" in Figure 10.1(d), respectively), and c represents the constituent label (e.g., PP). For the rest of this chapter we use C to denote the set of constituent labels, which consists of both phrase-level labels such as NP and token-level POS-tags such as NN. We can denote the subtree as $T(b, e, c)$, and its derivation probability as $P(T(b,e,c)) = \prod_{r \in T(b,e,c)} P(r)$, where r represents a grammar rule such as $NNS \rightarrow experts$. In this notation, we measure the probability of a derivation as the probability of a subtree.

Training PCFGs. Overall, a PCFG for binarised constituent trees consists of a single type of model parameter, namely $P(A \rightarrow \gamma)$. Given a training corpus $D = \{(W_i, T_i)\}|_{i=1}^{N}$, where W_i is a sentence and T_i is a manually labelled constituent tree for W_i, converted into a binary-branching form, each parameter instance can be estimated using

$$P(A \rightarrow \gamma) = P(\gamma|A) = \frac{count(A \rightarrow \gamma)}{count(A)}$$
$$= \frac{\sum_{i=1}^{N} count(A \rightarrow \gamma, T_i)}{\sum_{i=1}^{N} count(A, T_i)}. \tag{10.1}$$

Since D consists of trees, such corpora are also referred to as **treebank**s.

10.1.2 CKY Decoding

Given a trained PCFG model, we can use it for finding the most likely derivation given an input sentence. This process is also referred to as *parsing* or *inference*. Similar to sequence labelling and sequence segmentation, this decoding task is non-trivial since the number of possible outputs is exponential to the size of input (Exercise 10.2). Similar to the case of Viterbi decoding, a dynamic program can be used to solve the decoding problem in polynomial time. In particular, features as given in Eq 10.1 are local to each production rule according to PCFG, which enables optimal sub problems. Formally, consider a constituent span (b, e, c) with its subtree (e.g., the span $(6, 8, PP)$ in Figure 10.1(d)), where the topmost grammar rule is a binary rule $c \rightarrow c_1 c_2$ ($c, c_1, c_2 \in C$). Further, suppose that c_1 dominates a constituent span (b, k, c_1) (e.g., the span $(6, 6, of)$ in Figure 10.1(d)) and c_2 dominates a constituent span $(k+1, e, c_2)$ (e.g., the span $(7, 8, the\ experts)$ in Figure 10.1(d)). We can observe that $P(T(b,e,c)) = P(T(b,k,c_1))P(T(k+1,e,c_2))P(c \rightarrow c_1 c_2)$. This gives us a basis for finding optimal sub problem structures.

Denote the input sentence as $W_{1:n} = w_1 w_2 \ldots w_n$. Further, denote the most probable subtree over the span $w_b w_{b+1} \ldots w_e$ with a constituent label c as $\hat{T}(b,e,c)$, where $b \in [1, \ldots, n]$ and $e \in [1, \ldots, n-b+1]$ denote the start and size of the span. Considering a start index i and a span size s, we have

$$score(\hat{T}(i, i+s-1, c)) = \max_{c_1,c_2 \in C, j \in [i+1,\ldots,i+s-1]} \left(score(\hat{T}(i, j-1, c_1)) + score(\hat{T}(j, i+s-1, c_2)) \right.$$
$$\left. + \log P(c \rightarrow c_1 c_2) \right), \tag{10.2}$$

where j is the split point at which the span $w_i \ldots w_{s+i-1}$ is separated into two sub spans $w_i \ldots w_{j-1}$ and $w_j \ldots w_{s+i-1}$. The score of a derivation is expressed in log probability. A proof is straightforward by contradiction, which we leave to Exercise 10.3.

Equation 10.2 states that the most probable derivation must consist of the most probable sub derivations. Supposing that we only have binary non-terminal rules $c \rightarrow c_1 c_2$ and unary terminal rules $c \rightarrow w$, but do not have unary non-terminal rules $c \rightarrow c_1$, where $c, c_1, c_2 \in C$ and $w \in V$, we can iteratively find the most probable derivations of constituent spans bottom-up. In particular, a

---

Algorithm 10.1. CKY algorithm.

Input: $W_{1:n} = w_1 w_2 \ldots w_n$, PCFG model $P(c \to c_1 c_2)$, $P(c \to w)$;
Variables: *chart*, *bp*;
Initialisation:
for $i \in [1, \ldots, n]$ **do**   ▷ start index
   for $c \in C$ **do**   ▷ constituent label
      $chart[1][i][c] \leftarrow \log P(c \to w_i)$;
for $s \in [2, \ldots, n]$ **do**   ▷ size
   for $i \in [1, \ldots, n - s + 1]$ **do**   ▷ start index
      for $c \in C$ **do**   ▷ constituent label
         $chart[s][i][c] \leftarrow -\infty$;
         $bp[s][i][c] \leftarrow -1$;
Algorithm:
for $s \in [2, \ldots, n]$ **do**   ▷ size
   for $i \in [1, \ldots, n - s + 1]$ **do**   ▷ start index
      for $j \in [i + 1, \ldots, i + s - 1]$ **do**   ▷ split point
         for $c, c_1, c_2 \in C$ **do**   ▷ $c \to c_1 c_2$
            $score \leftarrow chart[j - i][i][c_1] + chart[s - j + i][j][c_2] + \log P(c \to c_1 \, c_2)$;
            if $chart[s][i][c] < score$ **then**
               $chart[s][i][c] \leftarrow score$;
               $bp[s][i][c] \leftarrow (j, c_1, c_2)$;
Output: FINDDERIVATION$\left(bp[n][1][\arg \max_c chart[n][1][c]] \right)$;

---

chart can be built bottom-up, with each cell storing the score of $\hat{T}(i, i + s - 1, c)$ for a specific combination of i, s and c. Pseudocode of this algorithm is shown in Algorithm 10.1, where *chart* corresponds to the score chart, and *bp* is a set of back pointers to find the highest scored derivation given *chart* (Exercise 10.4 discusses the back tracking algorithm). The algorithm enumerates i and s in the increasing order, building *chart* according to Eq 10.2. The time complexity of the algorithm is $O(n^3 |G|)$, where n is the length of the sentence and G is the set of grammar rules. The algorithm is named CKY, after its inventors Cocke, Kasami and Younger.

The grammar form above without unary non-terminal rules is also called the *Chomsky Normal Form* (CNF) of CFGs. It does not allow constituent trees with unary-branching nodes such as $VB \to VP \to S$ to be constructed. Exercise 10.5 discusses how unary rules can be added to the algorithm. Note that in theory, we can have a chain of infinite unary rule applications in a constituent tree, which makes the decoding time unbounded. There are two principled solutions to this issue. The first is to simply set a maximum limit for continuous unary rule applications, which can be decided according to the largest chain of unary rules in a training set. The second solution is to collapse all chains of unary rules into a single rule. For example, $VB \to VP \to S$ can be collapsed into $VB \to S$. Or alternatively, we can collapse $VB \to VP \to S$ into $VB|VP \to S$, where $VB|VP$ is treated as one label, thereby preserving the original structure by enlarging the constituent label set C. As a result, only one unary rule is allowed over each span of words. Note that the PCFG model builds a derivation top-down, generating a sentence from S. In contrast, the CKY decoding process is executed bottom-up, due the to need for finding the highest-scored derivation by table filling.

10.1.3 Evaluating Constituent Parser Outputs

The output of a constituent parser can be represented as a set of constituents (i.e., syntactic phrases) (b, e, c), where b, e and c are defined in the same way as in Section 10.1.1. According to this definition, the goal of evaluation is to calculate the degree of consistency between the set of constituents in a parser output and the set of constituents in a gold-standard tree. The *F-score* metric introduced in Chapter 8 can be used for this purpose, where the *precision* is defined as the percentage of constituents in the output set that are correct, and *recall* is defined as the percentage of gold-standard constituents that are identified in the parser output. Note that F-scores can be calculated by either considering constituent labels or not — *labelled F-score* considers a constituent as correct if both the span and the label are correct, while *unlabelled F-score* considers only the span.

10.1.4 Calculating Marginal Probabilities

We are interested in the marginal probability $P(T(i,j,c)|W_{1:n})$, $i \leq j$ and $c \in C$, which is the probability of the span $w_i w_{i+1} \ldots w_j$ having label c given the sentence $W_{1:n}$. According to the generative PCFG model, this probability can be calculated as $\frac{P(T(i,j,c),W_{1:n})}{\sum_{i',j'} P(T(i',j',c),W_{1:n})}$. In particular,

$$P(T(i,j,c), W_{1:n}) = P(S \stackrel{*}{\Rightarrow} w_1 w_2 \ldots w_{i-1} c w_{j+1} w_{j+2} \ldots w_n \stackrel{*}{\Rightarrow} W_{1:n})$$

$$= P(S \stackrel{*}{\Rightarrow} w_1 w_2 \ldots w_{i-1} c w_{j+1} w_{j+2} \ldots w_n) P(c \stackrel{*}{\Rightarrow} w_i w_{i+1} \ldots w_j) \quad (10.3)$$

$$\text{(independence assumption)}.$$

Equation 10.3 holds because the probability of a derivation is the product of all rule probabilities in it. In Eq 10.3, the second term

$$P(c \stackrel{*}{\Rightarrow} w_i w_{i+1} \ldots w_j) = \sum_{rules \in \text{GEN}(W_{i:j}(c))} P(c \stackrel{rules}{\Rightarrow} w_i w_{i+1} \ldots w_j)$$

$$= \sum_{rules \in \text{GEN}(W_{i:j}(c))} \prod_{r \in rules} P(r)$$

is named the **inside probability** of $T(i,j,c)$, which equals the total probability of all possible derivations $c \stackrel{*}{\Rightarrow} W_{i:j}$. It can also be viewed as the total probability of all possible tree structures $T(i,j,c)$ for the constituent span (i,j,c). Here $\text{GEN}(W_{i:j}(c))$ denotes all possible constituent trees over $w_i w_{i+1} \ldots w_j$ with label c.

The first term of Eq 10.3

$$P(S \stackrel{*}{\Rightarrow} w_1 w_2 \ldots w_{i-1} c w_{j+1} w_{j+2} \ldots w_n)$$

$$= \sum_{rules \in \text{GEN}(W_{1:n}(S)[c \stackrel{*}{\Rightarrow} W_{i:j}])} P(S \stackrel{rules}{\Rightarrow} w_1 w_2 \ldots w_{i-1} c w_{j+1} w_{j+2} \ldots w_n)$$

$$= \sum_{rules \in \text{GEN}(W_{1:n}(S)[c \stackrel{*}{\Rightarrow} W_{i:j}])} \prod_{r \in rules} P(r) \quad (10.4)$$

Algorithm 10.2. The outside algorithm.

Input: The sentence $W_{1:n} = w_1 w_2 \ldots w_n$, the PCFG model, the start index b, the end index e, the constituent label X;

Variables: *outside*;

Initialisation:

for $i \in [1, \ldots, n]$ **do**
  for $j \in [i, \ldots, n]$ **do**
    for $c \in C$ **do**
      $outside[i][j][c] \leftarrow 0$;
$outside[1][n][S] \leftarrow 1$;

Algorithm:

for $s \in [n, \ldots, 1]$ **do**
  for $i \in [1, \ldots, n - s + 1]$ **do**
    for $j \in [i + 1, \ldots, i + s - 1]$ **do**
      for $c, c_1, c_2 \in C$ **do** $\triangleright c \rightarrow c_1 c_2$
        $outside[i][j-1][c_1] \leftarrow outside[i][j-1][c_1] +$
        $outside[i][i+s-1][c] \times inside[j][i+s-1][c_2] \times P(c \rightarrow c_1 c_2)$;
        $outside[j][i+s-1][c_2] \leftarrow outside[j][i+s-1][c_2] + outside[i][i+s-1][c] \times inside[i][j-1][c_1] \times P(c \rightarrow c_1 c_2)$;

Output: $outside[b][e][X]$;

---

is named the **outside probability** of $T(i,j,c)$, which is the total probability of all possible derivations of $S \overset{*}{\Rightarrow} W_{1:i-1} c W_{j+1:n}$, which can also be denoted as $T(1,n,S)[c \overset{*}{\Rightarrow} W_{i:j}]$. The outside probability of $T(i,j,c)$ can also be viewed as the product of all the rule probabilities in $(1,n,S)$ except for those in (i,j,c). Here $\textsc{Gen}(W_{1:n}(S)[c \overset{*}{\Rightarrow} W_{i:j}])$ denotes all possible constituent trees over $w_1 \ldots w_n$ with label S and a subconstituent span (i,j,c).

Both the inside probability and the outside probability can be calculated in polynomial time using dynamic programming. Again let us assume that our grammar conforms to CNF. Denote $P(c \overset{*}{\Rightarrow} W_{i:j})$ as $inside(i,j,c)$. We have

$$inside(i,j,c)$$
$$= \sum_{k \in [i+1, \ldots j]} \sum_{c_1, c_2 \in C} inside(i, k-1, c_1) \times inside(k, j, c_2) \times P(c \rightarrow c_1 c_2). \quad (10.5)$$

Given that $inside(i,i,c) = P(c \rightarrow w_i) = P(w_i|c)$ if $c = \text{Pos}(w_i)$ (i.e., the POS of w_i) and 0 otherwise, we can find $inside(i, j, c)$ incrementally bottom-up, by building a chart $inside[i][j][c]$. Pseudocode of this algorithm is shown in Algorithm 10.2. It is named the **inside algorithm**.

The outside scores can be calculated top-down incrementally. Considering one incremental step. A constituent c over $W_{i:j}$ can be derived via a rule $c' \rightarrow c c_2$ or a rule $c' \rightarrow c_2 c$, depending on the relative position of c on the right-hand side of the grammar rule. In each case above, if the outside probability of c' is known, then the outside probability of c can be calculated by additionally multiplying the inside probability of c_2. As a result, enumerating c' and c_2 and combining

---

Algorithm 10.3. The outside algorithm.

Input: The sentence $W_{1:n} = w_1w_2\ldots w_n$, the PCFG model, the start index b, the end index e, the constituent label X;

Variables: *outside*;

Initialisation:

for $i \in [1,\ldots,n]$ **do**

    for $j \in [i,\ldots,n]$ **do**

        for $c \in C$ **do**

            $outside[i][j][c] \leftarrow 0$;

$outside[1][n][S] \leftarrow 1$;

Algorithm:

for $s \in [n,\ldots,1]$ **do**

    for $i \in [1,\ldots,n-s+1]$ **do**

        for $j \in [i+1,\ldots,i+s-1]$ **do**

            for $c, c_1, c_2 \in C$ **do** $\triangleright\ c \rightarrow c_1c_2$

                $outside[i][j-1][c_1] \leftarrow outside[i][j-1][c_1]+$

                $outside[i][i+s-1][c] \times inside[j][i+s-1][c_2] \times P(c \rightarrow c_1c_2)$;

                $outside[j][i+s-1][c_2] \leftarrow outside[j][i+s-1][c_2] + outside[i][i+s-$

                $1][c] \times inside[i][j-1][c_1] \times P(c \rightarrow c_1c_2)$;

Output: $outside[b][e][X]$;

---

their relevant probability (see Eq 10.4) scores gives the outside score. Now denoting the outside probability of $T(i,j,c)$ as $outside(i,j,c)$, we have

$$
\begin{aligned}
outside(i,j,c) \\
= \sum_{k\in[j+1,\ldots,n]} \sum_{c',c_2\in C} outside(i,k,c') \times inside(j+1,k,c_2) \times P(c' \rightarrow cc_2) \\
+ \sum_{k\in[1,\ldots,i-1]} \sum_{c',c_2\in C} outside(k,j,c') \times inside(k,i-1,c_2) \times P(c' \rightarrow c_2c).
\end{aligned}
\tag{10.6}
$$

Given that $outside(1,n,X) = 1$ if $X = S$ and 0 otherwise, we can build a chart $outside[i][j][X]$ top-down. Pseudocode of this algorithm is shown in Algorithm 10.3, where i and s denote the start and size of the current span, respectively. It is named the **outside algorithm**. Note that the order of enumerating relevant cells for each cell is different from Eq 10.6 (Exercise 10.6).

Since the marginal probabilities can be calculated as a product of inside probabilities and outside probabilities (Eq 10.3), the overall algorithm for finding marginal probabilities is called the **inside–outside algorithm**. The inside–outside algorithm is conceptually similar to the forward–backward algorithm for calculating marginal probabilities for sequence tasks. The main difference is that there are two subnodes for each constituent node, rather than one.

Algorithm 10.2 and Algorithm 10.3 consider CNF only. Exercise 10.5 discusses the inside and outside algorithms when unary rules are involved.

10.2 More Features for Constituent Parsing

As a generative model, PCFG offers a rather simple set of features for disambiguation, which limits its performance. There are several methods to integrate richer features into a constituent parser. First, we can extend the generative story of PCFGs. Second, we can use a discriminative model to accommodate overlapping features. This section begins by discussing a specific feature limitation of PCFGs, introducing a lexicalised PCFG version for allowing word-level features. Then we discuss how log-linear models and large-margin models can be constructed for tree-structured outputs.

10.2.1 Lexicalised PCFGs

One salient limitation of PCFGs is that grammar rules are isolated from lexical information, except for rules concerning leaf nodes in constituent trees. Take verb phrase rules for example. The rule $VP \rightarrow V\ NP$ can be used to describe a transitive verb and its object phrase, while the grammar rule $VP \rightarrow V$ can be used to describe an intransitive verb phrase. In a PCFG, the probabilities of these two rules are calculated irrespective of the actual verb. As a result, given a sentence with a transitive verb such as "*like*", it is impossible for a PCFG to tell that the former rule is more suitable for generating its verb phrase.

One way to solve this issue is to enrich PCFG constituent labels with lexical information. For example, the constituent label *VP* can be transformed into multiple constituent labels in the enriched version, including *VP[like]*, *VP[eat]*, *VP[understand]*, etc. The resulting grammar is a **lexicalised PCFG**. Again we assume that constituent trees are head-binarised, so that each grammar rule is either unary branching or binary branching. A head-lexicalised version of Figure 10.1(d) is shown in Figure 10.2. It can be seen that each constituent label in the tree is augmented with its corresponding head word. As a result, the constituent (3, 5 *NP*) in the original tree becomes (3, 5, *NP[contributions]*) in the head-lexicalised version, which provides us a basis for extracting richer features. For notational convenience, we denote the original unlexicalised label set still as C (i.e., {*NP*, *VBZ*, ...}), and the lexicalised label set as C_l (i.e., {*VP[like]*, *NP[contribution]*, ...}).

Given a head-lexicalised treebank D, suppose that we still use the same method to parameterise our PCFG model. The lexicalised PCFG model can be trained using Eq 10.1 over a lexicalised treebank. Due to the use of C_l instead of C, we have a much more fine-grained and much larger grammar. One example rule of this grammar is $S[are] \rightarrow VP[are]\ NP[contributions]$. Such features have much stronger disambiguation power compared to unlexicalised rules such as $S \rightarrow VP\ NP$. For example, $VP[eat] \rightarrow VB[eat]\ NP[pizza]$ should be more plausible compared to $VP[eat] \rightarrow VB[eat]\ NP[poster]$. On the other hand, they are much more sparse compared with the unlexicalised rules. To avoid zero probabilities, we can extract also coarser-grained rules by combining labels from C and C_l, using back-off to combine the probability of different grammar rule versions. For example, we can approximate $P(VP[eat] \rightarrow VB[eat]\ NP[pizza])$ by calculating $\lambda_1 P(VP[eat] \rightarrow VB[eat]\ NP[pizza]) + \lambda_2 P(VP[eat] \rightarrow VB[eat]\ NP) + \lambda_3 P(VP \rightarrow VB\ NP)$, where $\lambda_1 > 0$, $\lambda_2 > 0$ and $\lambda_3 > 0$ are hyper-parameters and $\lambda_1 + \lambda_2 + \lambda_3 = 1$.

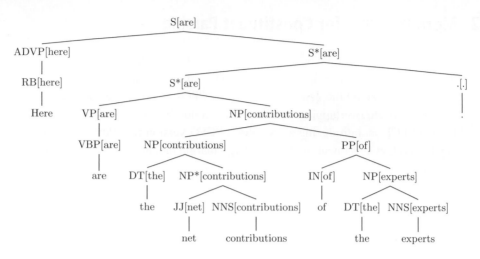

Figure 10.2 Head-lexicalised version of Fig 10.1(d).

The coarse-grained lexicalised grammar rules can still be estimated from a treebank using Eq 10.1. For example,

$$P(VP[like] \rightarrow VB[like] \ NP) = \frac{count(VP[like] \rightarrow VB[like] \ NP)}{count(VP[like])}$$

Decoding. Because the feature types of lexicalised PCFG are the same in form as PCFG, the same CKY algorithm in Algorithm10.1 can be used for decoding, by replacing C with C_l for the label set. However, $C_l >> C$ and is on the scale of the vocabulary V. This has implications for the decoding algorithm, which has a complexity of $O(n^3 C_l^3)$ according to Algorithm 10.1. At a closer inspection, enumeration of all non-terminals in C_l is unnecessary for line 16, because given a sentence, the head lexicon for a certain constituent span is restricted to be a word in the input rather than the whole vocabulary. As a result, for each cell, we only need to store an unlexicalised constituent label with a head word position in the input sentence. According to this observation, a modified version of the CKY decoder is shown in Algorithm 10.4. The algorithm uses the class C for constituent labels similar to Algorithm 10.1. However, different from Algorithm 10.1, we additionally maintain a head position for each chart cell, using $chart[s][i][c][h]$ to store the probability of the highest scored constituent $\hat{T}(i, i+s-1, c[w_h])$ over the text span $w_i \dots w_{i+s-1}$ with a constituent label c and a head index h.

Algorithm 10.4 additionally enumerates the head positions for building each chart cell. In particular, in the main algorithm, in addition to looping over the span size s, the start index i and the split point j, the algorithm also enumerates the head word index h_1 of the left span $W_{i:j-1}$ and the head word index h_2 of the right span $W_{j:i+s-1}$. Since the head word of the combined span must be propagated up from a sub span, we further enumerate h only in $\{h_1, h_2\}$. As a result, the complexity of the algorithm is $O(n^5 C^2)$, which is much smaller.

Despite the optimisation above, the complexity of Algorithm 10.4 is still significantly higher compared with Algorithm 10.1. One way of dealing with such high complexity is to use *beam-*

Algorithm 10.4. CKY algorithm for head lexicalised PCFG.

Input: $W_{1:n} = w_1 w_2 \ldots w_n$;

Variables: *chart*, *bp*;

Initialisation:

for $i \in [1, \ldots, n]$ **do**   ▷ start index

  for $c \in C$ **do**   ▷ constituent label

    $chart[1][i][c][i] \leftarrow \log P(c[w_i] \to w_i)$;

for $s \in [2, \ldots, n]$ **do**   ▷ size

  for $i \in [1, \ldots, n - s + 1]$ **do**   ▷ start index

    for $h \in [i, \ldots, i + s - 1]$ **do**   ▷ head

      for $c \in C$ **do**   ▷ constituent label

        $chart[s][i][c][h] \leftarrow -\infty$;

        $bp[s][i][c][h] \leftarrow -1$;

Algorithm:

for $s \in [2, \ldots, n]$ **do**   ▷ size

  for $i \in [1, \ldots, n - s + 1]$ **do**   ▷ start index

    for $j \in [i + 1, \ldots, i + s - 1]$ **do**   ▷ split point

      for $h_1 \in [i, \ldots, j - 1]$ **do**   ▷ left span head

        for $h_2 \in [j, \ldots, i + s - 1]$ **do**   ▷ right span head

          for $h \in \{h_1, h_2\}$ **do**   ▷ head

            for $c, c_1, c_2 \in C$ **do**   ▷ $c \to c_1 c_2$

              $score \leftarrow chart[j - i][i][c_1][h_1] + chart[s - j + i][j][c_2][h_2] +$

              $\log P(c[w_h] \to c_1[w_{h_1}] c_2[w_{h_2}])$;

              if $chart[s][i][c][h] < score$ **then**

                $chart[s][i][c][h] \leftarrow score$;

                $bp[s][i][c][h] \leftarrow (j, c_1, c_2, h_1, h_2)$;

Output: FINDDERIVATION$\left(bp[n][1][\arg\max_{c,h} chart[n][1][c][h]] \right)$;

---

search, storing the k highest scored constituents in each cell. This allows the reduction of the chart structure back to $chart[s][i][c]$, where s, i and c record the size, start and constituent label, respectively. Exercise 10.7 discusses this algorithm.

A lexicalised PCFG is still a generative model. As a result, overlapping features such as $VP[eat] \to VB[eat]\ NP$ and $VP \to VB\ NP$ can be captured only through engineering tricks such as back-off. In contrast, a discriminative model can handle these features more consistently in a training algorithm. We discuss discriminative constituent parser models in the next section.

10.2.2 Discriminative Linear Models for Constituent Parsing

Discriminative models map constituent trees for a given sentence into feature vectors before scoring them. Similar to discriminative models for classification, sequence labelling and sequence segmentation, feature engineering is important for constituent parsing. For example, we can use lexicalised and partially lexicalised grammar rules as feature templates. Feature instances according to such feature templates can include the patterns $VP[eat] \rightarrow VP[eat]\ NP[pizza]$, $VP[eat] \rightarrow VP[eat]\ NP$ and $VP \rightarrow VP\ NP$. In addition, we can define back-off feature templates by using X to denote an arbitrary constituent, or using prefixes and suffixes for representing words, resulting in feature instances such as $VP[eat] \rightarrow VP[eat]\ X$ and $VP[eat*] \rightarrow VP[eat*]\ NP[pizza]$, where * denotes an arbitrary string (e.g. "ed" and "ing") including the empty string. Exercise 10.8 further discusses features for constituent parsing.

Formally, given an input sentence $W_{1:n}$ and a constituent tree T over it, a linear model scores the input–output pair by first mapping $(W_{1:n}, T)$ into a global feature vector $\vec{\phi}(W_{1:n}, T)$, and then calculating:

$$score(W_{1:n}, T) = \vec{\theta} \cdot \vec{\phi}(W_{1:n}, T), \tag{10.7}$$

where $\vec{\theta}$ is the model parameter vector. This equation is consistent with the discriminative linear models for multi-class classification and structured prediction tasks that we have discussed in this book.

Feature locality. To allow efficient training and decoding, $\vec{\phi}(W_{1:n}, T)$ should be factorable into local feature components. Taking the same context range as PCFGs, we assume that features are local to each grammar rule. As a result, we have:

$$\vec{\phi}(W_{1:n}, T) = \sum_{r \in T} \vec{\phi}(W_{1:n}, r), \tag{10.8}$$

where r represents a rule in the derivation of T.

Given Eq 10.8, suppose that a subtree $T(i, j, c)$ consists of two subtrees $T(i, k, c_1)$ and $T(k + 1, j, c_2)$, generated according to $c \rightarrow c_1 c_2$. We have

$$score(T(i, j, c)) = score(T(i, k, c_1)) + score(T(k + 1, j, c_2)) + \vec{\theta} \cdot \vec{\phi}(W_{1:n}, c \rightarrow c_1 c_2).$$

Decoding. According to such feature locality, given a model $\vec{\theta}$, the highest scored output $\hat{T} = \arg\max_{T \in \text{GEN}(W_{1:n})} score(T)$ can be found using a dynamic program. In particular, since the score of a derivation can be calculated incrementally with each grammar rule, the task enjoys the optimal sub problem property. Denoting the highest-scored local parse tree over the text span $w_i w_{i+1} \ldots w_j$ with the constituent label being c and head word being w_h ($h \in [i, \ldots, j]$) as $\hat{T}(i, j, h, c)$, we have:

$$
\begin{aligned}
score(\hat{T}(i, j, h, c)) = \underset{k \in [i,\ldots,j-1], h_1 \in [i,\ldots,k], h_2 \in [k+1,\ldots,j], c_1, c_2 \in C}{\arg\max} & \left(score\left(\hat{T}(i, k, h_1, c_1)\right) \right. \\
& + score\left(\hat{T}(k + 1, j, h_2, c_2)\right) \\
& \left. + \vec{\theta} \cdot \vec{\phi}(W_{1:n}, c[w_h] \rightarrow c_1[w_{h_1}] c_2[w_{h_2}]) \right),
\end{aligned}
\tag{10.9}
$$

where h_1 and h_2 denote the head words of the two spans $w_1 \ldots w_k$ and $w_{k+1} w_{k+2} \ldots w_j$, respectively, c_1 and c_2 denote the constituent labels of the two spans, respectively, and k denotes the splitting index from (i, j, c) to (i, k, c_1) and $(k + 1, j, c_2)$ according to the binary rule $c \rightarrow c_1 c_2$.

Algorithm 10.5. CKY algorithm for discriminative linear parsing.

Input: $W_{1:n} = w_1 w_2 \ldots w_n$, $\vec{\theta}$ – model parameters;
Variables: *chart*, *bp*;
Initialisation:
for $i \in [1, \ldots, n]$ **do**   ▷ start index
  for $c \in C$ **do**   ▷ constituent label
    $chart[1][i][c][i] \leftarrow \vec{\theta} \cdot \vec{\phi}(W_{1:n}, c[w_i] \rightarrow w_i)$;
for $s \in [2, \ldots, n]$ **do**   ▷ size
  for $i \in [1, \ldots, n - s + 1]$ **do**   ▷ start index
    for $h \in [i, \ldots, i + s - 1]$ **do**   ▷ head
      for $c \in C$ **do**   ▷ constituent label
        $chart[s][i][c][h] \leftarrow -\infty$;
        $bp[s][i][c][h] \leftarrow -1$;
Algorithm:
for $s \in [2, \ldots, n]$ **do**   ▷ size
  for $i \in [1, \ldots, n - s + 1]$ **do**   ▷ start index
    for $j \in [i + 1, \ldots, i + s - 1]$ **do**   ▷ split point
      for $h_1 \in [i, \ldots, j - 1]$ **do**   ▷ left head
        for $h_2 \in [j, \ldots, i + s - 1]$ **do**   ▷ right head
          for $h \in \{h_1, h_2\}$ **do**   ▷ head
            for $c, c_1, c_2 \in C$ **do**   ▷ $c \rightarrow c_1 c_2$
              $score \leftarrow chart[j - i][i][c_1][h_1]$
              $+ chart[s - j + i][j][c_2][h_2] + \vec{\theta} \cdot \vec{\phi}(W_{1:n}, c[w_h] \rightarrow c_1[w_{h_1}] c_2[w_{h_2}])$;
              if $chart[s][i][c][h] < score$ **then**
                $chart[s][i][c][h] \leftarrow score$;
                $bp[s][i][c][h] \leftarrow (j, c_1, c_2, h_1, h_2)$;
Output: $\text{FindDerivation}\left(bp[n][1][\arg\max_{c,h} chart[n][1][c][h]]\right)$;

Accordingly, the CKY algorithm can be adapted as shown in Algorithm 10.5. Algorithm 10.5 is structurally similar to Algorithm 10.4, with the only difference being the scoring functions of grammar rules.

Training. The next two subsections discuss training of the model in Eq 10.7 using log-linear and large-margin objectives, respectively.

10.2.3 Training Log-Linear Models for Constituent Parsing

Given a sentence $W_{1:n}$ and a constituent tree T, a log-linear model calculates the conditional probability of T as:

$$P(T|W_{1:n}) = \frac{\exp(\vec{\theta} \cdot \vec{\phi}(W_{1:n}, T))}{\sum_{T' \in \text{Gen}(W_{1:n})} \exp(\vec{\theta} \cdot \vec{\phi}(W_{1:n}, T'))} \qquad (10.10)$$

where T' denotes all possible constituent trees over $W_{1:n}$. Since the form of Eq 10.10 is the same as CRF, such a log-linear model is also referred to as **tree CRF**.

Given a set of training data $D = \{(W_i, T_i)\}|_{i=1}^{N}$, where W_i is a sentence and T_i is a gold-standard constituent tree, the training objective is to maximise the log-likelihood of D:

$$
\begin{aligned}
\vec{\hat{\theta}} &= \arg\max_{\vec{\theta}} \log P(D) \\
&= \arg\max_{\vec{\theta}} \log \prod_i P(T_i|W_i) \quad (i.i.d.) \\
&= \arg\max_{\vec{\theta}} \sum_i \log \frac{\exp\left(\vec{\theta} \cdot \vec{\phi}(W_i, T_i)\right)}{\sum_{T' \in \text{GEN}(W_i)} \exp\left(\vec{\theta} \cdot \vec{\phi}(W_i, T')\right)} \\
&= \arg\max_{\vec{\theta}} \sum_i \left(\vec{\theta} \cdot \vec{\phi}(W_i, T_i) - \log \sum_{T' \in \text{GEN}(W_i)} \exp\left(\vec{\theta} \cdot \vec{\phi}(W_i, T')\right)\right).
\end{aligned}
$$
(10.11)

Using SGD, the local training objective for each training example is to maximise

$$
\log P(T_i|W_i) = \vec{\theta} \cdot \vec{\phi}(W_i, T_i) - \log\left(\sum_{T' \in \text{GEN}(W_i)} \exp\left(\vec{\theta} \cdot \vec{\phi}(W_i, T')\right)\right).
$$

Accordingly, the local gradient is

$$
\frac{\partial \log P(T_i|W_i)}{\partial \vec{\theta}} = \vec{\phi}(W_i, T_i) - \sum_{T' \in \text{GEN}(W_i)} P(T'|W_i)\vec{\phi}(W_i, T') \quad (\text{definition of } P(T'|W_i)). \quad (10.12)
$$

Similar to the training of log-linear models in Chapters 4, 8 and 9, there is an exponential number of candidate outputs T' given an input W_i, which makes the calculation of $\sum_{T'} P(T'|W_i)\vec{\phi}(W_i, T')$ computationally intractable. Again we resort to feature locality. In particular,

$$
\vec{\phi}(W_i, T') = \sum_{r \in T'} \vec{\phi}(W_i, r),
$$

where $r \in T'$ denotes a grammar rule in T'. As a result,

$$
\begin{aligned}
&\sum_{T' \in \text{GEN}(W_i)} P(T'|W_i)\vec{\phi}(W_i, T') \\
&= \sum_{T' \in \text{GEN}(W_i)} P(T'|W_i)\left(\sum_{r \in T'} \vec{\phi}(W_i, r)\right) \\
&= \sum_{T' \in \text{GEN}(W_i)} \sum_{r \in T'} P(T'|W_i)\vec{\phi}(W_i, r) \\
&= \sum_{r \in \text{GENR}(W_i)} \left(\sum_{T' \in \text{GEN}(W_i)} P(T'|W_i)\vec{\phi}(W_i, r) \cdot \mathbb{1}(r \in T')\right) \\
&= \sum_{r \in \text{GENR}(W_i)} E_{T' \sim P(T'|W_i)}\left(\vec{\phi}(W_i, r) \cdot \mathbb{1}(r \in T')\right).
\end{aligned}
$$
(10.13)

Equation 10.13 indicates that the expectation of the global feature vector $\vec{\phi}(W_i, r)$ over all T' is equal to the sum of expectations of each local feature vector $\vec{\phi}(W_i, r)$ over all possible T'. Here $\text{GENR}(W_i)$ represents the set of all possible grammar rules in all possible trees given the input W_i. For our current models, the grammar rules are lexicalised, taking the form $c[w_h] \rightarrow c_1[w_{h_1}]c_2[w_{h_2}]$ where $c, c_1, c_2 \in C$, and $h_0, h_1, h_2 \in [1, \ldots, |W_i|]$. The term $1(r \in T')$ equals 1 if $r \in T'$ and 0 otherwise.

Further, we have the following observation of expectation about T' and expectation over r:

$$\sum_{r \in \text{GENR}(W_i)} E_{T' \sim P(T'|W_i)}\Big(\vec{\phi}(W_i, r) \cdot 1(r \in T')\Big) = \sum_{r \in \text{GENR}(W_i)} E_{r \sim P(r|W_i)}\vec{\phi}(W_i, r). \qquad (10.14)$$

Therefore, if we can calculate the marginal probabilities $P(r|W_i)$ efficiently, then the expectation of $\vec{\phi}(W_i, r)$ over all possible T' is equivalent to the expectation over all possible r given W_i, namely $\sum_{r \in \text{GENR}(W_i)} P(r|W_i)\vec{\phi}(W_i, r)$.

Calculating marginal rule probabilities. Our goal is to efficiently calculate $P(r|W_{1:n})$, where the rule r can take the form $(b, b', e, h, h_1, h_2, c, c_1, c_2)$, where (b, e, c, h) represents the parent constituent, and $(b, b' - 1, c_1, h_1)$ and (b', e, c_2, h_2) represent the child constituents.

Since we know $P(T|W_{1:n})$ according to our log-linear model, $P(r|W_{1:n})$ can be calculated by summing up the conditional probabilities of all the constituent trees that contain r:

$$\begin{aligned} P(r|W_{1:n}) &= \sum_{T \in \text{GEN}(W_{1:n}) \text{ such that } r \in T} P(T|W_{1:n}) \\ &= \sum_{T \in \text{GEN}(W_{1:n}) \text{ such that } r \in T} \prod_{r' \in T} \exp\Big(\vec{\theta} \cdot \vec{\phi}(W_{1:n}, r')\Big) \end{aligned} \qquad (10.15)$$

Equation 10.15 is a sum of exponential terms, which can be divided into three components around r. For convenience of illustration, let us borrow terms from Section 10.1.4. In particular, use $\text{INSIDE}(b, e, c, h, W_{1:n})$ to denote the context of all derivations inside the subtree $T(b, e, c[w_h])$, namely within the derivation $c[w_h] \overset{*}{\Longrightarrow} w_b w_{b+1} \ldots w_e$, and $\text{OUTSIDE}(b, e, c, h, W_{1:n})$ to denote the context of all possible structures in the tree above $T(b, e, c[w_h])$, namely the derivation $S[w_*] \overset{*}{\Longrightarrow} w_1 w_2 \ldots w_{b-1} c w_{e+1} \ldots w_n$, where w_* denotes any head word in $W_{1:n}$.

Now defining

$$\begin{aligned} & \text{INSIDESCORE}(b, e, c, h, W_{1:n}) \\ &= \sum_{T(b,e,c[w_h]) \in \text{INSIDE}(b,e,c,h,W_{1:n})} \prod_{r' \in T(b,e,c[w_h])} \exp\Big(\vec{\theta} \cdot \vec{\phi}(W_{1:n}, r')\Big), \end{aligned}$$

and

$$\begin{aligned} & \text{OUTSIDESCORE}(b, e, c, h, W_{1:n}) \\ &= \sum_{\bar{T}(b,e,c[w_h]) \in \text{OUTSIDE}(b,e,c,h,W_{1:n})} \prod_{r' \in \bar{T}(b,e,c[w_h])} \exp\Big(\vec{\theta} \cdot \vec{\phi}(W_{1:n}, r')\Big), \end{aligned}$$

we have

$$\begin{aligned} P(r|W_{1:n}) \propto{} & \text{INSIDESCORE}(b, b' - 1, c_1, h_1, W_{1:n})\text{INSIDESCORE}(b', e, c_2, h_2, W_{1:n}) \\ & \text{OUTSIDE}(b, e, c, h, W_{1:n}) \exp\Big(\vec{\theta} \cdot \vec{\phi}(W_{1:n}, r)\Big). \end{aligned}$$

The calculation of $\textsc{InsideScore}(b, e, c, h, W_{1:n})$ and $\textsc{OutsideScore}(b, e, c, h, W_{1:n})$ can be performed by modifying Algorithms 10.2 and 10.3, which we leave to Exercise 10.10.

10.2.4 Training Large-Margin Models for Constituent Parsing

For both structured perceptron and SVM models, the training goal is to ensure a positive score margin between gold-standard outputs and incorrect outputs, given a set of training data $D = \{(W_i, T_i)\}|_{i=1}^{N}$. For structured perceptron, the training objective is to minimise:

$$\sum_{i=1}^{N} \max\left(0, \max_{T' \in \textsc{Gen}(W_i)} \left(\vec{\theta} \cdot \vec{\phi}(W_i, T')\right) - \vec{\theta} \cdot \vec{\phi}(W_i, T_i)\right). \tag{10.16}$$

For structured SVM, the training objective is to minimise:

$$\frac{1}{2}||\vec{\theta}||^2 + C\left(\sum_{i=1}^{N} \max\left(0, 1 - \vec{\theta} \cdot \vec{\phi}(W_i, T_i) + \max_{T' \neq T_i}\left(\vec{\theta} \cdot \vec{\phi}(W_i, T')\right)\right)\right), \tag{10.17}$$

where $T' \in \textsc{Gen}(W_i)$.

In both Eq 10.16 and Eq 10.17 above, calculating $\max_{T' \in \textsc{Gen}(W_i)} \left(\vec{\theta} \cdot \vec{\phi}(W_i, T')\right)$ involves the decoding process in Algorithm 10.5. This is similar to the case of sequence labelling, and sequence segmentation. However, due to differences in the definition of feature vectors, and incremental feature calculation, the decoding algorithm differs from the other structured prediction tasks.

10.3 Reranking

Similar to sequence labelling and sequence segmentation tasks, the time complexity of dynamic programs for constituent parsing is correlated with the context range of features. When the feature context is extended beyond a grammar rule, the asymptotic complexity of Algorithms 10.1, 10.2 and 10.3 can increase beyond $O(n^3)$. On the other hand, it has been shown that non-local features can be highly useful for structural disambiguation. For example, we can define a feature for *unbinarised rules*, which capture patterns of a collapsed *n*-ary rule, such as the rule $S \rightarrow ADVP\ VP\ NP$. in Figure 10.1, with the head being *VP*. A back-off version of this feature can cover the left-hand side of a rule (e.g. *S*) and *n*-grams on the right (e.g. *ADVP VP NP* .). In addition, as a second-order feature, a *grandparent feature* can be useful, which includes a grammar rule and the non-terminal above it. The feature can be further extended into a grammar rule and the entire rule above it, such as $S \rightarrow VP \rightarrow VBP$. Further, features from tree structures can also be useful. For example, it has been shown that constituent trees in English and other languages can have a right-branching bias, where the right subtree is larger than the left subtree for constituent nodes. Consequently, a "right branch" feature that counts the number of nodes on the rightmost branch of a constituent node can capture this tendency toward right-branching. As yet another example, the size (in terms of the number of words) and relative position of constituents can also serve as useful features. In the extreme case, the entire unlexicalised subtree can also serve as a feature! With regard to word–word relations, the head words between child nodes and a parent node can serve as a feature, and the pattern subject–verb–arguments in a sentence can also be useful for tree disambiguation. Exercise 10.8 discusses such features in more detail. Apparently, non-local features can disallow tractable dynamic programs.

Reranking is a technique for integrating such non-local features without introducing additional asymptotic complexity. The basic idea is to let a *base parser* with only local features provide a set of output candidates with the highest confidence (i.e., model score), given an input sentence. A separate *reranker model* is then used to rescore the set of candidates, by considering both the base parser model score and a set of additional non-local features, which cannot be easily integrated into the base parser. Now that the reranker explores only a small number of candidate outputs from the base parser, brute-force enumeration can be used to find the output with the highest reranking score. The reranker has a separate set of model parameters, and is trained after the base parser is trained.

Obtaining output candidates from a base parser. There are two major methods for obtaining the most confident output candidates from a base parser. The first is to obtain a fixed number of k-best candidates, and the second is to obtain a set of candidates that score higher than a threshold $\beta base\_score(\hat{T})$ by the base model, where $\hat{T}$ is the highest-scored output candidate. $base\_score(T)$ represents the score of T as given by the base model. $\beta \in (0, 1)$ is a hyper-parameter of the model. The value of β can be determined empirically. Typical values include 0.1, 0.001 etc. In order to obtain more than one best candidate output, the standard decoding algorithm such as the Viterbi algorithm and the CKY algorithm need to be modified. Exercise 10.11 discusses this problem.

Testing. Formally, the set of input data to the reranker can be denoted as $D = \{(W_i, TS_i)\}|_{i=1}^{N}$, where N is the total number of testing sentences. $TS_i = \{T_i^1, T_i^2, \ldots T_i^{n_i}\}$ is the set of n_i-best output candidates by the base parser. The score of a candidate output tree T_i^j given by the reranker can be defined as

$$score(T_i^j) = \alpha_0 \cdot base\_score(T_i^j) + \sum_{k=1}^{m} \alpha_k \cdot f_k(W_i, T_i^j) \tag{10.18}$$

where $f_k(W_i, T_i^j)$ $(k \in [1, \ldots, m])$ denotes a non-local feature by the reranker.

Equation 10.18 above is a linear model, taking features from the base model score and non-local feature templates. Denoting $\vec{\theta} = \langle \alpha_0, \alpha_1, \ldots, \alpha_m \rangle$, and $\vec{\phi}(W_i, T_i^j) = \langle base\_score(T_i^j), f_1(W_i, T_i^j), f_2(W_i, T_i^j), \ldots, f_m(W_i, T_i^j) \rangle$, we have

$$score(T_i^j) = \vec{\theta} \cdot \vec{\phi}(W_i, T_i^j). \tag{10.19}$$

It is worth noting that $base\_score(T_i^j)$ can take a real value, such as the log probability of T_i^j given W_i according to the base model. As discussed in Chapter 3, they are *real-valued features*, which differ from features in $f_k(W_i, T_i^j)$.

Training a reranking model using log-likelihood loss. Formally, the set of training data can be denoted as $D = \{(W_i, \{T_i\} \cup TS_i)\}|_{i=1}^{N}$, where N is the total number of training sentences. $TS_i = \{T_i^1, T_i^2, \ldots, T_i^{n_i}\}$ is the set of n_i-best *incorrect* output candidates by the base parser. Note that the gold-standard parse tree T_i may not be in the set of highest-scored base parses, in which case it should be added to the base output list in order for the reranker to learn gold-standard structures.

According to the MLE principle, the training objective is to maximise the likelihood $P(D) = \prod_i P(T_i|W_i)$. Here we take

$$P(T_i|W_i) = \frac{\exp\left(score(T_i)\right)}{\exp\left(score(T_i)\right) + \sum_{j\in[1,\ldots,n_i] \text{ such that } T_i^j\neq T_i} \exp\left(score(T_i^j)\right)}. \tag{10.20}$$

One thing to note is that in the definition above, the partition function $Z = \exp\left(score(T_i)\right) + \sum_{j\in[1,\ldots,n_i] \text{ such that } T_i^j\neq T_i} \exp\left(score(T_i^j)\right)$ contains only the gold-standard tree and the n_i incorrect output trees of the base parser, rather than the set of all valid constituent trees. This smaller sample space means that the reranker does not face challenges in time complexity.

Given the definition of $P(T_i|W_i)$ above, the training objective can be defined as maximising

$$\begin{aligned}
\log P(D) &= \sum_i \log P(T_i|W_i) \\
&= \sum_i \left(score(T_i) - \log\left(\exp\left(score(T_i)\right) + \sum_{j=1}^{n_i} \exp\left(score(T_i^j)\right)\right)\right).
\end{aligned} \tag{10.21}$$

SGD can be used for optimisation. For the ith training example the local gradient is

$$\begin{aligned}
\frac{\partial}{\partial\theta}\log P(T_i|W_i) &= \vec{\phi}(W_i, T_i) - \left(P(T_i|W_i)\cdot\vec{\phi}(W_i, T_i) + \sum_{j=1}^{n_i} P(T_i^j|W_i)\cdot\vec{\phi}(W_i, T_i^j)\right) \\
&= \left(1 - P(T_i|W_i)\right)\cdot\vec{\phi}(W_i, T_i) + \sum_{j=1}^{n_i} P(T_i^j|W_i)\cdot\vec{\phi}(W_i, T_i^j).
\end{aligned} \tag{10.22}$$

Training a reranking model using large-margin loss. The large-margin loss function discussed in Chapter 4 can also be used for reranking. The main goal is to maximise the score margins between T_i and $T' \in TS_i$ for all W_i. Take SVM for example: without considering regularisation, this objective function formally minimises the score margin function

$$\max\left(0, 1 + \max_{T'\in TS}\left(\vec{\theta}\cdot\vec{\phi}(W_i, T')\right) - \vec{\theta}\cdot\vec{\phi}(W_i, T_i)\right). \tag{10.23}$$

SGD can be used for optimisation. The local gradient for the ith training example is

$$\begin{cases}
0 & \text{if } \vec{\theta}\cdot\vec{\phi}(W_i, T_i) > \max_{T'\in TS_i}\vec{\theta}\cdot\vec{\phi}(W_i, T') + 1 \\
\vec{\phi}(W_i, T_i) - \max_{T'\in TS_i}\vec{\phi}(W_i, T') & \text{otherwise.}
\end{cases} \tag{10.24}$$

For training, we add the gold-standard constituent tree to the set of training examples for each W_i as required by Eq 10.21 and Eq 10.23. However, during test time, the gold-standard constituent tree may not be in the best output list of the base model. This can cause inconsistency for the training and test scenarios. One alternative way for training the reranker is to have the same TS_i settings as during testing. In this case, the "gold-standard" is chosen among TS_i, which can be the one that has the highest F-score. This "gold-standard" tree is also referred to as the **oracle** base output. Using the oracle base output for training may lead to penalisation of gold-tree features in non-oracle trees and rewarding of non-gold features in oracle trees. As a result, whether or not the gold-standard tree should be added to the reranker training instances is an empirical question.

10.4 Beyond Sequences and Trees

We have thus far discussed structured prediction models for sequence labelling, sequence segmentation and constituent tree prediction, for which common underlying modelling techniques have been used. For example, probability chain rule, independence assumptions and Bayes rule have been used for parameterising generative models, and dynamic programs have been used for decoding and for calculating the marginal probabilities in log-linear model training. These techniques are useful for designing structured prediction models for solving other NLP tasks.

As introduced in Chapter 1, dependency trees are another typical tree structure for representing syntax. Dynamic program decoders and large-margin discriminative models have been investigated in the research literature for this task. Similar to the tasks that we have seen in this book, a dynamic decoder for dependency parsing requires that features are local to a small context range. For example, an arc-factored model, which constrains features to individual dependency arcs, allows exact inference with $O(n^3)$ time complexity, where n is the size of the input sentence. Increasingly larger feature contexts lead to increasingly higher time complexity. To make better use of non-local information without compromising runtime efficiency, approximate inference algorithms have been exploited. The next chapter discusses a framework to this end, which uses learning-guided-search to address potential issues with inexact search.

Summary

In this chapter, we have learned:

- generative constituent parsing, binarisation, probabilistic context free grammars (PCFGs);
- CKY algorithms, inside–outside algorithms, lexicalised PCFGs;
- log-linear models for discriminative constituent parsing;
- large-margin models for discriminative constituent parsing;
- reranking.

Chapter Notes

Generative grammar was proposed by Chomsky (1957). Booth and Thompson (1973) and Grenander (1976) proposed probabilistic context free grammar (PCFG). Kasami (1966), Younger (1967),

Table 10.1 Head-finding rules for *NP* and *VP*.

Non-terminal	Rule
NP	r *POS NN NNP NNPS NNS*; r *NX*; r *JJR*; r *CD*;r *JJ*; r *JJS*; r *RB*; r *QP*; r *NP*; r
VP	l *VBD*; l *VBN*; l *MD*; l *VBZ*; l *VB*; l *VBG*; l *VBP*; l *VP*; l *ADJP*; l *NN*; l *NNS*; l *NP*; l

Cocke (1969) and Kay (1967) investigated the Cocke-Kasami-Younger (CKY) decoding algorithm. Aho and Ullman (1973) discussed algorithms for parsing computer languages which influenced research on constituent parsing. Statistical parsing was an important problem in structured prediction (Fujisaki et al., 1989; Schabes et al., 1993; Jelinek et al., 1994; Magerman, 1995; Collins, 1997; Charniak, 2000). Log-linear models were used for discriminative parsing (Abney, 1997; Della Pietra et al., 1997; Clark and Curran, 2003; Johnson et al., 1999). Rich lexicalised features (Magerman, 1995; Collins, 1996; Charniak, 2000) as well as unlexicalised features (Klein and Manning, 2003; Petrov and Klein, 2007) were investigated. Freund et al. (2003) addressed reranking problems, which were further explored by Collins and Koo (2005) for constituent parsing.

Exercises

10.1 Head-finding rules are useful for binarising constituent tree structures. Table 10.1 shows the head-finding rules of *NP* and *VP*. Take the rules for *NP* as an example. In the rule, there are several groups separated by ";". The algorithm starts by looking at the first group and continues to check the next group if the algorithm does not return a valid head word. Take the first group "r *POS NN NNP NNPS NNS*" for example: "r" denotes the searching direction; "*POS NN NNP NNPS NNS*" specifies a set of labels. The algorithm first traverses the children from right to left and tries to find a child labelled with *POS* or *NN* or *NNP* or *NNPS* or *NNS*. Otherwise, the same process will be applied to the second group. If the required label is a non-terminal, for example, *QP* or *NP*, the algorithm recursively applies the head-finding rules of *QP* or *NP* to find the head word. If the algorithm failed to find the head word after the group "r *NP*", a default rule will be used. The last group "r" means the head word of the rightmost child will be the default result.

(a) Given a constituent tree "(S (NP (DT The) (JJ little) (NN boy)) (VP (VBZ likes) (NP (JJ red) (NN tomatoes))) (. .))", annotate the head words of *NP* and *VP* in this tree using the rules in Table 10.1.
(b) Derive the head-finding rule for *ADJP*.
(c) How can you unbinarise a binarised tree in Figure 10.1(b), 10.1(c) and 10.1(d)?

10.2 Calculate the number of possible binarised trees given a sentence. (Hint: This is a Catalan number.)

10.3 Prove by contradiction that Eq 10.2 is true.

10.4 Describe the algorithm FINDDERIVATION for CKY when given the pointer bp. (Hint: Supposing $bp[s][i][c] = (j, c_1, c_2)$, recursively call FINDDERIVATION for the configurations $bp[j - i][i][c_1]$ and $bp[s - j + i][j][c_2]$.)

10.5 Algorithm 10.1, Algorithm 10.2 and Algorithm 10.3 consider only CNF while neglecting unary rules. Extend the algorithms when unary rules are allowed. For CKY (Algorithm 10.1), how should the backtrace algorithm be changed? How can looping rules (e.g., $NP \to NP$) negatively affect the algorithm and how can they be eliminated?

10.6 Show that Algorithm 10.3 calculates to Eq 10.6.

10.7 Beam search. By considering the head words of constituents, Algorithms 10.4 and 10.5 have a high time complexity of $O(n^5)$. This can make a parser intolerably slow in processing sentences of more than 20 words. One solution is to use beam search for approximate decoding. In particular, the enumeration of h_1, h_2 and h can be removed. Instead, the k highest-scored constituents among $\hat{T}(i, i + s - 1, c[w_h])$, with different h, are stored in each chart cell $chart[s][i][c]$. This new algorithm can be regarded as extending Algorithm 10.1 by modifying the chart cell structure, replacing a single local optimum with a beam of k local maxima, when additionally considering head information. Write pseudocode for the beam search decoder. What is its time complexity?

10.8 Features. Consider useful features for discriminative constituent parsing. What are useful syntactic patterns within a CFG rule? What are useful non-local patterns that span over more than one grammar rule?

10.9 One method of increasing the expressiveness of features in a PCFG is to enlarge the set of non-terminal symbols. Head lexicalistation can be understood as one typical example. A different strategy is to conduct **parent annotation** on each non-terminal symbol in a constituent tree. For example, in the constituent tree in Figure 10.1(a), the parent node of the NP over "*the net contributions of the experts*" is S. Therefore, the *NP* is relabelled as *NP@S*, with its parent information. Correspondingly, the grammar rule $NP \to NP\ PP$ now becomes $NP@S \to NP\ PP$. Different from head annotation, parent annotation effectively enlarges the context range of PCFG features, from a single rule to part of two consecutive rules. Now consider again the MLE training and CKY decoding algorithms PCFGs. How does parent annotation affect them? What is the smallest decoding time?

10.10 Extend the inside and outside algorithms (Algorithms 10.2 and 10.3) for calculating marginal rule probabilities in log-linear model training (Section 10.2.3). You need to consider the additional enumeration of head indices, and the replacement of PCFG probabilities with local feature scores.

10.11 Consider modifying Algorithm 10.5 for producing k-best output candidates rather than 1-best output for constituent parsing. In particular, when beam-search is used, a k best list can be found from the beam for S. Does this list consist of exactly the k highest-scored outputs? Can you think of a dynamic program to address the task?

10.12 PCFG can be viewed as a tree-structured version of HMM. In Chapter 7, we discussed unsupervised training for HMMs using EM. Now consider training PCFG from a raw text corpus $D = \{W_i\}|_{i=1}^{N}$, where W_i is a sentence. What are the hidden variables H, and what are the observed variables O? According to PCFG parameterisation, how do you define the Q function? What are the E-step and M-step that can be used to estimate parameters efficiently?

11 Transition-Based Methods for Structured Prediction

Thus far we have learned a range of discriminative models for structured prediction. In particular, given a specific task, a set of feature templates are defined for representing structured outputs in a feature space, so that a linear model can be used to score candidate structures. Dynamic programs are carefully designed to accommodate feature contexts, so that efficient training and decoding can be performed. This approach has been used to solve sequence labelling, sequence segmentation and tree prediction tasks, leading to CRF, semi-CRF and tree CRF models, as well as their structured perceptron and SVM counterparts.

For sequence segmentation and sequence labelling, we have seen in Chapter 9 one different discriminative approach, which uses learning-guided beam-search with early-update perceptron. The advantage is allowing rich features with linear runtime complexity. We have not yet discussed whether this type of approach can be applied to tree prediction tasks. To this end, this chapter generalises the sequential decision process of Chapter 9 into a state transition process, where a state represents a partially constructed output and transition actions incrementally build output structures. We show how this approach can be used to solve a range of parsing tasks in linear time complexity, enjoying competitive accuracies thanks to the freedom of using non-local features. The tasks cover constituent parsing, dependency parsing and joint parsing.

11.1 Transition-Based Structured Prediction

Given an input, a **transition-based structured prediction** model casts the output construction process into a state transition process, where a **state** represents partially constructed outputs and state **transition actions** represent incremental steps that build output structures. Formally, given an input X, a corresponding output is constructed from an **initial state** s_0, through a sequence of transition actions a_i, each advancing a state s_{i-1} into a next state s_i, until a **terminal state** $\bar{s}_{|S|}$ is reached, which corresponds to a full output structure. $|S|$ denotes the total number of states excluding s_0, or the total number of actions.

Taking word segmentation for example, a state can be formally denoted as $s = (\sigma, \omega, \beta)$, where σ represents a partial output, which is a list of words that have been recognised, ω represents the current partial word being constructed, and β represents the list of next incoming characters. Given an input sentence $X = C_{1:n} = c_1 c_2 \ldots c_n$, the initial state can be denoted as $s_0 = ([\,], \text{``''}, C_{1:n})$, with both the output word sequence and the current partial word being empty, and the incoming sequence consisting of all input characters. A final state takes the form $\bar{s} = (W_{1:|W|}, \text{``''}, [\,])$, where the segmented output $W_{1:|W|} = w_1 w_2 \ldots w_{|W|}$ covers all the input characters while the partial word ω and next inputs β are empty.

There are three possible actions for state transitions, namely:

- SEP, which moves ω onto σ, removes the front character β_0 from β, and takes β_0 as the new value of ω;
- APP, which removes the first character β_0 from β, and attaches it to the end of ω;
- FIN, which moves the current non-empty partial word ω onto σ when β is empty.

The above state transition system can be formalised as the deduction system shown in Figure 11.1. Given the input $C_1^7 =$ "以 (take) 前 (before) 天 (day) 下 (fall) 雨 (rain) 为 (be) 例 (example)" the sequence of actions $A_{1:7} = $ SEP, SEP, APP, SEP, APP, SEP, APP can be used to construct the output "以 (take) 前天 (the day before yesterday) 下雨 (rain) 为例 (for example)", as shown in Table 11.1.

Model. The goal of a transition-based structured prediction model is to learn to map an input to a sequence of state transitions, which correspond to the correct output structure. In this example, the input is $C_{1:7}$ and the output is $A_{1:7}$. Features are extracted from s_i for scoring a_{i+1} ($i \in [0, 7]$).

It is worth noting that this process can appear similar to a character tagging process in the sense that "separate" and "append" decisions are made on each character in the left-to-right

Axiom:	$([\ ], [\ ], \beta)$	APP:	$\dfrac{(\sigma, \omega, \beta_0 \mid \beta)}{(\sigma, \omega + \beta_0, \beta)}$
Goal:	$(\sigma, [\ ], [\ ])$		
SEP:	$\dfrac{(\sigma, \omega, \beta_0 \mid \beta)}{(\sigma \mid \omega, \beta_0, \beta)}$	FIN:	$\dfrac{(\sigma, \omega, [\ ])}{(\sigma \mid \omega, [\ ], [\ ])}$

Figure 11.1 State transition system for word segmentation, where | separates the head and tail of a list and $+$ indicates string concatenation. σ is a reversed list.

Table 11.1 Example transition-based word segmentation process for the sentence "以前天下雨为例 (take the rain on the day before yesterday for example)", which was also seen in Chapter 9.

Step	State $s_i = (\sigma, w, \beta)$	Next Action a_{i+1}
0	$([\ ], [\ ], [以, 前, 天, 下, 雨, 为, 例])$	SEP
1	$([\ ], [以], [前, 天, 下, 雨, 为, 例])$	SEP
2	$([以], [前], [天, 下, 雨, 为, 例])$	APP
3	$([以], [前天], [下, 雨, 为, 例])$	SEP
4	$([以, 前天], [下], [雨, 为, 例])$	APP
5	$([以, 前天], [下雨], [为, 例])$	SEP
6	$([以, 前天, 下雨], [为], [例])$	SEP
7	$([以, 前天, 下雨, 为], [例], [\ ])$	FIN
8	$([以, 前天, 下雨, 为, 例], [\ ], [\ ])$	

order, and can thus be seen on segmentation tags as characters. In practice, a transition-based model for sequence labelling may be effectively the same as a greedy sequence labeller we saw in Chapter 7 under certain feature settings. However, a transition-based model offers a theoretically different perspective in which we view the task, which brings unique benefits to highly complex structures such as trees and graphs. In particular, by transforming structures into action sequences, a transition-based model turns structural ambiguities into state transition ambiguities. Thus the target of modelling shifts from structural choices to action choices. Given an input, a transition-based model extracts features from states for scoring transition actions. Non-local features are typically extracted for scoring action sequences. We have seen example non-local features for sequence labelling in Chapter 9 (Section 9.3) and will see more of them for parsing later in this chapter. In contrast, a CRF sequence labeller model in Chapter 8 extracts features from output tag sequences directly, typically under the Markov assumption (Chapter 2) in order to allow dynamic programming. The scmi-CRF sequence segmentation algorithm and tree CRF constituent parsing algorithm that we discussed in Chapters 9 and 10 work in similar ways, directly extracting local structural features for directly over output graph structures. As a result, we name these algorithms **graph-based models** to contrast them with transition-based models.

Because features can be highly non-local for transition-based structured prediction models, dynamic programs are in general infeasible. In the next sections, we introduce a simple local model that considers each action individually, before introducing a global model that considers a sequence of actions as a whole.

11.1.1 Greedy Local Modelling

Formally, given a state s_{i-1}, our goal is to disambiguate all possible actions $a_i \in$ POSSIBLEACTIONS(s_{i-1}). This can be achieved by using a discriminative model to score transition actions. In particular, we can extract a feature vector $\vec{\phi}(s_{i-1}, a_i)$ for representing the input–output pair (s_{i-1}, a_i), and then using a linear model to score a_i:

$$score(a_i|s_{i-1}) = \vec{\theta} \cdot \vec{\phi}(s_{i-1}, a_i), \tag{11.1}$$

where $\vec{\theta}$ is the model parameter vector.

Taking the state transition process in Table 11.1 for example. At step 4 the current state $s_4 = ([以 前天], [下], [雨, 为, 例])$. One possible feature for scoring the action SEP is "$\sigma_0 = 前天, \omega = 下, \beta_0 = 雨$ and $a = $ APP".[1] The above features are effectively the same as the feature "$w_{j-1} = 前天, w_j = 下雨$" in Table 9.5 of Chapter 9 (feature template 2), both disambiguating a word bigram. On the other hand, rather than directly scoring the output structure, the transition-based model scores the next action a_5. To this goal, a non-local feature can be "$\sigma_{|\sigma|-1} = 以(take), \omega = 为(for), \beta_0 = 例(example), a = $ APP", which embodies the pattern "以 (take) ...为例 (for example)". A list of more feature templates are shown in Table 11.2. Note that all feature instances

---

[1] Words on σ are indexed such that the last word is σ_0 and the first word is $\sigma_{|\sigma|-1}$.

Table 11.2 Feature templates for transition-based segmentation. σ_0 – the top word on the stack; σ_{-1} – the bottom word on the stack; $\beta_0, \beta_1, \beta_2$ – the front characters on the buffer; ω – partial word; a – action. START, END and LEN return the beginning character, the end character and the size of a word, respectively.

ID	Feature	ID	Feature
1	ω and a	10	$\beta_0, \beta_1, \beta_2, a$
2	β_0 and a	11	$\text{END}(\sigma_0), \omega, \beta_0, a$
3	$\text{LEN}(\omega), \beta_0$ and a	12	$\text{START}(\sigma_0), \omega, \beta_0, a$
4	$\text{START}(\omega), \text{LEN}(\omega)$ and a	13	$\text{START}(\sigma_0), \text{START}(\omega), \beta_0, a$
5	ω, β_0 and a	14	$\text{LEN}(\sigma_0), \text{LEN}(\omega), \beta_0, a$
6	$\text{START}(\omega), \beta_0$ and a	15	$\text{END}(\sigma_0), \text{END}(\omega), \beta_0, a$
7	$\text{END}(\omega), \beta_0$ and a	16	$\sigma_0, \omega, \beta_0, a$
8	$\text{LEN}(\omega), \beta_0$ and a	17	$\sigma_1, \sigma_0, \omega, \beta_0, a$
9	$\text{END}(\omega), \beta_0, \beta_1$ and a	18	$\sigma_{-1}, \omega, \beta_0, a$

in a transition-based model must consist of both a state component and an action component, which serve as the input and output for action disambiguation, respectively.

Training and decoding. A conceptually simplest and most efficient decoding and training framework is a greedy local method. In particular, a local classifier is trained to decide the next action given a current state according to Eq 11.1. For testing, we use a greedy algorithm to build outputs by repeatedly applying the best action according to the local classifier.

Formally, for testing, given an input X, the decoder starts from the initial state $s_0(X)$, repeatedly finding $\hat{a}_i = \arg\max_a \vec{\theta} \cdot \vec{\phi}(s_{i-1}, a)$ using the model $\vec{\theta}$, until a terminal state is reached. For training, given a set of gold-standard data $D = \{(X_i, Y_i)\}|_{i=1}^{N}$, we break each training example (X_i, Y_i) down into a sequence of gold-standard state transitions $(s_{j-1}^{(i)}, a_j^{(i)})$, where $j \in [1, \dots, |S_i|]$. All such state–action pairs are then merged into a single training set. For training the classification model in Eq 11.1, discriminative models such as SVMs, perceptrons and log-linear models can be used.

The local model is conceptually simple, solving structured prediction tasks using a classifier. With the features in Table 11.2, a local greedy transition-based model can give similar accuracies compared to a semi-CRF segmentor discussed in Chapter 9, but runs much faster. However, for more complex problems such as constituent parsing, the accuracy of a local transition-based model can fall behind the best graph-based parsers, despite running orders of magnitudes faster. The reason for low accuracies can be explained in two aspects. First, for decoding, making greedy local decisions can lead to error propagation, since an incorrect action results in an incorrect state, which can negatively influence subsequent actions. This problem is significantly more severe for parsing tasks, which has stronger interdependencies between actions in a sequence compared with segmentation and sequence labelling tasks. Second, a local model does not consider structures as a whole. In particular, for transition-based structured prediction, a sequence of transition actions corresponds to a structured output as a whole unit. In a globally optimal action sequence, each action may not necessarily be the optimal choice when viewed locally. As a result, a local classification model may be inherently flawed for choosing the best action sequences. This is similar to the label bias problem discussed in Chapter 8. To address these problems, one solution is to use a globally trained model, which we discuss next.

11.1.2 Structured Modelling

Rather than making local decisions at each action, a global transition-based model scores a *sequence* of transition actions as a single unit, which corresponds to a global *structure*. Given an input X, a global transition-based model calculates $score(A|X)$ directly, where $A_{1:|A|} = a_1 a_2 \ldots a_{|A|}$ is a sequence of transition actions a_i for building an output structure for X. For word segmentation, for example, such a global model calculates $score(A_{1:n}|C_{1:n})$ for a given input $C_{1:n}$. For this task, the number of actions equals the number of characters n. For other tasks, $|A|$ may be different from $|X|$.

A global linear model can be used to calculate $score(A|X)$, based on a feature vector representation of A:

$$score(A|X) = \vec{\theta} \cdot \vec{\phi}(A, X),$$

where $\vec{\theta}$ is the model parameter vector.

To allow incremental decoding, $\vec{\phi}(A, X)$ can naturally be decomposed into feature vectors for individual actions:

$$\vec{\phi}(A, X) = \sum_{i=1}^{|A|} \vec{\phi}(s_{i-1}, a_i),$$

where s_{i-1} denotes the state in the $(i - 1)$th step and a_i denotes the action that changes s_{i-1} to s_i. The features $\vec{\phi}(s_{i-1}, a_i)$ can be defined in the same way as Eq 11.1.

Thus we can correspondingly decompose the global score $score(A|X)$:

$$score(A|X) = \vec{\theta} \cdot \vec{\phi}(A, X) = \vec{\theta} \cdot \left(\sum_{i=1}^{|A|} \vec{\phi}(s_{i-1}, a_i) \right) = \sum_{i=1}^{|A|} \left(\vec{\theta} \cdot \vec{\phi}(s_{i-1}, a_i) \right). \tag{11.2}$$

This incremental feature extraction and scoring process allows us to adapt the learning guided beam-search framework discussed in Chapter 9 for decoding and training. For decoding, beam-search can alleviate the error propagation problem compared with greedy search by simultaneously considering multiple highest-scored states at each step. For training, early-update perceptron allows us to train a model globally for scoring sequences of state transitions and minimising search errors.

Decoding. Algorithm 11.1 shows pseudocode of the decoder, which adapts Algorithm 9.6 of Chapter 9 by replacing the incremental structural feature extraction process with a process of incremental state transitions. In particular, given an input X, the decoder incrementally finds the output by using a beam of size K to record the highest-scored states at each step. *agenda*

Algorithm 11.1. Beam search decoding algorithm for transition-based structured prediction.

Inputs: $\vec{\theta}$ —discriminative linear model parameters;
X — task input;
K — beam size;
Initialization: $agenda \leftarrow [(\text{STARTSTATE}(X), 0)]$;
Algorithm:
while not ALLTERMINAL($agenda$) **do**
     $to\_expand \leftarrow agenda$;
     $agenda \leftarrow []$;
     for $(state, score) \in to\_expand$ **do**
         for $a \in$ POSSIBLEACTIONS($state$) **do**
             $new\_state \leftarrow$ EXPAND($state, a$);
             $new\_score \leftarrow score + \vec{\theta} \cdot \vec{\phi}(state, a)$;
             APPEND($agenda, (new\_state, new\_score)$);
     $agenda \leftarrow$ TOP-K($agenda, K$);
Output: TOP-K($agenda, 1$)[0];

---

represents the beam, which takes a list of (*state*, *score*) pairs. With the initial *agenda* consisting of only the initial state (i.e. STARTSTATE(X)), the algorithm repeatedly expands states on *agenda* using transition actions. At the step t, each state s_i^t ($i \in [1, \ldots, K]$) on *agenda* is expanded by applying all possible actions a, where each new state is incrementally scored by adding a new action score $\vec{\theta} \cdot \vec{\phi}(s_i^t, a)$ to the score of the expanded state s_i^t using Eq 11.2. After all the existing states are expanded, the K highest scored new states $s_1^{t+1}, \ldots, s_K^{t+1}$ are put back onto *agenda*. The same process repeats until *agenda* reaches a terminal condition (e.g., with all states in the beam being terminal states). Then the highest scored state on *agenda* is taken for output.

Training. Given a set of gold-standard data $D = \{(X_i, Y_i)\}|_{i=1}^{N}$, pseudocode of the training algorithm is shown in Algorithm 11.2, which adapts Algorithm 9.7 of Chapter 9. For each training example (X, Y), the gold-standard output structure Y is transformed into a gold-standard sequence of transition actions $G = g_1 g_2 \ldots g_{|G|}$. The training process goes over the set of training instances T iterations. When each training instance is processed, the decoding process is applied to X, with the initial *agenda* consisting of only the start state for X. Different from testing, however, an additional gold-standard state is maintained during the process, with the initial value being also the start state STARTSTATE(X). At each step, when the states in the beam are expanded using one transition action, the gold-standard state is advanced using the corresponding gold-standard action. At the end of the step, if the new gold state falls out of the beam, decoding is stopped, and a perceptron update is performed with the gold state being used as a positive example, and the highest-scored new state begin used as a negative example. As discussed in Chapter 9, this mechanism is called **early-stop** or **early-update**. If the gold states are not pruned throughout the decoding steps, a

---

Algorithm 11.2. Beam-search training algorithm for transition-based structured prediction.

Inputs: D – gold-standard training set;
K – beam size;
T – number of training iterations;
Initialisation: $\vec{\theta} \leftarrow 0$;
Algorithm:
for $t \in [1, \ldots, T]$ **do**
    for $(X, Y) \in D$ **do**
        $G \leftarrow$ GOLDACTIONSEQ(X, Y);
        $agenda \leftarrow [(\text{STARTSTATE}(X), 0)]$;
        $gold\_state \leftarrow$ STARTSTATE(X);
        $i \leftarrow 0$;
        while not ALLTERMINAL$(agenda)$ **do**
            $i \leftarrow i + 1$;
            $to\_expand \leftarrow agenda$;
            $agenda \leftarrow []$;
            for $(state, score) \in to\_expand$ **do**
                for $a \in$ POSSIBLEACTIONS$(state)$ **do**
                    $new\_state \leftarrow$ EXPAND$(state, a)$;
                    $new\_score \leftarrow score + \vec{\theta} \cdot \vec{\phi}(state, a)$;
                    APPEND$(agenda, (new\_state, new\_score))$;
            $agenda \leftarrow$ TOP-K$(agenda, K)$;
            $gold\_state \leftarrow$ EXPAND$(gold\_state, G[i])$;
            if not CONTAIN$(agenda, gold\_state)$ **then**
                $pos \leftarrow gold\_state$;
                 $neg \leftarrow$ TOP-K$(agenda, 1)[0]$;
                $\vec{\theta} \leftarrow \vec{\theta} + \vec{\phi}(pos) - \vec{\phi}(neg)$;
                return;
        if $gold\_state \neq$ TOP-K$(agenda, 1)[0]$ **then**
            $\vec{\theta} \leftarrow \vec{\theta} + \vec{\phi}(gold\_state) - \vec{\phi}(\text{TOP-K}(agenda, 1)[0])$;
Output: $\vec{\theta}$;

---

standard perceptron update is performed at the end, by comparing the gold final state with the highest scored final state on *agenda*. After T training iterations, the final model parameters are used for testing. In practice, the averaged perceptron algorithm discussed in Chapter 8 can be used to further improve the performance. Exercise 11.2 discusses this variation.

Application to specific tasks. For graph-based models, task-specific dynamic programs can be necessary for accommodating specific output structures and feature contexts for efficient training and decoding. In contrast, the training and decoding frameworks above work well for transition-based modelling of all different tasks, thanks to the fact that they allow arbitrary large feature contexts. Thus a transition-based model framework can be more easily applicable to new structured prediction tasks. In particular, given a new structured prediction task, the main things to do include (1) to find a state-transition process for building candidate outputs and (2) to define a set of feature templates for representing state transitions. In the following sections, we take various parsing tasks as examples to illustrate how these can be achieved.

11.2 Transition-Based Constituent Parsing

We discussed graph-based methods for constituent parsing in Chapter 10, where reranking is used to integrate non-local features into a model with dynamic programming. The transition-based structured prediction framework allows us to build a constituent parser with non-local features without doing reranking. As mentioned earlier, we need to find a state-transition process to build constituent trees. To this end, a **shift–reduce** parsing process can be directly applied, which uses a sequence of incremental left-to-right actions to build binarised parse trees. In particular, the term "shift" refers to incremental reading of a next input word from left to right, and the term "reduce" refers to the combination of two neighbouring constituents into a larger constituent. Below we discuss a shift–reduce constituent parser in our transition-based framework.

11.2.1 Shift–Reduce Constituent Parsing

Similar to Chapter 10, we work with binarised constituent trees. However, for now let us further simplify the task by assuming that POS-tagging has been performed before parsing, which means that a POS-tag is already assigned to each input word. This setting is also adopted by much parser research. We will move to the more challenging setting without input POS in Section 11.4.

Now we begin to build a transition-based constituent parser with the definition of a state-transition process. Formally, a state can be denoted as a tuple (σ, β), where σ represents a stack structure that holds a sequence of sub constituent trees that have been constructed, and β represents the list of incoming words that have not been processed. Given an input sentence $W_{1:n}$, the *initial state* consists of an empty stack, and a buffer that holds the full input sentence. In a state transition process, shift–reduce actions are used to incrementally consume words in the buffer and build outputs on the stack. Finally, a terminal state consists of a stack that contains a single constituent tree, and an empty buffer structure. The set of state transition actions include:

- SHIFT, which removes the front word from the buffer, pushing it onto the stack as a terminal node;
- REDUCE-L/R-X, which pops the top two nodes off the stack, making them children of a new parent node with constituent label X, and pushes the new node back onto the stack (L and R indicate that the lexical head word for the new node is from the left and right subnodes, respectively; the lexical head will be useful for extracting features);

Table 11.3 A transition-based constituent parsing example for the sentence *"The little boy likes red tomatoes."* The first six steps are shown. l and r in constituent labels indicate that the head word is from the left and right subnode, respectively.

Step	Stack	Buffer	Action
0		DT ADJ NN VV ADJ NNS . The little boy likes red tomatoes .	SHIFT
1	DT The	ADJ NN VV ADJ NNS . little boy likes red tomatoes .	SHIFT
2	DT ADJ The little	NN VV ADJ NNS . boy likes red tomatoes .	SHIFT
3	DT ADJ NN The little boy	VV ADJ NNS . likes red tomatoes .	REDUCE-R-NP*
4	DT / NP-r (ADJ NN: little boy) The	VV ADJ NNS . likes red tomatoes .	REDUCE-R-NP
5	NP-r (DT The / NP-r (ADJ NN: little boy))	VV ADJ NNS . likes red tomatoes .	SHIFT
6	NP-r (DT The / NP-r (ADJ NN: little boy)) VV likes	ADJ NNS . red tomatoes .	SHIFT

- UNARY-X, which pops the top node off the stack, making a new unary-branching parent node with constituent label X, and pushes the new node back onto the stack.

Given the sentence "*The little boy likes red tomatoes.*", the sequence of actions SHIFT, SHIFT, SHIFT, REDUCE-R-NP*, REDUCE-R-NP, SHIFT, SHIFT, SHIFT, REDUCE-R-NP, REDUCE-L-VP, SHIFT, REDUCE-L-S, REDUCE-R-S and IDLE can be used to construct its constituent tree. The first six steps are shown in Table 11.3, while Exercise 11.4 asks you to finish visualising the whole process. It can be shown that given an input sentence, every possible binarised constituent tree can be built using the above transition system.

Adding IDLE action. For working with the global model in Section 11.1.2, we add one additional action IDLE, which can be used on a terminal state, without changing the state. It is useful for dealing with unfair comparison caused by unary actions. Because of the existence of unary-branching nodes, the total number of nodes in different constituent trees can differ. Take the phrase "*address issues*" for example, as shown in Figure 11.3. It can form a constituent with three nodes (NP (NN *address*) (NNS *issues*)) or a constituent with four nodes (VP (VB *address*) (NP (NNS *issues*))). As a result, constituent trees for sentences containing the phrase can correspond to transition action sequences of different lengths. For fair comparison between different structures, it is desirable to have their feature vectors consisting of the same number of transition actions. As a result, IDLE actions can be used to advance terminal states with fewer shift–reduce actions, so that when all the states in *agenda* are terminal, they consist of the same number of transition actions.

A formal description of the transition system is shown as a deduction system in Figure 11.2.

Axiom:	$([\,], W_{1:n})$	SHIFT:	$(\sigma, w_0\|\beta)$
Goal:	$(\sigma, [\,])$		$(\sigma\|w_0, \beta)$
REDUCE-L-X:	$\dfrac{(\sigma\|s_1\|s_0,\ \beta)}{(\sigma\|\overset{X}{\overset{\diagup\ \diagdown}{s_1\qquad s_0}},\ \beta)}$	REDUCE-R-X:	$\dfrac{(\sigma\|s_1\|s_0,\ \beta)}{(\sigma\|\overset{X}{\overset{\diagup\ \diagdown}{s_1\qquad s_0}},\ \beta)}$
UNARY-X:	$\dfrac{(\sigma\|s_0,\ \beta)}{(\sigma\|\overset{X}{\underset{s_0}{\downarrow}},\ \beta)}$	IDLE:	$\dfrac{(\sigma, [\,])}{(\sigma, [\,])}$

Figure 11.2 Transition system for shift–reduce constituent parsing. Arrow indicates lexical head.

Figure 11.3 Constituent tree structure for the phrase "*address issues*".

Table 11.4 Feature templates for a shift-reduce constituent parser. s_0, s_1, s_2, s_3 – the top words on the stack; b_0, b_1, b_2, b_3 – the top words on the buffer; w – word; p – POS-tag; c – constituent label. For example, $w_0 w b_0 p$ denotes the pattern consisting of the top word on the stack and the POS-tag of the front word on the buffer. $_l$, $_r$ and $_u$ denote the left, right and only subnode of a constituent tree node, if any, respectively. For example, $s_{0.r}c$ denotes the constituent label of the right subnode of s_0.

Feature Type	Feature Template
unigrams	$s_0 pc$, $s_0 wc$, $s_1 pc$, $s_1 wc$, $s_2 pc$, $s_2 wc$, $s_3 pc$, $s_3 wc$, $b_0 wp$, $b_1 wp$, $b_2 wp$, $b_3 wp$, $s_{0.l}wc$, $s_{0.r}wc$, $s_{0.u}wc$, $s_{1.l}wc$, $s_{1.r}wc$, $s_{1.u}wc$
bigrams	$s_0 w s_1 w$, $s_0 w s_1 c$, $s_0 c s_1 w$, $s_0 c s_1 c$, $s_0 w b_0 w$, $s_0 w b_0 p$, $s_0 c b_0 w$, $s_0 c b_0 p$, $b_0 w b_1 w$, $b_0 w b_1 p$, $b_0 p b_1 w$, $b_0 p b_1 p$, $s_1 w b_0 w$, $s_1 w b_0 p$, $s_1 c b_0 w$, $s_1 c b_0 p$
trigrams	$s_0 c s_1 c s_2 c$, $s_0 w s_1 c s_2 c$, $s_0 c s_1 w b_0 p$, $s_0 c s_1 c s_2 w$, $s_0 c s_1 c b_0 p$, $s_0 w s_1 c b_0 p$, $s_0 c s_1 w b_0 p$, $s_0 c s_1 c b_0 w$

11.2.2 Feature Templates

A set of useful feature templates for the shift–reduce constituent parser is shown in Table 11.4, where $[\ldots, s_1, s_0]$ represents the top nodes on the stack, and $[b_0, b_1, \ldots]$ represents the front words on the buffer. xw denotes the word form of x, xp represents the part-of-speech of x (for a non-terminal node, word and POS refer to their head lexicon nodes) and xc represents the constituent label of a non-terminal node x, $x.l$, $x.r$ and $x.u$ denotes the left child, the right child and the unary child of x, respectively. For example, $s_0 w$ represents the top word on the stack.

As shown in the table, the set of features consists of combinations of word, POS and constituent label patterns of the top four nodes on the stack and the front four words on the buffer. Atomic features are combined in forming more sophisticated features for better disambiguation power. The feature templates are used to match each state and action pair (s_{i-1}, a_i) in a state transition process in order to instantiate a feature vector $\vec{\phi}(s_{i-1}, a_i)$ for Eq 11.2. For example, given the parsing example of Table 11.3, at the 6th step, the feature template $s_1 p s_1 c$ is instantiated to the feature instance $NN|NP$, because the second constituent on top of the stack has label NP, and the head word "boy" has a POS-tag NN. This feature instance is combined with the action a_i to derive a final feature instance in $\vec{\phi}(s_{i-1}, a_i)$, which contains instances of all feature templates in the above process.

Compared with the feature templates in Table 9.5 of Chapter 9, features in Table 11.4 can easily range beyond a single grammar rule. For example, at the 6th step in the transition-based example for sentence "*The little boy likes red tomatoes.*", the feature instance $\langle s_0 pc = VV|\text{NULL}, \ldots, s_1 pc = NN|NP, \ldots, s_{1.r}wc = boy|NP, \ldots, s_0 c s_1 c b_0 w = \text{NULL}|NP|red \rangle$ covers a context of the constituents $(4, 4, VV)$, $(1, 3, NP)$ and $(2, 3, NP)$ in the final constituent tree, which is far from being local. In general, given a dataset, feature engineering can be done for deriving a most effective set of feature templates, according to performances on a set of development data.

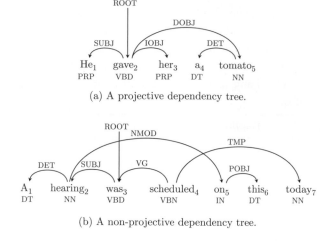

(a) A projective dependency tree.

(b) A non-projective dependency tree.

Figure 11.4 Dependency tree structures for "*He gave her a tomato*" and "*A hearing was scheduled on this today*". Words are indexed. Dependency arc labels can be found in Table 1.4 of Chapter 1.

11.3 Transition-Based Dependency Parsing

As shown in Chapter 1, dependency grammar is a formalism that focuses on the syntactic relations between word pairs. For example, in "*I ran .*", "*I*" serves as the subject, modifying the verb "*ran*". Given a sentence, there is one and only one syntactic root, which does not modify any word; all the other words modify exactly one head word. As a result, a dependency syntactic structure is a tree. Figure 11.4(a) gives the dependency tree structure for the sentence "*He gave her a tomato*".

Dependency trees can be *projective* or *non-projective*. In a projective dependency tree, any word and its recursive descendants form a contiguous word sequence. For example, in Figure 11.4(a), the word "*tomato*" is the root of a subtree over the noun phrase "*a tomato*" and the word "*gave*" is the root of a subtree over the phrase "*He gave her a tomato*". In a projective tree, there are no crossing arcs when the words are put in their linear order in the sentence. Non-projective trees, in contrast, have crossing arcs, which typically result from moving clauses. For example, in the sentence "*A hearing was scheduled on this today*", the modifier phrase "*on this*" for "*hearing*" was moved after the verb phrase "*was scheduled*", causing crossing arcs in its dependency tree, as shown in Figure 11.4(b). Non-projectivity is relatively rare in English sentences, but much more frequent in Czech, German and other morphologically rich languages, for which rich inflection allows grammatical relations to be expressed in relatively free word order.

Given a sentence with n words, where a POS-tag is assigned to each input word, the task of dependency parsing is to recover the dependency tree, which is essentially to find a set of $n - 1$ dependency arcs between words. Transition systems can be designed for both projective dependency parsing and non-projective dependency parsing.

11.3.1 Arc-Standard Dependency Parsing

A representative state transition system for projective dependency parsing is the *arc-standard* system, which is a shift–reduce dependency parser. Similar to shift–reduce constituent parsing in Section 11.2, an arc-standard dependency parser uses a stack to hold partially constructed output structures, and a buffer to maintain incoming words. Formally, in an arc-standard parser, a *state* is a tuple (σ, β, A), with σ representing the stack, β representing the buffer and A representing the set of dependency arcs that have been constructed.

Given an input sentence, the initial state consists of an empty stack, and a buffer that contains the full input sentence. A sequence of state transition actions are applied to incrementally consume input words and build the output. Finally, a terminal state consists of a stack with the root word, and an empty buffer. The set of transition actions include:

- SHIFT, which removes the front word from the buffer, pushing it onto the stack;
- LEFT-ARC-X, which constructs a dependency arc with label X between the top two words on the stack, with the top word being the head, and pops the second top word from the stack;

Axiom:	$([\,],\ W_{1:n},\ \phi)$	LEFT-ARC-X:	$\dfrac{(\sigma\|s_1\|s_0,\ \beta,\ A)}{(\sigma\|s_0,\ \beta,\ A \cup \{s_1 \overset{X}{\curvearrowleft} s_0\})}$
Goal:	$(\lfloor s_0\rfloor,\ \lfloor\ \rfloor,\ A)$		
SHIFT:	$\dfrac{(\sigma,\ b_0\|\beta,\ A)}{(\sigma\|b_0,\ \beta,\ A)}$	RIGHT-ARC-X:	$\dfrac{(\sigma\|s_1\|s_0,\ \beta,\ A)}{(\sigma\|s_1,\ \beta,\ A \cup \{s_1 \overset{X}{\curvearrowright} s_0\})}$

Figure 11.5 Deduction system for arc-standard dependency parsing.

Table 11.5 Arc-standard parsing for the sentence *"He gave her a tomato"*. In the state, 1, 2, 3, 4 and 5 represent *"He"*, *"gave"*, *"her"*, *"a"* and *"tomato"*, respectively.

Step	State	Action
0	([ ], [He, gave, her, a, tomato], { })	SHIFT
1	([He], [gave, her, a, tomato], { })	SHIFT
2	([He, gave], [her, a, tomato], { })	LEFT-ARC-SUBJ
3	([gave], [her, a, tomato], $\{1\overset{\text{SUBJ}}{\curvearrowleft}2\}$)	SHIFT
4	([gave, her], [a, tomato], $\{1\overset{\text{SUBJ}}{\curvearrowleft}2\}$)	RIGHT-ARC-IOBJ
5	([gave], [a, tomato], $\{1\overset{\text{SUBJ}}{\curvearrowleft}2, 2\overset{\text{IOBJ}}{\curvearrowright}3\}$)	SHIFT
6	([gave, a], [tomato], $\{1\overset{\text{SUBJ}}{\curvearrowleft}2, 2\overset{\text{IOBJ}}{\curvearrowright}3\}$)	SHIFT
7	([gave, a, tomato], [ ], $\{1\overset{\text{SUBJ}}{\curvearrowleft}2, 2\overset{\text{IOBJ}}{\curvearrowright}3\}$)	LEFT-ARC-DET
8	([gave, tomato], [ ], $\{1\overset{\text{SUBJ}}{\curvearrowleft}2, 2\overset{\text{IOBJ}}{\curvearrowright}3, 4\overset{\text{DET}}{\curvearrowleft}5\}$)	RIGHT-ARC-DOBJ
9	([gave], [ ], $\{1\overset{\text{SUBJ}}{\curvearrowleft}2, 2\overset{\text{IOBJ}}{\curvearrowright}3, 4\overset{\text{DET}}{\curvearrowleft}5, 2\overset{\text{DOBJ}}{\curvearrowright}5\}$)	

Table 11.6 Feature templates for arc-standard dependency parsing. s_0, s_1 – the top two elements of the stack; b_0 – front of the buffer; l–dependency label; The subscript $_l$ – leftmost dependent (if any); $_r$ – rightmost dependent (if any); $_{l_2}$ – second leftmost dependent (if any); $_{r_2}$ – second rightmost dependent (if any); w – word; p – POS-tag; d – number of words between s_0 and b_0; s_l set of dependency arc labels on the left dependents; s_r – set of dependency labels on the right dependents; v_l – number of dependents on the left; v_r – number of dependents on the right.

Feature Type	Feature Template	Feature Type	Feature Template
from single words	s_0wp; s_0w; s_0p; s_1wp; s_1w; s_1p; b_0wp; b_0w; b_0p; b_1wp; b_1w; b_1p; $s_{0.l}w$; $s_{0.l}p$; $s_{0.l}l$; $s_{0.r}w$; $s_{0.r}p$; $s_{0.r}l$; $s_{1.l}w$; $s_{1.l}p$; $s_{1.l}l$; $s_{1.r}w$; $s_{1.r}p$; $s_{1.r}l$; $s_{0.l2}w$; $s_{0.l2}p$; $s_{0.l2}l$; $s_{1.l2}w$; $s_{1.l2}p$; $s_{1.l2}l$; $s_{0.r2}w$; $s_{0.r2}p$; $s_{0.r2}l$; $s_{1.r2}w$; $s_{1.r2}p$; $s_{1.r2}l$;	from three words	$s_0ps_{0.l}ps_{0.l_2}p$; $s_0ps_{0.r}ps_{0.r_2}p$; $s_1ps_{1.l}ps_{1.l_2}p$; $s_1ps_{1.r}ps_{1.r_2}p$; $s_0ps_1ps_{0.l}p$; $s_0ps_1ps_{0.l_2}p$; $s_0ps_1ps_{0.r}p$; $s_0ps_1ps_{0.r_2}p$; $s_0ps_1ps_{1.l}p$; $s_0ps_1ps_{1.l_2}p$; $s_0ps_1ps_{1.r}p$; $s_0ps_1ps_{1.r_2}p$;
from word pairs	s_0wps_1wp; s_0wps_1w; s_0wps_1p; s_0ws_1wp; s_0ps_1wp; s_0ws_1w; s_0ps_1p;	valency	s_0wv_r; s_0pv_r; s_0wv_l; s_0pv_l; s_1wv_r; s_1pv_r; s_1wv_l; s_1pv_l;
distance	s_0wd; s_0pd; s_1wd; s_1pd; s_0ws_1wd; s_0ps_1pd;	label set	s_0ws_r; s_0ps_r; s_0ws_l; s_0ps_l; s_1ws_l; s_1ps_l

- RIGHT-ARC-X, which constructs a dependency arc with label X between the top two words on the stack, with the second word being the head, and pops the top word off the stack.

The above transition system can be formally described using the deduction system shown in Figure 11.5. Given the sentence "*He gave her a tomato*", the sequence of actions SHIFT, SHIFT, LEFT-ARC-SUBJ, SHIFT, RIGHT-ARC-IOBJ, SHIFT, SHIFT, LEFT-ARC-DET and RIGHT-ARC-DOBJ can be used to constructed its dependency tree, as shown in Figure 11.4(a). Table 11.5 shows the state transition sequences.

Feature templates. Given the state transition system, we are ready to adopt the local model in Section 11.1.1 or global model in Section 11.1.2 for building an arc-standard transition-based parser. As mentioned earlier, one additional thing to consider is a set of features. Table 11.6 shows a set of useful feature templates for disambiguating actions. These can be viewed as a combination of patterns over the state, and should be instantiated together with the next action to take. In particular, word (w), POS (p) and dependency label information (l) from the top words on the stack, as well as word and POS information from the front words on the buffer are combined. Such templates can be decided empirically by feature engineering.

Spurious ambiguities. Note that the transition system in Figure 11.5 allows many-to-one correspondences between transition action sequences and output dependency trees. In particular, for the sentence "*He likes tomatoes*", both the transition action sequence SHIFT, SHIFT, SHIFT, LEFT-ARC-OBJ, RIGHT-ARC-SUBJ and the sequence SHIFT, SHIFT, LEFT-ARC-SUBJ, SHIFT and RIGHT-ARC-OBJ can be used to build the same dependency tree, with different orders of arc prediction. Such ambiguities are referred to as **spurious ambiguities**, which are ambiguities in the transition system but not underlying structural ambiguities.

Intuitively, we want to build models to resolve structural ambiguities but not spurious ambiguities. To this end, one solution is to specify a set of **canonical action sequences**. For example, we can use hard rules to allow right modifiers to be built before left modifiers. Alternatively, we can allow any action sequence that leads to the correct parse tree to have higher scores than any action sequence that does not lead to the correct tree. This requires a slight modification of the training process. Exercise 11.13 gives more relevant discussion.

11.3.2 Evaluating Dependency Parsers Outputs

Dependency parsing performance can be evaluated by calculating the percentage of correctly identified dependency arcs on a test set. In particular, inclusive of a pseudo ROOT arc for each sentence, as shown in Figure 11.4, each word has exactly one incoming dependency arc. As a consequence, the accuracy can be calculated as the percentage of words that are assigned the correct head word, inclusive of the root word. Depending on whether the arc label is also considered, we can measure the *unlabelled attachment score* (UAS), which is the percentage without considering dependency arc labels, and the *labelled attachment score* (LAS), which counts a dependency arc as correct only when the head word and the arc label are both correctly identified.

11.3.3 Arc-Eager Projective Parsing

In addition to the arc-standard parser, a popular alternative dependency parser is the *arc-eager* parser, which takes a different order by building dependency arcs from left to right.

Similar to arc-standard parsing, the arc-eager parser state can be denoted using a tuple (σ, β, A), where σ denotes a stack of words being processed, β represents a buffer of next incoming words and A represents the set of dependency arcs that have been constructed. The initial state is the same as that for the arc-standard parser, consisting of an empty stack and a buffer that contains all the words. The goal state consists of a stack with only the root word and an empty buffer. The set of transition actions include:

- SHIFT, which removes the front word from the buffer and pushes it onto the stack;
- LEFT-ARC-X, which constructs a dependency arc of label X from the front word on the buffer to the top word on the stack, before popping the top word from the stack;
- RIGHT-ARC-X, which constructs a dependency arc of label X from the top word on the stack to the front word on the buffer, before pushing the front word of the buffer onto the stack;
- REDUCE, which pops the top word off the stack.

The transition system above can be formally described by the deduction system in Figure 11.6. Note that there is a pre-condition for the LEFT-ARC and REDUCE actions, with the former being applicable only when the top word on the stack does not already have a head, and the latter being

Axiom:	$([\,], W_{1:n}, \phi)$	LEFT-ARC-X:	$\dfrac{(\sigma\lvert s_0, b_0\lvert\beta, A), \text{ such that } \neg\left(\exists(k,\text{L})\ w_k \overset{\text{L}}{\frown} s_0 \in A\right)}{(\sigma, b_0\lvert\beta, A \cup \{s_0 \overset{\text{X}}{\frown} b_0\})}$
Goal:	$([s_0], [\,], A)$		
SHIFT:	$\dfrac{(\sigma, b_0\lvert\beta, \phi)}{(\sigma\lvert b_0, \beta, \phi)}$	RIGHT-ARC-X:	$\dfrac{(\sigma\lvert s_0, b_0\lvert\beta, A)}{(\sigma\lvert s_0\lvert b_0, \beta, A \cup \{s_0 \overset{\text{X}}{\frown} b_0\})}$
		REDUCE:	$\dfrac{(\sigma\lvert s_0, \beta, A), \text{ such that } \left(\exists(k,\text{L})\ w_k \overset{\text{L}}{\frown} s_0 \in A\right)}{(\sigma, \beta, A)}$

Figure 11.6 Deduction system for arc-eager dependency parsing.

applicable only when the top word on the stack already has a head word. Given the sentence "*He gave her a tomato*", the transition action sequence SHIFT, LEFT-ARC-SUBJ, SHIFT, RIGHT-ARC-IBOJ, REDUCE, SHIFT, LEFT-ARC-DET, RIGHT-ARC-DOBJ and REDUCE can be used to find its dependency tree (Exercise 11.5).

Both the arc-standard and the arc-eager parsers can be used to build projective dependency trees. The choice is empirical, depending also on factors such as features and the dataset. Exercise 11.6 discusses useful feature templates for the arc-eager parser.

11.3.4 Non-Projective Parsing Using the SWAP Action

Neither the arc-standard parser nor the arc-eager parser builds non-projective trees. This is because the transition systems construct dependency arcs between two words only after all words between them have been popped off the stack, therefore disallowing crossing arcs. As mentioned earlier, crossing arcs can be seen as being caused by movement of clauses. As a result, one way to achieve non-projective parsing is to swap the moved phrases to their projective locations, and then use projective parsers to obtain dependency arcs. For example, the non-projective sentence "*A hearing was scheduled on this today*" can be rephrased as the projective sentence "*A hearing on this was scheduled today*", which has a projective dependency tree. After projective parsing, we can restore the positions of moved clauses without affecting dependency relations. To achieve this, the arc-standard system can be extended by adding a new action:

- SWAP, which removes the second top word from the stack, putting it back to the buffer front.

The other actions are the same as arc-standard parsing. The resulting transition system can be formally shown in the deduction system in Figure 11.7. Given the sentence "*A hearing was scheduled on this today*", the action sequence SHIFT, SHIFT, LEFT-ARC-DET, SHIFT, SHIFT, SHIFT, SWAP, SWAP, SHIFT, SHIFT, SHIFT, SWAP, SWAP, RIGHT-ARC-POBJ, RIGHT-ARC-NMOD, SHIFT, LEFT-ARC-SUBJ, SHIFT, SHIFT, RIGHT-ARC-TMP and RIGHT-ARC-VG can be used to find its syntax, which effectively reorders the sentence into "*A hearing on this was scheduled today*". The state transition chain is illustrated in Table 11.7.

Table 11.7 Arc-standard parsing with Swap actions for the sentence "*A hearing was scheduled on this day*". SH–SHIFT; SW–SWAP; RA–RIGHT-ARC; LA–LEFT-ARC-SUBJ. In the state, 1, 2, 3, 4, 5, 6 and 7 represents "*A*", "*hearing*", "*was*", "*scheduled*", "*on*", "*this*" and "*day*", respectively.

State	Action
([ ], [A, hearing, was, scheduled, on, this, today], { })	SH
([A], [hearing, was, scheduled, on, this, today], { })	SH
([A, hearing], [was, scheduled, on, this, today], { })	LA-DET
([hearing], [was, scheduled, on, this, today], {1 ⌢^{DET} 2})	SH
([hearing, was], [scheduled, on, this, today], {1 ⌢^{DET} 2})	SH
([hearing, was, scheduled], [on, this, today], {1 ⌢^{DET} 2})	SH
([hearing, was, scheduled, on], [this, today], {1 ⌢^{DET} 2})	SW
([hearing, was, on], [scheduled, this, today], {1 ⌢^{DET} 2})	SW
([hearing, on], [was, scheduled, this, today], {1 ⌢^{DET} 2})	SH
([hearing, on, was], [scheduled, this, today], {1 ⌢^{DET} 2})	SH
([hearing, on, was, scheduled], [this, today], {1 ⌢^{DET} 2})	SH
([hearing, on, was, scheduled, this], [today], {1 ⌢^{DET} 2})	SW
([hearing, on, was, this], [scheduled, today], {1 ⌢^{DET} 2})	SW
([hearing, on, this], [was, scheduled, today], {1 ⌢^{DET} 2})	RA-POBJ
([hearing, on], [was, scheduled, today], {1 ⌢^{DET} 2, 5 ⌢^{POBJ} 6})	RA-NMOD
([hearing], [was, scheduled, today], {1 ⌢^{DET} 2, 5 ⌢^{POBJ} 6, 2 ⌢^{NMOD} 5})	SH
([hearing, was], [scheduled, today], {1 ⌢^{DET} 2, 5 ⌢^{POBJ} 6, 2 ⌢^{NMOD} 5})	LA-SUBJ
([was], [scheduled, today], {1 ⌢^{DET} 2, 5 ⌢^{POBJ} 6, 2 ⌢^{NMOD} 5, 2 ⌢^{SUBJ} 3})	SH
([was, scheduled], [today], {1 ⌢^{DET} 2, 5 ⌢^{POBJ} 6, 2 ⌢^{NMOD} 5, 2 ⌢^{SUBJ} 3})	SH
([was, scheduled, today], [ ], {1 ⌢^{DET} 2, 5 ⌢^{POBJ} 6, 2 ⌢^{NMOD} 5, 2 ⌢^{SUBJ} 3})	RA-TMP
([was, scheduled], [ ], {1 ⌢^{DET} 2, 5 ⌢^{POBJ} 6, 2 ⌢^{NMOD} 5, 2 ⌢^{SUBJ} 3, 4 ⌢^{TMP} 7})	RA-VG
([was], [ ], {1 ⌢^{DET} 2, 5 ⌢^{POBJ} 6, 2 ⌢^{NMOD} 5, 2 ⌢^{SUBJ} 3, 4 ⌢^{TMP} 7, 3 ⌢^{VG} 4})	

11.4 Joint Parsing Models

There are two important motivations for joint modelling of multiple NLP tasks. The first is information sharing. For example, tasks such as POS-tagging and syntactic parsing share common sources of information, such as lexical syntax. Jointly modelling such tasks can allow information from task-specific training data to fuse in a single model, leading to mutual benefits. The second motivation is reduction of error propagation. For example, pipelined sequential tasks such

Axiom:	$([\ ],\ W_{1:n},\ \phi)$	LEFT-ARC-X:	$\dfrac{([\sigma|s_1|s_0],\ \beta,\ A)}{([\sigma|s_0],\ \beta,\ A \cup \{s_1 \overset{\text{x}}{\frown} s_0\})}$
Goal:	$([s_0],\ [\ ],\ A)$		
SHIFT:	$\dfrac{(\sigma,\ [b_0|\beta],\ \phi)}{([\sigma|b_0],\ \beta,\ \phi)}$	RIGHT-ARC-X:	$\dfrac{([\sigma|s_1|s_0],\ \beta,\ A)}{([\sigma|s_1],\ \beta,\ A \cup \{s_1 \overset{\text{x}}{\frown} s_0\})}$
		SWAP:	$\dfrac{([\sigma|s_1|s_0],\ \beta,\ A),\ \text{such that } \text{IDX}(s_1) < \text{IDX}(s_0)}{([\sigma|s_0],\ [s_1|\beta],\ A)}$

Figure 11.7 Deduction system for arc-standard dependency parsing with a SWAP action for handling non-projective trees. $\text{IDX}(w)$ returns the index of w in the sentence $W_{1:n}$.

as word segmentation → POS-tagging → syntactic parsing and named entity recognition → relation extraction can suffer from error propagation because successor tasks take predecessor task outputs as inputs. Joint modelling of pipelined tasks benefits from both reduced error propagation and cross-task information fusion. We focus on joint parsing tasks in this section. Chapter 17 introduces more methods for joint NLP modelling.

Let us first consider joint POS-tagging and syntactic parsing. In this chapter we have assumed that inputs to a syntactic parser consist of POS-tagged words. However, POS-tagging errors can negatively affect parsing accuracies, since pipelined parsers do not fix POS errors. These issues can be solved by using a joint model to perform end-to-end parsing, where the input is a sequence of words and the output is a syntactic tree with POS labels. To this end, we can extend a transition-based parser with POS assignment functionalities. For instance, for dependency parsing, the arc-standard algorithm can be extended for joint POS-tagging and parsing, by replacing the original SHIFT action with

- SHIFT-X, which removes the front word from the buffer, assigning the POS label X to the word, and pushing it onto the stack.

With the same state definitions, the sentence "*John loves Mary*" can now be analysed using the action sequence SHIFT-PN, SHIFT-VBZ, LEFT-ARC-SUBJ, SHIFT-PN and RIGHT-ARC-DOBJ. Similar to Section 11.2.2, features can be extracted from words on the stack and buffer for disambiguation (Exercise 11.8). One potential disadvantage of this joint model is that no POS features are available on the buffer, which can negatively affect the accuracies of syntactic parsing. Whether this negative effect can outweigh the benefit of joint POS-tagging is an empirical question. Exercise 11.8 discusses potential solutions to this issue.

11.4.1 Joint Word Segmentation, POS-Tagging and Dependency Parsing

The word segmentation → POS-tagging → dependency parsing pipeline consists of three tasks, and thereby can suffer from more error propagation compared with a two-stage pipeline system. An end-to-end solution can alleviate this problem, while exploiting mutual benefits between segmentation and syntactic information. Below we consider extending the arc-eager parser for this purpose. Exercise 11.9 discusses its arc-standard alternative.

To make things more interesting, let us also consider internal structures of words. Characters can have syntactic relations when forming Chinese words. For example, in the word "考古 (archaeology)", the first character is a verb "考 (investigate)" and the second character serves as its object "古 (ancient)". They act as the predicate and its object syntactically. In the word "科技 (technology)", the two characters "科 (science)" and "技 (technology)" form a coordination structure. In the word "制服 (dominate)", the second character "服 (be convinced)" is a relative adverb of the verb "制 (control)". For simplicity, assume that syntactic relations between characters in a word are unlabelled, while word relations are labelled as for the standard dependency parsing task.

Now we build a state transition system that constructs the joint structure, which consists of a word-level dependency tree, POS on words and internal unlabelled character dependency trees within words. The base parser to extend, namely the arc-eager parser, builds dependency arcs between words. Given that our inputs are characters, the main idea is to add a mechanism for recognising words from a character sequence, and then making use of the arc-eager parser for building inter-word dependencies. In addition, in order to build inter-character dependencies within words, the arc-eager system can also be used.

In particular, a partial-word buffer δ can be added between the stack σ and the buffer β, which serves as the stack for parsing character dependencies, as well as the buffer for parsing word dependencies. Formally, a state is now defined as a tuple $(\sigma, \delta, \beta, A_c, A_w)$, where A_c and A_w denote the sets of character dependencies and word dependencies, respectively. Two sets of arc-eager actions are necessary, for building character dependencies between δ and β, and word dependencies between σ and δ, respectively. In addition, a POP action is defined to recognise the character dependency subtree in δ as a full word, assigning a POS to it.

Formally, the actions include:

- SHIFT-C, which pops the front character off β, pushing it onto δ;
- LEFT-ARC-C, which pops the last character off δ, adding it as a dependent word to the front character on β;
- RIGHT-ARC-C, which moves the front character of β onto δ, adding it as a dependent to the current last character on δ;
- REDUCE-C, which pops the last character off δ;
- POP-X, which pops the only character off δ, recognising the subtree that it dominates as a full word, assigning the POS label X to it, and pushing it as the only item onto δ;
- SHIFT, which removes the only word from δ, pushing it onto σ;
- LEFT-ARC-X, which pops the top word off σ, attaching it as a dependent word to the only word in δ, assigning the dependency label X to the new arc;
- RIGHT-ARC-X, which pushes the only word in δ onto σ, assigning it as a dependent word to the current top word on σ and assigning the new dependency arc with label X;
- REDUCE, which pops the top word off σ.

Axiom:	$([\,],[\,],\,C_{1:n},\,\phi,\,\phi)$
Goal:	$([S_0],[\,],[\,],\,A_c,\,A_w)$
Left-arc-c:	$\dfrac{(\sigma,\,\delta\vert d_0,\,b_0\vert\beta,\,A_c,\,A_w)\text{ such that }\neg(\exists d,\in\delta,d\frown d_0\in A_c)}{(\sigma,\,\delta,\,b_0\vert\beta,\,A_c\cup\{d_0\frown b_0\},\,A_w)}$
Left-arc-X:	$\dfrac{(\sigma\vert s_0,\,[d_0],\,\beta,\,A_c,\,A_w)\text{ such that }\neg(\exists s,\in\sigma,s\frown s_0\in A_w)}{(\sigma,\,[d_0],\,\beta,\,A_c,\,A_w\cup\{s_0\frown d_0\})}$
Shift:	$\dfrac{(\sigma,\,[d_0],\,\beta,\,A_c,\,A_w)}{(\sigma\vert d_0,\,[\,],\,\beta,\,A_c,\,A_w)}$
Shift-c:	$\dfrac{(\sigma,\,\delta,\,b_0\vert\beta,\,A_c,\,A_w)}{(\sigma,\,\delta\vert b_0,\,\beta,\,A_c,\,A_w)}$
Right-arc-c:	$\dfrac{(\sigma,\,\delta\vert d_0,\,b_0\vert\beta,\,A_c,\,A_w)}{(\sigma,\,\delta[d_0]b_0,\,\beta,\,A_c\cup\{d_0\frown b_0\},\,A_w)}$
Right-arc-X:	$\dfrac{(\sigma\vert s_0,\,[d_0],\,\beta,\,A_c,\,A_w\cup\{s_0\frown d_0\})}{(\sigma\vert s_0\vert d_0,\,[\,],\,\beta,\,A_c,\,A_w)}$
Pop-X:	$\dfrac{(\sigma,\,[d_0],\,\beta,\,A_c,\,A_w)}{(\sigma,\,[\textsc{Subtree}(d_0,\,A_c)/X],\,\beta,\,A_c,\,A_w)}$
Reduce-c:	$\dfrac{(\sigma,\,\delta\vert d_0,\,\beta,\,A_c,\,A_w)\text{ such that }\exists d\in\delta,d\frown d_0\in A_c}{(\sigma,\,\delta,\,\beta,\,A_c,\,A_w)}$
Reduce:	$\dfrac{(\sigma\vert s_0,\,\delta,\,\beta,\,A_c,\,A_w)\text{ such that }\exists s\in\sigma,s\frown s_0\in A_w}{(\sigma,\,\delta,\,\beta,\,A_c,\,A_w)}$

Figure 11.8 Deduction system for joint word segmentation, POS-tagging and arc-eager dependency parsing.

Figure 11.8 shows a deduction system that describes the transition system above. Given the sentence "我 (I) 来 (come) 到 (arrive) 会 (meet) 客 (guest) 室 (room)", for which the segmentation output is "我 (I) 来到 (come to) 会客室 (reception room)", the sequence of transition actions to find its end-to-end syntactic tree is shown in Table 11.8.

Table 11.9 shows the set of feature templates for the joint segmentation, POS-tagging and parsing model. It contains word, character, POS-tag and dependency structure features between s_0, δ and b_0. In addition, there are combinations of atomic features such as s_0cp (i.e., the character and POS-tag of s_0) and $s_0c\delta c$ (i.e., the head characters of s_0 and δ). As can be seen from the table, useful feature templates can be highly complex for effective parsing. In practice, heavy feature engineering can be necessary for deriving a set of most effective features on a development set. The challenge can be increasingly large when the output structure goes increasingly complex. Chapter 15 introduces neural alternatives to linear models for transition-based structured prediction, which frees us from defining complex feature templates.

11.4.2 Discussion

We have used various parsing tasks as the main examples for illustrating transition-based structured prediction. Nevertheless, the local and global model frameworks that we discussed in Section 11.1 can be applied to tasks beyond parsing. For example, they have given state-of-the-art results in named entity recognition, relation extraction, event detection, abstract meaning representation (AMR) semantic parsing and other tasks also. It turns out that for most structured

Table 11.8 Transition-based systems for joint word segmentation, POS-tagging and dependency parsing for the sentence "我来到会客室 (I came to the reception)". SHC–SHIFT-C; P–POP; SW–SHIFT-W; LAC–LEFTARC-C; RAC–RIGHTARC-C; RC–REDUCE-C; LA–LEFTARC; RA–RIGHTARC; SH–SHIFT; R–REDUCE.

Step	State	Action
0	[[ ], [ ], [我, 来, 到, 会, 客, 室], ϕ, ϕ]	SHC
1	[[ ], [我], [来, 到, 会, 客, 室], ϕ, ϕ]	P-PN
2	[[ ], [我/PN], [来, 到, 会, 客, 室], ϕ, ϕ]	SW
3	[[我/PN], [ ], [来, 到, 会, 客, 室], ϕ, ϕ]	SHC
4	[[我/PN], [来], [到, 会, 客, 室], ϕ, ϕ]	LAC
5	[[我/PN], [来], [到, 会, 客, 室], [来⌢到], ϕ]	P-VV
6	[[我/PN], [来到/VV], [会, 客, 室], [来⌢到], ϕ]	LA-SUBJ
7	[], [来到/VV], [会, 客, 室], [来⌢到], [我/PN ⌢ᴿ^{ˢᵁᴮᴶ} 来到/VV]]	SH
8	[来到/VV], [], [会, 客, 室], [来⌢到], [我/PN ^{SUBJ}⌢ 来到/VV]]	SHC
9	[来到/VV], [会], [客, 室], [来⌢到], [我/PN ^{SUBJ}⌢ 来到/VV]]	RAC
10	[来到/VV], [会, 客], [室], [来⌢到, 会⌢客], [我/PN ^{SUBJ}⌢ 来到/VV]]	RC
11	[来到/VV], [会], [室], [来⌢到, 会⌢客], [我/PN ^{SUBJ}⌢ 来到/VV]]	LAC
12	[来到/VV], [], [室], [来⌢到, 会⌢客, 会⌢室], [我/PN ^{SUBJ}⌢ 来到/VV]]	SHC
13	[来到/VV], [室], [], [来⌢到, 会⌢客, 会⌢室], [我/PN ^{SUBJ}⌢ 来到/VV]]	P-NN
14	[来到/VV], [会客室/NN], [], [来⌢到, 会⌢客, 会⌢室], [我/PN ^{SUBJ}⌢ 来到/VV, 来到/VV ⌢ 会客室/NN]]	RA-DOBJ
15	[来到/VV, 会客室/NN], [], [], [来⌢到, 会⌢客, 会⌢室], [我/PN ^{SUBJ}⌢ 来到/VV, 来到/VV ^{SUBJ}⌢ 会客室/NN]]	R
16	[来到/VV], [], [], [来⌢到, 会⌢客, 会⌢室], [我/PN ^{SUBJ}⌢ 来到/VV, 来到/VV ^{SUBJ}⌢ 会客室/NN]]	

prediction problems in NLP, one can find a state-transition system to describe the output-building process.

Compared to a graph-based model for structured prediction, a transition-based model has two main advantages. First, it allows arbitrary non-local features, which can be highly useful for improving model performance. Second, it runs in linear time with respect to the number of state transitions, which is also typically linear to the input size. Take constituent parsing for example, the CKY algorithms in Chapter 10 can run in $O(n^5)$ while a transition-based parser can run in $O(n)$. This means that transition-based parsing can be orders of magnitude faster compared with a graph-based parser. One relative disadvantage of transition-based models is that the search algorithm is inexact, which means that the decoder cannot guarantee to find the output with the highest

Table 11.9 Feature templates for joint word segmentation, POS-tagging and dependency parsing. l_1 and r_1 denote the closest left and right children, respectively; l_2 and r_2 denote the second leftmost and rightmost children, respectively. For example, $s_{0.l_1}$ denotes the leftmost child of the top word on the stack; w denotes word; c and p denote to the head-character and POS-tag, respectively. For example, $\delta_{r_1}cp$ denotes the head-character and POS-tag for the rightmost child of δ.

Feature Type	Feature Template
from single nodes	$s_0c, s_0cp, \delta c, \delta cp, b_0c, b_0cp, s_{0.l_1}c, s_{0.r_1}c, \delta_{l_1}c, \delta_{r_1}c, b_{0.l_1}c, s_{0.l_1}cp, s_{0.r_1}cp, \delta_{l_1}cp, \delta_{r_1}cp,$ $b_{0.l_1}cp,$
from nodes pairs	$s_0c\delta c, s_0c\delta w, s_0w\delta c, s_0cp\delta w, s_0wp\delta c, s_0w\delta cp, s_0c\delta wp, \delta cb_0c, \delta cb_0w, \delta wb_0c,$ $\delta cpb_0w, \delta wpb_0c, \delta wb_0cp, \delta cb_0wp,$
from three nodes	$s_0c\delta cs_{0.l_1}c, s_0c\delta cs_{0.r_1}c, s_0c\delta cs_{0.l_2}c, s_0c\delta cs_{0.r_2}c, s_0c\delta c\delta_{l_1}c, s_0c\delta c\delta_{l_2}c, \delta cb_0c\delta_{l_1}c,$ $\delta cb_0c\delta_{r_1}c, \delta cb_0c\delta_{l_2}c, \delta cb_0c\delta_{r_2}c, \delta cb_0cb_{0.l_1}c, \delta cb_0cb_{0.l_2}c.$

model score. This is true for both the greedy local model and the global model with beam-search. However, thanks to methods such as the perceptron guided by beam search (Section 11.1.2) and neural networks (see Part III of this book), transition-based methods give competitive performance in practice compared to graph-based methods.

Summary

In this chapter, we have learned:

- transition-based structured prediction with greedy local modelling and structured modelling;
- shift–reduce constituent parsing;
- shift–reduce dependency parsing;
- joint word segmentation, POS-tagging and dependency parsing.

Chapter Notes

Arc-standard dependency parsing was proposed by Yamada and Matsumoto (2003) and arc-eager dependency parsing by Nivre (2003). Sagae and Lavie (2005) were among the first to use a transition-based algorithm for constituent parsing. Alternative state transition systems were proposed for dependency parsing (Nivre, 2008, 2009; Choi and McCallum, 2013) and constituent parsing (Zhu et al., 2013; Dyer et al., 2016; Liu and Zhang, 2017) subsequently. Beam-search with early update (Collins and Roark, 2004) was first investigated for transition-based structured prediction by Zhang and Clark (2011). In addition to parsing, transition-based methods see their use in joint NLP tasks (Bohnet and Nivre, 2012; Hatori et al., 2012; Qian and Liu, 2012; Zhang et al., 2014; Wang et al., 2018; Zhang et al., 2018a).

Exercises

11.1 Consider the set of feature templates for transition-based word segmentation in Table 11.2, Compared with the feature templates in Table 9.5, what are the similarities and what are the differences? These differences show the different nature in transition-based feature definitions as compared with their graph-based counterparts.

11.2 Give pseudocode for an averaged perceptron algorithm that extends Algorithm 11.2.

11.3 Define a state transition system for joint word segmentation and POS-tagging. Given an input sentence, the output is a sequence of words, each having a POS label. What features can be useful for the task?

11.4 Draw the stack and buffer for each state during shift-reduce parsing of the sentence "*The little boy likes red tomatoes.*" in Section 11.2.1 by completing Table 11.3.

11.5 Draw the arc-eager parsing process for the sentence "*He gave her a tomato*" in the format of the example in Table 11.3.

11.6 Design a set of features for arc-standard dependency parsing by consulting Table 11.4.

11.7 The arc-standard parser corresponds naturally to the shift–reduce constituent parser in Section 11.2 in that it attaches modifier words to their syntactic head words in a bottom-up order. The only difference is that dependency trees are relatively more flat compared to constituent trees in losing phrase structure hierarchies. Draw a constituent tree for the sentence in Figure 11.4(a), comparing it with the dependency tree in the figure. Compare the arc-standard parsing process and shift-reduce constituent parsing process for the sentence.

11.8 Design a set of feature templates for the joint POS-tagging and parsing model in Section 11.4.1. Can part-of-speech information be leveraged for words on the buffer? How can the transition system be extended for accommodating such features? (Hint: One solution can be to design a dequeue structure between the stack and buffer for holding a few tagged words.)

11.9 Design a transition system for joint segmentation, POS-tagging and arc-standard dependency parsing.

11.10 Design a transition system for joint named entity recognition and targeted sentiment. Here the input is a sentence and the output consists of a set of entity mentions and a sentiment polarity towards each entity mention. Each entity mention is a text span in the input. Sentiment polarities can be the set {*positive, negative, neutral*}. The task is also called open-domain targeted sentiment as discussed in Chapter 1.

11.11 Design a transition system for joint semantic role labelling and syntactic parsing. (Hint: Two stacks can be necessary for holding syntax and semantics structures, respectively.)

11.12 Design a transition system for joint named entity recognition and relation extraction (Chapter 1). Here the input is a sentence and the output is a set of entity mentions and a set of relations between them. Each entity mention is a span in the input sentence, labelled with a type such as "person", "organisation" and "location", and each relation is a tuple (e_1, r, e_2) where e_1 and e_2 denote two entities and r denotes a relation type such as "social relation" and "affiliation".

11.13 If there is more than one gold-standard sequence of actions that correspond to the same gold structure, how can Algorithm 11.2 be adapted? (Hint: Consider early update criteria and the choice of positive example in parameter update.) Does the decoder in Algorithm 11.1 need to change?

12 Bayesian Network

Thus far, we have seen a range of generative models, such as Naïve Bayes (Chapter 2), PLSA (Chapter 6) and HMMs (Chapter 7). These models can be generalised into a probabilistic graph model, namely a Bayesian network. A Bayesian network can model complex joint probability distributions among a set of random variables in a compact way based on their conditional independence. We start by discussing how to represent a task using a Bayesian network, and then move on to show training methods for Bayesian network models. In particular, we have so far seen maximum likelihood estimation (MLE) for supervised settings. When dealing with hidden variables in unsupervised settings we can use expectation maximisation (EM). In this chapter, we introduce another two parameter estimation methods, namely maximum a posteriori (MAP) and Bayesian estimation. For the latter, we discuss how to calculate marginal probabilities in a Bayesian network with both observed and hidden variables. Specifically, we show Gibbs sampling for approximate inference and parameter estimation. For applications, we will see Bayesian versions of unigram language models, IBM model 1, HMMs and PLSA, which is also known as Latent Dirichlet Allocation (LDA).

12.1 A General Probabilistic Model

A **Bayesian network** is a general form of probabilistic model for structured prediction, which describes parameterisation according to probability chain rule and independence assumptions. n-gram language models, Naïve Bayes text classifiers, PLSA models and HMMs are all instances of Bayesian networks, where the model parameters consist of different conditional probability factors. As we have seen for those models, general problems over a Bayesian network include supervised and unsupervised learning, as well as calculating marginal probabilities. We start defining Bayesian network by reviewing the role of probability chain rule and conditional independence for parameterising a joint probability of a full structure. Formally, a Bayesian network models a set of random variables $\{x_1, x_2, \ldots, x_n\}$, for which the joint probability distribution $P(x_1, x_2, \ldots, x_n)$ can be highly complex to parameterise. For example, supposing that every random variable takes a Boolean variable, we need $2^n - 1$ parameters in total to define the joint probability distribution without any prior knowledge among the variables, since we need to enumerate all possible joint values. Now using the probability chain rule, $P(x_1, x_2, \ldots, x_n)$ can be rewritten as

$$P(x_1, x_2, \ldots, x_n) = \prod_{i=1}^{n} P(x_i | x_1, \ldots, x_{i-1}).$$

We learned in Chapter 2 how to simplify conditional probabilities with independence assumptions. For example, in the extreme case, we can build a naïve model by simplifying the above equation with a bag-of-feature assumption:

$$P(x_1, x_2, \ldots, x_n) = \prod_{i=1}^{n} P(x_i).$$

As a second example, we can make $x_2, \ldots, x_n$ independent conditioned on x_1:

$$P(x_1, x_2, \ldots, x_n) = P(x_1) \prod_{i=2}^{n} P(x_i | x_1).$$

Here **conditional independence** among random variables is used as a tool for reducing the model size. For three random variables x_1, x_2 and x_3, x_2 is conditionally independent of x_3 given x_1 if and only if $P(x_2, x_3 | x_1) = P(x_2 | x_1) P(x_3 | x_1)$. We denote this as $x_2 \perp\!\!\!\perp x_3 | x_1$. Intuitively, given knowledge of x_1, conditional independence between x_2 and x_3 indicates that the value of x_2 does not affect that of x_3 and vice versa.

Bayesian network represents the probabilistic relationships among a set of random variables using a directed acyclic graph based on their conditional dependence. Nodes in the graph are random variables, and edges denote conditional dependencies. If there is an edge from node x_i to node x_j, then x_i is a *parent node* of x_j, and correspondingly x_j is a *child node* of x_i. The edge denotes that the value of x_j depends on the value of x_i.

Figure 12.1 shows an example of Bayesian network for modelling stock price change. For a certain company, either "releasing a new product" (x_1) or "appointing a new CEO" (x_2) can lead to the increasing of the stock price (x_3). The price increment can cause a person A to buy (x_4) or a person B to buy (x_5) stock shares of this company. Here $x_1, \ldots, x_5$ are Boolean random variables representing whether an event occurs. In this case, the conditional dependence between variables reflects a "cause–effect" relationship.

Factorisation. According to the probability chain rule and conditional independence, a Bayesian network allows us to decompose the joint probability distribution into probability factors. Denote the set of parent nodes of x_i as $x_{\pi(i)}$. For example, in Figure 12.1, $\pi(1) = \phi$, $\pi(3) = \{1, 2\}$. For a Bayesian network over $x_1, x_2, \ldots, x_n$, the joint probability can be rewritten as

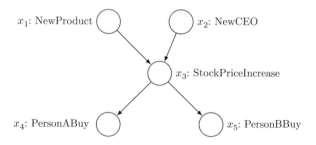

Figure 12.1 A Bayesian network for modelling stock price change.

Table 12.1 Local conditional probability table for Figure 12.1.

x_1	$P(x_1)$	x_2	$P(x_2)$	x_1, x_2	$P(x_3 = T\|x_1, x_2)$
T	0.1	T	0.05	F, F	0.02
x_3	$P(x_4 = T\|x_3)$	x_3	$P(x_5 = T\|x_3)$	T, F	0.6
T	0.8	T	0.9	F, T	0.3
F	0.4	F	0.55	T, T	0.99

$$P(x_1, x_2, \ldots, x_n) = \prod_{i=1}^{n} P(x_i | x_{\pi(i)}). \tag{12.1}$$

Here $P(x_i | x_{\pi(i)})$ is the local conditional probability distribution of the random variable x_i given its parents $x_{\pi(i)}$. Intuitively, Eq 12.1 says that the joint probability distribution can be factored as the product of the local conditional probability of each variable.

Based on Eq 12.1, we can write out the joint probability distribution in any Bayesian network according to the topological order of the random variables in the graph. For example, for Figure 12.1, the joint probability is

$$\begin{aligned} P(x_1, x_2, x_3, x_4, x_5) &= \prod_{i=1}^{5} P(x_i | x_{\pi(i)}) \\ &= P(x_1)P(x_2)P(x_3 | x_1, x_2)P(x_4 | x_3)P(x_5 | x_3). \end{aligned}$$

Table 12.1 shows the local conditional probabilities for Figure 12.1. In this table, some probability items are omitted since they can be induced from the constraint that the sum of a discrete probability distribution is 1. For example, given that we know $P(x_4 = T | x_3 = T) = 0.8$, we can infer that $P(x_4 = F | x_3 = T) = 1 - P(x_4 = T | x_3 = T) = 0.2$. According to the table, we can calculate joint probabilities such as

$$\begin{aligned} &P(x_1 = T, x_2 = F, x_3 = T, x_4 = T, x_5 = F) \\ &= P(x_1 = T)P(x_2 = F)P(x_3 = T | x_1 = T, x_2 = F) \\ &\quad P(x_4 = T | x_3 = T)P(x_5 = F | x_3 = T) \\ &= 0.1 \times (1 - 0.05) \times 0.6 \times 0.8 \times (1 - 0.9) = 0.00456. \end{aligned}$$

In this example, with strong independence assumptions, the number of model parameters necessary for describing a joint distribution of five Boolean variables is reduced from $2^5 - 1$ to 10. When the number of random variables is large, such reduction of model size can be drastic.

Probabilistic dependence of non-directly connected nodes. In a Bayesian network, the relationships between directly connected nodes are explicitly specified. However, we do not immediately know the conditional independence relationships between any two random variables given a certain condition. For example, we might want to know whether x_1 and x_5 in Figure 12.1 are independent, namely $x_1 \perp\!\!\!\perp x_5$. Further, given the evidence of x_3, will x_1 and x_5 be conditionally independent, namely $x_1 \perp\!\!\!\perp x_5 | x_3$? We introduce two theorems that cover the typical situations.

The first rule is based on **Markov blanket**, which is the set of a node's *parent nodes*, *child nodes* and *co-parent* nodes. A co-parent node refers to the node that shares at least one child with the target node. For example, the Markov blankets of x_3 and x_4 are $\{x_1, x_2, x_4, x_5\}$ and $\{x_3\}$ in Figure 12.1, respectively.

Theorem 12.1. Given a node x_i's Markov blanket $\text{MB}(x_i)$, x_i is conditionally independent of all other nodes Y. Formally,

$$P(x_i|\text{MB}(x_i), Y) = P(x_i|\text{MB}(x_i)). \tag{12.2}$$

According to Eq 12.2, in Figure 12.1, with evidence of x_3, x_4 is independent of x_1, x_2 and x_5.

The second rule is based on the *descendants* and *nondescendants* of a node x_i. Descendants of x_i refers to the set of nodes that can be reached from x_i with a directed path. On the other hand, nondescendants of x_i are nodes in the graph that are not descendants of x_i. For example, in Figure 12.1, the descendants of x_2 are $\{x_3, x_4, x_5\}$, and nondescendants of x_3 are $\{x_1, x_2\}$. Note that parents and co-parents of x_i are both its nondescendants.

Theorem 12.2. Given a node x_i's parents $A(x_i)$, x_i is conditionally independent of its nondescendants $\text{ND}(x_i)$. Formally,

$$P(x_i|A(x_i), \text{ND}(x_i)) = P(x_i|A(x_i)). \tag{12.3}$$

According to Eq 12.3, in Figure 12.1, x_2 is independent of x_1, and x_5 is conditionally independent of x_4 given x_3.

We will see applications of these two theorems in Section 12.3.

12.2 Training Bayesian Networks

Given a certain model structure, one important question for a Bayesian network is how to estimate model parameters from data. For example, given the model in Figure 12.1 and a set of observations of the random variables, how can we obtain the conditional probability tables such as Table 12.1 from training data? We have discussed MLE in Chapter 2 when all variables are observed in training data, and EM in Chapter 6 when some variables are hidden variables. Bayesian networks including Naïve Bayes and HMM can be trained using both methods. In this chapter, we discuss three general methods for training a Bayesian network, in which MLE and EM belong to one method.

Formally, denote the set of model parameters in a Bayesian network as Θ. The parameter estimation methods that we have seen so far treat Θ as a unknown constant, trying to find its values given a set of training data D. In Bayesian models, in contrast, we treat Θ itself as a random variable, just as the other variables in a Bayesian network. The training goal is to find the **value distributions** of Θ instead of a single value. In particular, our goal is to estimate $P(\Theta|D)$. According to the Bayes rule, we have

$$P(\Theta|D) = \frac{P(\Theta)P(D|\Theta)}{P(D)}. \tag{12.4}$$

Here $P(\Theta)$ is the **prior distribution** of Θ, $P(D|\Theta)$ is the **data likelihood** and $P(D)$ is the **evidence**. They together define the **posterior distribution** $P(\Theta|D)$, namely the training goal. The prior distribution can reflect our knowledge or experience before seeing the training data, while the posterior distribution reflects our final belief after seeing the evidence. For example, the prior can be our belief that a coin is totally fair, or the knowledge that the frequency of words in natural text should meet the power-law distribution, or the data sparsity preference that a document usually contains only a few topics.

It is worth noting that the prior distributions of model parameters are typically continuous random variables, rather than discrete random variables. For example, as mentioned in Chapter 2, $\theta = P(head)$ for coin tossing takes a real value in $[0, 1]$. As a result, its distribution is described as a probability density function $P(\theta)$, and we can obtain the probability of θ falling in the range $[0.4, 0.6]$ by finding $\int_{0.4}^{0.6} P(\theta)d\theta$.

We consider three estimation methods for Θ here. In particular, the first method is **maximum likelihood estimation** (MLE), which focuses only on the likelihood $P(D|\Theta)$. This method finds the model parameters according to $\Theta^{MLE} = \arg\max_\Theta P(D|\Theta)$. We have seen examples without hidden variables, where relative frequency counting is used (Chapter 2), and with hidden variables, where EM is used (Chapter 6). The second method is **maximum a posteriori** (MAP), which considers both the prior distribution $P(\Theta)$ and the likelihood $P(D|\Theta)$, finding the model parameters by $\Theta^{MAP} = \arg\max_\Theta P(\Theta)P(D|\Theta)$. The third method is **Bayesian estimation**, which treats the parameter set Θ itself as random variables, looking for the posterior distribution $P(\Theta|D)$ for the parameters instead of point estimations. In contrast, the estimations returned by both MLE and MAP are constants.

12.2.1 Maximum Likelihood Estimation

Assuming that there is a set of unknown best model parameters Θ, we find the parameters by maximising the likelihood of the observed data D using

$$\theta^{MLE} = \arg\max_\Theta P(D|\Theta).$$

This objective can be intuitively understood as finding Θ that can best generate D. Further assume that there are K random variables in the model, namely $x_1, x_2, \ldots, x_K$. Let us review settings with and without hidden variables.

Without hidden variables. If all the nodes in a Bayesian network are observed in the training data, we can directly maximise the data likelihood. In particular, let the training dataset be $D = \{X_i\}|_{i=1}^N$, where the ith training example $X_i = x_1^i, x_2^i, \ldots, x_K^i$. Let the model parameters be $\Theta = \{\theta_k\}|_{k=1}^K$, where θ_k represents the local conditional probability distribution for the random variable x_k given its parents $\pi(k)$, namely $P(x_k|\pi(k)), k \in \{1, \ldots, K\}$. The model log-likelihood function is then

$$\begin{aligned}\Theta^{MLE} &= \arg\max_\Theta \sum_{i=1}^N \log P(x_1^i, x_2^i, \ldots, x_K^i|\Theta) \\ &= \arg\max_\Theta \sum_{i=1}^N \sum_{k=1}^K \log P(x_k^i|x_{\pi(k)}^i, \theta_k),\end{aligned}$$

(12.5)

where $x^i_{\pi(k)}$ denotes the values of the parent variables $\pi(k)$ for the variable x_k in the ith training instance. As discussed in Chapters 2, 7 and 10, for Bernoulli and categorical distributions, we can obtain the optimal parameters by counting relative frequencies:

$$\theta^{MLE}_k(x_k = v | x_{\pi(k)} = v_\pi) = \frac{\#(x_k = v, x_{\pi(k)} = v_\pi)}{\#(x_{\pi(k)} = v_\pi)}, \tag{12.6}$$

where v and v_π denote specific values x_k and $x_{\pi(k)}$, respectively.[1]

With hidden variables. Without loss of generality, suppose that $x_1, x_2, \ldots, x_j$ are hidden variables and $x_{j+1}, \ldots, x_K$ are observed variables. The likelihood function of the observed variables is

$$\Theta^{MLE} = \arg\max_\Theta \sum_{i=1}^N \log P(x^i_{j+1}, x^i_{j+2}, \ldots, x^i_K | \Theta)$$

$$= \arg\max_\Theta \sum_{i=1}^N \log \left(\sum_{x^i_1} \sum_{x^i_2} \cdots \sum_{x^i_j} P(x^i_1, x^i_2, \ldots, x^i_K | \Theta) \right)$$

$$= \arg\max_\Theta \sum_{i=1}^N \log \left(\sum_{x^i_1} \sum_{x^i_2} \cdots \sum_{x^i_j} \prod_{k=1}^K P(x^i_k | x^i_{\pi(k)}, \theta_k) \right),$$

where $\sum_{x^i_u}$ denotes summation over all possible values of $x^i_u, u \in [1, \ldots, j]$. We discussed in Chapter 6 how EM approximately solves this optimisation problem.

Coin tossing example. Similar to Chapter 2, let us use a coin tossing example to illustrate different parameter estimation methods. Suppose that we independently toss a coin 8 times, where the observed sequence is $D = HTHTHTTT$ ("H" and "T" indicate a heads event and a tails event, respectively). Let the model parameter θ denote the probability of the heads event. As shown in Chapter 2, each coin toss is a Bernoulli experiment. The likelihood of the data is $P(D|\theta) = \theta^{\#(H)}(1-\theta)^{\#(T)}$. Using MLE, we have

$$\theta^{MLE} = \arg\max_\theta \theta^{\#(H)}(1-\theta)^{\#(T)}$$
$$= \frac{\#(H)}{\#(H) + \#(T)} = \frac{3}{8} = 0.375. \tag{12.7}$$

12.2.2 Maximum a Posteriori

Now we move on to the second training method for Bayesian networks, namely **maximum a posteriori** (MAP). Similar to MLE and EM, MAP finds the best possible parameters given a set

[1] Note that for notational convenience we assumed that each unique variable occurs exactly once in each training data instance in the data likelihood function, which means that models such as HMM cannot be directly represented in Eq 12.5, which contains repeated variable (e.g., word and POS-tag) instances in each training sentence.

of training data D. Formally, according to Eq 12.4, the optimal parameter Θ^{MAP} is obtained by

$$\Theta^{MAP} = \arg\max_{\Theta} P(\Theta|D)$$

$$= \arg\max_{\Theta} \frac{P(D|\Theta)P(\Theta)}{P(D)}$$

$$= \arg\max_{\Theta} P(\Theta)P(D|\Theta),$$

where the last equality holds because D is constant across all values of Θ.

For a Bayesian network, we can find Θ^{MAP} by

$$\Theta^{MAP} = \arg\max_{\Theta} \log\left(P(\Theta)P(D|\Theta)\right)$$

$$- \arg\max_{\Theta} \left(\log P(\Theta) + \log P(D|\Theta)\right)$$

$$= \arg\max_{\Theta} \left(\log P(\Theta) + \sum_{i=1}^{N}\sum_{k=1}^{K} \log P(x_k|x_{\pi(k)}, \theta_k)\right).$$

Compared with MLE, the prior distribution $P(\Theta)$ plays a role here. It enables us to incorporate prior knowledge of parameter distributions into each local data distribution $P(x_k|x_{\pi(k)})$.

Coin tossing example continued. From Eq 12.7 we see that MLE gives an estimation $\theta^{MLE} = 0.375$. Different from MLE, MAP maximises $P(\theta|D)$ by further considering a prior $P(\theta)$. Intuitively, prior knowledge on θ can change our estimation. For instance, if we believe that the coin is fair, namely $P(\theta) = 1$ if $\theta = 0.5$ and 0 otherwise, then the final estimation according to $P(\theta|D)$ should be more than 0.375. Below we show that this is true by introducing a detailed calculation of θ^{MAP}.

Rather than using one specific distribution $P(\theta)$, we look at a family of distributions. In particular, let us consider the **Beta distribution** family, which makes optimisation easy for the coin tossing problem. Formally, for $P(\theta)$ we can have

$$Beta(\theta|\alpha, \beta) = \frac{\theta^{\alpha-1}(1-\theta)^{\beta-1}}{B(\alpha, \beta)}. \tag{12.8}$$

Here α, β are two positive hyper-parameters that can control the distribution shape and the normalisation constant $B(\alpha, \beta)$ is the *beta function*:

$$B(\alpha, \beta) = \frac{\Gamma(\alpha)\Gamma(\beta)}{\Gamma(\alpha + \beta)}, \tag{12.9}$$

where $\Gamma(x)$ is the *Gamma function*, which is a generalised form of the factorial function $\Gamma(n+1) = n!$ over real numbers. Formally, we have

$$\Gamma(x) = \int_0^\infty y^{x-1}e^{-y}dy.$$

One important property of $\Gamma(x)$ is:

$$\Gamma(x + 1) = x\Gamma(x). \tag{12.10}$$

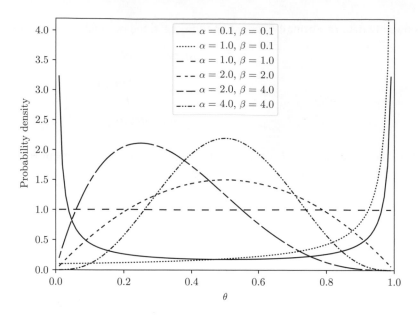

Figure 12.2 Example Beta distributions.

Figure 12.2 shows a range of Beta distributions, each with a specific combination of α and β. When $\alpha = 1$ and $\beta = 1$, the beta distribution is the uniform distribution. When α and β are both small (e.g., $\alpha = 0.1$ and $\beta = 0.1$), the beta distribution can be highly sparse. When α and β are both large, the distribution can be more spiky or centred.

With $B(\alpha, \beta)$ being a constant, $Beta(\theta|\alpha, \beta) \propto \theta^{\alpha-1}(1 - \theta)^{\beta-1}$. It gives a convenient form of the posterior distribution of θ given D:

$$P(\theta|D, \alpha, \beta) \propto P(\theta|\alpha, \beta)P(D|\theta)$$
$$\propto \theta^{\alpha-1}(1 - \theta)^{\beta-1} \cdot \theta^{\#(H)}(1 - \theta)^{\#(T)} \tag{12.11}$$
$$= \theta^{\#(H)+\alpha-1}(1 - \theta)^{\#(T)+\beta-1}.$$

Ignoring the normalising term, Eq 12.11 can be regarded as the likelihood function of the observations with $(\#(H) + \alpha - 1)$ heads and $(\#(T) + \beta - 1)$ tails. Because of this, α and β are also called *pseudo-counts*. Therefore, we can derive the MAP estimation θ^{MAP} in a similar way to Eq 12.7:

$$\theta^{MAP} = \frac{\#(H) + \alpha - 1}{\#(H) + \alpha - 1 + \#(T) + \beta - 1}. \tag{12.12}$$

Now if we believe that the coin is fair, we can set both α and β to 4, which gives the distribution a high probability around 0.5 as shown in Figure 12.2. In this case, the estimated value of θ^{MAP} is

$$\theta^{MAP} = \frac{3 + 4 - 1}{3 + 4 - 1 + 5 + 4 - 1} = \frac{3}{7} = 0.429.$$

Compared with $\theta^{MLE} = 0.375$, θ^{MAP} is much closer to 0.5, reflecting a bias towards our belief that the coin is fair. This demonstrates how MAP provides a means for prior knowledge or belief to be included in parameter estimation. In case that the dataset is small and insufficient for deriving a reliable model, a proper prior can play an important role in finding a better model.

12.2.3 Conjugate Priors

Let us look at the posterior distribution $P(\theta|D, \alpha, \beta)$ in Eq 12.11 again. In particular,

$$
\begin{aligned}
P(\theta|D, \alpha, \beta) &\propto \theta^{\#(H)+\alpha-1}(1-\theta)^{\#(T)+\beta-1} \\
&\propto \frac{\theta^{\#(H)+\alpha-1}(1-\theta)^{\#(T)+\beta-1}}{B(\#(H)+\alpha, \#(T)+\beta)} \\
&= Beta(\theta|\#(H)+\alpha, \#(T)+\beta).
\end{aligned}
\tag{12.13}
$$

As we have seen in Chapter 2, the data likelihood of coin tossing is proportional to binomial distributions. Given the underlying connections between binomial distributions and Beta priors, the posterior function above is also a Beta distribution. Eq 12.13 is similar in form to the likelihood function in Eq 12.7. It allows θ^{MAP} to be calculated using the same algorithm as θ^{MLE}, which brings much computational convenience. When the posterior distribution and the prior distribution have the same form, the prior is called a **conjugate prior** of the likelihood function. Conjugate priors can greatly simplify the computation efforts of inferring the posterior distributions.

Beta-Binomial conjugate. In the coin tossing example, the data likelihood is proportional to a binomial distribution $Bin(n_1, n_2|\theta)$, i.e.,

$$
P(D|\theta) \propto \theta^{n_1}(1-\theta)^{n_2}.
$$

Here $n_1 = \#(H)$ and $n_2 = \#(T)$, denoting the number of successes and failures of Bernoulli experiments, respectively. The **Beta-Binomial conjugate** can be described as

$$
Beta(\theta|\alpha, \beta) \cdot Bin(n_1, n_2|\theta) \propto Beta(\theta|\alpha + n_1, \beta + n_2)
\tag{12.14}
$$

where $Beta(\theta|\alpha, \beta) = \frac{\theta^{\alpha-1}(1-\theta)^{\beta-1}}{B(\alpha,\beta)}$ as in Eq 12.8 and $B(\alpha, \beta) = \frac{\Gamma(\alpha)\Gamma(\beta)}{\Gamma(\alpha+\beta)}$ as in Eq 12.9.

Dirichlet-Multinomial conjugate. Now let us move from Bernoulli random variables to categorial random variables. Let us consider a categorial random variable e with K possible values $\imath_1, \imath_2, \ldots, \imath_K$, which is parameterised with a vector $\vec{\theta} = \langle \theta_1, \theta_2, \ldots, \theta_K \rangle$, where $P(e = \imath_k) = \theta_k$ and $\sum_{k=1}^{K} \theta_k = 1$. As we discussed in Chapter 2, the random event of casino dice casting can be modelled by a categorial random variable, and the data likelihood of a set of *i.i.d.* dice casting experiments is proportional to a multinomial distribution $Mult(\vec{n}|\vec{\theta})$:

$$
P(D|\vec{\theta}) \propto \prod_{i=1}^{K} \theta_k^{n_k},
$$

where n_k in $\vec{n} = \langle n_1, n_2, \ldots, n_K \rangle$ denotes the count of the kth value $\imath_k$ in the data.

Dirichlet distributions serve as conjugate priors for multinomial distributions. Parameterised with hyper-parameter vector $\vec{\alpha} = \langle \alpha_1, \alpha_2, \ldots, \alpha_K \rangle$, the Dirichlet distribution defines a probability distribution family over $\vec{\theta}$:

$$P(\vec{\theta}|\vec{\alpha}) = Dir(\vec{\theta}|\vec{\alpha}) = \frac{1}{\Delta(\vec{\alpha})} \prod_{k=1}^{K} \theta_k^{\alpha_k-1}, \tag{12.15}$$

with the normalisation constant $\Delta(\vec{\alpha})$ being:

$$\Delta(\vec{\alpha}) = \frac{\prod_{k=1}^{K} \Gamma(\alpha_k)}{\Gamma(\sum_{k=1}^{K} \alpha_k)}, \tag{12.16}$$

where $\Gamma(x)$ is the Gamma function as defined in Eq 12.10.

$\Delta(\vec{\alpha})$ can be regarded as a generalisation of the Beta function $B(\alpha, \beta)$ to the multidimensional space. Further, since $P(\vec{\theta}|\vec{\alpha})$ is a probability distribution, we have

$$\int_{\theta_1} \int_{\theta_2} \cdots \int_{\theta_K} P(\vec{\theta}|\vec{\alpha})d\theta_1 d\theta_1 \ldots d\theta_K = \int_{\vec{\theta}} P(\vec{\theta}|\vec{\alpha})d\vec{\theta} = \int_{\vec{\theta}} \frac{1}{\Delta(\vec{\alpha})} \prod_{k=1}^{K} \theta_k^{\alpha_k-1} d\vec{\theta} = 1,$$

from which we can see that the normalising constant is

$$\Delta(\vec{\alpha}) = \int_{\vec{\theta}} \prod_{k=1}^{K} \theta_k^{\alpha_k-1} d\vec{\theta}. \tag{12.17}$$

After specifying the data likelihood $P(D|\vec{\theta})$ and the prior $P(\vec{\theta}|\vec{\alpha})$, we now compute the posterior distribution of our parameter vector $\vec{\theta}$:

$$\begin{aligned} P(\vec{\theta}|\vec{n}, \vec{\alpha}) &= P(\vec{\theta})P(D|\vec{\theta}) \\ &\propto Dir(\vec{\theta}|) \cdot Mult(\vec{n}|\vec{\theta}) \\ &\propto \prod_{k=1}^{K} \theta_k^{\alpha_k-1} \cdot \prod_{i=1}^{K} \theta_k^{n_k} = \prod_{k=1}^{K} \theta_k^{n_k+\alpha_k-1} \\ &\propto Dir(\vec{\theta}|\vec{\alpha} + \vec{n}). \end{aligned} \tag{12.18}$$

According to Eq 12.18, the **Dirichlet-Multinomial conjugate** can be described as:

$$Dir(\vec{\theta}|\vec{\alpha}) \cdot Mult(\vec{n}|\vec{\theta}) \propto Dir(\vec{\theta}|\vec{\alpha} + \vec{n}). \tag{12.19}$$

MAP estimation is typically made with conjugate priors. Since conjugate priors are families of distributions, they involve hyper-parameters such as α, β and $\vec{\alpha}$ in the equations above. While they represent prior knowledge about parameter distributions, their values can also be adjusted empirically. Similar to this section, we include these hyper-parameters in conditional probability notations for the rest of this chapter to highlight their influence.

12.2.4 Bayesian Estimation

As the third parameter estimation method in this chapter, **Bayesian estimation** differs from likelihood and MAP estimation methods in treating the model parameters as random variables, estimating the probability distribution of the model parameters, rather than their best values. In particular, Bayesian estimation uses the same posterior distribution $P(\Theta|D)$ as MAP to quantify the model parameters. According to Eq 12.20, we have

$$P(\Theta|D) = \frac{P(\Theta)P(D|\Theta)}{P(D)} = \frac{P(\Theta)P(D|\Theta)}{\int_\Theta P(\Theta)P(D|\Theta)d\Theta}. \tag{12.20}$$

Different from MAP, the normalisation constant $P(D)$ is not ignored in Eq 12.20. Therefore, the calculation of $P(\Theta|D)$ is precise. In addition, unlike MLE and MAP, an optimisation process is unnecessary because rather than one optimal Θ value, Bayesian estimation of model parameters calculates the distribution of Eq 12.20 as the final result. This can lead to many benefits. First, the probability distribution of Θ tells us more about the uncertainty in the parameters. For example, we can know the mean and the variance of estimated model parameters. Second, when using a model for testing, we can take expectations over Θ to average out the uncertainty, which can reduce prediction risks by taking all possibilities of Θ into consideration. For testing, in general, given the model Eq 12.20 and a test input x, the probabilities of output y should be calculated as:

$$P(y|x, D) = \int_\Theta P(y, \Theta|x, D)d\Theta = \int_\Theta P(y|x, \Theta)P(\Theta|D)d\Theta, \tag{12.21}$$

where $P(y|x)$ represents the model probability of the output.

Coin tossing example continued. Let us still use the coin tossing problem as an example. For predicting the outcome of a new coin toss given the observed training data D, we can calculate:

$$P(H|D) = \int_\theta P(H|\theta)P(\theta|D)d\theta, \tag{12.22}$$

where $P(H|D)$ deotes the probability of heads in a test sample.

Given that $P(H|\theta) = \theta$ and $P(\theta|D) = Beta\left(\theta|\#(H)+\alpha, \#(T)+\beta\right)$, Eq 12.22 can be rewritten as

$$P(H|D) = \int_\theta \theta \cdot Beta\left(\theta|\#(H)+\alpha, \#(T)+\beta\right)d\theta. \tag{12.23}$$

For a Beta distribution $Beta(\theta|\alpha, \beta)$, we have:

$$\int_\theta Beta(\theta|\alpha, \beta)d\theta = \int_\theta \frac{\theta^{\alpha-1}(1-\theta)^{\beta-1}}{B(\alpha, \beta)}d\theta = 1.$$

Therefore, we have

$$B(\alpha, \beta) = \int_\theta \theta^{\alpha-1}(1-\theta)^{\beta-1}d\theta. \tag{12.24}$$

As a result, given any $\theta \in [0, 1]$, we have

$$
\begin{aligned}
\int_\theta \theta \cdot Beta(\theta | \alpha, \beta) d\theta &= \int_\theta \theta \cdot \frac{\theta^{\alpha-1}(1-\theta)^{\beta-1}}{B(\alpha, \beta)} d\theta \\
&= \frac{1}{B(\alpha, \beta)} \int_\theta \theta^{\alpha+1-1}(1-\theta)^{\beta-1} d\theta \\
&= \frac{1}{B(\alpha, \beta)} \cdot B(\alpha+1, \beta) \quad \text{(Using Eq 12.24)} \\
&= \frac{\Gamma(\alpha+\beta)}{\Gamma(\alpha)\Gamma(\beta)} \cdot \frac{\Gamma(\alpha+1)\Gamma(\beta)}{\Gamma(\alpha+\beta+1)} \quad \text{(Using Eq 12.9)} \\
&= \frac{\alpha}{\alpha+\beta} \quad \text{(Using Eq 12.10).}
\end{aligned}
\tag{12.25}
$$

Equation 12.25 is general to all α and β values. Consequently, the estimation for the coin tossing example in Eq 12.23 is given by

$$
\begin{aligned}
P(H|D) &= \int_\theta \theta \cdot Beta(\theta | \alpha + \#(H), \beta + \#(T)) d\theta \\
&= \frac{\#(H) + \alpha}{\#(H) + \alpha + \#(T) + \beta} = \frac{3+4}{3+4+5+4} = 0.438.
\end{aligned}
$$

Expectation of parameters. Equation 12.25 calculates the expectation of $\theta \sim Beta(\theta | \alpha, \beta)$. In general, the calculation of the parameter expectation $\theta^{Expect} = E_{\theta \sim P(\theta | D)}(\theta) = \int_\theta \theta \cdot P(\theta | D) d\theta$ can be useful for Bayesian models, as we will see later in this chapter.

For a Dirichlet distribution $Dir(\vec{\theta} | \vec{\alpha})$, we have the expectation as a vector

$$
E(\vec{\theta}) = \langle \frac{\alpha_1}{\sum_{k=1}^K \alpha_k}, \frac{\alpha_2}{\sum_{k=1}^K \alpha_k}, \dots, \frac{\alpha_K}{\sum_{k=1}^K \alpha_k} \rangle.
\tag{12.26}
$$

We leave the proof to Exercise 12.2.

Correlation with MLE and MAP. Θ^{Expect} is by definition a mean of Θ. It can be used as a fixed estimated parameter value to make output prediction, similar to Θ^{MLE} and Θ^{MAP}. MLE does not incorporate the prior distribution and might overfit on small data. When an event fails to occur in the training data, such as a word in the test data that does not exist in training data for a unigram language model (Chapter 2), MLE assigns zero probability. However, the prior distribution in MAP and Bayesian estimation can help smooth the probability distribution, giving non-zero probabilities for an unseen observation in the training data. In the coin tossing example, when the number of experiments increases, Θ^{MLE}, Θ^{MAP} and Θ^{Expect} converge to the same value. Although sufficient for estimating the outcome of a new test case in our coin tossing example, using Θ^{Expect} instead of $P(\Theta | D)$ for a Bayesian model in general loses information. In general, given a task, we should use Eq 12.21 to find the output. Due to the necessity of maintaining a full posterior distribution, the runtime cost of training and testing can be higher for Bayesian estimation compared with MLE and MAP. The next section discusses one example model with Bayesian estimation.

12.2.5 Bayesian Unigram Language Model

As discussed in Chapter 2, given a sentence $s = w_1w_2 \ldots w_n$, a unigram LM calculates $P(s) = \prod_{j=1}^{n} P(w_j)$. Denoting the set of model parameters $\vec{\theta} = \langle P(w_1), P(w_2), \ldots, P(w_{|V|}) \rangle$, where V is the vocabulary, the likelihood of a corpus D can be written as

$$P(D|\vec{\theta}) = \prod_{i=1}^{|V|} P(w_i)^{n_i},$$

where n_i is the total count of the ith vocabulary word w_i in the corpus. According to the equation, $P(D|\vec{\theta})$ is proportional to a multinomial distribution $Mult(\vec{n}|\vec{\theta})$, where $\vec{n} = \langle n_1, n_2, \ldots, n_{|V|} \rangle$ are the counts of each vocabulary word in D. As a result, we can apply the Dirichlet prior $Dir(\vec{\theta}|\vec{\alpha}) = \frac{1}{\Delta(\vec{\alpha})} \prod_{i=1}^{|V|} P(w_i)^{\alpha_i - 1}$ for $P(\vec{\theta})$, so that the Dirichlet-Multinomial conjugate in Eq 12.18 and Eq 12.15 gives the posterior distribution

$$P(\vec{\theta}|D) \propto Dir(\vec{\theta}|\vec{n} + \vec{\alpha}) = \frac{1}{\Delta(\vec{n} + \vec{\alpha})} \prod_{i=1}^{|V|} P(w_i)^{n_i + \alpha_i - 1} \tag{12.27}$$

where $\Delta(\vec{n} + \vec{\alpha}) = \int_{\vec{\theta}} \prod_{i=1}^{|V|} \theta_i^{n_i + \alpha_i - 1} d\vec{\theta}$ according to Eq 12.17.

Equation 12.27 gives the Bayesian unigram language model. Let us use the model to do two tasks. First, let us take a look at the posterior distribution $P(\vec{\theta}|D)$. It is straightforward to show that the posterior unigram probabilities correspond to the expectations of $\vec{\theta}$ (see Exercise 12.7). Using Eq 12.26, we can obtain the expectation of $\vec{\theta}$ as the following vector

$$E(\vec{\theta}) = \langle \frac{n_1 + \alpha_1}{\sum_{i=1}^{|V|}(n_i + \alpha_i)}, \frac{n_2 + \alpha_2}{\sum_{i=1}^{|V|}(n_i + \alpha_i)}, \ldots, \frac{n_{|V|} + \alpha_{|V|}}{\sum_{i=1}^{|V|}(n_i + \alpha_i)} \rangle. \tag{12.28}$$

If we apply symmetric priors by setting each $\alpha_i = \alpha$, $E(\vec{\theta})$ can be rewritten as

$$E(\vec{\theta}) = \langle \frac{n_1 + \alpha}{N + \alpha|V|}, \frac{n_2 + \alpha}{N + \alpha|V|}, \ldots, \frac{n_{|V|} + \alpha}{N + \alpha|V|} \rangle, \tag{12.29}$$

where $N = \sum_{i=1}^{|V|} n_i$ represents the total number of words. Equation 12.29 is exactly the estimation of unigram models using **add-α smoothing** introduced in Chapter 2. Thus, we find a Bayesian explanation for add-α smoothing. In fact, smoothing can be regarded as a prior knowledge for expressing the intuition that even if an n-gram fails to occur in the training data, we should assign a small probability to it.

As the second task, let us calculate the probability of the whole corpus $P(D|\vec{\alpha})$ using our model Eq 12.27 by integrating out the parameter $\vec{\theta}$:

$$P(D|\vec{\alpha}) = \int_{\vec{\theta}} P(D|\vec{\theta}) P(\vec{\theta}|\vec{\alpha}) d\vec{\theta} = \int_{\vec{\theta}} \prod_{i=1}^{|V|} \theta_i^{n_i} \frac{1}{\Delta(\vec{\alpha})} \cdot \prod_{i=1}^{|V|} \theta_i^{\alpha_i - 1} d\vec{\theta}$$

$$= \frac{1}{\Delta(\vec{\alpha})} \int_{\vec{\theta}} \prod_{i=1}^{|V|} \theta_i^{n_i + \alpha_i - 1} d\vec{\theta} = \frac{\Delta(\vec{n} + \vec{\alpha})}{\Delta(\vec{\alpha})}, \tag{12.30}$$

where $\theta_i = P(w_i)$. The last step is obtained using Eq 12.17, by replacing $\vec{\alpha}$ with $\vec{n} + \vec{\alpha}$:

$$\Delta(\vec{n} + \vec{\alpha}) = \int_{\vec{\theta}} \prod_{i=1}^{|V|} \theta_i^{n_i + \alpha_i - 1} d\vec{\theta}. \tag{12.31}$$

With $P(D|\vec{\alpha})$, we can calculate the perplexity of this language model. The derivation process of Eq 12.30 is general. It works not only for the Bayesian unigram language model but also for other Dirichlet-Multinomial conjugate structures. We will see more applications later.

12.3 Inference

Bayesian networks can be used to infer the probabilities of some variables given observations on others in a particular structured sample. We have seen simple examples with only one variable such as coin tossing and unigram language modelling. For a more complicated example, the Bayesian network in Figure 12.1 can help us to answer questions such as "If the person A bought the stock, what is the probability that the company has released a new product?" and "If the company hired a new CEO, what is the probability that the person B will buy the stock of this company?" To answer these questions, we need to calculate the marginal probabilities, which requires **inference** techniques.

Formally, given a Bayesian network with all conditional probabilities being specified, we consider a dataset with observed variables and unobserved variables. The inference task finds the marginal probability $P(X|E = e)$ of a query variable X given some evidence variables $E = e$. In general, $P(X|E = e)$ can be calculated using

$$P(X|E = e) = \frac{P(X, E = e)}{P(E = e)}. \tag{12.32}$$

Both $P(X, E = e)$ and $P(E = e)$ should be estimated efficiently. Depending on the number of variables and the structure of the Bayesian network, exact computation can be tractable or intractable. Sections 12.3.1 and 12.3.2 show exact methods and approximate methods for inference, respectively.

12.3.1 Exaction Inference

Enumeration. When the numbers of variables and their possible values are small, we can use the marginalisation method discussed in Chapter 2 for finding $P(X, E = e)$ and $P(E - e)$ from joint probabilities. This exact method is typically referred to as *enumeration*. Formally, letting Z be all the random variables in the Bayesian network except E and X, we have

$$P(X|E = e) = \frac{P(X, E = e)}{P(E = e)} = \frac{\sum_Z P(X, E = e, Z)}{\sum_{Z,X} P(X, E = e, Z)} \propto \sum_Z P(X, E = e, Z). \tag{12.33}$$

For example, the distribution $P(x_2|x_4 = T)$ can be calculated by:

$$P(x_2|x_4 = T) \propto P(x_2, x_4 = T)$$
$$= \sum_{x_1, x_3, x_5} P(x_1, x_2, x_3, x_4 = T, x_5) \qquad (12.34)$$
$$= \sum_{x_1, x_3, x_5} P(x_1)P(x_2)P(x_3|x_1, x_2)P(x_4 = T|x_3)P(x_5|x_3).$$

By looking up Table 12.1 for $P(x_1)$, $P(x_2)$, $P(x_3|x_1, x_2)$, $P(x_4|x_3)$ and $P(x_5|x_3)$, we can calculate $P(x_2 = T, x_4 = T)$ and $P(x_2 = F, x_4 = T)$, and then normalise them into a sum of 1 to obtain $P(x_2|x_4 = T)$.

Variable Elimination. Similar to the ideas of forward–backward (Chapter 7) and inside-outside (Chapter 10) algorithms, the variable elimination method exploits the Bayesian network structure by using a dynamic program to carry out summation operations variable by variable, storing intermediate results in tables to save computation efforts. For example,

$$P(x_2, x_4 = T) = \sum_{x_1, x_3, x_5} P(x_1)P(x_2)P(x_3|x_1, x_2)P(x_4 = T|x_3)P(x_5|x_3)$$
$$= P(x_2) \sum_{x_1} P(x_1) \sum_{x_3} P(x_3|x_1, x_2)P(x_4 = T|x_3) \sum_{x_5} P(x_5|x_3)$$
$$= P(x_2) \sum_{x_1} P(x_1) \sum_{x_3} P(x_3|x_1, x_2)P(x_4 = T|x_3)s_{x_5}[x_3] \qquad (12.35)$$
$$= P(x_2) \sum_{x_1} P(x_1)s_{x_3}[x_1, x_2]$$
$$= P(x_2)s_{x_1}[x_2].$$

Here $s_x[y]$ denotes a table of sums over x by each y, and $s_x[y, z]$ denotes a table of sums over x by each combination of (y, z). For example, $s_{x_5}[x_3]$ stores the sums $\sum_{x_5} P(x_5|x_3)$ according to each x_3 value (i.e. T and F). $s_x[y]$ and $s_x[y, z]$ eliminate x from further computation. Equation 12.35 is more efficient to compute compared with Eq 12.34 thanks to the use of tables for storing sums.

In this particular example, $s_{x_5}[x_3] = 1$ for both $x_3 = T$ and $x_3 = F$, which indicates that x_5 is irrelevant to this marginal probability. In general, a random variable y is irrelevant unless y belongs to the ancestors of X and E.

12.3.2 Gibbs Sampling

When the Bayesian network structure becomes complex and the number of random variables is large, the computation cost for exact inference can be highly expensive. When the random variables are continuous-valued rather than discrete, the sum operations become integral operations, which does not allow exact inference. In the above situations, approximate inference is necessary.

One idea is sampling, which is to randomly draw samples according to the joint distribution $P(X, E = e)$. Suppose that we randomly generated 100 samples, 60 of which with evidence e. If the event $(X = x, E = e)$ appears 28 times, then probability $P(X = x, E = e) \approx \frac{28}{60}$ by counting relative frequencies. The more samples we create, the more accurate the approximation can be.

A key problem in sampling is how to draw structured instances $\langle x'_1, x'_2, \dots, x'_n \rangle$ according to the joint probability distribution $P(x_1, x_2, \dots, x_n)$. To this end, **Gibbs sampling** is a useful sampling method for distributions with multiple random variables. It deals with random variables in a Bayesian network one by one. The main idea of Gibbs sampling is to assume that the values of the other variables are fixed when sampling one variable. In particular, Gibbs sampling starts with a random assignment of all the variables, and then goes through each variable in turn. For the variable x_i, the Gibbs sampler assumes that the other variables are fixed to their last-drawn values, drawing a sample of x_i according to the marginal distribution $P(x_i | x_1, x_2, \dots, x_{i-1}, x_{i+1}, \dots, x_n)$. After processing x_i, the Gibbs sampler turns to sample a next random variable, such as x_{i+1}. At this time, the sampler uses the distribution $P(x_{i+1} | x_1, x_2, \dots, x'_i, x_{i+2}, \dots, x_n)$, where x'_i is the new sample of x_i. In theory, the distribution estimated by Gibbs sampling is guaranteed to converge to the joint distribution $P(x_1, x_2, \dots, x_n)$.

Algorithm 12.1 shows the Gibbs sampling algorithm for general joint distributions $P(x_1, x_2, \dots, x_n)$. The algorithm first randomly chooses an initial point $x^{(0)} = \langle x_1^{(0)}, x_2^{(0)}, \dots, x_n^{(0)} \rangle$, where $x_n^{(t)}$ means the sample value of x_n at the tth iteration. It then iteratively generates the sample $x_i^{(t)}$ according to the marginal distribution $P(x_i | X^{-i})$, where X^{-i} denotes variables excluding x_i. The algorithm can stop after T iterations.

For efficiently computing $P(x_i | X^{-i})$, the marginal probability can be simplified according to the conditional independence. In particular, according to Theorem 12.1, denote the Markov blanket of x_i as $MB(x_i)$. Further denote its parents, co-parents and children as $A(x_i)$, $C(x_i)$ and $H(x_i)$, respectively. We have:

$$
\begin{aligned}
P(x_i | X^{-i}) &= P\Big(x_i | MB(x_i), Y\Big) \qquad (Y = X - MB(x_i) - \{x_i\}) \\
&= P(x_i | MB(x_i)) \qquad \text{(Eq 12.2)} \\
&= P\Big(x_i | A(x_i), C(x_i), H(x_i)\Big) \\
&= \frac{P\Big(x_i, H(x_i) | C(x_i), A(x_i)\Big)}{P\Big(H(x_i) | C(x_i), A(x_i)\Big)} \\
&= \frac{P\Big(x_i | C(x_i), A(x_i)\Big) P\Big(H(x_i) | x_i, C(x_i), A(x_i)\Big)}{P\Big(H(x_i) | C(x_i), A(x_i)\Big)} \qquad (12.36) \\
&\propto P\Big(x_i | C(x_i), A(x_i)\Big) P\Big(H(x_i) | x_i, C(x_i), A(x_i)\Big) \\
&\qquad\qquad (H(x_i), C(x_i) \text{ and } A(x_i) \text{ are fixed}) \\
&= P\Big(x_i | A(x_i)\Big) P\Big(H(x_i) | x_i, C(x_i)\Big) \qquad \text{(Eq 12.3)} \\
&= P(x_i | x_{\pi(i)}) \prod_{j : x_i \in x_{\pi(j)}} P(x_j | x_{\pi(j)}) \qquad \text{(Eq 12.1)}.
\end{aligned}
$$

Algorithm 12.1. Gibbs sampling.

Initialisation: Create a random sample $X^{(0)} = \langle x_1^{(0)}, x_2^{(0)}, \ldots, x_n^{(0)} \rangle$;
Algorithm:
$t \leftarrow 0$;
for $t \in [1, \ldots, T]$ **do**
    for $i \in [1, \ldots, n]$ **do**
        Sample $x_i^{(t)} \sim P(X_i | x_1^{(t)}, x_2^{(t)}, \ldots, x_{i-1}^{(t)}, x_{i+1}^{(t-1)}, x_{i+2}^{(t-1)}, \ldots, x_n^{(t-1)})$;

$X - \mathrm{MB}(x_i) - \{x_i\}$ refers to all the other variables after excluding x_i and $\mathrm{MB}(x_i)$. According to Eq 12.36, for sampling x_i, we need to consider both what can directly affect x_i and what can be directly affected by x_i. $P(x_i | x_{\pi(i)})$ is the probability distribution that affects x_i given its parent variables. For all x_j such that $x_i \in x_{\pi(j)}$, $P(x_j | x_{\pi(j)})$ is the local probability distribution that can be affected by x_i. For example, for sampling x_4 in Figure 12.1, we can directly use $P(x_4 | x_3)$. For sampling x_3, we need to calculate $P(x_3 | x_1, x_2) P(x_4 | x_3) P(x_5 | x_3)$.

Gibbs sampling and hidden variables. Sampling can serve as a useful tool when training Bayesian models with hidden variables. As mentioned at the beginning of Chapter 6, with the counts of hidden variables being unavailable during training, we cannot define a full data likelihood function. One strategy for training a model with hidden variables is to randomly initialise their counts, so that an initial version of the likelihood function can be defined, which leads to an initial model. Then we can use Gibbs sampling to obtain new samples according to the initial model, so that new counts can be obtained. Next, a better model can be defined using the new counts. This process can be iteratively executed until convergence, and the final model can be used for testing. We will see one detailed example in the next section.

12.4 Latent Dirichlet Allocation

Equipped with inference techniques, we can now consider training Bayesian networks when the training data contains hidden variables. We have seen the Naïve Bayes model in Chapter 2, which is trained by MLE via relative frequencies. Introducing latent variables into the Naïve Bayes model results in the PLSA model discussed in Chapter 6, which is trained with EM. Here we extend the PLSA model with Bayesian estimation to introduce sparse priors, assuming that a document often only contains a few topics and only a few keywords are highly relevant for a topic.

Latent Dirichlet allocation (LDA) is a Bayesian network for document topic modelling, which assumes that each document contains a mixture of latent topics and each word is generated from a topic. We start by briefly reviewing PLSA. In PLSA, given a word w_j ($j \in [1, \ldots, N_d]$) in a document d, the probability $P(w_j | d)$ is

$$P(w_j | d) = \sum_{k=1}^{K} P(w_j | z_j = k) P(z_j = k | d), \tag{12.37}$$

where N_d is the total number of words in d, K is the total number of topics, z_j is the latent topic of w_j, $P(w_j|z_j = k)$ is the kth "topic–word" distribution, and $P(z_j = k|d)$ is the "document-topic" distribution for d. Suppose that the topics $\vec{z}_d = \langle z_1, z_2, \ldots, z_{N_d} \rangle$ for words $\vec{w}_d = \langle w_1, w_2, \ldots, w_{N_d} \rangle$ in the document d are already known.[2] Assuming that the words are conditionally independent given d, the joint probability of the topics and the words in d is

$$P(\vec{z}_d, \vec{w}_d) = \prod_{j=1}^{N_d} P(w_j|z_j)P(z_j|d)$$
$$= \prod_{k=1}^{K} \left(P(z = k|d)^{n_{d,k}} \prod_{i=1}^{|V|} P(w_i|z = k)^{c_{d,k,i}} \right). \tag{12.38}$$

Here V is the vocabulary, w_i denotes the ith word in the vocabulary, $n_{d,k}$ denotes the number of times the kth topic appears in d, and $c_{d,k,i}$ denotes the number of times the ith vocabulary word w_i is generated from the kth topic in d.

Now suppose that we have a corpus D of multiple documents. Since the generation process of one document is independent of the other documents, the probability of the whole corpus is

$$P(D) = \prod_{d=1}^{|D|} P(\vec{z}_d, \vec{w}_d) = \prod_{d=1}^{|D|} \left(\prod_{k=1}^{K} P(z = k|d)^{n_{d,k}} \prod_{i=1}^{|V|} P(w_i|z = k)^{c_{d,k,i}} \right)$$
$$= \prod_{d=1}^{|D|} \left(\left(\underbrace{\prod_{k=1}^{K} P(z = k|d)^{n_{d,k}}}_{\propto \text{ per-document multinomial}} \right) \cdot \left(\underbrace{\prod_{k=1}^{K} \prod_{i=1}^{|V|} P(w_i|z = k)^{c_{k,i}}}_{\propto \text{ per-topic multinomial}} \right) \right), \tag{12.39}$$

where $|D|$ is the document count, and $c_{k,i} = \sum_{d=1}^{|D|} c_{d,k,i}$ denotes the total number of times that the ith vocabulary word w_i is generated from the kth topic in D.

Unfortunately, given a set of text documents, we do not have the counts $c_{d,k,i}$ or $n_{d,k}$ because z is not observable. PLSA addresses this problem by casting the topic as hidden variable, using EM to train $P(w|z)$ and $P(z|d)$. LDA models the same topic–word and document–topic distributions, both being categorical distributions, with the topics being hidden variables, yet uses a Bayesian estimation method instead of EM, with prior distributions over the model parameters. In particular, according to Eq 12.39, the data likelihood consists of two distribution terms which are both proportional to multinomial distributions. Consequently, LDA puts Dirichlet priors both on the topic–word distribution parameters and the document–topic distribution parameters.

Figure 12.3 shows the Bayesian network structure for LDA. Here $\vec{\Phi} = \langle \vec{\varphi}_1, \vec{\varphi}_2, \ldots, \vec{\varphi}_K \rangle$ denotes the set of topic–word distributions, where $\vec{\varphi}_k$ is the kth topic–word distribution ($k \in \{1, \ldots, K\}$). In particular,

$$\vec{\varphi}_k = \langle P(w_1|z = k), P(w_2|z = k), \ldots, P(w_{|V|}|z = k) \rangle, k \in \{1, \ldots, K\}.$$

---

[2] As mentioned in Chapter 6, d here is a symbolic representation of the document, for which we induce the topics. Consequently, we use $\vec{w}_d$ to denote the word sequence in d.

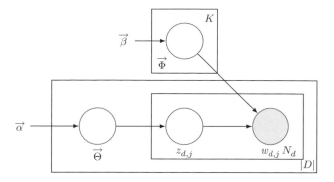

Figure 12.3 Nested plate notation for LDA.

$\vec{\beta}$ parameterises a Dirichlet prior $Dir(\vec{\beta})$, which is shared by all topic–word distributions $\vec{\varphi}_k$, with $|\vec{\beta}| = |V|$. Each hyper-parameter β_i can be regarded as a pseudo prior count for the number of times word i occurred in a topic before seeing any actual observations.

$\vec{\Theta} = \langle \vec{\theta}_1, \vec{\theta}_2, \ldots, \vec{\theta}_{|D|} \rangle$ denotes the set of document–topic distributions, where $\vec{\theta}_d$ represents the dth document–topic distribution. In particular,

$$\vec{\theta}_d = \langle P(z = 1|d), P(z = 2|d), \ldots, P(z = K|d) \rangle.$$

$\vec{\alpha}$ parameterises a Dirichlet prior $Dir(\vec{\alpha})$, which is shared by all document-topic distributions $\vec{\theta}$, with $|\vec{\alpha}| = K$. Every hyper-parameter α_k can be imagined as a pseudo prior count for the number of times topic k appeared in a document d before seeing any actual words from d.

In LDA, empirically setting the priors $Dir(\vec{\alpha})$ and $Dir(\vec{\beta})$ to be symmetric priors $Dir(\alpha)$ and $Dir(\beta)$ where $\alpha = \frac{K}{50}$ and $\beta = 0.05$ can encode sparsity, requiring that a document only contains a few topics and each topic only consists of a few keywords.

The generative story of LDA can be described as follows:

1. For each topic k, generate the topic–word distribution $\vec{\varphi}_k$ according to $Dir(\vec{\varphi}_k|\vec{\beta})$. In total, we generate K topic–word distributions.
2. For each document $d \in D$,
   (a) Generate the document–topic distribution $\vec{\theta}_d$ according to $Dir(\vec{\theta}_d|\vec{\alpha})$.
   (b) For each position $j \in N_d$,
      i. Generate the topic $z_{d,j} = k$ according to $\vec{\theta}_d$;
      ii. Generate the word $w_{d,j}$ according to $\vec{\varphi}_k$.

12.4.1 Training with Hidden Variables

Given the generative story above, we want to fully specify our model using Bayesian estimation, namely to find out two posterior model parameter probability distributions: $P(\vec{\theta}_d|D, \vec{\alpha})$ and $P(\vec{\varphi}_k|D, \vec{\beta})$. Unlike the case for the Bayesian unigram language model, however, one challenge here is that our data D is not fully observed because of the hidden variable z. This prevents the model posterior from being calculated directly, which is the product of model prior and data likelihood (Eq 12.4).

Our overall strategy is to first specify the posteriors of model parameters with relevant counts being used as variables. In particular, the counts $n_{d,k}$ and $c_{k,i}$ are treated as variables in multinomial distributions, so that the data likelihood in Eq 12.39 can be used directly for deriving the full model. As shown earlier in this chapter, the data likelihood and conjugate priors can be used to derive the posteriors $P(\vec{\theta}_d|D, \vec{\alpha})$ for each d and $P(\vec{\varphi}_k|D, \vec{\beta})$ for each k. Using these model posteriors we can define the full Bayesian network, still with the counts being variables. For training, the count variables can be randomly initialised, and the following two steps are iteratively executed until convergence. First, the posterior distributions are calculated using the current counts. Second, the counts are updated by Gibbs sampling using the current posteriors.

Posterior distribution of parameters. There are two types of count variables according to Eq 12.39, namely $\vec{n}_d$, which is the frequency vector of topics in d, and $\vec{c}_k$, which is the frequency vector of words which are assigned to the topic k. Formally we have $\vec{n}_d = \langle n_{d,1}, n_{d,2}, \ldots, n_{d,K} \rangle$ and $\vec{c}_k = \langle c_{k,1}, c_{k,2}, \ldots, c_{k,|V|} \rangle$. We can specify the model posteriors with the count variables. Specifically, for each document d, the generative model $\vec{\alpha} \to \vec{\theta}_d \to \vec{z}_d$ is a Dirichlet-Multinomial conjugate structure. The likelihood $P(z = k|d) = \theta_{d,k}^{n_{d,k}}$ with $n_{d,k}$ being a count variable. According to Eq 12.18, the posterior $P(\vec{\theta}_d|D, \vec{\alpha})$ is

$$P(\vec{\theta}_d|D, \vec{\alpha}) = Dir(\vec{\theta}_d|\vec{n}_d + \vec{\alpha}).$$

For the topic k, the generative model $\vec{\beta} \to \vec{\varphi}_k \to \vec{w}_k$ is a Dirichlet-Multinomial conjugate structure. According to Eq 12.18, the posterior distribution $P(\vec{\varphi}_k|D, \vec{\beta})$ is

$$P(\vec{\varphi}_k|D, \vec{\beta}) = Dir(\vec{\varphi}_k|\vec{c}_k + \vec{\beta})$$

Calculating joint distribution. Based on the generative process specified in Figure 12.3, given D, the joint probability distribution of the full Bayesian network is

$$P(\vec{\Theta}, \vec{\Phi}, \vec{Z}, \vec{W}|\vec{\alpha}, \vec{\beta})$$
$$= \prod_{d=1}^{|D|} Dir(\vec{\theta}_d|\vec{\alpha}) \prod_{i=1}^{N_d} P(z_{d,i}|\vec{\theta}_d) \prod_{k=1}^{K} Dir(\vec{\varphi}_k|\vec{\beta}) P(w_{d,i}|\vec{\varphi}_{z_{d,i}}), \tag{12.40}$$

where $\vec{W}$ is the observed words in each document $d \in [1, \ldots, D]$, $\vec{W} = \langle \vec{w}_1, \vec{w}_2, \ldots, \vec{w}_{|D|} \rangle$, and $\vec{Z}$ is the topic assignment in each $d \in [1, \ldots, D]$. $\vec{Z} = \langle \vec{z}_1, \vec{z}_2, \ldots, \vec{z}_{|D|} \rangle$. $\vec{z}_d$ and $\vec{w}_d$ are defined at the beginning of this section.

Given the joint distribution, we can now consider Gibbs sampling for finding the counts. In practice, however, it can be easier to sample topic assignments according to the distribution $P(Z, W|\vec{\alpha}, \vec{\beta})$ instead of the full joint distribution, since the parameters $\vec{\Theta}$ and $\vec{\Phi}$ are continuous. As a result, we want to find out $P(Z, W|\vec{\alpha}, \vec{\beta})$ given the joint distribution, still with $n_{d,k}$ and $c_{k,i}$ being variables in them. This is a standard marginalisation process, which can be done by integrating out the values of $\vec{\Theta}$ and $\vec{\Phi}$. However, a simpler solution is feasible given the structure of Eq 12.39. We can obtain the joint distribution $P(\vec{Z}, \vec{W}|\vec{\alpha}, \vec{\beta})$ through the understanding of the Dirichlet-Multinomial conjugate structures instead of using direct mathematical integral calculations.

According to the conditional independences in Figure 12.3, $P(\vec{Z}, \vec{W}|\vec{\alpha}, \vec{\beta}) = P(\vec{Z}|\vec{\alpha})P(\vec{W}|\vec{Z}, \vec{\beta})$. This can be intuitively understood as concatenating all the documents into a single document, and then generating the topics for the concatenated document using the probability distribution $P(\vec{Z}|\vec{\alpha})$. Then given the topics, we generate all the words according to the probability distribution $P(\vec{W}|\vec{Z}, \vec{\beta})$.

The generation of topics in one document is independent of the other documents. Therefore, $P(\vec{Z}|\vec{\alpha})$ can be decomposed to

$$P(\vec{Z}|\vec{\alpha}) = \prod_{d=1}^{|D|} P(\vec{z}_d|\vec{\alpha}).$$

Given that $P(\vec{\theta}_d|D, \vec{\alpha}) = Dir(\vec{\theta}_d|\vec{n}_d + \vec{\alpha})$, we can follow the derivation of Eq 12.30 for Dirichlet-Multinomial distributions to obtain

$$P(\vec{z}_d|\vec{\alpha}) = \int_{\vec{\theta}_d} P(\vec{z}_d|\vec{\theta}_d)P(\vec{\theta}_d|D, \vec{\alpha})d\vec{\theta}_d = \frac{\Delta(\vec{n}_d + \vec{\alpha})}{\Delta(\vec{\alpha})},$$

where

$$\Delta(\vec{\alpha}) = \int_{\vec{\theta}_d} \prod_{z=1}^{K} \theta_{d,z}^{\alpha_z-1} d\vec{\theta}_d$$

and

$$\Delta(\vec{n}_d + \vec{\alpha}) = \int_{\vec{\theta}_d} \prod_{z=1}^{K} \theta_{d,z}^{n_{d,z}+\alpha_z-1} d\vec{\theta}_d$$

according to Eq 12.17. Therefore we have

$$P(\vec{Z}|\vec{\alpha}) = \prod_{d=1}^{|D|} \frac{\Delta(\vec{n}_d + \vec{\alpha})}{\Delta(\vec{\alpha})}, \tag{12.41}$$

which is the product of $|D|$ independent Dirichlet-Multinomial conjugates.

$P(\vec{W}|\vec{Z}, \vec{\beta})$ can be factored into the product of K independent Dirichlet-Multinomial conjugate structures in a similar way. In particular, the word generation of each topic is independent of the other topics. Therefore, we process the word generation topic by topic. Formally, for the topic k, the posterior distribution of parameters $P(\vec{\varphi}_k|D, \vec{\beta}) = Dir(\vec{\varphi}_k|\vec{c}_k + \vec{\beta})$. Similar to Eq 12.41, $P(\vec{W}|\vec{Z}, \vec{\beta})$ is given by

$$P(\vec{W}|\vec{Z}, \vec{\beta}) = \prod_{k=1}^{K} \frac{\Delta(\vec{c}_k + \vec{\beta})}{\Delta(\vec{\beta})} \tag{12.42}$$

where

$$\Delta(\vec{\beta}) = \int_{\vec{\varphi}_k} \prod_{i=1}^{|V|} \varphi_{k,i}^{\beta_i-1} d\vec{\varphi}_k$$

and

$$\Delta(\vec{c}_k + \vec{\beta}) = \int_{\vec{\varphi}_k} \prod_{i=1}^{|V|} \varphi_{k,i}^{c_{k,i}+\beta_i-1} d\vec{\varphi}_k$$

according to Eq 12.17.

Combining Eq 12.41 and Eq 12.42, we have

$$P(\vec{Z}, \vec{W} | \vec{\alpha}, \vec{\beta}) = P(\vec{Z} | \vec{\alpha}) P(\vec{W} | \vec{Z}, \vec{\beta})$$
$$= \prod_{d=1}^{|D|} \frac{\Delta(\vec{n}_d + \vec{\alpha})}{\Delta(\vec{\alpha})} \prod_{k=1}^{K} \frac{\Delta(\vec{c}_k + \vec{\beta})}{\Delta(\vec{\beta})}. \tag{12.43}$$

In this equation, both $\vec{n}_d$ and $\vec{c}_k$ are calculated according to a given $\vec{z}$.

Gibbs sampling. In Eq 12.43, the hidden variables $\vec{\Theta}$ and $\vec{\Phi}$ are marginalised out. The only remaining hidden variables in our LDA model are the topics $\vec{z}$ in the training data. They directly decide all the count variables in the posterior model distributions. Let us use Gibbs sampling discussed in Section 12.3.2 to sample the hidden topics for each input word. Formally, in order to sample the topic of each word $w_{d,j}$ for each word position j in each document d, we need to define the marginal probability distribution $P(z_I | \vec{Z}^{\neg I}, \vec{W}, \vec{\alpha}, \vec{\beta})$, where $I = (d, j)$ and $\neg I$ denotes all the positions except for I. We further use i to denote the index of the word $w_{d,j}$ in the vocabulary. $n_{d,k}^{\neg I}$ and $c_{k,i}^{\neg I}$ denote the counts $n_{d,k}$ and $c_{k,i}$ with I being excluded, respectively. We have $n_{d,k'}^{\neg I} = n_{d,k'} - \delta(k', k)$ and $c_{k,i'}^{\neg I} = c_{k,i'} - \delta(i', i)$. Formally, fixing the values of $\vec{Z}^{\neg I}$, $\vec{W}$, $\vec{\alpha}$ and $\vec{\beta}$ for sampling z_I, the marginal distribution is given by

$$P(z_I = k | \vec{Z}^{\neg I}, \vec{W}, \vec{\alpha}, \vec{\beta}) = \frac{P(\vec{Z}, \vec{W} | \vec{\alpha}, \vec{\beta})}{P(\vec{Z}^{\neg I}, \vec{W} | \vec{\alpha}, \vec{\beta})} \quad \left(P(\vec{Z}, \vec{W} | \vec{\alpha}, \vec{\beta}) = P(\vec{Z}^{\neg I}, \vec{W} | \vec{\alpha}, \vec{\beta}) \cdot P(z_{\neg I} | \vec{Z}^{\neg I}, \vec{W}, \vec{\alpha}, \vec{\beta}) \right)$$

$$= \frac{P(\vec{Z}, \vec{W} | \vec{\alpha}, \vec{\beta})}{P(\vec{Z}^{\neg I}, \vec{W}^{\neg I}, w_I | \vec{\alpha}, \vec{\beta})} = \frac{P(\vec{Z}, \vec{W} | \vec{\alpha}, \vec{\beta})}{P(\vec{Z}^{\neg I}, \vec{W}^{\neg I} | \vec{\alpha}, \vec{\beta}) P(w_I | \vec{Z}^{\neg I}, \vec{W}^{\neg I}, \vec{\alpha}, \vec{\beta})} \quad \text{(chain rule)}$$

$$\propto \frac{P(\vec{Z}, \vec{W} | \vec{\alpha}, \vec{\beta})}{P(\vec{Z}^{\neg I}, \vec{W}^{\neg I} | \vec{\alpha}, \vec{\beta})} \quad (\vec{Z}^{\neg I}, \ \vec{W}^{\neg I}, \ \vec{\alpha}, \ \vec{\beta}, \ w_I \text{ are constants to } z_I)$$

$$= \frac{\prod_{d'=1}^{|D|} \frac{\Delta(\vec{n}_{d'} + \vec{\alpha})}{\Delta(\vec{\alpha})} \prod_{k'=1}^{K} \frac{\Delta(\vec{c}_{k'} + \vec{\beta})}{\Delta(\vec{\beta})}}{\prod_{d'=1}^{|D|} \frac{\Delta(\vec{n}_{d'}^{\neg I} + \vec{\alpha})}{\Delta(\vec{\alpha})} \prod_{k'=1}^{K} \frac{\Delta(\vec{c}_{k'}^{\neg I} + \vec{\beta})}{\Delta(\vec{\beta})}} \quad \text{(Eq 12.43)}$$

$$= \frac{\Delta(\vec{n}_d + \vec{\alpha})}{\Delta(\vec{n}_d^{\neg I} + \vec{\alpha})} \frac{\Delta(\vec{c}_k + \vec{\beta})}{\Delta(\vec{c}_k^{\neg I} + \vec{\beta})} \quad (\vec{n}_{d'} \text{ differs from } \vec{n}_{d'}^{\neg I} \text{ only when } d' = d)$$

$$= \frac{\prod_{k'=1}^{K} \Gamma(n_{d,k'} + \alpha_{k'})}{\Gamma(\sum_{k'=1}^{K} (n_{d,k'} + \alpha_{k'}))} \frac{\Gamma(\sum_{k'=1}^{K} (n_{d,k'}^{\neg I} + \alpha_{k'}))}{\prod_{k'=1}^{K} \Gamma(n_{d,k'}^{\neg I} + \alpha_{k'})}$$

$$\frac{\prod_{i'=1}^{|V|} \Gamma(c_{k,i'} + \beta_{i'})}{\Gamma(\sum_{i'=1}^{|V|} (c_{k,i'} + \beta_{i'}))} \frac{\Gamma(\sum_{i'=1}^{|V|} (c_{k,i'}^{\neg I} + \beta_{i'}))}{\prod_{i'=1}^{V} \Gamma(c_{k,i'}^{\neg I} + \beta_{i'})} \quad \text{(Eq 12.16)}$$

$$= \frac{\Gamma(n_{d,k} + \alpha_k)}{\Gamma(n_{d,k}^{-I} + \alpha_k)} \frac{\Gamma(\sum_{k'=1}^{K} (n_{d,k'}^{-I} + \alpha_{k'}))}{\Gamma(\sum_{k'=1}^{K} (n_{d,k'} + \alpha_{k'}))} \quad (n_{d,k'} \text{ differs from } n_{d,k'}^{-I} \text{ only when } k' = k)$$

$$\frac{\Gamma(c_{k,i} + \beta_i)}{\Gamma(c_{k,i}^{-I} + \beta_i)} \frac{\Gamma(\sum_{i'=1}^{|V|} (c_{k,i'}^{-I} + \beta_{i'}))}{\Gamma(\sum_{i'=1}^{|V|} (c_{k,i'} + \beta_{i'}))} \quad (c_{k,i'} \text{ differs from } c_{k,i'}^{-I} \text{ only when } i' = i)$$

$$= \frac{\Gamma(n_{d,k}^{-I} + \alpha_k + 1)}{\Gamma(n_{d,k}^{-I} + \alpha_k)} \frac{\Gamma(\sum_{k'=1}^{K} (n_{d,k'}^{-I} + \alpha_{k'}))}{\Gamma(\sum_{k'=1}^{K} (n_{d,k'}^{-I} + \alpha_{k'}) + 1)} \quad (n_{d,k} = n_{d,k}^{-I} + 1 \text{ excluding } z_j = k) \quad (12.44)$$

$$\frac{\Gamma(c_{k,i}^{-I} + \beta_i + 1)}{\Gamma(c_{k,i}^{-I} + \beta_i)} \frac{\Gamma(\sum_{i'=1}^{|V|} (c_{k,i'}^{-I} + \beta_{i'}))}{\Gamma(\sum_{i'=1}^{|V|} (c_{k,i'}^{-I} + \beta_{i'}) + 1)} \quad (c_{k,i} = c_{k,i}^{-I} + 1 \text{ excluding } w_j = w_i)$$

$$= \frac{n_{d,k}^{-I} + \alpha_k}{\sum_{k'=1}^{K} (n_{d,k'}^{-I} + \alpha_{k'})} \cdot \frac{c_{k,i}^{-I} + \beta_i}{\sum_{i'=1}^{|V|} (c_{k,i'}^{-I} + \beta_{i'})} \quad \text{(Eq 12.10)}$$

The result is quite intuitive. The first term is the document–topic distribution and the second term the topic–word distribution after excluding the pair $(z_j = k, w_j = w_i)$ from document d.

Algorithm 12.2 shows the training algorithm for LDA based on Gibbs sampling. The algorithm starts by randomly choosing a topic for each word in each document as the initial topic assignment. Then the sampling process begins, which iteratively samples a new topic for each word based on the current values of the count variables, and then updates the count variables by decreasing the relevant count variables for the old topic by 1 and increasing the counts for the new topic by 1. The convergence can be empirically detected by checking the likelihood function (Eq 12.43).

12.4.2 Using LDA

Similar to PLSA, LDA can be applied to document clustering, information retrieval, machine translation and keyword mining, estimating the document–topic distributions and the topic–word distributions. The document–topic distribution is a distributed representation for a document, which can be used to measure the similarities of documents. The topic–word distribution can help to extract informative words from each document.

To this end, we need fixed values of $\vec{\theta}_d$ and $\vec{\phi}_k$. Using the estimated counts obtained in Algorithm 12.2, we can know the posterior distributions $P(\vec{\theta}_d|D, \vec{\alpha})$ and $P(\vec{\phi}_k|D, \vec{\beta})$ of the model parameters. To obtain an estimated value of each model parameter, we can take the expectation over the posterior distributions of the model parameters (Section 12.4.1) as outputs for every t iterations. According to Eq 12.26, we have

$$E(\vec{\theta}_d) = \langle \frac{n_{d,1} + \alpha_1}{\sum_{k=1}^{K} (n_{d,k} + \alpha_k)}, \frac{n_{d,2} + \alpha_2}{\sum_{k=1}^{K} (n_{d,k} + \alpha_k)}, \dots, \frac{n_{d,K} + \alpha_K}{\sum_{k=1}^{K} (n_{d,k} + \alpha_k)} \rangle$$

$$E(\vec{\phi}_k) = \langle \frac{c_{k,1} + \beta_1}{\sum_{i=1}^{V} (c_{k,i} + \beta_i)}, \frac{c_{k,2} + \beta_2}{\sum_{i=1}^{V} (c_{k,i} + \beta_i)}, \dots, \frac{c_{k,|V|} + \beta_{|V|}}{\sum_{i=1}^{V} (c_{k,i} + \beta_i)} \rangle. \quad (12.45)$$

Algorithm 12.2. Gibbs sampling algorithm for LDA.

Input: A document set D, the priors $\vec{\alpha}$, $\vec{\beta}$, the topic number K;

Initialisation:

Set the document-topic count $n_{d,k}$, the document-topic sum count n_d, the topic–word count $c_{k,i}$ and the topic–word sum count c_k to zero.

for $d \in [1, \ldots, |D|]$ **do**

    for $j \in [1, \ldots, N_d]$ **do**

        $k \leftarrow$ random choice of $[1, \ldots, K]$;

        $z_j \leftarrow k$;

        $i \leftarrow$ index of w_j in vocabulary;

        $c_{k,i} \leftarrow c_{k,i} + 1; c_k \leftarrow c_k + 1$;

        $n_{d,k} \leftarrow n_{d,k} + 1; n_d \leftarrow n_d + 1$;

Algorithm:

repeat

    for $d \in [1, \ldots, |D|]$ **do**

        for $j \in [1, \ldots, N_d]$ **do**

            $k \leftarrow z_j$;

            $i \leftarrow$ index of w_j in vocabulary;

            $c_{k,i} \leftarrow c_{k,i} - 1; c_k \leftarrow c_k - 1$;

            $n_{d,k} \leftarrow n_{d,k} - 1; n_d \leftarrow n_d - 1$;

            Sample $z_j = k'$ according to Eq 12.44 using $(c_{k,i} + \beta_i)$ as $(c_{k,i}^{-I} + \beta_i)$,

            $(n_{d,k} + \alpha_k)$ as $(n_{d,k}^{-I} + \alpha_k)$, $(n_d + \sum_{k'=1}^{K} \alpha_{k'})$ as $\sum_{k'=1}^{K}(n_{d,k'}^{-I} + \alpha_{k'})$ and

            $(c_k + \sum_{i'=1}^{|V|} \beta_{i'})$ as $\sum_{i'=1}^{|V|}(c_{k,i'}^{-I} + \beta_{i'})$;

            $c_{k',i} \leftarrow c_{k',i} + 1; c_{k'} \leftarrow c_{k'} + 1$;

            $n_{d,k'} \leftarrow n_{d,k'} + 1; n_d \leftarrow n_d + 1$;

until $\textsc{Converge}(P(\vec{Z}, \vec{W} | \vec{\alpha}, \vec{\beta}))$;

The different model parameters obtained at different iterations can be averaged for better performances. Topics cluster words according to topic–word distributions, where the most probable words under a topic can define the meaning of the topic.

12.4.3 Topic Evaluation

Normalised pointwise mutual information (NPMI) between all the pairs of words in a set of topics can be used to evaluate the topic quality. For each topic t, the top M most probable words $[w_1, \ldots, w_M]$ are selected to compute the NPMI. The measurement of NPMI for topic t is:

$$NPMI(t) = \sum_{i,j \leq M;\, j \neq i} \frac{\log \frac{P(w_i, w_j)}{P(w_i)P(w_j)}}{-\log P(w_i, w_j)}. \tag{12.46}$$

The overall NPMI score for a topic model is the average score for all topics. Larger NPMI scores indicate more coherent and better topic models.

12.5 Bayesian IBM Model 1

As a second example for Bayesian learning with hidden variables, consider IBM Model 1 in Chapter 6, which uses EM for parameter estimation. Let us define a Bayesian version of this model here. Given a bilingual parallel corpus $D = \{(X_i, Y_i)\}|_{i=1}^{N}$, we need to estimate the probabilities $P(x|y)$, where x is a source word and y is a target word.

For training, let us consider a single sentence pair. In particular, let $X = \{x_i\}|_{i=1}^{N_x}$, $Y = \{y_j\}|_{j=1}^{N_y}$ be a pair of source input and target output, N_x and N_y are the corresponding lengths of the source input and the target output, and A be the alignment between X and Y. As shown in Chapter 6, the joint probability is

$$P(X, Y, A|\vec{\Theta}) = \frac{\prod_{i=1}^{N} P(x_i|y_{a_i})}{(|Y| + 1)^{N_x}} \propto \prod_{i=1}^{N} P(x_i|y_{a_i}) = \prod_{j=1}^{|V_y|} \prod_{i=1}^{|V_x|} P(x_i|y_j)^{c_{y_j,x_i}},$$

where $c_{y,x}$ is the overall counts of x being aligned to y. Given the sentence pair (X, Y), we can execute Gibbs sampling to sample alignment between each word pair (x_i, y_j). In particular, for each target word y, the source word generation likelihood is proportional to a categorical distribution $P(x|y)$. Let $\vec{\theta}_y = \langle P(x_1|y), P(x_2|y), \ldots, P(x_{|V_x|}|y)\rangle$, we have $\vec{\Theta} = \langle \vec{\theta}_1, \vec{\theta}_2, \ldots, \vec{\theta}_{|V_y|}\rangle$, where V_x is the source language vocabulary and V_y is the target language vocabulary. We can put a symmetric Dirichlet prior $Dir(\alpha)$ on each $\vec{\theta}_y$. Similar to Eq 12.44, it can be shown that the marginal probability distribution for Gibbs sampling is

$$P(\alpha_j = i|X, Y, A^{-j}, \vec{\alpha}) \propto \frac{c_{y_j,x_i}^{-j} + \alpha}{\sum_{v=1}^{|V_x|}(c_{y_j,x_v}^{-j} + \alpha)},$$

where A^{-j} represents the alignments except for the jth position, and c_{y_j,x_i}^{-j} represents the count of the target word y_j being aligned to some source word x_i in (X, Y) without considering the specific pair (y_j, x_i) at the ith position in X and jth position in Y.

Thus training can be conducted with a random initial alignment, going through each y_i and resampling the alignment according to $P(a_j = i|X, Y, A^{-j}, \vec{\alpha})$. Each $P(x|y, D)$ can be estimated by the generated alignment samples. These posterior distributions can be directly used for Bayesian inference.

Similar to Bayesian unigram LM, it can be useful to alternatively calculate the expectation of the posterior distribution $P(\vec{\theta}_y)$ using Eq 12.28

$$E(\vec{\theta}_y) = \langle \frac{c_{y,x_1} + \alpha}{c_y + |V_x|\alpha}, \frac{c_{y,x_2} + \alpha}{c_y + |V_x|\alpha}, \ldots, \frac{c_{y,x_{|V_x|}} + \alpha}{c_y + |V_x|\alpha}\rangle. \tag{12.47}$$

Summary

In this chapter we have introduced:

- Bayesian network;
- maximum a posteriori and Bayesian estimation;
- Gibbs sampling;
- latent Dirichlet allocation;
- Bayesian unigram LMs, Bayesian IBM Model 1.

Chapter Notes

Pearl (1985) originally proposed Bayesian network, and Jensen et al. (1996) gave a thorough introduction to the model. Neapolitan et al. (2004) discussed how to estimate the parameters of Bayesian network. With regard to inference, Dempster (1968) gave a generalisation of Bayesian inference, and Gelfand et al. (1990) used Gibbs sampling to perform Bayesian inference. For text clustering, Blei et al. (2003) introduced latent Dirichlet allocation. Griffiths and Steyvers (2004) presented Gibbs sampling for LDA models. Heinrich (2005) gave an introduction of Bayesian parameter estimation for text analysis. Porteous et al. (2008) presented a faster collapsed Gibbs sampling algorithm. Riley and Gildea (2012) used Bayesian methods to improve the IBM word alignment models. Ghahramani (2001) introduced Bayesian Hidden Markov Models. Goldwater and Griffiths (2007) presented a Bayesian approach to unsupervised part-of-speech tagging. Bayesian models were also widely explored in unsupervised word segmentation (Goldwater et al., 2009), unsupervised grammar induction (Johnson et al., 2007; Borensztajn and Zuidema, 2007; Post and Gildea, 2009), language modelling (Neubig et al., 2012) and CCG parsing (Garrette et al., 2015).

Exercises

12.1 If $x_2 \perp\!\!\!\perp x_3|x_1$, show that $P(x_2|x_1, x_3) = P(x_2|x_1)$.

12.2 Prove Eq 12.26 using similar techniques as Eq 12.25.

12.3 Consider the Bayesian network as shown in Figure 12.4. Every node indicates a Boolean variable.

(a) Are x_1 and x_2 conditionally independent given the evidence of x_5?
(b) What is the Markov blanket of x_3?
(c) How many parameters are necessary for describing this model?
(d) Calculate the joint distribution $P(x_1, x_2, x_3, x_4, x_5)$ using the probabilities as shown in Table 12.2.

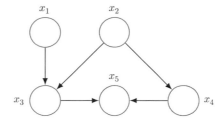

Figure 12.4 An example of Bayesian network.

Table 12.2 The local conditional probabilities tables for Figure 12.4.

	$P(\cdot)$		$P(x_4 = T\|x_2)$
$x_1 = T$	0.5	$x_2 = T$	0.8
$x_2 = T$	0.5	$x_2 = F$	0.2
	$P(x_3 = T\|x_1, x_2)$		$P(x_5 = T\|x_3, x_4)$
F, F	0.09	F, F	0.02
T, F	0.01	T, F	0.6
F, T	0.1	F, T	0.4
T, T	0.9	T, T	0.06

(e) Write a program to approximate the joint distribution $P(x_1, x_2, x_3, x_4, x_5)$ with Gibbs sampling, given the probability table (Table 12.2). In particular, what is the posterior distribution for sampling x_4?

(f) Compute the marginal distribution $P(x_1, x_2, x_3, x_5|x_4 = T)$ both with exact inference and Gibbs sampling.

12.4 For the coin toss example, suppose that we immediately estimate the model parameters after each observation, and obtain a sequence of estimation results.

(a) What is the sequence of estimated parameters using MLE?

(b) What is the sequence of estimated parameters using MAP?

(c) Draw the posterior distribution after each toss and observe the probability density changes of the posterior distribution.

12.5 For the M-step in EM, can we use MAP or Gibbs sampling to choose the model parameters? Why?

12.6 Consider the Naïve Bayes model. Try to add priors to the model parameters and show how to do model inferences.

12.7 Show that for a Bayesian unigram language model, the posterior unigram probabilities correspond to the expectations of $\vec{\theta}$.

12.8 Consider a Bayesian version of the first-order HMM model for POS-tagging in Chapter 7. In particular, both emission and transition probabilities follow categorical distributions, and we can add separate Dirichlet priors to them. Given a raw set of sentences, can you use Gibbs sampling to estimate the parameters for this model?

12.9 Consider a Bayesian version of the PCFG model for constituent parsing in Chapter 10. In particular, the grammar rule probabilities follow a categorical distribution, and we can add a Dirichlet prior to denote the prior probability of each non-terminal symbol. Given a set of raw sentences, can you use Gibbs sampling to estimate the parameters for this model?

Part III

Deep Learning

13 Neural Network

As shown in Chapter 4, discriminative models can be viewed as scoring functions, trained to assign higher scores to more correct output structures given an input. The primary basis for calculating model scores is *feature vectors*, which represent input–output pairs in the vector space according to their most salient characteristics. The models we have seen so far in the book are linear models, which score a candidate output by the inner product of its feature vector representation and a model weight vector, which effectively gives a weighted sum of all the features.

Intuitively, linear models have limited power. They can differentiate feature vectors only if they are separable by a hyperplane. In this chapter, we introduce neural networks as a a major type of non-linear models, using text classification as the main task for discussion. In particular, we begin by showing how a neural network text classifier can be built by extending the generalised perceptron model of Chapter 4 with multiple layers. A new set of notations are introduced for denoting neural networks and SGD training of multiple layers is discussed. Then we make a paradigm shift in model design, by representing words using dense vectors and introducing a range of neural network structures for obtaining vector representations of a word sequence. This paradigm shift frees us from manually designing sparse indicator features, thus avoiding the effort of feature engineering. However, it can make parameter estimation more difficult. Towards the end of the chapter, we discuss several optimisation techniques for better training neural networks.

13.1 From One Layer to Multiple Layers

Let us derive a non-linear model from our known linear models by extending a perceptron into a neural network. In particular, let us consider the task of binary text classification, where the input is a text and the output is a class layer $y \in \{+1, -1\}$. Recall the generalised linear model in Chapter 4, which assigns a score y according to an input vector $\vec{\phi}$ via $y = f(\vec{\theta} \cdot \vec{\phi})$, where $\vec{\theta}$ is the model parameter vector and f is the activation function. Below we denote the input feature vector as $\vec{x}$ and thus the model is:

$$y = f(\vec{\theta} \cdot \vec{x}) \tag{13.1}$$

where y indicates the score of $\vec{x}$ belonging to the class +1. Here let us take $f = sigmoid$ for example. In this case, y indicates the probability of $\vec{x}$ belonging to +1. Figure 13.1(a) shows this linear model, which is also referred to as a generalised *perceptron*. Despite that f can be a non-linear function, the model can express only a linear mapping between $\vec{x}$ and y (Exercise 13.1).

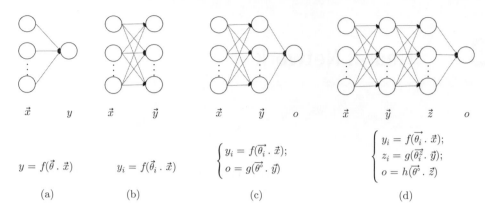

$$y = f(\vec{\theta} \cdot \vec{x})$$

$$y_i = f(\vec{\theta}_i \cdot \vec{x})$$

$$\begin{cases} y_i = f(\vec{\theta}_i \cdot \vec{x}); \\ o = g(\vec{\theta}^o \cdot \vec{y}) \end{cases}$$

$$\begin{cases} y_i = f(\vec{\theta}_i \cdot \vec{x}); \\ z_i = g(\vec{\theta}_i^z \cdot \vec{y}); \\ o = h(\vec{\theta}^o \cdot \vec{z}) \end{cases}$$

(a)   (b)   (c)   (d)

Figure 13.1 From one layer to three layers.

Now suppose that there is more than one text classification task, with outputs $y_1, y_2, \ldots, y_m$, respectively. For example, if $\vec{x}$ is a text document, then y_1 can be "whether $\vec{x}$ is related to sports", y_2 can be "whether $\vec{x}$ contains a positive sentiment" and y_3 can be "whether $\vec{x}$ is from Twitter". As shown in Figure 13.1(b), the outputs can be regarded as a vector $\vec{y} = [y_1, y_2, \ldots, y_m]^T \in \mathbb{R}^m$, where

$$y_i = f(\vec{\theta}_i \cdot \vec{x}).$$

In the figure, each y_i is calculated according to the same input $\vec{x}$ and a separate set of model parameters $\vec{\theta}_i$. Similar to the scalar output case in Figure 13.1(a), the model in Figure 13.1(b) can only express a linear mapping between the input vector $\vec{x}$ and the output vector $\vec{y}$. The vector $\vec{y}$ reflects the validities of $\vec{x}$ with regard to a set of m classes, and is therefore a form of abstract feature representation of $\vec{x}$. It can be fed as inputs to another generalised perceptron, for deriving a score o for a more abstract text classification task (i.e., "Things that John likes to read."):

$$o = g(\vec{\theta}^o \cdot \vec{y})$$

where g is an activation function and $\vec{\theta}^o$ is a model parameter vector.

The model structure is shown in Figure 13.1(c). It has two *perceptron layers*; one calculates $\vec{x} \rightarrow \vec{y}$ and the other $\vec{y} \rightarrow o$. It can also be viewed as consisting of three *node layers*, namely $\vec{x}$, $\vec{y}$ and o, respectively. This **multi-layer perceptron** (MLP) model can learn non-linear mappings between the input $\vec{x}$ and the output o

$$o = g\left(\vec{\theta}^o \cdot f(\vec{\theta}^y \cdot \vec{x})\right). \tag{13.2}$$

f and g can be the sigmoid function or other non-linear activation functions. Now suppose that the MLP in Eq 13.2 models input–output pairs $(\vec{x}, o)$ directly, without needing the values of $\vec{y}$. Therefore, $\vec{y}$ in this model is also called a **hidden layer**. Correspondingly, o is called the **output layer**.

Table 13.1 Activation functions for neural networks.

Name	Function
identity	$identity(x) = x$
rectify	$ReLU(x) = \max(x, 0)$
tanh	$tanh(x) = \frac{e^x - e^{-x}}{e^x + e^{-x}}$
sigmoid	$\sigma(x) = \frac{1}{1 + e^{-x}}$
softmax	$softmax(x_1, x_2, \ldots, x_n) = \left[\frac{e^{x_1}}{\sum_{k=1}^{n} e^{x_k}}, \frac{e^{x_2}}{\sum_{k=1}^{n} e^{x_k}}, \ldots, \frac{e^{x_n}}{\sum_{k=1}^{n} e^{x_k}} \right]$
ELU	$ELU(x) = \begin{cases} x, & \text{if } x > 0 \\ \alpha(e^x - 1) & \text{if } x \leq 0. \end{cases}$
softplus	$softplus(x) = \log(1 + e^x)$

In the training of an MLP, which we will see in Section 13.1.2, supervision signal (i.e., loss) is given on the output layer nodes only. Hidden layer nodes are trained to minimise loss on the output layer nodes, and do not receive direct supervision signal. Thus we can no longer make sure that they represent text features such as the "class" and "sentiment", as in the earlier case. Instead, they can be seen as automatically induced higher-level features over the input features x_i, where each y_i represents a combination of all the features in $\vec{x}$. These nodes are rather abstract features, with real values instead of integer values.

We can stack more layers of perceptrons. For example, Figure 13.1(d) consists of one more layer compared with Figure 13.1(c), where

$$z_i = g(\vec{\theta}_i^z \cdot \vec{y}) \qquad o = h(\vec{\theta}^o \cdot \vec{z}).$$

Intuitively, with more layers with non-linear activation functions, a multi-layer perceptron can potentially express increasingly complex mapping functions between the output layer and the input feature vector.

Activation functions. Table 13.1 shows six activation functions. In particular, when applied to vectors, the functions are used element-wise except for *softmax*. As shown in the table, the *identity* function is a linear function, and others are non-linear functions. The *rectify* function keeps only the positive elements of the input vectors, while setting the others to zero. It is commonly used in building very deep neural networks due to its fast speed. The *tanh* function maps the input to the $[-1, 1]$ range. The *sigmoid* function does a transformation $\mathbb{R} \to [0, 1]$, which normalises the output feature to a probabilistic space. As shown in Chapter 3, it is typically used for binary classification. The role of the *softmax* function is similar to that of the *sigmoid* function, normalising real-valued features into the probabilistic space for multi-label classification. The *ELU* function differs from the *rectify* function by giving negative elements non-zero values. The *softplus* function is a smooth approximation to *ReLU* and its value range is $[0, +\infty)$.

In summary, a multi-layer perceptron consists of an *input layer*, an *output layer* and a number of *hidden layers*. The input layer receives input data and represents them using vectors. The hidden layer induces useful non-linear features from the input vectors. The output layer makes predictions according to the features extracted from the hidden layers. In Figure 13.1(c), $\vec{x}$ is an input layer,

o is an output layer and $\vec{y}$ is a hidden layer. In this model, the **input size** is n, the **hidden size** is m and the **output size** is 1. In Figure 13.1(d), $\vec{x}$ is the input layer, o is the output layer and $\vec{y}$, $\vec{z}$ are two hidden layers. The network structure and capacity design (e.g., the number of layers and the number of features in each layer) can reflect fitting and generalisation powers (Chapter 4) on specific tasks or problems.

13.1.1 Multi-Layer Perceptrons for Text Classification

Neural network notation. The literature has a set of notational conventions for denoting neural network models, which differs from our notation above, derived from linear models. In this section, we make a change of notation by first discussing model parameters and then node layers. In particular, the mapping function of each neural layer can be written in a matrix-vector notation. For the remainder of this book, let us assume that vectors are by default *column vectors*. For example, in Figure 13.1(b), defining

$$\mathbf{W}^y = [\vec{\theta}_1; \vec{\theta}_2; \ldots; \vec{\theta}_m]^T,$$

where $[\vec{\theta}_1; \vec{\theta}_2; \ldots; \vec{\theta}_m]$ denotes juxtaposition of column vectors into a matrix, we have

$$\vec{y} = f(\mathbf{W}^y \vec{x}),$$

where each $\vec{\theta}_i$ is an n dimensional column vector, $\mathbf{W}^y$ is an m by n matrix. $\mathbf{W}^y \in \mathbb{R}^{m \times n}$ and f is applied element-wise to a vector.

For the remainder of this book, we use bold font letters to denote vectors and matrices. Thus

$$\mathbf{y} = f(\mathbf{W}^y \mathbf{x}) \tag{13.3}$$

is used for representing Figure 13.1(b), where $\mathbf{x} \in \mathbb{R}^n$ is a column vector, and $\mathbf{W}^y \in \mathbb{R}^{m \times n}$ is a parameter matrix.

Similarly, Figure 13.1(c) can be represented using

$$\mathbf{y} = f(\mathbf{W}^y \mathbf{x}) \qquad o = g(\mathbf{u}^T \mathbf{y}), \tag{13.4}$$

where $\mathbf{u} = \vec{\theta}^o$, $\mathbf{u} \in \mathbb{R}^m$ and $\mathbf{y} \in \mathbb{R}^m$ are column vectors.

Figure 13.1(d) can be represented using

$$\mathbf{y} = f(\mathbf{W}^y \mathbf{x}) \qquad \mathbf{z} = g(\mathbf{W}^z \mathbf{y}) \qquad o = h(\mathbf{v}^T \mathbf{z}) \tag{13.5}$$

where $\mathbf{v} = \vec{\theta}^o$.

Now with regard to the naming of node layers, $\mathbf{h}$ are typically used for denoting hidden layers. In this notation, Eq 13.5 can be rewritten as:

$$\mathbf{h}^1 = f(\mathbf{W}^y \mathbf{x}) \qquad \mathbf{h}^2 = g(\mathbf{W}^z \mathbf{h}^1) \qquad o = h(\mathbf{v}^T \mathbf{h}^2).$$

MLP for multi-class classification. So far, all the MLP models that we have constructed are for binary classification. For multi-class classification, we can replace the output layer, calculating a score for each text class. Formally, denote the set of output classes as $C = \{c_1, c_2, \ldots, c_m\}$. Given the feature vector $\mathbf{h}$ of the last hidden layer, we compute

$$o_1 = \mathbf{v}_1^T \mathbf{h} \quad o_2 = \mathbf{v}_2^T \mathbf{h} \quad \ldots \quad o_m = \mathbf{v}_m^T \mathbf{h}, \tag{13.6}$$

where $o_1, o_2, \ldots, o_m$ denote the scores for $c_1, c_2, \ldots, c_m$, respectively. $\mathbf{v}_1, \mathbf{v}_2, \ldots, \mathbf{v}_m$ denote the corresponding model weight vectors.

The above equations can be written as a single equation by merging $o_1, o_2, \ldots, o_m$ into a vector $\mathbf{o} = \langle o_1, o_2, \ldots, o_m \rangle$ and correspondingly $\mathbf{v}_1, \mathbf{v}_2, \ldots, \mathbf{v}_m$ into a matrix $\mathbf{W}^o = [\mathbf{v}_1; \mathbf{v}_2; \ldots; \mathbf{v}_m]^T$. As a result,

$$\mathbf{o} = \mathbf{W}^o \mathbf{h}. \tag{13.7}$$

For obtaining a probability distribution over the class labels, we can apply a *softmax* activation function, as we discussed in Chapter 4:

$$\mathbf{p} = softmax(\mathbf{o}), \tag{13.8}$$

where $\mathbf{p}$ denotes the probability distribution of the class labels, with the ith element $\mathbf{p}[i]$ denoting $P(c_i|\mathbf{x})$.

Correlation with linear classifier. When we compare Eqs 13.6–13.8 with Eq 3.11 in Chapter 3, we can find a salient difference between the way we handled multi-class classification for single-layer perceptrons and MLPs. In particular, for the former models, we integrate the class label (c) into all feature instances, effectively duplicating the feature representation $\vec{\phi}(x)$ of the input text into m copies $\vec{\phi}(x, c_i)$ ($i \in [1, \ldots, m]$), each copy representing the text in a specific class. In contrast, for MLP models, we duplicated the *model parameter* of the output layer m times (i.e. $\mathbf{v}_1, \ldots, \mathbf{v}_m$), keeping the input representation vector $\mathbf{h}$ unchanged.

At a closer look, the two strategies can be the same. In particular, for a single-layer perceptron, a scalar weight in $\vec{\theta}$ is assigned to each feature instance in $\vec{\theta} \cdot \vec{\phi}(x)$, which serves as the model parameter for the instance. Thus duplicating the input feature vector m times also leads to the duplication of the model parameter vector $\vec{\theta}$ m times. In addition, for each input–output pair (x, c), only the feature instances with the class label c have non-zero values in $\vec{\phi}(x, c)$, among all $c' \in C$. As a result, we can view the single-layer perceptron also as duplicating only model parameters. Formally, the scoring of

$$score(c_1) = \vec{\theta} \cdot \vec{\phi}(x, c_1)$$
$$score(c_2) = \vec{\theta} \cdot \vec{\phi}(x, c_2)$$
$$\ldots$$
$$score(c_m) = \vec{\theta} \cdot \vec{\phi}(x, c_m)$$

can be rewritten as

$$score(c_1) = \vec{\theta}_1 \cdot \vec{\phi}(x)$$
$$score(c_2) = \vec{\theta}_2 \cdot \vec{\phi}(x)$$
$$\ldots$$
$$score(c_m) = \vec{\theta}_m \cdot \vec{\phi}(x),$$

where $\vec{\phi}(x)$ denotes the input feature representation without combining the class label, and $\vec{\theta}_i$ denotes the corresponding weight vector for $\vec{\phi}(x, c_i), i \in [1, \ldots, m]$. Thus for both binary classification and multi-class classification, MLP are the same as linear perceptrons in using a linear output layer. MLP differs from linear perceptron only in the use of hidden layers.

Characteristics of neural hidden layers and their representation power. The analogy above sheds light on a comparison between the input features for single-layer perceptrons and MLPs, and between discrete linear models and neural network models in general. In particular, given that the output layers are the same in MLP and single-layer perceptron, let us take the last hidden layer in an MLP as the final input representation, which is used for output prediction. Compared with a feature vector $\vec{\phi}(x)$ in a linear model, it has the following salient differences. First, it is low dimensional, typically in the scales of 10s to 100s, as compared with millions to billions in its discrete counterpart. Second, it is dense, with nodes in real numbers, as compared to its discrete counterparts, which contains integers typically (although for cases such as *TF-IDF* and *PMI* they can also be real-valued also). Third, and most importantly, it is dynamically calculated rather than being manually specified. Thus it potentially frees us from feature engineering when building neural network models, as we will see later.

As discussed earlier, a neural network model can be stronger than a linear model for text classification. This can be seen in Eq 13.2, where a neural network model learns a non-linear mapping between the input and the output. With more hidden layers, a neural network can be more powerful in fitting input–output mapping functions. It has been shown that with more than three layers, a neural network can learn arbitrary mapping functions between inputs and outputs.

The above power can be understood from a vector space perspective also. While a linear model separates data in a vector space using a hyperplane, non-linear models can separate data using a more flexible hypersurface. As shown in Figure 13.2(a), a non-linear model can separate non-linearly-separable data. Since the output layer of an MLP text classifier is identical to that of a discrete linear model, the key to the separation power is in the hidden representation. As shown in Figure 13.2(b), a neural network can effectively transfer a non-linearly-separable dataset in the

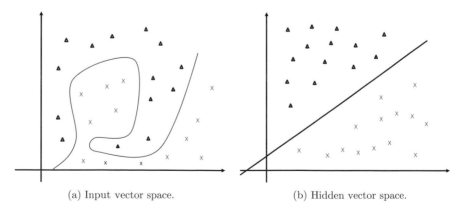

(a) Input vector space.   (b) Hidden vector space.

Figure 13.2 The effect of hidden layer representation (e.g., ▲ and × denote denotes two classes of inputs).

input vector space into a linearly separable one in the hidden vector space, so that a linear output layer can be effective. In this process, more abstract features can be induced from input features.

While hidden layer nodes can potentially capture very subtle combinations of input features, their meaning can be difficult to interpret directly. In this respect, hidden layer nodes in an MLP and in general in deep neural networks are very different from the discrete-valued indicator features that we have been working with in the book. We will make discuss their interpretation further in the next chapter.

Deep multi-layer perceptrons. Deep MLP can consist of a large number of hidden layers. Such networks can be conveniently denoted layerwise. In particular, the mapping function from the lth node layer to the $(l+1)$th node layer can be described as

$$\mathbf{h}^l = f(\mathbf{W}^l\mathbf{h}^{l-1} + \mathbf{b}^l), \tag{13.9}$$

where $\mathbf{h}^0 = \mathbf{x}$ represents the input vector and $\mathbf{h}^K$ for a K layer network denotes the output, which can be a scalar for binary classification. Later in this chapter and subsequent chapters we will see neural network structures that are different from MLP. However, we will stick to the notation convention of using $\mathbf{h}$ for denoting hidden layers and using $\mathbf{W}$ / $\mathbf{b}$ to denote weight matrices and bias vectors, respectively.

13.1.2 Training a Multi-Layer Perceptron

Given a training set $D = \{(\mathbf{x}_i, c_i)\}|_{i=1}^n$ and a neural network, where $\mathbf{x}_i$ is an input feature vector and c_i is the gold-standard output label, we want to find the values of all the neural networks parameters by minimising a loss function over D. We have seen several ways to define training objective functions in Chapter 4, such as the log-likelihood (i.e., cross-entropy) and max-margin losses, as well as several regularisation functions such as L_2 regularisation. Take log-likelihood loss with L_2 regularisation for example. The overall loss function is

$$L = -\log P(D) + \lambda||\Theta||^2 = -\sum_{i=1}^{N} \log P(c_l|\mathbf{x}_l) + \lambda||\Theta||^2,$$

where $P(c_i|\mathbf{x}_i)$ is given by the neural network model and Θ denotes the set of all model parameters. λ is a hyper-parameter. For example, in the model of Figure 13.1(c), $P(c_i|\mathbf{x}_i)$ is calculated according to Eq 13.4, and the model parameters consist of $\mathbf{W}^y$ and $\mathbf{u}$; in the model of Figure 13.1(d), $P(c_i|\mathbf{x}_i)$ is calculated according to Eq 13.5, and the model parameters consist of $\mathbf{W}^y$, $\mathbf{W}^z$, $\mathbf{v}$. The regularisation term $||\Theta||^2$ in the equation above refers to the sum of the square of each element in the parameter matrices and vectors.

It turns out that the underlying principles of training the generalised perceptron model discussed in Chapter 4 can still be applied for the training of multi-layer perceptrons. In particular, Algorithm 4.9 defines a general online learning framework under SGD. Given a training set D, the algorithm goes through all the training instances for multiple iterations. For each training instance, it calculates the gradient of a local loss with respect to each model parameter, before updating the model parameters with their respective gradients, possibly with a learning rate factor. We can also use this algorithm to train an MLP.

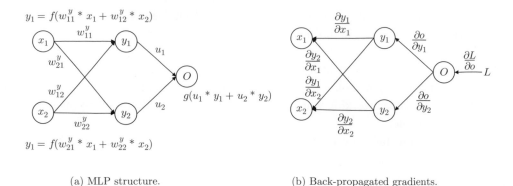

(a) MLP structure.   (b) Back-propagated gradients.

Figure 13.3 Computation graph for a neural network.

Without loss of generality, let us use the model in Figure 13.1(c) for example. Further, let us assume that all the layers consist of only two nodes, namely $\mathbf{x} = \langle x_1, x_2 \rangle$ and $\mathbf{y} = \langle y_1, y_2 \rangle$. The resulting neural network structure is shown in Figure 13.3(a). Further assume that f is the *square* function and g is the *sigmoid* function. We have:

$$y_1 = (w^y_{11}x_1 + w^y_{12}x_2)^2$$
$$y_2 = (w^y_{21}x_1 + w^y_{22}x_2)^2$$
$$o = \sigma(u_1y_1 + u_2y_2).$$

In this model, the set of parameters is $\Theta = \{w^y_{11}, w^y_{12}, w^y_{21}, w^y_{22}, u_1, u_2\}$. It is worth noting that the values of y_1 and y_2 contain the product x_1x_2, which can be seen as combined input features. It is easy to see that when the input contains more than two features, a *square* activation function induces combined features over all possible pairs of input nodes. Further, a *cube* activation function can induce combination of three input features. Due to the possibility of using Taylor expansion for approximating arbitrary non-linear functions, we conclude that all non-linear activation functions have the power of achieving automatic feature combination.

Now given a training instance $(\mathbf{x}_i, c_i)$, the loss is

$$L(\mathbf{x}_i, c_i, \Theta) = -\log P(c_i|\mathbf{x}_i) + \lambda||\Theta||^2$$
$$= -\log \sigma(u_1y_1 + u_2y_2) + \lambda||\Theta||^2$$
$$= -\log \sigma\left(u_1(w^y_{11}x_1 + w^y_{12}x_2)^2 + u_2(w^y_{21}x_1 + w^y_{22}x_2)^2\right)$$
$$+ \lambda\left((w^y_{11})^2 + (w^y_{12})^2 + (w^y_{21})^2 + (w^y_{22})^2 + (u_1)^2 + (u_2)^2\right),$$

The local gradients are

$$\frac{\partial L(\mathbf{x}_i, c_i, \Theta)}{\partial u_1} = \frac{\partial - \log o}{\partial u_1} + \frac{\partial||\Theta||^2}{\partial u_1}$$
$$= -\frac{\partial\left((u_1y_1 + u_2y_2) - \log\left(1 + \exp(u_1y_1 + u_2y_2)\right)\right)}{\partial u_1} + 2\lambda u_1$$

$$= -\left(y_1 - \frac{\exp(u_1 y_1 + u_2 y_2)}{1 + \exp(u_1 y_1 + u_2 y_2)} y_1\right) + 2\lambda u_1$$

$$= -(1 - o)y_1 + 2\lambda u_1$$

$$\frac{\partial L(\mathbf{x}_i, c_i, \Theta)}{\partial u_2} = -(1 - o)y_2 + 2\lambda u_2$$

$$\frac{\partial L(\mathbf{x}_i, c_i, \Theta)}{\partial w_{11}^y} = -(1 - o) \cdot \left(u_1 \cdot 2(w_{11}^y x_1 + w_{12}^y x_2) \cdot x_1\right) + 2\lambda w_{11}^y$$

$$= -2(1 - o)\left(u_1(w_{11}^y x_1 + w_{12}^y x_2) \cdot x_1\right) + 2\lambda w_{11}^y$$

$$\frac{\partial L(\mathbf{x}_i, c_i, \Theta)}{\partial w_{12}^y} = -2(1 - o)\left(u_1(w_{11}^y x_1 + w_{12}^y x_2) \cdot x_2\right) + 2\lambda w_{12}^y$$

$$\frac{\partial L(\mathbf{x}_i, c_i, \Theta)}{\partial w_{21}^y} = -2(1 - o)\left(u_2(w_{21}^y x_1 + w_{22}^y x_2) \cdot x_1\right) + 2\lambda w_{21}^y$$

$$\frac{\partial L(\mathbf{x}_i, c_i, \Theta)}{\partial w_{22}^y} = -2(1 - o)\left(u_2(w_{21}^y x_1 + w_{22}^y x_2) \cdot x_2\right) + 2\lambda w_{22}^y. \tag{13.10}$$

Matrix-vector notation of gradients. Equation 13.10 can be written concisely using matrix-vector notation. In particular,

$$\frac{\partial L(\mathbf{x}_i, c_i, \Theta)}{\partial \mathbf{u}} = \left\langle \frac{\partial L(\mathbf{x}_i, c_i, \Theta)}{\partial u_1}, \frac{\partial L(\mathbf{x}_i, c_i, \Theta)}{\partial u_2} \right\rangle$$

$$= \langle -(1 - o)y_1 + 2\lambda u_1, -(1 - o)y_2 + 2\lambda u_2 \rangle$$

$$= -(1 - o)\mathbf{y} + 2\lambda \mathbf{u}.$$

$\frac{\partial L(\mathbf{x}_i, c_i, \Theta)}{\partial \mathbf{W}^y}$ can be denoted similarly

$$\frac{\partial L(\mathbf{x}_i, c_i, \Theta)}{\partial \mathbf{W}^y} = \begin{pmatrix} \frac{\partial L(\mathbf{x}_i, c_i, \Theta)}{\partial w_{11}^y}, \frac{\partial L(\mathbf{x}_i, c_i, \Theta)}{\partial w_{12}^y} \\ \frac{\partial L(\mathbf{x}_i, c_i, \Theta)}{\partial w_{21}^y}, \frac{\partial L(\mathbf{x}_i, c_i, \Theta)}{\partial w_{22}^y} \end{pmatrix}$$

$$= -2(1 - o)\begin{pmatrix} u_1(w_{11}^y x_1 + w_{12}^y x_2)x_1, u_1(w_{11}^y x_1 + w_{12}^y x_2)x_2 \\ u_2(w_{21}^y x_1 + w_{22}^y x_2)x_1, u_2(w_{21}^y x_1 + w_{22}^y x_2)x_2 \end{pmatrix}$$

$$+ 2\lambda \begin{pmatrix} w_{11}^y, w_{12}^y \\ w_{21}^y, w_{22}^y \end{pmatrix} \qquad \text{(according to Eq 13.10)} \tag{13.11}$$

$$= -2(1 - o) \cdot \left\langle \begin{matrix} u_1(w_{11}^y x_1 + w_{12}^y x_2) \\ u_2(w_{21}^y x_1 + w_{22}^y x_2) \end{matrix} \right\rangle \langle x_1, x_2 \rangle$$

$$+ 2\lambda \mathbf{W}^y$$

$$= -2(1 - o) \cdot \left(\mathbf{u} \otimes (\mathbf{W}^y \mathbf{x})\right)\mathbf{x}^T + 2\lambda \mathbf{W}^y.$$

The matrix-vector notation above is general, and does not depend on the sizes of $\mathbf{u}$, $\mathbf{W}^y$, $\mathbf{x}$ and $\mathbf{y}$. Thus we stick to this notation further on.

Back-propagation. Given the gradients, we can calculate the incremental update of each parameter in Θ for SGD training by multiplying the local loss L and the gradients. One limitation of such direct calculation, however, is that it is network-specific, difficult to generalise across different neural network structures, and can be tedious when the number of layers is large. Thanks to the chain rule of derivatives, we can find a more principled solution for calculating derivatives across layers, namely **back-propagation**.

The central idea of back-propagation is to perform modularised and incremental gradient calculation. In particular, taking the network of Figure 13.1(c) for instance, suppose that we want to calculate $\frac{\partial L(\mathbf{x}_i, c_i, \Theta)}{\partial w_{11}^y}$. It can be broken into $\frac{\partial L(\mathbf{x}_i, c_i, \Theta)}{\partial o} \cdot \frac{\partial o}{\partial y_1} \cdot \frac{\partial y_1}{\partial w_{11}^y}$. As a result, disregarding the regularisation term, gradients can be first calculated for the output layer, where $\frac{\partial L(\mathbf{x}_i, c_i, \Theta)}{\partial o} = -\frac{1}{o}$, and then for the hidden layer nodes $\frac{\partial L(\mathbf{x}_i, c_i, \Theta)}{\partial o} \cdot \frac{\partial o}{\partial y_1} = -(1-o) \cdot u_1$, before finally for the hidden layer model parameter $-(1-o) \cdot u_1 \cdot 2(w_{11}^y x_1 + w_{12}^y x_2)x_1$. In this way, we can factorise back-propagated gradients into components.

We want to denote the above process in a matrix-vector notation. Without losing generality, let us denote the input and output for each layer as vectors $\mathbf{v}_i$ and $\mathbf{v}_o$, respectively, and the parameters as $\mathbf{W}$. For our network, in the $\mathbf{x} \to \mathbf{y}$ layer, $\mathbf{v}_i$ is $\mathbf{x}$ and $\mathbf{v}_o$ is $\mathbf{y}$ and $\mathbf{W}$ is $\mathbf{W}^y$, and in the $\mathbf{y} \to o$ layer, $\mathbf{v}_i$ is $\mathbf{y}$, $\mathbf{v}_o$ is o and $\mathbf{W}$ is $\mathbf{u}$. Now for each layer, if we know the value of $\frac{\partial L}{\partial \mathbf{v}_o}$ as a vector, we can easily compute $\frac{\partial L}{\partial \mathbf{W}}$ and $\frac{\partial L}{\partial \mathbf{v}_i}$, where $\frac{\partial L}{\partial \mathbf{v}_i}$ serves as $\frac{\partial L}{\partial \mathbf{v}_o}$ to the layer below. As a result, back-propagation works by calculating $\frac{\partial L}{\partial \mathbf{v}_o}$ incrementally for each layer.

Still take Figure 13.3 for example. We have for the MLP

$$\mathbf{y} = (\mathbf{W}^y \mathbf{x})^2, \qquad o = \sigma(\mathbf{u}^T \cdot \mathbf{y}).$$

For SGD, the local loss is

$$L(\mathbf{x}, c, \Theta) = L^o + ||\Theta||^2,$$

where $L^o = -\log o$. We consider the back-propagation of L^o only, since $\frac{\partial ||\Theta||^2}{\partial \Theta}$ is straightforward to compute. We specify the local gradients in matrix-vector notation, based on element-wise derivatives. In particular, for the layer $\mathbf{y} \to o$, the input gradient is $\frac{\partial L^o}{\partial o}$, given which we have

$$\begin{aligned} \frac{\partial L^o}{\partial \mathbf{u}} &= \frac{\partial L^o}{\partial o} \cdot o(1-o)\mathbf{y} \\ \frac{\partial L^o}{\partial \mathbf{y}} &= \frac{\partial L^o}{\partial o} \cdot o(1-o)\mathbf{u}. \end{aligned} \tag{13.12}$$

For the layer $\mathbf{x} \to \mathbf{y}$, the input gradient is $\frac{\partial L^o}{\partial \mathbf{y}}$, given which we have

$$\frac{\partial L^o}{\partial \mathbf{W}^y} = \frac{\partial L^o}{\partial \mathbf{y}} \otimes (2\mathbf{W}^y \mathbf{x}) \cdot \mathbf{x}^T. \tag{13.13}$$

Equation 13.13 can be derived in a similar way as the derivation of Eq 13.11, which is based on element-wise calculation of Eq 13.10. Exercise 13.4 discusses the detailed derivation. Given Eq 13.12 and Eq 13.13, we can derive the gradients in Eq 13.10 incrementally from $\partial L_o / \partial o =$

Algorithm 13.1. Back-propagation for calculating gradients for arbitrary network.

Inputs: a network of M layers, each with a FORWARDCOMPUTE function and a BACKPROPAGATE function; the set of model parameters for the ith layer Θ_i; a gold-standard output $\mathbf{y}$ at the output layer; an input $\mathbf{x}$;

Initialisation: $\mathbf{h}_0 \leftarrow \mathbf{x}$;

for $l \in [1, \ldots, M]$ **do**   ▷ forward computation
  | $\mathbf{h}_l \leftarrow$ FORWARDCOMPUTE$(\mathbf{h}_{l-1}, \Theta_l)$

$L \leftarrow$ COMPUTELOSS$(\mathbf{h}_M, \mathbf{y})$;

$\mathbf{g}_M \leftarrow L$;

for $l \in [M, \ldots, 1]$ **do**   ▷ back-propagation
  | $\mathbf{g}_{l-1}, \mathbf{g}_l^{\Theta} \leftarrow$ BACKPROPAGATE$(\mathbf{g}_l, \Theta_l)$

Output: $\{\mathbf{g}_l^{\Theta}\}|_{l=1}^M$;

$-1/o$. Exercise 13.5 verifies the correctness of the incremental back-propagation calculation. In addition, Exercise 13.6 discusses a method of empirical verification of gradient calculation in general.

Back-propagation allows modularisation of neural network components in deep networks. In particular, for each neural network layer or component, as long as we know the forward computation (e.g., $\mathbf{y} = \mathbf{W}^y\mathbf{x}$), and the back-propagation rule (i.e., (1) the partial derivative of the output (e.g., $\mathbf{y}$ with respect to the model parameters (e.g., $\mathbf{W}^y$) and (2) the partial derivative of the output with respect to the input layer (e.g., $\mathbf{x}$)), the neural network layer can be assembled with other neural network layers and components without worrying about synchronised training. Algorithm 13.1 shows pseudocode of the gradient calculation process for arbitrary neural networks, where FORWARDCOMPUTE and BACKPROPAGATE are the forward computation and back-propagation functions that need to be specified by each network layer. $\mathbf{g}_l$ denotes the local gradients on the output of a current layer, which is used to derive $\mathbf{g}_{l-1}$ and $\mathbf{g}_l^{\Theta}$, the gradient over the model parameters in the current layer. Later in this chapter and in this book, we will learn a range of different neural network components other than an MLP layer, for each of which we specify the forward computation and the back-propagation rules (1), (2) above. In the end we need $\mathbf{g}_l^{\Theta}$ for all $l \in [1, \ldots, M]$.

Parameter initialisation. Now that we are equipped with a powerful tool to calculate local gradients with respect to each model parameter, we are ready to apply Algorithm 4.9 for model training. However, one more thing should be considered, namely the initialisation. For the generalised linear model all parameters are initialised as 0s. However, it does not work for our neural network. Intuitively, the two hidden layer nodes y_1 and y_2 in Figure 13.3(a) should capture different features about $\mathbf{x}$, so as to work together as a useful feature vector. However, if the two rows in $\mathbf{W}^y$ are identical during initialisation and the two elements of $\mathbf{u}$ are similarly identical, then the values y_1 and y_2 as well as their local derivatives for all training instances will remain identical throughout the training process. What is worse, at a closer examination, if the initial values of all the parameters are 0s, Eq 13.10 tells us that the derivatives will be all 0s throughout the training process!

To avoid the undesired situation, we need to initialise the parameters with different values. Random initialisation is a practical solution. Given a model parameter $\mathbf{W}$ at the lth layer and $\mathbf{W} \in \mathbb{R}^{d_l \times d_{l-1}}$, where d_l denotes the hidden vector size of the lth layer, common methods for initialisation of each element in $\mathbf{W}$ include

1 Xavier Uniform Initialisation. $\mathbf{W} \sim \mathcal{U}(-\sqrt{\frac{6}{d_l+d_{l-1}}}, \sqrt{\frac{6}{d_l+d_{l-1}}})$.
2 Xavier Normal Initialisation. $\mathbf{W} \sim \mathcal{N}(0, \frac{2}{d_l+d_{l-1}})$.
3 Kaiming Uniform Initialisation. $\mathbf{W} \sim \mathcal{U}(-\sqrt{\frac{6}{d_{l-1}}}, \sqrt{\frac{6}{d_{l-1}}})$.
4 Kaiming Normal Initialisation. $\mathbf{W} \sim \mathcal{N}(0, \frac{2}{d_{l-1}})$.

Here $\mathcal{U}[-a, a]$ is the uniform distribution in $[-a, a]$, $\mathcal{N}(0, \sigma^2)$ is the zero-mean Gaussian distribution with variance σ^2. Xavier uniform initialisation is also known as *Glorot initialisation*. For hidden layers with *ReLU* activation functions, Kaiming uniform initialisation and Kaiming normal initialisation are recommended choices. For hidden layers with *tanh* activation functions, both Xavier uniform initialisation and Xavier normal initialisation are empirically competitive options.

Random initialisation has several implications for the resulting model. First, we cannot make sure that each dimension in a hidden layer learns the same feature across two separate training processes. This adds to the difficulty of feature interpretation. Second, the test results can be different every time we train a model. This means that given a test set, the performance of a model can vary from time to time! The variation can be rather significant. One solution to this problem is to repeat the same experiment several times (e.g. 5 or 10), reporting the mean performance and the standard deviation. We will see later that neural network model training is sensitive not only to random initialisation, but also to other hyper-parameter settings such as the size of the hidden vectors, the regularisation constant λ, the number of hidden layers and the learning rate. There will be more discussion of training tricks in Section 13.3 and the next chapter.

13.2 Building a Text Classifier without Manual Features

We have now seen a neural network model for text classification, which uses a multi-layer perceptron to replace a linear perceptron for calculating scores. The model is more powerful, but the input features are manually designed over a sentence. We have seen some examples in Chapter 3, such as word count vectors, word-bigram features (Eq 3.10) and *TF-IDF* vectors. They are sparse and high-dimensional, which is inconsistent with the dense and low-dimensional hidden and output layers. Now that a powerful neural network allows us to automatically combine atomic features and even induce more abstract features, we want to minimise the effort of manual feature engineering.

One principled solution is to represent each word in the sentence also using a dense low-dimensional vector, and then design a neural network to combine the dense word vectors into

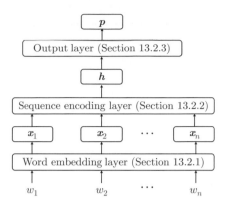

Figure 13.4 A neural text classifier.

a dense sentence vector representation. In this way, both the input and the hidden layers are represented consistently. Given this observation, Figure 13.4 shows the structure of a neural network text classifier, which is conceptually very different from the linear text classifiers that we have discussed. In particular, given a sequence of words $W_{1:n} = w_1 w_2 \ldots w_n$, we first transform them into a sequence of low-dimensional real-valued vectors $\mathbf{x}_1, \mathbf{x}_2, \ldots, \mathbf{x}_n$, before learning a single sentence-level feature vector by transforming $\mathbf{x}_1, \mathbf{x_2}, \ldots, \mathbf{x}_n$ into a single hidden layer $\mathbf{h}$. Finally, we apply an output layer to predict a text class distribution $\mathbf{p}$ according to the hidden feature nodes $\mathbf{h}$. This section introduces such a neural network by first discussing dense word vectors (Section 13.2.1), and then introducing various neural network structures to induce sentence-level representations (Sections 13.2.2), before finally discussing the output layer (Section 13.2.3), and training (Section 13.2.4).

13.2.1 Word Embeddings

We have seen several methods for representing a word in Chapter 5, including one-hot feature vectors and vectors based on PMI between words. For neural networks such as MLP, words can be represented using 50- to 200-dimensional real-valued vectors instead, which are generally referred to as **word embeddings**. Each element in a word embedding encodes a certain attribute or feature of the word. If words are similar in meaning, their corresponding vectors are close in the vector space. It has been shown that dense embeddings offer a better semantic similarity measure compared to sparse vectors.

Word embedding vectors can be stored in a lookup table and obtained using a corresponding one-hot vector in the input layer, which is also called the **embedding layer**. In addition, given a one-hot column vector $\mathbf{x} \in \mathbb{R}^{|V|}$ for the word x, the embedding vector of x can be defined by

$$emb(x) = \mathbf{W}\mathbf{x}. \tag{13.14}$$

Here $\mathbf{W} \in \mathbb{R}^{d \times |V|}$ is the **word embedding matrix**, where d is the dimension size of the embedding vector. Each column in $\mathbf{W}$ is the embedding vector of a specified word in the vocabulary V. $\mathbf{Wx}$ yields the column that corresponds to $\mathbf{x}$. $\mathbf{W}$ is also called the **embedding lookup table**.

Word embedding vectors are a part of the model parameters in a neural network. They can be randomly initialised, just as the other model parameters, and then jointly trained with the other parameters during model training. Alternatively, their initial values can also be separately trained over large raw texts before being used in an NLP task, so as to obtain useful information even before model training. For example, if we can load a model with word vectors such that $emb(\text{``}cat\text{''})$ is similar to $emb(\text{``}dog\text{''})$, the model can have prior knowledge on words, which facilitates further training for a specific task such as NER. This is referred to as **pre-training**. Chapter 17 discusses pre-training techniques in detail.

13.2.2 Sequence Encoding Layers

A sequence encoder is a subnetwork that transforms a sequence of dense vectors into a single dense vector that represents features over the whole sequence. It can consist of one or more neural network layers. There are a number of alternative neural network structures to this end, such as the pooling and convolutional network structures that we discuss in this section, and the recurrent neural network and attentional neural network structures, which will be discussed later in the book. It is worth noting that some sequence encoders compute a sequence of sequence-level feature vectors instead of one vector. However, for the purpose of building a text classifier, we restrict ourself to computing a single hidden vector in this section.

Pooling. Similar to the case of statistical models, the simplest neural network for representing a sentence is a "bag-of-words" model, which is also known as a **pooling** function over a set of vectors. Figure 13.5 shows a pooling based sequence representation, where the pooling operations includes **sum pooling**, **averaging pooling**, **max pooling** and **min pooling**. Formally, given a sentence $W_{1:n} = w_1 w_2 \dots w_n$, with the corresponding word vectors being $\mathbf{X}_{1:n} = \mathbf{x}_1, \mathbf{x}_2, \dots, \mathbf{x}_n$ and each $\mathbf{x}_i \in \mathbb{R}^d$, the pooling operations aggregate $\mathbf{X}_{1:n}$ into a single vector $\mathbf{h} = pool(\mathbf{X}_{1:n})$. Specific *pooling* instances include:

$$sum(\mathbf{X}_{1:n}) = \sum_{i=1}^{n} \mathbf{x}_i \text{ (sum pooling)}$$

$$avg(\mathbf{X}_{1:n}) = \frac{1}{n} \sum_{i=1}^{n} \mathbf{x}_i \text{ (average pooling)}$$

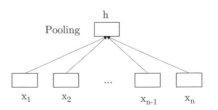

Figure 13.5 Deep averaging network (DAN).

$$max(\mathbf{X}_{1:n}) = \langle \max_{i=1}^{n} \mathbf{x}_i[1], \max_{i=1}^{n} \mathbf{x}_i[2], \ldots, \max_{i=1}^{n} \mathbf{x}_i[d] \rangle^T \text{ (max pooling)}$$

$$min(\mathbf{X}_{1:n}) = \langle \min_{i=1}^{n} \mathbf{x}_i[1], \min_{i=1}^{n} \mathbf{x}_i[2], \ldots, \min_{i=1}^{n} \mathbf{x}_i[d] \rangle^T \text{ (min pooling)}, \quad (13.15)$$

where $\mathbf{x}_i[j]$ denotes the jth element of $\mathbf{x}_i$, $j \in [1, \ldots, d]$.

Pooling is simple and fast, introducing no additional model parameters. Using the matrix notation, the pooling methods are column-wise vector operations. Intuitively, sum pooling aggregates the input feature vectors element-wise. Suppose that the first element among all $\mathbf{x}_i$ represents the positive sentiment,[1] the first element in $sum(\mathbf{X}_{1:n})$ shows the total positivity in the feature vectors. Average pooling can be seen as a normalised version of sum pooling. In contrast to sum pooling and average pooling, max pooling extracts only the most salient feature element, such as the value of the most positive sentiment, for representing the input. min pooling works in the opposite direction. While sum pooling is the most commonly used among these functions, comparison between different pooling functions can be empirical. A concatenation of different pooling result vectors can give a richer hidden feature vector.

For back-propagation, we only need to consider output–input gradients since there are no parameters. In particular, given a local loss L, suppose that we have obtained $\frac{\partial L}{\partial \mathbf{h}}$ as a constant vector in $\mathbb{R}^d$ during back-propagation. Now we need to compute $\frac{\partial L}{\partial \mathbf{X}_{1:n}}$. For sum pooling, $\frac{\partial L}{\partial \mathbf{x}_i} = \frac{\partial L}{\partial \mathbf{h}}$ for all $\mathbf{x}_i$ ($i \in [1, \ldots, n]$). For average pooling, $\frac{\partial L}{\partial \mathbf{x}_i} = \frac{1}{n} \frac{\partial L}{\partial \mathbf{h}}$. For maximum pooling, we need to consider each element in $\mathbf{x}_i$ separately for obtaining subgradients. In particular,

$$\frac{\partial L}{\partial \mathbf{x}_i[j]} = \begin{cases} \frac{\partial L}{\partial \mathbf{h}}[j] & \text{if } i = \arg\max_{i' \in [1,\ldots,n]} \mathbf{x}_{i'}[j], (i \in [1, \ldots, n], j \in [1, \ldots, d]) \\ 0 & \text{otherwise.} \end{cases}$$

The partal derivatives of minimum pooling can be defined similarly.[2]

For Algorithm 13.1, the function FORWARDCOMPUTE($\mathbf{X}_{1:n}$) returns values specified by Eq 13.15, and the BACKPROPAGATE($\mathbf{g}$) function returns $\left(\overset{n}{\underset{i=1}{;}} \left(\frac{\partial \mathbf{h}}{\partial \mathbf{x}_i} \cdot \mathbf{g} \right), \text{NULL} \right)$, where ; denotes vector juxtaposition and $\mathbf{g}$ denotes a constant vector in $\mathbb{R}^d$, which represents the back-propagated gradient $\frac{\partial L}{\partial \mathbf{h}}$ given a local loss L.

Compared with MLP, which requires a fixed-sized input vector, pooling can work with a variable-sized set of input vectors, aggregating them into a fixed-sized output. Sum pooling has the identical aggregation function compared with discrete bag-of-words models such as Naïve Bayes discussed in Chapter 2. Pooling networks for sequence representation are also called **deep averaging networks** (DAN).

---

[1] As mentioned earlier we cannot verify the meaning of automatically induced neural features, but our example here makes the intuition simpler to convey.

[2] In the rare case where $\mathbf{x}_{i_1}[j] = \mathbf{x}_{i_2}[j] = \max_{i' \in [1,\ldots,n]} \mathbf{x}_{i'}[j]$, a random choice should be made between i_1 and i_2 as the maximum element.

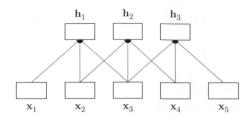

Figure 13.6 Convolutional neural network.

Convolutional neural network (CNN). A drawback of pooling-based representation is that it captures only uni-gram features and does not consider word order information. A convolutional neural network (CNN) uses *convolutional filters* to extract n-gram features, where each CNN filter calculates a vector representation of a local K-word window. Figure 13.6 shows an example CNN with window-size $K = 3$ filters. The input is $\mathbf{X}_{1:5} = \mathbf{x}_1, \mathbf{x}_2, \mathbf{x}_3, \mathbf{x}_4, \mathbf{x}_5$, and the output is $\mathbf{H}_{1:3} = \mathbf{h}_1, \mathbf{h}_2, \mathbf{h}_3$. Three CNN filters are present, calculating $\mathbf{h}_1$ according to $\mathbf{x}_1, \mathbf{x}_2, \mathbf{x}_3$, $\mathbf{h}_2$ according to $\mathbf{x}_2, \mathbf{x}_3, \mathbf{x}_4$ and $\mathbf{h}_3$ according to $\mathbf{x}_3, \mathbf{x}_4, \mathbf{x}_5$. In a CNN, each input vector $\mathbf{x}_i$ is also called an *input channel* and each output vector $\mathbf{h}_j$ an *output channel*.

Formally, given a filter with window size K, supposing that the input channel and the output channel dimensions are d_I and d_O, respectively, the convolution operation for a sequence of input vectors $\mathbf{X}_{1:n} = \mathbf{x}_1, \mathbf{x}_2, \ldots, \mathbf{x}_n$ can be described as

$$\mathbf{H}_{1:n-K+1} = \text{CNN}(\mathbf{X}_{1:n}, K, d_O) = \mathbf{W} \circledast \mathbf{X}_{1:n} + \mathbf{b}, \tag{13.16}$$

where $\circledast$ denotes the overall convolution operation. $\mathbf{W} \in \mathbb{R}^{d_O \times K d_I}$ and $\mathbf{b} \in \mathbb{R}^{d_O}$ denote the model parameters shared by each convolution filter. Now the set of size-K convolution filters are as follows:

$$
\begin{aligned}
\mathbf{h}_1 &= \mathbf{W}(\mathbf{x}_1 \oplus \mathbf{x}_2 \oplus \cdots \oplus \mathbf{x}_{1+K-1}) + \mathbf{b} \\
\mathbf{h}_2 &= \mathbf{W}(\mathbf{x}_2 \oplus \mathbf{x}_3 \oplus \cdots \oplus \mathbf{x}_{2+K-1}) + \mathbf{b} \\
&\cdots \\
\mathbf{h}_i &= \mathbf{W}(\mathbf{x}_i \oplus \mathbf{x}_{i+1} \oplus \cdots \oplus \mathbf{x}_{i+K-1}) + \mathbf{b} \\
&\cdots \\
\mathbf{h}_{n-K+1} &= \mathbf{W}(\mathbf{x}_{n-K+1} \oplus \mathbf{x}_{n-K+2} \oplus \cdots \oplus \mathbf{x}_n) + \mathbf{b},
\end{aligned}
\tag{13.17}
$$

where $\oplus$ denotes the column-wise concatenation of column vectors. The $n - K + 1$ filters can be briefly denoted as $\mathbf{H}_{1:n-K+1} = \mathbf{W} \circledast \mathbf{X}_{1:n} + \mathbf{b} = \mathbf{h}_1, \mathbf{h}_2, \ldots, \mathbf{h}_{n-K+1}$. $\mathbf{H}_{1:n-K+1} \in \mathbb{R}^{(n-K+1) \times d_O}$ consists of $n - K + 1$ column vectors each with size d_O.

In Eq 13.17, each convolution feature is a standard perceptron layer with the *identity* activation function. As a result, a convolutional neural network layer can be seen as a sequence of perceptron layers over a sequential input. For back-propagation, given a local loss L and $\frac{\partial L}{\partial \mathbf{H}_{1:n-K+1}}$, namely $\frac{\partial L}{\partial \mathbf{h}_i}$ ($i \in [1, \ldots, n - K + 1]$) as input ($\frac{\partial L}{\partial \mathbf{h}_i}$ is a back-propagated constant vector in $\mathbb{R}^{d_O}$), we need to calculate $\frac{\partial L}{\partial \mathbf{x}_i}$ ($i \in [1, \ldots, n]$) as well as $\frac{\partial L}{\partial \mathbf{W}}$ and $\frac{\partial L}{\partial \mathbf{b}}$. We leave the former to Exercise 13.9. For the latter, noticing that $\mathbf{W}$ and $\mathbf{b}$ are shared among all convolution filters, we have:

$$\frac{\partial L}{\partial \mathbf{W}} = \sum_{i=1}^{n-K+1} \left(\frac{\partial L}{\partial \mathbf{h}_i} (\mathbf{x}_i \oplus \mathbf{x}_{i+1} \oplus \ldots \oplus \mathbf{x}_{i+K-1})^T \right)$$

$$\frac{\partial L}{\partial \mathbf{b}} = \sum_{i=1}^{n-K+1} \frac{\partial L}{\partial \mathbf{h}_i} \cdot 1 = (n - K + 1) \cdot \frac{\partial L}{\partial \mathbf{h}_i}.$$

For Algorithm 13.1, the function FORWARDCOMPUTE($\mathbf{X}_{1:n}$) returns $\mathbf{H}_{1:n-K+1}$, and the function BACKPROPAGATE $\left(\left\{ \frac{\partial L}{\partial \mathbf{h}_i} \right\} |_{i=1}^{n-K+1} \right)$ returns $\left(\left\{ \frac{\partial L}{\partial \mathbf{x}_i} \right\} |_{i=1}^{n}, \langle \frac{\partial L}{\partial \mathbf{W}}, \frac{\partial L}{\partial \mathbf{b}} \rangle \right)$ as calculated above.

Comparison with discrete n-gram features. The correlation between a size K convolution filter output and a one-hot n-gram feature is analogous to the correlation between a word embedding vector and a one-hot word vector. While both represent a certain n-gram, the former is dense and low-dimensional, dynamically computed and adjustable during model training. Thus it has stronger representation power.

13.2.3 Output Layer

A CNN calculates a sequence of vectors $\mathbf{H}_{1:n-K+1}$ given a sequence of vectors $\mathbf{X}_{1:n}$. To derive a single vector representation of $\mathbf{X}_{1:n}$, a pooling layer can be used after the convolution layer (Exercise 13.8). For a given sentence $\mathbf{X}_{1:n}$, CNN and pooling give a vector representation $\mathbf{h}$, which is a dense and more abstract representation of $\mathbf{X}_{1:n}$. Now suppose that the output classes are $C = \{c_1, \ldots, c_{|C|}\}$. We use the aforementioned *softmax* multi-class output layer for calculating the classification probability distribution:

$$\begin{aligned} \mathbf{o} &= \mathbf{W}^o \mathbf{h} + \mathbf{b}^o \\ \mathbf{p} &- softmax(\mathbf{o}), \end{aligned} \tag{13.18}$$

where $\mathbf{W}^o$ and $\mathbf{b}^o$ are the model parameters of the softmax classifier. $\mathbf{p} \in \mathbb{R}^{|C|}$ is the model probability, where the ith element in $\mathbf{p}$ is $P(c_i | \mathbf{X}_{1:n})$.

Similar to log-linear models, for decoding, we do not need to apply the *softmax* activation function for selecting the most probable output class because $\arg\max_i \mathbf{o}[i] = \arg\max_i \mathbf{p}[i]$. When the number of output classes is large (e.g., the vocabulary), this can make the algorithm more efficient.

When $|C| = 2$, we can also use a *sigmoid* output layer, as we have in Eq 13.4 and Eq 13.5 at the beginning of the chapter. In this case,

$$\mathbf{p} = \sigma(\mathbf{u}^o \mathbf{x} + \mathbf{b}^o),$$

where $\mathbf{p}$ represents $P(y = +1 | \mathbf{X}_{1:n})$. However, the multi-class classification output layer in Eq 13.18 is more dominantly used for neural NLP. Thus we stick to Eq 13.18 for a default output layer.

13.2.4 Training

Equation 13.18 makes our classifier inherently a probabilistic model, for which a natural loss is the cross-entropy loss, or log-likelihood loss, as discussed in Chapters 4 and 5. In particular, given a set of training samples $\{(\mathbf{X}_i, c_i)\}|_{i=1}^{N}$, the cross-entropy loss is:

$$L = -\sum_{i=1}^{n} \log \mathbf{p}[c_i]$$

where $\mathbf{p}[c_j]$ denotes the c_jth element of the vector $\mathbf{p}$, $c_j \in C$. In addition, regularisation such as L_2 can be further used.

In theory, we can also choose $\mathbf{o}$ in Eq 13.18 as the output layer, without *softmax* normalisation, using a max-margin loss such as the SVM or perceptron losses discussed in Chapter 4 as the loss function. However, empirically the performance can be worse than using $\mathbf{p}$ with a cross-entropy loss. One possible reason is that a cross-entropy loss on $\mathbf{p}$ allows non-zero loss values on each element of $\mathbf{o}$. In contrast, a max-margin loss allows at most two elements in $\mathbf{o}$ to have non-zero loss values (Exercise 13.10 discusses this in detail). As a result, a cross-entropy loss function gives a more fine-grained supervision signal, which is more suitable for training the more expressive neural model.

Having defined the loss function, the training procedure can follow the SGD framework in Algorithm 4.9 in Chapter 4, where the local gradients on each model parameter are calculated using back-propagation discussed earlier in Section 13.1.2. In particular, for each training instance, loss will back-propagate from the *softmax* output layer to $\mathbf{h}$, and then to the sequence encoding layer (e.g., CNN) model parameters, and the word embedding lookup table. The word embedding lookup table is a special type of model parameter in the sense that it can be pre-trained (see Chapter 17) before the text classifier is trained. In this case, whether the values of word embeddings should be adjusted during text classification training is an empirical question. Such adjustment is also called **fine-tuning** in differentiation to pre-training.

13.3 Improving Neural Network Training

Due to increased power, neural network models turn out to be much more difficult to train compared with linear models. Intuitively, we no longer work with linear hyperplanes as we did in Chapter 3, but can train arbitrary hyper-surface shapes in a high-dimensional vector space for separating different data instances. This makes the training data more separable (Chapter 4). However, it can be much more difficult to find an arbitrary curve shape for separating training data as compared to finding a hyperplane. This implies much increased difficulty in training neural networks. The challenge is saliently reflected by back-propagated gradients, which can become negligibly small through layers. In addition, the strong fitting power of neural network can lead to a tendency of overfitting, thereby affecting generalisability (Chapter 4). In this section, we discuss several practical techniques to facilitate neural network training, which range from architecture changes to parameter and setting adjustments.

13.3.1 Short-Cut Connections

Short-cut connections refer to extensions to feed-forward network structures by adding cross-layer connections. They solve gradient diminishing issues in deep neural networks by providing direct links between non-adjacent node layers. As a result, in addition to layer-wise back-propagation, nodes can receive gradients also from distant top layers during training.

A **residual network** extends a baseline network by adding a direct connection between the input layer and the output layer. Formally, for a given input vector $\mathbf{x}$, denote a baseline network as $g(\mathbf{x})$, where g is a non-linear transformation for $\mathbf{x}$. A residual network $\text{RESIDUAL}(\mathbf{x}, g)$ is given by

$$\mathbf{h} = g(\mathbf{x}) + \mathbf{x}. \tag{13.19}$$

For training, given a local loss L and back-propagated gradients $\frac{\partial L}{\partial \mathbf{h}}$, we can calculate $\frac{\partial L}{\partial \mathbf{x}}$ as $\frac{\partial L}{\partial \mathbf{x}}[g] + \frac{\partial L}{\partial \mathbf{h}}$, where $\frac{\partial L}{\partial \mathbf{x}}[g]$ is the gradient $\frac{\partial L}{\partial \mathbf{x}}$ calculated by the original network $g(\mathbf{x})$ according to $\frac{\partial L}{\partial \mathbf{h}}$. The additional path of the residual network allows $\frac{\partial L}{\partial \mathbf{h}}$ itself to be accummulated to $\frac{\partial L}{\partial \mathbf{x}}[g]$, preventing failure of training if $\frac{\partial L}{\partial \mathbf{x}}[g]$ is too small. In practice, residual networks are effective for training very deep neural networks.

13.3.2 Layer Normalisation

Layer normalisation is another architecture change for better training. In a deep neural network, given an input vector to the whole network, the input vector of each layer depends on the parameters of all the preceding layers. Slightly changing one parameter of a layer can greatly affect the distribution of the node values in the subsequent layers, particularly when the network becomes deep. This means that a layer needs to continuously fit new input–output mappings during training, which increases the training difficulty. The phenomenon of changing input distributions with respect to internal nodes in a neural network is referred as **internal covariate shift**. One idea to remedy this problem is to keep the input distribution of each layer relatively stable over time and independent of all the other layers. With this, training can also be more efficient. In addition, making the training and test data share the same distribution over each node layer can improve the performance of neural networks as well.

Formally, for a certain hidden layer, suppose that the output feature vector is $\mathbf{z} \in \mathbb{R}^d$. **Layer normalisation** calculates the mean and variance statistics over $\mathbf{z}$ itself directly for defining a mapping function $LayerNorm : \mathbb{R}^d \to \mathbb{R}^d$. Formally, $LayerNorm(\mathbf{z}; \boldsymbol{\alpha}, \boldsymbol{\beta})$ is given by

$$\mu = \frac{1}{d} \sum_{i=1}^{d} \mathbf{z}[i],$$

$$\sigma = \sqrt{\frac{1}{d} \sum_{i=1}^{d} (\mathbf{z}[i] - \mu)} \tag{13.20}$$

$$LayerNorm(\mathbf{z}; \boldsymbol{\alpha}\boldsymbol{\beta}) = \frac{\mathbf{z} - \mu}{\sigma} \otimes \boldsymbol{\alpha} + \boldsymbol{\beta}$$

where μ is the estimated mean of $\mathbf{z}$ and σ^2 is the estimated variance of $\mathbf{z}$. α and β are two sets of adjustable model parameters. The initial values for α and β are a vector of ones and a vector of zeros, respectively. α and β are multiplicative and additive parameters to ensure that the normalised vector and the original vector have the same representation power. The vector α is called the *gains* and β is called the *biases*.

13.3.3 Dropout

Dropout is a training setting for neural networks to prevent overfitting. It randomly sets the values of nodes or node connections (i.e., parameter matrices) to zeros with a probability during training. Intuitively, this prevents the co-adaptations between nodes and creates an effective ensemble of less-connected neural network structures for training, improving the neural network performances in a simple and effective way. Formally, given a vector $\mathbf{x} \in \mathbb{R}^d$ and a dropout probability p, the function $\text{DROPOUT}(\mathbf{x}, p)$ is defined as

$$\mathbf{m} \sim Bernoulli(p) \quad \text{(sample a 1/0 vector from Bernoulli distribution)}$$
$$\hat{\mathbf{m}} = \frac{\mathbf{m}}{1-p} \tag{13.21}$$
$$\text{DROPOUT}(\mathbf{x}, p) = \mathbf{x} \otimes \hat{\mathbf{m}}.$$

In the above equations, $\mathbf{m}$ is the dropout mask. The size of $\mathbf{m}$ is identical to $\mathbf{x}$. $\hat{\mathbf{m}}$ is the scaled mask. Dropout is used only for training. The dropout probability p is an important hyper-parameter for neural network training, which can be chosen using a development dataset. For different vectors, the dropout probabilities can be different. $p = 0.5$ can be the default choice.

13.3.4 Improving SGD Training for Neural Networks

Thus far, we have been using SGD to train convex objective functions of discriminative models such as perceptrons, log-linear models and SVMs, as well as non-convex objective functions for neural networks, which are more challenging to optimise, requiring more techniques. Suppose that the set of model parameters is Θ and the loss function is $L(\Theta)$. The general updating rules of the time step t for SGD are

$$\mathbf{g}_t = \frac{\partial L(\Theta_{t-1})}{\partial \Theta_{t-1}} \tag{13.22}$$
$$\Theta_t = \Theta_{t-1} - \eta \mathbf{g}_t,$$

where $\mathbf{g}_t$ is the gradient with respect to the set of parameters Θ at the time step t and η is the learning rate. Different from Chapter 4, where a fixed learning rate $\alpha = \alpha_o$ is used throughout the SGD training process, for training neural networks it can be useful to adjust the learning rate η at different time steps for better training of neural networks. We will discuss some of these techniques later in this section and more of them in Chapter 14. For neural network training, $\mathbf{g}_t$ can be calculated on a mini-batch of training examples.

SGD goes over a set of training instances for multiple iterations. The number of training iterations, or epochs, can be fixed to a certain number, or selected according to development experiments also. In part I of the book we determine the best number of training iterations for the perceptron model (Chapter 3) and for SGD training in general (Chapter 4) according to development experiments. For neural models, we can do the same, simply stop training when the development data performance plateaus. This method is referred to as **early stopping**.

Below we discuss several techniques for improving SGD training of neural networks.

Learning Rate Decay. Intuitively, the training of SGD is sensitive to the learning rate. Reducing the learning rate over time is helpful for training deep networks. In particular, at the beginning, a high learning rate is useful for accelerating the training process. As the training procedure continues, the learning rate decreases with a decay schedule to carefully explore the loss surface for spotting the minimum point. Common decay methods include *step decay*, *exponential decay* and *inverse decay*. For step decay, the learning rate decreases by a factor τ ($\tau < 1$) every few epochs, or by a factor according to the performance on a development set. When the training performance is stuck on the development set, the learning rate can be scaled down. For exponential decay, the learning rate is multiplied by an exponential decay factor. Formally, the learning rate of the epoch t is set to $\eta_t = \eta e^{-\tau t}$, where τ is a hyper-parameter and η is the initial learning rate. For inverse decay, the learning rate of the epoch t is set to $\eta_t = \frac{\eta}{1+\tau t}$. Inverse decay is found to be useful for many NLP tasks. The values of τ can be chosen from $\{0.05, 0.08, 0.1\}$.

SGD with Momentum. The hypersurface shape for a training objective can be highly complex in high-dimensional spaces, where the gradient can be steep in one direction but gentle in the other directions. For these scenarios, SGD can face many up-and-down oscillations, especially when the learning rate is large. Momentum is a way to soften such oscillations, accelerating the converging process. The basic idea is to maintain a short-memory of the history gradients. The parameter update considers not only the immediate gradient but also the history gradients. Formally, the update rules for momentum SGD are

$$\mathbf{g}_t = \frac{\partial L(\Theta_{t-1})}{\partial \Theta_{t-1}}$$
$$\mathbf{v}_t = \gamma \mathbf{v}_{t-1} + \eta \mathbf{g}_t \qquad\qquad (13.23)$$
$$\Theta_t = \Theta_{t-1} - \mathbf{v}_t.$$

Here $\mathbf{v}_t$ is the *memory vector*, which is typically called the *velocity vector*. The initial velocity is zero. γ is the *momentum* hyper-parameter or the *friction* parameter, which can be set to 0.5, 0.9 or 0.99. Intuitively, $\mathbf{v}_t$ keeps the running average of the history gradients, which can be regarded as the momentum. At the beginning, the previous velocity vector is zero and the current velocity vector is the gradient vector alone, which makes the parameter update the same as that of SGD. During training, when the direction of the velocity vector is the same as that of the gradient vector, the update will be accelerated. Otherwise, the update will be reduced. This reduces oscillations. In addition, there are many possible saddle points in the high-dimensional error surface, where the gradients are zero in many directions. Momentum also helps the SGD optimiser escape from the saddle points since even when the gradient vector is zero, the velocity vector accumulated from the past can still exist. Similarly, momentum can help SGD roll over small valleys which contain local optimums, leading to better chances for reaching the global optimum.

Gradient clipping. Gradient clipping is a regularisation method to prevent the gradient being too large by consulting hard threshold values. One common clipping method is based on the gradient norms. Once the gradient norm exceeds a predefined maximum threshold τ, the clipping method rescales the gradients to match τ. Formally, the $L2$-norm clipping method is given by

$$\mathbf{g} = \frac{\min(||\mathbf{g}||^2, \tau)}{||\mathbf{g}||^2}\mathbf{g}.$$

Gradient clipping can reduce the effect of extremely large gradients and make the training of neural networks more stable. Common values for τ include 1.0, 3.0, 5.0 and 10.0.

13.3.5 Hyper-Parameter Search

There are many hyper-parameters for neural network training, such as the hidden sizes, the number of stacked layers, the learning rates, the momentum hyper-parameter and the $L2$ regularisation weight and the dropout rate. They should be determined using development experiments. This process is referred to as **hyper-parameter search**. *Grid search* is a representative hyper-parameter search method. To use grid search, we first specify a set of candidate values for each hyper-parameter. Then, we build a model for every combination of the specified hyper-parameters and evaluate the performance of each model. The combination which gives the best performance on the development set is used as the final hyper-parameter configuration. Grid search is easy to use but requires expensive computation. A more efficient way is *random search*, which considers random combinations of hyper-parameters instead of exhaustively exploring all the combinations. As mentioned earlier in the book, feature engineering can be the most time-consuming part in tuning a discrete linear statistical model. In contrast, hyper-parameter search can be the most time-consuming in tuning a neural model.

Summary

In this chapter, we have learned:

- multi-layer perceptrons and deep neural networks;
- convolutional neural networks for text classification;
- residual network, dropout and layer normalisation;
- SGD with momentum.

Chapter Notes

Rosenblatt (1958) discussed multilayer perceptron. Rumelhart et al. (1986) introduced the back-propogation algorithm to learn internal representations of neural networks. Hornik et al. (1989) investigated the representation power of neural networks with different numbers of layers, demonstrating that a neural network with more than three layers can be used to approximate arbitrary functions. Convolutional neural network (CNN) was among the first influential network structures for learning sentence representations (Kim, 2014; Kalchbrenner et al., 2014; Yin et al., 2017).

Highway network (Srivastava et al., 2015) and residual network (He et al., 2016) are used as short-cut layers to train deep networks. Batch normalisation (Ioffe and Szegedy, 2015) and layer normalisation (Ba et al., 2016) are used as normalisation layers for improving deep network training. Srivastava et al. (2014) proposed dropout as a simple way to prevent neural networks from overfitting. Bottou (2010) discussed using SGD for learning parameters in neural networks.

Exercises

13.1 Specify the Taylor expansion of the *sigmoid* activation function, demonstrating that it achieves both pair-wise and triple-wise combinations of automatic features. Such non-linear feature combination power takes effect only when a neural network has more than two layers. Why do they not work for single-layer models?

13.2 The *swish* activation function is defined as $swish(x) = x \cdot sigmoid(\beta x)$, where β is a hyper-parameter.

(a) Derive the gradient of $swish(x)$ with respect to x.
(b) Compare *swish* with *ReLU*, *LeakyReLU* and *ELU*.

13.3 According to Figure 13.3, rewrite Eq 13.12 and Eq 13.13 for $\frac{\partial L}{\partial y_1}$, $\frac{\partial L}{\partial y_2}$, $\frac{\partial L}{\partial x_1}$, $\frac{\partial L}{\partial x_2}$, $\frac{\partial L}{\partial u_1}$, $\frac{\partial L}{\partial u_2}$, $\frac{\partial L}{\partial w_{11}^y}$, $\frac{\partial L}{\partial w_{12}^y}$, $\frac{\partial L}{\partial w_{21}^y}$ and $\frac{\partial L}{\partial w_{22}^y}$ assuming that f and g are both *sigmoid* functions. What are the input and hidden sizes? Show that if all parameters are initiated as $\mathbf{0}$s, SGD can fail to learn a useful model.

13.4 Following the derivation of Eq 13.10 and Eq 13.11, derive Eq 13.12 and Eq 13.13 by taking element-wise derivatives.

13.5 Show for the model in Figure 13.3 that calculation of derivatives using back-propagation in the notation of Eq 13.12 and Eq 13.13 gives the same results as direct calculation in Eq 13.10 and Eq 13.11.

13.6 Gradient check. Back-propagation allows us to modularise network components by specifying how loss should be propagated from the output layer back to the input layer. We can use gradient check to verify empirically that the gradient on each model parameter is correct. In particular, suppose that we have a neural network with a parameter matrix $\mathbf{W}$. For a training instance, we have a given input and the network computes an output value. Now we can make a small change Δw_{ij} to $\mathbf{W}[i][j]$ and recalculate the output value, thus obtaining a difference Δo. We can verify whether the calculation of $\frac{\partial o}{\partial \mathbf{W}[i][j]}$ is correct by comparing Δo with $\Delta w_{ij} \times \frac{\partial o}{\partial \mathbf{W}[i][j]}$. If they are identical, then the partial derivative is correct. This verification cannot be precise. Typically we deem the gradient as correct as long as the difference between the compared values is below 10^{-9}. Why? What is the requirement for the change Δw_{ij}?

13.7 Back-propagation allows modularisation of network components, where a large network can be seen as the composition of smaller layer components, for which the forward computation and back-propagation equations are easy to compute. For the MLP model in Section 13.1.2, we modularised the network layerwise. A more fine-grained way to modularise the model is to take activation functions as additional layers. As a result, the example in Figure 13.3 can be written as

$$\mathbf{t}_y = \mathbf{W}^y \mathbf{x}, \ \mathbf{y} = \mathbf{t}_y^2, \ t_o = \mathbf{u}^T \mathbf{y}, \ o = \sigma(t_o).$$

Derive back-propagation functions for each of the four layers above. What is the advantage of such modularisation?

13.8 Add a pooling layer after the convolutional neural network in Eq 13.16 for deriving a sentence-level vector $\mathbf{h}$ given $\mathbf{X}_{1:n}$. How does back-propagation training work?

13.9 Calculate the partial derivatives $\frac{\partial \mathbf{H}_{1:n-K+1}}{\partial \mathbf{x}_i} (i \in [1, \dots, n])$ for the CNN model in Section 13.2.2. (Hint: how many convolution filters does each $\mathbf{x}_i$ contribute to?)

13.10 Show that in Eq 13.18, a cross-entropy loss defined on $\mathbf{p}$ allows non-zero loss values on each element of $\mathbf{o}$, while a perceptron loss defined on $\mathbf{o}$ directly allows non-zero loss on either 0 or 2 elements of $\mathbf{o}$.

13.11 Consider CNN in Section 13.2.2:

(a) By default, the number of output vectors is different from the number of input vectors using our convolution of neural network with convolution filter size K. To make the output size the same as the input size, zero vectors can be added to the beginning of the input matrix. Discuss how this can be implemented.

(b) How can the CNN layers be stacked to capture more powerful representations?

(c) CNN can use multiple filters with different window sizes and outputs sizes, extracting features from various perspectives. Discuss how to merge multiple filters' outputs for text classification.

13.12 The hidden vector $\mathbf{h}$ in Eq 13.18 and the topic distribution of PLSA in Chapter 6 (Section 6.2.3) are both dense low-dimensional vector representations of documents. What are their differences?

13.13 As a variant of layer normalisation, **batch normalisation** is a method that normalises layer inputs by fixing the means and variances of a layer based on the statistics within an input mini-batch during mini-batch SGD training. Formally, given a mini-batch of inputs $\mathbf{X} = \mathbf{x}[1], \mathbf{x}[2], \dots, \mathbf{x}[m]$, batch normalisation is given by

$$\boldsymbol{\mu}_B = \frac{1}{m} \sum_{i=1}^{m} \mathbf{x}[i], \ \sigma_B = \frac{1}{m} \sum_{i=1}^{m} (\mathbf{x}[i] - \boldsymbol{\mu}_B)^2$$

$$\hat{\mathbf{x}}[i] = \frac{\mathbf{x}[i] - \boldsymbol{\mu}_B}{\sqrt{\sigma_B^2 + \epsilon}}, \ y_i = \gamma \hat{\mathbf{x}}[i] + \beta,$$

$$BatchNorm(\mathbf{X}, \gamma, \beta) = y_i,$$

$$(13.24)$$

where m is the batch size, μ_B and σ_B^2 are the estimated mean and estimated variance of the input mini-batch, respectively, and $\hat{\mathbf{x}}[i]$ ($i \in [1, \ldots, m]$) denote the normalised inputs. γ and β are model parameters to scale and shift the normalised inputs, ensuring that the returned input after normalisation can have the same representation power as before normalisation. ϵ is a hyper-parameter for numerical stability.

1 The above batch normalisation applies to each feature independently. For an MLP $\mathbf{h} = g(\mathbf{Wx} + \mathbf{b})$, the batch normalised version is

$$\mathbf{h} = g(BN(\mathbf{Wx}; \boldsymbol{\gamma}, \boldsymbol{\beta}) + \mathbf{b}) \qquad (13.25)$$

In Eq 13.25, batch normalisation is used for each dimension of the vector $\mathbf{h}$. Suppose that $\mathbf{h} \in \mathbb{R}^d$, we have $\boldsymbol{\gamma} \in \mathbb{R}^d$ and $\boldsymbol{\beta} \in \mathbb{R}^d$. $\boldsymbol{\gamma}[i]$ and $\boldsymbol{\beta}[i]$ are the scale and shift parameters for the i-th feature dimension of $\mathbf{h}$, respectively.

During testing, how can you obtain the estimated mean and variance of each feature?

2 For CNNs, batch normalisation is applied per feature map rather than per feature. For example, suppose that the batch size is m, the CNN feature map size is $p \times q$. To apply batch normalisation, we can treat the new batch size as $m \times p \times q$ and use one pair of parameters $\boldsymbol{\gamma}$ and $\boldsymbol{\beta}$ rather than $p \times q$ pairs. Fully specify batch normalised version of a CNN.

13.14 Derive back-propagation gradients for *LayerNorm* in Section 13.3.

14   Representation Learning

We have seen several neural network models for text classification, including CNN/pooling over word embeddings. Compared with the generalised perceptron model in Chapter 4, the output layers are identical for both binary classification and multi-class classification (see Section 13.1.1). The biggest difference is in the representation of the input text, where neural models make use of multiple hidden layers with non-linear activation functions to calculate a dense vector representation. The strong power of neural text classification models lies in the strong representation power. Thus representation learning is a central topic for neural NLP.

This chapter looks at more neural network structures for learning representations. First, we begin with recurrent neural networks, which calculate representations of sequences that contain global features. Second, we discuss neural attention, which can be seen as an alternative to pooling for aggregating a set of representation vectors. We show how a sequence encoding network can be built by using attention as the main component. Third, intuitively, explicit syntactic and semantic structures of input texts, which can be obtained using parser systems, can provide useful features for better classification. We have not discussed discrete text classification given tree structured inputs because it mainly involves feature engineering, which is not a main topic of this book. In contrast, neural representation of trees and graphs can be both theoretically more interesting and empirically much stronger, which we discuss in this chapter. Towards the end of the chapter, we discuss more variants of standard SGD training for improved neural network optimisation.

14.1   Recurrent Neural Network

We have thus far learned two sequence encoder networks, namely CNN and pooling. However, only pooling aggregates a variable-sized set of dense vectors into one. Intuitively, pooling has limited representation power: it is insensitive to the input order, and cannot capture non-linear interactions between different input vectors. CNN can learn strong non-linear representations of *n*-grams, but it cannot capture long-range dependencies between input vectors. Ideally, we want to find a neural network that is adaptive to variable-sized inputs, while being able to capture long-range syntactic patterns such as "*one of the ...among ...*", semantic dependencies such as predicate–argument structures and discourse relations such as "*if ..., then ...*"

To this end, we can consider a recurrent state-transition process for left-to-right reading of the input sequence, where the state is an incrementally updated hidden layer vector, which represents the syntactic, semantic and discourse context from the beginning until the current input, and a state transition step integrates the current input word into the state. The state can serve as a memory, which allows patterns to be remembered over long-range contexts. A dense vector state can potentially remember multiple syntactic and semantic patterns simultaneously.

Recurrent neural network (RNN) achieves this functionality. In particular, a vanilla RNN model uses a standard perceptron layer with non-linear activation to achieve the recurrent state-input combination function. There are several variants of RNNs, which turn out to have stronger representation power. We discuss them in this section.

14.1.1 Vanilla RNNs

A vanilla RNN calculates an output sequence $\mathbf{h}_1, \mathbf{h}_2, \ldots, \mathbf{h}_n$ given an input sequence $\mathbf{X}_{1:n} = \mathbf{x}_1, \ldots, \mathbf{x}_n$ recurrently from an initial state $\mathbf{h}_0$, where each $\mathbf{h}_t$ ($t \in [1, \ldots, n]$) is calculated according to the previous state $\mathbf{h}_{t-1}$ and the current input $\mathbf{x}_t$. Formally, a RNN step can be written as:

$$
\begin{aligned}
\mathbf{h}_t &= \text{RNN\_STEP}(\mathbf{x}_t, \mathbf{h}_{t-1}) \\
&= f(\mathbf{W}^h \mathbf{h}_{t-1} + \mathbf{W}^x \mathbf{x}_t + \mathbf{b}),
\end{aligned}
\tag{14.1}
$$

where f is a non-linear activation function, such as *tanh* (or other activation functions discussed in Table 13.1). $\mathbf{W}^h$, $\mathbf{W}^x$ and $\mathbf{b}$ are model parameters shared among different time steps.

The above process can be illustrated by Figure 14.1(a). Briefly, the steps

$$
\begin{aligned}
\mathbf{h}_1 &= \text{RNN\_STEP}(\mathbf{x}_1, \mathbf{h}_0), \\
\mathbf{h}_2 &= \text{RNN\_STEP}(\mathbf{x}_2, \mathbf{h}_1), \\
&\cdots \\
\mathbf{h}_n &= \text{RNN\_STEP}(\mathbf{x}_n, \mathbf{h}_{n-1}),
\end{aligned}
\tag{14.2}
$$

can be written as one function $\mathbf{H} = [\mathbf{h}_1; \mathbf{h}_2; \ldots; \mathbf{h}_n] = RNN(\mathbf{X})$. The initial hidden vector $\mathbf{h}_0$ can be set to zero or can be defined as a randomly initialised model parameter. The final vector $\mathbf{h}_n$ can be used for representing $\mathbf{X}_{1:n}$.

Layers and time steps. RNNs look very different from MLPs and CNNs due to the recurrent time steps. In particular, we have learned how to model a multi-layer neural network, for which the output of a lower layer is fed as input to an upper layer. However, we have not learned conceptually what happens when the output of a network layer is wired back as input to itself. We are not yet fully certain of the implications. For example, the lack of a layer order can make back-propagation training difficult.

A better understanding of RNNs can be achieved by exchanging time for space. In particular, if we do not wipe away the previous state $\mathbf{h}_{t-1}$ when calculating $\mathbf{h}_t$ but instead record all the history states, we can effectively "unfold" the recurrent state-transition process into a linear chain, as illustrated in Figure 14.1(b). Now this unfolded version of RNN is a standard multi-layer perceptron with lower layers towards the left and upper layers towards the right. Each layer corresponds to a RNN_STEP function. The only difference between this and a standard MLP is that the size of the network dynamically grows with the size of the input sequence. The trick for RNN achieving

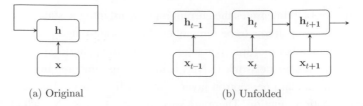

(a) Original   (b) Unfolded

Figure 14.1 Recurrent neural network.

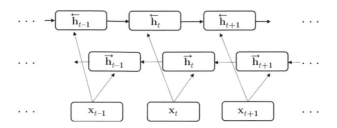

Figure 14.2 Bi-directional RNN.

dynamic size is the sharing of model parameters across layers (i.e., $\mathbf{W}^h$, $\mathbf{W}^x$ and $\mathbf{b}$ in Eq 14.1). In this light, all that is necessary for understanding a RNN model is our understanding of an MLP model, which we have in Section 13.1, and back-propagation training is feasible. When the input size is large, the very large number of layers can make RNN training difficult. We will discuss this more in Section 14.1.2.

Bi-directional RNNs. A characteristic of RNNs is that a hidden vector $\mathbf{h}_t$ is calculated for each input vector $\mathbf{x}_t$. $\mathbf{h}_t$ can be regarded as a feature vector for the tth position, representing the historical context from the first word to the tth word. To also consider future information when extracting features for the tth position, a bi-directional RNN can be built. In particular, the left-to-right RNN ($\overrightarrow{RNN}$) is responsible for capturing history information and a right-to-left RNN ($\overleftarrow{RNN}$) is further used to model future information. The latter executes RNN steps in the order of $\mathbf{x}_n, \mathbf{x}_{n-1}, \ldots, \mathbf{x}_1$. Thus history features in $\overleftarrow{RNN}$ correspond to future features in the left-to-right direction. Formally, denote a bi-directional RNN by the function $BiRNN(\mathbf{X})$. We have

$$\overrightarrow{\mathbf{H}} = \overrightarrow{RNN}(\mathbf{X}) = [\overrightarrow{\mathbf{h}}_1; \overrightarrow{\mathbf{h}}_2; \ldots; \overrightarrow{\mathbf{h}}_n]$$
$$\overleftarrow{\mathbf{H}} = \overleftarrow{RNN}(\mathbf{X}) = [\overleftarrow{\mathbf{h}}_1; \overleftarrow{\mathbf{h}}_2; \ldots; \overleftarrow{\mathbf{h}}_n] \tag{14.3}$$
$$BiRNN(\mathbf{X}) = \overrightarrow{\mathbf{H}} \oplus \overleftarrow{\mathbf{H}} = [\overrightarrow{\mathbf{h}}_1 \oplus \overleftarrow{\mathbf{h}}_1; \overrightarrow{\mathbf{h}}_2 \oplus \overleftarrow{\mathbf{h}}_2; \ldots; \overrightarrow{\mathbf{h}}_n \oplus \overleftarrow{\mathbf{h}}_n],$$

where $\oplus$ denotes the vector concatenation operation. The model parameters of $\overrightarrow{RNN}$ and $\overleftarrow{RNN}$ can be different.

The model structure above is shown in Figure 14.2. A concatenation of the left-to-right feature vector $\overrightarrow{\mathbf{h}}_t$ and the right-to-left feature vector $\overleftarrow{\mathbf{h}}_t$ gives the final representation of the tth word. At the sentence-level, concatenating $\overrightarrow{\mathbf{h}}_n$ and $\overleftarrow{\mathbf{h}}_1$ gives a single-vector sentence representation, which can be used for classification.

14.1.2 Training RNNs

Denote the input sequence as $\mathbf{X}_{1:n}$ and the RNN output sequence as $\mathbf{H}_{1:n}$. Further, suppose that $\mathbf{h} = \mathbf{h}_n$ is used for representing the sentence in classification. RNNs can be trained using unfolded representation as shown in Figure 14.1(b). This method is also referred to as **back-propagation through time** (BPTT). As mentioned earlier, the training is identical to MLP except that the number of layers is dynamic to the input and can be large. Below we show the gradients and potential challenges for RNN training caused by very large layer numbers.

In Figure 14.1(b), each RNN layer is specified by Eq 14.1, where $\mathbf{h}_t = f(\mathbf{W}^h \mathbf{h}_{t-1} + \mathbf{W}^x \mathbf{x}_t + \mathbf{b})$. Let us assume that $f = \tanh$; thus for the tth layer, FORWARDCOMPUTE$(\mathbf{h}_{t-1}, \mathbf{x}_t)$ returns $\tanh(\mathbf{W}^h \mathbf{h}_{t-1} + \mathbf{W}^x \mathbf{x}_t + \mathbf{b})$. The parameters include $\mathbf{W}^h$, $\mathbf{W}^x$ and $\mathbf{b}$.

For back-propagation, given a vector value $\frac{\partial L}{\partial \mathbf{h}_t}$ passed down from layers above, we need to calculate $\frac{\partial L}{\partial \mathbf{x}_t}$, $\frac{\partial L}{\partial \mathbf{h}_{t-1}}$, $\frac{\partial L}{\partial \mathbf{W}^h}$, $\frac{\partial L}{\partial \mathbf{W}^x}$ and $\frac{\partial L}{\partial \mathbf{b}}$. In particular, the activation function *tanh* has $\frac{\partial \tanh(x)}{\partial x} = 1 - \tanh(x)^2$, which is applied element-wise. As a result, we have

$$\frac{\partial L}{\partial \mathbf{x}_t} = (\mathbf{W}^x)^T \cdot \left(\frac{\partial L}{\partial \mathbf{h}_t} \otimes (1 - \mathbf{h}_t^2) \right)$$
$$\frac{\partial L}{\partial \mathbf{h}_{t-1}} = (\mathbf{W}^h)^T \cdot \left(\frac{\partial L}{\partial \mathbf{h}_t} \otimes (1 - \mathbf{h}_t^2) \right)$$
$$\frac{\partial L}{\partial \mathbf{W}^h} = \left(\frac{\partial L}{\partial \mathbf{h}_t} \otimes (1 - \mathbf{h}_t^2) \right) \cdot \mathbf{h}_{t-1}^T \qquad (14.4)$$
$$\frac{\partial L}{\partial \mathbf{W}^x} = \left(\frac{\partial L}{\partial \mathbf{h}_t} \otimes (1 - \mathbf{h}_t^2) \right) \cdot \mathbf{x}_t^T$$
$$\frac{\partial L}{\partial \mathbf{b}} = \frac{\partial L}{\partial \mathbf{h}_t} \otimes (1 - \mathbf{h}_t^2),$$

where $\otimes$ denotes element-wise vector product. BACKPROPAGATE$\left(\frac{\partial L}{\partial \mathbf{h}_t} \right)$ thus returns $\left\langle \left(\frac{\partial L}{\partial \mathbf{x}_t}, \frac{\partial L}{\partial \mathbf{h}_{t-1}} \right), \left(\frac{\partial L}{\partial \mathbf{W}^h}, \frac{\partial L}{\partial \mathbf{W}^x}, \frac{\partial L}{\partial \mathbf{b}} \right) \right\rangle$ as calculated in Eq 14.4. For the entire RNN, gradients on $\frac{\partial L}{\partial \mathbf{W}^h}$, $\frac{\partial L}{\partial \mathbf{W}^x}$ and $\frac{\partial L}{\partial \mathbf{b}}$ should be accumulated across all layers, since the same parameters are shared by each layer.

Gradient issues. RNNs can be difficult to train using SGD due to gradient exploding and vanishing problems. The reason can be understood as follows. First, consider $\frac{\partial L}{\partial \mathbf{h}_{n-t}}$ where t is a relatively large number. We have

$$\frac{\partial L}{\partial \mathbf{h}_{n-t}} = (\mathbf{W}^h)^T \cdot \left(\frac{\partial L}{\partial \mathbf{h}_{n-t+1}} \otimes (1 - \mathbf{h}_{n-t+1}^2) \right)$$
$$= (\mathbf{W}^h)^T \cdot \left((\mathbf{W}^h)^T \cdot \left(\frac{\partial L}{\partial \mathbf{h}_{n-t+2}} \otimes (1 - \mathbf{h}_{n-t+2}^2) \right) \otimes (1 - \mathbf{h}_{n-t+1}^2) \right)$$
$$= \dots \qquad (14.5)$$
$$= \left((\mathbf{W}^h)^T \right)^t \cdot \frac{\partial L}{\partial \mathbf{h}_n} \left(\otimes_{j=1}^t (1 - \mathbf{h}_{n-t+j}^2) \right).$$

Each $\mathbf{h}_{n-t+j}$ is obtained by the *tanh* function and $\tanh(x) \in [-1, 1]$, which means that $1 - h_{n-t+j}^2 \in [0, 1]$. If for every $j \in [1, \dots, t]$, $(1 - \mathbf{h}_{n-t+j}^2)$ are small, then $\otimes_{j=1}^t (1 - \mathbf{h}_{n-t+j}^2)$ can be extremely small, leading to **vanishing gradients**. In addition, if the value $(\mathbf{W}^h)^T$ is small, $((\mathbf{W}^h)^T)^t$ can also be small, which is another potential reason for gradient vanishing. In the reverse case, when $(\mathbf{W}^h)^T$ is not initialised properly and $(\mathbf{W}^h)^T$ is large, then $((\mathbf{W}^h)^T)^t$ can be extremely large, causing **exploding gradients**.

To avoid the gradient exploding and vanishing problems, some training tricks can be applied. For example, to mitigate the gradient exploding problem, we can use *truncated BPTT* by setting a maximum allowed back-propagation step T. In addition, using appropriate weight initialisations can diminish the gradient exploding and vanishing problems of RNNs. Finally, alternative RNN models such as GRUs and LSTMs alleviate these gradient training problems by specific architecture design, which we will discuss in the next section.

Training bi-directional RNNs. The training of BiRNNs differs from the training of vanilla RNNs in two aspects. First, for an input $\mathbf{x}_1, \ldots, \mathbf{x}_n$, both $\overrightarrow{\mathbf{h}}_n$ and $\overleftarrow{\mathbf{h}}_1$ receive back-propagated gradients, since $\overrightarrow{\mathbf{h}}_n \oplus \overleftarrow{\mathbf{h}}_1$ is used as the output. Second, as shown in Figure 14.2, each $\mathbf{x}_i$ ($i \in [1, \ldots, n]$) receives back-propagated gradients from both $\overrightarrow{\mathbf{h}}_i$ and $\overleftarrow{\mathbf{h}}_i$. These two gradients should be summed as the final gradient. The rest of back-propagation is identical to vanilla RNN in each BiRNN component.

14.1.3 Long-Short-Term Memory and Gated Recurrent Units

Long-short-term memory (LSTM) is an RNN variant which allows better SGD training by better control of back-propagation gradients over a large number of network layers. In particular, a standard LSTM splits the hidden state of each recurrent step into a *state vector* and a *memory cell vector*. Given an input $\mathbf{X}_{1:n}$, the state vectors $\mathbf{H}_{1:n}$ correspond to the hidden state vectors $\mathbf{H}_{1:n}$ for RNN, while the cell vectors $\mathbf{C}_{1:n}$ represent a recurrent memory in LSTM. Formally, a standard LSTM recurrent step can be written as $\mathbf{h}_t, \mathbf{c}_t = \mathrm{LSTM\_STEP}(\mathbf{x}_t, \mathbf{h}_{t-1}, \mathbf{c}_{t-1})$, where

$$
\begin{aligned}
\mathbf{i}_t &= \sigma(\mathbf{W}^{ih}\mathbf{h}_{t-1} + \mathbf{W}^{ix}\mathbf{x}_t + \mathbf{b}^i) \\
\mathbf{f}_t &= \sigma(\mathbf{W}^{fh}\mathbf{h}_{t-1} + \mathbf{W}^{fx}\mathbf{x}_t + \mathbf{b}^f) \\
\mathbf{g}_t &= \tanh(\mathbf{W}^{gh}\mathbf{h}_{t-1} + \mathbf{W}^{gx}\mathbf{x}_t + \mathbf{b}^g) \\
\mathbf{c}_t &= \mathbf{i}_t \otimes \mathbf{g}_t + \mathbf{f}_t \otimes \mathbf{c}_{t-1} \\
\mathbf{o}_t &= \sigma(\mathbf{W}^{oh}\mathbf{h}_{t-1} + \mathbf{W}^{ox}\mathbf{x}_t + \mathbf{b}^o) \\
\mathbf{h}_t &= \mathbf{o}_t \otimes \tanh(\mathbf{c}_t).
\end{aligned}
\tag{14.6}
$$

In Eq 14.6, $\mathbf{W}^{ih}$, $\mathbf{W}^{ix}$, $\mathbf{b}^i$, $\mathbf{W}^{fh}$, $\mathbf{W}^{fx}$, $\mathbf{b}^f$, $\mathbf{W}^{gh}$, $\mathbf{W}^{gx}$, $\mathbf{b}^g$, $\mathbf{W}^{oh}$, $\mathbf{W}^{ox}$ and $\mathbf{b}^o$ are model parameters. $\mathbf{g}_t$ performs a non-linear transformation for better representing the input $\mathbf{x}_t$. $\mathbf{i}_t$, $\mathbf{f}_t$ and $\mathbf{o}_t$ are a set of input gate, forget gate and output gate, respectively. σ is the *sigmoid* function and $\otimes$ is the element-wise multiplication (i.e., Hadamard product) operation.

LSTM recurrent steps are characterised by the use of gates through the Hadamard product operation. Each element in a **gate vector** takes a real value between 0 and 1. Intuitively, the element-wise product of a gate vector and a feature vector filters each feature with a decay. In the extreme cases, the feature is fully "blocked" when the corresponding gate element is 0, and fully "passes through" when the gate element is 1. Now consider the $\otimes$ operators in Eq 14.6. The input gate controls the reading process of the current input for calculating a cell. The forget gate selectively keeps the history in a memory cell, and the output gate decides the mapping from a memory cell to a hidden vector.

In the cell computation $\mathbf{c}_t = \mathbf{i}_t \otimes \mathbf{g}_t + \mathbf{f}_t \otimes \mathbf{c}_{t-1}$, $\mathbf{i}_t$ decides how much information of the input representation $\mathbf{g}_t$ can be written to $\mathbf{c}_t$ and $\mathbf{f}_t$ controls how much information of $\mathbf{c}_{t-1}$ can be preserved for $\mathbf{c}_t$. This is the key step for *recurrent state transition* in LSTM, which differs from the vanilla RNN step, using gates for fine-grained control of "remembered" and "forgotten" information by each feature (i.e., corresponding elements in $\mathbf{g}_t$ and $\mathbf{c}_t$).

In Eq 14.6, the calculating of $\mathbf{i}_t, \mathbf{f}_t, \mathbf{g}_t$ and $\mathbf{o}_t$ can also be written concisely as

$$\begin{pmatrix} \mathbf{i}_t \\ \mathbf{f}_t \\ \mathbf{g}_t \\ \mathbf{o}_t \end{pmatrix} = \sigma(\mathbf{W}^h \mathbf{h}_{t-1} + \mathbf{W}^x \mathbf{x}_t + \mathbf{b}), \tag{14.7}$$

where $\mathbf{W}^h = \begin{pmatrix} \mathbf{W}^{ih} \\ \mathbf{W}^{fh} \\ \mathbf{W}^{gh} \\ \mathbf{W}^{oh} \end{pmatrix}$, $\mathbf{W}^x = \begin{pmatrix} \mathbf{W}^{ix} \\ \mathbf{W}^{fx} \\ \mathbf{W}^{gx} \\ \mathbf{W}^{ox} \end{pmatrix}$ and $\mathbf{b} = \begin{pmatrix} \mathbf{b}^i \\ \mathbf{b}^f \\ \mathbf{b}^g \\ \mathbf{b}^o \end{pmatrix}$.

Similar to Eq 14.2, we define the *LSTM* function as a new feature extractor for the whole input sequences, summarising

$$\begin{aligned} \mathbf{h}_1, \mathbf{c}_1 &= \text{LSTM\_STEP}(\mathbf{x}_1, \mathbf{h}_0, \mathbf{c}_0) \\ \mathbf{h}_2, \mathbf{c}_2 &= \text{LSTM\_STEP}(\mathbf{x}_2, \mathbf{h}_1, \mathbf{c}_1) \\ &\cdots \\ \mathbf{h}_n, \mathbf{c}_n &= \text{LSTM\_STEP}(\mathbf{x}_n, \mathbf{h}_{n-1}, \mathbf{c}_{n-1}) \end{aligned} \tag{14.8}$$

into $\mathbf{H} = [\mathbf{h}_1; \mathbf{h}_2; \ldots; \mathbf{h}_n] = LSTM(\mathbf{X})$. $\mathbf{h}_0$ are $\mathbf{c}_0$ are the initial state and cell vectors, which are model parameters.

Compared with vanilla RNN, the LSTM gates and the memory cell allow better back-propagation through large numbers of steps. Exercise 14.1 discusses the back-propagated gradients of each LSTM time step.

Bi-directional extension. Similar to bi-directional RNNs, we can define **bi-directional LSTMs** (BiLSTM). Formally,

$$\begin{aligned} \overrightarrow{\mathbf{H}} &= \overrightarrow{LSTM}(\mathbf{X}) = [\overrightarrow{\mathbf{h}}_1; \overrightarrow{\mathbf{h}}_2; \ldots; \overrightarrow{\mathbf{h}}_n], \\ \overleftarrow{\mathbf{H}} &= \overleftarrow{LSTM}(\mathbf{X}) = [\overleftarrow{\mathbf{h}}_1; \overleftarrow{\mathbf{h}}_2; \ldots; \overleftarrow{\mathbf{h}}_n], \\ BiLSTM(\mathbf{X}) &= \overrightarrow{\mathbf{H}} \oplus \overleftarrow{\mathbf{H}} = [\overrightarrow{\mathbf{h}}_1 \oplus \overleftarrow{\mathbf{h}}_1; \overrightarrow{\mathbf{h}}_2 \oplus \overleftarrow{\mathbf{h}}_2; \ldots; \overrightarrow{\mathbf{h}}_n \oplus \overleftarrow{\mathbf{h}}_n], \end{aligned} \tag{14.9}$$

where $\overrightarrow{LSTM}$ and $\overleftarrow{LSTM}$ are the left-to-right and the right-to-left LSTMs, respectively, which can have different parameters.

Gated recurrent units. LSTMs empirically give better results compared with vanilla RNNs, but are much slower due to increased model parameters and computation steps. **Gated recurrent units** (GRU) simplify LSTM by removing the cell structure, and using only two gates, namely a reset gate and a forget gate, instead of three. Formally, given an input $\mathbf{X}_{1:n} = \mathbf{x}_1, \ldots, \mathbf{x}_n$, a standard GRU cell $\mathbf{h}_t = \text{Gru\_Step}(\mathbf{x}_t, \mathbf{h}_{t-1})$ is given by

$$
\begin{aligned}
\mathbf{r}_t &= \sigma(\mathbf{W}^{rh}\mathbf{h}_{t-1} + \mathbf{W}^{rx}\mathbf{x}_t + \mathbf{b}^r) \\
\mathbf{z}_t &= \sigma(\mathbf{W}^{zh}\mathbf{h}_{t-1} + \mathbf{W}^{zx}\mathbf{x}_t + \mathbf{b}^z) \\
\mathbf{g}_t &= \tanh\left(\mathbf{W}^{hh}(\mathbf{r}_t \otimes \mathbf{h}_{t-1}) + \mathbf{W}^{hx}\mathbf{x}_t + \mathbf{b}^h\right) \\
\mathbf{h}_t &= (\mathbf{1.0} - \mathbf{z}_t) \otimes \mathbf{h}_{t-1} + \mathbf{z}_t \otimes \mathbf{g}_t,
\end{aligned}
\tag{14.10}
$$

where $\mathbf{W}^{rh}$, $\mathbf{W}^{rx}$, $\mathbf{b}^r$, $\mathbf{W}^{zh}$, $\mathbf{W}^{zx}$, $\mathbf{b}^z$, $\mathbf{W}^{hh}$, $\mathbf{W}^{hx}$ and $\mathbf{b}^h$ are model parameters. $\mathbf{r}_t$ is the reset gate, and $\mathbf{z}_t$ is the forget gate. The last step in Eq 14.10 controls the balance between input reading and memory keeping.

Both GRUs and LSTMs can better deal with back-propagation gradients compared with RNNs, while GRU is faster than LSTM. For a large dataset, GRU can be a better choice. The decision should be made empirically.

14.1.4 Stacked LSTMs

Thanks to the fact that the output sequence of vectors have the same size as the input sequence, recurrent neural networks such as LSTMs can be stacked to multiple layers to improve the representation power, with each layer feeding its output vectors as input to the next layer in the bottom-up direction. Take deep BiLSTMs with l layers for example. The stacking method can be written as

$$
\begin{aligned}
\overrightarrow{\mathbf{H}}^0 &= \mathbf{X}, \ \overleftarrow{\mathbf{H}}^0 = \mathbf{X} \\
\overrightarrow{\mathbf{H}}^1 &= \overrightarrow{LSTM}_1(\overrightarrow{\mathbf{H}}^0), \ \overrightarrow{\mathbf{H}}^2 = \overrightarrow{LSTM}_2(\overrightarrow{\mathbf{H}}^1), \ \ldots, \ \overrightarrow{\mathbf{H}}^l = \overrightarrow{LSTM}_l(\overrightarrow{\mathbf{H}}^{l-1}) \\
\overleftarrow{\mathbf{H}}^1 &= \overleftarrow{LSTM}_1(\overleftarrow{\mathbf{H}}^0), \ \overleftarrow{\mathbf{H}}^2 = \overleftarrow{LSTM}_2(\overleftarrow{\mathbf{H}}^1), \ \ldots, \ \overleftarrow{\mathbf{H}}^l = \overleftarrow{LSTM}_l(\overleftarrow{\mathbf{H}}^{l-1}) \\
\mathbf{H} &= \overrightarrow{\mathbf{H}}^l \oplus \overleftarrow{\mathbf{H}}^l = [\overrightarrow{\mathbf{h}}^l_1 \oplus \overleftarrow{\mathbf{h}}^l_1; \ \overrightarrow{\mathbf{h}}^l_2 \oplus \overleftarrow{\mathbf{h}}^l_2; \ldots; \ \overrightarrow{\mathbf{h}}^l_n \oplus \overleftarrow{\mathbf{h}}^l_n].
\end{aligned}
$$

Here $\mathbf{h}^j_t$ denotes the output hidden vector of the tth word at the jth layer, $\mathbf{H}^j$ denotes the output hidden vectors of the whole sequence at the jth layer and $\mathbf{H}$ is the final output vectors. $\overrightarrow{LSTM}_j$ and $\overleftarrow{LSTM}_j$ denote the left-to-right LSTM and the right-to-left LSTM at the jth layer, respectively. The stack of the model is shown in Figure 14.3. The LSTM parameters at different layers or different directions can be the same or different. It should be decided empirically.

14.2 Neural Attention

Neural **attention** is an alternative method to pooling operations for aggregating a set of vectors. It can be used to find a single vector representation of a sentence, given a sequence of word-level vectors such as word embeddings or CNN, LSTM and GRU outputs. Different from pooling, attention finds a weighted sum of vectors in a sequence with regard to certain targets. For example, given a comment about a restaurant "*great service but the price is very high*", when we are

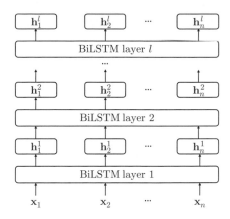

Figure 14.3 Stacked BiLSTMs.

concerned about the service, the comment is positive by focusing on the word "*great*". However, if we refer to the price, the comment is negative as indicated by "*high*". For the same sequence, attention mechanisms return different vectors given different targets.

Formally, given a target vector $\mathbf{q}$ and a list of content vectors $\mathbf{H} = \mathbf{h}_1, \mathbf{h}_2, \cdots, \mathbf{h}_n$, where $\mathbf{q} \in \mathbb{R}^d$, $\mathbf{h}_i \in \mathbb{R}^d$ and d is the dimension size, we define a function *attention* over $\mathbf{q}$ and $\mathbf{H}$:

$$s_i = score(\mathbf{q}, \mathbf{h}_i) \quad (i \in [1, \dots, n])$$
$$\alpha_i = \frac{\exp(s_i)}{\sum_{i=1}^{N} \exp(s_i)} \quad \text{(softmax normalisation)} \tag{14.11}$$
$$\mathbf{c} = \sum_{i=1}^{n} \alpha_i \times \mathbf{h}_i \quad \text{(weighted sum)},$$

where $\mathbf{c}$ is taken as the output of *attention*$(\mathbf{q}, \mathbf{H})$ in Eq 14.11. s_i is a relevance score between $\mathbf{q}$ and $\mathbf{h}_i$. The *score* function can be parameterised using various neural networks. It is called the *attention score function* or the *alignment function*. We will discuss more details about it later. α_i are normalised relevance scores based on s_i. The normalised score vector $\alpha = \langle \alpha_1, \alpha_2, \dots, \alpha_n \rangle$ gives a probability distribution over the content vectors. Thus $\mathbf{c}$ is a weighted sum of the content vectors, with each vector $\mathbf{h}_i$ being weighted by the corresponding attention score α_i.

The resulting vector $\mathbf{c}$ can be used as a context-aware feature representation of $\mathbf{q}$. For example, suppose that the input is $W_{1:n} =$"*great service but the price is high*", and $\mathbf{H}_{1:n} = \mathbf{h}_1, \mathbf{h}_2, \dots, \mathbf{h}_n$ is its BiLSTM representation. When the target is "*service*", the expected attention weights for "*great*" and "*high*" can be "0.95" and "0.001", respectively, which can ensure that the sentiment of the "*service*" target is dominated by the word "*great*".

Now we introduce four choices for the *score* function in Eq 14.11:

1. **Dot-product attention.** The dot-product attention function defines the score between the target vector $\mathbf{q}$ and the context vector $\mathbf{h}$ by:

$$score(\mathbf{q}, \mathbf{h}) = \mathbf{q}^T \mathbf{h}. \tag{14.12}$$

This score function introduces no model parameters; it intuitively measures the similarity between $\mathbf{q}$ and $\mathbf{h}$.

2. **Scaled dot-product attention.** This function scales the dot-product attention score by $\frac{1}{\sqrt{d}}$, where d is the dimension of $\mathbf{q}$ and $\mathbf{h}$:

$$score(\mathbf{q}, \mathbf{h}) = \frac{\mathbf{q}^T \mathbf{h}}{\sqrt{d}}. \tag{14.13}$$

3. **General attention.** This method introduces a parameter matrix $\mathbf{W}$ to capture the interaction between each element in $\mathbf{q}$ and each element in $\mathbf{h}$, where $\mathbf{q} \in \mathbb{R}^{d_1}$, $\mathbf{h} \in \mathbb{R}^{d_2}$ and $\mathbf{W} \in \mathbb{R}^{d_1 \times d_2}$:

$$score(\mathbf{q}, \mathbf{h}) = \mathbf{q}^T \mathbf{W} \mathbf{h}. \tag{14.14}$$

4. **Additive attention.** The method first makes a concatenation of $\mathbf{q}$ and $\mathbf{h}$, and then applies a feed-forward neural layer before multiplying the resulting vector with a parameter vector $\mathbf{v}$:

$$score(\mathbf{q}, \mathbf{h}) = \mathbf{v}^T \tanh\left(\mathbf{W}(\mathbf{q} \oplus \mathbf{h}) + \mathbf{b}\right), \tag{14.15}$$

where $\mathbf{v}$, $\mathbf{W}$ and $\mathbf{b}$ are model parameters. $\oplus$ denotes concatenation.

In order to use dot-production attention and scaled dot-production attention, $\mathbf{q}$ and $\mathbf{h}$ must have the same dimension size. For general attention and additive attention, the dimensions of $\mathbf{q}$ and $\mathbf{h}$ can be different. We leave the calculation of back-propagated gradients with respect to $\mathbf{q}$, $\mathbf{h}$ and $\mathbf{W}$, $\mathbf{b}$ to Exercise 14.8.

Correlation with gating functions. We discussed gating functions in Section 14.1.3 as a component in LSTM. Gating functions are naturally a tool for calculating weighted sums of a set of vectors also. In particular, given a set of hiddden vectors $\mathbf{H}_{1:n} = \mathbf{h}_1, \mathbf{h}_2, \ldots, \mathbf{h}_n$, and a target vector $\mathbf{q}$, we can calculate a set of gate vectors for aggregating $\mathbf{H}_{1:n}$:

$$
\begin{aligned}
\mathbf{s}_i &= \mathbf{W}^q \mathbf{q} + \mathbf{W}^h \mathbf{h}_i \\
\mathbf{g}_i &= softmax(\mathbf{s}_1, \mathbf{s}_2, \ldots \mathbf{s}_n) \quad \text{(element-wise softmax)} \\
\mathbf{c} &= \sum_{i=1}^{n} \mathbf{g}_i \otimes \mathbf{h}_i,
\end{aligned}
\tag{14.16}
$$

where $\mathbf{W}^q$ and $\mathbf{W}^h$ are model parameters, and $\otimes$ denotes element-wise multiplication. Equation 14.16 calculates a score vector $\mathbf{s}_i$ for each hidden vector $\mathbf{h}_i$, before normalising $\mathbf{s}_i$ for all $i \in [1, \ldots, n]$ element-wise, by applying *softmax* across each row of $[\mathbf{s}_1; \mathbf{s}_2; \ldots; \mathbf{s}_n]$. Finally, the normalised score vectors are used as gates for aggregating $\mathbf{h}_1, \ldots, \mathbf{h}_n$. In this aggregation step, each element of $\mathbf{c}$ is a weighted sum of the corresponding element in $\mathbf{h}_1, \ldots, \mathbf{h}_n$. Compared with attention aggregation, **gating aggregation** offers more fine-grained combination of input vectors, but is also computationally more expensive with more model parameters.

14.2.1 Query–Key–Value Attention

In database queries, we use a *key*, such as a student ID, to retrieve a *value*, such as a student name. For neural attention, when the contexts contain a set of key-value pairs, it is useful to decompose each context vector into a key vector and a value vector. In this case, the context vectors can be regarded as associated memories. Given a target query, we compare the query vector with a list of key vectors and return the aggregation of their corresponding value vectors. Formally, suppose that the query vector is $\mathbf{q}$, the key vectors are $\mathbf{K}_{1:n} = [\mathbf{k}_1; \mathbf{k}_2; \ldots; \mathbf{k}_n]$, and the value vectors are $\mathbf{V}_{1:n} = [\mathbf{v}_1; \mathbf{v}_2; \ldots; \mathbf{v}_n]$. For each key vector $\mathbf{k}_i$, the corresponding value vector is $\mathbf{v}_i$. The query-key-value attention function $attention(\mathbf{q}, \mathbf{K}, \mathbf{V})$ is given by

$$
\begin{aligned}
s_i &= score(\mathbf{q}, \mathbf{k}_i) \quad (i \in [1, \ldots, n]) \\
\alpha_i &= \frac{\exp(s_i)}{\sum_{i=1}^{N} \exp(s_i)} \quad \text{(softmax normalisation)} \\
\mathbf{c} &= \sum_{i=1}^{n} \alpha_i \mathbf{v}_i \quad \text{(weighted sum)},
\end{aligned}
\tag{14.17}
$$

where $\mathbf{c}$ is used as the output of $attention(\mathbf{q}, \mathbf{K}, \mathbf{V})$, s_i is the attention score between the query vector $\mathbf{q}$ and the ith key vector $\mathbf{k}_i$, and $\mathbf{c}$ is the weighted sum of the value vectors with the ith weight score being s_i. When $\mathbf{K} = \mathbf{V}$, $attention(\mathbf{q}, \mathbf{K}, \mathbf{K})$ in Eq 14.17 becomes $attention(\mathbf{q}, \mathbf{K})$ defined in Eq 14.11. Thus $attention(\mathbf{q}, \mathbf{K}, \mathbf{V})$ is more general than $attention(\mathbf{q}, \mathbf{K})$.

Query–key–value attention with a sequence of queries. In the above method for calculating attention weights, we only deal with one query vector. Sometimes we need to consider a *sequence* of queries. For example, given an input query sentence, we might want to find the attentive representation of a document with respect to each word in the input query. This may help us better capture the interaction between the document and the query. One simple way to deal with a sequence of queries is to call the attention function separately for each query, and then return a list of results. Suppose that the sequence of queries is $\mathbf{Q}_{1:l} = [\mathbf{q}_1; \mathbf{q}_2; \ldots; \mathbf{q}_l]$ and the key vectors $\mathbf{K}$ and the value vectors $\mathbf{V}$ are defined in the same way as in Eq 14.17, the attention function $attention(\mathbf{Q}, \mathbf{K}, \mathbf{V})$ is given by

$$
\begin{aligned}
\mathbf{c}_1 &= attention(\mathbf{q}_1, \mathbf{K}, \mathbf{V}) \\
\mathbf{c}_2 &= attention(\mathbf{q}_2, \mathbf{K}, \mathbf{V}) \\
&\cdots \\
\mathbf{c}_l &= attention(\mathbf{q}_l, \mathbf{K}, \mathbf{V}) \\
attention(\mathbf{Q}, \mathbf{K}, \mathbf{V}) &= [\mathbf{c}_1; \mathbf{c}_2; \cdots; \mathbf{c}_l],
\end{aligned}
$$

where each column vector $\mathbf{c}_i \in \mathbb{R}^d$ is the attentive result of the ith query by calling the attention function in Eq 14.17.

Calling the attention function once for each query is computationally expensive. In fact, we can use matrix multiplications to enable parallel computations. In this way, a better way to calculate the attention function $attention(\mathbf{Q}, \mathbf{K}, \mathbf{V})$ is

$$\mathbf{S} = score(\mathbf{Q}, \mathbf{K})$$
$$\mathbf{A} = softmax_1(\mathbf{S}). \tag{14.18}$$

The final result $\mathbf{C} = \mathbf{V}\mathbf{A}^T$, where $\mathbf{C}$ is taken as the result of $attention(\mathbf{Q}, \mathbf{K}, \mathbf{V}) \in \mathbb{R}^{d \times l}$. Here $\mathbf{Q} \in \mathbb{R}^{d \times l}$, $\mathbf{K} \in \mathbb{R}^{d \times n}$ and $\mathbf{V} \in \mathbb{R}^{d \times n}$. $\mathbf{S} \in \mathbb{R}^{l \times n}$ is a score matrix, with $\mathbf{S}[i][j]$ (also denoted as s_{ij}) being the relevance score of the $\mathbf{q}_i$ and $\mathbf{k}_j$. $softmax_1(\mathbf{S})$ refers to applying the $softmax$ function to normalise each column in $\mathbf{S}$. The resulting matrix $\mathbf{A}$ is the attention score matrix and $\mathbf{A} \in \mathbb{R}^{l \times n}$. In the attentive results matrix $\mathbf{C} \in \mathbb{R}^{d \times l}$, the ith column represents the attentive result vector of $\mathbf{q}_i$. The $score$ function can be defined via matrix multiplication. For example, based on the dot-product score function, $score(\mathbf{Q}, \mathbf{K}) = \mathbf{Q}^T\mathbf{K}$.

14.2.2 Self-Attention-Network (SAN)

By itself, attention is similar to pooling in that it aggregates a set of vectors. On the other hand, it can be useful to design an attention network structure that produces a sequence of output vectors $\mathbf{H}_{1:n} = \mathbf{h}_1, \mathbf{h}_2, \ldots, \mathbf{h}_n$ given a sequence of input vectors $\mathbf{X}_{1:n} = \mathbf{x}_1, \mathbf{x}_2, \ldots, \mathbf{x}_n$. To this end, we can make use of query–key–value attention, finding the output representation $\mathbf{h}_i$ for each $\mathbf{x}_i$ by taking $\mathbf{x}_i$ as the query for aggregating $\mathbf{X}_{1:n}$:

$$\mathbf{H}_{1:n} = attention(\mathbf{X}_{1:n}, \mathbf{X}_{1:n}, \mathbf{X}_{1:n}).$$

Intuitively, each $\mathbf{h}_i$ is an attentive representation of $\mathbf{X}_{1:n}$ by using $\mathbf{x}_i$ as a query; it can also be viewed as a representation of $\mathbf{x}_i$ in the sentence-level context. Similar to bi-directional LSTMs, SANs can be stacked for several layers, with the output of one layer being fed as input to the subsequent layer in the bottom-up direction.

Comparison with bi-directional RNN variants. SANs have two salient advantages compared with bi-directional RNN variants such as BiRNNs, BiGRUs and BiLSTMs. First, SANs allow the representation $\mathbf{h}_i$ in each layer to take into consideration all $\mathbf{x}_i$s globally. In contrast, bi-directional RNN variants has information only about the history vectors $\mathbf{x}_1, \ldots, \mathbf{x}_{i-1}$ for calculating $\mathbf{h}_i$, and *indirectly* via $\mathbf{h}_{i-1}$, in the forward direction. The backward component suffers from the same issue in the reverse direction, which makes RNNs relatively weaker in capturing long-range dependencies between input vectors. Second, the computation of $\mathbf{H}_{1:n}$ from $\mathbf{X}_{1:n}$ in each direction is sequential in nature, with the value of $\mathbf{h}_i$ depending upon the value of $\mathbf{h}_{i-1}$ in the forward direction. Thus the time complexity of RNNs is $O(n)$ for computing $\mathbf{H}_{1:n}$. In contrast, for SAN, the *attention* function for each $\mathbf{h}_i$ is independent, which allows strong parallelisation in computation. The asymptotic complexity of calculating $\mathbf{H}_{1:n}$ in each layer is $O(n^2)$ but can be parallelised. Despite the theoretic advantages, whether SANs outperform RNN variants is ultimately an empirical question. We will see a more powerful variant of the vanilla SAN in Chapter 16.

14.3 Representing Trees

Sequence encoders such as CNNs, RNNs and SANs are useful for encoding both sentences (as word sequences) and words (as character sequences). In NLP, trees, directed acyclic graphs (DAGs) and cyclic graph structures are useful for representing syntax, semantics, etc. For example, constituent trees and dependency trees provide syntactic features. To make use of such information for text classification, we can first run a syntactic or semantic parser over the input text, obtaining its explicit structure. Then a neural network can be used to represent the structure that we have obtained, namely to calculate a dense vector $\mathbf{h}$ that captures the most useful features for text classification. Finally, a standard output layer can be added on top of $\mathbf{h}$ for making prediction, as we have seen in Chapter 13. We introduce several methods that extend sequence representation models for representing more complex graph structures.

Let us start with trees. Tree LSTMs can be constructed by extending a sequence LSTM model. In particular, recurrent time steps can be taken in the bottom-up direction for calculating hidden state vectors for each node. The idea is to allow each node to receive information from its subnodes recurrently, so that the top tree node can contain features over the entire tree structure. As shown in Figure 14.4, bottom-up time steps along a tree can be similar to left-to-right time steps along a sequence. However, a salient difference is that, each node has only one predecessor in a sequence LSTM model, but multiple predecessors in a tree LSTM model. Depending on whether the number of child nodes for a given tree node is fixed, different methods can be devised for building a tree LSTM. Below we begin with a more general tree LSTM structure (Section 14.3.1), and then discuss a specific variant for binary trees (Section 14.3.2).

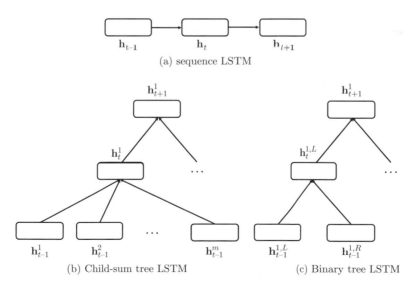

Figure 14.4 Sequence (a) and tree LSTMs (b and c).

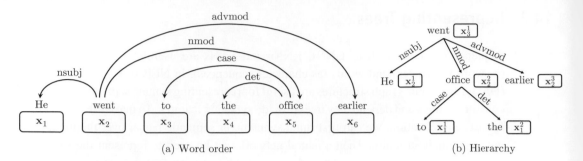

Figure 14.5 Dependency tree in word order (a) and hierarchical order (b).

14.3.1 Child-Sum Tree LSTM

Child-sum tree LSTM models can be used to represent arbitrary trees. The basic idea is to turn multiple child nodes into one by summing up their hidden states, so that a tree structure is reduced to a sequence structure in recurrent state computation. Let us use dependency trees as an example to illustrate these models. In particular, given a sentence $W_{1:n} = w_1, w_2, \ldots, w_n$, we use embedding vectors $\mathbf{X}_{1:n} = \mathbf{x}_1, \mathbf{x}_2, \ldots, \mathbf{x}_n$ to represent words. A sequence of hidden state vectors $\mathbf{h}_1, \mathbf{h}_2, \ldots, \mathbf{h}_n$ is calculated for representing $\mathbf{x}_1, \ldots, \mathbf{x}_n$, respectively, according to the syntactic structure of $W_{1:n}$.

For bottom-up recurrent computation of hidden states, the input is first rearranged hierarchically from the root. Figure 14.5 shows the dependency syntax of the sentence "*He went to the office earlier*" in its word order (a) and hierarchical form (b). In the latter case, words are re-indexed in the bottom-up order as $\mathbf{x}_t^i$, where t denotes the layer index from the bottom, and i represents the index within the layer. The numbers of child nodes for different tree nodes can vary.

The values of hidden nodes $\mathbf{h}_t^i$ for each $\mathbf{x}_t^i$ in Figure 14.5(b) are calculated layer by layer, with increasing t. A special initial state $\mathbf{h}_s$ is used as the predecessor state for leaf nodes. At each time step t, for a node $\mathbf{x}_t^i$, the hidden states of all its child nodes are summed up into a single state $\mathbf{h}_{t-1}^i$, which is used together with the current input $\mathbf{x}_t^i$ for calculating the current hidden state $\mathbf{h}_t^i$. Such calculation can follow the recurrent time step of sequence LSTM from leaf nodes to the root of the tree, so that a hidden state is calculated for each input word.

Formally, for a given node $\mathbf{x}_t^i$, the predecessor node hidden states can be denoted as $\mathbf{h}_{t-1}^{c(t,i,1)}, \mathbf{h}_{t-1}^{c(t,i,2)}, \ldots, \mathbf{h}_{t-1}^{c(t,i,m_t^i)}$, and the corresponding cell states as $\mathbf{c}_{t-1}^{c(t,i,1)}, \mathbf{c}_{t-1}^{c(t,i,2)}, \ldots, \mathbf{c}_{t-1}^{c(t,i,m_t^i)}$, where m_t^i represents the number of child nodes of $\mathbf{x}_t^i$, and $c(t,i,j)$ represents the index of the jth child node of $\mathbf{x}_t^i$ among nodes on the $(t-1)$th layer. For example, in Figure 14.5, $c(3,1,2) = 2$ and $c(2,2,1) = 1$; $\mathbf{x}_2^{c(3,1,2)}$ is $\mathbf{x}_2^2$ ("*office*") and $\mathbf{x}_1^{c(2,2,1)}$ is $\mathbf{x}_1^1$ ("*to*"). Summing up $\mathbf{h}_{t-1}^{c(t,i,j)}$ ($j \in [1, \ldots, m_t^i]$) as $\mathbf{h}_{t-1}^i$, we have:

$$\mathbf{h}_{t-1}^i = \sum_{j=1}^{m_t^i} \mathbf{h}_{t-1}^{c(t,i,j)}. \tag{14.19}$$

We then calculate the hidden state $\mathbf{h}_t^i$ by calculating a set of gate vectors and a cell state, including an input gate, an output gate and a set of forget gates, in the same way as for sequence LSTM. In particular, an input gate $\mathbf{i}_t^i$ and an output gate $\mathbf{o}_t^i$ are calculated according to $\mathbf{h}_{t-1}^i$ and $\mathbf{x}_t^i$:

$$
\begin{aligned}
\mathbf{i}_t^i &= \sigma(\mathbf{W}^{ih}\mathbf{h}_{t-1}^i + \mathbf{W}^{ix}\mathbf{x}_t^i + \mathbf{b}^i) \\
\mathbf{o}_t^i &= \sigma(\mathbf{W}^{oh}\mathbf{h}_{t-1}^i + \mathbf{W}^{ox}\mathbf{x}_t^i + \mathbf{b}^o),
\end{aligned}
\tag{14.20}
$$

where $\mathbf{W}^{ih}$, $\mathbf{W}^{ix}$, $\mathbf{b}^i$, $\mathbf{W}^{oh}$, $\mathbf{W}^{ox}$ and $\mathbf{b}^o$ are model parameters (i in $\mathbf{b}^i$ is not a variable).

In addition, m_t^i forget gates are calculated, each for a cell state $\mathbf{c}_{t-1}^{c(t,i,j)}$ ($j \in [1, \ldots, m_t^i]$), respectively:

$$
\mathbf{f}_t^{i,j} = \sigma(\mathbf{W}^{fh}\mathbf{h}_{t-1}^{c(t,i,j)} + \mathbf{W}^{fx}\mathbf{x}_t^i + \mathbf{b}^f),
\tag{14.21}
$$

where $\mathbf{W}^{fh}$, $\mathbf{W}^{fx}$ and $\mathbf{b}^f$ are model parameters.

According to the gate vector values, a cell state $\mathbf{c}_t$ is computed as follows:

$$
\begin{aligned}
\mathbf{g}_t^i &= \tanh(\mathbf{W}^{gh}\mathbf{h}_{t-1}^i + \mathbf{W}^{gx}\mathbf{x}_t^i + \mathbf{b}^g) \\
\mathbf{c}_t^i &= \mathbf{i}_t^i \otimes \mathbf{g}_t + \sum_{j=1}^{m_t^i} \mathbf{f}_t^{i,j} \otimes \mathbf{c}_{t-1}^{c(t,i,j)},
\end{aligned}
\tag{14.22}
$$

where $\mathbf{W}^{gh}$, $\mathbf{W}^{gx}$ and $\mathbf{b}^g$ are model parameters. $\mathbf{g}_t^i$ serves to represent a new cell state with the input $\mathbf{x}_t^i$ being considered; it is integrated with previous cell states by input and forget gates. $\otimes$ denotes Hadamard product.

Finally, $\mathbf{h}_t^i$ is calculated from $\mathbf{c}_t^i$ through the output gate:

$$
\mathbf{h}_t^i = \mathbf{o}_t^i \otimes \tanh(\mathbf{c}_t^i).
\tag{14.23}
$$

14.3.2 Binary Tree LSTM

As shown in Figure 14.4(c), in a binary tree, each node has at most two child nodes. This allows the hidden state of each child node to be considered separately in computing gate and cell values for more fine-grained features of hidden state values as compared to child-sum LSTMs.

Let us take constituent syntax in CNF as an example. Figure 14.6 shows the tree for the sentence "*The little boy likes red tomatoes*". As discussed in Chapter 10, CNF consists of binary nodes and unary nodes only, and several methods can be applied for binarising a constituent tree. For simplicity, we consider binary trees that do not contain unary-branching nodes (see Exercise 14.10 for adding unary nodes). Thus each non-terminal node in a tree has exactly two child nodes. Similar to Figure 14.5, we label each node according to the bottom-up layer index t and the in-layer node index i. The goal is to calculate a hidden vector $\mathbf{h}_t^i$ for each node in a tree LSTM.

Similar to dependency tree LSTMs, the computation can be performed in a bottom-up timeline. In particular, for a node i on level t, we calculate its cell state $\mathbf{c}_t^i$ and hidden state $\mathbf{h}_t^i$ using the hidden state values $\mathbf{h}_{t-1}^{b(t,i,L)}$, $\mathbf{h}_{t-1}^{b(t,i,R)}$ and the cell values $\mathbf{c}_{t-1}^{b(t,i,L)}$, $\mathbf{c}_{t-1}^{b(t,i,R)}$ of its left and right child nodes, respectively. Here $b(t, i, L)$ and $b(t, i, R)$ represent the index of the left and right child of x_t^i among nodes on the $(t-1)$th layer, respectively. In particular, $b(t, i, L) = c(t, i, 1)$ and $b(t, i, R) = c(t, i, 2)$

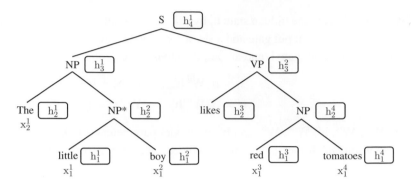

Figure 14.6 A constituent tree in CNF.

in the $c(t, i, j)$ notation in Eq 14.19. For example, in Figure 14.6, $b(4, 1, L) = 1$ (i.e., "*NP*" on the third level over "*The little boy*"), $b(3, 1, R) = 2$ (i.e., "*NP*∗" on the second level over "*little boy*") and $b(2, 4, L) = 3$ (i.e., "*red*" on the first level). For binary tree LSTM, recurrent LSTM steps follow sequential LSTM cell computation but differentiating the two predecessor states of each node $\mathbf{h}_t^i$. In particular, an input gate $\mathbf{i}_t^i$ and two forget gates $\mathbf{f}_t^{i,L}$, $\mathbf{f}_t^{i,R}$ are computed as follows:

$$\mathbf{i}_t^i = \sigma(\mathbf{W}_L^{ih}\mathbf{h}_{t-1}^{b(t,i,L)} + \mathbf{W}_R^{ih}\mathbf{h}_{t-1}^{b(t,i,R)} + \mathbf{W}_L^{ic}\mathbf{c}_{t-1}^{b(t,i,L)} + \mathbf{W}_R^{ic}\mathbf{c}_{t-1}^{b(t,i,R)} + \mathbf{b}^i)$$

$$\mathbf{f}_t^{i,L} = \sigma(\mathbf{W}_L^{f_l h}\mathbf{h}_{t-1}^{b(t,i,L)} + \mathbf{W}_R^{f_l h}\mathbf{h}_{t-1}^{b(t,i,R)} + \mathbf{W}_L^{f_l c}\mathbf{c}_{t-1}^{b(t,i,L)} + \mathbf{W}_R^{f_l c}\mathbf{c}_{t-1}^{b(t,i,R)} + \mathbf{b}^{f_l}) \quad (14.24)$$

$$\mathbf{f}_t^{i,R} = \sigma(\mathbf{W}_L^{f_r h}\mathbf{h}_{t-1}^{b(t,i,L)} + \mathbf{W}_R^{f_r h}\mathbf{h}_{t-1}^{b(t,i,R)} + \mathbf{W}_L^{f_r c}\mathbf{c}_{t-1}^{b(t,i,L)} + \mathbf{W}_R^{f_r c}\mathbf{c}_{t-1}^{b(t,i,R)} + \mathbf{b}^{f_r}),$$

where $\mathbf{W}_L^{ih}$, $\mathbf{W}_R^{ih}$, $\mathbf{W}_L^{ic}$, $\mathbf{W}_R^{ic}$, $\mathbf{b}^i$, $\mathbf{W}_L^{f_l h}$, $\mathbf{W}_R^{f_l h}$, $\mathbf{W}_L^{f_l c}$, $\mathbf{W}_R^{f_l c}$, $\mathbf{b}^{f_l}$, $\mathbf{W}_L^{f_r h}$, $\mathbf{W}_R^{f_r h}$, $\mathbf{W}_L^{f_r c}$, $\mathbf{W}_R^{f_r c}$, $\mathbf{b}^{f_l}$ and $\mathbf{b}^{f_r}$ are model parameters. Note that for non-terminal nodes, there is no input $\mathbf{x}_t^i$.

The cell state and hidden state values are calculated as follows:

$$\mathbf{g}_t^i = \tanh(\mathbf{W}_L^{gh}\mathbf{h}_{t-1}^{b(t,i,L)} + \mathbf{W}_R^{gh}\mathbf{h}_{t-1}^{b(t,i,R)} + \mathbf{b}^g)$$

$$\mathbf{c}_t^i = \mathbf{i}_t^i \otimes \mathbf{g}_t^i + \mathbf{f}_t^{i,R} \otimes \mathbf{c}_{t-1}^{b(t,i,R)} + \mathbf{f}_t^{i,L} \otimes \mathbf{c}_{t-1}^{b(t,i,L)}$$

$$\mathbf{o}_t^i = \sigma(\mathbf{W}_L^{oh}\mathbf{h}_{t-1}^{b(t,i,L)} + \mathbf{W}_R^{oh}\mathbf{h}_{t-1}^{b(t,i,R)} + \mathbf{W}^{oc}\mathbf{c}_t^i + \mathbf{b}^o) \quad (14.25)$$

$$\mathbf{h}_t^i = \mathbf{o}_t \otimes \tanh(\mathbf{c}_t^i),$$

where $\mathbf{W}_L^{gh}$, $\mathbf{W}_R^{gh}$, $\mathbf{b}^g$, $\mathbf{W}_L^{oh}$, $\mathbf{W}_R^{oh}$, $\mathbf{W}^{oc}$ and $\mathbf{b}^o$ are model parameters.

14.3.3 Tree LSTM Features and Sequence LSTM Features

A sentence can be represented both using a sequence LSTM and using a tree LSTM given its syntactic structure. In both forms of representation, the LSTM network plays the role of integrating local word-level features into hidden representations that reflect a sentence-level context. The role of syntax and tree LSTMs here is to control the process of information integration, whereby syntactically correlated words are integrated before unrelated words. This can potentially be stronger than a sequence LSTM in capturing long-range syntactic dependencies. The representation power of tree LSTMs can be further combined with that of sequence LSTMs by stacking a tree LSTM on top of a sequence LSTM, feeding the hidden states of a sequence encoder as input to the tree encoder.

14.4 Representing Graphs

In this section, we discuss the representation of more general graph structures. Figure 14.7(a) shows an example of an abstract meaning representation (AMR) graph, which corresponds to the sentence "*The boy wants to go*". In this AMR graph, the node "*boy*" is the agent for both the node "*want-01*" and the node "*go-01*". In addition, the node "*go-01*" is the patient of the node "*want-01*". This results in a directed acyclic graph (DAG) structure, which cannot be directly modelled by tree LSTMs. However, since the graph is directed, it still allows a recurrent timeline to be defined for hidden state computation (such time steps are left-to-right in a sequence LSTM and bottom-up in a tree LSTM, through which information is passed down through different nodes for learning global features). In fact, DAGs can be modelled by a slight adaptation of sequence and tree LSTM structures. Exercise 14.10 discusses extension of tree LSTMs to DAG structures. **DAG LSTMs** are also referred to as **lattice LSTMs**.

Figure 14.7(b) shows a more general semantic graph, which is cyclic, and more challenging to represent compared to trees and DAGs. In particular, cycles cause difficulty in finding a natural order of nodes in a graph, which serves as a basis for defining recurrent time steps for calculating hidden states. To address this issue, hidden state computation for graph nodes can be made independent of a node order. Recall that for sequence and tree LSTMs, hidden states are calculated for representing a current input in the context of a long-term memory. For cyclic graphs, we also want a hidden state to represent a node in a large graph-level context. To this end, each node can

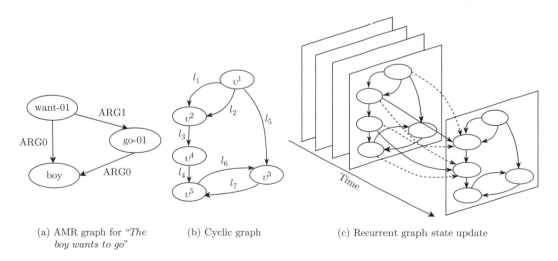

(a) AMR graph for "*The boy wants to go*"   (b) Cyclic graph   (c) Recurrent graph state update

Figure 14.7 Cyclic graph representations.

collect information from its neighbours recurrently, in order to gain insight of an increasing larger context.

As shown in Figure 14.7(c), to achieve the above goal, time steps can be taken in a direction that is orthogonal to the graph edges so that node hidden states exchange information recurrently according to the graph structure. Figure 14.7(c) can be viewed as taking a sequence of "snapshots" of the graph structure in Figure 14.7(b), each corresponding to a recurrent time step. At each time step, the hidden state representation of each node is updated by collecting information from the hidden states of itself and its neighbours in the previous time step. Here neighbouring nodes can be the nodes that are connected by one edge. Each recurrent time step can also be viewed as a *message passing* time step, where each node collects information from its neighbours as a *message* for updating its own state. In this way, node states are recurrently updated with increasing context information. In particular, each node state captures context within a 1-edge, 2-edge and 3-edge radius after 1, 2 and 3 recurrent steps, respectively.

Formally, denote a graph as $\{V, E\}$, where $V = \{v_1, v_2, \ldots v_{|V|}\}$ represents the set of nodes in the graph and $E = \{e_1, e_2, \ldots, e_{|E|}\}$ represents the set of edges. $e_i = (v_i^1, l_i, v_i^2)$ connects two nodes v_i^1 and v_i^2 with an edge labelled l_i ($i \in [1, \ldots, |E|]$). For directed graphs, we assume that e_i points from v_i^1 to v_i^2. For example, in this notation, a dependency tree can be represented as a graph (V, E), where V consists of words in the sentence and E consists of dependency arcs. In the AMR graph in Figure 14.7(a), V represents the set of concepts, such as "*boy*", "*want-01*" and "*go-01*", and E includes all edges, such as "ARG0" and "ARG1".

A **graph neural network** (GNN) assigns an initial hidden state vector $\mathbf{h}_0^i$ for each v_i ($i \in [1, \ldots, |V|]$), and then recurrently calculates $\mathbf{h}_1^i, \mathbf{h}_2^i, \ldots, \mathbf{h}_T^i$ as the hidden state for representing v_i. Here $\mathbf{h}_t^i$ represents the hidden state for node i at step t. The total number of time steps T can be decided empirically according to the performance of a task that uses the representation. Below we discuss how recurrent functions (Section 14.4.1), convolution functions (Section 14.4.2) and attention functions (Section 14.4.3) can be used for incrementally calculating the states $\mathbf{h}_t^i$, respectively.

14.4.1 Graph Recurrent Neural Network (GRN)

A graph recurrent neural network (GRN) can follow a standard RNN in defining time steps. Here we still use LSTM for example. The basic idea is similar to that of child-sum tree LSTM, in that by aggregating multiple predecessor states, a standard LSTM recurrent step can be used. In particular, the hidden states $\mathbf{h}_1^i, \mathbf{h}_2^i, \ldots, \mathbf{h}_T^i$ for a node v_i are calculated in a recurrent process, in which each $\mathbf{h}_t^i$ ($t \in [1, \ldots, T]$) is calculated according to an aggregated previous state $\mathbf{m}_{t-1}^i$ and a current input $\mathbf{x}^i$:

$$\mathbf{h}_t^i = \text{LSTM\_STEP}(\mathbf{m}_{t-1}^i, \mathbf{x}^i), \tag{14.26}$$

where $\mathbf{m}_{t-1}^i$ and $\mathbf{x}^i$ denote the aggregation vector of the previous hidden states and input representation over the neighbours of v_i, respectively.

In light of the aforementioned message passing view, $\mathbf{m}_t^i$ can be regarded as the message received by v_i at time t. Denote the neighbours of node v_i as $\Omega(i)$. For undirected graphs, or disregarding edge directions in directed graphs, $\mathbf{m}_{t-1}^i$ can be represented by summing the previous hidden states of v_i's neighbours:

$$\mathbf{m}_{t-1}^i = \sum_{k \in \Omega(i)} \mathbf{h}_{t-1}^k. \tag{14.27}$$

$\mathbf{x}^i$ represent inherent natures of the graph node v_i. It can be defined for integrating both node and edge information:

$$\mathbf{x}^i = \sum_{k \in \Omega(i)} \left(\mathbf{W}^x \Big(emb(v_i) \oplus emb^e\big(l(i,k)\big) \oplus emb(v_k) \Big) + \mathbf{b}^x \right), \tag{14.28}$$

where emb denotes the embedding for a node and emb^e denotes the embedding for an edge. $l(i,k)$ denotes the edge label between v_i and v_k. $\mathbf{W}^x$ and $\mathbf{b}^x$ are model parameters.

Differentiating edge directions. The above model captures rather crude features by aggregating node and message structures. For directed graphs, neighbour nodes can be grouped by the edge direction for more fine-grained representation, where $\mathbf{m}_t^i$ for v_i is calculated as:

$$\mathbf{m}_{t-1}^{i\uparrow} = \sum_{k \in \Omega_\uparrow(i)} \mathbf{h}_{t-1}^k$$

$$\mathbf{m}_{t-1}^{i\downarrow} = \sum_{k \in \Omega_\downarrow(i)} \mathbf{h}_{t-1}^k \tag{14.29}$$

$$\mathbf{m}_{t-1}^i = \mathbf{m}_{t-1}^{i\uparrow} \oplus \mathbf{m}_{t-1}^{i\downarrow}.$$

In Eq 14.29, $\Omega_\uparrow(i)$ and $\Omega_\downarrow(i)$ represent all incoming and outgoing neightbors, respectively. As a result, $\mathbf{m}_{t-1}^{i\uparrow}$ and $\mathbf{m}_{t-1}^{i\downarrow}$ represent previous states from ncighbours with incoming and outgoing edges, respectively. $\mathbf{m}_{t-1}^i$ is the concatenation of $\mathbf{m}_{t-1}^{i\uparrow}$ and $\mathbf{m}_{t-1}^{i\downarrow}$.

$\mathbf{x}_t^i$ can be defined by similarly combining up information in both edge directions:

$$\mathbf{x}_t^{i\uparrow} = \sum_{k \in \Omega_\uparrow(i)} \left(\mathbf{W}_{x\uparrow} \Big(emb(v_k) \oplus emb\big(l(i,k)\big) \oplus emb(v_i) \Big) + \mathbf{b}_{x\uparrow} \right)$$

$$\mathbf{x}_t^{i\downarrow} = \sum_{k \in \Omega_\downarrow(i)} \left(\mathbf{W}_{x\downarrow} \Big(emb(v_k) \oplus emb\big(l(i,k)\big) \oplus emb(v_i) \Big) + \mathbf{b}_{x\downarrow} \right) \tag{14.30}$$

$$\mathbf{x}_t^i = \mathbf{x}_t^{i\uparrow} \oplus \mathbf{x}_t^{i\downarrow},$$

where $\mathbf{W}_{x\uparrow}, \mathbf{b}_{x\uparrow}, \mathbf{W}_{x\downarrow}, \mathbf{b}_{x\downarrow}$ are model parameters. Similar to Eq 14.28, $l(k,i)$ denotes the label of the edge from v_k to v_i.

More fine-grained control. The above model uses the standard LSTM_STEP function in Eq 14.6 for message passing. Inspired by child-sum tree LSTMs, we can also use a separate gate for controlling information flow from each neighbour individually. Exercise 14.11(b) discusses this in detail.

14.4.2 Graph Convolutional Neural Network (GCN)

The recurrent nature of RNNs makes them suitable for modelling the recurrent message passing process for GNNs. We have shown earlier that there is a connection between layers and time steps when discussing RNN, where different layers can be used to represent different time steps. As a consequence, we can also make use of multi-layer CNNs to model the recurrent information-exchange process. Given a node v_i, a graph convolutional neural network (GCN) uses a convolution function to calculate $\mathbf{h}_t^i$ based on $\mathbf{h}_{t-1}^i$. Assume that the context for information exchange is identical to the case of GRN in Section 14.4.1. We calculate $\mathbf{m}_t^i$ and $\mathbf{x}_t^i$ by using Eqs 14.27–14.28 or Eqs 14.29–14.30. The main difference between GCN and GRN is the way for updating node states. While GRN adopts LSTM operations (Eq 14.26), GCN can use a convolution function:

$$\mathbf{h}_t^i = \sigma(\mathbf{W}^m \mathbf{m}_{t-1}^i + \mathbf{W}^x \mathbf{x}_t^i + \mathbf{b}), \tag{14.31}$$

where $\mathbf{W}^m$, $\mathbf{W}^x$ and $\mathbf{b}$ are model parameters.

Differentiating edge labels. A variant of GCN collects information separately from different neighbours, using different weights for edges with different labels. Formally, denote the edge label between v_i and v_k as $l(i, k)$ and the edge direction between v_i and v_k as $dir(i, k)$. A GCN can be defined by replacing Eq 14.31 with:

$$\mathbf{h}_t^i = \sigma\left(\sum_{k \in \Omega(i)} \left(\mathbf{W}_{l(i,k),dir(i,k)}^m \mathbf{h}_{t-1}^k + \mathbf{W}_{l(i,k),dir(i,k)}^x \mathbf{x}_t^k + \mathbf{b}_{l(i,k),dir(i,k)} \right) \right)$$
$$\mathbf{x}_t^k = \left(emb(v_k) \oplus emb^e\left(l(i, k) \right) \oplus emb(v_i) \right), \tag{14.32}$$

where $\mathbf{W}_{l(i,k),dir(i,k)}^m$ are $|L| \times 2$ sets of model parameters to replace a single $\mathbf{W}^m$ in Eq 14.31. Similar extensions apply to $\mathbf{W}^x$ and $\mathbf{b}$. L is the set of edge labels.

Adding gates. One more variant of GCN adds a gate value to Eq 14.32 in order to control the amount of information passed from each $\mathbf{h}^k (k \in \Omega(i))$ to $\mathbf{h}^i$. In particular, using $|L| \times 2$ more sets of parameters $\mathbf{W}_{l(i,k),dir(i,k)}^g$ and $\mathbf{b}_{l(i,k),dir(i,k)}^g$, the value of a gate $\mathbf{g}_t^{i,k}$ can be defined as

$$\mathbf{g}_t^{i,k} = \sigma\left(\mathbf{W}_{l(i,k),dir(i,k)}^g \mathbf{h}_{t-1}^k + \mathbf{b}_{l(i,k),dir(i,k)}^g \right), \tag{14.33}$$

which is used to extend Eq 14.32 as follows:

$$\mathbf{h}_t^i = \sigma\left(\sum_{k \in \Omega(i)} \mathbf{g}_t^{i,k} \otimes \left(\mathbf{W}_{l(i,k),dir(i,k)}^m \mathbf{h}_{t-1}^k + \mathbf{W}_{l(i,k),dir(i,k)}^x \mathbf{x}_t^k + \mathbf{b}_{l(i,k),dir(i,k)} \right) \right). \tag{14.34}$$

14.4.3 Graph Attentional Neural Network

Graph attentional neural networks (GAT) are another variation of graph neural network, which uses attention functions for aggregating information from neighbour states at each recurrent step. Similar to CNNs, multiple layers of attention aggregation are used to reflect multiple recurrent time steps. In particular, for calculating $\mathbf{h}_t^i$ for v_t at the step t, we find a weighted sum of the neighbour previous states:

$$\mathbf{h}_t^i = \sum_{k \in \Omega(i)} \alpha_{ik} \mathbf{h}_{t-1}^k. \tag{14.35}$$

The weights α_{ik} above can be calculated by normalising a set of attention scores, each calculated using the previous hidden states $\mathbf{h}_{t-1}^i$ and $\mathbf{h}_{t-1}^k$:

$$s_{ik} = \sigma\left(\mathbf{W}(\mathbf{h}_{t-1}^i \oplus \mathbf{h}_{t-1}^k)\right)$$
$$\alpha_{ik} = \frac{\exp(s_{ik})}{\sum_{k' \in \Omega(i)} \exp(s_{ik'})}, \tag{14.36}$$

where $\mathbf{W}$ is a model parameter.

14.4.4 Feature Aggregation

Unlike tree LSTMs, for which the hidden state of the top-level node can be used for representing the whole tree, graph neural networks calculate a hidden state for each node in a graph structure. In order to obtain a single vector representation of the whole graph, we can add one aggregation layer on top of the final $\mathbf{h}_i$ ($i \in [1, \ldots, |V|]$). Pooling and attention aggregation are both feasible. For the latter, a query vector $\mathbf{q}$ is necessary as shown in Eq 14.11. This query vector can be a randomly initialised model parameter. Thus we obtain a text classifier that has a similar structure to Figure 13.3 in Chapter 13, but by replacing the sequence encoding layer with a graph encoding layer given a semantic graph structure.

14.5 Analysing Representation

As discussed in Chapter 13 and this chapter, the neural representation vector $\mathbf{h}$ for a text can contain automatic combinations of input features, capturing syntactic and semantic information. On the other hand, they are dynamically computed and not easily interpretable. There are two indirect ways to analyse learned representation vectors, which we discuss below.

First, visualisation is a qualitative method for analysing representation vectors. In particular, we want to project hidden representations into a two-dimensional figure to better understand their correlations. To this end, a useful tool is **t-distributed stochastic neighbour embedding** (**t-SNE**), which is a non-linear dimensionality reduction technique that aims to preserve the distance correlation between vectors in the original high-dimensional vector space and the projected two-dimensional space.

By examining the geometric correlation between vector representations of different inputs, we can gain knowledge about the characteristics of the representation vectors. For example, suppose that we use the text classifier shown in Figure 13.4 for sentiment classification. We can tell whether the hidden representation captures sentiment attributes over input texts by checking whether the hidden vectors for positive texts and negative texts are well separated in the vector space. Figure 14.8 shows the t-SNE visualisation of a set of documents through their hidden representations.

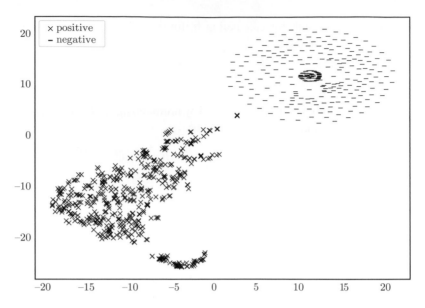

Figure 14.8 t-SNE visualisation of positive and negative documents.

We can see that positive documents and negative documents reside on different clusters in the vector space, which demonstrates that the vector representation captures sentiment information. We will see more examples of t-SNE visualisation in Chapter 17 for word embeddings.

Second, a quantitative method to analyse learned representations is to use **probing tasks**. Here probing tasks refers to auxiliary tasks that predict the features that we expect a learned representation to capture. For example, if we expect that a vector representation of texts contains sentiment features, we can add a sentiment prediction task as the probing task. Probing tasks can be achieved using the following procedure. (1) given a set of documents with gold-standard outputs (i.e., sentiment labels), we split the documents into training, development and test sets; (2) we run the representation model and dump the vector representation for each training and test instance; (3) we train a very simple classification model, such as an MLP with one or two layers, with the dumped representation vectors as inputs, and the probed task (e.g., sentiment classification) as the output; (4) the more accurate the trained simple model is, the more confident we are that the representation vectors contain relevant information.

14.6 More on Neural Network Training

As discussed in Chapter 13, neural network training can be much more challenging compared with the training of linear models. A key to successful representation learning is the optimisation technique. As the neural network structure becomes increasingly deep and complex, the standard SGD algorithm may not give the best optimisation towards a training objective. As shown in Chapter 13, several tricks can be added to SGD for better training. Now we discuss more alternatives to SGD for optimisation.

14.6.1 AdaGrad

As discussed earlier, for non-convex optimisation, we can set different learning rates for different parameters so that each can be better optimised. Intuitively, a slower learner is a better choice for frequently updated parameters and a faster learner is more suitable for parameters which are updated less frequently. AdaGrad is an optimisation algorithm that adaptively sets the learning rate for each parameter based on the gradient.

Formally, following Chapter 13, still denote the set of model parameters as Θ and the corresponding set of gradients as $\mathbf{g}$. For each parameter $\theta_i \in \Theta$ ($i \in [1, \ldots, |\Theta|]$), AdaGrad maintains an accumulated squared gradient sg_i from the start of training to estimate the per-parameter learning rate. The learning rate η_i for θ_i is inversely proportional to the root of sg_i. Intuitively, if the value of $sg_{t,i}$ is large, the value change along the ith dimension is quick, AdaGrad uses a small learning rate to carefully modify θ_i. When $sg_{t,i}$ is small, the learning rate is large, performing aggressive update. The update rules of AdaGrad can be written as

$$
\begin{aligned}
\mathbf{g}_t &= \frac{\partial L(\Theta_{t-1})}{\partial \Theta_{t-1}} \\
sg_{t,i} &= sg_{t-1,i} + g_{t,i}^2 \\
\theta_{t,i} &= \theta_{t-1,i} - \frac{\eta}{\sqrt{sg_{t,i} + \epsilon}} g_{t,i},
\end{aligned}
\tag{14.37}
$$

where L represents the loss, ϵ is a hyper-parameter for numerical stability. t represents the time step number in parameter update. $sg_{t,i}$ is the sum of squares of the gradient with respect to θ_i, namely $sg_{t,i} = \sum_{k-1}^{t} g_{k,i}^2$. Common hyper-parameter settings for AdaGrad are $\epsilon = 1e^{-8}$ and $\eta = 0.01$.

14.6.2 RMSProp

One problem of AdaGrad is that the learning rate decreases monotonically and aggressively, which can lead to early and suboptimal convergence. This is because the squares of the gradients are always positive and their sum does not decrease. Another problem of AdaGrad is that it is sensitive to initial gradients. If the initial gradients are too large, the learning rate decreases too quickly. RMSProp solves the problems of AdaGrad by using attention to a limited history window instead of all history gradients. The gradients far in the past are ignored. In this way, the accumulated gradient estimation does not increase monotonically. In addition, the initial gradient does not greatly affect the learning rate of future time steps. Formally, the update rules for RMSProp are

$$
\begin{aligned}
\mathbf{g}_t &= \frac{\partial L(\Theta_{t-1})}{\partial \Theta_{t-1}} \\
\mathbb{E}\,|\mathbf{g}^2|_t &= \rho\,\mathbb{E}\,|\mathbf{g}^2|_{t-1} + (1 - \rho)\mathbf{g}_t^2
\end{aligned}
$$

$$RMS|\mathbf{g}|_t = \sqrt{\mathbb{E}\,|\mathbf{g}^2|_t + \epsilon}$$

$$\Theta_t = \Theta_{t-1} - \frac{\eta}{RMS|\mathbf{g}|_t}\mathbf{g}_t. \qquad (14.38)$$

Equation 14.38 is written in a matrix-vector multiplicate form. Here $\mathbb{E}\,|\mathbf{g}^2|_t$ denotes the dynamic average of the squares of the gradients. ρ is a hyper-parameter, controlling the percentage of the previous average and the current gradient. In RMSProp, the root square $RMS|\mathbf{g}|_t$ replaces the role of $\sqrt{\mathbf{sg}_t + \epsilon}$ in AdaGrad. The remaining of the RMSProp updating rules are the same as AdaGrad. $\rho = 0.9$ and $\eta = 0.001$ are typical hyper-parameter settings.

14.6.3 AdaDelta

AdaDelta is similar to RMSProp in dealing with the learning rate decay problem of AdaGrad, with an exponentially running average of the square of history gradients. In addition, AdaDelta eliminates the need for manual selection of the initial learning rate η in AdaGrad. The key idea of AdaDelta is to make the parameter update $\Delta\Theta$ proportional to the parameter Θ itself, which allows larger updates for larger Θ_i components. In AdaGrad and RMSProp, the final update rules are both $\Theta_t = \Theta_{t-1} - \frac{\eta}{f(\mathbf{g}_t)}\mathbf{g}_t$. For RMSProp, both $\mathbf{g}_t$ and $f(\mathbf{g}_t)$ are proportional to Θ. As a result, $\Delta\Theta = \frac{\eta}{f(\mathbf{g}_t)}\mathbf{g}_t$ is not proportional to Θ. AdaDelta replaces η with an estimation of $\Delta\Theta_t$ at the tth timestep, which is proportional to Θ. In particular, it maintains the running average of the squares of the parameter update by defining

$$\mathbb{E}\,|\Delta\Theta^2|_t = \rho\,\mathbb{E}\,|\Delta\Theta^2|_{t-1} + (1-\rho)\Delta\Theta_t^2$$

$$RMS|\Delta\Theta|_t = \sqrt{\mathbb{E}\,|\Delta\Theta^2|_t + \epsilon}.$$

Here $\Delta\Theta$ denotes the parameter change and $\mathbb{E}\,|\Delta\Theta^2|$ represents the exponential running averaging of the squares of the parameter change. $RMS|\Delta\Theta|$ is proportional to Θ. Replacing the learning rate η using $RMS|\Delta\Theta|$ makes $\Delta\Theta$ proportional to the original parameter vector. However, $RMS|\Delta\Theta|_t$ remains unknown before calculating $\Delta\Theta_t$. AdaDelta approximates $RMS|\Delta\Theta|_t$ with the previous timestep estimations $RMS|\Delta\Theta|_{t-1}$ by assuming the $RMS(\cdot)$ function is locally smooth, resulting in the following update rule for $\Delta\Theta_t$,

$$\Delta\Theta_t = -\frac{RMS|\Delta\Theta|_{t-1}}{RMS|\mathbf{g}|_t}\mathbf{g}_t.$$

The numerator $RMS|\Delta\Theta|_{t-1}$ can be regarded as an acceleration term, summarising the history parameter update within a recent window. The computation of $\mathbf{g}_t$, $\mathbb{E}\,|\mathbf{g}^2|_t$ and $RMS|\mathbf{g}|_t$ is the same as that in RMSProp. The hyper-parameter ρ and ϵ can also be set to 0.9 and $1e^{-6}$, respectively.

14.6.4 Adam

Adam integrates the ideas of momentum SGD and RMSProp. In order to provide adaptive learning rates, Adam maintains the exponentially running averages of both the first-order moment and the second-order moment. Here moment is a mathematical tool for quantitative description of the shape of the gradient function. In particular, the first-order moment in Adam records the moving average of history gradients and the second-order moment in Adam accumulates the moving average of history squared gradients. Formally, the two gradient estimations are defined as

$$
\mathbf{g}_t = \frac{\partial L(\Theta_{t-1})}{\partial \Theta_{t-1}}
$$
$$
\mathbf{v}_t = \beta_1 \mathbf{v}_{t-1} + (1 - \beta_1)\mathbf{g}_t \tag{14.39}
$$
$$
\mathbb{E}\,|\mathbf{g}^2|_t = \beta_2\, \mathbb{E}\,|\mathbf{g}^2|_{t-1} + (1 - \beta_2)\mathbf{g}_t^2.
$$

In Eq 14.39, $\mathbf{v}$ is a first-order moment estimation, acting as the momentum. $\mathbb{E}\,|\mathbf{g}^2|$ is a second-order moment estimation, representing the running expectation of the squares of the gradients as in RMSProp. β_1 and β_2 are two hyper-parameters, which are both recommended to be set close to 1. For example, we can define $\beta_1 = 0.9$ and $\beta_2 = 0.999$. The initial values of $\mathbf{v}$ and $\mathbf{g}$ are both zeros. At time step t, $\mathbf{v}_t$ is given by

$$
\mathbf{v}_1 = \beta_1 \mathbf{v}_0 + (1 - \beta_1)\mathbf{g}_1 = (1 - \beta_1)\mathbf{g}_1
$$
$$
\mathbf{v}_2 = \beta_1 \mathbf{v}_1 + (1 - \beta_1)\mathbf{g}_2 = \beta_1(1 - \beta_1)\mathbf{g}_1 + (1 - \beta_1)\mathbf{g}_2
$$
$$
= (1 - \beta_1)(\beta_1 \mathbf{g}_1 + \mathbf{g}_2)
$$
$$
\cdots
$$
$$
\mathbf{v}_t = (1 - \beta_1)(\beta_1^{t-1}\mathbf{g}_1 + \beta_1^{t-2}\mathbf{g}_2 + \cdots + \mathbf{g}_t).
$$

$\mathbf{v}_t$ is a weighted sum of gradients within time step t. Now let us consider the sum of the weights of the gradients $\mathbf{g}_1, \mathbf{g}_2, \ldots, \mathbf{g}_t$, denoted as b_t:

$$
b_t = (1 - \beta_1)(\beta_1^{t-1} + \beta_1^{t-2} + \cdots + 1) = (1 - \beta_1)\sum_{i=1}^{t}\beta_1^{t-i}
$$
$$
= \sum_{i=1}^{t}\beta_1^{t-i} - \sum_{i=1}^{t}\beta_1^{t+1-i} \tag{14.40}
$$
$$
= 1 - \beta_1^t,
$$

which is not equal to 1. When β_1 is large and t is relatively small, b_t is also small. This indicates that Adam is biased towards zero parameter update in the beginning steps. For example, when $t = 1$ and $\beta = 0.9$, we have $\mathbf{v}_1 = 0.1\mathbf{g}_1$. To remedy these biases, Adam uses bias-corrected estimations:

$$
\hat{\mathbf{v}}_t = \frac{\mathbf{v}_t}{1 - \beta_1^t}. \tag{14.41}
$$

In this way, the sum of the weights of the gradients in $\mathbf{v}_t$ can be 1. Similarly, the bias-corrected estimation for the second-order moment is

$$
\hat{\mathbb{E}}|\mathbf{g}^2|_t = \frac{\mathbb{E}\,|\mathbf{g}^2|_t}{1 - \beta_2^t}. \tag{14.42}
$$

The final update rule for Adam applied to θ_t is similar to the one used in AdaGrad

$$\Theta_t = \Theta_{t-1} - \frac{\eta}{\sqrt{\hat{\mathbb{E}}|\mathbf{g}^2|_t + \epsilon}} \hat{\mathbf{v}}_t. \tag{14.43}$$

The default values for ϵ and η are $1e^{-8}$ and $1e^{-3}$ respectively.

14.6.5 Choosing a Training Method

The main difference between the adaptive learners is how they compute the per-parameter learning rate. The performance of these adaptive gradient optimisers can vary with different datasets and hyper-parameter choices. As a result, the choice of the optimiser itself can be viewed as a hyper-parameter, which is decided empirically. In practice, Adam is the most popular choice of the adaptive gradient optimisers. SGD with momentum discussed in Chapter 13 can often obtain good or even better performances with careful learning rate decay compared to Adam. On the other hand, Adam converges much faster than SGD with momentum.

Summary

In this chapter we have learned:

- recurrent neural network (RNN);
- neural attention and self-attention-network (SAN);
- child-sum tree LSTM and binary tree LSTM;
- graph recurrent network, graph convolutional network and graph attentional network;
- AdaGrad, RMSProp, AdaDelta and Adam.

Chapter Notes

Sutskever et al. (2014) discussed the use of RNN (Elman, 1990; Mikolov et al., 2010) for sentence representation. Attention (Bahdanau et al., 2015; Yang et al., 2016) has been widely used by NLP models for feature aggregation. LSTM (Hochreiter and Schmidhuber, 1997), GRU (Cho et al., 2014), CNN (LeCun et al., 1998; Kim, 2014) and SAN (Vaswani et al., 2017) are among the most frequently used sequence encoders in NLP (Ma and Hovy, 2016; Lample et al., 2016; Chung et al., 2014).

Tree LSTMs (Tai et al., 2015; Zhu et al., 2016) have been used for representing syntax for tasks such as relation extraction (Miwa and Bansal, 2016). DAG LSTMs have been used for directed acyclic graphs (Zhu et al., 2015; Peng et al., 2017) and character-word lattice (Chen et al., 2015; Zhang and Yang, 2018). Sperduti and Starita (1997) first applied neural networks to directed acyclic graphs, which motivated early studies on GNNs. The notion of graph neural networks was introduced by Gori et al. (2005), and further elaborated by Scarselli et al. (2008). GCN

(Niepert et al., 2016; Kipf and Welling, 2016) was an early and influential GNN model for NLP. It was used for semantic role labelling (Marcheggiani and Titov, 2017), text generation (Bastings et al., 2017), relation extraction (Zhang et al., 2018b) and many other tasks. GRN (Song et al., 2018; Beck et al., 2018) and GAT (Veličković et al., 2017; Xu et al., 2018) were introduced to the NLP field thereafter.

AdaGrad (Duchi et al., 2011), RMSProp (Tieleman and Hinton, 2012), AdaDelta (Zeiler, 2012) and Adam (Kingma and Ba, 2014) are commonly used optimisers for training neural NLP models.

Exercises

14.1 Specify BACKPROPAGATE($\mathbf{g}_t$) for LSTM steps in Eq 14.6, where $\mathbf{g}_t$ denotes the back-propagated gradient on $\mathbf{h}_t$. Compare the gradient with the RNN gradients. Discuss why LSTMs allow better back-propagation.

14.2 Formally specify bi-directional GRUs and a neural network with mulitple layers of bi-GRUs.

14.3 Recall the stacked BiLSTM method in Section 14.1.4. One alternative method does the concatenation of hidden vectors at each layer and then feeds the combined vectors as the inputs for the next layer. Formally, the second stacking method is given by

$$\mathbf{H}_c^0 = \mathbf{X}$$
$$\overrightarrow{\mathbf{H}}^1 = \overrightarrow{LSTM}_1(\mathbf{H}_c^0), \ \overleftarrow{\mathbf{H}}^1 = \overleftarrow{LSTM}_1(\mathbf{H}_c^0)$$
$$\mathbf{H}_c^1 = \overrightarrow{\mathbf{H}}^0 \oplus \overleftarrow{\mathbf{H}}^0 = [\overrightarrow{\mathbf{h}}_1^1 \oplus \overleftarrow{\mathbf{h}}_1^1; \overrightarrow{\mathbf{h}}_2^1 \oplus \overleftarrow{\mathbf{h}}_2^1; \dots; \overrightarrow{\mathbf{h}}_n^1 \oplus \overleftarrow{\mathbf{h}}_n^1]$$
$$\overrightarrow{\mathbf{H}}^2 = \overrightarrow{LSTM}_2(\mathbf{H}_c^1), \ \overleftarrow{\mathbf{H}}^2 = \overleftarrow{LSTM}_2(\mathbf{H}_c^1)$$
$$\mathbf{H}_c^2 = \overrightarrow{\mathbf{H}}^2 \oplus \overleftarrow{\mathbf{H}}^2 = [\overrightarrow{\mathbf{h}}_1^2 \oplus \overleftarrow{\mathbf{h}}_1^2; \overrightarrow{\mathbf{h}}_2^2 \oplus \overleftarrow{\mathbf{h}}_2^2; \dots; \overrightarrow{\mathbf{h}}_n^2 \oplus \overleftarrow{\mathbf{h}}_n^2]$$
$$\dots$$
$$\overrightarrow{\mathbf{H}}^l = \overrightarrow{LSTM}_l(\mathbf{H}_c^{l-1}), \ \overleftarrow{\mathbf{H}}^l = \overleftarrow{LSTM}_l(\mathbf{H}_c^{l-1})$$
$$\mathbf{H}_c^2 = \overrightarrow{\mathbf{H}}^l \oplus \overleftarrow{\mathbf{H}}^l = [\overrightarrow{\mathbf{h}}_1^l \oplus \overleftarrow{\mathbf{h}}_1^l; \overrightarrow{\mathbf{h}}_2^l \oplus \overleftarrow{\mathbf{h}}_2^l; \dots; \overrightarrow{\mathbf{h}}_n^l \oplus \overleftarrow{\mathbf{h}}_n^l].$$

Here $\mathbf{H}_c^i$ is the concatenation of the hidden vectors of the ith layer. In this way, the ith layer is aware of both the left-to-right and the right-to-left information of the $(i-1)$th layer. Compare the advantages and disadvantages of the two methods.

14.4 A document is composed by a sequence of sentences and a sentence consists of a sequence of words. Thus the document context contains a hierarichical structure.

(a) Define hierarichical LSTMs for documents.
(b) How can you encode a document by additionally using the attention mechanism?

14.5 Highway networks modify a feed-forward network by directly carrying information from the input to the output. Formally, for a given input vector $\mathbf{x}$, a feed-forward network calculates

$$FF(x) = g(\mathbf{W}^H \mathbf{x} + \mathbf{b}^H)$$

where $\mathbf{W}^H$ and $\mathbf{b}^H$ are model parameters and g is a non-linear function.

A highway network $\text{HIGHWAY}(\mathbf{x})$ is given by

$$\text{HIGHWAY}(\mathbf{x}) = \mathbf{t} \otimes g(\mathbf{W}^H \mathbf{x} + \mathbf{b}^H) + (1 - \mathbf{t}) \otimes \mathbf{x}$$
$$\mathbf{t} = \sigma(\mathbf{W}^T \mathbf{x} + \mathbf{b}^T), \tag{14.44}$$

where $\mathbf{W}^H$, $\mathbf{W}^T$, $\mathbf{b}^H$ and $\mathbf{b}^T$ are model parameters and g is a non-linear activation function (typically *ReLU*). Information flow between the original output $g(\mathbf{W}^H \mathbf{x} + \mathbf{b}_H)$ and the shortcut input is controlled by a *gate* $\mathbf{t}$, which is similar to a gate in LSTM models. $\mathbf{t}$ and $1 - \mathbf{t}$ control information flow between the original $FF(\mathbf{x})$ network and the shortcut from x. $\mathbf{t}$ is named the *transformation gate*, which reflects the mapping function of FF, and $1 - \mathbf{t}$ the *carrying gate*, allowing input information to be adaptively connected to the output in a direct way. During training, gradients from the output layer can be passed down to the input layers via the carrying gate. Therefore, highway networks are useful for training very deep networks. Derive back-propagation rules for highway networks. Compare highway networks with residual networks in Section 13.3.1. What are the similarities? What are the differences?

14.6 Dropout for RNNs. As discussed in Chapter 13 (Section 13.3.3), dropout is a useful training technique to reduce overfitting. There are two types of connections in RNNs, namely input-to-hidden connections and hidden-to-hidden connections. Applying dropout in Eq 13.21 to the input-to-hidden connections is safe. However, using the naïve dropout method for the hidden-to-hidden connections can cause damage to the model, which affects the representation ability of RNNs. **Variational dropout** is a variant of dropout for RNNs. It can be applied to both input-to-hidden connections and hidden-to-hidden connections. Different from the naïve dropout method, which uses *different* dropout masks for different inputs, variational dropout adopts *the same* masks for each timestep. Formally, variational dropout for RNN is given by

$$\mathbf{m}_x \sim \text{Bernoulli}(p_x) \quad \text{(masks for input-to-hidden connections)}$$
$$\mathbf{m}_h \sim \text{Bernoulli}(p_h) \quad \text{(masks for hidden-to-hidden connections)}$$
$$\hat{\mathbf{m}}_x = \frac{\mathbf{m}_x}{1 - p_x}, \ \hat{\mathbf{m}}_h = \frac{\mathbf{m}_h}{1 - p_h} \tag{14.45}$$
$$\hat{\mathbf{x}}_t = \mathbf{x}_t \otimes \hat{\mathbf{m}}_x, \ \hat{\mathbf{h}}_{t-1} = \mathbf{h}_{t-1} \otimes \hat{\mathbf{m}}_h$$
$$\mathbf{h}_t = RNN(\hat{\mathbf{x}}_t, \hat{\mathbf{h}}_{t-1}),$$

where p_x and p_h are the dropout probabilities for input-to-hidden connections and hidden-to-hidden connections, respectively. $\mathbf{m}_x$ and $\mathbf{m}_h$ are the masks for input-to-hidden connections and hidden-to-hidden connections across the time steps, respectively. Why does naïve dropout not work? How does variational dropout solve the issue?

14.7 Layer normalisation can be used for recurrent neural networks such as LSTMs and GRUs. For cxample, a layer normalised LSTM can be:

$$\begin{pmatrix} \mathbf{i}_t \\ \mathbf{f}_t \\ \mathbf{g}_t \\ \mathbf{o}_t \end{pmatrix} = LayerNorm(\mathbf{W}^x \mathbf{x}_t; \alpha_1, \beta_1) + LayerNorm(\mathbf{W}^2 \mathbf{h}_{t-1}; \alpha_2, \beta_2) + \mathbf{b}$$

$$\mathbf{c}_t = \sigma(\mathbf{i}_t) \otimes \tanh(\mathbf{g}_t) + \sigma(\mathbf{f}_t) \otimes \mathbf{c}_{t-1}$$
$$\mathbf{o}_t = \sigma(\mathbf{o}_t) \otimes \tanh(LayerNorm(\mathbf{c}_t; \alpha_3, \beta_3)),$$

where three *LayerNorm* functions with different parameters are applied. Can you apply *LayerNorm* to self-attention network?

14.8 Specify the back-propagation gradients of dot-product attention, scaled dot-product attention, general attention and additive attention with respect to the input vectors and parameter matrices/vectors, respectively.

14.9 Consider again Eq 14.16. Can you think of alternative methods for calculating s_i? What are their relative advantages?

14.10 On tree-structured LSTM:

(a) For both child-sum tree LSTMs and binary tree LSTMs, discuss different ways to calculate the hidden and cell states for leaf nodes, setting necessary model parameters.
(b) Design a child-sum tree LSTM for a constituent tree. What is the main difference from the dependency-tree child-sum tree LSTM in Section 14.3.1? What do you think is the most suitable input value $\mathbf{x}_t$ to each node?
(c) Extend the binary tree LSTM in Section 14.3.2 for handling unary-branching nodes.
(d) Extend a binary tree LSTM to a more general N-ary tree LSTM. Can your model handle cases where nodes can have varying number of child nodes? (Hint: a vector can be made $\vec{0}$ for non-existent nodes.)
(e) Extend the child-sum tree LSTM in Section 14.3.1 to DAG LSTM, which can handle DAG structures such as Figure 14.7(a). (Hint: tree LSTMs extend sequence LSTMs by allowing more than one incoming edge for each node. DAG LSTMs further extend tree LSTMs by allowing multiple outgoing edges. How can such edges be handled?)

14.11 On graph neural network:

(a) We have seen a graph recurrent neural network formulation by extending LSTM in Section 14.4.1. Can you design a graph neural network by extending GRU discussed in Chapter 13?
(b) Extend the graph recurrent neural network discussed in Section 14.4.1, by extending the standard LSTM step, using a separate gate to control messages from each neighbour. Can edge information be integrated through this channel too?

(c) Graphs include trees and sequences. Thus in theory, GNNs can be used to represent trees and sequences also. Discuss how multi-layer CNNs and SANs can be viewed as forms of GCNs and GATs, respectively. What are the graph structures?

(d) Equation 14.35 considers only the neighbour node previous states when calculating the hidden states for a node in GAT. Design a version that also includes the previous state of the node itself.

(e) Discuss possible ways for representing a text document using GNN. For instance, a document can be viewed as a flat sequence of words. Alternatively, it can be viewed as a sequence of sentences, where each sentence can be represented as a vector. A sequence network can be used to integrate sentence-level information. Discourse relations can be added between sentences. Discuss graph structures for representing documents. Add entity, coreference and other features that you can think of by defining nodes and edges.

14.12 We have learned several methods for representing structures. Now consider the case where there are multiple syntactic structures and semantic structures available for the sentence, such as constituent trees, dependency trees and AMR graphs. How can a representation be learnt jointly for all the structures and the original sequence? Think of several alternative methods and compare their relative advantages.

14.13 AdaMax. Adam calculates the second-order statistics using the L_2 norm (Eq 14.39). AdaMax replaces the L_2 norm in Adam with the L_∞ norm of history gradients. Formally, AdaMax cancels out $\hat{\mathbb{E}}|g^2|_t$ and introduces $\mathbf{n}_t$ to record the L_∞ norm. The updating rule of AdaMax is given by

$$\mathbf{n}_t = \max(\beta_2 \mathbf{n}_{t-1}, |\mathbf{g}_t|)$$
$$\Theta_t = \Theta_{t-1} - \frac{\eta}{\mathbf{n}_t + \epsilon}\hat{\mathbf{v}}_t. \tag{14.46}$$

Here $\hat{\mathbf{v}}_t$ is defined in the same way as Adam. Compare AdaMax with Adam with regard to complexity and optimisation effectiveness.

15 Neural Structured Prediction

We have seen neural network models for text classification in Chapters 13 and 14. Compared with discrete statistical text classifiers in Chapters 3 and 4, neural classifiers differ mainly in the feature representation – instead of a high-dimensional hard-coded sparse vector, a low-dimensional dense vector is dynamically calculated given word embeddings for representing the input text, which can capture deep semantic information. The output layers are identical in discrete linear models and neural models, as discussed in Section 13.2.

Chapters 8 to 11 showed discriminative linear models for various structured prediction tasks, including sequence segmentation, sequence labelling and tree prediction. For structured prediction tasks, discrete statistical models rely heavily on features that represent the *output*, so that structure can be scored according to explicit patterns. In contrast, the strong *input* representation power of neural models allow highly lightweight output representation: they enable the scoring of structures by scoring highly local components individually. We show in this chapter how graph-based (Chapters 8–10) and transition-based (Chapter 11) neural models can be built in this spirit. Towards the end of the chapter, we show for both types of methods how to further integrate representation of output structures on top of input representations.

15.1 Local Graph-Based Models

Discrete structured prediction models can be seen as natural extensions of discrete multi-class text classifiers, both of which score input-output pairs by extracting features for representing their characteristics (Chapter 3). Before building a neural structured prediction model, let us recall the neural multi-class classification model in Chapter 13. In particular, we used an output layer with a *softmax* activation function for calculating the distribution of output class labels, given a hidden input representation vector. Intuitively, the same principle can be applied for *local* sequence labelling also: given the hidden representation of a word in a sentential context (e.g., the hidden state of a RNN), an output layer can be added for predicting the local output label. Going one step further, the same principle can be adapted for handling structures beyond sequences.

Interestingly, for multi-class classification, we have seen at the end of Section 13.1.1 that a log-linear model (Chapter 3) can also be viewed as a multi-dimensional perceptron output layer with *softmax* activation on top of a vector representation of the input. Therefore, a multi-layer perceptron classifier (Chapter 13) differs from a discrete log-linear model only in the input representation. For a linear structured prediction model, however, we have seen in Chapter 7 that a local model based on the input representation alone, as we consider here for neural structured

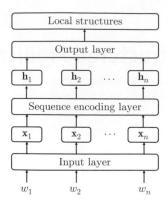

Figure 15.1 A general network structure for neural structured prediction.

prediction, does not give competitive performance – features need to be defined for representing inter-correlations between output sub structures also. In contrast, for a neural model, a strong representation of the input allows local decisions to give highly accurate structures, with efficient greedy search decoding.

We introduce two general approaches to local neural structured prediction, namely a graph-based method (this section) and a transition-based method (Section 15.2). Their discrete linear model counterparts are discussed in Chapters 8–10 and Chapter 11, respectively. In particular, the former decomposes an output structure to atomic or small local components, independently predicting each local structure, and the latter makes a sequence of state transition decisions, each building a small incremental part of the output. Similar to Part II of the book, we take sequence and tree structures for discussing structured prediction.

Local graph-based models. As shown in Figure 15.1, the typical structure of a local neural graph-based model consists of three main layers, including an input layer, a sequence encoding layer and an output layer. Given an input sentence $W_{1:n} = w_1, w_2, \ldots, w_n$, the input layer calculates a representation $\mathbf{x}_i$ for each word w_i ($i \in [1, \ldots, n]$). The sequence encoding layer learns more contextualised representations $\mathbf{h}_1, \ldots, \mathbf{h}_n$ given $\mathbf{x}_1, \ldots, \mathbf{x}_n$, through the use of network layers such as bi-directional LSTM and self-attention network, as discussed in Chapter 14. The output layer makes local predictions, where label sequences can be broken down into individual labels, dependency trees can be broken into individual arcs, and constituent trees into individual spans.

15.1.1 Sequence labelling

Given an input sentence $W_{1:n} = w_1, w_2, \ldots, w_n$, the output for **sequence labelling** can be denoted as $T_{1:n} = t_1, t_2, \ldots, t_n$, where t_i is the output label for w_i, $i \in [1, \ldots, n]$. We introduce each layer below according to Figure 15.1.

Input layer. The input layer can simply represent each word w_i using its embedding $emb(w_i)$. However, for tasks such as POS-tagging, morphological features can also be a useful source of information. For example, prefix and suffix patterns have been used as a typical feature in statistical models, as shown in Table 8.1. For neural sequence labelling, such information can be represented by using a neural network to encode the character sequence of a word. This can be done in two steps, namely a character embedding step and a character sequence encoding step.

Character-enriched word representation. First, denote $w_i = C^i_{1:|w_i|} = c^i_1, c^i_2, \ldots, c^i_{|w_i|}$, where c^i_j is a character in the word, $|w_i|$ is the number of characters in w_i and $j \in [1, \ldots, |w_i|]$. Each c^i_j can be represented using a **character embedding** vector $emb^c(c^i_j)$, obtained by using a lookup table $E_c \in \mathbb{R}^{K_c \times |C|}$. E_c consists of $|C|$ columns, each containing an embedding vector of K_c dimensions, where C represents the set of characters. E_c is typically randomly initialised as a part of the model parameters.

Second, the character sequence $C^i_{1:|w_i|}$ can be represented using a neural network *encoder* for sequence structures, such as CNN or LSTM:

$$\mathbf{x}^c_{w_i} = [emb^c(c^i_1); \ldots; emb^c(c^i_{|w_i|})]$$
$$chr(w_i) = \text{ENCODER}(\mathbf{x}^c_{w_i}). \tag{15.1}$$

The character encoder parameters, including E_c, can be fine-tuned during model training. The resulting hidden vector $chr(w_i)$ contains dense spelling information useful for the end-task. It can be concatenated with the word embedding of w_i for a final representation of the word:

$$\mathbf{x}_i = chr(w_i) \oplus emb(w_i), \tag{15.2}$$

where $\oplus$ denotes vector concatenation.

Sequence representation layer. As shown in Figure 14.1(a), on top of the sequence of input vectors $\mathbf{X}_{1:n} = \mathbf{x}_1, \mathbf{x}_2, \ldots, \mathbf{x}_n$, a sequence encoder network can be used for extracting dense sentence-level features, deriving a sequence of vectors $\mathbf{H}_{1:n} = \mathbf{h}_1, \mathbf{h}_2, \ldots, \mathbf{h}_n$, each corresponding to an input word given its sentential context. For example, if bi-directional LSTM is used, we have:

$$\mathbf{H}_{1:n} = BiLSTM(\mathbf{X}_{1:n}). \tag{15.3}$$

As discussed in Chapter 14, each bi-directional hidden state $\mathbf{h}_i = [\overrightarrow{\mathbf{h}}_i; \overleftarrow{\mathbf{h}}_i]$ contains contextual information over the whole sentence. In particular, $\overrightarrow{\mathbf{h}}_i$ is the left-to-right LSTM hidden state, which contains context from $w_1, \ldots, w_{i-1}$, and $\overleftarrow{\mathbf{h}}_i$ is the right-to-left LSTM hidden state, which contains context from $w_{i+1} \ldots w_n$.

Multiple layers of sequence encoders can be used, with the hidden vectors $\mathbf{h}_i$ from one layer being used as input to a subsequent layer. The number of layers can be set empirically according to a development dataset. Each layer can have a different set of model parameters, or share the same LSTM parameters. This can also be determined empirically.

Output layer. For the local model, the output tag t_i for each word w_i is decided individually by adding a classification layer on $\mathbf{h}_i$:

$$\mathbf{o}_i = \mathbf{W}\mathbf{h}_i + \mathbf{b}$$
$$\mathbf{p}_i = softmax(\mathbf{o}_i), \tag{15.4}$$

where $\mathbf{W}$ and $\mathbf{b}$ are model parameters shared by all the words. $\mathbf{p}_i$ gives a local label probability distribution over the label set L for the input word w_i. In particular, the jth element in $\mathbf{p}_i$, denoted as $\mathbf{p}_i[\ell_j]$, represents $P(t_i = \ell_j | W_{1:n})$, $\ell_j \in L$.

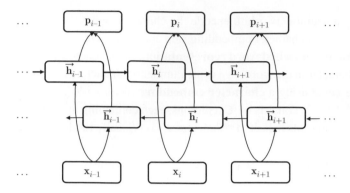

Figure 15.2 A one-layer local sequence labeller using a BiLSTM encoder.

The structure of the model above using a single-layer BiLSTM is shown in Figure 15.2.

Training. Given a set of gold-standard samples $\{(W_i, T_i)\}|_{i=1}^{N}$, where $W_i = w_1^i, w_2^i, \ldots, w_n^i$ denotes a sentence and $T_i = t_1^i, t_2^i, \ldots, t_n^i$ denotes the corresponding gold-standard label sequence, the training objective can be to minimise the negative log-likelihood of each local label. The loss is thus:

$$L = - \sum_{i}^{N} \sum_{j=1}^{|W_i|} \log(\mathbf{p}_j^i[t_j^i]) \tag{15.5}$$

where $\mathbf{p}_j^i[t_j^i]$ represents $P(t_j^i | W_i)$ as given by the model in Eq 15.4.

We can use SGD and its variants discussed in Section 13.3 and Section 14.6 in the previous chapters for optimisation. In particular, for each training instance, local gradients are calculated for each model parameter using back-propagation. Different from classification tasks, there are multiple outputs on the sequence encoder. As shown in Figure 15.2, for each hidden state $\overrightarrow{\mathbf{h}}_i$, there are back-propagated loss values from both $\mathbf{p}_i$ and $\overrightarrow{\mathbf{h}}_{i+1}$. The input nodes $\mathbf{x}_i$ similarly receive back-propagated gradients from two sources, namely $\overrightarrow{\mathbf{h}}_i$ and $\overleftarrow{\mathbf{h}}_i$. We discussed the case for the input nodes $\mathbf{x}_i$ of BiLSTM inputs in Section 14.1. The hidden nodes $\overrightarrow{\mathbf{h}}_i$ (and $\overleftarrow{\mathbf{h}}_i$) here should be processed similarly – the two loss values from $\mathbf{p}_i$ and $\overrightarrow{\mathbf{h}}_{i+1}$ should be summed up as input to BACKPROPAGATE to the hidden layer of the left-to-right LSTM layer. To avoid overfitting, L_2-normalisation and dropout discussed in the previous chapter can be applied to the input layer, the sequence encoding layer and the output layer. Other training techniques such as gradient clipping and layer normalisation can be used according to development performance.

15.1.2 Dependency Parsing

We first discussed dependency parsing in Chapter 11, where transition-based models were used. Here let us discuss a graph-based neural model. Similar to Chapter 11, assume that POS-tagging is taken as a pre-processing step. An example is shown in Figure 15.3(a). Given an input sentence $S = (w_1, t_1), (w_2, t_2), \ldots, (w_n, t_n)$, where w_i denotes the ith word and t_i denotes the ith POS-tag ($i \in$

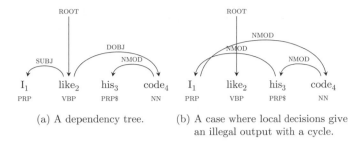

(a) A dependency tree.   (b) A case where local decisions give an illegal output with a cycle.

Figure 15.3 Dependency parsing examples.

$[1, \ldots, n])$, the output can be denoted as $\{(i, h_i, l_i)\}|_{i=1}^{n}$, where $h_i \in [0, \ldots, n]$ represents the head index of w_i, and l_i represents the dependency label of the arc from w_{h_i} to w_i. As discussed in Chapter 11 and shown in Figure 15.3(a), dependency arcs in a sentence form a tree structure, where there is only one root word in the sentence, for which the head index is 0 (i.e., $w_0 =$ ROOT is a pseudo root word).

We build a local model following the structure of Figure 15.1. Compared with the POS-tagging model in Section 15.1.1, the dependency parser differs mainly in the output layer.

Input and sequence encoding layers. The input layer computes a sequence of word representations $\mathbf{X}_{1:n} = \mathbf{x}_1, \mathbf{x}_2, \ldots, \mathbf{x}_n$. Given the input POS labels $T_{1:n} = t_1 t_2, \ldots, t_n$, the word representations can be additionally augmented with POS information. In particular, we can have:

$$\mathbf{x}_i = emb(w_i) \oplus chr(w_i) \oplus emb^p(t_i), \tag{15.6}$$

where similar to character embeddings, emb^p is calculated according to a **POS embedding** table, which can be randomly initialised as a part of the model parameters. Similar to word embedding tables and character embedding tables, a POS embedding table contains $|L|$ columns, where each column is the embedding of a specific POS-tag $\ell \in L$. L is the POS-tag set.

Following Figure 15.1, on top of $\mathbf{X}_{1:n}$, a sequence encoding neural network is then used to induce the representation of each word under its sentence-level context. Still using BiLSTM as an example, we obtain a sequence of hidden states $\mathbf{H}_{1:n} = \mathbf{h}_1, \mathbf{h}_2, \ldots, \mathbf{h}_n$ via:

$$\mathbf{H}_{1:n} = BiLSTM(\mathbf{X}_{1:n}). \tag{15.7}$$

Similar to sequence labelling, a number of BiLSTM layers can be stacked for empirically optimal results.

Output layer. The output task can be defined as finding the most likely head word for each word w_i in the sentence. To this purpose, a score can be computed between w_i and each w_j ($j \in [0, ..., n], j \neq i$), which are represented by $\mathbf{h}_i$ and $\mathbf{h}_j$, respectively.

In particular, the score of $h_i = j$ can be computed as follows:

$$s_{i,j} = \mathbf{h}_i^T \mathbf{U} \mathbf{h}_j + \mathbf{v}^T(\mathbf{h}_i \oplus \mathbf{h}_j), \tag{15.8}$$

where $\mathbf{h}_i^T \mathbf{U} \mathbf{h}_j$ is a bi-affine tensor product, and $\mathbf{v}^T(\mathbf{h}_i \oplus \mathbf{h}_j)$ is a standard vector dot product. $\mathbf{U}$ and $\mathbf{v}$ are model parameters. Due to the use of the bi-affine scoring function, the local parser can be referred to as a **bi-affine parser**. For each word w_i, $s_{i,j}$ ($j \in [0, \ldots, n], j \neq i$) can be normalised into a distribution $\mathbf{p}_i^{arc} \in \mathbb{R}^{n+1}$, where each dimension $\mathbf{p}_i^{arc}[j]$ indicates the probability $P(h_i = j)$:

$$
\begin{aligned}
\mathbf{o}_i^{arc} &= \langle s_{i,1}, s_{i,2}, \ldots, s_{i,n} \rangle \\
\mathbf{p}_i^{arc} &= softmax(\mathbf{o}_i^{arc}).
\end{aligned} \tag{15.9}
$$

The most likely head h_i can then be calculated as:

$$
h_i = \arg \max_h \mathbf{p}_i^{arc}[h]. \tag{15.10}
$$

The set of arcs consisting of the most likely head for each word can be used directly as the output. However, they do not necessarily correspond to a projective dependency tree structure. As shown in Figure 14.5, the set of heads for each word can make a graph with cycles. We can obtain an unlabelled dependency tree with proper constraints by using the maximum spanning tree (MST) algorithm, which is a greedy algorithm to find a highest-scored spanning tree given arc scores in a fully connected graph. See Exercise 15.3 for more discussion.

So far we have obtained an unlabelled dependency tree. The last step is to assign a dependency arc label to each arc in the tree. This task can be achieved using a bi-affine classifier given a word w_i and the predicted head w_{h_i}:

$$
\begin{aligned}
\mathbf{o}_i^{label} &= \mathbf{h}_i^T \mathbf{U}' \mathbf{h}_{h_i} + \mathbf{V}'(\mathbf{h}_i \oplus \mathbf{h}_{h_i}) + \mathbf{b}' \\
\mathbf{p}_i^{label} &= softmax(\mathbf{o}_i^{label})
\end{aligned} \tag{15.11}
$$

where $\mathbf{U}', \mathbf{V}'$ and $\mathbf{b}'$ are model parameters. $\mathbf{p}_i^{label}[l_i]$ represents the probability distribution of l_i on the arc from w_{h_i} to w_i, according to which the most likely label can be chosen.

Training. Given a set of training data $D = \{(S_i, T_i)\}|_{i=1}^N$, where S_i dentoes the ith input sentence, and T_i denotes its dependency tree structure, we use a cross-entropy loss function to train the bi-affine parser. $T_i = \{(j, h_j^i, l_j^i)\}|_{j=1}^{|S_i|}$, where h_j^i denotes the head index of w_j^i and l_j^i denotes the label of the arc from $w_{h_j^i}^i$ to w_j^i. Given each input S_i, the dependency arcs $h_1^i, \ldots, h_{|S_i|}^i$ and their labels $l_1^i, \ldots, l_{|S_i|}^i$ are predicted separately, using Eq 15.10 and Eq 15.11, respectively. Thus there is a loss value for each task. Training for the dependency arc and dependency arc label prediction tasks can be performed jointly for each training instance. We minimise the accumulated loss

$$
L = - \sum_i^N \sum_{j=1}^{|W_i|} \left(\log \left((\mathbf{p}_j^i)^{arc}[h_j^i] \right) + \log \left((\mathbf{p}_j^i)^{label}[l_j^i] \right) \right).
$$

Optimisation is similar to text classifiers and the POS-tagger. When calculating back-propagated gradients for each training instance, each hidden vector receives multiple gradients, including arc loss when $\mathbf{h}_i$ is the head or the dependent (Eq 15.8), and arc label loss when $\mathbf{h}_i$ is the head or the dependent (Eq 15.11). Such signals are accumulated before being back-propagated. They allow the neural network to learn an input representation that integrates information from different perspectives for mutual benefit.

Representation learning with multi-task information. As mentioned earlier, two different types of outputs are produced on a shared hidden representation $\mathbf{H}_{1:n} = \mathbf{h}_1, \ldots, \mathbf{h}_n$, namely arc prediction and arc label prediction. Thus the hidden representation should contain both arc information and arc label information, possibly with necessary interaction features. This is enabled by

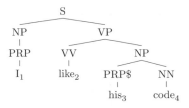

Figure 15.4 Constituent parsing example.

loss from both the arc and arc label output layers onto the shared hidden representations during training, which mix into the representation network layers during back-propagation. The structure is called **multi-task learning** by **parameter sharing**, which will be discussed further in Chapter 17. Neural representation gives an advantage to multi-task learning. Note that when compared with joint models discussed in Chapter 11, multi-task learning benefits only from information integration. However, our local parser does not predict the arc and label structures jointly, and therefore can still suffer from error propagation in a pipeline, where incorrectly predicted arcs lead to lower labelled arc scores.

15.1.3 Constituent Parsing

We have discussed both graph-based models (Chapter 10) and transition-based models (Chapter 11) for constituent parsing. Here let us discuss a neural graph-based constituent parser. Similar to the dependency parser in the previous section, assume that POS-tagging is performed as a pre-processing step. Given an input sentence $S = (w_1, t_1), (w_2, t_2), \ldots, (w_n, t_n)$, where w_i denotes the ith word and t_i denotes the POS tag of the ith word, the output constituent tree can be factored as a set of triples $T = \{(b, e, c)\}$. For each triple, $1 \leq b \leq n$, $b \leq e \leq n$, and c denotes the constituent label of the text span $W_{b:e} = w_b \ldots w_e$. An example is shown in Figure 15.4. Similar to Chapter 10, we assume that the constituent trees are binarised. In addition, unary nodes are collapsed by merging the constituent labels. For example, if a text span corresponds to the unary rule $S \rightarrow VP$, we merge the rule into a single constituent label $S|VP$. If a span in the sentence does not correspond to a constituent, the corresponding label is set to a special label ϕ. There are $\frac{n(n+1)}{2}$ spans to be considered in total.

Input layer. The input layer consists of three types of representation vectors, including word embeddings, char-based representation vectors and POS-tag embeddings. The word embedding $emb(w_i)$ is obtained by using a lookup table. The char-based representations are given by Eq 15.1. This time suppose that a BiLSTM encoder is used, where the last output vectors of the left-to-right and right-to-left char LSTMs are $\mathbf{ch}_i^l$ and $\mathbf{ch}_i^r$, respectively. The POS-tag embeddings $emb^p(t_i)$ are obtained by using a lookup table $E_p \in \mathbb{R}^{d_p \times |L|}$, where $|L|$ is the number of POS tags and d_p is the dimension of POS embeddings. The final input vector $\mathbf{x}_i$ is given by

$$chr(w_i) = \tanh(\mathbf{W}_e^{char}\mathbf{ch}_i^l + \mathbf{W}_r^{char}\mathbf{ch}_i^r + \mathbf{b}^{char})$$
$$\mathbf{x}_i = emb(w_i) \oplus chr(w_i) \oplus emb^p(t_i),$$

where $\mathbf{W}_e^{char}$, $\mathbf{W}_r^{char}$ and $\mathbf{b}^{char}$ are model parameters.

Sequence encoding layer. Similar to dependency parsing, bi-directional LSTM layers are used to extract sentence-level features. The output hidden vectors of the left-to-right LSTM and the right-to-left LSTM for $w_1, w_2, \ldots, w_n$ are denoted as $\overrightarrow{\mathbf{h}}_1, \overrightarrow{\mathbf{h}}_2, \ldots, \overrightarrow{\mathbf{h}}_n$ and $\overleftarrow{\mathbf{h}}_1, \overleftarrow{\mathbf{h}}_2, \ldots, \overleftarrow{\mathbf{h}}_n$, respectively. We further calculate a representation vector $\mathbf{s}[b, e]$ of the span $W_{b:e} = w_b \ldots w_e$ by simply concatenating the bi-directional output vectors at the input word b and the input word e:

$$\mathbf{s}[b, e] = \overrightarrow{\mathbf{h}}_b \oplus \overleftarrow{\mathbf{h}}_b \oplus \overrightarrow{\mathbf{h}}_e \oplus \overleftarrow{\mathbf{h}}_e. \tag{15.12}$$

$\mathbf{s}[b, e]$ contains information about the span $W_{b:e}$ because the hidden vectors $\overrightarrow{\mathbf{h}}_b, \overrightarrow{\mathbf{h}}_e, \overleftarrow{\mathbf{h}}_b$ and $\overleftarrow{\mathbf{h}}_e$ encode the sequential context for all the words between w_b and w_e. Back-propagation training allows $\mathbf{s}[b, e]$ to automatically capture relevant features from these words for optimising the parser.

Output Layer. $\mathbf{s}[b, e]$ is then passed through a non-linear transformation layer and the probability distribution $P(c|S, b, e)$ is given by

$$\begin{aligned} \mathbf{h}[b, e] &= \tanh(\mathbf{W}^h \mathbf{s}[b, e] + \mathbf{b}^h) \\ \mathbf{o}[b, e] &= \mathbf{W}^o \mathbf{h}[b, e] + \mathbf{b}^o \\ \mathbf{p}[b, e] &= softmax(\mathbf{o}[b, e]), \end{aligned} \tag{15.13}$$

where $\mathbf{p}[b, e][c]$ represents $P(c|S, b, e)$, which is the probability of the span $W_{b:e}$ having label c. $\mathbf{W}^h, \mathbf{b}^h, \mathbf{W}^o$ and $\mathbf{b}^o$ are model parameters. $c = \phi$ if the span $W_{b:e}$ is not a constituent.

Decoding. For decoding, one simple method is to assign every span a label according to the label probability distribution defined in Eq 15.13 using the argmax operation. However, similar to the case of dependency parsing, this decoding method cannot ensure that the result is a valid constituent tree. Instead, we can use the CKY algorithm discussed in Chapter 10 for decoding. In particular, we follow the local dependency parser in Section 15.1.2 by first performing unlabelled constituent parsing, and then assigning a constituent label on each constituent span. For the first task, we calculate the probability of a span $W_{b:e}$ being a constituent span, denoted as $y_{b,e} = 1$, using

$$\begin{aligned} P(y = 1|S, b, e) &= \sum_{c, c \neq \phi} P(c|S, b, e) \\ P(y = 0|S, b, e) &= P(\phi|S, b, e), \end{aligned}$$

where c denotes a constituent label. In this equation, the probability of a span being a constituent span takes all possible syntactic labels into consideration. The span production probability for the rule $W_{b:e} \to W_{b:b'-1} W_{b':e}$ given by the binary classification model is

$$P(r|S, b, e) = P(y = 1|S, b, b' - 1) P(y = 1|S, b', e).$$

Using the rule production probabilities, we can find the optimal unlabelled binarised parse tree using the CKY algorithm. Note that since the model is local and does not involve grammar rules, this model can be regarded as a 0th-order constituent tree model, which is the most *local*. As a result, a simple version of the CKY algorithm can be derived (see Exercise 15.5). All structural relations in a constituent tree must be implicitly captured by the BiLSTM encoder over the sentence alone. After obtaining the unlabelled binaried parsing tree, the constituent label for each span $W_{b:e}$ in the tree can be calculated as:

$$\hat{c} = \arg\max_{c, c \neq \phi} P(c|S, b, e). \tag{15.14}$$

Training. Given a set of sentences with manually labelled constituent trees $D = \{(S_i, T_i)\}|_{i=1}^{N}$, where $S_i = (w_1^i, t_1^i), \ldots, (w_{|S_i|}^i, t_{|S_i|}^i)$ and $T_i = \{(b_k^i, e_k^i, l_{b_k^i, e_k^i}^i)\}|_{k=1}^{|T_i|}$, training loss is to minimise the negative log-likelihood of the label distributions

$$L = -\sum_{i=1}^{N} \sum_{1 \leq b \leq |S_i|, b \leq e \leq |S_i|} \log P(c|S, b, e),$$

where the inside sum traverses over all the spans for a single sentence. Here $c = l_{b,e}$ if $(b, e, c) \in T_i$ and ϕ otherwise. The outside sum considers all the training sentences. Given the calculation of $P(c|S, b, e)$ in Eq 15.13, back-propagation training can be performed.

15.1.4 Comparison with Linear Models

The local neural models above do not learn explicit correlations between output sub structures, such as the dependency between two consecutive POS tags, and the dependency between two sibling dependency arcs. However, they empirically outperform discrete linear models. How is this achieved? Generally speaking, knowledge on interdependencies between output sub structures is gained implicitly during representation learning. In particular, the local output layers on different sub structures share the same sequence encoding layer. During training, loss back-propagated from different local predictions are mixed in the encoding layer, where they interact and enable the network to learn a representation of the input that implicitly contains interdependent sub structure information. The representation is global in the sense that it covers the hidden state for every input word. A local model enjoys the flexibility of dealing with arbitrary output structures easily, as compared to a structured model with dynamic programming decoding such as CRF. So far we have used sequences and trees to discuss structured prediction in the book. On the other hand, many structured prediction problems discussed in Chapter 1 involve more general graph structures. Exercise 15.4 discusses building a local neural model for relation extraction.

The strong representation power endows a neural model with better capabilities to fit a set of training data, yet can also lead to strong overfitting, reducing the generalisation power. Techniques such as $L2$ normalisation and dropout can be useful to address this issue. In addition, compared with a discrete linear model, which uses directly interpretable feature patterns to score the output, neural structured prediction models are relatively less interpretable, which is a disadvantage.

15.2 Local Transition-Based Models

As first discussed in Chapter 11, a transition-based model for structured prediction casts the output-building process into a state transition process, where each *state* represents a partially

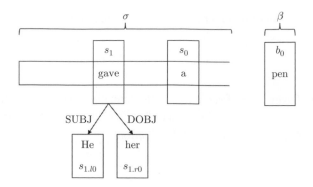

Figure 15.5 A state in arc-standard transition-based dependency parsing.

constructed output and transition *actions* represent incremental steps for building structures. Given a specific input, the start state represents an empty output, a terminal state corresponds to a full output structure, and the role of a model is to predict a sequence of transition actions for finding the most likely output structure. A neural transition-based model can be built by adapting a statistical counterpart, using neural feature representations and a network for scoring transition actions.

Take dependency parsing for example, which was first discussed in Section 11.3. Here we briefly review the method using the arc-standard parser (Section 11.3.1). Formally, denote each state as $s = (\sigma, \beta, A)$, where $\sigma = [\ldots, s_1, s_0]$ and $\beta = [b_0, b_1, \ldots]$ represent the stack of partially built output and buffer of next incoming words, respectively. A represents the set of dependency arcs that has been recognised. An example state during the parsing of "*He gave her a pen*" is shown in Figure 15.5, where σ=[gave, a], β=[pen] and A={(He $\overset{\text{SUBJ}}{\frown}$ gave), (gave $\overset{\text{DOBJ}}{\frown}$ her)}. A transition-based neural model calculates the score of possible transition actions a given a state s.

The key problem for the design of a transition-based parser is how to represent s so that a can be predicted the most effectively. Below we introduce three incrementally more complex neural models, which score transition actions locally at each step.

15.2.1 Model 1

Let us start by adapting the discrete linear parser in Chapter 11 into a neural counterpart, replacing discrete features with neural features, and a linear model with a multi-layer perceptron. In particular, consider the arc-standard parser in Section 11.3, which represents s by consulting the feature templates in Table 11.6. Because neural networks are capable of automatically combining input features, we select only the atomic features, such as $s_0 w$ (word on top of the stack) and $s_{1.r1} p$ (POS of the second rightmost child of the second word on the stack), etc.. The list of selected features is shown in Table 15.1, which serves as a basis for computing a hidden representation of the state.

The structure of the model is shown in Figure 15.6(a), where $W_{1:n}$ and $P_{1:n}$ represent the input word and POS sequences, respectively. s represents the state and a represents the next action. As shown in the figure, features from s are represented as embedding vectors, which are concatenated into a single long vector, and then fed as input to a multi-layer perceptron for learning a non-linear

Table 15.1 Feature templates for a neural transition-based dependency parser. $s_0, s_1, \ldots$ – top items on the stack; $b_0, b_1 \ldots$ – front items on the buffer; w – word; p – POS; l – arc label; subscript l – left child; subscript r – right child. For example, $s_{0.l0}$ indicates the leftmost child s_0, and $s_{0.l0.r0}$ indicates the rightmost child $s_{0.l0}$; n_w, n_p, n_l indicate the number of feature templates for words, POS and arc labels, respectively. (Because a non-linear neural network automatically concatenates atomic features, combined features such as $s_0 p s_{0.r} p s_{0.r_2} p$ in Table 11.6 are not necessary here.)

Type	Feature template
word features (n_w=18)	$s_0 w, s_1 w, s_2 w, b_0 w, b_1 w, b_2 w$
	$s_{0.l0} w, s_{0.l1} w, s_{1.l0} w, s_{1.l1} w, s_{0.r0} w, s_{0.r1} w, s_{1.r0} w, s_{1.r1} w$
	$s_{0.l0.l0} w, s_{0.r0.l0} w, s_{0.l0.r0} w, s_{0.r0.r0} w$
POS features (n_p=18)	$s_0 p, s_1 p, s_2 p, b_0 p, b_1 p, b_2 p$
	$s_{0.l0} p, s_{0.l1} p, s_{1.l0} p, s_{1.l1} p, s_{0.r0} p, s_{0.r1} p, s_{1.r0} p, s_{1.r1} p$
	$s_{0.l0.l0} p, s_{0.r0.l0} p, s_{0.l0.r0} p, s_{0.r0.r0} p$
arc features (n_l=12)	$s_{0.l0} l, s_{0.l1} l, s_{1.l0} l, s_{1.l1} l, s_{0.r0} l, s_{0.r1} l, s_{1.r0} l, s_{1.r1} l$
	$s_{0.l0.l0} l, s_{0.r0.l0} l, s_{0.l0.r0} l, s_{0.r0.r0} l$

representation $\mathbf{h}$. $\mathbf{h}$ is then used as input to a *softmax* output layer for predicting a. Below we discuss the features and prediction layers, respectively.

Feature representation. Formally, denote the word features in Table 15.1 as $S^w = \{wf_1 = s_0 w, wf_2 = s_1 w, \ldots, wf_{n_w} = s_{0.r0.r0} w\}$, the POS features as $S^p = \{pf_1 = s_0 p, pf_2 = s_1 p, \ldots, pf_{n_p} = s_{0.r0.r0} p\}$ and the arc label features $S^l = \{lf_1 = s_{0.l0} l, lf_2 = s_{0.l1} l, \ldots, lf_{n_l} = s_{0.r0.r0} l\}$, where $n_w = 18$, $n_p = 18$ and $n_l = 12$, as shown in Table 15.1. Their neural representations can be defined as the concatenation of atomic feature embeddings:

$$
\begin{aligned}
\mathbf{x}^w &= \mathrm{emb}(wf_1) \oplus \cdots \oplus \mathrm{emb}(wf_{n_w}) \\
\mathbf{x}^p &= \mathrm{emb}^p(pf_1) \oplus \cdots \oplus \mathrm{emb}^p(pf_{n_p}) \\
\mathbf{x}^l &= \mathrm{emb}^l(lf_1) \oplus \cdots \oplus \mathrm{emb}^l(lf_{n_l}),
\end{aligned}
\tag{15.15}
$$

where the word embeddings $\mathrm{emb}()$ can be initialised randomly or using pre-trained embedding tables, while the POS embeddings $\mathrm{emb}^p()$ and the label embeddings $\mathrm{emb}^l()$ can be randomly initialised and fine-tuned during parser training. All the embeddings serve as model parameters.

A hidden state is calculated by using a feed-forward layer with a non-linear activation f, which serves as a final combined feature vector:

$$
\mathbf{h} = f(\mathbf{W}^w \mathbf{x}^w + \mathbf{W}^p \mathbf{x}^p + \mathbf{W}^l \mathbf{x}^l + \mathbf{b}_h),
\tag{15.16}
$$

where $\mathbf{W}^w, \mathbf{W}^p, \mathbf{W}^l$ and $\mathbf{b}_h$ are model parameters. $\mathbf{W}^w \mathbf{x}^w$ is a compact way of writing $\sum_{i=1}^{n_w} \mathbf{W}^w[i] \times \mathrm{emb}(wf_i)$, where

$$
\mathbf{W}^w = [\mathbf{W}^w[1]; \mathbf{W}^w[2]; \ldots; \mathbf{W}^w[n_w]] \quad (n_w = 18)
$$

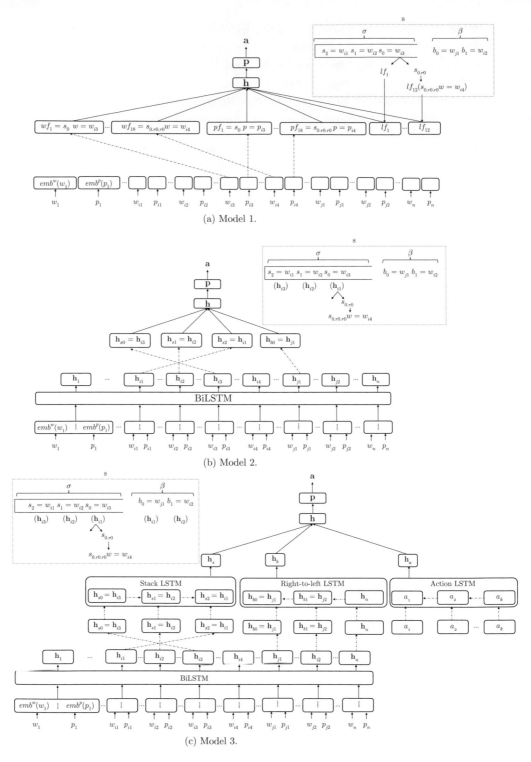

Figure 15.6 Three transition-based models for dependency parsing ($i1, i2, \ldots$ denote word indices on the stack; $j1, j2, \ldots$ denote word indices on the buffer).

is the concatenation of $\mathbf{W}^w[i]$, each of which represent the weight matrix for $emb(wf_i)$, $i \in [1, \ldots, n_w]$ and $\mathbf{x}^w$ is described in Eq 15.15.

Action prediction. A *softmax* output layer is used to calculate the action probabilities according to $\mathbf{h}$:

$$\begin{aligned} \mathbf{o} &= \mathbf{W}^o\mathbf{h} + \mathbf{b}^o \\ \mathbf{p} &= softmax(\mathbf{o}), \end{aligned} \tag{15.17}$$

where $\mathbf{W}^o$ and $\mathbf{b}^o$ are model parameters. Each element in $\mathbf{p}$ gives the probability of a specific action, such as SHIFT, LEFTARC-NSUBJ and RIGHTARC-DOBJ (Chapter 11), according to which the most likely next action can be chosen.

The above neural network model resembles its statistical counterpart in Chapter 11, essentially performing local classification tasks to determine each action in a sequence of state transitions. The accuracy is significantly higher, which shows the strength of neural feature representation and non-linear feature combination power. Note that a cube activation function $f(x) = x^3$ in Eq 15.16 in the hidden layer has been shown to outperform *sigmoid* or *tanh* activation empirically, which demonstrates the importance of hyper-parameter selection in deep learning models.

Training. Given a set of training data $D = \{(W_i, T_i)\}|_{i=1}^N$, where W_i denotes the ith training feature and T_i denotes its corresponding gold-standard tree, we first transform each T_i into a sequence of gold-standard state transitions

$$\langle(s_0^i, a_1^i), (s_1^i, a_2^i), \ldots, (s_{2|W_i|-2}^i, a_{2|W_i|-1}^i)\rangle. \tag{15.18}$$

The overall loss function can then be the total negative log-likelihood of each state transition

$$L = -\sum_{i=1}^N \sum_{j=1}^{2|W_i|-1} \log P(a_j^i|s_{j-1}^i), \tag{15.19}$$

given that there are $2|W_i| - 1$ transition actions to build a dependency tree for W_i with the arc-standard system.

15.2.2 Model 2

One limitation of model 1 is that it represents each word independently using its word embedding, without considering sentence-level contexts. To further leverage the strength of neural networks in representing global contextual information, a sequence network can be used to encode the input sentence, before making a prediction of the next action.

The structure of such a model is shown in Figure 15.6(b). In particular, given an input sentence $w_1, w_2, \ldots, w_n$ together with the corresponding POS tags $t_1, t_2, \ldots, t_n$, each word w_i is represented by the concatenation of the word embedding and the corresponding POS embedding:

$$\mathbf{x}_i = emb(w_i) \oplus emb^p(t_i). \tag{15.20}$$

A BiLSTM is then used to encode the whole sentence:

$$\mathbf{H}_{1:n} = BiLSTM(\mathbf{X}_{1:n}). \tag{15.21}$$

The use of BiLSTM encoding allows simpler feature representation by using fewer but stronger features to replace the long list of features in Table 15.1. In particular, the corresponding hidden state of the three words on the top of the stack ($\mathbf{h}_{s_0}, \mathbf{h}_{s_1}, \mathbf{h}_{s_2}$) and the first word in the buffer ($\mathbf{h}_{b_0}$) can then be fed into a feed-forward layer for action classification:

$$\begin{aligned}
\mathbf{h} &= \mathbf{h}_{s_0} \oplus \mathbf{h}_{s_1} \oplus \mathbf{h}_{s_2} \oplus \mathbf{h}_0 \\
\mathbf{o} &= \mathbf{W}^o \tanh(\mathbf{W}^h \mathbf{h} + \mathbf{b}^h) + \mathbf{b}^o \\
\mathbf{p} &= softmax(\mathbf{o}),
\end{aligned} \tag{15.22}$$

where $\mathbf{W}^o, \mathbf{b}^o, \mathbf{W}^h$ and $\mathbf{b}^h$ are model parameters. Similar to Eq 15.17, $\mathbf{p}$ gives the probabilities of transition actions. The training process of model 2 can be the same as model 1.

Comparison between model 1 and model 2. The differences between model 1 and model 2 represent core distinctions in design principles between neural modelling and statistical modelling. Model 1 is close in spirit to a statistical transition-based parser, which manually designs a set of rich features that represent a state. In contrast, model 2 first represents the whole input sentence using a sequence encoding network (i.e., BiLSTM), and is thus less independent of manual features. However, the stack is still represented by using three independent features (i.e., $\mathbf{h}_{s_0}, \mathbf{h}_{s_1}$ and $\mathbf{h}_{s_2}$), rather than one hidden vector that represents its global information. To this end, we can take one step further by finding a neural representation of the stack structure explicitly.

15.2.3 Model 3

Model 3 further improves upon model 2 by calculating single-vector representations of the stack, the buffer and the action history, respectively, thereby finding a more succinct representation of the state s. The structure of the model is shown in Figure 15.6(c). Compared with model 2, one additional LSTM is used to represent the stack structure, by treating the items on the stack as a sequence and applying recurrent time steps from the bottom of the stack to the top. Correspondingly, words on the buffer are also represented by applying an LSTM, this time from right to left. As shown in the figure, the last hidden states $\mathbf{h}_s$ and $\mathbf{h}_b$ can be used as global representations of the stack and buffer, respectively.

In a similar way, the sequence of actions $a_1, a_2, \ldots, a_k$ that have been used to build the current state can also be embedded into a list of vectors $emb^a(a_1), emb^a(a_2), \ldots, emb^a(a_k)$, and represented using an LSTM from a_1 to a_k. The last hidden state from this LSTM, $\mathbf{h}_a$ can be used to represent the action history. Similar to POS and dependency label embeddings, action embeddings can be achieved through a lookup table $E_a \in \mathbb{R}^{d_a \times |A|}$, which consists of $|A|$ columns, each containing an embedding vector of d_a dimensions. Here A represents the set of actions. E_a can be randomly initialised as a part of the model parameters.

The final feature representation of the parser state can then be:

$$\mathbf{h} = \mathbf{h}_s \oplus \mathbf{h}_b \oplus \mathbf{h}_a \tag{15.23}$$

from which the next action can be predicted as for model 2:

$$\mathbf{o} = \mathbf{W}^o \tanh(\mathbf{W}^h \mathbf{h} + \mathbf{b}^h) + \mathbf{b}^o$$
$$\mathbf{p} = softmax(\mathbf{o}), \tag{15.24}$$

where $\mathbf{W}^o$, $\mathbf{b}^o$, $\mathbf{W}^h$ and $\mathbf{b}^h$ are model parameters.

Dynamic updates of neural network components. One thing to note is that the stack, buffer and sequence of actions change dynamically during the parsing process of a given input sentence. As a result, $\mathbf{h}_s$, $\mathbf{h}_b$ and $\mathbf{h}_a$ need to be dynamically computed. Intuitively, none of them should be computed from scratch at each incremental state transition step, which will lead to unnecessary loss of computation efficiency. Instead, we should be able to incrementally update the representations as the parser state is updated incrementally through the output construction process. Among the three features, the buffer representation $\mathbf{h}_b$ changes at each SHIFT action only, which moves the front of the buffer one word to the right. As a result, a buffer LSTM representation can be computed once before parsing starts:

$$\mathbf{h}_n^b, \mathbf{h}_{n-1}^b, \dots, \mathbf{h}_1^b = LSTM(\mathbf{h}_n, \mathbf{h}_{n-1}, \dots, \mathbf{h}_1) \tag{15.25}$$

where $\mathbf{h}_1, \dots, \mathbf{h}_n$ come from Eq 15.21.

The LSTM is applied to the input sequence in the reverse direction so that $\mathbf{h}_i^b$ is independent of $\mathbf{h}_1 \dots \mathbf{h}_{i-1}$. This facilitates popping, which is the only operation for the buffer. At the initial state when parsing starts, $\mathbf{h}_b = \mathbf{h}_1^b$, which represents the whole buffer from w_1 to w_n. During the parsing process, for each SHIFT action, $\mathbf{h}_b$ is updated from $\mathbf{h}_i^b$ to $\mathbf{h}_{i+1}^b$, which represents the part of the buffer from w_{i+1} to w_n. LEFTARC and RIGHTARC actions does not lead to buffer change.

In the reverse direction to the buffer LSTM, the action history LSTM is incremented with one additional action after every state transition step. Only pushing is taken. Thus its representation can be initialised using a fixed start vector and updated incrementally with a recurrent LSTM step each time. In particular, denote the hidden state that represents $a_1, a_2, \dots, a_k$ as $\mathbf{h}_1^a, \mathbf{h}_2^a, \dots, \mathbf{h}_k^a$, respectively. At step k, $\mathbf{h}_a = \mathbf{h}_k^a$. Suppose that the next action taken is a_k, we have:

$$\mathbf{h}_{k+1}^a = \text{LSTM\_STEP}(\mathbf{h}_k^a, emb(a_k))$$
$$\mathbf{h}_a = \mathbf{h}_{k+1}^a. \tag{15.26}$$

The initial action history state $\mathbf{h}_0^a$ can be set to an all-zero vector.

Stack LSTM. The stack representation is more challenging compared to the buffer and the action history, since both pushing and popping operations can be applied. It turns out that dynamically updating a stack LSTM representation can be made in $O(1)$ runtime complexity also, just as the updating for the buffer and the action history. The process is shown in Figure 15.7. In particular, for the start state, the stack is empty, and thus can be represented using a zero vector $\mathbf{h}_s = \mathbf{h}_0^s = \vec{0}$. At a time step where $\mathbf{h}_s = \mathbf{h}_i^s$, when one item $\mathbf{x}$ is pushed onto the stack, an LSTM step can be taken for integrating it into the current stack representation:

$$\mathbf{h}_{i+1}^s = \text{LSTM\_STEP}(\mathbf{h}_i^s, \mathbf{x})$$
$$\mathbf{h}_s = \mathbf{h}_{i+1}^s. \tag{15.27}$$

This process is shown in Figure 15.7(a).

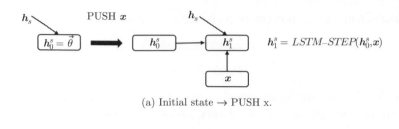

(a) Initial state → PUSH x.

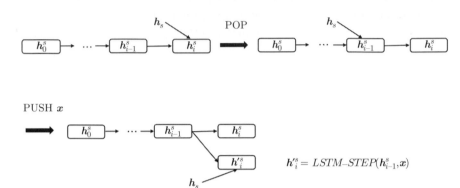

(b) POP → PUSH x.

Figure 15.7 Stack LSTM.

Now when an item is popped off the stack, we simply need to change $\mathbf{h}_s$ from $\mathbf{h}_i^s$ back to $\mathbf{h}_{i-1}^s$, which represents all the items on the stack from the bottom to $\mathbf{h}_{i-1}^s$. This process is shown in Figure 15.7(b), which is similar to the udpate of $\mathbf{h}_b$ when a SHIFT action is taken. From this representation, if a new item $\mathbf{x}$ is pushed onto the stack again, a new branch is made from $\mathbf{h}_{i-1}^s$, resulting in

$$\mathbf{h}_s = \mathbf{h}_i'^s = \text{LSTM\_STEP}(\mathbf{h}_{i-1}^s, \mathbf{x}) \tag{15.28}$$

At this step, the value of $\mathbf{h}_i^s$ is obsolete, since it was popped off the stack. The training process of model 3 can be the same as model 1 and model 2.

15.3 Global Structured Models

In this section, we discuss neural models that take into consideration output structures. To this end, the same thinking discussed in Part II of this book can be applied. In particular, for graph based models, a CRF layer can be used to replace a local *softmax* output layer for capturing Markov dependencies between consecutive labels in a sequence or a tree (Section 15.3.1). For transition-based models, we can consider global normalisation, namely to predict the probability of a sequence of transition actions as a unit (Section 15.3.2).

15.3.1 Neural CRF

To capture dependencies between output labels, conditional random fields (Chapter 8) can be integrated with neural network representations, resulting in **neural CRF** structures. Neural CRFs can be intuitively viewed from two perspectives. First, they can be regarded as replacing a set of local output prediction layers in the models of Section 15.1 with a single structured output CRF layer. Second, they can also be regarded as replacing the feature representation of local cliques in discrete CRFs in Chapter 8 with neural hidden layer representations. For both sequence structures and tree structures, we have discussed CRF models in Part II of the book. Here we discuss their neural CRF versions. Recall the CRF model discussed in Chapter 8. Formally, given a word sequence $W_{1:n} = w_1, w_2, \ldots, w_n$ and a label sequence $T_{1:n} = t_1, t_2, \ldots, t_n$, a first-order CRF model calculates $P(T_{1:n}|W_{1:n})$ using:

$$P(T_{1:n}|W_{1:n}) = \frac{\exp\left(\vec{\theta} \cdot \vec{\phi}(T_{1:n}, W_{1:n})\right)}{\sum_{T'_{1:n}} \exp\left(\vec{\theta} \cdot \vec{\phi}(T'_{1:n}, W_{1:n})\right)}, \tag{15.29}$$

where $T'_{1:n}$ represents one from all possible label sequences, $\vec{\phi}$ is a feature representation of the input–output pair and $\vec{\theta}$ is the model parameter vector. With first-order Markov assumptions, the global feature vector $\vec{\phi}(T'_{1:n}, W_{1:n})$ can be broken down into the sum of local feature vectors $\vec{\phi}(t_i, t_{i-1}, W_{1:n})$, which is limited to a tag bi-gram $t_{i-1}t_i$:

$$\vec{\theta} \cdot \vec{\phi}(T_{1:n}, W_{1:n}) = \sum_{i=1}^{n} \vec{\theta} \cdot \vec{\phi}(t_i, t_{i-1}, W_{1:n}). \tag{15.30}$$

With this, Eq 15.29 can be rewritten as:

$$P(T_{1.n}|W_{1:n}) = \frac{\exp\left(\sum_{i=1}^{n} \vec{\theta} \cdot \vec{\phi}(t_i, t_{i-1}, W_{1:n})\right)}{\sum_{T'_{1:n}} \exp\left(\sum_{i=1}^{n} \vec{\theta} \cdot \vec{\phi}(t'_i, t'_{i-1}, W_{1:n})\right)}. \tag{15.31}$$

A **simple neural CRF** model can be constructed by replacing $\vec{\phi}(t_i, t_{i-1}, W_{1:n})$ with $\mathbf{h}_i = f(W_{1:n}, i)$, which is a dense feature vector representation of the local input w_i in its sentence-level context. Here we use a standard multi-layer perceptron as an example for the neural function f. Given $emb(w_i)$, we can calculate $\mathbf{h}_i$ based on representation of a five-word window:

$$\begin{aligned} \mathbf{X}_{i-2:i+2} &= emb(w_{i-2}) \oplus emb(w_{i-1}) \oplus emb(w_i) \oplus emb(w_{i+1}) \oplus emb(w_{i+2}) \\ \mathbf{h}_i &= f(W_{1:n}, i) = \tanh(\mathbf{W}^x \mathbf{X}_{i-2:i+2} + \mathbf{b}^x), \end{aligned} \tag{15.32}$$

where $\mathbf{W}^x$ and $\mathbf{b}^x$ are model parameters. As a result, the probability of $T_{1:n}$ given $W_{1:n}$ can be calculated by:

$$P(T_{1:n}|W_{1:n}) = \frac{\exp\left(\sum_{i=1}^{n} \left(\mathbf{u}(t_i)^T \mathbf{h}_i + b(t_i, t_{i-1})\right)\right)}{\sum_{T'_{1:n}} \left(\exp\left(\sum_{i=1}^{n} \left(\mathbf{u}(t'_i)^T \mathbf{h}_i + b(t'_i, t'_{i-1})\right)\right)\right)}. \tag{15.33}$$

Here $\mathbf{u}(t_i)$ and $b(t_i, t_{i-1})$ are parameters for emission and transition features, respectively. $\mathbf{u}(t_i)$ is a vector model parameter specific to a label t_i, and $b(t_i, t_{i-1})$ is a scalar parameter specific to two consecutive labels t_i and t_{i-1}. $\mathbf{u}(t_i)$ serves to map the feature vector t_i into a scalar score value, and $b(t_i, t_{i-1})$ serves as the only parameter for representing tag transitions.

Training neural CRF. The training of neural CRF models can be performed using SGD given a log-likelihood loss L over a set of training data D, where gradients are calculated on model parameters by standard back-propagation. In particular, $\mathbf{h}_i$ can be viewed as a dense feature vector, where each element represents a feature instance. Gradients can be calculated by taking the derivative of L with respect to each $\mathbf{h}_i$. Then standard back-propagation can be applied to further pass the gradients down to the neural network parameters that give $\mathbf{h}_i$. Similarly, $\mathbf{u}(t_i)$ and $b(t_i, t_{i-1})$ can be updated by taking derivatives of L respectively.

Formally, denote $D = \{(W_i, T_i)\}|_{i=1}^{N}$. The training objective is to minimise the cross-entropy loss

$$
\begin{aligned}
L(W_i, T_i, \Theta) &= -\frac{1}{N} \sum_{i=1}^{N} \log P(T_i | W_i) \\
&= -\frac{1}{N} \sum_{i=1}^{N} \log \frac{\exp\left(\sum_{j=1}^{|W_i|} \left(\mathbf{u}(t_j^i)^T \mathbf{h}_j^i + b(t_j^i, t_{j-1}^i) \right) \right)}{\sum_{T'} \left(\exp\left(\sum_{j=1}^{|W_j|} \left(\mathbf{u}(t_j')^T \mathbf{h}_j^i + b(t_j', t_{j-1}') \right) \right) \right)} \\
&= -\frac{1}{N} \left(\sum_{i=1}^{N} \left(\sum_{j=1}^{|W_i|} \left(\mathbf{u}(t_j^i)^T \mathbf{h}_j^i + b(t_j^i, t_{j-1}^i) \right) \right) \right. \\
&\qquad \left. - \log \sum_{T'} \exp\left(\sum_{j=1}^{|W_i|} \left(\mathbf{u}(t_j')^T \mathbf{h}_j + b(t_j', t_{j-1}') \right) \right) \right).
\end{aligned}
\tag{15.34}
$$

For each training instance (W_i, T_i), the local gradient with respect to the model parameter $\mathbf{U}(\ell_k)$ $(\ell_k \in L)$ is:

$$
\begin{aligned}
\frac{\partial L(W_i, T_i, \Theta)}{\partial \mathbf{u}(\ell_k)} &= -\left(\sum_{j=1}^{|W_i|} \mathbf{h}_j^i \delta(t_j^i = \ell_k) \right. \\
&\qquad \left. - \sum_{T'} \frac{\exp\left(\sum_{j=1}^{|W_i|} \left(\mathbf{u}(t_j')\mathbf{h}_j^i + b(t_j', t_{j-1}') \right) \right)}{\sum_{T''} \left(\exp\left(\sum_{j=1}^{|W_i|} \left(\mathbf{u}(t_j'')\mathbf{h}_j^i + b(t_j'', t_{j-1}'') \right) \right) \right)} \sum_{j=1}^{|W_i|} \mathbf{h}_j \delta(t_j' = \ell_k) \right) \\
&= -\left(\sum_{j=1}^{|W_i|} \mathbf{h}_j^i \delta(t_j^i = \ell_k) - \sum_{T'} P(T'|W_i) \mathbf{h}_j^i \delta(t_j' = \ell_k) \right) \\
&= -\sum_{j=1}^{|W_i|} \left(\mathbf{h}_j^i \delta(t_j^i = \ell_k) - \sum_{T'} (P(T'|W_i) \mathbf{h}_j^i \delta(t_j' = \ell_k) \right) \\
&= -\sum_{j=1}^{|W_i|} \left(\mathbf{h}_j^i \delta(t_j^i = \ell_k) - \mathbb{E}_{T' \sim P(T'|W_i)} \mathbf{h}_j^i \delta(t_j' = \ell_k) \right).
\end{aligned}
$$

$$
\tag{15.35}
$$

where $\ell_k \in L$ is a label from the label set L. Note that $\mathbf{h}_j^i$ is dependent on W_i only, but not on T_i or T' or T''. $\delta(x)$ returns 1 if x is true and 0 otherwise. Equation 15.35 calculates two terms for each word $w_j^i \in W_i$, $j \in [1, \ldots, |W_i|]$, including a term $\mathbf{h}_j\delta(t_j = \ell_k)$ about the gold-standard output T_i, and a term $E_{T' \sim P(T'|W_i)}\mathbf{h}_j\delta(t_j' = \ell_k)$ about all possible outputs T' over W_i. Similar to Section 8.3.4, the expectation over all possible output sequences can be transformed into the expectation over marginal probabilities

$$\mathbb{E}_{T' \sim P(T'|W_i)}\mathbf{h}_j^i\delta(t_j' = \ell_k) = \mathbb{E}_{t_j' \sim P(t_j'|W_i)}\mathbf{h}_j^i\delta(t_j' = \ell_k). \tag{15.36}$$

The forward–backward algorithm discussed in Algorithm 8.4 can then be used to calculate $P(t_j'|W_i)$ (see Exercise 15.10). Similarly, the local derivative for $\mathbf{h}_j$ in (W_i, T_i) can be calculated as follows:

$$\begin{aligned}
\frac{\partial L(W_i, T_i, \Theta)}{\partial \mathbf{h}_j^i} &= \mathbf{u}(t_j^i) - \frac{\exp\left(\sum_{j=1}^{|W_i|}\left(\mathbf{u}(t_j^i)^T\mathbf{h}_j^i + b(t_j^i, t_{j-1}^i)\right)\right)}{\sum_{T'}\left(\exp\left(\sum_{j=1}^{|W_i|}\left(\mathbf{u}(t_j')^T\mathbf{h}_j^i + b(t_j', t_{j-1}')\right)\right)\right)}\mathbf{u}(t_j') \\
&= \mathbf{u}(t_j^i) - \sum_{T'} P(T'|W_i)\mathbf{u}(t_j') \\
&= \mathbf{u}(t_j^i) - \mathbb{E}_{T' \sim P(T'|W_i)}\mathbf{u}(t_j') \\
&= \mathbf{u}(t_j^i) - \mathbb{E}_{t_j' \sim P(t_j'|W_i)}\mathbf{u}(t_j').
\end{aligned} \tag{15.37}$$

Note that the derivation of the gradients above is similar to the derivation of gradients for discrete CRF training discussed in Section 8.3.4 in Chapter 8, in particular Eqs 8.14 and 8.15, because of the inherent similarities in the output CRF layer.

BiLSTM-CRF. The neural CRF model in Eq 15.32 and Eq 15.33 treats each word locally by encoding a five-word context window. This representation is weaker compared to the local model in Section 15.1.1. A stronger representation of $W_{1:n}$ such as BiLSTM can be used for obtaining $\mathbf{h}_i$. For example, in a BiLSTM-CRF structure, we can have:

$$\mathbf{H}_{1:n} = BiLSTM(\mathbf{X}_{1:n}) \tag{15.38}$$

still with

$$P(T_{1:n}|W_{1:n}) = \frac{\exp\left(\sum_{i=1}^n\left(\mathbf{u}(t_i)^T\mathbf{h}_i + b(t_i, t_{i-1})\right)\right)}{\sum_{T'}\left(\exp\left(\sum_{i=1}^n\left(\mathbf{u}(t_i')^T\mathbf{h}_i + b(t_i', t_{i-1}')\right)\right)\right)}. \tag{15.39}$$

The training of a BiLSTM-CRF model can be the same as the training of the neural CRF model above with the same loss L and the same gradients $\frac{\delta L}{\delta \mathbf{h}_i}$. The only difference is that gradients from $\mathbf{h}_i$ back-propagate to the BiLSTM layer instead of the feed-forward feature combination layer.

Compared with the naïve neural CRF model, a BiLSTM-CRF model is much stronger in calculating emission features thanks to the context representation of BiLSTM, and therefore can give significantly better results on sequence labelling. BiLSTM-CRF models can be regarded as adding a CRF output layer to the local sequence labelling model in Section 15.1.1 and Figure 15.1, which captures tag–tag dependencies explicitly.

Tree CRF. The tree CRF model discussed in Section 10.2.2 can be extended into a neural tree CRF in a similar way. In particular, given a sentence W and a corresponding constituent tree T, the discrete linear tree CRF model calculates the probability of T as:

$$P(T|W) = \frac{\exp\left(\vec{\theta} \cdot \vec{\phi}(W, T)\right)}{\sum_{T' \in \text{GEN}(W)} \exp\left(\vec{\theta} \cdot \vec{\phi}(W, T')\right)}, \tag{15.40}$$

where $\vec{\phi}(W, T)$ is a global feature vector of T over W, $\text{GEN}(W)$ represents all possible trees for W, and $\vec{\theta}$ is the model parameter vector. $\vec{\phi}(W, T)$ can be further decomposed into the sum of local features over each rule:

$$\vec{\phi}(W, T) = \sum_{r \in T} \vec{\phi}(W, r), \tag{15.41}$$

where r represents a grammar rule in T.

As a result, the probability of T conditioned on W is:

$$P(T|W) = \frac{\exp\left(\sum_{r \in T} \vec{\theta} \cdot \vec{\phi}(W, r)\right)}{\sum_{T' \in \text{GEN}(W)} \exp\left(\sum_{r' \in T'} \vec{\theta} \cdot \vec{\phi}(W, r')\right)}. \tag{15.42}$$

Now a simple neural tree CRF model can be constructed by replacing the discrete scoring function $\vec{\theta} \cdot \vec{\phi}(W, r)$ with a neural network function f, similar to the case of sequence structure CRF. To this end, we can reuse the neural network structure in Section 15.1.3.

For the neural network model, the probability of T conditioned on W can be given by:

$$P(T|W) = \frac{\exp\left(\sum_{r \in T} f(W, r)\right)}{\sum_{T' \in \text{GEN}(W)} \exp\left(\sum_{r' \in T'} f(W, r')\right)}, \tag{15.43}$$

where f is the neural network based scoring function.

The whole scores for a tree can be decomposed to the sum of the local scoring function $f(W, r)$ for each local rule. Each grammar rule r covering the span $w_b, w_{b+1}, \ldots, w_e$ can be specified by a tuple (b, b', e, c, c_1, c_2), where $c \to c_1 c_2$ is the label production rule, and indices b, b' and e denote the span production rule: $W_{b:e} \to W_{b:b'-1} W_{b':e}$. Here b' is the splitting point of the span. The corresponding constituent labels for the three spans $W_{b:e}$, $W_{b:b'-1}$ and $W_{b':e}$ are c, c_1 and c_2, respectively. The scoring function $f(W, r)$ can be defined as

$$f(W, r) = f(W, c \to c_1 c_2, b, b', e; \vec{\theta})$$
$$= \vec{\tau}(W, b, b', e)^T \mathbf{W}^f \vec{\gamma}(c \to c_1 c_2),$$

where $\mathbf{W}^f$ is a model parameter, the feature vector $\vec{\tau}$ is used to extract surface and partition features for the span production rule over the sentence and the function $\vec{\gamma}$ denotes features for the rule $c \to c_1 c_2$.

$\vec{\tau}$ can be defined using the BiLSTM output features:

$$\vec{\tau}(W, b, b', e) = ReLU(\mathbf{W}^w(\mathbf{h}_b \oplus \mathbf{h}_{b'-1} \oplus \mathbf{h}_e)),$$

where each $\mathbf{x}_i$ and $\mathbf{h}_i$ is defined in the same way as Section 15.1.3, with $\mathbf{h}_i$ being $\overrightarrow{\mathbf{h}}_i \oplus \overleftarrow{\mathbf{h}}_i$, and $\mathbf{W}^w$ is a trainable model parameter.

$\vec{\gamma}$ can be defined as a one-hot mapping or a lookup table for obtaining rule embeddings. For the rule embedding, the lookup table for rules is $E_r \in \mathbb{R}^{d_r \times |G|}$, where $|G|$ is the grammar size and d_r is the dimension of rule embeddings. In addition, the vector $\vec{\gamma}$ can be defined in a compositional way by considering the constituent labels of each rule. For example, the representation vector of the rule $c \rightarrow c_1 c_2$ can be given by:

$$\vec{\gamma}(c \rightarrow c_1 c_2) = ReLU\big(\mathbf{W}^a emb^s(c) + \mathbf{W}^l emb^s(c_1) + \mathbf{W}^r emb^s(c_2) + \mathbf{b}\big),$$

where $\mathbf{W}^a$, $\mathbf{W}^l$, $\mathbf{W}^r$ and $\mathbf{b}$ are model parameters. $emb^s(c)$ is the syntactic constituent label embedding of $c \in C$, which can be obtained from a lookup table $E_p \in \mathbb{R}^{d_e \times |C|}$, where $|C|$ is the number of constituent labels and d_e is the dimension size of constituent label embeddings. C denotes the set of constituent labels.

Training. To train the neural tree CRF models, we can use back-propagation to calculate the gradients in the same way as for neural CRFs. The training objective is to maximise the log-likelihood, with the loss being

$$
\begin{aligned}
L &= -\frac{1}{N} \sum_{i=1}^{N} \log P(T_i | W_i) \\
&= -\frac{1}{N} \sum_{i=1}^{N} \log \frac{\exp\left(\sum_{r \in T_i} \vec{\tau}(r)^T \mathbf{W}^f \vec{\gamma}(r)\right)}{\sum_{T_i' \in \text{Gen}(W_i)} \exp\left(\sum_{r' \in T_i'} \vec{\tau}(r')^T \mathbf{W}^f \vec{\gamma}(r')\right)},
\end{aligned}
\tag{15.44}
$$

where $\vec{\tau}(r)$ and $\vec{\gamma}(r)$ denote $\vec{\tau}(W_i, b, b', e)$ and $\vec{\gamma}(c \rightarrow c_1 c_2)$. The local gradient $\frac{\partial L}{\partial \mathbf{W}^f}$ is

$$
\begin{aligned}
\frac{\partial L}{\partial \mathbf{W}^f} &= -\left(\sum_{r \in T_i} \vec{\tau}(r) \vec{\gamma}(r)^T - \sum_{T_i' \in \text{Gen}(W_i)} P(T_i'|W_i) \sum_{r' \in T_i'} \vec{\tau}(r') \vec{\gamma}(r')^T \right) \\
&= -\left(\sum_{r \in T_i} \vec{\tau}(r) \vec{\gamma}(r)^T - \mathbb{E}_{T_i' \sim P(T_i'|W_i)} \sum_{r' \in T_i'} \vec{\tau}(r') \vec{\gamma}(r')^T \right) \\
&= -\left(\sum_{r \in T_i} \vec{\tau}(r) \vec{\gamma}(r)^T - \mathbb{E}_{r' \sim P(r'|W_i)} \sum_{r' \in T_i'} \vec{\tau}(r') \vec{\gamma}(r')^T \right),
\end{aligned}
\tag{15.45}
$$

which contains an expectation of the marginal probability $P(r'|W_i)$ for all possible rules $r' \in \text{GenR}(W_i)$, namely all possible rules in all possible trees in W_i. This expectation can be efficiently calculated using the inside–outside algorithms discussed in Section 10.1.4. Similarly, to update the parameters involved in $\vec{\tau}$ and $\vec{\gamma}$, we need to consider the gradients $\frac{\partial L}{\partial \vec{\tau}(r)}$ and $\frac{\partial L}{\partial \vec{\gamma}(r)}$ (Exercise 15.12), which can be achieved in a similar way as calculating $\frac{\partial L}{\partial \mathbf{W}^f}$. For example, the gradient $\frac{\partial L}{\partial \vec{\tau}(r)}$ is given by

$$
\begin{aligned}
\frac{\partial L}{\partial \vec{\tau}(r)} &= -\left(\sum_{r \in T_i} \mathbf{W}^f \vec{\gamma}(r) - \sum_{r' \in \text{GenR}(W_i)} P(r'|W_i) \mathbf{W}^f \vec{\gamma}(r') \right) \\
&= -\left(\sum_{r \in T_i} \mathbf{W}^f \vec{\gamma}(r) - \mathbb{E}_{r' \sim P(r'|W_i)} \mathbf{W}^f \vec{\gamma}(r') \right).
\end{aligned}
\tag{15.46}
$$

After obtaining the gradients of $\frac{\partial L}{\partial \vec{\tau}(r)}$ and $\frac{\partial L}{\partial \vec{\gamma}(r)}$, we can use back-propagation to find gradients for the model parameters $\mathbf{W}^w$, $\mathbf{W}^a$, $\mathbf{W}^l$, $\mathbf{W}^r$ and $\mathbf{b}$.

Large-margin alternatives to neural CRF. For both sequence and tree structures we have discussed large-margin models such as structured perceptron and structured SVM as alternatives to CRF in Part II of the book. For neural network models, large-margin training objectives are relatively little used, just as they are not much used for classification tasks, which we discussed in Chapter 13 (Section 13.2.4). As a result, we focus on probabilistic modelling (i.e., CRF) as for other problems in this part of the book.

15.3.2 Neural Transition-Based Models with Global Normalisation

The transition-based models in Section 15.2 are essentially greedy local classifiers that predict the most suitable next action given a current state. Such models can potentially suffer from two problems. First, the sequence of actions with the highest total score may not necessarily correspond to the sequence of actions each with its highest local score. This problem is a modelling (normalisation) issue, which is similar to the label bias problem discussed in Section 8.2.[1] Second, errors in preceding steps propagate to subsequent steps. This issue concerns both training and decoding. For training, local models see only gold-standard states, and therefore do not learn how to deal with states that correspond to *incorrect* partial parses that result from earlier mistakes. For decoding, greedy search is the main reason for error propagation. As discussed in Section 11.1.2 in Chapter 11, global training addresses all these issues. The main idea is to model a sequence of transition actions as a whole, which corresponds to a structured output.

For discrete linear models, we discussed an algorithm framework that uses perceptron-guided beam search (Section 11.1.2) for global training and decoding. This model calculates the score of an action sequence as the total score of each individual action in the sequence. Beam-search is applied to find a highest-scored action sequence, where an agenda is used to record the K highest-scored partial sequence at each state-transition step (Algorithm 11.1). Online training is used to guide the beam search algorithm, where an initial model is repeatedly updated by decoding each training sentence. At each decoding step, if the gold-standard sequence of actions falls out of the agenda, the model makes a search error. Consequently, decoding for the training instance is stopped and a perceptron update is executed by using the gold-standard sequence of actions as a positive example, and the current highest-scored sequence of actions in the agenda as a negative example (Algorithm 11.2). This update is called *early update*. In case no early update happens for a training instance, the training algorithm follows the standard perceptron, where a parameter update is performed when the final model output differs from the gold-standard output. This update is called *final update*, to differentiate it from early update.

For a neural transition-based model, similar ideas can be applied. For a local model in Section 15.2, given a state s, the scores of possible actions are calculated as a vector $\mathbf{o}$, and then

---

[1] Note that given a neural model such as model 3 in Section 15.2, which represents a state with global information on the parser configuration, the problem of label bias can be to some extent alleviated, since the label bias problem occurs when identical local contexts exist in different global sequences. Stack LSTM represents global context instead. However, for models such as model 1, the problem can still exist.

normalised into a probability distribution **p** by using *softmax*. This is local normalisation (see Eq 15.17). Let us take model 1 in Section 15.2.1 as the base local parser, extending it for global modelling.

Now we want to score a *sequence* of state transitions $A_{1:i} = a_1, a_2, \ldots, a_i$, which transforms a start state s_0 into a sequence of incremental new states $s_1, s_2, \ldots, s_i$. In this process, we record the sequence of score vectors $\mathbf{o}_1, \mathbf{o}_2, \ldots, \mathbf{o}_i$ for each respective action (Eq 15.17). The score of $A_{1:i}$ can then be calculated as:

$$score(A_{1:i}) = \sum_{j=1}^{i} score(a_j) = \sum_{j=1}^{i} \mathbf{o}_j[a_j], \qquad (15.47)$$

where $score(a_j) = \mathbf{o}_j[a_j]$ is read from the corresponding element in $\mathbf{o}_j$. Without being normalised into a probability distribution, this score can be used for scoring a_j in incremental decoding.

Decoding. We follow the beam-search decoding process in Figure 15.8, which is formally described by Algorithm 11.1. When the beam size K is set to 1, the decoding process is the same as the greedy decoder for the models in Section 15.2. When K increases, the decoder is increasingly capable of leveraging action sequence scores, so that locally low-scored gold-standard actions do not prevent the gold-standard sequence of actions from being predicted with the highest overall score in the end.

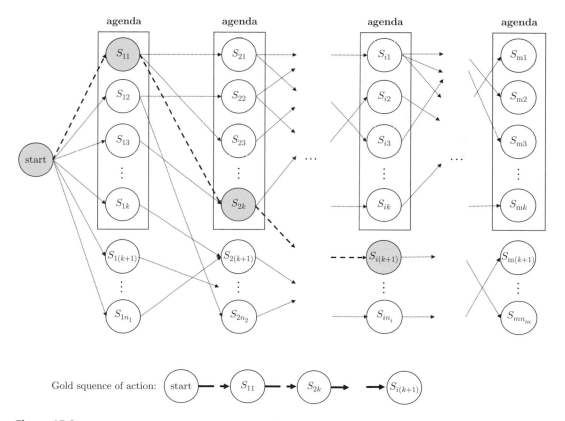

Figure 15.8 Transition-based structured prediction with global normalisation.

Training. Now let us consider training with beam-search, as described by Figure 15.8 and formally by Algorithm 11.2. As mentioned earlier, there are two forms of parameter updates, including early update and final update, respectively. In each update, a loss function should be defined for SGD training with back-propagation.

The discrete linear model in Chapter 11 uses a perceptron loss for parameter update, considering the most violated constraints by choosing the highest-scored structure as the only negative example. However, as mentioned earlier, for neural network models a probabilistic (i.e., cross-entropy) loss function empirically works better. We describe the update method using this loss. First, rather than locally normalising each action score into a probability distribution, as the local model in Eq 15.17 does, we want to normalise the scores of full sequences of actions into a probability distribution. Thus the score of a sequence of actions is:

$$P(A_{1:i}|W_{1:n}) = softmax_{\text{GEN}(W_{1:n},i)}(A_{1:i}) = \frac{\exp\left(\sum_{j=1}^{i} \mathbf{o}_j[a_j]\right)}{\sum_{A'_1{}^i} \exp\left(\sum_{j=1}^{i} \mathbf{o}'_j[a_j]\right)} \tag{15.48}$$

where $A'_{1:i} \in \text{GEN}(W_{1:n}, i)$ denotes the set of all possible action sequences from s_0 with length i. This is global normalisation.

Second, for back-propagation, the local log-likelihood loss is defined as $L = -\log P(A_{1:i}|W_{1:n})$

$$\begin{aligned} L &= -\log P(A_{1:i}|W_{1:n}) \\ &= -\log \frac{\exp(\sum_{j=1}^{i} \mathbf{o}_j[a_j])}{\sum_{A'_{1:i}} \exp(\sum_{j=1}^{i} \mathbf{o}'_j[a_j])} \\ &= -\log \frac{\exp(\sum_{j=1}^{i} \mathbf{o}_j[a_j])}{Z} \\ &= \log Z - \sum_{j=1}^{i} \mathbf{o}_j[a_j], \end{aligned} \tag{15.49}$$

where Z is the partition function:

$$Z = \sum_{A'_{1:i}} \exp(\sum_{j=1}^{i} \mathbf{o}_j[a'_j]). \tag{15.50}$$

However, the number of possible action sequences $A'_{1:i}$ is exponential to i, which makes the summation intractable. Here we use **contrastive estimation** for solving this problem, approximately calculating Z by summing up the probabilities of all $A'_{1:i} = a'_1, a'_2, \ldots, a'_i$ that we know, namely the set of states in the current agenda $\{s_{i,1}, \ldots, s_{i,n_i}\}$ in Figure 15.8:

$$Z'(x_i, \theta) = \sum_{A'_1 \in [s_{i,1}, \ldots, s_{i,n_i}]} \exp(\sum_{j=1}^{i} \mathbf{o}_j[a'_j]), \tag{15.51}$$

so that a log-likelihood loss can be calculated.

Given a local loss of each training instance, standard back-propagation can then be used for SGD training, where gradients back-propagate from $\mathbf{o}_j$ to the neural parameters in Eqs 15.15–15.17. Exercise 15.16 discusses pseudocode for the complete algorithm.

Summary

In this chapter we have learned:

- local neural models for sequence labelling, dependency parsing and constituent parsing;
- neural CRF and BiLSTM-CRF;
- neural transition-based structured prediction.

Chapter Notes

Both local softmax classifiers (Ling et al., 2015) and CRF models (Wang, et al., 2013; Huang et al., 2015; Ma and Hovy, 2016; Lample et al., 2016) have been used for neural sequence labelling, typically combined with a BiLSTM sequence encoder. Kiperwasser and Goldberg (2016) and Dozat and Manning (2017) investigated local models for dependency parsing. Kitaev and Klein (2018) and Teng and Zhang (2018) worked on local models for constituent parsing. Durrett and Klein (2015) investigated neural CRF parsing.

Chen and Manning (2014), Dyer et al. (2015) and Kiperwasser and Goldberg (2016) discussed local transition-based dependency parsing. Transition-based models with global normalisation was investigated for parsing by Zhou et al. (2015) and Watanabe and Sumita (2015). Andor et al. (2016) show the theoretical advantages of global normalisation compared to greedy local models.

Exercises

15.1 Compare the sequence labelling models in Section 15.1.1 and Section 15.3.1. On which layer do they differ in Figure 15.1? Why can a CRF output layer be more accurate compared to a local classification output layer? What is the trade-off in runtime complexity?

15.2 Recall the biaffine scoring function in Eq 15.8. A simpler way to integrate $\mathbf{h}_i$ and $\mathbf{h}_j$ is

$$s_{i,j} = \mathbf{W}(\mathbf{h}_i \oplus \mathbf{h}_j) + \mathbf{b}.$$

What is the advantage of Eq 15.8 compared to the function above? Are there alternative functions to integrate information from $\mathbf{h}_i$ and $\mathbf{h}_j$ that you can think of? What are their advantages and disadvantages?

15.3 Consider the decoding problem of the dependency parser in Section 15.1.2 again. Several maximum spanning tree algorithms are available in the algorithms literature, such as the Prim algorithm, the Kruskal algorithm and the Chu–Liu–Edmond algorithm. Which algorithm do you think is the most useful for the parser in consideration in terms of both accuracy and efficiency? Does the choice of decoding algorithm affect the training of the parser?

15.4 Consider the task of relation extraction, which is to predict relation links over given entities in a sentence. In particular, denoting an entity span over a given sentence $W_{1:n}$ as $S = W_{b:e}$, where $1 \leq b \leq e \leq n$, the set of outputs for the task is $R = \{(S_k^1, S_k^2, r_k)\}|_{k=1}^{|R|}$, where S_k^1 and S_k^2 are two entities and r_k is the relation between S_k^1 and S_k^2. Can the dependency parsing model in Section 15.1.2 be adapted to this task? What type of additional knowledge is useful? Can you think of how to integrate dependency syntax as input features? (See also Exercise 15.15 for span encoding.)

15.5 Write pseudocode for the dynamic program for the 0th-order CKY decoder in Section 15.13.

15.6 Consider the task of constituent parsing in Section 15.1.3. Can you think of a method to deal with unary rules without using the collapsed rule representations? Instead of using the span classification model to simulate the unlabelled span production probability $P(W_{b:e} \rightarrow W_{b:b'-1}W_{b':e}|S)$, can you propose a method to directly model this probability distribution with a local classification model using the the biaffine scoring method in Section 15.1.2 for dependency parsing?

15.7 Compare model 1 and model 2 for transition-based dependency parsing in Figure 15.6. What features are missing from model 2 as compared with model 1? Which of the missing features do you think can be added to model 2 for improving its performance? How can you add them to the model? (The effectiveness should ultimately be verified empirically.)

15.8 Recall model 2 for transition-based dependency parsing in Figure 15.6(b), which integrates hidden representations $\mathbf{h}_{i_3}, \mathbf{h}_{i_2}, \mathbf{h}_{i_1}$ and $\mathbf{h}_{j_1}$ for representing s. Are i_1, i_2, i_3 and j_1 static or dynamic? Draw the back-propagation path given a training instance. The BiLSTM representation is updated for optimising the accuracy of action prediction. How does the model learn to coordinate BiLSTM sentence representation with stack information for optimal action prediction?

15.9 Recall Eq 15.31 for neural CRF, where the only parameter for transition scores is $b(t_i, t_{i-1})$. How many parameter instances are in b? Can you extend the transition scoring so that information about the input words can be combined with b?

15.10 Consider Eq 15.35 for training a neural CRF model, which requires the calculation of $P(t_j'|W_i)$. Derive a forward–backward algorithm by consulting Algorithm 8.2 and Algorithm 8.3 of Chapter 8.

15.11 Derive the partial derivative $\partial L(W_i, T_i, \Theta)/\partial b(\ell, \ell')$ for all $\ell, \ell' \in L$ for Eq 15.34.

15.12 In Eq 15.46, we define the local gradients with respect to the hidden vectors $\vec{\tau}(r)$. Similarly, derive the local gradients of Eq 15.44 with respect to $\vec{\gamma}(r)$.

15.13 Derive the back-propagation function BACKPROPAGATE for the bi-affine parser output layer in Eq 15.8–Eq 15.10.

15.14 Character augmented word representation. As shown in Eq 15.1, given a sentence $W_{1:n} = w_1 w_2 \ldots w_n$, we can enhance the representation of a word by augmenting its word embedding $emb(w_i)$ with a character sequence representation $chr(w_i)$. Equation 15.1 concatenates the two representations as the final representation. Alternatively, we can also simply add them together if their dimension sizes are identical: $emb(w_i) + chr(w_i)$. What sources of information does this representation lose compared with the concatenated version? Empirically it can work just as well. What can be the reason? Give the function BACKPROPAGATE for each case.

15.15 Span representation. Equation 15.12 gives the representation of a span in a sentence $W_{1:n} = w_1 w_2 \ldots w_n$ encoded using bi-directional RNN. What are the alternatives to this representation? Can you use pooling functions over all the words in the span? How about attention functions? In fact, you can also use a minus function $\overrightarrow{\mathbf{h}}_e - \overrightarrow{\mathbf{h}}_b$ for representing the span $W_{b:e}$ in the left-to-right direction. Compare these representations, which can empirically give similar performances. What other structured prediction tasks can benefit from span representation?

15.16 Specify a training algorithm for neural transition-based structured prediction with global normalisation (Section 15.3.2) by modifying Algorithm 11.2 in Chapter 11.

16 Working with Two Texts

We have thus far discussed neural models for both text classification and structured prediction, both by learning a text representation. This allows a single base model structure such as the ones in Figure 13.4 and Figure 15.1 to deal with multiple problems. In addition to individual tasks, dense representation also enables conceptually simpler *end-to-end* systems to be built for large-scale downstream NLP problems such as machine translation, text summarisation, machine reading comprehension, question answering and automatic conversation, which are traditionally solved using a pipelined approach, so that entity, coreference, syntax and other necessary linguistic information can be obtained using sub-systems and represented in carefully hand-crafted features. Compared to a pipeline system, an end-to-end neural model learns the mapping between inputs and outputs directly through representation learning, without explicitly considering intermediate structures.

In light of this, this chapter discusses neural architectures that handle two texts, which we have not discussed for discrete linear models. The first architecture deals with text-to-text tasks such as machine translation and summarisation, where the input is a text and the output is another. The second architecture deals with text-matching tasks such as reading comprehension and natural language inference, for which the input consists of two texts. For both types of tasks above, neural models offer conceptually simpler solutions compared with discrete linear models. Through the discussion, we introduce more neural network components, including (1) more neural sequence encoders, (2) neural decoders, which generate word sequences, and (3) neural encoders for two texts.

16.1 Sequence-to-Sequence Models

Neural **sequence-to-sequence** (seq2seq) models offer a conceptually simple framework for text-to-text tasks such as machine translation, summarisation and dialogue. The goal is to map an input text into an output text. For machine translation, for example, the input is a source language sentence and the output is its translation. For dialogue systems, the input can be a user utterance and the output is a system response. A neural seq2seq model works by first finding a neural representation of the input, and then incrementally generating the output word by word.

The structure of a seq2seq model consists of two components: an **encoder** for learning a neural input representation, and a **decoder** for constructing the output sequence. Both RNNs and SANs have been used for building seq2seq encoders and decoders. According to the characteristics of a specific task, the encoder and decoder structures can vary slightly. For example, for a

summarisation system, the encoder should consider multiple sentences and their discourse relations rather than a single sentence input; for a restaurant booking dialogue system, given a user
utterance, the decoder can generate a belief of user intention before generating a response sentence. Without losing generality, we introduce the basic structure, where both the encoder and the
decoder work with one single sentence.

16.1.1 Model 1: seq2seq Using LSTM

Let us first consider a seq2seq model using LSTM for encoding and decoding. Following Chapter
6, for machine translation, we can use X and Y to denote the input and output, respectively.

Encoder. The encoder is the same as the BiLSTM sequence encoder in the previous chapters.
Given an input sentence $X_{1:n} = x_1, x_2, \ldots, x_n$, a BiLSTM is used to obtain its deep hidden representation, which contains its syntactic and semantic information. In particular, we have in each
direction:

$$\overrightarrow{\mathbf{h}}_i^{enc} = \text{LSTM\_STEP}\left(\overrightarrow{\mathbf{h}}_{i-1}^{enc}, emb(x_i)\right)$$
$$\overleftarrow{\mathbf{h}}_i^{enc} = \text{LSTM\_STEP}\left(\overleftarrow{\mathbf{h}}_{i+1}^{enc}, emb(x_i)\right).$$

(16.1)

There are two things to consider for the start states for both the forward and the backward
directions. First, it is a useful practice to add pseudo start and end tokens (i.e., $\langle s \rangle$ and $\langle /s \rangle$) to
the beginning and end of the input sentence, respectively, as we did in Chapter 2 for language
modelling. Second, the start hidden states $\overrightarrow{\mathbf{h}}_0^{enc}$ and $\overleftarrow{\mathbf{h}}_{n+1}^{enc}$ in both directions can be set to $\mathbf{0}$. However, for encoding more information about the source sentence, it has been shown useful to use
$\sum_{i=1}^{n} emb(x_i)$ as their values.

The last hidden states in both directions, namely $\overrightarrow{\mathbf{h}}_n^{enc}$, $\overleftarrow{\mathbf{h}}_1^{enc}$, are concatenated as the final input
representation $\mathbf{h}^{enc} = \overrightarrow{\mathbf{h}}_n^{enc} \oplus \overleftarrow{\mathbf{h}}_1^{enc}$. $\mathbf{h}^{enc}$ is then passed to the decoder for generating an output
$Y_{1:m} = y_1, y_2, \ldots, y_m$.

Decoder. We have not yet discussed a neural decoder, the goal of which is to generate a sequence
of words given an initial hidden vector. This is achieved by generating a sequence of hidden vectors
first, and then generating a word from each hidden vector as a classification task. In particular, our
current model uses an LSTM for modelling the recurrent generation of $Y_{1:m}$, where in each step
i ($i \in [1, \ldots, m]$) we predict y_i given $y_1, \ldots, y_{i-1}$. Formally, a hidden $\mathbf{h}_{i-1}^{dec}$ is used to represent the
generation history from y_1 to y_{i-1} so that y_i can be generated using y_{i-1} and $\mathbf{h}_{i-1}^{dec}$.

For the first step, $\mathbf{h}^{enc}$ is used as an initial state $\mathbf{h}_0^{dec}$. y_1 is predicted by first calculating $\mathbf{h}_1^{dec}$
given $\mathbf{h}_0^{dec}$ and $\langle s \rangle$:

$$\mathbf{h}_1^{dec} = \text{LSTM\_STEP}\left(\mathbf{h}_0^{dec}, emb'(\langle s \rangle)\right).$$

(16.2)

In this equation, the special symbol $\langle s \rangle$ is used as the pseudo-word for representing the start of
a sentence, similar to the encoder. Depending on the task (e.g. translation and summarisation), the
embedding emb' for the target sentence can be different from that (i.e., emb) for the source.

$\mathbf{h}_1^{dec}$ is used for predicting y_1 in the output sequence, through the use of a feed-forward output layer with *softmax* activation:

$$\mathbf{o}_1 = \mathbf{W}\mathbf{h}_1^{dec} + \mathbf{b}$$
$$\mathbf{p}_1 = softmax(\mathbf{o}_1), \tag{16.3}$$

in which each element in the output vector $\mathbf{p}_1 \in \mathbb{R}^{|V|}$ represents the probability of a particular word from the vocabulary:

$$P(y_1|X_{1:n}) = \mathbf{p}_1[y_1],$$

where $\mathbf{p}_1[y_1]$ denotes the value of the element in $\mathbf{p}_1$ that corresponds to a specific output y_1. $\mathbf{W}$ and $\mathbf{b}$ are model parameters. According to $\mathbf{p}_1$, the most probable word y_1 can be selected.

In each subsequent step i, the previous output word y_{i-1} and hidden state $\mathbf{h}_{i-1}^{dec}$ are used as input for generating $\mathbf{h}_i^{dec}$, and then subsequently y_i:

$$\mathbf{h}_i^{dec} = \text{LSTM\_STEP}\left(\mathbf{h}_{i-1}^{dec}, emb'(y_{i-1})\right)$$
$$\mathbf{o}_i = \mathbf{W}\mathbf{h}_i^{dec} + \mathbf{b}$$
$$\mathbf{p}_i = softmax(\mathbf{o}_i). \tag{16.4}$$

Similar to Eq 16.3, we have $P(y_i|X_{1:n}, Y_{1:i-1}) = \mathbf{p}_i[y_i]$, where $\mathbf{W}$ and $\mathbf{b}$ are the same model parameters as in Eq 16.3.

Decoding. Given an input $X_{1:n}$, the decoding process is a greedy local search process, where in each step the system yields

$$y_i = \underset{y_i'}{\arg\max}\, P(y_i'|X_{1:n}, Y_{1:i-1}) \tag{16.5}$$

according to the probability distribution $\mathbf{p}_i$ in Eq 16.4. In order not to restrict the size of output m as a constant, the same process can repeat until a special end-of-sentence $\langle/s\rangle$ token is generated, or a maximum size m is reached.

Training. Given a set of input–output pairs $D = \{(X_i, Y_i)\}|_{i=1}^N$, where $X_i = x_1, x_2, \dots, x_{n_i}$ and $Y_i = y_1^i, y_2^i, \dots, y_{m_i}^i$, the above sequence-to-sequence model can be trained by maximising the log-likelihood of all $y_j^i \in Y_i$ ($i \in [1, \dots, N], j \in [1, \dots, m_i]$):

$$L = -\sum_{i=1}^{N}\sum_{j=1}^{m_i} \log\left(P(y_j^i|X_i, Y_{1:j-1}^i)\right), \tag{16.6}$$

where $Y_{1,j-1}^i$ denotes $y_1^i, y_2^i, \dots, y_{j-1}^i$ and $P(y_j^i|X_i, Y_{i:j-1}^i)$ is the model probability as defined earlier. SGD and its variants can be used for optimisation, where standard back-propagation can be used for calculating gradients on model parameters.

The target vocabulary. Unlike the classification and structured prediction tasks that we saw in the previous two chapters, a seq2seq model outputs a target word from a vocabulary at each time step. This means that the number of classes can be relatively large, in the scale of 10^4. It is a useful practice to restrict the vocabulary so that the model can be smaller and the runtime efficiently higher. For example, we can remove highly infrequent words. This, however, can result in a situation where some words in the training data are out of the vocabulary, making Eq 16.6 undefined.

To address this issue, we can expand the vocabulary by adding a special token $\langle \text{UNK} \rangle$ for representing unknown words in the training data. All OOV words are replaced by the token during training, so that gradients can be computed at each output word. During testing, $\langle \text{UNK} \rangle$ can be the most probable output at certain time steps, which leads to unfriendly results. One solution is to further disallow the $\langle \text{UNK} \rangle$ from being generated during testing. However, since the generation of the next word depends on the current output word (Eq 16.4), this strategy may lead to inconsistency between training and test scenarios, which is harmful. As one alternative solution, post-processing can be conducted to handle $\langle \text{UNK} \rangle$ tokens in the system output.

Beam-search. One disadvantage of greedy decoding is that it can suffer from error propagation. In order to avoid an incorrectly chosen word from affecting a whole sequence of target words to follow, beam-search can be applied. In particular, denote the probability of an output sequence $P(Y_{1:i}|X_{1:n}) = P(y_1|X_{1:n})P(y_2|X_{1:n}, y_1) \dots P(y_i|X_{1:n}, Y_{1:i-1})$. A beam of size K can be used to store the K highest-scored sequences $Y_{1:i}$ at each incremental decoding step i. Then for enumerating $Y_{1:i+1}$, all $Y_{1:i}$ in the beam are expanded by adding a new word y_{i+1} from the vocabulary. In particular, given each $Y_{1:i}$ in the beam, the highest scored M (typically $M = 2K$) y_{i+1} candidates are considered, leading to M new $Y_{1:i+1}$ candidates. As a result, with K candidates in the beam, we have KM new candidates for $Y_{1:i+1}$. From these, the K highest scored candidates are kept for the next incremental step. This process repeats until the highest-scored output sequence in the beam contains $\langle /s \rangle$, or a maximum output size m is reached.

Note that the above beam-search algorithm is slightly different from the beam-search algorithm earlier in this book. In particular, when $Y_{1:i+1}$ is generated from $Y_{1:i}$, enumeration of all possible y_{i+1} gives $|V|$ new candidates, thus would result in a naïve beam-search algorithm with $mK|V|$ time complexity (where m is the number of words in the output sequence). However, the magnitude of $|V|$ can make the naïve algorithm prohibitively slow. It is therefore reasonable to conduct pruning, keeping only the top $M \propto K$ candidates, thus making the number of new candidates scale with the beam size. A typical value of K in practice is 6.

16.1.2 Model 2: Adding More Source Features Using Target-to-Source Attention

Model 1 works by encoding semantic information from a source text $X_{1:n}$ into a hidden state vector $\mathbf{h}^{enc} = \overrightarrow{\mathbf{h}}_n^{enc} \oplus \overleftarrow{\mathbf{h}}_1^{enc}$, which is then used as the starting point of a recurrent decoding process to generate $Y_{1:m}$. This method can empirically give strong results for machine translation and abstractive summarisation. However, the performances do not match up with the best discrete linear models.

As one important limitation, the only connection point between source encoding and target decoding is the source representation vector $\mathbf{h}^{enc}$. When m is large, RNNs face challenges in maintaining long-range dependencies between target and source words. One way to solve this problem is to keep the source hidden states at hand when generating each target word, rather than letting

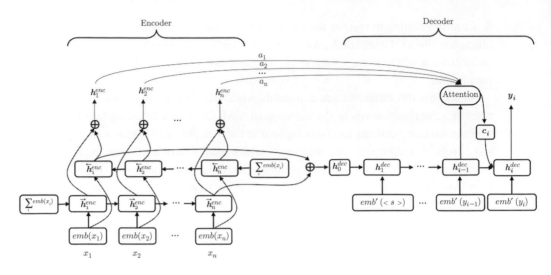

Figure 16.1 Seq2seq model 2 yielding the output y_i.

$\mathbf{h}^{enc}$ become a far-away history when moving down a target sentence. In addition, to avoid loss of long-range semantic dependencies in the source itself when n is large, we would like to consider the hidden states for each source word simultaneously, rather than using only the last hidden states $\mathbf{h}^{enc} = \overrightarrow{\mathbf{h}}_n^{enc} \oplus \overleftarrow{\mathbf{h}}_1^{enc}$ to represent the whole source sentence.

For the above purposes, the attention mechanism introduced in Chapter 14 can be used. In particular, when generating y_i, the previous decoder hidden state $\mathbf{h}_{i-1}^{dec}$ is used to attend over the encoder hidden states over all input words $\mathbf{h}_1^{enc}, \mathbf{h}_2^{enc}, \dots, \mathbf{h}_n^{enc}$ for constructing a context vector $\mathbf{c}_i$, as shown in Figure 16.1. The computation process can be formally described as:

$$\mathbf{c}_i = \sum_{j=1}^{n} \alpha_{ij}\mathbf{h}_j^{enc},$$

where

$$\alpha_{ij} = \frac{\exp(s_{ij})}{\sum_{k=1}^{n} \exp(s_{ik})} \tag{16.7}$$
$$s_{ij} = \mathbf{v}_a^T \tanh(\mathbf{W}^a\mathbf{h}_{i-1}^{dec} + \mathbf{U}^a\mathbf{h}_j^{enc}).$$

$\mathbf{v}^a, \mathbf{W}^a$ and $\mathbf{U}^a$ are model parameters.

Taking the context vector $\mathbf{c}_i$ into consideration, the decoder LSTM time step calculates the hidden state $\mathbf{h}_i^{dec}$ by:

$$
\begin{aligned}
\mathbf{i}_i &= \sigma(\mathbf{W}^i emb'(y_{i-1}) + \mathbf{W}^{ih}\mathbf{h}_{i-1}^{dec} + \mathbf{W}^{ic}\mathbf{c}_i) \\
\mathbf{f}_i &= \sigma(\mathbf{W}^f emb'(y_{i-1}) + \mathbf{W}^{fh}\mathbf{h}_{i-1}^{dec} + \mathbf{W}^{fc}\mathbf{c}_i) \\
\mathbf{o}_i &= \sigma(\mathbf{W}^o emb'(y_{i-1}) + \mathbf{W}^{oh}\mathbf{h}_{i-1}^{dec} + \mathbf{W}^{oc}\mathbf{c}_i) \\
\tilde{\mathbf{c}}_i^{dec} &= \mathbf{i}_i \otimes \tanh(\mathbf{W}^h emb'(y_{i-1}) + \mathbf{W}^{hh}\mathbf{h}_{i-1}^{dec} + \mathbf{W}^{hc}\mathbf{c}_i) + \mathbf{f}_i \otimes \tilde{\mathbf{c}}_{i-1}^{dec} \\
\mathbf{h}_i^{dec} &= \mathbf{o}_i \otimes \tanh(\tilde{\mathbf{c}}_i^{dec}),
\end{aligned}
\tag{16.8}
$$

where $\mathbf{i}_i$, $\mathbf{f}_i$, $\mathbf{o}_i$ are a set of input, forget, output gates for the ith output, respectively. $\tilde{\mathbf{c}}_i^{dec}$ is a cell state. $\mathbf{W}^i$, $\mathbf{W}^f$, $\mathbf{W}^o$, $\mathbf{W}^{ih}$, $\mathbf{W}^{fh}$, $\mathbf{W}^{oh}$, $\mathbf{W}^{ic}$, $\mathbf{W}^{fc}$, $\mathbf{W}^{oc}$, $\mathbf{W}^h$, $\mathbf{W}^{hh}$ and $\mathbf{W}^{hc}$ are model parameters. Equation 16.8 extends the standard LSTM time step discussed in Chapter 14, introducing the context $\mathbf{c}_i$ into the computation of input, forget, output gates and the cell state, respectively.

Given $\mathbf{h}_i^{dec}$, the generation of a target word can be the same as model 1:

$$\begin{aligned} \mathbf{o}_i' &= \mathbf{W}\mathbf{h}_i^{dec} + \mathbf{b} \\ \mathbf{p}_i &= softmax(\mathbf{o}_i'), \end{aligned} \tag{16.9}$$

where $P(y_i|X_{1:n}, Y_{1:i-1}) = \mathbf{p}_i[y_i]$ is the local probability for a specific output word y_i, and $\mathbf{W}$ and $\mathbf{b}$ are model parameters.

16.1.3 Model 3: Copying from the Source

In many cases, text-to-text tasks involve copying words from the source into the target. For example, in a summarisation system, important phrases from a source document can be directly copied into the target summary. In dialogue systems, part of the user utterance can be directly included in a system response for echoing its mention. In machine translation, copying is also useful since certain source terms such as original terminologies and quoted texts can be better left not translated. Both model 1 and model 2 generate target words directly from a target vocabulary, without considering the copying of source words. We build model 3 by integrating copying into model 2.

The basic idea is to allow a source word copying probability to be interpolated with a vocabulary level generation probability when generating each target word. To this end, two things must be considered, namely an expansion of the target vocabulary in consideration of potential source words to be copied (which may not be in the target vocabulary, especially for cross-lingual tasks such as machine translation) and the integration of copy probabilities into generation probabilities. Still denote a source input as $X_{1:n}$ and its target output as $Y_{1:m}$; further denote the target vocabulary as V. Now with source copying, the target vocabulary should be extended with all the words in the source sentence. Denoting the set of unique words in $X_{1:n}$ as U, we have a new target vocabulary for the specific source input, namely $U \cup V$.

The encoder is the same as LSTM seq2seq model 1 in Eq 16.1. Suppose that the current decoding step is to generate y_i. The probability of generation can be the same as model 2, namely Eq 16.9:

$$score_g(y_i = v_j) = \mathbf{p}_i[v_j], v_j \in V. \tag{16.10}$$

In contrast to the generation probability, the copy probability is a distribution over U instead of V. It can be calculated by integrating information from the target hidden state $\mathbf{h}_{i-1}^{dec}$ and each source hidden state $\mathbf{h}_k^{enc}$ ($k \in [1, \dots, n]$), so that a score can be given to represent the probability of each source word being copied to y_i. There are two variations to this end: the **pointer network** and **copying network**. The former reuses the attention weights α_{ij} in Eq 16.7 as a distribution over U, while the latter takes a dedicated neural network layer for calculating the copy score.

Pointer network. We can take α_{ij} in Eq 16.7 as the distribution of a pointer from $\mathbf{h}_i^{dec}$ to a source word, calculating

$$score_c(y_i = x_k) = \alpha_{ik}, k \in [1, \ldots, n]. \tag{16.11}$$

The pointers to the same word in the source vocabulary U are then aggregated so that a distribution over U can be calculated:

$$score_c(y_i = u_j) = \sum_{k:x_k=u_j} \alpha_{ik}, u_j \in U, j \in [1, \ldots, |U|], \tag{16.12}$$

where u_j denotes the jth vocabulary word from U.

Finally, for the generation of y_i, the generation probability and the copy probability are linearly interpolated as the final score:

$$score(y_i) = \lambda score_g(y_i) + (1 - \lambda)score_c(y_i), \tag{16.13}$$

where λ is a weight for controlling the contribution between generation and copying mechanisms. $\lambda \in [0, 1]$ can be calculated dynamically according to information over $\mathbf{h}_{i-1}^{dec}$ and y_{i-1}:

$$\lambda = \sigma(\mathbf{W}^{\lambda h}\mathbf{h}_{i-1}^{dec} + \mathbf{W}^{\lambda y}emb'(y_{i-1}) + b^\lambda), \tag{16.14}$$

where $\mathbf{W}^{\lambda h}$, $\mathbf{W}^{\lambda y}$ and b^λ are model parameters.

Copying network. A copying network calculates $score_c$ directly, by taking the current decoding state $\mathbf{h}_{i-1}^{dec}$ and the encoder hidden state of a source word $\mathbf{h}_j^{enc}$ ($j \in [1, \ldots, n]$) as input, and giving the score for y_i being the copy of x_j. For example, we can use the following network:

$$score_c(y_i = u_k) = \sum_{j:x_j=u_k} \tanh(\mathbf{h}_j^{enc}\mathbf{W}^c)\mathbf{h}_{i-1}^{dec}, \tag{16.15}$$

where $\mathbf{W}^c$ is a model parameter, $u_k \in U, j \in [1, \ldots, n], k \in [1, \ldots, |U|]$.

The probability of generating a target word y_i is calculated by the sum of a generate probability and a copy probability:

$$P(y_i|X_{1:n}, Y_{1:i-1}) = P_g(y_i|X_{1:n}, Y_{1:i-1}) + P_c(y_i|X_{1:n}, Y_{1:i-1}), \tag{16.16}$$

where P_g and P_c represent normalised versions of $score_g$ and $score_c$, respectively, which are a part of a distribution P of the generation and copy, respectively. In particular,

$$P_g(y_i = v_j|X_{1:n}, Y_{1:i-1}) = \begin{cases} \frac{1}{Z}\exp(score_g(y_i = v_j)), y_i \in V \\ 0, y_i \notin V \end{cases} \tag{16.17}$$

$$P_c(y_i = u_k|X_{1:n}, Y_{1:i-1}) = \begin{cases} \frac{1}{Z}\exp(score_c(y_i = u_k)), y_i \in U \\ 0, y_i \notin U \end{cases} \tag{16.18}$$

where v_j denotes the jth vocabulary word in V and u_k denotes the kth vocabulary word in U. $Z = \sum_{v \in V}\exp(score_g(v)) + \sum_{u \in U}\exp(score_c(u))$ is the partition function.

16.1.4 Using Subwords

So far, models 1, 2 and 3 use a special token ⟨UNK⟩ to represent OOV words on the target side. However, the ⟨UNK⟩ token does not contain fine-grained information about the unknown word. In contrast, spelling information such as the case, the prefix and the suffix can give us hints about the meaning of a word. Inspired by this, we can make use of **subwords** to enrich both the source and the target vocabulary in a seq2seq system, treating both X and Y as subword sequences.

The first thing to consider is how to obtain subwords. Morphological segmentation is one solution. However, segmentation of unknown words can be ambiguous, and known morphemes do not cover all words in a vocabulary. Instead, information theory can be used for finding potentially more meaningful subwords automatically from a large corpus. One useful algorithm is **byte-pair encoding** (BPE), a data compression algorithm. The original BPE algorithm uses unused codes (i.e., the character codes which do not appear in the text) to replace the most frequent pair of two consecutive characters, so that one character is reduced. The same replacement action can be repeated until no frequent pairs appear in the text or all character codes are used, and the data receives maximum compression.

Suppose that we want to compress the following text using BPE:

aabaadaab.

The byte-pair "**aa**" is the most frequent pair, which can be replaced by an unused code "**Z**":

ZbZdZb

Then we repeat the process through replacing "**Zb**" by "**Y**":

YZdY.

"**YZdY**" is the final representation, since there are now no more character pairs that occur more than once.

Expanding the vocabulary using BPE. BPE provides a natural way for collecting subwords. In particular, we can run BPE over a large corpus. In each merge operation, BPE finds a new frequent character n-gram, which can be taken as a subword. As a result, after the BPE procedure, we collect a set of subwords. The final vocabulary size is equal to the size of the original vocabulary, plus the number of merge operations. We record the frequency of each word and subword in the vocabulary. Compressed sentences are not used.

Transforming a corpus for eliminating OOV words. Now that we have a new vocabulary with both words and subwords, we can transform words in a corpus into known subwords. A greedy algorithm can be used to this end. In particular, for a given word, we first split it into a sequence of characters, each serving as a subword. Then a recurrent merging process is taken, merging a pair of consecutive subwords into a larger subword in each step. More specifically, among the possible new subwords that can be derived by merging two consecutive subwords, the one with the highest frequency in the lexicon is chosen for each merging step. The same process repeats until no further merging is feasible, namely when the merging results in the original full word, or none of the new candidate subwords are in the subword vocabulary. After the transformation algorithm, if more than one subword is left in a word, all partial words except for the last one are augmented with a "internal subword" symbol "@@", so as to restore the original word information.[1]

For example, suppose that the word to transform is "*aabd*", which is an OOV word, and the subword vocabulary contains "*aa*", "*aab*" and "*bd*" as relevant subwords, with frequencies 5, 4 and 2, respectively. The transformation algorithm first splits the OOV word into a list of subwords ["*a*", "*a*", "*b*", "*d*"]. Then recurrent merging is executed. In the first step, subwords "*aa*", "*ab*" and "*bd*" are considered for merging consecutive subwords, among which "*aa*" has the highest frequency. "*ab*" has a frequency of 0, being out of the vocabulary. Thus we obtain ["*aa*", "*b*", "*d*"] as the new list. In the next step, "*aab*" and "*bd*" are considered as new subword candidates, and "*aab*" is chosen due to higher frequency. The resulting list ["*aab*", "*d*"] cannot be further merged. As a result, we split the word "*aabd*" into "*aab*@@" and "*d*", with "@@" being added to the subword "*aab*" for representing non-ending of a word, retaining the original word information.

Applications to seq2seq systems. Using the above algorithm, we can transform a corpus into a subword-based corpus. From this transformed corpus, we recollect the source and target vocabularies, which now contain words and subwords with and without "@@" ending. The encoder and decoder for a seq2seq system work with the new vocabulary, thus addressing OOV problems. After obtaining a target output sequence, a post-processing step should be taken, merging subwords that end with "@@" with their successor subwords.

16.1.5 seq2seq Using Self-Attention Network

Self-attention networks have been shown to be a competitive alternative to recurrent networks for building sequence-to-sequence models. Here we introduce a framework named Transformer, which uses an extension to the standard self-attention network (SAN) discussed in Chapter 14 for both encoding and decoding. Figure 16.2 shows the architecture, which extends the layer structure of the naïve SAN for better performance. We introduce the encoder and decoder respectively below.

In particular, the structure of the encoder is shown on the left, which consists of K self-attention layers. Each self-attention layer consists of two sub layers, which include a **multi-head self-attention** sub layer, and a standard feed-forward network at each word. K can be decided empirically; a typical value is 6 for machine translation.

Encoder layer structure. Formally, denote the input of an encoder layer as $\mathbf{H}^{\text{in}} = [\mathbf{h}_1^{\text{in}}; \mathbf{h}_2^{\text{in}}; \ldots; \mathbf{h}_n^{\text{in}}] \in \mathbb{R}^{n \times d_h}$ and the output as $\mathbf{H}^{\text{out}} = [\mathbf{h}_1^{\text{out}}; \mathbf{h}_2^{\text{out}}; \ldots; \mathbf{h}_n^{\text{out}}]$. We discuss the encoder layer structure by the sublayer, namely multi-head self-attention, layer normalisation and feed-forward function.

(1) *Multi-head attention sublayer.* Let us first define the multi-head attention function. *Multi-head self-attention* is an extension to the standard self-attention function for extracting

---

[1] Alternatively, one can also choose to add "@@" to the beginning of all subwords except for the first one, achieving the same goal.

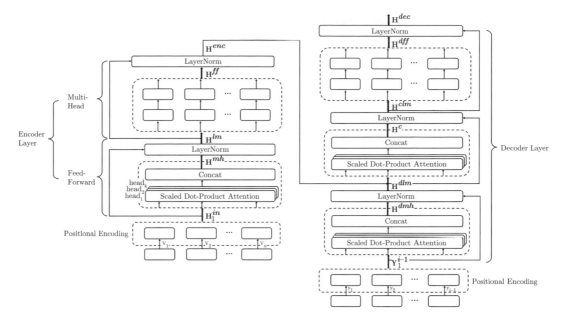

Figure 16.2 Transformer architecture.

richer features. Formally, denote the input to a self-attention layer as a sequence of vectors $\mathbf{V}_{1:n} = \mathbf{v}_1 \mathbf{v}_2 \ldots \mathbf{v}_n$, where $\mathbf{v}_i$ is a d_h-dimensional vector and $\mathbf{V}_{1:n} \in \mathbb{R}^{d_h \times n}$. As mentioned in Chapter 13, standard self-attention represents $\mathbf{v}_i$ by using $\mathbf{v}_i$ to attend over $\mathbf{V}_{1:n}$:

$$attention(\mathbf{V}_{1:n}, \mathbf{V}_{1:n}, \mathbf{V}_{1:n}). \tag{16.19}$$

Multi-head attention extends standard attention by projecting each input $\mathbf{v}_i$ linearly into k feature vectors, each in d_h/k dimensions. A naïve implementation has:

$$\begin{aligned} \mathbf{head}_{ij} &= \mathbf{W}_j \mathbf{v}_i, i \in [1, ..., n], j \in [1, ..., k] \\ \mathbf{head}_j &= attention(\mathbf{W}_j \mathbf{V}_{1:n}, \mathbf{W}_j \mathbf{V}_{1:n}, \mathbf{W}_j \mathbf{V}_{1:n}), \end{aligned} \tag{16.20}$$

where $\mathbf{W}_j \in \mathbb{R}^{d_h/k \times d_h}$ is a parameter matrix.

The smaller hidden size d_h/k of $\mathbf{head}_{ij}$ reduces the computation cost as compared with the original $\mathbf{h}_i$ ($i \in [1, \ldots, n]$). Further, for differentiating features that serve as the query term, key and value in the attention network, we use $\mathbf{W}_j^{query}$, $\mathbf{W}_j^{key}$ and $\mathbf{W}_j^{value}$ for projecting each $\mathbf{v}_i$ into the jth query feature, the jth key feature and the jth value feature, respectively. Therefore, we have instead of Eq 16.20:

$$\mathbf{head}_j = attention(\mathbf{W}_j^{query} \mathbf{V}_{1:n}, \mathbf{W}_j^{key} \mathbf{V}_{1:n}, \mathbf{W}_j^{value} \mathbf{V}_{1:n}) \tag{16.21}$$

where $\mathbf{W}_j^{query}$, $\mathbf{W}_j^{key}$ and $\mathbf{W}_j^{value} \in \mathbb{R}^{d_h/k \times d_h}$ are model parameters, $j \in [1, ..., k]$.

The final multi-head attention output can thus be obtained as the concatenation of all k single-head attention outputs:

$$MultiHead(\mathbf{V}_{1:n}, \mathbf{V}_{1:n}, \mathbf{V}_{1:n}) = \mathbf{W}^o[\mathbf{head}_1; \ldots; \mathbf{head}_k], \tag{16.22}$$

where $\mathbf{W}^o \in \mathbb{R}^{d_h \times d_h}$ is a model parameter.

Now back to the encoder layer structure. Given an encoder layer input $\mathbf{H}^{in} = [\mathbf{h}_1^{in}; \mathbf{h}_2^{in}; \ldots; \mathbf{h}_n^{in}]$, the multi-head self-attention sublayer yields $\mathbf{H}^{mh} \in \mathbb{R}^{d_h \times n}$

$$\mathbf{H}^{mh} = MultiHead(\mathbf{H}^{in}, \mathbf{H}^{in}, \mathbf{H}^{in}). \tag{16.23}$$

(2) *Layer normalisation.* Transformer uses additional layer normalisation over the attention results to reduce overfitting. In particular, a residual connection, which is illustrated in Chapter 13, is used on top of the self-attention function:

$$\mathbf{H}^{lm} = LayerNorm(\mathbf{V}_{1:n} + \mathbf{H}^{mh}), \tag{16.24}$$

where *LayerNorm* is the layer normalisation function introduced in Chapter 13.

(3) *Feed-forward sub-layer.* A feed-forward sub-layer is added on each attention layer to increase non-linearity. Here in each layer, the standard feed-forward network consists of two linear layers, with a *ReLU* activation function in between:

$$\begin{aligned} \mathbf{H}^{ff'} &= ReLU(\mathbf{W}^{ff'} \mathbf{H}^{lm} + \mathbf{b}^{ff'}) \\ \mathbf{H}^{ff} &= \mathbf{W}^{ff} \mathbf{H}^{ff'} + \mathbf{b}^{ff}, \end{aligned} \tag{16.25}$$

where $\mathbf{W}^{ff'}$, $\mathbf{b}^{ff'}$, $\mathbf{W}^{ff}$ and $\mathbf{b}^{ff}$ are model parameters.

Again a residual connection and layer normalisation are used on top of the multi-layer perceptron:

$$\mathbf{H}^{out} = LayerNorm(\mathbf{H}^{ff} + \mathbf{H}^{lm}). \tag{16.26}$$

The encoder. The input representation of Transformer is slightly different from that for models 1, 2 and 3 discussed earlier. Since SAN does not capture explicit order information, word embeddings for a source sequence are augmented with their position information. In particular, given a source sequence $X_{1:n} = x_1, x_2, \ldots, x_n$, the vector representation of each word can be:

$$\mathbf{x}_i = emb(x_i) + \mathbf{V}_i^p, \tag{16.27}$$

where the position encoding component is a hard-coded vector:

$$\begin{aligned} \mathbf{V}_i^p[2j] &= \sin(i/10000^{2j/d_h}) \\ \mathbf{V}_i^p[2j+1] &= \cos(i/10000^{2j/d_h}). \end{aligned} \tag{16.28}$$

Here $i \in [1, \ldots, n]$ is the position of a word in the sentence and $j \in [1, \ldots, d_h]$ is the dimension index in the positional encoding. As mentioned earlier, the encoder is a K-layer network, which takes $\mathbf{X}_{1:n} = \mathbf{x}_1, \mathbf{x}_2, \ldots, \mathbf{x}_n$ as $\mathbf{H}_1^{in}$, calculating $\mathbf{H}_1^{out}$ according to Eqs 16.20 to 16.26. Then for the ith layer, the input $\mathbf{H}_i^{in} = \mathbf{H}_{i-1}^{out}$. The final $\mathbf{H}_k^{out}$ is taken as the encoder hidden states $\mathbf{H}^{enc}$. Note that each encoder layer can have a different set of parameters.

The decoder. The decoder uses the same self-attention function as described above, with layer structure consisting of three sublayers. As shown on the right of Figure 16.2, the first sub layer is a self-attention layer over existing target output words (namely a partially generated target sentence), the second sub layer is an encoder–decoder attention layer over both source and target words, and the top sub layer is a feed-forward sub layer.

Formally, given a source sequence $X_{1:n}$ and a partially generated target sequence $Y_{1:i-1}$, we use the embeddings to represent $Y_{1:i-1}$

$$\mathbf{Y}_{1:i-1} = [emb'(y_1); emb'(y_2); ...; emb'(y_{i-1})], \tag{16.29}$$

where emb' denotes target side embeddings. The first sub layer (target self-attention with layer normalisation) can be described as:

$$\begin{aligned}\mathbf{H}^{dmh} &= MultiHead(\mathbf{Y}_{1:i-1}, \mathbf{Y}_{1\cdot i-1}, \mathbf{Y}_{1:i-1}) \\ \mathbf{H}^{dlm} &= LayerNorm(\mathbf{Y}_{1:i-1} + \mathbf{H}^{dmh}).\end{aligned} \tag{16.30}$$

The second sub layer (target to source attention with layer normalisation) can be described as:

$$\begin{aligned}\mathbf{H}^c &= MultiHead(\mathbf{H}^{dlm}, \mathbf{H}^{enc}, \mathbf{H}^{enc}) \\ \mathbf{H}^{clm} &= LayerNorm(\mathbf{H}^c + \mathbf{H}^{dlm}).\end{aligned} \tag{16.31}$$

Finally, the last sub layer is an MLP layer:

$$\begin{aligned}\mathbf{H}^{dff'} &= ReLU(\mathbf{W}^{dff'}\mathbf{H}^{clm} + \mathbf{b}^{dff'}) \\ \mathbf{H}^{dff} &= \mathbf{W}^{dff}\mathbf{H}^{dff'} + \mathbf{b}^{dff} \\ \mathbf{H}^{dout} &= LayerNorm(\mathbf{H}^{dff} + \mathbf{H}^{clm}),\end{aligned} \tag{16.32}$$

where $\mathbf{W}^{dff'}$, $\mathbf{b}^{dff'}$, $\mathbf{W}^{dff}$ and $\mathbf{b}^{dff}$ are model parameters.

The decoder layer structure can also be stacked into multiple layers (typically 6), each having a separate set of parameters, and $\mathbf{H}^{out}$ of the top layer is taken as $\mathbf{H}^{dec}$.

Now with $\mathbf{H}^{dec} = [\mathbf{h}_1^{dec}; \mathbf{h}_2^{dec}; \dots ; \mathbf{h}_{i-1}^{dec}]$, we can obtain the next target word y_i by:

$$\begin{aligned}\mathbf{o}_i &= \mathbf{W}^{dec}\mathbf{h}_{i-1}^{dec} + \mathbf{b}^{dec} \\ \mathbf{p}_i &= softmax(\mathbf{o}_i),\end{aligned} \tag{16.33}$$

where $P(y_i|X_{1:n}, Y_{1:i-1}) = \mathbf{p}_i[y_i]$ for a specific output y_i. $\mathbf{W}^{dec}$ and $\mathbf{b}^{dec}$ are model parameters.

Training. Similar to the LSTM seq2seq models in Sections 16.1.1–16.1.3, given a set of input–output pairs $D = \{(X_i, Y_i)\}|_{i=1}^N$, where $X_i = x_1, x_2, \dots, x_{n_i}$ and $Y_i = y_1^i, y_2^i, \dots, y_{m_i}^i$, Transformer can be trained by maximising the log-likelihood of all $y_j^i \in Y_i$ ($i \in [1, ..., N], j \in [1, ..., m_i]$):

$$L = -\sum_{i=1}^N \sum_{j=1}^{m_i} \log(\mathbf{p}_j[y_j^i]) = -\sum_{i=1}^N \sum_{j=1}^{m_i} \log\left(P(y_j^i|X_i, Y_{1:j-1}^i)\right). \tag{16.34}$$

Comparison with RNN models. Compared to LSTM seq2seq models, Transformer has two salient advantages. The first is that SAN enables a higher degree of parallelisation. Recurrent time steps are inherently sequential, making the asymptotic time complexity for encoding a sentence linear to the number of words. In contrast, self-attention operations can be done in

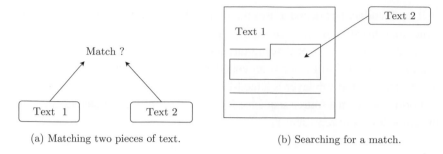

(a) Matching two pieces of text.   (b) Searching for a match.

Figure 16.3 Semantic matching.

parallel on each word, thereby improving the efficiency. The second is a shorter path length between two distantly dependent words. For LSTMs, the encoding of such dependency involves a number of recurrent steps that scales with the word-to-word distance. In contrast, in SAN there is direct interaction between every two words in the sentence at each self-attention layer.

16.2 Text Matching Models

Matching between two pieces of text is useful for making comparison between texts, which is useful for paraphrase detection and machine reading comprehension. Neural representations allow semantic matching by making use of dense representations of words and sequences. In this section, we discuss two basic forms of semantic matching. The first is to decide whether two pieces of text semantically match each other. Examples include paraphrase detection and text entailment detection. This task is illustrated in Figure 16.3(a). The second is to find a section in a given piece of text that matches the meaning of another piece of text. A typical example is reading comprehension, where the algorithm is expected to find a span from a reference document that answers a question. This task is illustrated in Figure 16.3(b).

Both tasks rely on effective encoding of two texts. The key factors to consider include how to represent both pieces of text, and how to represent their correlation. For the former, sequence representation networks that have been discussed earlier are a strong tool. For the latter, techniques range from simple calculation of cosine similarity between representation vectors to more complex iterative processes based on neural attention. We discuss the two tasks in Section 16.2.1 and Section 16.2.2, respectively, before introducing memory networks as a method to solve the second task in Section 16.2.3.

16.2.1 Matching Two Texts in Symmetry

Siamese network. A simple method for matching two sentences, Siamese network applies identical encoders to represent both sentences. The structure of a Siamese network is shown

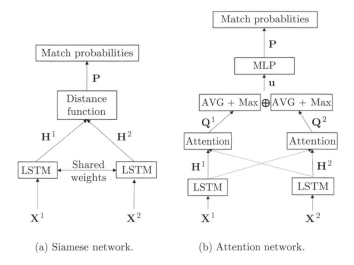

(a) Siamese network.   (b) Attention network.

Figure 16.4 Two types of network structures for text matching.

in Figure 16.4(a). In particular, given two sentences $W^1_{1:n_1} = w^1_1, w^1_2, \ldots, w^1_{n_1}$ and $W^2_{1:n_2} = w^2_1, w^2_2, \ldots, w^2_{n_2}$, we find their respective word embedding representation:

$$emb(W^1) = [emb(w^1_1); emb(w^1_2); \ldots; emb(w^1_{n_1})]$$
$$emb(W^2) = [emb(w^2_1); emb(w^2_2); \ldots; emb(w^2_{n_2})],$$

(16.35)

where $emb(w^1_i) \in \mathbb{R}^{d_h}$ ($i \in [1, \ldots, n_1]$) and $emb(w^2_i) \in \mathbb{R}^{d_h}$ ($i \in [1, \ldots, n_2]$). Then a sequence network can be used to find their deep hidden representations, respectively. Take BiLSTM for example, we have:

$$\mathbf{H}^1 = BiLSTM\left(emb(W^1)\right)$$
$$\mathbf{H}^2 = BiLSTM\left(emb(W^2)\right),$$

(16.36)

where both BiLSTMs of Eq 16.36 use the same model parameters.

The hidden representations $\mathbf{H}^1 \in \mathbb{R}^{d_h \times n_1}$ and $\mathbf{H}^2 \in \mathbb{R}^{d_h \times n_2}$ are used for predicting the matching between W^1 and W^2. In particular, for finding a fixed-sized representation of the two sequences $\mathbf{H}^1 = [\overrightarrow{\mathbf{h}}^1_1 \oplus \overleftarrow{\mathbf{h}}^1_1; \overrightarrow{\mathbf{h}}^1_2 \oplus \overleftarrow{\mathbf{h}}^1_2; \ldots; \overrightarrow{\mathbf{h}}^1_{n_1} \oplus \overleftarrow{\mathbf{h}}^1_{n_1}]$ and $\mathbf{H}^2 = [\overrightarrow{\mathbf{h}}^2_1 \oplus \overleftarrow{\mathbf{h}}^2_1; \overrightarrow{\mathbf{h}}^2_2 \oplus \overleftarrow{\mathbf{h}}^2_2; \ldots; \overrightarrow{\mathbf{h}}^2_{n_2} \oplus \overleftarrow{\mathbf{h}}^2_{n_2}]$, $\mathbf{h}^1 = \overrightarrow{\mathbf{h}}^1_{n_1} \oplus \overleftarrow{\mathbf{h}}^1_1$ and $\mathbf{h}^2 = \overrightarrow{\mathbf{h}}^2_{n_2} \oplus \overleftarrow{\mathbf{h}}^2_1$ can be used, respectively. The correlation between $\mathbf{h}^1$ and $\mathbf{h}^2$ can be used for representing the matching relation between $\mathbf{W}^1$ and $\mathbf{W}^2$. Take paraphrase detection for example, which is a binary classification task that decides whether W^1 and W^2 have the same meaning. For this goal, we can measure the distance between $\mathbf{h}^1$ and $\mathbf{h}^2$. Formally, the distance function $dist(\mathbf{h}^1, \mathbf{h}^2) \in \mathbb{R}$ can be defined simply as a cosine distance between $\mathbf{h}^1$ and $\mathbf{h}^2$, namely $\cos(\mathbf{h}^1, \mathbf{h}^2)$.

Alternatively, we can calculate the match probability between W^1 and W^2 directly using a network. In particular, a multi-layer perceptron can be first used to match $\mathbf{h}^1$ and $\mathbf{h}^2$ by taking the concatenation of the hidden vector as input. Then, given the MLP output, a logistic function can be used to calculate the probability whether both the sentences have same meaning:

$$\mathbf{o} = MLP(\mathbf{h}^1 \oplus \mathbf{h}^2)$$
$$P(match(W^1, W^2)) = \sigma(\mathbf{o}). \tag{16.37}$$

The *sigmoid* activation function σ is used to map the matching probability value into the range $[0, 1]$.

Equation 16.37 allows supervised training for flexible semantic relations. Given a set of labelled training data $D = \{(W_i^1, W_i^2, y_i)\} |_{i=1}^N$, where $y_i \in [0, 1]$ is the true label for instance i, the training objective function can be to minimise the negative log-likelihood loss function:

$$L = - \sum_{i=1}^N \left(y_i \log P(match(W_i^1, W_i^2)) + (1 - y_i) \log \left(1 - P(match(W_i^1, W_i^2))\right) \right), \tag{16.38}$$

where $P(match(W_i^1, W_i^2))$ is calculated according to Eq 16.36 and Eq 16.37.

Attention matching network. Alternative to Siamese network, attention networks can be used to extract correlation information between two sentences, which serves to measure the semantic distance. The key idea is to find representations of each sentence conditioned on the other sentence by the use of neural attention. The structure of a matching network using attention is shown in Figure 16.4(b). In particular, given two sentences $W_{1:n_1}^1 = w_1^1, w_2^1, \ldots, w_{n_1}^1$ and $W_{1:n_2}^2 = w_1^2, w_2^2, \ldots, w_{n_2}^2$, a sequence encoder layer such as Eq 16.36 can be used to obtain their hidden representation $\mathbf{H}^1 = \mathbf{h}_1^1, \mathbf{h}_2^1, \ldots, \mathbf{h}_{n_1}^1$ and $\mathbf{H}^2 = \mathbf{h}_1^2, \mathbf{h}_2^2, \ldots, \mathbf{h}_{n_2}^2$, respectively. Then, in order to obtain a representation $\hat{\mathbf{h}}_i^1$ that contains matching information with W^2, the hidden state $\mathbf{h}_i^1$ of each word w_i^1 is used as the key to attend over all words in W^2. In particular, we calculate a score s_{ij} for representing $\mathbf{h}_i^1$ combined with $\mathbf{h}_j^2$:

$$s_{ij} = \mathbf{v}^T \tanh(\mathbf{W}^1 \mathbf{h}_i^1 + \mathbf{W}^2 \mathbf{h}_j^2 + \mathbf{b}), \tag{16.39}$$

where $\mathbf{v} \in \mathbb{R}^{d_h}, \mathbf{W}^1 \in \mathbb{R}^{d_h \times d_h}, \mathbf{W}^2 \in \mathbb{R}^{d_h \times d_h}$ and $\mathbf{b} \in \mathbb{R}^{d_h}$ are model parameters. s_{ij} values are normalised into a distribution α_{ij} ($j \in [1, \ldots, n_2]$) using *softmax*:

$$\alpha_{ij} = \frac{\exp(s_{ij})}{\sum_{k=1}^{n_2} \exp(s_{ik})}. \tag{16.40}$$

Finally, $\hat{\mathbf{h}}_i^1$ is calculated as a weighted sum of $\mathbf{h}_j^2$ using α_{ij}:

$$\hat{\mathbf{h}}_i^1 = \sum_{j=1}^{n_2} \alpha_{ij} \mathbf{h}_j^2. \tag{16.41}$$

After obtaining $\hat{\mathbf{h}}_i^1$ for all w_i^1 ($i \in [1, \ldots, n_1]$), we obtain a sentence representation $\hat{\mathbf{H}}^1 = \hat{\mathbf{h}}_1^1, \hat{\mathbf{h}}_2^1, \ldots, \hat{\mathbf{h}}_{n_1}^1$ for W^1, which contains matching information over W^2. The above process can be denoted as:

$$\hat{\mathbf{H}}^1 = sent\_att(\mathbf{H}^1, \mathbf{H}^2). \tag{16.42}$$

The same method can be used to match each word w_j^2 ($j \in [1, \ldots, n_2]$) to all words in W^1, for obtaining a matched hidden representation:

$$\hat{\mathbf{H}}^2 = sent\_att(\mathbf{H}^2, \mathbf{H}^1). \tag{16.43}$$

We concatenate the original vectors and the matching vectors as final representations:

$$\begin{aligned}
\mathbf{Q}^1 &= [\mathbf{h}_1^1 \oplus \hat{\mathbf{h}}_1^1; \mathbf{h}_2^1 \oplus \hat{\mathbf{h}}_2^1; \ldots; \mathbf{h}_{n_1}^1 \oplus \hat{\mathbf{h}}_{n_1}^1] \\
\mathbf{Q}^2 &= [\mathbf{h}_1^2 \oplus \hat{\mathbf{h}}_1^2; \mathbf{h}_2^2 \oplus \hat{\mathbf{h}}_2^2; \ldots; \mathbf{h}_{n_2}^2 \oplus \hat{\mathbf{h}}_{n_2}^2].
\end{aligned} \tag{16.44}$$

$\mathbf{Q}^1$ and $\mathbf{Q}^2$ are then used for calculating the matching between W^1 and W^2. To this end, we obtain a fixed-size representation by aggregating the vectors in $\mathbf{Q}^1$ and $\mathbf{Q}^2$. Take average and max pooling for example. Denoting the bitwise average pooling function and max pooling function as $avg()$ and $max()$, respectively, we have:

$$\mathbf{u} = avg(\mathbf{Q}^1) \oplus max(\mathbf{Q}^1) \oplus avg(\mathbf{Q}^2) \oplus max(\mathbf{Q}^2). \tag{16.45}$$

$\mathbf{u}$ can be fed into a final multilayer perceptron for obtaining the probability whether the sentences match each other:

$$P\left(match(W^1, W^2)\right) = \sigma\left(MLP(\mathbf{u})\right). \tag{16.46}$$

Given a set of training data $D = \{(W_i^1, W_i^2, y_i)\}|_{i=1}^N$, where $y_i \in [0, 1]$ is the true matching label of the ith instance, we can train the matching network by minimising the negative log probabilities of the output P, in the same way as the Siamese model in Eq 16.38.

Bi-directional attention matching network. In the above attention matching network, we calculate attention from $\mathbf{H}^1$ to $\mathbf{H}^2$ (Eq 16.42) and $\mathbf{H}^2$ to $\mathbf{H}^1$ (Eq 16.43), respectively. *Bi-directional attention*, also named **co-attention** can be used to extract the mutual information between $\mathbf{H}^1$ and $\mathbf{H}^2$ by sharing a similarity matrix. The key is to calculate a similarity matrix in which each element represents a similarity score between a certain pair of words between W^1 and W^2. Formally, we calculate the similarity matrix $\mathbf{S} \in \mathbb{R}^{n_1 \times n_2}$, where $\mathbf{S}[i][j]$ denotes the similarity score between w_i^1 and w_j^2, $i \in [1, \ldots, n_1], j \in [1, \ldots, n_2]$. The calculation of $\mathbf{S}$ is based on information from $\mathbf{H}^1$ and $\mathbf{H}^2$, which is similar to the case of the uni-directional attention network discussed earlier. For bi-directional attention, we want to cast both $\mathbf{H}^1$ and $\mathbf{H}^2$ into third-order tensors, so that they have compatible dimensionality, and matching operations can be performed conveniently. To this end, we duplicate $\mathbf{H}^1$ n_2 times, and $\mathbf{H}^2$ n_1 times to extend the two matrices into third-order tensors:

$$\begin{aligned}
\tilde{\mathbf{H}}^1 &= \text{Dup}(\mathbf{H}^1, n_2) \\
\tilde{\mathbf{H}}^2 &= \text{Dup}(\mathbf{H}^2, n_1).
\end{aligned} \tag{16.47}$$

In the above equation, $\tilde{\mathbf{H}}^1 \in \mathbb{R}^{d_h \times n_1 \times n_2}$ and $\tilde{\mathbf{H}}^2 \in \mathbb{R}^{d_h \times n_2 \times n_1}$. The matrix-to-tensor extension process is shown in Figure 16.5. With $\mathbf{H}^1$ and $\mathbf{H}^2$, we want to align them by transposing the latter in the n_1- and n_2-sized dimensions. This is denoted as $(\mathbf{H}^2)^{T_{2,3}}$. To capture the interactions between each element in $\mathbf{H}^1$ and $\mathbf{H}^2$, we further calculate the element-wise product between $\mathbf{H}^1$ and

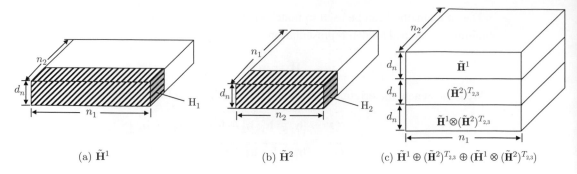

Figure 16.5 Visualisation of Eq 16.47 and Eq 16.48 (shaded shape denotes the original matrix, and full shape denotes the tensor after duplication).

$(\mathbf{H}^2)^{T_{2,3}}$, piling the resulting third-order tensor with $\mathbf{H}^1$ and $(\mathbf{H}^2)^{T_{2,3}}$, as shown in Figure 16.5(c), and then using a linear layer as follows:

$$\mathbf{S} = avg_1\left(\mathbf{V}\left(\tilde{\mathbf{H}}^1 \oplus (\tilde{\mathbf{H}}^2)^{T_{2,3}} \oplus (\tilde{\mathbf{H}}^1 \otimes (\tilde{\mathbf{H}}^2)^{T_{2,3}})\right)\right) \tag{16.48}$$

where $\tilde{\mathbf{H}}^1 \otimes \tilde{\mathbf{H}}^2$ captures the interaction between $\tilde{\mathbf{H}}^1$ and $\tilde{\mathbf{H}}^2$, $\mathbf{V} \in \mathbb{R}^{3d_h \times 3d_h}$, and $\otimes$ represents element-wise product. avg_1 denotes average pooling along the first tensor dimension, namely squeezing a tensor in $\mathbb{R}^{d_h \times n_1 \times n_2}$ into a matrix in $\mathbb{R}^{n_1 \times n_2}$. $\mathbf{S} \in \mathbb{R}^{n_1 \times n_2}$ is a score matrix, where $\mathbf{S}[i][j]$ represents matching information between $\mathbf{h}_i^1$ and $\mathbf{h}_j^2 (i \in [1, \ldots, n_1], j \in [1, \ldots, n_2])$.

Then an $\mathbf{H}^1$ to $\mathbf{H}^2$ attention signifies which words in $\mathbf{H}^2$ are most relevant to each word in $\mathbf{H}^1$. In particular, one attention weight matrix $\alpha_1 \in \mathbb{R}^{n_1 \times n_2}$ is calculated

$$\alpha_1 = softmax_2(\mathbf{S}), \tag{16.49}$$

based on which we calculate $\hat{\mathbf{H}}^1 = \mathbf{H}^2 \alpha_1^T, \hat{\mathbf{H}}^1 \in \mathbb{R}^{d_h \times n_1}$, where $softmax_2$ represents calculating $softmax$ function across each row.

In the reverse direction, a $\mathbf{H}^2$ to $\mathbf{H}^1$ attention weight matrix $\alpha_2 \in \mathbb{R}^{n_2 \times n_1}$ is calculated

$$\alpha_2 = softmax_2(\mathbf{S}^\mathbf{T}) \tag{16.50}$$

based on which we calculate $\hat{\mathbf{H}}^2 = \mathbf{H}^1 \alpha_2^T, \hat{\mathbf{H}}^2 \in \mathbb{R}^{d_n \times n_2}$.

Intuitively, the roles of $\hat{\mathbf{H}}^1$ and $\hat{\mathbf{H}}^2$ are similar to Eq 16.42 and Eq 16.43, with the former being a representation of W^1 that contains matching information with W^2, and the latter being a representation of W^2 that contains matching information with W^1. Given these representation matrices, the same process as in Eq 16.44 to Eq 16.46 can be used to find the final matching probabilities.

Comparison with attention matching. Compared with naïve attention matching, co-attention matching uses one scoring matrix $\mathbf{S}$ for calculating both α_1 and α_2, which makes the attention scores in both directions closely coupled. In fact, the same functionality of Eq 16.46 can also be achieved using separate attention functions in two directions (see Exercise 16.9 for a detailed discussion). Compared with using separate attentions, Eq 16.46 is also more centralised, allowing varieties of bi-directional scoring calculation to be investigated by changing Eq 16.48 alone.

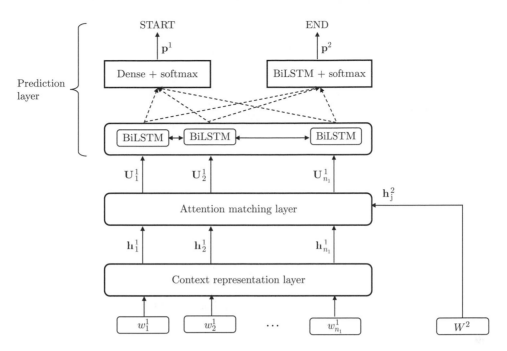

Figure 16.6 Network structure searching for a match.

16.2.2 Searching for a Match

Formally, given a reference text $W^1_{1:n_1} = w^1_1, w^1_2, \ldots, w^1_{n_1}$ and query $W^2_{1:n_2} = w^2_1, w^2_2, \ldots, w^2_{n_2}$, the task is to find an answer span $Y = W^1_{b:e} = w^1_b, \ldots, w^1_e$ from W^1 that matches W^2, where $b, e \in [1, \ldots, n_1], b \leq e$. Borrowing the idea from the previous sections, attention matching can be used to find the indices b and e, respectively. Such a model can consist of three main layers, including a context representation layer, an attention matching layer and a prediction layer, as shown in Figure 16.6.

The *context representation layer* maps each word to a contextualised representation. Similar to the previous section, word embedding can be used to represent each input word, before a network layer is used to extract sentence-level features $\mathbf{H}^1_{1:n_1} \in \mathbb{R}^{d_h \times n_1}$ and $\mathbf{H}^2_{1:n_2} \in \mathbb{R}^{d_h \times n_2}$. Take bi-directional LSTM for example, we have:

$$
\begin{aligned}
\mathbf{H}^1 &= BiLSTM\Big(emb(W^1)\Big) \\
\mathbf{H}^2 &= BiLSTM\Big(emb(W^2)\Big).
\end{aligned}
\tag{16.51}
$$

The *attention matching layer* is responsible for linking and fusing information from the context words $\mathbf{h}^1_i$ ($i \in [1, \ldots, n_1]$) and the query words $\mathbf{h}^2_j$ ($j \in [1, \ldots, n_2]$). First, we calculate a matching score s_{ij} for $\mathbf{h}^1_i$ and $\mathbf{h}^2_j$:

$$
s_{ij} = \mathbf{v}^T \tanh(\mathbf{W}^1 \mathbf{h}^1_i + \mathbf{W}^2 \mathbf{h}^2_j + \mathbf{b}),
\tag{16.52}
$$

where $\mathbf{v} \in \mathbb{R}^{d_h}, \mathbf{W}^1 \in \mathbb{R}^{d_h \times d_h}, \mathbf{W}^2 \in \mathbb{R}^{d_h \times d_h}$ and $\mathbf{b} \in \mathbb{R}^{d_h}$ are model parameters. Then s_{ij} are normalised into a distribution α_{ij} using *softmax*:

$$\alpha_{ij} = \frac{\exp(s_{ij})}{\sum_{k=1}^{n_2} \exp(s_{ik})}. \tag{16.53}$$

Finally, for each hidden state $\mathbf{h}_i^1$ in $\mathbf{H}^1$, the attention vector $\hat{\mathbf{h}}_i^1$ is calculated as a weighted sum of $\mathbf{h}_j^2$:

$$\hat{\mathbf{h}}_i^1 = \sum_{j=1}^{n_2} \alpha_{ij} \mathbf{h}_j^2. \tag{16.54}$$

The original context embeddings $\mathbf{H}^1$ and the matching attention vectors $\hat{\mathbf{H}}^1$ are combined to yield a final representation of W^1:

$$\mathbf{U}^1 = [\mathbf{h}_1^1 \oplus \hat{\mathbf{h}}_1^1; \mathbf{h}_2^1 \oplus \hat{\mathbf{h}}_2^1; \dots; \mathbf{h}_{n_1}^1 \oplus \hat{\mathbf{h}}_{n_1}^1]. \tag{16.55}$$

The *prediction layer* finds a sub sequence of the paragraph W^1 to answer the query by predicting the start and end indices b and e for the answer, respectively. This is achieved in two steps. First, a sequence encoding layer is used to extract further abstract features from $\mathbf{U}^1$:

$$\mathbf{M}^b = BiLSTM(\mathbf{U}^1). \tag{16.56}$$

$\mathbf{U}^1 = [\mathbf{u}_1^1; \mathbf{u}_2^1; \dots; \mathbf{u}_{n_1}^1]$ and $\mathbf{M}^b = [\mathbf{m}_1^b; \mathbf{m}_2^b; \dots; \mathbf{m}_{n_1}^b]$ can be concatenated by each position:

$$\mathbf{Q}^b = [\mathbf{u}_1^1 \oplus \mathbf{m}_1^b; \mathbf{u}_2^1 \oplus \mathbf{m}_2^b; \dots; \mathbf{u}_{n_1}^1 \oplus \mathbf{m}_{n_1}^b]. \tag{16.57}$$

The resulting $\mathbf{Q}^b$ is used for calculating the probability $\mathbf{p}^b$ of each word in W^1 being the start index b by:

$$\begin{aligned} \mathbf{s}^b[i] &= (\mathbf{v}^b)^T \mathbf{Q}^b[i], i \in [1, ..., n_1] \\ \mathbf{p}^b &= softmax(\mathbf{s}^b), \end{aligned} \tag{16.58}$$

where $\mathbf{v}^b \in \mathbb{R}^{3d_h}$ is a model parameter. $\mathbf{p}^b[i]$ denotes $P(b = w_i^1)$ $(i \in [1, \dots, n_1])$.

Second, $\mathbf{M}^b$ is passed to another bi-directional LSTM layer to obtain $\mathbf{M}^e = BiLSTM(\mathbf{M}^b)$. We concatenate $\mathbf{U}^1$ and $\mathbf{M}^e$ element-wise to obtain:

$$\mathbf{Q}^e = [\mathbf{u}_1^1 \oplus \mathbf{m}_1^e; \mathbf{u}_2^1 \oplus \mathbf{m}_2^e; \dots; \mathbf{u}_{n_1}^1 \oplus \mathbf{m}_{n_1}^e]. \tag{16.59}$$

$\mathbf{Q}^e$ can then be used to obtain the probability distribution $\mathbf{p}^e$ of the end index e:

$$\begin{aligned} \mathbf{s}^e[i] &= (\mathbf{v}^e)^T \mathbf{Q}^e[i], i \in [1, ..., n_1] \\ \mathbf{p}^e &= softmax(\mathbf{s}^e) \end{aligned} \tag{16.60}$$

where $\mathbf{v}^e \in \mathbb{R}^{3d_h}$ is a trainable weight vector. $\mathbf{p}^e[i]$ denotes $P(e = w_i^1)$ $(i \in [1, \dots, n_1])$.

Intuitively, $\mathbf{M}^b$ serves as a representation of $\mathbf{U}^1$ specifically for finding b, and $\mathbf{s}^b[i]$ is a score representation by projecting $\mathbf{q}_i^b$ into a scalar using $\mathbf{v}^b$. $\mathbf{M}^e$ serves as a representation of $\mathbf{U}^1$ specifically

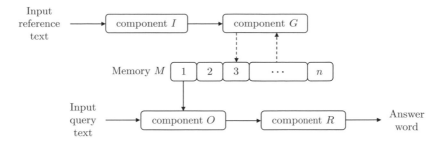

Figure 16.7 Memory network structure.

for finding e. Since the end index e should be highly correlated with the start index b, $\mathbf{M}^e$ is calculated based on the value of $\mathbf{M}^b$.

Given a set of training samples $D = \left\{ (W_i^1, W_i^2, b_i, e_i) \right\} |_{i=1}^N$, where b_i and e_i are gold-standard start and end indices when matching W_i^2 to W_i^1, respectively, the training loss can be defined as the sum of the negative log probabilities of the true start and end indices according to the model distributions, averaged over all samples:

$$L = -\frac{1}{N} \sum_{i=1}^N \left(\log(\mathbf{p}^b[b_i]) + \log(\mathbf{p}^e[e_i]) \right),\tag{16.61}$$

where N is the number of samples in the dataset.

16.2.3 Memory Network

The method discussed in the previous section is useful for question answering by machine reading. For instance, if $W^1 =$ "*Wolfgang Amadeus Mozart (27 January 1756–5 December 1791), baptised as Johannes Chrysostomus Wolfgangus Theophilus Mozart, was a prolific and influential composer of the classical era.*" and $W^2 =$ "*When was Wolfgang Mozart born?*", the algorithm can identify "*27 January 1756*" as the match. However, in many cases, the correct answer to a question cannot be directly read off W^1, but multi-stage inference is required instead. For instance, suppose that the document is "*Joe travelled to the office. Joe left the milk. Joe went to the bathroom.*" In order to answer the question "*Where is the milk now?*", one needs to find out the most relevant fact, "*Joe left the milk*" in this case. Then, one needs to consider the second relevant fact, "*Joe travelled to the office*", before finding a word from the vocabulary to describe the answer "*office*".

Memory network reasons with inference components combined with a long-term memory component that represents the input reference document, learning how to use these components jointly. The long-term memory can be read from and written to, with the goal of facilitating prediction. Formally, a memory network consists of a memory M and four components I (input feature map), G (generalisation), O (output feature map) and R (response). I encodes the reference document into hidden representations; G stores relevant hidden representations into memory; O is responsible for reading from the memory and performing inference; R produces the final response. The flow of the model is shown in Figure 16.7. The components can be trained end-to-end in a text-matching task.

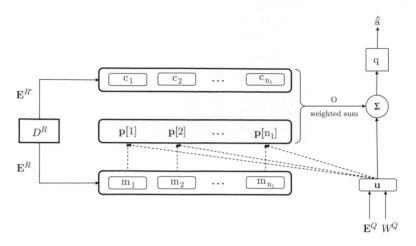

Figure 16.8 End-to-end memory network for question answering.

Formally, given an input document D^R and a query sentence W^Q, let us suppose that the task is to find a word $a \in V$ that answers W^Q according to D^R. Slightly different from the setting earlier, the answer a is from the vocabulary V and not necessarily from D^R. Denote $D^R_{1:n_R} = W^1, W^2, \ldots, W^{n_R}$, where $W^i = w^i_1, w^i_2, \ldots, w^i_{n_i}$, and n_i is the number of words in W^i. Similarly, $W^Q = w^Q_1, w^Q_2, \ldots, w^Q_{n_Q}$ is the query sentence and w^Q_j is a word in $W^Q, j \in [1, \ldots, n_Q]$.

Below we discuss how memory network can be used to match inference.

Input representation. We convert the sentence representation W^i into memory vectors $\mathbf{m}_i$ by embedding each W^i in a vector space (see Figure 16.8). In the simplest case, we use an embedding matrix $\mathbf{E}^R \in \mathbb{R}^{d_h \times |V|}$ with sum pooling to obtain a bag-of-words representation of the sentence:

$$\mathbf{m}_i = \sum_{j=1}^{n_i} emb^{\mathbf{E}^R}(w^i_j). \tag{16.62}$$

One limitation of Eq 16.62 is that it cannot capture the order of words in the sentence. To address this issue, we can further encode the position of words in the representation:

$$\mathbf{m}_i = \sum_{j=1}^{n_i} l^i_j \cdot emb^{\mathbf{E}^R}(w^i_j) \tag{16.63}$$

where $l^i_j = (1 - j/n_i) - (i/d_h)(1 - 2j/n_i)$ is a scalar position encoding, n_i is the number of words in the sentence, and d_h is the dimension of the embedding. $\mathbf{M} = [\mathbf{m}_1; \ldots; \mathbf{m}_{n_R}]$ serves as a memory representation of R for matching with W^Q.

Query representation. The query W^Q is similarly turned into a hidden representation $\mathbf{u}$ using a different embedding matrix $\mathbf{E}^Q \in \mathbb{R}^{d_h \times |V|}$:

$$\mathbf{u} = \sum_{i=1}^{n_Q} l^Q_i \cdot emb^{\mathbf{E}^Q}(W^Q_i), \tag{16.64}$$

where $l^Q_i = (1 - i/n_Q) - (1/d_h)(1 - 2i/n_Q)$ is a scalar position encoding.

Given $\mathbf{m}_i$ ($i \in [1, \ldots, n_Q]$) and $\mathbf{u}$, subsequent layers work by first finding the most relevant evidence from the input memory $\mathbf{M}$, which are then used to form a memory representation vector $\mathbf{o}$. $\mathbf{o}$ is integrated into the query representation $\mathbf{u}$ for deriving a representation that consists of both the original query information and the most relevant evidence. The final representation is then used for directly predicting one answer word from the vocabulary V. Below we discuss these three steps, respectively.

Matching. First, the most relevant memory blocks are found by calculating a distribution $\mathbf{p}$ over the memory cells $\mathbf{m}_i$ using the query representation $\mathbf{u}$. To this end, we first compute a score s_i between $\mathbf{u}$ and each memory cell $\mathbf{m}_i$ by taking the dot-product:

$$s_i = \mathbf{u}^T \mathbf{m}_i. \tag{16.65}$$

s_i are normalised into a distribution $\mathbf{p}$ using *softmax*:

$$\mathbf{p}[i] = \frac{\exp(s_i)}{\sum_{k=1}^{n_R} \exp(s_k)}. \tag{16.66}$$

Second, we calculate a context vector $\mathbf{o}$ by representing R in accordance with $\mathbf{p}$. This is achieved by calculating a weighted sum of the memory vectors using $\mathbf{p}$. In order not to affect the memory cells $\mathbf{m}_i$, a separate representation of each W^i is calculated, which can be done simply by encoding W^i using a separate embedding matrix $\mathbf{E}^{R'} \in \mathbb{R}^{d_h \times |V|}$, resulting in:

$$\mathbf{c}_i = \sum_{j=1}^{n_i} l_j^i \cdot emb^{\mathbf{E}^{R'}}(w_j^i) \tag{16.67}$$

where l_j^i are the same as in Eq 16.63. $\mathbf{o}$ can then be calculated as the weighted sum of $\mathbf{c}_i$ ($i \in [1, \ldots, n]$):

$$\mathbf{o} = \sum_{i=1}^{n_Q} \mathbf{p}[i]\mathbf{c}_i. \tag{16.68}$$

Response. The sum of $\mathbf{o}$ and $\mathbf{u}$ is passed through a final weight matrix $\mathbf{W}$ to obtain a combined representation $\mathbf{q} \in \mathbb{R}^{|V|}$, the columns of which are normalised into a distribution $\hat{\mathbf{a}}$ using softmax:

$$\begin{aligned} \mathbf{q} &= \mathbf{W}(\mathbf{o} + \mathbf{u}) \\ \hat{\mathbf{a}} &= softmax(\mathbf{q}), \end{aligned} \tag{16.69}$$

where $\hat{\mathbf{a}}[i]$ represents the probability of the ith word from the vocabulary being the answer word. $\hat{\mathbf{a}} \in \mathbb{R}^{|V|}$.

Multi-hop inference. As mentioned at the beginning of this section, more reasoning steps can be necessary for inferring the most direct evidence in the input paragraph for making prediction. To this end, we can leverage the existing evidence vector $\mathbf{o}$ to find a new distribution $\mathbf{p}$ over the memory cells, which in turn results in a new context representation of $\mathbf{o}$. This process is typically called a *hop* in the inference process.

To allow multiple inference hops, we take the original query representation as $\mathbf{U}_1$, and the resulting context vector $\mathbf{o}$ as $\mathbf{o}_1$ for the first hop. Then given the kth hop ($k \in [1, \ldots, K-1]$, $K \in D$), we can update the query vector by integrating the existing evidence $\mathbf{o}_k$ and query $\mathbf{u}_k$:

$$\mathbf{u}_{k+1} = \mathbf{u}_k + \mathbf{o}_k. \tag{16.70}$$

After obtaining a new value of $\mathbf{u}_{k+1}$, the same process of calculating the context vector $\mathbf{o}_{k+1}$ can be achieved by using Eqs 16.65 to 16.68. The same inference hops can repeat for K iterations.

At the top of the network, the system combines the input and the output of the top memory layers:

$$\mathbf{q}_K = \mathbf{W}(\mathbf{o}_K + \mathbf{u}_K), \tag{16.71}$$

where $\mathbf{W} \in \mathbb{R}^{|V| \times d_h}$ is the same parameter as Eq 16.69. Using $\mathbf{q}_K$ as input, the response prediction layer that calculates $\hat{\mathbf{a}}$ is the same as Eq 16.69.

Training. Given a set of training data $D = \{(D_i^R, W_i^Q, a_i)\}|_{i=1}^N$, the three embedding matrices $\mathbf{E}^R, \mathbf{E}^Q$ and $\mathbf{E}^{R'} \in \mathbb{R}^{d_h \times |V|}$ as well as $\mathbf{W} \in \mathbb{R}^{|V| \times d_h}$ are jointly learned by minimising a standard cross-entropy loss:

$$L = -\sum_i^N \log\left(\hat{\mathbf{a}}_i[a_i]\right), \tag{16.72}$$

where N is the number of samples in the dataset. $\hat{\mathbf{a}}_i$ is calculated by Eq 16.69 and $\hat{\mathbf{a}}_i[a_i]$ represents the element in $\hat{\mathbf{a}}_i$ that corresponds to a_i.

Summary

In this chapter we have learned:

- characteristics of neural end-to-end models;
- neural sequence-to-sequence models using recurrent and self-attention networks;
- copying and pointer network;
- subword embedding and BPE;
- Siamese network, attention network and co-attention network for text matching;
- memory network.

Chapter Notes

Sequence-to-sequence models were first investigated for machine translation by Cho et al. (2014) and Sutskever et al. (2014), and subsequently applied to text summarisation (Rush et al., 2015) and other NLP tasks. Bahdanau et al. (2015) first explored attention mechanism for NMT, and

Sennrich et al. (2015) adapted BPE (Shibata et al., 1999) to NMT. Pointer network and copy network were proposed by Vinyals et al. (2015) and Gu et al. (2016), respectively. See et al. (2017) used pointer-generator network for summarisation. Transformer was proposed by Vaswani et al. (2017) for machine translation.

Siamese network was originally introduced by Bromley et al. (1993). In NLP, Hu et al. (2014) developed a Siamese network with convolutional layers for sentence matching, and Neculoiu et al. (2016) used Siamese recurrent networks for learning text similarity. Yin et al. (2016) and Parikh et al. (2016) used a decomposable attention model for text matching in natural language inference. Attention for reading comprehension was first used by Hermann et al. (2015), and then extended by subsequent research (Chen et al. , 2014; Cui et al., 2016; Seo et al., 2017). Cheng et al. (2016) and Miller et al. (2018) explored memory network for reading comprehension.

Exercises

16.1 Consider Eq 16.16 again. Can you introduce a weight factor λ similar to the pointer network in Eq 16.14? Work out a new normalisation equation to make P a probability distribution.

16.2 Recall model 1 for seq2seq tasks in Section 16.1. The decoder generates different target sentences given different source sentences, because the LSTM initial hidden state depends on the source. Such a process is also referred to as **conditioned generation**. Its encoding counterpart, namely an LSTM encoder that represents the same sentence differently given different initial states, is called a **conditioned encoder**. Discuss possible applications of conditioned encoding and conditioned decoding. Model 2 can be viewed as a more controlled form of conditional decoding using attention. Can similar ideas be used for conditioned encoding?

16.3 Transformer uses multi-layer SAN for both encoding and decoding. However, models 1, 2 and 3 use only one-layer BiLSTM for encoding. Can multi-layer BiLSTMs be used instead? What are the advantages and disadvantages?

16.4 Seq2seq models and structured prediction.

(a) Can sequence-to-sequence models be used for sequence labelling? What are the advantages compared with the local model discussed in Chapter 15? What are the disadvantages? Discuss the similarities and differences between sequence labelling tasks and sequence-to-sequence tasks.

(b) Can sequence-to-sequence models be used for transition-based structured prediction? Compare the sequence-to-sequence models discussed in this chapter and the transition-based dependency parser discussed in the previous chapter. What are the similarities and what are the differences?

16.5 Consider how sequence-to-sequence models can be used for dialogue systems.

(a) A simple method is to take only the most recent utterance as the input, generating a response utterance as the output sequence. What is the disadvantage of such a model? Is it more useful for chitchat or for task-oriented dialogue?

(b) Now try to extend the model above by modelling the dialogue history. What models can be used for integrating more than one utterance?

(c) External knowledge can play an important role in dialogue systems, offering context for making sensible responses. For example, given an utterance *"I want to find a restaurant."*, the response *"I saw a noodle bar across the road."* requires knowledge that a noodle bar is a restaurant. Discuss possible ways for representing knowledge that are useful for a dialogue system. A useful way to integrate such knowledge into a sequence-to-sequence dialogue system is to use the attention mechanism discussed in Section 16.1.2. In particular, a context vector can be calculated by using the current decoder state to attend over a knowledge representation, and then used for generating the next word. Discuss in more detail how this can be achieved.

(d) Can you use a memory network as discussed in Section 16.2.3 to extend the attention mechanism in (c)? What are the advantages of doing this?

16.6 Some researchers perform AMR parsing (introduced in Chapter 1) using seq2seq methods, by first predicting a sequence of nodes and then predicting a sequence of edges between the nodes. Discuss how a neural network can be built for end-to-end AMR parsing using the above method. Compare the model with a greedy local structure prediction model discussed in Chapter 15 and a transition-based model.

16.7 Consider again Siamese networks discussed in Section 16.2.1. If cosine distance is used for calculating the matching probability of two texts, how can you define a training objective function over data, and BACKPROPAGATE from the output layer to the hidden layers $\mathbf{h}^1$ and $\mathbf{h}^2$?

16.8 In Eq 16.37, $\mathbf{h}^1 = \overrightarrow{\mathbf{h}}^1_{n_1} \oplus \overleftarrow{\mathbf{h}}^1_1$ and $\mathbf{h}^2 = \overrightarrow{\mathbf{h}}^1_{n_2} \oplus \overleftarrow{\mathbf{h}}^2_1$ are used for representing W^1 and W^2, respectively. Alternatively, the average of $\mathbf{h}^1_i = \overrightarrow{\mathbf{h}}^1_i \oplus \overleftarrow{\mathbf{h}}^1_i$ ($i \in [1, \ldots, n_1]$) and $\mathbf{h}^2_j = \overrightarrow{\mathbf{h}}^2_j \oplus \overleftarrow{\mathbf{h}}^2_j$ ($j \in [1, \ldots, n_2]$) can be used instead. What advantage can the averaged representation bring to text matching? Design an aggregation layer using neural attention. Why can you expect a better performance compared to simple averaging?

16.9 Similar to using Eqs 16.39–16.41 for the details of Eq 16.42, describe the details of Eq 16.47 to Eq 16.50 using $\mathbf{h}^1_1, \mathbf{h}^1_2, \ldots, \mathbf{h}^1_{n_1}$ and $\mathbf{h}^2_1, \mathbf{h}^2_2, \ldots, \mathbf{h}^2_{n_2}$. What advantages does $\mathbf{S}$ bring to bi-directional attention in comparison with naïve attention matching?

16.10 Consider again attention matching using Eq 16.46. Some researchers propose an enhanced method for computing sentence-level attention. In particular, $\mathbf{H}^1$-to-$\mathbf{H}^2$ attention signifies which words of $\mathbf{H}^2_{1:n_2} = \mathbf{h}^2_1, \mathbf{h}^2_2, \ldots, \mathbf{h}^2_{n_2}$ are most relevant to each word of $\mathbf{H}^1_{1:n_1} = \mathbf{h}^1_1, \mathbf{h}^1_2, \ldots, \mathbf{h}^1_{n_1}$. $\mathbf{H}^2$-to-$\mathbf{H}^1$ attention signifies which words of $\mathbf{H}^1_{1:n_1}$ have the closest similarity to one of the words of $\mathbf{H}^2_{1:n_2}$.

According to Eq 16.39, we can obtain a matrix $\mathbf{S} \in \mathbb{R}^{n_1 \times n_2}$, where $\mathbf{S}[i][j] = s_{ij}$, $i \in [1, \ldots, n_1]$ and $j \subset [1, \ldots, n_2]$. Now consider the attention weights by $MAX_{row}(\mathbf{S}) \in \mathbb{R}^{n_1}$, where the maximum function (MAX_{row}) is performed across the row. We can have

$$m_i = MAX_{row}(\mathbf{S}[i])$$

$$\beta_i = \frac{\exp(m_i)}{\sum_{k=1}^{n_1} \exp(m_k)} \tag{16.73}$$

$$\tilde{\mathbf{h}}^1 = \sum_{i=1}^{n_1} \beta_i \mathbf{h}_i^1.$$

The vector $\tilde{\mathbf{H}}^1 \in \mathbb{R}^{d_h}$ indicates the weighted sum of the most important words in the $\mathbf{H}^1$ with respect to the $\mathbf{H}^2$. $\tilde{\mathbf{h}}^1$ can be repeated to derive $\mathbf{Q}^1 = [\mathbf{h}_1^1 \oplus \hat{\mathbf{h}}_1^1 \oplus \tilde{\mathbf{h}}^1; \mathbf{h}_2^1 \oplus \hat{\mathbf{h}}_2^1 \oplus \tilde{\mathbf{h}}^1; \ldots; \mathbf{h}_{n_1}^1 \oplus \hat{\mathbf{h}}_{n_1}^1 \oplus \tilde{\mathbf{h}}^1]$. The same can be done for $\mathbf{H}^2$-to-$\mathbf{H}^1$ attention. Try to perform semantic matching tasks using the above for Eq 16.44. What is the advantage of this method?

16.11 For attention-based text matching (such as Eq 16.39 and Eq 16.52), changing the attention function may affect the result. What are the relative advantages of the mechanisms below by intuition?

Bilinear attention:

$$s_{ij} = \mathbf{h}_i^{1^T} \mathbf{W} \mathbf{h}_j^2. \tag{16.74}$$

Dot-product attention:

$$s_{ij} = \mathbf{h}_i^{1^T} \mathbf{h}_j^2. \tag{16.75}$$

Additive attention:

$$s_{ij} = \mathbf{v}^T \tanh\left(\mathbf{W}_1 \mathbf{h}_i^1 + \mathbf{W}_2 \mathbf{h}_j^2\right). \tag{16.76}$$

Given a dataset, the effectiveness should ultimately be verified empirically.

16.12 Recall a multi-hop memory network model in Section 16.2.3. Discuss back-propagation during its training. Intuitively, how can such a memory network learn to make evidence inference?

17 Pre-training and Transfer Learning

We have thus far used dense embeddings to represent words, characters, parts-of-speech, dependency arcs and other sources of information in neural models. Such vectors can be randomly initialised, and then tuned along with other parameter matrices and vectors during training, as a part of the model. But as mentioned in Chapter 13, a better method is to pre-train word embeddings, typically over large-scale raw texts. The resulting vectors are then used as the initial embedding values for a model, which empirically serve as better starting points for fine-tuning. Containing distributed knowledge from a corpus that is significantly larger than that of a typical labelled training set (e.g., a treebank), pre-trained word embedding values can also be used without being fine-tuned during model training.

Seminal work on training word embeddings arises from investigation of neural language models. Starting with a simple neural LM, this chapter discusses various approaches to training word and character embeddings, which allow very fast pre-training of word embeddings over large raw texts. We then discuss more complex neural LMs, showing that hidden vectors from these language models can also be used as pre-trained representations. In particular, both recurrent network LM and self-attention network LM can provide contextualised embeddings of words, which offer significantly richer information for NLP tasks, but can be much more demanding on computational resources due to much higher model complexities. At the end of this chapter, we show that pre-training is a special form of transfer learning, and discuss more neural methods for transfer learning.

17.1 Neural Language Models and Word Embedding

Recall n-gram language models discussed in Chapter 2, which are used to estimate the probability of a word given its $n - 1$ predecessors. A statistical n-gram language model learns a probability lookup table that consists of all the n-grams in a training corpus, estimating the probability of each n-gram using MLE. In this section, we show how a neural network can be used for n-gram language modelling, with its unique advantages. Being a part of the model parameters, word embeddings can be obtained as a by-product of LM training (Section 17.1.1). There has been work that simplifies neural language models for more efficient training of word embeddings (Sections 17.1.3 – 17.1.5), which has become widely adopted in practice. We then show how to evaluate (Section 17.1.6) and use (Section 17.1.7) word embeddings.

17.1.1 Neural *n*-gram Language Modelling

Formally, an *n*-gram language model calculates $P(w_i|w_{i-n+1}, \ldots, w_{i-1})$, where w_i is a word in a natural language sentence and $w_{i-n+1}, \ldots, w_{i-1}$ are its $n-1$ predecessors. Below we make a neural *n*-gram language model by using a feed-forward network to predict a distribution of $w_i \in V$ given $w_{i-1}, \ldots, w_{i-n+1}$.

To parameterise this model, we first use a mapping function *emb* to transform each word into a *d*-dimensional dense embedding vector. Here *d* typically takes a value between 50 and 300. To predict w_i, we can arrange $emb(w_{i-n+1}), \ldots, emb(w_{i-1})$ into a vector sequence, finding their concatenation

$$\mathbf{x} = emb(w_{i-n+1}) \oplus \ldots \oplus emb(w_{i-1}), \tag{17.1}$$

based on which we further use a standard feed-forward network to calculate the probability of w_i, where

$$\begin{aligned}
\mathbf{h} &= \tanh(\mathbf{W}^h \mathbf{x} + \mathbf{b}^h) \\
\mathbf{o} &= \mathbf{W}^o \mathbf{h} + \mathbf{b}^o \\
\mathbf{p} &= softmax(\mathbf{o}).
\end{aligned} \tag{17.2}$$

Here $\mathbf{p}[w_i]$ denotes the value of the element in $\mathbf{p}$ that corresponds to w_i, which represents $P(w_i|w_{i-n+1}, \ldots, w_{i-1})$. $\mathbf{W}^h, \mathbf{W}^o, \mathbf{b}^h$ and $\mathbf{b}^o$ are model parameters.

The overall structure of the neural *n*-gram language model is shown in Figure 17.1(a), which can be viewed as an MLP classifier over *V*. The model consists of its embedding lookup table of size $d \times |V|$ (see Chapter 13), a hidden layer $\mathbf{W}^h$ of size $d_h \times d$ and an output layer $\mathbf{W}^o$ of size $|V| \times d_h$. Since d_h can typically range from 50 to 1000, $|V| \times d_h$ can be large.

Model variation. A shortcut connection from the first layer to the last layer (Figure 17.1(b)) can empirically give better results by facilitating back-propagation training. Formally,

$$\begin{aligned}
\mathbf{h} &= \tanh(\mathbf{W}^h \mathbf{x} + \mathbf{b}^h) \\
\mathbf{o} &= \mathbf{U}\mathbf{x} + \mathbf{W}^o \mathbf{h} + \mathbf{b}^o \\
\mathbf{p} &= softmax(\mathbf{o}),
\end{aligned} \tag{17.3}$$

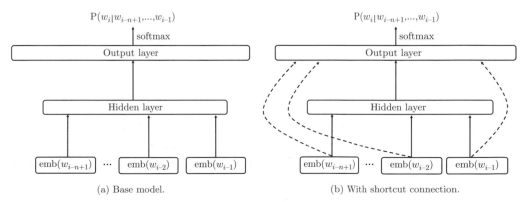

(a) Base model. (b) With shortcut connection.

Figure 17.1 Neural *n*-gram language models.

where $\mathbf{p}[w_i]$ represents $P(w_i|w_{i-n+1},\ldots,w_{i-1})$. $\mathbf{U},\mathbf{W}^h,\mathbf{W}^o,\mathbf{b}^h$ and $\mathbf{b}^o$ are model parameters. Equation 17.3 has one additional term $\mathbf{U}x$ in the hidden layer compared with Eq 17.2, which represents the shortcut connection from the word features to the output.

Training. Given a large raw text corpora D, we denote all the n-grams as $T = \{(w_1^i,w_2^i,\ldots,w_n^i)\}|_{i=1}^{|T|}$. A neural language model can be trained over T using a maximum log-likelihood training objective, where the loss is

$$L = -\frac{1}{|T|}\sum_{i=1}^{|T|}\log\left(P(w_n^i|w_1^i,\ldots,w_{n-1}^i)\right).\tag{17.4}$$

SGD and its variants discussed in Chapter 13 and Chapter 14 can be used for optimisation, where the initial values for the *emb* vectors can be set randomly. In particular, for the ith training instance, denote $w = w_n^i$ and $c = w_1^i, w_2^i,\ldots,w_{n-1}^i$. According to this notation, the local probability $P(w_n^i|w_1^i,\ldots,w_{n-1}^i)$ can be written as $P(w|c) = \mathbf{p}[w] = \frac{\exp(\mathbf{o}[w])}{\sum_{w'\in V}\exp(\mathbf{o}[w'])}$, which is given by the model in Eq 17.2 or Eq 17.3.

Comparison with statistical LM. Embedding vectors capture distributed semantic information of words, and therefore words with related meaning are expected to stay close with each other in the vector space. This allows neural language models to better deal with unseen n-grams as compared with their statistical counterparts, which use one-hot word representations. For example, suppose that the n-gram "*the cat ran away*" is seen in the training corpus but the n-gram "*the emu ran away*" is not. A statistical language model uses back-off smoothing to estimate $P(away|the\ emu\ ran)$ according to $P(away|\ ran)$ and $P(away)$, losing information about "*emu*". In contrast, a neural language model can give a rather accurate estimation if "*emu*" is in the embedding vocabulary (namely the word embedding training data). In particular, the probability of $P(away|the\ emu\ ran)$ can be similar to that of $P(away|the\ cat\ ran)$, since the vector representation of "*emu*" is expected to be similar to that of "*cat*". The example shows the advantage of dense word vector representations over sparse representations.

17.1.2 Noise Contrastive Estimation

The training objective in Eq 17.4 can also be viewed as maximising the log likelihood

$$J = \frac{1}{|T|}\sum_{i=1}^{|T|}\log\left(P(w_n^i|w_1^i,\ldots,w_{n-1}^i)\right).\tag{17.5}$$

For SGD training, given a training instance (w,c), the local derivative with respect to the neural network parameter θ is

$$\begin{aligned}\frac{\partial}{\partial\theta}J &= \frac{\partial}{\partial\theta}\log P(w|c) = \frac{\partial}{\partial\theta}\log\frac{\exp(\mathbf{o}[w])}{\sum_{w'\in V}\exp(\mathbf{o}[w'])}\\ &= \frac{\partial}{\partial\theta}\mathbf{o}[w] - \sum_{w'\in V}\frac{\exp(\mathbf{o}[w'])}{\sum_{w''\in V}\exp(\mathbf{o}[w''])}\frac{\partial}{\partial\theta}\mathbf{o}[w']\\ &= \frac{\partial}{\partial\theta}\mathbf{o}[w] - \sum_{w'\in V}P_\theta(w'|c)\frac{\partial}{\partial\theta}\mathbf{o}[w'].\end{aligned}\tag{17.6}$$

The log-likelihood objective computes the probability $P(w_n^i|w_{n-1}^i, ..., w_1^i) = P_\theta(w_n^i|c) = \mathbf{p}[w_n^i] = \frac{\exp(\mathbf{o}[w_n^i])}{Z(c)}$ according to Eq 17.2. One thing worth noting is that the (context-dependent) partition function $Z(c) = \sum_{w' \in V} \exp(\mathbf{o}[w'])$ can be relatively expensive to calculate due to enumeration of all words in the vocabulary. **Noise contrastive estimation** (NCE) is one technique for addressing this issue.

NCE approximates MLE by drawing negative samples and calculating the probability whether a sample is a positive (real) sample or a negative (out of data) sample. In particular, at each step, we sample a positive sample from an empirical (data) distribution $\tilde{P}(w|c)$ and k negative samples from a distribution Q for words over the vocabulary V. In practice, Q can be a uniform or empirical unigram distribution, which can be given by a unigram language model discussed in Chapter 2. Further, use $d \in \{0, 1\}$ to denote whether a word sample comes from the data distribution, where $d = 1$ denotes a positive sample and $d = 0$ denotes a negative sample. According to the sampling process above, given c, the joint probability of (d, w) is:

$$P(d, w|c) = \begin{cases} \frac{k}{1+k} & \times & Q(w) & \text{if } d = 0 \\ \frac{1}{1+k} & \times & \tilde{P}(w|c) & \text{if } d = 1 \end{cases}. \qquad (17.7)$$

By the definition of conditional probability, we further have:

$$P(d|c, w) = \frac{P(d, w|c)}{P(w|c)} = \frac{P(d, w|c)}{\sum_{d' \in \{0,1\}} P(d', w|c)}. \qquad (17.8)$$

Thus:

$$P(d = 0|c, w) = \frac{\frac{k}{1+k} \times Q(w)}{\frac{1}{1+k} \times \tilde{P}(w|c) + \frac{k}{1+k} \times Q(w)}$$
$$= \frac{k \times Q(w)}{\tilde{P}(w|c) + k \times Q(w)} \qquad (17.9)$$
$$P(d = 1|c, w) = \frac{\tilde{P}(w|c)}{\tilde{P}(w|c) + k \times Q(w)}.$$

Next we try to achieve the same training goal as MLE by inserting the neural LM into Eq 17.9. In particular, to parameterise the model, NCE replaces the empirical distribution $\tilde{P}(w|c)$ with the model distribution $P_\theta(w|c)$. Intuitively, $P_\theta(w|c) = \frac{\exp(\mathbf{o}[w])}{Z(c)}$ is the original probability that requires evaluating the partition function. To avoid computing the partition function $Z(c)$, NCE treats $Z(c)$ as a set of context-dependent model parameters (i.e., one sparse parameter for each context n-gram). We can therefore rewrite Eq 17.9 as:

$$P(d = 0|c, w) = \frac{k \times Q(w)}{P_\theta(w|c) + k \times Q(w)}$$
$$P(d = 1|c, w) = \frac{P_\theta(w|c)}{P_\theta(w|c) + k \times Q(w)}. \qquad (17.10)$$

Now given $T = \{(w_1^i, w_2^i, \ldots, w_n^i)\}|_{i=1}^{|T|}$, a maximum likelihood training objective of this binary classification problem for NCE is to maximise:

$$J_{NCE} = \frac{1}{|T|} \sum_{i=1}^{|T|} \left(\log P(d_i = 1 | c_i, w_i) + \sum_{j=1, w_j \sim Q}^{k} \log P(d_i = 0 | c_i, w_j) \right). \tag{17.11}$$

Comparing NCE with MLE. Again using w to represent w_i and c to represent c_i, the local partial derivatives of J_{NCE} with respect to θ can be written as:

$$
\begin{aligned}
\frac{\partial}{\partial \theta} J_{NCE} =& \frac{\partial}{\partial \theta} \log \left(\frac{P_\theta(w|c)}{P_\theta(w|c) + kQ(w)} \right) + \sum_{j=1, w_j \sim Q}^{k} \log \left(\frac{kQ(w_j)}{P_\theta(w_j|c) + kQ(w_j)} \right) \\
=& \frac{\partial}{\partial \theta} \log \left(\frac{\exp(\mathbf{o}[w])}{\exp(\mathbf{o}[w]) + kQ(w)Z(c)} \right) + \sum_{j=1, w_j \sim Q}^{k} \log \left(\frac{kQ(w_j)Z(c)}{\exp(\mathbf{o}[w_j]) + kQ(w_j)Z(c)} \right) \\
=& \frac{\partial}{\partial \theta} \mathbf{o}[w] - \frac{\exp(\mathbf{o}[w])}{\exp(\mathbf{o}[w]) + kQ(w)Z(c)} \frac{\partial}{\partial \theta} \mathbf{o}[w] \\
& + \sum_{j=1, w_j \sim Q}^{k} \left(-\frac{\exp(\mathbf{o}[w_j])}{\exp(\mathbf{o}[w_j]) + kQ(w_j)Z(c)} \frac{\partial}{\partial \theta} \mathbf{o}[w_j] \right) \\
=& \frac{kQ(w)Z(c)}{\exp(\mathbf{o}[w]) + kQ(w)Z(c)} \frac{\partial}{\partial \theta} \mathbf{o}[w] \\
& + \sum_{j=1, w_j \sim Q}^{k} \left(-\frac{\exp(\mathbf{o}[w_j])}{\exp(\mathbf{o}[w_j]) + kQ(w_j)Z(c)} \frac{\partial}{\partial \theta} \mathbf{o}[w_j] \right).
\end{aligned}
\tag{17.12}
$$

When $k \to \infty$, we have

$$
\begin{aligned}
\frac{\partial}{\partial \theta} J_{NCE} \overset{k \to \infty}{=}& \frac{kQ(w)Z(c)}{\exp(\mathbf{o}[w]) + kQ(w)Z(c)} \frac{\partial}{\partial \theta} \mathbf{o}[w] \\
& - k\mathbb{E}_{w' \sim Q} \frac{\exp(\mathbf{o}[w'])}{\exp(\mathbf{o}[w']) + kQ(w')Z(c)} \frac{\partial}{\partial \theta} \mathbf{o}[w'] \\
\overset{k \to \infty}{=}& \frac{kQ(w)Z(c)}{\exp(\mathbf{o}[w]) + kQ(w)Z(c)} \frac{\partial}{\partial \theta} \mathbf{o}[w] \\
& - \sum_{w' \in V} Q(w') \frac{k \times \exp(\mathbf{o}[w'])}{\exp(\mathbf{o}[w']) + kQ(w')Z(c)} \frac{\partial}{\partial \theta} \mathbf{o}[w'] \\
\overset{k \to \infty}{=}& \frac{kQ(w)Z(c)}{\exp(\mathbf{o}[w]) + kQ(w)Z(c)} \frac{\partial}{\partial \theta} \mathbf{o}[w] \\
& - \sum_{w' \in V} \frac{kQ(w')\exp(\mathbf{o}[w'])}{\exp(\mathbf{o}[w']) + kQ(w')Z(c)} \frac{\partial}{\partial \theta} \mathbf{o}[w'] \\
\overset{k \to \infty}{=}& \frac{\partial}{\partial \theta} \mathbf{o}[w] - \sum_{w' \in V} \frac{\exp(\mathbf{o}[w'])}{Z(c)} \frac{\partial}{\partial \theta} \mathbf{o}[w'] \\
\overset{k \to \infty}{=}& \frac{\partial}{\partial \theta} \mathbf{o}[w] - \sum_{w' \in V} P_\theta(w'|c) \frac{\partial}{\partial \theta} \mathbf{o}[w'].
\end{aligned}
\tag{17.13}
$$

Comparing Eq 17.13 with Eq 17.6, it can be seen that the NCE derivative approximates the MLE derivative when $k \to \infty$. By using a relatively small value of k (e.g., $k = 5$), NCE provides a faster but inexact alternative to MLE via sampling. After training, the resulting embedding lookup table $\mathbf{E}$ gives a set of word vectors.

In NCE, we have another set of parameters, namely $Z(c)$, which can be learned similarly using SGD, by taking the partial derivative of Eq 17.11 with respect to $Z(c)$. However, one issue is that $Z(c)$ is sparse, making the resulting model unable to handle n-grams unseen in training data. In practice, it has been shown that simply setting all Z_c to 1 gives competitive results. Therefore we can avoid the sparsity issue. In this way, we effectively force θ to be trained so that $\exp(\mathbf{o}[w])$ is a **self-normalised** probability value. Thus when using NCE, we can change Eq 17.10 into

$$P(d = 0|c, w) = \frac{k \times Q(w)}{\exp(\mathbf{o}[w]) + k \times Q(w)}$$
$$P(d = 1|c, w) = \frac{\exp(\mathbf{o}[w])}{\exp(\mathbf{o}[w]) + k \times Q(w)}.$$

17.1.3 Optimising Neural Language Models

In practice, we want to make a language model as fast as possible in order to train the model over as many sentences as feasible. Noise contrastive estimation can be viewed as one way of optimising the training speed compared with maximum likelihood. However, it does not change the model itself. A big computational bottleneck of the neural network language model in the previous section is the output layer ($|V| \times d_h$ in Eq 17.2 and Eq 17.3), which has a *softmax* function over the whole vocabulary. Below we introduce two techniques to make the model smaller.

Hierarchical softmax. One way to reduce the size of the output layer is to organise the vocabulary into a hierarchy. In particular, suppose that we can arrange the vocabulary into a hierarchy of two layers, with the first layer containing M categories, and the second layer containing $\lceil |V|/M \rceil$ words in each category. Two steps can be taken for predicting a word, by first predicting a category out of M using a *softmax* function, and then predicting a word from the category. Formally, denoting the last hidden layer in Eq 17.2 as $\mathbf{h}$, we have

$$\begin{aligned}\mathbf{p}^c &= softmax(\mathbf{W}^c\mathbf{h} + \mathbf{b}^c) \\ \mathbf{p} &= softmax(\mathbf{W}\mathbf{p}^c + \mathbf{b}),\end{aligned} \tag{17.14}$$

where $\mathbf{p}^c$ represents the distribution $P(t_i|w_{i-n+1}, ..., w_{i-1})$ and $\mathbf{p}$ represents the distribution $P(w_i|t_i, w_{i-n+1}, ..., w_{i-1})$, where we assume that given t_i the distribution of w_i is independent of $w_{i-n+1}, \ldots, w_{i-1}$, and t_i is the word category. $\mathbf{W}^c, \mathbf{W}, \mathbf{b}^c$ *and* $\mathbf{b}$ are model parameters. In this case, the parameter size of the output layer becomes $M \times d_h + |V| \times M$, which can be much smaller compared with $|V| \times d_h$.

One alternative to using a two-level hierarchy is to use a binary tree to represent all words in the vocabulary, which is more efficient. Here each leaf represents one word. Each word has a unique path from the root to its corresponding leaf. The probability of a word can be computed by the product of conditional probabilities of the corresponding category nodes along the path. The binary tree structure thus decreases the computational complexity per instance from $O(|V|)$ to $O(\log|V|)$. Exercise 17.2 discusses more details.

Log-bilinear model. Hierarchical softmax reduces the language model by changing the *output* layer. We can also reduce the model size by reducing the number of *hidden* layers. Log-bilinear models are such examples. In a log-bilinear model, $emb(w_i)$ is used directly for computing the probability $P(w_i|w_{i-n+1}, \ldots, w_{i-1})$, through a bi-linear similarity function with the context word vectors $emb(w_{i-n+1}), \ldots, emb(w_{i-1})$. In particular, the embeddings of context words are linearly combined into a context vector

$$\mathbf{c} = \sum_{j=i-n+1}^{i-1} s_j \cdot emb(w_j) \qquad (17.15)$$

before a similarity score between $\mathbf{c}$ and $emb(w_i)$ is calculated via dot-product:

$$sim\Big(\mathbf{c}, emb(w_i)\Big) = \mathbf{c}^T \cdot emb(w_i). \qquad (17.16)$$

In Eq 17.15, s_j are weights for each context position j, which can be all 1s or differ by the position. In Eq 17.16, $\cdot$ represents dot-product.

The similarity scores are directly normalised to obtain the distribution of the predicted word $w_i = w$

$$\mathbf{p} = softmax\Big(sim\Big(\mathbf{c}, emb(w)\Big)\Big), \qquad (17.17)$$

where $\mathbf{p}[w]$ represents $P(w_i = w|w_{i-n+1}, \ldots, w_{i-1}), w \in V$. Log-bilinear models are orthogonal to and thus can be combined with hierarchical softmax for building faster language models.

17.1.4 Distributed Word Representations

For the purpose of training word embeddings, we do not necessarily need to train a highly accurate neural language model. Instead, language models can be further simplified for faster training speed. This can result in a simpler way of obtaining word vectors.

Continuous bag of words. A simple and fast method for training word vectors is the **continuous bag of words** (CBOW) model. It can be regarded as a further simplification of the log-bilinear model in Section 17.1.3 with NCE. In the name "CBOW", "continuous" indicates the use of word embeddings rather than discrete word vectors for representing words, and "BOW" represents a model with *i.i.d.* (Chapter 2) assumptions between words. As shown in Figure 17.2(a), the training objective is to predict a word given its neighbours in a size C window. To this purpose, two sets of embedding vectors are used for each word, one (*emb*) for representing a word as the output target, and the other (*emb'*) for representing a word in the context.

Formally, given a set of context words $w_{I,1}, \ldots, w_{I,2C}$, and a target word w_O, we aim to train the embedding of w_O given the context embeddings of $w_{I,1}, w_{I,2}, \ldots, w_{I,2C}$. Here $w_{I,1}, w_{I,2}, \ldots, w_{I,2C}$ can be a surrounding window of w_O. For example, given an *n*-gram

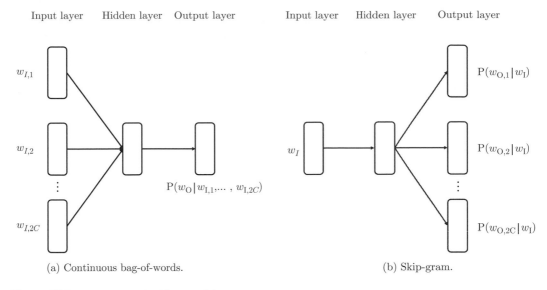

(a) Continuous bag-of-words.   (b) Skip-gram.

Figure 17.2 Two word embedding models.

$w_{i-C}, \ldots, w_{i-1}, w_i, w_{i+1}, \ldots, w_{i+C}$, w_O is w_i and $w_{I,1}, w_{I,2}, \ldots, w_{I,2C}$ is $w_{i-C}, \ldots, w_{i-1}, w_{i+1}, \ldots,$ w_{i+C}. The probability of the target word $P(w_O|w_{I,1}, \ldots, w_{I,2C})$ is calculated by:

$$
\begin{aligned}
\mathbf{h} &= \frac{1}{2C}\Big(emb(w_{I,1}) + \ldots + emb(w_{I,2C})\Big) \\
\mathbf{u}^o &= emb'(w_O) \cdot \mathbf{h} \\
\mathbf{p} &= softmax(\mathbf{u}^o),
\end{aligned}
\tag{17.18}
$$

where *emb* and *emb'* represent context and target embeddings, respectively. $\mathbf{p}[w_O]$ denotes $P(w_O|w_{I,1}, \ldots, w_{I,2C})$. $\cdot$ denotes dot-product.

Given a training set $T = \{(w_{I,1}^i, \ldots, w_{I,2C}^i, w_O^i)\}|_{i=1}^{|T|}$, denote $c_i - w_{I,1}^i, \ldots, w_{I,2C}^i$. NCE is used for training *emb* and *emb'*. In particular, for each training instance $(w_{I,1}^i, \ldots, w_{I,2C}^i, w_O^i)$, we sample k random words as negative samples $w_1, \ldots, w_k$. Using $d = 1$ to represent a positive sample and $d = 0$ to represent a negative sample, the NCE training objective for CBOW is to maximise:

$$
J = \frac{1}{T}\sum_{i=1}^{|T|}\Big(\log P(d_i = 1|c_i, w_O^i) + \sum_{j=1, w_j \sim Q}^{k} \log P(d_i = 0|c_i, w_j)\Big)
\tag{17.19}
$$

where

$$
\begin{aligned}
P(d = 1|c, w) &= \frac{\exp(\mathbf{u}^o)}{\exp(\mathbf{u}^o) + k \times Q(w)} \\
P(d = 0|c, w) &= \frac{k \times q(w)}{\exp(\mathbf{u}^o) + k \times Q(w)}.
\end{aligned}
\tag{17.20}
$$

$\mathbf{u}^o$ is defined by the model in Eq 17.18. Similar to Section 17.1.2, Q can be a uniform distribution or empirical unigram distribution. In practice, C is typically 2 for CBOW. k is typically in the range

5–20 and 2–5 for small training datasets and large training datasets, respectively. After optimising J in Eq 17.19, the target embedding vectors *emb* are taken as the final word embeddings. The context embedding vectors *emb'* here are model parameters and not included into the final set of trained embeddings.

Skip-gram. One slightly different variant of CBOW is the *skip-gram* model (Figure 17.2(b)), which takes the opposite direction in making word predictions. In particular, the target word is at the input layer and the context words are at the output layer.

Formally, denote the context window of a word as $w_{O,1}, w_{O,2}, \ldots, w_{O,2C}$, and the input word as w_I. $w_{O,1}, \ldots, w_{O,2C}$ are typically the surrounding words of w_I. A set of *context embedding vectors* $emb'(w_{O,j})$ $(j \in [1, \ldots, 2C])$ and a set of *target embedding vectors* $emb(w_I)$ are used to compute the probability of the context word $P(w_{O,j}|w_I)$:

$$\begin{aligned} \mathbf{u}_j^o &= emb'(w_{O,j}) \cdot emb(w_I) \\ \mathbf{p} &= softmax(\mathbf{u}_j^o), \end{aligned} \tag{17.21}$$

where $w_{O,j}$ is the jth word in the output layer. $\cdot$ denotes dot-product. $P(w_{O,j}|w_I) = \mathbf{p}[w_{O,j}]$.

Given a training corpus $T = \{(w_I, w_{O,1}, \ldots, w_{O,2C})\}|_{i=1}^{|T|}$, NCE is used to find the embedding tables for *emb* and *emb'*, respectively, under the same setting as CBOW, where the training objective is to maximise:

$$J = \frac{1}{|T|} \sum_{i=1}^{|T|} \sum_{j=1}^{2C} \left(\log P(d_i = 1|w_I^i, w_{O,j}^i) + \sum_{m=1, w_m \sim Q}^{k} \log P(d_i = 0|w_I^i, w_m) \right). \tag{17.22}$$

Here k is the number of negative samples, $d = 1$ represents a positive sample and $d = 0$ represents a negative sample.

$$\begin{aligned} P(d = 1|w_I, w_{O,j}) &= \frac{\exp(\mathbf{u}_j^o)}{\exp(\mathbf{u}_j^o) + k \times Q(w_{O,j})} \\ P(d = 0|w_I, w_{O,j}) &= \frac{k \times Q(w)}{\exp(\mathbf{u}_j^o) + k \times Q(w_{O,j})}. \end{aligned} \tag{17.23}$$

The negative distribution $Q(w)$ can be a uniform or empirical unigram distribution. The choice of k can be the same as CBOW. A context window with $C = 5$ empirically gives strong results. After optimising J in Eq 17.22, the target embedding vectors *emb* are taken as the final word embeddings.

Comparison between CBOW and skip-gram. In CBOW, each target word is predicted once conditioned on the context window. The time complexity is $O(|V|)$. In skip-gram, in contrast, each target word is used to predict $2C$ context words, respectively, and therefore the time complexity is $O(2C|V|)$. During training, CBOW is faster than skip-gram. Skip-gram has been shown comparable or sightly more accurate empirically compared to CBOW.

17.1.5 Word Embeddings using Global Statistics (GloVe)

CBOW and skip-gram make weak use of global corpus-level information since they train word vectors based on local context windows. To address this issue, a different approach is to train embeddings on global word–word co-occurrence counts in a corpus. Formally, use a matrix X to denote word–word co-occurrence counts, where $X[i][j] - X_{ij}$ represents the number of times a word $w_j \in V$ occurs in the context of a word $w_i \in V$. Here a context window can be defined similarly as CBOW and skip-gram. A context window of 10 words empirically gives competitive results. Further use $emb(w_i)$ and $emb'(w_j)$ to denote the target embedding of a target word w_i and the context embedding of a context word w_j, respectively. The word vectors are learned so that the dot-product scales with the probabilities

$$emb(w_i)^T emb'(w_j) + b_i + b_j = \log(X_{ij}), \qquad (17.24)$$

where b_i and b_j represent bias terms for w_i and w_j, respectively. Given a training corpus, we first obtain X_{ij} for every word pair in the vocabulary by counting. The training objective is to minimise the loss function

$$L = \sum_{i=1}^{|V|} \sum_{j=1}^{|V|} f(X_{ij}) \left(emb(w_i)^T emb'(w_j) + b_i + b_j - \log X_{ij} \right)^2, \qquad (17.25)$$

where V denotes the vocabulary. $f(X_{ij})$ is a weighting function,

$$f(X_{ij}) = \begin{cases} (\frac{X_{ij}}{X_{\max}})^\alpha & \text{if } X_{ij} < X_{\max} \\ 1 & \text{otherwise} \end{cases}. \qquad (17.26)$$

$X_{\max}$ and α are hyper-parameters, $X_{\max} = 100$ and $\alpha = 3/4$ empirically gives competitive results. After training, $emb(w) + emb'(w)$ is taken as the final word embeddings for w.

17.1.6 Word Embedding Evaluation

Now that language modelling is not the primary goal, how can we know the quality of the word embedding vectors obtained using different methods? One way to evaluate word embeddings is to measure the performances of downstream tasks when they are used as input representations. To this end, typical tasks include classification tasks such as sentiment classification, and sequence labelling tasks such as part-of-speech tagging. Such evaluation is extrinsic and indirect in the sense that additional parameters are necessary for modelling end tasks. Alternatively, capturing distributed semantic information, word embeddings can also be evaluated *intrinsically* using lexical semantics tasks. Here we list two of them.

The first task is **word similarities**. In particular, there have been corpora that contain words and their related words, such as "*eat : ate, eating, edible, eaten*", each with a similarity score given by a number of human experts. Table 17.1 shows a fraction of such a corpus, which can be used for evaluating word vectors by finding the correlation between embedding-based similarity scores and human-given similarity scores.

We can evaluate the quality of word embeddings by comparing word similarities calculated by embedding vectors and word similarities given by human annotators. In particular, the cosine similarity between embedding vectors is typically used to calculate the similarity between two words. Given the similarity scores X by embeddings and Y by humans over a set of word pairs,

Table 17.1 Corpus containing two sets of English word pairs along with human-assigned similarity scores.

word1	word2	similarity
computer	*keyboard*	7.62
computer	*internet*	7.58
plane	*car*	5.77
train	*car*	6.31

Table 17.2 Similarities given by human and model.

	model (X)	human (Y)
banking–investment	0.5	0.6
telephone–mobile	0.8	0.9
beer–drink	0.7	0.5
animal–human	0.7	0.8
horse–house	0.4	0.2
leg–finger	0.8	0.8

where both X and Y are a list of real numbers, the **Pearson correlation coefficient**, which measures the linear correlation between two variables, can be used as the evaluation metric:

$$\rho_{(X,Y)} = \frac{E[(X - \mu_X)(Y - \mu_Y)]}{\sigma_X \sigma_Y} \tag{17.27}$$

where E denotes mathematical expectation, μ_X and μ_Y are the means of X and Y, respectively, and σ_X and σ_Y are the standard deviations of X and Y, respectively.

Table 17.2 shows a specific example including six sets of scores Y given by human evaluators, and the corresponding cosine similarities X between word pairs from a word embedding model. The Pearson's correlation between X and Y is:

$$\mu_X = E[X] = \frac{0.5 + 0.8 + 0.7 + 0.7 + 0.4 + 0.8}{6} = 0.65$$

$$\mu_Y = E[Y] = \frac{0.6 + 0.9 + 0.5 + 0.8 + 0.2 + 0.8}{6} = 0.6333$$

$$\sigma_X = \sqrt{E[X^2] - E[X]^2} = 0.15$$

$$\sigma_Y = \sqrt{E[Y^2] - E[Y]^2} = 0.2357$$

$$\rho_{(X,Y)} = \frac{E[XY] - E[X]E[Y]}{\sqrt{E[X^2] - E[X]^2}\sqrt{E[Y^2] - E[Y]^2}} = 0.849.$$

The Pearson correlation value of 0.849 shows that word embeddings well capture word relations. Note that the cosine similarity between word embeddings typically capture word *relatedness* rather than *similarity* in its strict sense, because embeddings are trained to learn distributed

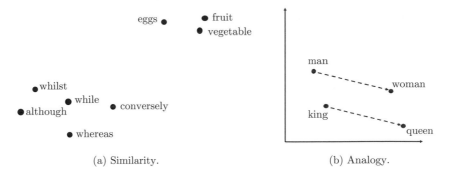

(a) Similarity.   (b) Analogy.

Figure 17.3 Visualisation of skip-gram embeddings.

similarities given a context window. Antonyms are typically highly related just as synonyms are, since they also share similar contexts.

The second lexical semantics task is **analogy**, where a word pair such as "*king – queen*" and a third word such as "*man*" are given, and a fourth word is sought for making an analogy "(*king – queen*) vs (*man –* ?)". In this example, the correct answer can be "*woman*". This test was originally proposed for evaluating skip-gram embeddings, which allows the word vectors to follow $emb(king) - emb(queen) \approx emb(man) - emb(woman)$.

More embedding evaluation methods are discussed in Exercise 17.5.

Visualisation can be used to qualitatively evaluate word embedding vectors. Given that the dimensionality of word embeddings is much larger than 3, they cannot be directly visualised in a 2D or 3D space. t-SNE discussed in Chapter 14 can be used to map word embeddings into 2D spaces. Examples of t-SNE visualised embeddings using skip-gram are shown in Figure 17.3. In particular, from Figure 17.3(a), we can see that words with similar meanings such as "*food*" and "*discourse markers*" are typically close to each other in the embedding space. In Figure 17.3(b), with skip-gram embeddings, word pairs with similar meanings have similar spatial correlations.

17.1.7 Embeddings and Unknown Words

Pre-trained embeddings can be directly used as input word representations in NLP tasks. In this case, the vocabulary V_p for pre-trained embeddings and the vocabulary V_t for a dataset of the end task can be different. Typically, $|V_p|$ is much larger compared with $|V_t|$. On the other hand, there can also be words in V_t that do not exist in V_p. This causes unknown words in two directions. Let us consider the potential impact of $V_p - V_t$ and $V_t - V_p$, namely words in V_p but not V_t and words in V_t but not V_p, respectively.

The former case affects fine-tuning of pre-trained embeddings during model training. First, suppose that pre-trained embeddings are not fine-tuned during model training for the end task. In this case, all word embeddings conform to their pre-trained distributed similarity relations. The model behavior is expected to be consistent on the word embedding level for both in-domain and cross-domain test sets, since words in V_t are in the same embedding space as new test words in $V_p - V_t$. In contrast, if word embeddings are fine-tuned, then words in V_t will change their positions in the embedding space, which makes their semantic subspace different from words in $V_p - V_t$, which are not fine-tuned. This can increase in-domain performance since embeddings in V_t contribute to the set of tuned parameters. However, it can also decrease the generalisation power of the model across domains, where the test data contain many $V_p - V_t$ words. As a result, on a particular NLP dataset, whether or not to fine-tune word embeddings is an empirical question.

Now with regard to the latter case, $V_t - V_p$, the task data can contain words that do not exist in an embedding lookup table. As a result, no embedding vectors are available for their representation. There are several possible strategies for dealing with such OOV words. For example, they can be uniformly cast as a special word $\langle \text{UNK} \rangle$, and assigned an embedding vector. While the value of $emb(\langle \text{UNK} \rangle)$ can simply be set to $\mathbf{0}$ or a random vector, a more useful strategy is to try to learn it from embedding training. This can be achieved by randomly flipping low-frequency words to $\langle \text{UNK} \rangle$ when training word embeddings. In particular, different random samples can be drawn from each sentence at different training iterations. Alternatively, the embeddings of OOV words can be derived from their characters and subwords, which we will discuss in Section 17.1.8.

17.1.8 Character n-Gram Based Word Embedding

As discussed in Chapter 13, the process of word embedding lookup can be viewed as a matrix vector multiplication process, $emb(w) = \mathbf{E}\mathbf{v}$, where the matrix $\mathbf{E}$ is an embedding lookup table and $\mathbf{v}$ is a one-hot vector word representation. The one-hot vector $\mathbf{v}$ can be regarded as an indicator feature vector for representing a word, which is highly sparse. One way to reduce its sparsity is to break the one-hot vector into a discrete feature vector of character n-grams in the word, in which each dimension represents the count of a certain character n-gram in the word. Still using a matrix vector multiplication to find the embedding of a word w, we have:

$$emb(w) = \mathbf{E}\mathbf{v}^{ng}, \tag{17.28}$$

where $\mathbf{E}$ is the embedding lookup table, each column in which can be regarded as the embedding of a character n-gram. $\mathbf{v}^{ng}$ is a vector of character n-gram counts in the word w, where each dimension of $\mathbf{v}^{ng}$ stores the count of a unique character n-gram.

The resulting embedding of w can be regarded as the sum of all character n-gram embeddings in w. Formally, suppose that $w = c_1, \ldots, c_m$, where m is the word size. $C_{i:j} = c_i, \ldots, c_j$ denotes the subsequence of characters from position i to position j. The embedding of w can be written as:

$$
\begin{aligned}
emb(w) &= \mathbf{E}\mathbf{v}^{ng} \\
&= \mathbf{E}\left(\sum_{i=1}^{m-n+1} \mathbf{1}[\text{IDX}(C_{i:i+n-1})] \right) \\
&= \sum_{i=1}^{m-n+1} \mathbf{E} \cdot \mathbf{1}[\text{IDX}(C_{i:i+n-1})] \\
&= \sum_{i=1}^{m-n+1} emb^c(C_{i:i+n-1})
\end{aligned}
\tag{17.29}
$$

where $\mathbf{1}[k]$ denotes a one-hot vector where the element k is 1. $\text{IDX}(C_{i:i+n-1})$ denotes the index of $C_{i:i+n-1}$ in the character n-gram vocabulary. emb^c represents a character n-gram embedding using the lookup table $\mathbf{E}$.

In Eq 17.29, n can be 1, 2, 3, etc., leading to word embeddings based on character unigrams, bigrams, trigrams, etc. Alternatively, we can also sum up embeddings of n-grams of different lengths:

$$emb(w) = \sum_{n=1}^{4} \sum_{i=1}^{m-n+1} emb^c(C_{i:i+n-1}). \tag{17.30}$$

The character n-gram embedding lookup table $\mathbf{E}$ can be randomly initialised and trained in a downstream task via back-propagation.

17.2 Contextualised Word Representations

So far, word embeddings are trained to be invariant across different sentences. More sophisticated LMs allow more contextualised embeddings. For example, as a more computation-intensive alternative to n-gram LMs, recurrent neural networks and self-attention-networks can be used to build language models that capture a history beyond n-grams for predicting the next word. Such language models can be used for pre-training contextualised word embeddings, which are word embeddings that can vary according to sentence-level contexts.

17.2.1 Recurrent Neural Language Models

The strong representation power of neural networks allows us to build neural language models that consider context information beyond n-grams. A recurrent neural LM uses RNN to model a history context from the beginning of the sentence until the previous word when estimating the probability of a word. Below we introduce a RNN LM that uses character embeddings to represent a word.

Formally, denote a sentence as $W_{1:n} = w_1, \ldots, w_n$. We use CNNs for encoding the character sequence of a word. Given a word $w_i = c_1^i, c_2^i, \ldots, c_{|w_i|}^i$, we use a character embedding lookup table for finding $emb^c(c_j^i)$ for each c_j^i in the word. For CNN encoding, we can have

$$\begin{aligned} \mathbf{x}_i &= [emb^c(c_1^i); \ldots; emb^c(c_{|w_i|}^i)] \\ \mathbf{H}_i^c &= \text{CNN}(\mathbf{x}_i, k, d_c) \\ \mathbf{h}_i^c &= max(\mathbf{H}_i^c) \\ emb(w_i) &= \text{HIGHWAY}(\mathbf{h}_i^c), \end{aligned} \tag{17.31}$$

where k is the filter size and d_c is the output dimension of the convolution layer.

On the sequence level, $P(w_i|w_1, w_2, \ldots, w_{i-1})$ is calculated by encoding $emb(w_1), \ldots, emb(w_{i-1})$ using RNN, and then predicting w_i as a classification task over V:

$$\begin{aligned} \mathbf{h}_i &= \textsc{Rnn\_Step}(emb(w_{i-1}), \mathbf{h}_{i-1}) \\ \mathbf{p} &= softmax(\mathbf{W}^o \mathbf{h}_i), \end{aligned} \tag{17.32}$$

where $P(w_i|w_1, w_2, \ldots, w_{i-1})$ is represented by $\mathbf{p}[w_i]$. $\mathbf{W}^o$ is a model parameter.

Multiple layers of RNNs can be stacked for better representation power by treating the hidden states $\mathbf{h}_i$ as $\mathbf{h}_i^0$, and adding more layers $\mathbf{h}_i^1, \mathbf{h}_i^2, \ldots$ on top of each other:

$$\begin{aligned} \mathbf{h}_i^0 &= \textsc{Rnn\_Step}(emb(w_{i-1}), \mathbf{h}_{i-1}^0) \\ \mathbf{h}_i^j &= \textsc{Rnn\_Step}(\mathbf{h}_i^{j-1}, \mathbf{h}_{i-1}^j) \ j \in [1, \ldots, k] \\ \mathbf{p} &= softmax(\mathbf{W}^o \mathbf{h}_i^k), \end{aligned} \tag{17.33}$$

where $\mathbf{W}^o$ is a model parameter, $\mathbf{p}[w_i]$ represents $P(w_i|w_1, w_2, \ldots, w_{i-1})$. $\mathbf{h}_i^j$ denotes the ith hidden state of the jth layer and k is the number of further stacked LSTM layers.

17.2.2 Contextualised Word Embeddings

When trained over a large corpus, a recurrent language model can glean complex semantic knowledge through the representation layers. As a result, given a new sentence $W_{1:n}$, the hidden states $\mathbf{h}_i^j$ ($i \in [1, \ldots, n], j \in [1, \ldots, k]$) of RNN LMs capture sentential contexts for representing input words, which can be useful for disambiguating the meaning of polysemous words, expressing syntactic and semantic characteristics of the sentence context, and even demonstrating commonsense knowledge. As a result, given a sentence $W_{1:n} = w_1, w_2, \ldots, w_n$, the hidden states $\mathbf{h}_i^0$ ($i \in [1, \ldots, n]$) of a single-layer RNN LM can be used instead of the input embeddings $\mathbf{x}_i$ ($i \in [1, \ldots, n]$) as the representation of each word in the sentence. Due to the modelling of context, such word representation is referred to as **contextualised word embeddings**.

When there are multiple hidden layers in a pre-trained RNN LM, the hidden states for a word in each layer can be integrated using linear interpolation for contextualised word embeddings:

$$\mathbf{H} = \sum_{j=1}^{k} s^j \mathbf{H}^j, \tag{17.34}$$

where $\mathbf{H}^j = [\mathbf{h}_1^j, \ldots, \mathbf{h}_n^j]$. s^j are weights that add up to 1, which can be hyper-parameters of the model. For example, if only the last hidden layer is used, $[s^0, s^1, \ldots, s^{k-1}, s^k] = [0, 0, \ldots, 0, 1]$.

Bi-directional extension. One potential issue of the above embeddings, however, is that they capture only the left context of each word. To address this limitation, bi-directional RNN can be used, where a second RNN LM is trained in the reverse order, capturing sentential contexts right-to-left. Denoting the hidden states of the left-to-right RNN for each word w_j as $\overrightarrow{\mathbf{H}}^j$

and the right-to-left RNN as $\overleftarrow{\mathbf{H}}^j$, the hidden states can be concatenated for representing each word:

$$\mathbf{H}^j = [\overrightarrow{\mathbf{h}}_1^j \oplus \overleftarrow{\mathbf{h}}_1^j; \overrightarrow{\mathbf{h}}_2^j \oplus \overleftarrow{\mathbf{h}}_2^j; \ldots; \overrightarrow{\mathbf{h}}_n^j \oplus \overleftarrow{\mathbf{h}}_n^j], \tag{17.35}$$

where $\oplus$ denotes vector concatenation. Eq 17.34 can be further applied for obtaining contextualised word representation.

Comparison with skip-gram and GloVe embeddings. In contrast to skip-gram and GloVe embeddings, which are fixed after training, contextualised embeddings are calculated dynamically given a sentence. For skip-gram and GloVe, each vocabulary word has a fixed vector representation across sentences. In contrast, contextualised embeddings for each word vary from sentence to sentence. Similar to skip-gram and GloVe embeddings, contextualised embeddings can also be fine-tuned, the decision of which should be empirical. However, different from skip-gram and GloVe, for which the embedding parameters are constrained to an embedding lookup table, parameters in contextualised embedding models consist of weights and biases in RNN layers also. During training, these parameters should be updated using back-propagation, as a part of the the model parameters. The model in Eqs 17.34 and 17.35 is also referred to as Embeddings from Language Models (**ELMo**).

17.2.3 Contextualised Embeddings using Self-Attention

SANs are sequence encoder networks just like RNNs. As a result, we can build SAN counterparts to RNNs for both neural language modellings contextualised embeddings.

Self-attention-network language models. As an alternative to RNN LM, a muliti-layer SAN can also be used to estimate the probability of a word. As shown in Figure 17.4(a), given a sequence of words $W_{1:i-1} = w_1, w_2, \ldots, w_{i-1}$, a k-layer SAN LM predicts the next word w_i by:

$$\begin{aligned}
\mathbf{H}^0 &= [emb(w_1); \ldots; emb(w_{i-1})] + \mathbf{V}^p \\
\mathbf{H}^j &= \text{SAN\_ENCODER\_L}(\mathbf{H}^{j-1}) \ j \in [1, \ldots, k] \\
\mathbf{p} &= softmax(\mathbf{W}\mathbf{h}_i^k),
\end{aligned} \tag{17.36}$$

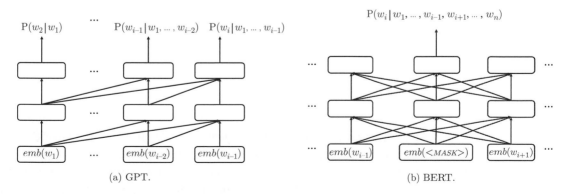

(a) GPT.   (b) BERT.

Figure 17.4 Contextualised word embeddings using SAN.

where $\mathbf{W}$ is a model parameter. k denotes the number of SAN layers. $\mathbf{p}[w_i]$ represents $P(w_i|w_1, w_2, \ldots, w_{i-1})$. $\mathbf{V}^p$ is a position embedding matrix. In particular, for a word w_i, the position encoding $\mathbf{V}^p[i]$ is calculated by:

$$
\begin{aligned}
\mathbf{V}^p[i][2j] &= \sin(i/10000^{2j/|\mathbf{V}^p|}) \\
\mathbf{V}^p[i][2j+1] &= \cos(i/10000^{2j/|\mathbf{V}^p|}),
\end{aligned}
\tag{17.37}
$$

where $2j$ and $2j+1$ denotes an element in $\mathbf{V}^p[i]$, $j \in [1, \ldots, |\mathbf{V}^p|/2]$.

In Eq 17.36, the function SAN_ENCODER_L corresponds to a self-attention-network layer for sequence encoding, which can be implemented through the Transformer architecture discussed in Chapter 16. However, for language modelling, we use each word w_i as a query vector to attend to only key vectors of its preceding words $w_1, w_2, \ldots, w_{i-1}$, but not its succeeding words. In this way, we effectively make a prediction for each word according to the preceding context, calculating $P(w_i|w_1, w_2, \ldots, w_{i-1})$ as we do for RNN LMs.

Similar to RNN LMs, the above SAN LM can be trained over large-scale texts. Formally, denoting a training set as $D = \{W_i\}|_{i=1}^N$, where $W_i = w_1^i, w_2^i, \ldots, w_{|W_i|}^i$, we minimise the negative log-likelihood of all words

$$
L = -\sum_{i=1}^{N} \sum_{j=1}^{|W_i|} \log P(w_j^i|w_1^i, \ldots, w_{j-1}^i).
\tag{17.38}
$$

Contextualised embeddings using SAN LM. After LM training, given a sentence $W_{1:n} = w_1, \ldots, w_n$, we use Eq 17.36 to calculate hidden states, and the top hidden layer representation $\mathbf{h}_i^k$ of a word w_i can be used as the contextualised representation of the word. This method has been used as a principle behind the Generative Pre-Training (GPT) model, which is built using the Transformer architecture.

17.2.4 Bi-directional Self-Attention-Network LMs

Masked langauge modelling. Intuitively, sentence-level information from both the left and right context can be useful for predicting a word. For example, given the sentence "*I went to the* ⟨MASK⟩ *to get some food.*", we can predict that the masked word ⟨MASK⟩ can be some location that a person visits according to the left context. However, if we further know the right context, we can better guess that the word is likely "*restaurant*", "*pizzeria*", "*store*", "*cafe*" or "*pub*", where food is sold. This provides a third option for defining a language model, in addition to the n-gram LM and RNN LMs we have seen earlier. Let us consider using SAN for building such a model. As shown in Figure 17.4(b), we represent each word by jointly considering both its left and right context in each SAN layer. To train a language model, we repeatedly mask a randomly chosen token as a special symbol ⟨MASK⟩ (or a random word), and predict the masked token in the input sentence. This training objective is referred as the **masked language model** (MLM).

In particular, given $w_1, w_2, \ldots, w_n$, suppose that a certain token w_i ($i \in [1, \ldots, n]$) is masked. We predict w_i using:

$$
\begin{aligned}
\mathbf{H}^0 &= [emb(w_1); \ldots; emb(w_{i-1}); emb(\langle \text{MASK} \rangle); emb(w_{i+1}); \ldots; emb(w_n)] + \mathbf{V}^p \\
\mathbf{H}^j &= \text{SAN\_ENCODER}(\mathbf{H}^{j-1}) \quad j \in [1, \ldots, k] \\
\mathbf{p} &= softmax(\mathbf{W}\mathbf{h}_i^k),
\end{aligned}
\tag{17.39}
$$

where $\mathbf{V}_p$ is the position embedding matrix in Eq 17.37 and $\mathbf{W}$ is a model parameter. Similar to Eq 17.36, k denotes the number of SAN layers. $\mathbf{p}[w_i]$ denotes $P(w_i|w_1, \ldots, w_{i-1}, \langle \text{MASK} \rangle, w_{i+1}, \ldots, w_n)$. Different from Eq 17.36, SAN_ENCODER here is the standard SAN encoder without constraints on attention targets (i.e. to the left only).

The above model can be trained over large unlabelled text. Formally, given $D = \{W_i\}|_{i=1}^N$, we first perform masking to derive training instances with $\langle \text{MASK} \rangle$ symbols. In particular, we can randomly choose $\alpha\%$ of the words in D and mask them. A typical value of α is 15. Given the resulting corpus, we minimise

$$
L = -\sum_{i=1}^{N} \sum_{j=1}^{|W_i|} \log \left(P(w_j^i | w_1^i, \ldots, w_{j-1}^i, \langle \text{MASK} \rangle, w_{j+1}^i, \ldots, w_{|W_i|}^i) \right). \tag{17.40}
$$

Contextualised embeddings using masked LM. After LM training, given a new sentence $W_{1:n} = w_1, \ldots, w_n$, we use the pre-trained model to calculate hidden states, where

$$
\begin{aligned}
\mathbf{H}^0 &= [emb(w_1); \ldots; emb(w_n)] + \mathbf{V}^p \\
\mathbf{H}^j &= \text{SAN\_ENCODER}(\mathbf{H}^{j-1}) \quad j \in [1, \ldots, k].
\end{aligned}
\tag{17.41}
$$

$\mathbf{V}^p$ is defined similarly as Eq 17.37. $\mathbf{h}_i^k$ ($i \in [1, \ldots, n]$) is used as the contextualised embedding for w_i.

Note that Eq 17.41 is slightly different from Eq 17.39. Here inconsistency arises between training and testing scenarios because of masking during training – in order not to simply copy a word for predicting itself, we replace a word to be predicted with a $\langle \text{MASK} \rangle$ token. In this way each word is predicted solely based on its left and right context words. However, at test time, our goal is to calculate a contextualised embedding for each word in a given sentence, and therefore we cannot mask any word.

To solve this problem, the testing scenario should be reflected in the training process as much as possible. One strategy is to integrate different settings during training, by replacing the masked token with the special $\langle \text{MASK} \rangle$ token, a random word and the original word, respectively, with a 80%: 10%: 10% ratio, for predicting the token. Thus 10% of the training samples have identical settings as the test samples, which provides a chance for the model to gain consistency. In addition, 80% of the samples are still masked, so that the model will not learn to superficially copy the input. Finally, we combine the above strategy with the original sampling strategy for pre-processing a corpus D. In particular, $\alpha\%$ of the words in D are first randomly selected for being predicted. Then for each word to be predicted, the 80% / 10% / 10% masking strategy is further applied, resulting in a set of training instances. For example, suppose that a training sentence is "*I went to the supermarket to buy a can of beans*", a pre-processed version can be "*I went to the* $\langle \text{MASK} \rangle$

to buy a <u>dog</u> of <u>beans</u>", where the underlined words are the words to predict in masked language model training.

The above contextualised embedding method has been used as a principle behind the Bidirectional Encoder Representations from Transformers (**BERT**) model.

SAN LM vs RNN LM. Compared with contextualised representations using RNN LM, those with SAN LM enjoy the following relative advantages. First, SAN aggregates information from all words in a sentence simultaneously, and can therefore be better at capturing long-range semantic dependencies. Second, SAN allows better parallelisation and therefore can be faster to train. In order to reduce sparsity, BPE (Chapter 16) can be used to make subwords the basic unit of contextualised language models rather than words. When this is the case, embedding of the first subword can be used as the word representation.

17.2.5 Using Contextualised Embeddings

As mentioned earlier, contextualised embeddings can be used to replace static embeddings such as skip-gram and GloVe for input representation, where fine-tuning of RNN/SAN parameters can be done during training. Due to the strong representation power of contextualised embedding models, it turns out that they allow light-weight output layers to achieve competitive results for NLP tasks. For example, for text classification, given a word sequence $W_{1:n}$, a competitve sequence labeller can be built by using a local MLP output layer on top of the contextualised embedding $\mathbf{h}_i$ of each word w_i ($i \in [1, ..., n]$), without using additional sequence encoding layers.

A main reason behind the above observation is that contextualised embeddings contain rich knowledge automatically learned from large texts, which can cover syntax, semantics and even commonsense knowledge. To empirically verify to what extent a specific type of knowledge is contained in a contextualised embedding model, *probing tasks* discussed in Chapter 14 can be used. For example, when probing hidden representations from a multi-layer BERT model, people found that the lower layer representations contain more shallow syntactic knowledge, while the higher layers contain more abstract semantic knowledge.

17.3 Transfer Learning

Transfer learning makes use of knowledge from one particular task, domain or language to help improve performance on a different task, domain or language. For discrete linear models, transfer learning is typically performed by extracting shared features across tasks, or defining cross-task output features explicitly. For neural models, in contrast, transfer learning can be achieved by sharing representation of input structures.

Pre-training techniques discussed earlier can be viewed as a form of transfer learning, which applies knowledge learned from the task of language modelling to a subsequent NLP task. In particular, the same model parameters are shared between a pre-trained language model and a subsequent task, where pre-training serves to bring LM knowledge into the parameters for a better starting point of the subsequent task. We have seen two main types of pre-trained parameters. One, as exemplified by skip-gram, consists of a set of embedding vectors, which can be used via table lookup. The other, as exemplified by ELMo and BERT, consists of a deep neural network, through which contextualised vector representations are computed given an input.

Pre-training beyond LM. The idea of pre-training can be applied beyond language modelling, for transferring knowledge from resource-rich tasks, domains, languages and annotation standards to low-resource ones. For example, syntactic resources can be used to pre-train models for semantic role labelling. Relatively larger corpora in the news domain can be used to pre-train models for low-resource domains such as social media. In neural machine translation, there has been work using resource-rich language pairs such as English–French for pre-training a model for low-resource language pairs such as English–Uzbek.

Beyond pre-training. The idea of parameter sharing can also be implemented by methods beyond pre-training. This section discusses various forms of multi-task learning through representation learning. We use the term *task* to describe transfer learning methods, although it can also stand for *domain, language, annotation standard*, etc.

17.3.1 Multi-Task Learning

Multi-task learning exploits parameter sharing for seeking mutual benefits between tasks. It is correlated with pre-training in the sense that both transfer knowledge from task to task via shared representation parameters. Figure 17.5(a) shows a pre-training example, where knowledge from a language modelling task is transferred to a sequence labelling task. In particular, given a word sequence $W_{1:n} = w_1, \ldots, w_n$, a standard LSTM is used to obtain a hidden state sequence

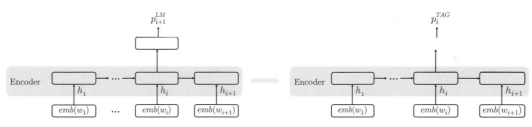

(a) Language modeling pre-training for better sequence labelling.

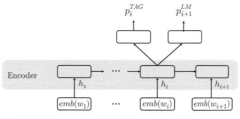

(b) Multi-task learning for LM and sequence labelling.

Figure 17.5 Transfer learning by parameter sharing.

$\mathbf{h}_1, \ldots, \mathbf{h}_n$. Two types of outputs are computed over $\mathbf{h}_1, \ldots, \mathbf{h}_n$. The first is for LM, which is to predict the next word given each hidden state $\mathbf{h}_i$:

$$\mathbf{p}_{i+1}^{\text{LM}} = softmax(\mathbf{W}^{\text{LM}}\mathbf{h}_i + \mathbf{b}^{\text{LM}}), \tag{17.42}$$

where $\mathbf{W}^{\text{LM}}$ and $\mathbf{b}^{\text{LM}}$ are model parameters. $P(w_{i+1} = w|w_1 \ldots w_i)$ is represented by $\mathbf{p}_{i+1}^{\text{LM}}[w]$, $w \in V$.

The second output is for sequence labelling, where

$$\mathbf{p}_i^{\text{TAG}} = softmax(\mathbf{W}^{\text{TAG}}\mathbf{h}_i + \mathbf{b}^{\text{TAG}}), \tag{17.43}$$

where $\mathbf{W}^{\text{TAG}}$ and $\mathbf{b}^{\text{TAG}}$ are model parameters. $\mathbf{P}(t_i = \ell|W_{1:i})$ is represented by $\mathbf{p}_i^{\text{TAG}}[\ell]$, $\ell \in L$. In practice, bi-directional LSTM encoding can be used, which allows us to compute $P(w_{i+1}|w_1 \ldots w_i)$ using the left-to-right component, $P(w_{i-1}|w_i \ldots w_n)$ using the right-to-left component and $P(t_i|W_{1:i})$ using both components.

Training is performed in two stages, by first running a pre-training step over a set of LM training data $D^{\text{LM}} = \{W_i^{\text{LM}}\}|_{i=1}^{N}$, where W_i^{LM} denotes the ith training sentence, before running a fine-tuning step over a set of sequence labelling training data $D^{\text{TAG}} = \{(W_i^{\text{TAG}}, T_i^{\text{TAG}})\}|_{i=1}^{M}$, where W_i^{TAG} denotes the ith training sentence and T_i^{TAG} denotes its gold-standard label sequence. During pre-training, loss from the LM task back-propagates to the encoder parameters and the word embedding table from each $\mathbf{h}_i$ in Eq 17.42. Thus sequence labelling can benefit from LM by having more informed starting parameters. Note that the training data for the two tasks do not need to overlap – LM can be trained over different sentences compared with sequence labelling data.

This scenario can be viewed as a special case of a more general setting of **multi-task learning** by parameter sharing, with one task being used to train the set of shared parameters before another, so that the performance of the second task is optimised. Alternatively, if we want to exploit *mutual* benefit between the two tasks, we can train the two tasks simultaneously. To this end, if the training data of the two tasks overlap, then a total loss can be computed for each training instance. Still taking LM and sequence labelling for example, as shown in Figure 17.5(b), if the training data for both tasks is $D^{\text{TAG}} = \{(W_i, T_i)\}|_{i=1}^{N}$, we can simultaneously predict the next word w_{i+1} and current label t_i from the hidden state $\mathbf{h}_i$ in Eqs 17.42 and 17.43. Loss over both tasks can be summed up on $\mathbf{h}_i$ for this training instance, before gradients being back-propagated to model parameters in the shared layers.

If the training data for the two tasks do not overlap, gradients cannot be accumulated on an instance-by-instance basis. Instead, we can alternate the optimisation for LM and sequence labelling. In principle, the model can be trained on a few LM training examples and then on a few sequence labelling examples, before moving back to new LM training examples, and so on. This process is similar to the pre-training process in making switches of tasks during training, but different in that rather than finishing LM training before moving on to sequence labelling, we move back and forth between training examples for the two tasks for seeking their mutual benefit. In the SGD optimisation process for the two tasks, gradients from both tasks are accumulated on the shared neural model parameters, which integrate knowledge of both tasks.

When batch training is used, another way of joint training is to mix the two tasks in the batch level, where each batch of training samples consists of instances from the LM task and instances from the sequence labelling task. In each batch, loss over the two tasks are accumulated for back-propagation through to the shared model parameters.

More than two tasks. A key factor that enables the above multi-task learning strategy is representation learning, and in particular the fact that hidden representation vectors are calculated dynamically. In contrast, it would be much more difficult for hard-coded indicator features to support such transfer learning. With neural transfer learning, multi-task learning can also be carried out between more than two tasks. For example, it has been shown that POS-tagging, syntactic chunking and NER are mutually beneficial by parameter sharing. The techniques discussed for LM and sequence labelling apply here, where all the tasks share a set of common model parameters, and are optimised simultaneously during training. The shared model parameters provide a channel for information integration.

17.3.2 Selecting Parameters for Sharing

Multi-task learning does not always bring benefit to each task involved. Sometimes the performance of a task can drop when jointly trained with other tasks. This is because different tasks can have varying amounts of information overlap, and the training of some tasks can bring more noise than relevant features to a task. Whether a given set of tasks are suitable for multi-task learning needs to be verified both intuitively and empirically. In addition, in a neural network with multiple representation vectors, we can also choose which representation vectors are shared for better cross-task performance. Two examples are discussed below.

Selecting shared layers. Depending on the task, it can be useful to choose what parameters to share. Take a multi-layer BiLSTM encoder for example. Each layer of BiLSTM makes a different level of abstraction over the input sequence. Suppose that multi-task learning between POS-tagging and dependency parsing is performed on a two-layer BiLSTM encoder. It has been shown that a POS-tagging output layer on the first BiLSTM layer and a syntactic parsing output layer on the second BiLSTM layer (Figure 17.6(b)) give better results than setting the output layers of both tasks on the second BiLSTM layer (Figure 17.6(a)). This is likely because sequence labelling benefits from more shallow contextual information, which is better captured in lower LSTM layers.

Multi-task learning via shared heads in SAN. Let us consider multi-head attention discussed in Chapter 16 as a second example, where each attention head uses a different parameter matrix to

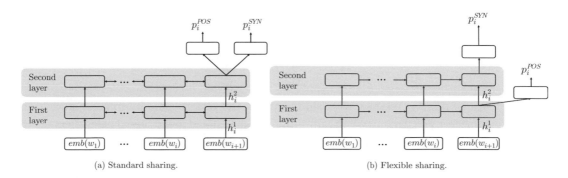

(a) Standard sharing.   (b) Flexible sharing.

Figure 17.6 Multi-task learning structures for POS-tagging and parsing.

project input vectors into a head-specific feature space. As a result, different heads can be used to capture different aspects of the input, and it can be beneficial to use different heads for extracting knowledge of different tasks. For example, for multi-task learning that involves dependency parsing and POS-tagging, one dot-product attention head can be replaced by the bi-affine attention to predict syntactic dependencies, while a different head can be used for predicting POS labels. Exercise 17.10 discusses more details.

17.3.3 Shared–Private Network Structure

As mentioned earlier, sharing model parameters across tasks can potentially suffer from information conflict. We want to minimise such conflict while maximising the mutual benefit between tasks via common information. To this end, one solution is to learn a set of shared parameters across tasks, while keeping a separate copy of parameters for each task. This method is called the **shared–private network** structure.

Take classification for example, where parameters can be shared for different tasks such as sentiment classification, stance classification and emotion detection, etc. Formally, for M tasks, the shared–private network structure consists of $M+1$ copies of encoder parameters, in which one common set of parameters, Θ^{shared} is shared between all tasks, and one set of specific parameters Θ^i is allocated for each task i ($i \in [1, \ldots, M]$). The shared parameters are used to calculate a shared representation $\mathbf{h}^{shared}$, and the private parameters for each task are used to calculate a private representation $\mathbf{h}^i$ ($i \in [1, \ldots, M]$) for the task. Given an input sentence W^i from task i, we calculate its representations from the shared network $\mathbf{h}^{shared}$ and the private network $\mathbf{h}^i$ as follows:

$$
\begin{aligned}
\mathbf{h}^{shared} &= \text{ENCODER}(W^i, \Theta^{shared}) \\
\mathbf{h}^i &= \text{ENCODER}(W^i, \Theta^i),
\end{aligned}
\tag{17.44}
$$

where ENCODER denotes the function for both the shared and private networks. $\mathbf{h}^{shared}$ and $\mathbf{h}^i$ are concatenated and used for making a prediction:

$$
\mathbf{p}^i = g(\mathbf{h}^{shared} \oplus \mathbf{h}^i),
\tag{17.45}
$$

where g represents the output layer. $\mathbf{p}^i$ is the output label distribution.

Separating shared and private information. Given a set of training data $\{D_i\}|_{i=1}^{M}$, where $D_i = \{(W_j^i, y_j^i)\}|_{j=1}^{|D_i|}$, W_j^i denotes the jth training example in D_i, and $y_j^i \in L_i$ is the gold-stand output class label in the label set L_i. The training objective is to minimise

$$
L^{\text{TASK}} = \sum_{i=1}^{M} L_i^{\text{TASK}} = \sum_{i=1}^{M} \sum_{j=1}^{|D_i|} - \log \mathbf{p}_j^i[y_j^i].
\tag{17.46}
$$

In the training process, we want to enforce that task-specific information goes to the private parameters, and that no task-specific information is stored in the shared parameters Θ^{shared}. To this purpose, **adversarial training** can be used. In particular, one auxiliary task $\mathbf{p}^{task}$ is made using the shared representation $\mathbf{h}^{shared}$, which is to predict the task where the input is from. This task is a standard M-way classification task. We want to ensure that $\mathbf{h}^{shared}$ contains no task-specific information through $\mathbf{p}^{task}$. As shown in Figure 17.7, a special adversarial loss L^{ADV} is used to train

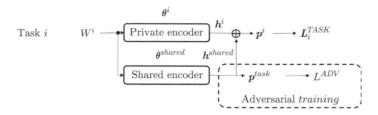

Figure 17.7 Adversarial shared–private network.

a classifier so that it *cannot* predict the task for the input instance. Correspondingly, given a set of training data $\{D_i\}|_{i=1}^{M}$, the cross-entropy between the task prediction output and the correct task class label is maximised rather than minimised:

$$L^{\text{ADV}} = \sum_{i=1}^{M} \sum_{j=1}^{|D_i|} \log(\mathbf{p}^{task})_j^i[i], \tag{17.47}$$

where i denotes the task of the current instance, and $|D_i|$ denotes the number of training instance for task i. $(\mathbf{p}^{task})_j^i[i]$ denotes the probability of the ith task as given by the distribution $\mathbf{p}^{task}$ for the jth training example from D_i.

The total loss is:

$$L = \sum_{i=1}^{M} L_i^{\text{TASK}} + L^{\text{ADV}}. \tag{17.48}$$

One thing to note is that optimising L from the very beginning of training may not lead to fast convergence or improved performance. Instead, a practical trick is to train the shared–private model by maximising L^{ADV} first, for a few training iterations, before starting to minimise it as described in L. The main reason is that, at the very beginning, the randomly initialised model is unable to perform reliable task classification. At this stage "confusing" the task classifier does not bring insight to the model, since there is no task classifier at all. By maximising L^{ADV} for a few iterations, we maximise the log-likelihood for task classification, thereby obtaining a reasonable task classifier model, particularly by training the output parameters for $\mathbf{p}^{task}$. The trained task classifier output layer gives us a channel through which we can drive out task-specific information from the shared parameters Θ^{shared} by confusing the task classifier.

Summary

In this chapter we have learned:

- neural n-gram language models and recurrent neural language models;
- noise contrastive estimation;
- word embeddings as distributed word representations;
- contextualised word embeddings;
- pre-training and transfer learning.

Chapter Notes

Neural *n*-gram language model was proposed by Bengio et al. (2003). Collobert et al. (2011) showed the utility of word embeddings for representing input in neural NLP. Hierachical softmax (Morin and Bengio, 2005) and log-bilinear models (Mnih and Hinton, 2007) inspired CBOW and skip-gram models (Mikolov et al., 2013). Word embeddings and their evaluations attracted much attention (Turian et al., 2010; Collobert et al., 2011; Pennington et al., 2014; Tang et al., 2014; Iacobacci et al., 2015; Goldberg and Levy, 2014). Starting from ELMo (Peters et al., 2018), contextualised embeddings such as GPT (Radford et al., 2018), BERT (Devlin et al., 2018), XLM (Lample and Conneau, 2019), XLNet (Yang et al., 2019) and RoBERTa (Liu et al., 2019b) outperformed static word embeddings across a wide range of NLP tasks.

Caruana (1997) empirically demonstrated the advantages of multi-task learning over a single-task neural architecture on various learning problems. Collobert and Weston (2008) explored sequence labelling tasks jointly using a CNN-style network. Rei (2017) jointly learned language models and sequence labelling models by sharing BiLSTM parameters. This method inspired ELMo (Peters et al., 2018). Søgaard and Goldberg (2016) explored parameter sharing across different layers for parsing and POS tagging. Strubell et al. (2018) addressed multi-task learning using different heads in Transformer. Shared–private network was used for transfer learning between domains and tasks (Yang et al., 2017).

Exercises

17.1 Compare the model structures of neural *n*-gram LM in Section 17.1 and recurrent neural LM in Section 17.3. Can RNNs be used for *n*-gram neural language modelling? Can MLP be used for recurrent neural language modelling? Why?

17.2 Recall hierarchical softmax discussed in Section 17.1.3. Formally define a hierarchical output layer using a binary tree, given a representation vector **h** as input.

17.3 Skip-gram uses a local context window, without considering syntactic information. Intuitively, syntactically related words can better serve as context words by bringing close long-range dependency information. Consider the dependency syntax. If a treebank is obtained by automatically parsing a large raw text corpus into dependency trees, how can the skip-gram method be extended so that context words are defined as words directly connected with the target word by a dependency arc?

17.4 Skip-gram treats all context words equally, disregarding the relative position in a context window when predicting a context word. However, words in different relative positions can have different semantic relations to the target word. One way to integrate the relative position into training of word embeddings is to augment context words with their relative position index. For example, given the *n*-gram "*A dog is sitting under the tree in the garden*", if the target word is "*sitting*", then the context words in a size $C = 5$ window include "A_{-3}", "dog_{-2}", "is_{-1}", "$under_1$", "the_2", "$tree_3$", "in_4", "the_5". Compared with the naïve skip-gram method, the context embedding table is effectively enlarged by a factor of $2C$ while the target embedding table remains the same. What are the relative advantages and disadvantages of this method?

17.5 Consider the following evaluation methods for word embeddings:

(a) A lexical semantics task is **thematic fit**, which evaluates how well word embeddings can find semantically similar nouns that play certain semantic roles for certain verbs. For example, given a verb "*cut*" and a pre-defined thematic role *patient*, the *patient* role is expected to be fulfilled by something that is cuttable. The most expected noun is "*cake*" rather than "*cat*". Thus the pair "*cut*" and "*cake*" would have a higher score by an embedding model. Discuss how word embeddings can be used for thematic fit.

(b) A lexical semantics is **outlier word detection**. Given a set of words "*cat*", "*dog*", "*bird*", "*laptop*", "*horse*", "*sheep*", which are mostly animals, "*laptop*" would be an outlier. Outliers are expected to be better detected using better embeddings. Discuss how embeddings can be used for outlier detection.

17.6 Given the following three sequences of scores:

(a) 0.55 0.65, 0.8, 0.2, 0.99, 0.1
(b) 0.52, 0.43, 0.75, 0.1, 0.875, 0
(c) 0.6, 0.7, 0.3, 0.1, 0.99, 0.22

What is the Pearson's correlation coefficient between (a) and (b) and between (a) and (c), respectively?

17.7 Similar to word embeddings, sentence representations can also be pre-trained. The basic idea is to predict the representation of neighbouring sentences using the representation of the current sentence. Can sentence embeddings be trained directly using a sentence lookup table? Why? Discuss representing a sentence using both a bag-of-word pooling method and a sequence encoding network.

17.8 Can contextualised word embeddings such as ELMo, GPT and BERT be used directly for calculating word similarities and detecting analogy? Why?

17.9 It has been shown that contextualised embeddings such as ELMo, GPT and BERT offer syntactic and semantic knowledge when used as input to a model for a downstream task. Discuss how probing tasks can be defined for verifying such knowledge quantitatively. (Hint: consider tasks such as dependency parsing, semantic role labelling and word sense disambiguation.)

17.10 Recall the discussion of multi-task learning in SAN in Section 17.3.2. Fully specify a multi-task learning SAN network for POS-tagging and dependency parsing by using the Transformer encoder discussed in Chapter 16 and the local output layers for the two tasks discussed in Chapter 15.

17.11 Parameter generation network is useful for multi-task learning. The main idea is to use a set of *meta parameters* for generating a set of model parameters given a specific input. For example, supposing that we want to build models for solving M classification tasks, extracting shared information for mutual benefit between tasks. We can represent each task using a *task vector*. Given a sentence $W_{1:n}$, a task-specific classifier is built by using the meta parameter and the relevant task vector to generate a set of text classification model parameters. Now consider a BiLSTM softmax model structure for sequence labelling (Section 15.1). To generate such a set of model parameters, the meta parameters can consist of tensors, which can be multiplied with task vectors to obtain parameter matrices and vectors in the classifier. Specify such a parameter generation network. Comapre it with the shared–private network structure in Section 17.3.3. Why can it work better than naïve multi-task learning?

17.12 Consider the local structured prediction models in Section 15.1 again. The prediction of different local structures are synchronised thanks to a shared representation of the input. Can you draw correlations between the training of those models and multi-task learning discussed in Section 17.3.1? Identify similarities in gradient back-propagation and the function of encoder parameters.

17.13 Dynamic masking. Consider again BERT in Section 17.2.4. So far we have prepared training data by taking masking as a static pre-processing step. One relative disadvantage of the strategy, however, is that each training sentence offers only a fixed set of predicted words. A relatively more effective way to make use of training sentences is to allow *dynamic masking*, where words are sampled and masked dynamically over each training iteration, so that different training instances can be derived from the same training sentence at different training iterations. Dynamic masking can still be achieved through static pre-processing. In particular, we can prepare m different training instances from a training sentence by applying the process of random masking m times, using each for a different training iteration. Write pseudocode for this algorithm. This is the motivation behind the Robustly Optimised BERT Pre-training Approach (RoBERTa) model.

18   Deep Latent Variable Models

We have discussed *models with hidden variables* such as IBM model 1 and HMM in Chapter 6 and LDA in Chapter 12. In this chapter, we combine the advantages of deep neural networks with hidden (i.e., latent) variables, leading to **deep latent variable models**. On one hand, deep neural networks can be used as strong function approximators to infer latent variables from data. On the other hand, latent variables can help deep neural networks to explicitly model compositional factors to generate data. In this way, linguistic prior knowledge can be injected to deep neural network models, increasing both the performance and the interpretability of deep neural models.

Deep latent variable models are more challenging to learn compared to models with fully observed data, because latent variables introduce challenges to SGD and back-propagation. We introduce approximate methods for learning and inference. Useful applications include variational autoencoders for text generation and neural topic models for document modelling.

18.1   Introducing Latent Variables into a Neural Network Model

Similar to discrete linear models, neural network models can benefit from hidden variables, such as the topic of a document and the word alignment between a sentence pair. Hidden variables are also referred to as **latent variables**. To avoid confusion with neural hidden layers in neural networks, we adopt the second terminology in this chapter. In addition, rather than using O and H to denote observed and latent variables, respectively, we follow the research literature and use X and Z, respectively, to avoid confusion with hidden and output layer representations.

Similar to the latent variable models we discussed in Chapters 6 and 12, and similar to most neural models we discussed in this part of the book, let us consider a probabilistic generative model. Formally, throughout this chapter, we consider models that describe the generative probability $P(X)$ of some observed variables X. We extend such a model by introducing latent variables Z. When Z denotes discrete categorical variables, $P(X)$ is given by

$$P(X|\Theta) = \sum_Z P(X, Z|\Theta) = \sum_Z P(Z|\Theta)P(X|Z, \Theta), \qquad (18.1)$$

where Θ denotes the set of model parameters, $P(X, Z|\Theta)$ is the joint likelihood of X and Z, $P(Z|\Theta)$ is the prior distribution of the latent variable and $P(X|Z, \Theta)$ is the conditional generative probability distribution of X given Z.

Equation 18.1 is similar to the models we discussed in Chapters 6 and 12 in considering discrete valued latent variables. Most of the random variables we have seen in this book are categorical random variables, such as a word from the vocabulary and a label from a tagset. On the other hand, in this part of the book it has been shown that real-valued features such as dense embeddings endow models with stronger representation power. Thus for deep latent variable models, it is worth considering continuous latent variables also. When Z is a continuous variable, $P(X)$ is given by

$$P(X|\Theta) = \int_Z P(X, Z|\Theta) dZ = \int_Z P(Z|\Theta) P(X|Z, \Theta) dZ. \tag{18.2}$$

With regard to parameterisation, the models that we discuss in this chapter extend a neural model that calculates $P(X)$, and are thus parameterised by a neural network. This is different from the models in Chapters 6 and 12, for which parameterisation is achieved by breaking the model probability into a set of basic probability factors (i.e., $P(w|c)$ and $P(c)$ in a Naïve Bayes model), which serve as model parameters.

As we have learned earlier in this part of the book, a neural network can be used to represent sequences, trees and more complex graph structures in a dense hidden vector. A model that calculates $P(X)$ learns a representation that fits the distribution of observed data, which can be highly complex. Introducing Z results in a structured generative model, which can consist of simpler distributions for both $P(Z)$ and $P(X|Z)$. In particular, it has been shown that even when $P(X|Z, \Theta)$ is simple (e.g., a Gaussian distribution), Eq 18.1 can represent powerful distributions. Introducing latent variables can also increase the interpretability of neural models.

When both $P(Z)$ and $P(X|Z)$ are parameterised by deep neural networks, it can be ideal that SGD and back-propagation can be applied to train the model end-to-end. To this goal, one intuitive solution is to maximise the likelihood of a training dataset of observed variables X using SGD. As we will see in Section 18.2, this method leads to the need for calculating the posterior distribution of Z given X. We call the problem **posterior inference**, which is a key to the training of deep latent variable models.

Depending on the type of Z, exact (Section 18.2 and Section 18.3) or approximate posterior inference (Section 18.4) can be used, which are the main techniques that we discuss in this chapter. Among the three general training techniques for Bayesian networks (i.e. MLE, MAP and Bayesian learning) discussed in Chapter 12, the training methods of this chapter fall into the maximum likelihood category. Given that there are latent variables, the training algorithm is inherently connected with EM. Discussion of the other two types of training methods, namely MAP and Bayesian learning for neural models, is beyond the scope of this book.

18.2 Working with Categorical Latent Variables

We worked with categorical latent variables for discrete linear models in Chapters 6 and 12. Examples include PLSA and topic models. They can be useful for document clustering. The discrete models are parameterised by using the Bayes rule, the probability chain rule and making independence assumptions for deriving parameter probability distributions such as topic probabilities and word probabilities conditioned on topics. In this section, let us discuss how neural network parameterisation can be used for such models. In particular, let us start with a model framework trained using SGD and back-propagation, before discussing text modelling.

18.2.1 Model with SGD Training

We take Eq 18.1 to build our model, considering Z as a categorical random variable. In particular, $Z \in \{1, \ldots, K\}$. To optimise the log-likelihood in Eq 18.1, we can directly apply stochastic gradient descent (SGD) (Chapter 4) and its variants (Chapters 13 and 14). Formally, given a dataset $D = \{X_i\}|_{i=1}^{N}$, the gradient of the log marginal likelihood of D with respect to Θ is given by

$$
\begin{aligned}
\frac{\partial P(D|\Theta)}{\partial \Theta} &= \frac{\partial \sum_{i=1}^{N} \log P(X_i|\Theta)}{\partial \Theta} = \sum_{i=1}^{N} \frac{\partial \log P(X_i|\Theta)}{\partial \Theta} \\
&= \sum_{i=1}^{N} \frac{\frac{\partial P(X_i|\Theta)}{\partial \Theta}}{P(X_i|\Theta)} = \sum_{i=1}^{N} \frac{\sum_Z \frac{\partial P(X_i,Z|\Theta)}{\partial \Theta}}{P(X_i|\Theta)} \\
&= \sum_{i=1}^{N} \frac{\sum_Z P(X_i,Z|\Theta) \frac{\partial \log P(X_i,Z|\Theta)}{\partial \Theta}}{P(X_i|\Theta)} \\
&\quad \left(\frac{\partial \log P(X_i,Z|\Theta)}{\partial \Theta} = \frac{1}{P(X_i,Z|\Theta)} \frac{\partial P(X_i,Z|\Theta)}{\partial \Theta} \right) \\
&= \sum_{i=1}^{N} \sum_Z \frac{P(X_i,Z|\Theta)}{P(X_i|\Theta)} \frac{\partial \log P(X_i,Z|\Theta)}{\partial \Theta} \\
&= \sum_{i=1}^{N} \sum_Z P(Z|X_i,\Theta) \frac{\partial \log P(X_i,Z|\Theta)}{\partial \Theta} \\
&= \sum_{i=1}^{N} E_{Z \sim P(Z|X_i,\Theta)} \frac{\partial \log P(X_i,Z|\Theta)}{\partial \Theta}.
\end{aligned}
\tag{18.3}
$$

Using this gradient, Θ can be updated using SGD if our model $P(X,Z|\Theta)$ is differentiable. In particular, for each training example X_i the local update is:

$$
\Theta \leftarrow \Theta + \eta E_{Z \sim P(Z|X_i,\Theta)} \frac{\partial \log P(X_i,Z|\Theta)}{\partial \Theta}
\tag{18.4}
$$

where η is the learning rate.

To calculate the gradient $E_{Z \sim P(Z|X_i,\Theta)} \frac{\partial \log P(X_i,Z|\Theta)}{\partial \Theta}$, we need to know the posterior distribution $P(Z|X_i, \Theta)$, and then calculate an expectation of a gradient function of the joint log-likelihood $\log P(X_i,Z|\Theta)$ with respect to the posterior distribution. When Z represents a discrete latent variable (or a set of discrete variables), $P(Z|X, \Theta)$ can be explicitly calculated by:

$$
P(Z|X, \Theta) = \frac{P(Z,X|\Theta)}{P(X|\Theta)} = \frac{P(Z|\Theta)P(X|Z, \Theta)}{\sum_{Z'} P(Z'|\Theta)P(X|Z', \Theta)}.
\tag{18.5}
$$

In Eq 18.5, both $P(Z|\Theta)$ and $P(X|Z, \Theta)$ are parameterised model probabilities. With the posterior distribution $P(Z|X, \Theta)$, the expectation of Eq 18.3 can be calculated by enumerating all values of the categorical random variable Z. Thus we arrive at a SGD training algorithm for the model.

Correlation with EM. Recall the EM algorithm discussed in Chapter 6, where the M-step maximises the expectation function $Q(\Theta, \Theta^t)$ to find the optimal Θ^{t+1} at iteration t. According to Eq 6.9, $Q(\Theta, \Theta^t)$ is given by

$$Q(\Theta, \Theta^t) = \sum_{i=1}^{N} E_{Z \sim P(Z|X_i, \Theta^t)} \log P(X_i, Z|\Theta). \tag{18.6}$$

Taking the gradient of $Q(\Theta, \Theta^t)$ directly with respect to Θ leads to

$$\frac{\partial Q(\Theta, \Theta^t)}{\partial \Theta} = \sum_{i=1}^{N} E_{Z \sim P(Z|X_i, \Theta^t)} \frac{\partial \log P(X_i, Z|\Theta)}{\partial \Theta}, \tag{18.7}$$

which allows us to optimise $Q(\Theta, \Theta^t)$ using SGD, if the parameterisation of our model is differentiable (e.g. neural network). We call this method gradient-based EM, or **generalised EM**. In particular, starting from a randomly initialised Θ, generalised EM repeatedly calculates:

$$\Theta^{t+1} = \Theta^t + \eta \frac{\partial Q(\Theta, \Theta^t)}{\partial \Theta}. \tag{18.8}$$

Equation 18.7 is the same as Eq 18.4 except for being defined with a global loss over D, rather than a local loss over X_i. This builds an intuitive connection between SGD optimisation for deep latent variable models and EM. For an M-step in Chapter 6, we used Lagrange multipliers to obtain closed-form solutions for Θ^{t+1} that maximise Eq 18.6. In contrast, generalised EM increases $Q(\Theta, \Theta^t)$ using an iterative numerical process. Interestingly, optimising $Q(\Theta, \Theta^t)$ using generalised EM is equivalent to directly optimising the log marginal likelihood $P(D|\Theta)$ using gradient ascent, without the approximation step according to Jensen's inequality discussed in Section 6.3.

The EM algorithm discussed in Chapter 6 updates model parameters based on the whole set of training examples. With gradient-based optimisation, we can use mini-batch gradient ascent to update model parameters. From the perspective of the EM algorithm, this training schedule interleaves the E-step and M-step for each mini-batch. This training schedule is referred to as **online update**. Alternatively, we can also perform **offline update**, where the E-step is first executed for all training examples and then the M-step is repeated to train using mini-batch gradient ascent until convergence based on the estimated posterior distribution of the E-step. In practice, for efficiency considerations, the M-step can be trained for only a single iteration over all training examples, instead of to convergence before the next E-step.

18.2.2 A Bag-of-Words Model for Text Clustering

The SGD training framework in the previous section allows us to parameterise latent variable models using neural network. In particular, both $P(Z|\Theta)$ and $P(X|Z, \Theta)$ should be explicitly modelled. For a first example, let us consider a neural bag-of-words model with a latent topic, which is structurally similar to the PLSA model in Chapter 6.

The structure of the model is shown in Figure 18.1(a). Formally, we have a latent categorical random variable $z \in \{1, \ldots, K\}$, distributed by $\pi = \langle P(z = 1), P(z = 2), \ldots, P(z = K) \rangle$. Similar to PLSA, z serves as a latent topic, according to which a document can be generated.

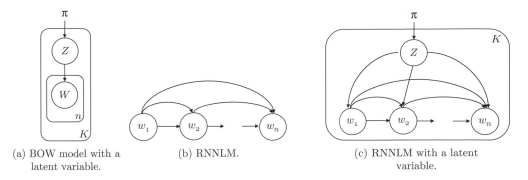

(a) BOW model with a   (b) RNNLM.   (c) RNNLM with a latent
    latent variable.   variable.

Figure 18.1 Bayesian network structures of a BOW model with a categorical latent variable (a), an RNNLM (b) and an RNNLM with a categorical latent variable (c), in nested plate notation.

In particular, given a specific topic z, the distribution of a word w is given by $P(w|z)$, and the probability of a document $d = W_{1:n} = w_1 w_w \ldots w_n$ is given by $\prod_{i=1}^{n} P(w_i|z)$. Now different from PLSA, which directly takes $P(w|z)$ as the model parameter, let us use a neural network to parameterise $P(w|z)$.

In particular, let us first consider a baseline model to calculate $P(w)$ without considering z. Given a one-hot vector representation $\mathbf{v}(w)$ of w, we use an embedding lookup table $\mathbf{E}$ to obtain a dense vector

$$\mathbf{x} = emb(w) = \mathbf{E}\mathbf{v}(w).$$

Then a hidden layer representation can be calculated by using a *sigmoid* layer

$$\mathbf{h} = \sigma(\mathbf{W}\mathbf{x} + \mathbf{b}).$$

Finally, a *softmax* output layer can be used to calculate the probability

$$P(w) = softmax(\mathbf{U}\mathbf{h} + \mathbf{b}^u).$$

The above model can be written concisely as $P(w) = MLP(\mathbf{v}(w)|\Theta)$, where $\Theta = \{\mathbf{E}, \mathbf{W}, \mathbf{b}, \mathbf{U}, \mathbf{b}^u\}$ is the set of model parameters.

Now to integrate z into $P(w)$ for calculating $P(w|z)$, we can make Θ depend on z. In particular, K sets of model parameters $\Theta_1, \Theta_2, \ldots, \Theta_K$ can be used, where each Θ_k ($k \in \{1, \ldots, K\}$) corresponds to a specific value of z. In addition, to avoid duplicating the embedding table, which has a large number of parameters, we can allow all Θ_k to share the same $\mathbf{E}$.

As a result, our final model calculates two probability distributions:

$$\begin{aligned} P(z) &= \pi[z] \\ P(w_i|z) &= MLP(\mathbf{v}(w_i)|\Theta_z), \end{aligned} \tag{18.9}$$

where the set of model parameters is $\Theta = \{\pi\} \cup \Theta_1 \cup \ldots \cup \Theta_K$.

The final probability of a word is the mathematical expectation over all z, as indicated by Eq 18.1 earlier:

$$P(w_i) = \sum_z P(z)P(w_i|z).$$

Given a set of documents $D = \{d_i\}|_{i=1}^{N}$, we train the model by maximising

$$P(D) = \prod_{i=1}^{N} P(d_i) = \prod_{i}\prod_{j=1}^{|d_i|} P(w_j^i) = \prod_{i}\prod_{j=1}^{|d_i|} \left(\sum_{z_i} P(z_i)P(w_j^i|z_i, \Theta_z) \right), \qquad (18.10)$$

where $|d_i|$ denotes the number of words in d_i.

For SGD training, we directly take the partial derivatives of Eq 18.10 with respect to every parameter in Θ. In particular, the gradients with respect to π (i.e., $P(z)$) are straightforward, while the gradients with respect to $\Theta_1, \ldots, \Theta_K$ can be calculated using back-propagation. Thus the training of the latent variable model is no more difficult compared with the training of an MLP discussed in Chapter 13.

We can then calculate the posterior $P(z|d_i)$ for each document and use the distribution as a vector representation of d_i.

18.2.3 Considering Sequence Information

The model in the previous section is structurally highly similar to PLSA. However, compared with a sparse model using individual $P(w|z)$ ($w \sim V, z \sim \{1, \ldots, K\}$) as model parameters, the neural model above allows similar words such as "*cat*" and "*crane*" to have correlated distributions through their embedding similarity (Eq 18.9). Neural parameterisation further allows more complex sequence-level features to be integrated for strong representation of text. For instance, a sequence encoding network can be used to replace the bag-of-words model. In this section, let us consider using LSTM to encode a word sequence.

Still without considering a hidden variable, an RNN language model can be represented by the Bayesian network structure of Figure 18.1(b), which is also shown in Figure 2.1(a) in Chapter 2. Compared with n-gram language models, this model generates each word according to all the preceding words, rather than making Markov assumptions. Formally, given a sequence of words $W_{1:n} = w_1 \ldots w_n$, we calculate $P(w_i|W_{1:i-1})$ for $i \in [1, \ldots, n]$ by feeding the corresponding embedding vector sequence $\mathbf{X}_{1:n} = \mathbf{x}_1\mathbf{x}_2 \ldots \mathbf{x}_n$ as input to a LSTM sequence encoder to find a sequence of hidden vectors

$$\mathbf{H}_{1:n} = \mathbf{h}_1\mathbf{h}_2 \ldots \mathbf{h}_n = LSTM(\mathbf{X}_{1:n}, \Theta^{\text{LSTM}}),$$

where Θ^{LSTM} denotes the LSTM parameters.

$P(w_i|W_{1:i-1})$ is then given by

$$P(w_i|W_{1:i-1}) = softmax(\mathbf{W}\mathbf{h}_i + \mathbf{b}),$$

where $\mathbf{W}$ and $\mathbf{b}$ are model parameters. Thus for the model $\Theta = \Theta^{\text{LSTM}} \cup \{\mathbf{E}, \mathbf{W}, \mathbf{b}\}$, where $\mathbf{E}$ is the embedding lookup table.

Now with a categorical random variable $z \in \{1, \ldots, K\}$, the generative story can be shown in Figure 18.1(c). In particular, we first generate z before generating $W_{1:n}$ from left to right, conditioned on z. The model calculates two probabilities: $P(z)$ and $P(w_i|W_{1:i-1}, z)$. Similar to the model in the previous section, $P(z)$ is parameterised by a discrete vector $\pi = \langle P(z = 1), P(z = 2), \ldots, P(z = K) \rangle$.

Now with regard to the parameterisation of $P(w_i|W_{1:i-1}, z)$, we take the same strategy as the previous section. For each value of z, we use a separate set of LSTM parameters Θ_k^{LSTM} ($k \in \{1, \ldots, K\}$) for encoding $\mathbf{X}_{1:n}$, resulting in $\mathbf{H}_{1:n}^k = \mathbf{h}_1^k \ldots \mathbf{h}_n^k = LSTM(\mathbf{X}_{1:n}, \Theta_k^{LSTM})$. Accordingly, the probability distribution of w_i is:

$$P(w_i|W_{1:i-1}, z=k) = softmax(\mathbf{W}_k \mathbf{h}_i^k + \mathbf{b}_k).$$

For this model, the set of parameters is

$$\Theta = \left(\cup_{k=1}^K \Theta^{LSTM_k} \right) \cup \{\mathbf{E}\} \cup \left(\cup_{k=1}^K \{\mathbf{W}_k, \mathbf{b}_k\} \right).$$

Given a set of sentences $D = \{W_i\}|_{i=1}^N$, we train the model by maximising

$$P(D) = \prod_{i=1}^N P(W_i|\Theta)$$

using SGD (Section 18.2.1), where for each sentence $W_i = w_1^i \ldots w_{|W_i|}^i$ we have

$$P(W_i|\Theta) = \sum_z P(z|\Theta)P(W_i|z, \Theta) = \sum_z P(z|\Theta) \prod_{j=1}^{|W_i|} P(w_j^i|w_1^i, \ldots, w_{j-1}^i, z, \Theta_z)$$

for $z \in \{1, \ldots, K\}$. The calculation of gradients is similar to the model of the previous section, except that back-propagation is performed on the LSTM sequence encoder also (see Chapter 14 for more details).

For clustering, the posterior distribution $P(z|D, \Theta)$ can be used, which can be calculated as

$$P(z|D, \Theta) = \frac{P(z|\Theta)P(D|z, \Theta)}{\sum_{z'} P(z'|\Theta)P(D|z', \Theta)}.$$

18.3 Working with Structured Latent Variables

In Chapter 6, we modelled the alignment between a translation pair as a latent variable for IBM model 1. In this case, the latent variable contains multiple elements, each denoting the alignment between a source word and a target word. Since the alignment links are correlated with each other, the latent variables are *structured*. More examples of structured latent variables include latent sequences, trees and graphs over input sentences.

Using structured latent variables is an effective way to introduce structural biases into neural network models. Taking the latent tree as an example. For many NLP tasks, considering the syntax of the sentence as a feature can be beneficial. One way to obtain the syntactic tree of a sentence is to use an off-the-shelf parser. However, parsing errors can negatively affect the sentiment classifier. Another possible solution is to jointly learn a *latent* task-specific syntactic tree as a part of model training for the end-task. This method has several potential advantages in addition to avoiding error propagation. For example, it is independent of manually labelled resources for training a parser. In addition, the induced latent tree is optimised for the end-task objective, and thus can be adjusted for better end-to-end performance. Following the order of Chapters 8, 9 and 10 for discrete models, and the order of Chapter 14 for neural models without latent variables, we discuss latent sequence labelling, sequence segmentation and constituent trees in Sections 18.3.2, 18.3.3 and 18.3.4, respectively.

18.3.1 Introducing Structured Latent Variables

Formally, let the input sentence representation be $\mathbf{X} = \mathbf{x}_1, \mathbf{x}_2, \ldots, \mathbf{x}_n$, with each $\mathbf{x}_i$ ($i \in [1, \ldots, n]$) being a vector representation of a corresponding input word, which can be the output hidden representation vector from a sequence encoding network (e.g., bi-directional RNN or SAN), and the latent variable be $Z = z_1, z_2, \ldots, z_m$, which denotes a certain structure.

Given $\mathbf{X}$, we can compute the distribution of Z by modelling $P(Z|\mathbf{X}, \Theta)$, where Θ are model parameters for the neural network models. In addition, for each value of the structure Z, we encode the original input $\mathbf{X}$ and the latent variable Z using a neural network function $f(\mathbf{X}, Z|\Theta)$, resulting in a dense feature vector. Here f is also called an *annotation function*, which gives a latent feature. We can take the expectation of the annotation function with respect to the posterior distribution of the latent variable Z to obtain a context vector $\mathbf{c}$:

$$\mathbf{c} = E_{Z \sim P(Z|\mathbf{X}, \Theta)} f(\mathbf{X}, Z|\Theta). \tag{18.11}$$

$f(\mathbf{X}, Z|\Theta)$ can be a scalar or a dense vector. When $f(\mathbf{X}, Z|\Theta)$ is a scalar, it can be interpreted as $\log P(\mathbf{X}, Z|\Theta)$. In this case if Z contains only one element, $\mathbf{c}$ turns out to be the Q function defined in Eq 18.6 for $\mathbf{X}$. We therefore obtain a version of Eq 18.1 with structured latent variables. This model consists of $P(Z|\mathbf{X}, \Theta)$ and $P(\mathbf{X}, Z|\Theta)$, which are both neural networks and can be optimised using Eq 18.1. However, unlike the models in Section 18.2, because the number of possible Z given $\mathbf{X}$ can be exponential or even more, dynamic programming can be necessary for calculating Eq 18.11. We will see more details later.

When $f(\mathbf{X}, Z|\Theta)$ is a vector, $\mathbf{c}$ can be viewed as a neural representation of $\mathbf{X}$ enriched with a latent structure Z, which provides prior knowledge. In this case, $\mathbf{c}$ serves as features for an NLP task such as sentiment classification where additional output layers should be added. In such cases, f should be optimised via back-propagation losses from the end task. Because we introduce external output variables, the loss function is no longer Eq 18.1. However, similar to generalised EM, SGD can be used to train our latent variable models.

Correlation with attention. Recall the attention function discussed in Chapter 14, which calculates a weighted aggregation of a set of input vectors. The attention weights are not trained by supervision, and thus can be viewed as latent variables. In fact, Eq 18.11 can be regarded as a neural network layer, where the input is $\mathbf{X}$ and the output is $\mathbf{c}$. This layer is referred to as a **structured attention layer** since $P(Z|\mathbf{X}, \Theta)$ can be considered as a set of attention scores over structures Z. In particular, recall the standard attention function, where the context vector is

$$\mathbf{c} = \sum_{i=1}^{n} \alpha_i \mathbf{x}_i,$$

$$\alpha_1, \alpha_2, \ldots, \alpha_n = softmax\Big(g(\mathbf{X}|\Theta)\Big). \tag{18.12}$$

α_i is the attention score of the ith input according to the score function $g(\mathbf{X}|\Theta)$. By setting Z to be a categorical latent variable z, the assignments of z to be $\{1, 2, \ldots, n\}$, $P(z = i|\mathbf{X}, \Theta) = \alpha_i$ and $f(\mathbf{X}, Z|\Theta) = \mathbf{x}_z$, Eq 18.11 becomes the standard attention function.

Dynamic programming for structured attention. To calculate Eq 18.11, we need to enumerate Z for calculating the expectation over $P(Z|\mathbf{X}, \Theta)$. As mentioned earlier, it can be intractable to enumerate all the assignments of the structured latent variable and we can use dynamic programming algorithms for efficient solutions. The algorithms depend on the independence assumptions such as Markov assumptions in CRFs discussed in Chapter 8. Formally, $P(Z|\mathbf{X}, \Theta)$ is given by

$$P(Z|\mathbf{X}, \Theta) = \frac{1}{\mathcal{Z}} \exp \left(\sum_C \psi(Z_C, \mathbf{X}|\Theta) \right)$$
$$\mathcal{Z} = \sum_{Z'} \exp \left(\prod_C \psi(Z'_C, \mathbf{X}|\Theta) \right), \tag{18.13}$$

where C represents an individual clique, Z_C is the sub structure of Z with the clique C, $\psi(Z_C, \mathbf{X}|\Theta)$ is the log potential function of the clique C and $\mathcal{Z}$ is the partition function.

Further, the annotation function f in Eq 18.11 is also assumed to be the sum of annotations of each clique, namely $f(\mathbf{X}, Z|\Theta) = \sum_C f(\mathbf{X}, Z_C|\Theta)$. Using these assumptions, Eq 18.11 can be rewritten as

$$\mathbf{c} = E_{Z \sim P(Z|\mathbf{X}, \Theta)} f(\mathbf{X}, Z|\Theta) = \sum_C E_{Z_C \sim P(Z_C|\mathbf{X}, \Theta)} f_C(\mathbf{X}, Z_C|\Theta), \tag{18.14}$$

where $P(Z_C|\mathbf{X}, \Theta)$ is the marginal posterior distribution of the clique C. Below we discuss specific examples of Z_C for various structures.

18.3.2 Sequence Labelling

We discussed unsupervised learning of HMMs using EM in Chapter 6, which can be used for unsupervised sequence labelling. Here let us consider a neural counterpart, where emission and transition probabilities are not parameterised as discrete conditional probabilities, but using a neural network. In particular, the input to our model is a sequence of representation vectors $\mathbf{X} = \mathbf{x}_1 \ldots \mathbf{x}_n$, which can be the hidden states of a BiLSTM, and the output is a latent tag sequence $Z_{1:n} = z_1 \ldots z_n$, where z_i denotes the tag for $\mathbf{x}_i$ ($i \in [1, \ldots, n]$).

For a first-order Markov model, each z_C is defined as two consecutive tags, and the log potential function is the sum of two components:

$$\psi(z_{i-1}z_i, \mathbf{X}|\Theta) = \psi_E(z_i, \mathbf{X}|\Theta) + \psi_T(z_{i-1}z_i, \mathbf{X}|\Theta), \tag{18.15}$$

where $\psi_E(z_i, \mathbf{X}|\Theta)$ corresponds to the emission $z_i \rightarrow w_i$ and $\psi_T(z_{i-1}z_i, \mathbf{X}|\Theta)$ corresponds to the transition $z_{i-1} \rightarrow z_i$. Exercise 18.2 discusses parameterisation of the two scores.

Given the log clique potential functions, we can find the conditional probability $P(Z_{1:n}|\mathbf{X}, \Theta)$ as

$$P(Z_{1:n}|\mathbf{X}, \Theta) = \frac{1}{\mathcal{Z}} \exp \left(\sum_{i=1}^n \psi(z_{i-1}z_i, \mathbf{X}|\Theta) \right), \tag{18.16}$$

where $\mathcal{Z}$ is the partition function, $z_0 = \langle B \rangle$ is a special label for the beginning of the sentence, following Chapter 7. The above equation resembles the CRF models discussed in Chapters 8 and 15.

Now given $\psi(z_{i-1}z_i, \mathbf{X}|\Theta)$, we can turn Eq 18.14 into

$$
\begin{aligned}
\mathbf{c} &= \sum_C E_{z_C \sim P(z_C|\mathbf{X},\Theta)} f_C(\mathbf{X}, z_C|\Theta) \\
&= \sum_{i=1}^n P(z_{i-1}z_i|\mathbf{X}, \Theta) \cdot (\mathbf{x}_{i-1} \oplus \mathbf{x}_i),
\end{aligned}
\tag{18.17}
$$

where the annotation function $f_C(\mathbf{X}, z_C|\Theta)$ for $C = z_{i-1}z_i$ is defined as the concatenation of $\mathbf{x}_{i-1}$ and $\mathbf{x}_i$. More complex networks can also be considered for f_C. $P(z_{i-1}z_i|\mathbf{X}, \Theta)$ can be calculated according to $P(Z_{1:n}|\mathbf{X}, \Theta)$ using the forward–backward algorithm (Chapter 8). Exercise 18.3 discusses more details on the back-propagation training process.

18.3.3 Sequence Segmentation

A **segmentation attention layer** considers contiguous subsequences of an input sequence. As discussed in Chapter 9, sequence segmentation can be presented using segmentation labels on each input. Here let us consider a simple label set, consisting of binary labels indicating separation of the current input from its predecessor. The number of latent variables is equal to the input length. Each latent variable $z_i \in \{1, 0\}$ indicates whether the ith word begins a new contiguous subsequence or not.

Now let us specify Z_C as a special case of Eq 18.14, where $C \in \{1, \ldots, n\}$ and $f(\mathbf{X}, Z_C|\Theta) = \delta(z_C, 1)\mathbf{x}_i$. $\delta(z_i, 1)$ tests whether z_i is equal to 1. We have:

$$
\begin{aligned}
\mathbf{c} &= E_{Z \sim P(Z|\mathbf{X},\Theta)} f(\mathbf{X}, Z|\Theta) \\
&= \sum_{i=1}^n E_{z_i \sim P(z_i|\mathbf{X},\Theta)} f(\mathbf{X}, i, z_i|\Theta) \quad \text{(Eq 18.14)} \\
&= \sum_{i=1}^n \Big(P(z_i = 1|\mathbf{X}, \Theta)\delta(z_i = 1, 1)\mathbf{x}_i + \underbrace{P(z_i = 0|\mathbf{X}, \Theta)\delta(z_i = 0, 1)\mathbf{x}_i}_{0} \Big) \\
&= \sum_{i=1}^n P(z_i = 1|\mathbf{X}, \Theta)\mathbf{x}_i.
\end{aligned}
\tag{18.18}
$$

Similar to Eq 18.12, $\mathbf{c}$ given by Eq 18.18 is a weighted sum of the input vectors. However, the weights in Eq 18.18 are not normalised over the input elements, thus enabling multiple individual inputs to receive high weights. In Eq 18.18, we essentially use the start of each subsequence to represent the span. This is reasonable since $\mathbf{x}_i$ can be the output of a sequence encoder layer such as BiLSTM, which contains global information (see also Exercise 18.4).

In Eq 18.18 we made a 0th-order Markov assumption between consecutive segments. As a result, the marginal probability $P(z_i = 1|\mathbf{X}, \Theta)$ can be simply calculated using a log potential function $\psi_U(z_i, \mathbf{X}|\Theta)$, where ψ_U denotes the potential score for a segment that begins with $\mathbf{x}_i$. In particular, ψ_U can be defined as

$$\psi_U(z_i = 1, \mathbf{X}|\Theta) = \mathbf{u}\mathbf{x}_i + b^u$$
$$\psi_U(z_i = 0, \mathbf{X}|\Theta) = 0 \tag{18.19}$$

where $\mathbf{u}$ and b^u are model parameters, and

$$P(z_i = 1, \mathbf{X}|\Theta) = \frac{1}{\mathcal{Z}} \exp\left(\psi_U(z_i, \mathbf{X}, \Theta)\right). \tag{18.20}$$

As we discussed in Chapter 15, local models can work well for structured prediction thanks to the representation power of neural network encoders. On the other hand, similar to Chapter 9, we can define higher-order semi-CRF models to capture dependencies of consecutive segments also, which we leave to Exercise 18.5.

18.3.4 Constituent Parsing

The segmentation attention layer uses a linear-chain CRF to model the sequential label dependencies of latent variables. Similarly, we can define a constituent parser to learn the probability of syntactic spans as latent variables. Let us consider a 0th-order parser, which is similar to the local parser in Chapter 15. Formally, given an input representation sequence $\mathbf{X}_{1:n} = \mathbf{x}_1 \ldots \mathbf{x}_n$, for all $1 \leq i \leq j \leq n$, each latent variable $z_{ij} \in \{0, 1\}$ indicates whether the span $\mathbf{X}_{i:j}$ belongs to a constituent tree. A constituent attention layer is defined by

$$\mathbf{c} = \sum_{i=1}^{n} \sum_{j=i}^{n} P(z_{ij} = 1|\mathbf{X}, \Theta)\mathbf{v}_{ij}, \tag{18.21}$$

where $\mathbf{v}_{ij}$ is a representation vector of the span $\mathbf{X}_{i:j}$. Exercise 18.6 discusses neural encoders for computing $\mathbf{v}_{ij}$ given $\mathbf{X}$ as inputs. Given a latent variable $Z = \{z_{11}, z_{12}, \ldots, z_{nn}\}$, which represents a valid binarised constituent tree, the posterior probability of Z is given by

$$P(Z|\mathbf{X}, \Theta) = \frac{1}{\mathcal{Z}} \exp\left(\sum_{z_{ij} \in Z} \psi_S(z_{ij}, \mathbf{X}|\Theta)\right), \tag{18.22}$$

where $\psi_S(z_{ij}, \mathbf{X}|\Theta)$ is the log potential of the span $\mathbf{X}_{i:j}$, which is defined as

$$\psi_S(z_{ij} = 1, \mathbf{X}|\Theta) = \boldsymbol{\theta}^S \mathbf{v}_{ij} + b$$
$$\psi_S(z_{ij} = 0, \mathbf{X}|\Theta) = 0. \tag{18.23}$$

$\boldsymbol{\theta}^S \in \mathbb{R}^{1 \times d}$ and $b \in \mathbb{R}$ are model parameters and d is the dimension size of $\mathbf{v}_{ij}$. Using these definitions, the marginal distribution $P(z_{ij} = 1|\mathbf{X}, \Theta)$ can be calculated directly according to $P(z_{ij} = 1|\mathbf{X}, \Theta) = \frac{1}{\mathcal{Z}'} \exp\left(\psi_S(z_{ij} = 1, \mathbf{X}|\Theta)\right)$, where $\mathcal{Z}'$ is the partition function. Similar to Chapter 10, we can define higher-order tree CRF models by considering the dependencies of z_{ij}. For example, a first-order model can model the dependencies as a CFG rule. In this case, a clique is a grammar rule and the inside–outside algorithm in Chapter 10 can be used to find clique marginal distributions. We leave this to Exercise 18.8.

18.4 Variational Inference

So far we have discussed EM training for a range of latent variable neural models, where expectations over the posterior $P(Z|X, \Theta)$ can be calculated exactly. To this end, either brute-force enumeration or dynamic programming has been used. For some situations, however, the expectation function cannot be precisely calculated. For instance, when Z involves continuous variables, Eq 18.5 becomes:

$$P(Z|X, \Theta) = \frac{P(Z, X|\Theta)}{P(X|\Theta)} = \frac{P(Z|\Theta)P(X|Z, \Theta)}{\int_{Z'} P(Z'|\Theta)P(X|Z', \Theta)dZ'},$$

which typically does not have a closed-form solution.

One idea for dealing with intractable posterior inference is to approximate it with a tractable proxy. **Variational inference** (VI) is such a method by optimising a lower bound of $\log P(X)$ with a surrogate of the exact posterior $P(Z|X, \Theta)$.

18.4.1 Evidence Lower Bound

Recall that in Section 6.3 of Chapter 6, we derived a lower bound of $\log P(X)$ for discrete latent variable models by using Jensen inequality:

$$\log P(X|\Theta) \geq \sum_{Z} P_C(Z) \log \frac{P(X, Z|\Theta)}{P_C(Z)} = E_{P_C(Z)} \log \frac{P(X, Z|\Theta)}{P_C(Z)},$$

where $P_C(Z)$ is a proxy for the exact posterior $P(Z|X, \Theta)$. This lower bound is named the **evidence lower bound** (ELBO). While $P_C(Z)$ can be an arbitrary distribution, we showed in Chapter 6 that the condition $P_C(Z) = P(Z|X, \Theta)$ gives the maximum lower bound value. This result cannot help us here, however, since we assume that $P(Z|X, \Theta)$ is intractable. Instead, we turn to less tight bounds, regularising the posterior $P(Z|X, \Theta)$ to a family of simpler distributions $\mathcal{Q}$ over Z (e.g., Gaussian distributions). Typically, $P(Z|X, \Theta)$ does not belong to $\mathcal{Q}$. Each distribution in $\mathcal{Q}$ is represented as $q_\lambda(Z)$, where λ denotes a set of **variational parameters** (e.g., μ and σ^2 in Gaussian distributions). The key to variational inference is to allow flexible variational parameters to be set specifically for each training instance so that the simple distribution family $q_\lambda(z)$ can approximate $P(Z|X, \Theta)$. Using the **variational posterior** $q_\lambda(Z)$, the lower bound can be written as

$$ELBO(X|\lambda, \Theta) = E_{q_\lambda(Z)} \log \frac{P(X, Z|\Theta)}{q_\lambda(Z)}, \qquad (18.24)$$

which is the expectation of $\log \frac{P(X,Z|\Theta)}{q_\lambda(Z)}$ over the distribution $q_\lambda(Z)$. This conclusion holds for both discrete and continuous latent variables. We assume that latent variables are continuous for the remaining of this section.

Similar to Eq 6.31, it can be shown that the difference between the evidence and the evidence lower bound is the KL divergence of the approximate posterior and the true posterior. Formally,

$$ELBO(X|\lambda, \Theta) = \log P(X|\Theta) - KL\Big(q_\lambda(Z), P(Z|X, \Theta)\Big). \qquad (18.25)$$

Now instead of directly optimising $\log P(X|\Theta)$, we turn to maximising the lower bound $ELBO(X|\boldsymbol{\lambda}, \Theta)$, which is intuitively equivalent to choosing a probability distribution from $\mathcal{Q}$ which is the closest to $P(Z|X, \Theta)$ according to the distance measured by $KL(q_{\boldsymbol{\lambda}}(Z), P(Z|X, \Theta))$.

The variational parameter $\boldsymbol{\lambda}$ is dependent on the data instance since for each training instance the posterior distribution $P(Z|X, \Theta)$ can be different. Given a dataset $D = \{x_i\}|_{i=1}^{N}$, for the ith input x_i, let its variational parameter be $\boldsymbol{\lambda}_i$. The log marginal likelihood of the whole dataset is

$$
\begin{aligned}
\log P(D|\boldsymbol{\Lambda}, \Theta) &= \sum_{i=1}^{N} \log P(x_i|\boldsymbol{\lambda}_i, \Theta) \\
&\geq \sum_{i=1}^{N} ELBO(x_i|\boldsymbol{\lambda}_i, \Theta) = \sum_{i=1}^{N} E_{q_{\boldsymbol{\lambda}_i}(Z)}\left(\log \frac{P(x_i, Z|\Theta)}{q_{\boldsymbol{\lambda}_i}(Z)}\right) \\
&= ELBO(D|\boldsymbol{\Lambda}, \Theta),
\end{aligned}
\tag{18.26}
$$

where $\boldsymbol{\Lambda} = \{\boldsymbol{\lambda}_1, \boldsymbol{\lambda}_2, \ldots, \boldsymbol{\lambda}_N\}$. The lower bound of the whole dataset is the aggregate ELBO of each data point. Intuitively, the lower bound depends on the choice of the distribution $q_{\boldsymbol{\lambda}}(Z)$, where a more complex $q_{\boldsymbol{\lambda}}(Z)$ can potentially better approximate the true $P(Z|X, \Theta)$. In the next three sections, we discuss three optimisation methods for Eq 18.26, respectively. The first two techniques correspond to the standard and generalised EM algorithms for exact posteriors discussed in Chapter 6 and Section 18.1, respectively.

18.4.2 Coordinate Ascent Variational Inference

For each input x_i, there are two types of parameters, namely $\boldsymbol{\lambda}_i$ and Θ. In order to optimise ELBO, we can apply coordinate ascent discussed in Chapter 6, first keeping Θ fixed while updating $\boldsymbol{\lambda}_i$ and then keeping $\boldsymbol{\lambda}_i$ fixed while updating Θ. This learning procedure, which is known as **coordinate ascent VI** (CAVI), resembles EM and is also called **variational EM**. The second name reflects underlying connections between EM and CAVI – they differ only in the optimisation goal (i.e., true posterior v.s. ELBO).

Variational E-step. Similar to the E-step in EM algorithms, which finds the posterior latent variable distribution with respect to fixed model parameters, the variational E-step finds the optimal variational posterior distribution $q_{\boldsymbol{\lambda}_i}(Z)$ for each input x_i by assuming that Θ are constants. Formally, $\boldsymbol{\lambda}_i$ is given by

$$
\begin{aligned}
\boldsymbol{\lambda}_i &= \arg\max_{\boldsymbol{\lambda}_i'} ELBO(x_i|\boldsymbol{\lambda}_i', \Theta) \\
&= \arg\max_{\boldsymbol{\lambda}_i'} \left(\log P(x_i|\Theta) - KL(q_{\boldsymbol{\lambda}_i'}(Z), P(Z|x_i, \Theta))\right) \text{ (Using Eq 18.24)} \\
&= \arg\min_{\boldsymbol{\lambda}_i'} KL(q_{\boldsymbol{\lambda}_i'}(Z), P(Z|x_i, \Theta)).
\end{aligned}
\tag{18.27}
$$

The last equation above holds because $\log P(x_i|\Theta)$ is independent of $\boldsymbol{\lambda}_i'$ when Θ is fixed.

Variational M-step. The variational M-step optimises Θ to maximise the ELBO of the whole dataset by fixing each λ_i to its corresponding value obtained in the variational E-step

$$
\begin{aligned}
\Theta &= \arg\max_{\Theta'} ELBO(D|\Lambda, \Theta') = \arg\max_{\Theta'} \sum_{i=1}^{N} ELBO(x_i|\lambda_i, \Theta) \\
&= \arg\max_{\Theta'} \sum_{i=1}^{N} E_{q_{\lambda_i}(Z)} \left(\log \frac{P(x_i, Z|\Theta')}{q_{\lambda_i}(Z)} \right) \\
&= \arg\max_{\Theta'} \sum_{i=1}^{N} E_{q_{\lambda_i}(Z)} \left(\log P(x_i, Z|\Theta') - q_{\lambda_i}(Z) \right) \\
&= \arg\max_{\Theta'} \sum_{i=1}^{N} E_{q_{\lambda_i}(Z)} \log P(x_i, Z|\Theta').
\end{aligned}
\tag{18.28}
$$

The last step above holds because the entropy term $-\sum_{i=1}^{N} E_{q_{\lambda_i}(Z)} q_{\lambda_i}(Z)$ does not depend on Θ'.

The variational M-step is similar to the M-step in EM, which optimises Θ by maximising the expectation of the complete data log likelihood $\sum_{i=1}^{N} E_{P(Z|x_i, \Theta)} \log P(x_i, Z|\Theta')$ with regard to the true posterior $P(Z|x_i, \Theta)$. The variational M-step performs the same maximisation with respect to the variational posterior $q_{\lambda_i}(Z)$ instead of the true posterior. In the extreme case, when $q_\lambda(Z)$ is carefully chosen such that $P(Z|x_i, \Theta)$ belongs to the variational family, we have $q_{\lambda_i}(Z) = P(Z|x_i, \Theta)$ since in the variational E-step the KL divergence is zero, which makes the variational EM process become EM.

18.4.3 Stochastic Variational Inference

In CAVI, the E-step traverses all the training data to calculate the posterior distribution of each training instance, which can be inefficient. Instead we can apply gradient-based optimisation using mini-batch. In this way, we approximate the E-step and the M-step by stochastic gradient ascent, which is similar to the M-step in generalised EM. This learning algorithm is named **stochastic VI** (SVI). We consider a batch of M examples to illustrate the updating procedure of SVI.

Gradient-based E-step. The gradient-based E-step updates the variational parameter λ_i for the ith training instance by the gradient $\frac{\partial ELBO(x_i|\lambda_i, \Theta)}{\partial \lambda_i}$

$$
\begin{aligned}
\lambda_i^{t+1} &= \lambda_i^t + \eta \frac{\partial ELBO(x_i|\lambda_i, \Theta)}{\partial \lambda_i} \\
&= \lambda_i^t - \eta \frac{\partial KL(q_{\lambda_i}(Z), P(Z|x_i, \Theta))}{\partial \lambda_i}.
\end{aligned}
\tag{18.29}
$$

Here η is the learning rate. In each mini-batch, the initial parameter λ_i^0 can be randomly initialised. Then the gradient-based E-step for each training instance is performed for K steps to make λ_i^K a good approximation.

Gradient-based M-step. Using the learned variational parameters $\{\lambda_1^K, \lambda_2^K, \ldots, \lambda_M^K\}$, the gradient-based M-step updates Θ by the gradient $\frac{\partial \sum_{i=1}^{M} ELBO(x_i|\lambda_i^K, \Theta)}{\partial \Theta}$:

$$
\begin{aligned}
\Theta^{t+1} &= \Theta^t + \eta \frac{\partial \sum_{i=1}^{M} ELBO(x_i|\lambda_i^K, \Theta)}{\partial \Theta}, \\
&= \Theta^t + \eta \sum_{i=1}^{M} E_{q_{\lambda_i^K}(Z)} \frac{\partial \log P(x_i, Z|\Theta)}{\partial \Theta}.
\end{aligned}
\tag{18.30}
$$

Compared to CAVI, SVI iteratively updates model parameters using mini-batch training samples, which does not require closed-form solutions of λ and Θ for the whole training dataset.

18.4.4 Amortised Variational Inference

Both CAVI and SVI optimise **instance-specific** variational parameters by maximising ELBO. There are three potential issues. First, the number of variational parameters is linear to the training data size, which does not scale for large datasets. Second, for a new test sample, the optimisation process is again necessary in order to obtain the variational parameter. Third, the optimisation for a single example can be expensive because there are typically no closed-form solutions for variational parameters of deep generative models when using CAVI, and the gradient calculation $\frac{\partial ELBO(x_i|\lambda_i, \Theta)}{\partial \lambda_i}$ in SVI can induce highly expensive computation.

To alleviate these issues, **amortised variational inference** (Amortised VI) restricts the variational distribution family to a certain distribution parameterised by deep neural networks, which are called **recognition network**, **inference network** or **encoders**. Instead of learning one set of variational parameters for each training instance, amortised VI learns a *globally shared* set of neural network parameters to *predict* the variational parameter λ_i of each instance. Particularly, we denote the inference network as $\text{INFNET}(x_i; \phi)$, where ϕ are the model parameters of the inference network. The variational parameter of x_i is dynamically decided by $\lambda_i = \text{INFNET}(x_i; \phi)$. Given the training set $D = \{x_i\}|_{i=1}^{N}$, we can optimise the shared parameter set ϕ by maximising the aggregate ELBO of the whole dataset where the loss is

$$
L = -\sum_{i=1}^{N} ELBO(x_i|\text{INFNET}(x_i; \phi), \Theta).
\tag{18.31}
$$

For simplicity, we denote $ELBO(x_i|\text{INFNET}(x_i; \phi), \Theta)$ as $ELBO(x_i|\phi, \Theta)$. Using the above learning objective, we can use mini-batch stochastic gradient ascent to alternatively optimise ϕ and Θ:

$$
\begin{aligned}
\phi^{t+1} &= \phi^t + \eta \frac{\partial \sum_{i=1}^{M} ELBO(x_i|\phi, \Theta^t)}{\partial \phi} \\
\Theta^{t+1} &= \Theta^t + \eta \frac{\partial \sum_{i=1}^{M} ELBO(x_i|\phi^t, \Theta)}{\partial \Theta}.
\end{aligned}
\tag{18.32}
$$

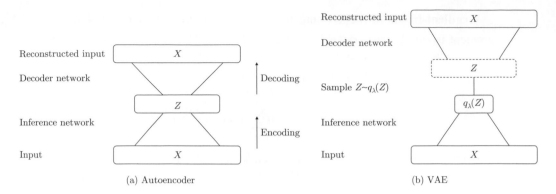

Figure 18.2 Autoencoder and variational autoencoder (VAE).

In this way, we jointly learn ϕ and Θ. Compared to CAVI and SVI, amortised VI is less expressive since it introduces one more constraint that the variation posterior distribution λ_i is a parameterised mapping from the observation data x_i. The gap between free-form VI (e.g., CAVI and SVI) and amortised VI is called the **amortisation gap**. In practice, amortised VI can be much faster than CAVI and SVI due to the fact that we can simply run the encoder over the input samples to obtain the variational parameters. When the encoder is well designed and trained, the variational parameters learned by the encoder can represent good variational posterior distributions, which can well approximate the true posterior. Amortised VI also bridges deep neural networks and efficient VI for massive datasets. The next section discusses a typical use of amortised VI.

18.4.5 Variational Autoencoders

Variational autoencoders (VAEs) are applications of amortised VI for unsupervised representation learning using latent variables based on an **autoencoder** framework. The goal of an autoencoder (Figure 18.2(a)) is to train a model that can **encode** an input x into a representation z and then reconstruct (i.e, **decode**) x from z. The representation z is typically a more compact representation of x that contains all information about x. Preservation of information is ensured through the reconstruction training objective. The structure of a typical autoencoder is shown in Figure 18.2. While z can be a deterministic hidden vector in a neural autoencoder (Figure 18.2 (a)), VAEs (Figure 18.2(b)) make z a stochastic variable instead.

For decoding, VAEs are trained to generate samples from a continuous space. To generate a sample x using VAEs, we first sample a random vector $\mathbf{z}$ from the prior distribution $P(\mathbf{z}|\Theta)$ and then use a **decoder network** $P(x|\mathbf{z}, \Theta)$ to construct x from $\mathbf{z}$.

For encoding, given an input x, we find a distribution $q_\lambda(\mathbf{Z})$, where the variational parameters ($\boldsymbol{\lambda}$) are predicted by an **inference network** with parameters ϕ (i.e. $\boldsymbol{\lambda} = \text{INFNET}(x; \phi)$). Thus $q_\lambda(\mathbf{Z})$ is a posterior conditioned on x, similiar to Section 18.4.4. In particular, we denote the variational posterior distribution $q_\lambda(Z)$ over the latent variable $\mathbf{z}$ as $q(\mathbf{z}|x, \phi)$. To ensure the random vector $\mathbf{z}$ from the prior $P(\mathbf{z}|\Theta)$ can encode meaningful representations of the input, the posterior $q(\mathbf{z}|x, \phi)$ are enforced to match $P(\mathbf{z}|\Theta)$ during training. Θ and ϕ are jointly trained using Eq 18.32 to maximise the ELBO of x, which now can be rewritten as

$$
\begin{aligned}
ELBO(x|\phi, \Theta) &= E_{q(\mathbf{z}|x,\phi)} \left[\log \frac{P(x, \mathbf{z}|\Theta)}{q(\mathbf{z}|\phi)} \right] \\
&= E_{q(\mathbf{z}|x,\phi)} \left[\log \frac{P(x|\mathbf{z}, \Theta) P(\mathbf{z}|\Theta)}{q(\mathbf{z}|\phi)} \right] \\
&= \underbrace{E_{q(\mathbf{z}|x,\phi)} \log P(x|\mathbf{z}, \Theta)}_{\text{reconstruction loss}} - \underbrace{KL\left(q(\mathbf{z}|x, \phi), P(\mathbf{z}|\Theta) \right)}_{\text{regulariser}}.
\end{aligned}
\tag{18.33}
$$

The first term $E_{q(\mathbf{z}|x,\phi)} \log P(x|\mathbf{z}, \Theta)$ can be regarded as a reconstruction loss. The encoder first generates latent random vectors $\mathbf{z}$ according to the posterior distribution $q(\mathbf{z}|x, \phi)$. The latent random vector $\mathbf{z}$ is trained to best reconstruct x by maximising the log-likelihood $P(x|\mathbf{z}, \Theta)$. The second term $KL\left(q(\mathbf{z}|x; \phi), P(\mathbf{z}; \Theta) \right)$ is a regulariser, which forces the posterior distribution to be similar to the prior distribution. The posterior distribution and the prior distribution can typically be chosen from the same type of distribution with different parameters, which can make optimisation easier.

For example, we can apply multivariate Gaussian distributions (Chapter 2) with diagonal covariance matrices as the posterior distributions and prior distributions. In particular, $P(\mathbf{z}|\Theta) = \mathcal{N}(\mathbf{z}|\mathbf{0}, \mathbf{I})$ and $q(\mathbf{z}|x, \phi) = \mathcal{N}(\mathbf{z}|\boldsymbol{\mu}, \text{diag}(\boldsymbol{\sigma}^2))$, where $\boldsymbol{\mu}$ and $\boldsymbol{\sigma}$ are predicted by an inference network over x, $\boldsymbol{\mu} \in \mathbb{R}^d$ and $\boldsymbol{\sigma} \in \mathbb{R}^d$:

$$
\begin{aligned}
\boldsymbol{\mu} &= \text{INFNET}^{\mu}(x, \phi^{\mu}) \\
\boldsymbol{\sigma}^2 &= \text{INFNET}^{\sigma}(x, \phi^{\sigma}),
\end{aligned}
\tag{18.34}
$$

where INFNET^{μ} and INFNET^{σ} are two separate networks parameterised by ϕ^{μ} and ϕ^{σ}, respectively, both of which can be MLPs. Thus $\text{INFNET} = \text{INFNET}^{\mu} \cup \text{INFNET}^{\sigma}$ and $\phi = \phi^{\mu} \cup \phi^{\sigma}$.

Training. To train the decoder, we update Θ using the gradient $\frac{\partial ELBO(x|\phi, \Theta)}{\partial \Theta}$, which is similar to Eq 18.30:

$$
\frac{\partial ELBO(x|\phi, \Theta)}{\partial \Theta} = E_{q(\mathbf{z}|x,\phi)} \left[\frac{\partial \log P(x, \mathbf{z}|\Theta)}{\partial \Theta} \right].
\tag{18.35}
$$

Equation 18.35 is the expectation of the gradients of the complete data log-likelihood $\log P(x, \mathbf{z}|\Theta)$ with respect to Θ according to the variational posterior $q(\mathbf{z}|x, \phi)$. To estimate the intractable expectation term, we can approximate the gradient by generating M samples of $\mathbf{z}$ from $q(\mathbf{z}|x, \phi)$, namely $\mathbf{z}_1, \mathbf{z}_2, \ldots, \mathbf{z}_M$:

$$
E_{q(\mathbf{z}|x,\phi)} \left[\frac{\partial \log P(x, \mathbf{z}|\Theta)}{\partial \Theta} \right] \approx \frac{1}{M} \sum_{i=1}^{M} \frac{\partial \log P(x, \mathbf{z}_i|\Theta)}{\partial \Theta}.
\tag{18.36}
$$

In practice, M can typically be set to 1 for a balance of efficiency and accuracy. Similarly, we can optimise the inference network parameter ϕ by using the gradient $\frac{\partial ELBO(x|\phi,\Theta)}{\partial\phi}$, which is given by

$$
\begin{aligned}
\frac{\partial ELBO(x|\phi,\Theta)}{\partial\phi} &= \frac{\partial E_{q(\mathbf{z}|x,\phi)} \log \frac{P(x,\mathbf{z}|\Theta)}{q(\mathbf{z}|x,\phi)}}{\partial\phi} \\
&= \frac{\partial E_{q(\mathbf{z}|x,\phi)} \log P(x,\mathbf{z}|\Theta)}{\partial\phi} - \frac{\partial E_{q(\mathbf{z}|x,\phi)} \log q(\mathbf{z}|x,\phi)}{\partial\phi}.
\end{aligned}
\tag{18.37}
$$

The calculation of $\frac{\partial E_{q(\mathbf{z}|x,\phi)} \log P(x,\mathbf{z}|\Theta)}{\partial\phi}$ and $\frac{\partial E_{q(\mathbf{z}|x,\phi)} \log q(\mathbf{z}|x,\phi)}{\partial\phi}$ are similar. Consider the second term first, where

$$
\begin{aligned}
\frac{\partial E_{q(\mathbf{z}|x,\phi)} \log q(\mathbf{z}|x,\phi)}{\partial\phi} &= \frac{\partial \int \log q(\mathbf{z}|x,\phi)q(\mathbf{z}|x,\phi)d\mathbf{z}}{\partial\phi} \\
&= \int \frac{\partial\Big(\log q(\mathbf{z}|x,\phi)q(\mathbf{z}|x,\phi)\Big)d\mathbf{z}}{\partial\phi} \\
&= \int q(\mathbf{z}|x,\phi)\frac{\partial\log q(\mathbf{z}|x,\phi)}{\partial\phi} + \log q(\mathbf{z}|x,\phi)\frac{\partial q(\mathbf{z}|x,\phi)}{\partial\phi}d\mathbf{z} \\
&= \int \frac{\partial q(\mathbf{z}|x,\phi)}{\partial\phi}d\mathbf{z} + \int \log q(\mathbf{z}|x,\phi)\frac{\partial q(\mathbf{z}|x,\phi)}{\partial\phi}d\mathbf{z} \\
&= 0 + \int \log q(\mathbf{z}|x,\phi)\frac{\partial q(\mathbf{z}|x,\phi)}{\partial\phi}d\mathbf{z} \\
&= \int \log q(\mathbf{z}|x,\phi)q(\mathbf{z}|x,\phi)\frac{\partial\log q(\mathbf{z}|x,\phi)}{\partial\phi}d\mathbf{z} \\
&= E_{q(\mathbf{z}|x,\phi)}\Big[\log q(\mathbf{z}|x,\phi)\frac{\partial\log q(\mathbf{z}|x,\phi)}{\partial\phi}\Big].
\end{aligned}
\tag{18.38}
$$

Similarly, we can obtain the first term above, $\frac{\partial E_{q(\mathbf{z}|x,\phi)} \log P(x,\mathbf{z}|\Theta)}{\partial\phi}$, as

$$
\frac{\partial E_{q(\mathbf{z}|x,\phi)} \log P(x,\mathbf{z}|\Theta)}{\partial\phi} = E_{q(\mathbf{z}|x,\phi)}\Big[\log P(x,\mathbf{z}|\Theta)\frac{\partial\log q(\mathbf{z}|x,\phi)}{\partial\phi}\Big].
$$

Therefore, $\frac{\partial ELBO(x|\phi,\Theta)}{\partial\phi}$ is finally given by

$$
\begin{aligned}
\frac{\partial ELBO(x|\phi,\Theta)}{\partial\phi} &= E_{q(\mathbf{z}|x,\phi)}\Big[\log P(x,\mathbf{z}|\Theta)\frac{\partial\log q(\mathbf{z}|x,\phi)}{\partial\phi}\Big] \\
&\quad - E_{q(\mathbf{z}|x,\phi)}\Big[\log q(\mathbf{z}|x,\phi)\frac{\partial\log q(\mathbf{z}|x,\phi)}{\partial\phi}\Big] \\
&= E_{q(\mathbf{z}|x,\phi)}\Big[\log \frac{P(x,\mathbf{z}|\Theta)}{q(\mathbf{z}|x,\phi)}\frac{\partial\log q(\mathbf{z}|x,\phi)}{\partial\phi}\Big].
\end{aligned}
\tag{18.39}
$$

Again, using M random samples, we can approximate $\frac{\partial ELBO(x|\phi,\Theta)}{\partial\phi}$ by

$$
\frac{\partial ELBO(x|\phi,\Theta)}{\partial\phi} \approx \frac{1}{M}\sum_{i=1}^{M} \log \frac{P(x,\mathbf{z}_i|\Theta)}{q(\mathbf{z}_i|x,\phi)}\frac{\partial\log q(\mathbf{z}_i|x,\phi)}{\partial\phi}.
\tag{18.40}
$$

18.4.6 Reparameterisation

For the VAE gradient estimators in the previous section, we generate M samples to estimate expectations of gradients. For example, when we try to update the parameters for the inference network, the gradients are calculated using Eq 18.40. In this process, we first calculate a posterior distribution of the latent variables $\mathbf{z}$, based on which we sample a latent variable instance, before calculating gradients of the ELBO function. Now the sampling process depends on the parameter ϕ of the inference network itself. In theory, gradients should be back-propagated through the sampling process also to ϕ so as to adjust the sampling distribution for better ELBO optimisation. However, the sampling process is a discrete-valued function that is non-differentiable. One natural question that arises is whether we can ensure that all the parameters are updated during SGD training wherever they play a role.

One idea is to remove the parameter ϕ from the sampling process, so that a sample is drawn independently of all model parameters. In this way, we are safe ignoring the sampling process when back-propagating the gradients of ELBO. To this goal, **reparameterisation** of the posterior distribution can help us. In particular, we want to make the posterior distribution $q(\mathbf{z}|x, \phi)$ a deterministic, invertible and differentiable transformation f_ϕ to a specific base distribution $q(\epsilon)$, which does not depend on ϕ. In this way, a random sample $\mathbf{z}$ is calculated by first drawing a sample ϵ using $q(\epsilon)$:

$$
\begin{aligned}
\epsilon &\sim q(\epsilon) \\
\mathbf{z} &= f_\phi(\epsilon)
\end{aligned}
\tag{18.41}
$$

$f_\phi(\epsilon)$ is typically the inverse function of a **standardisation function** $s_\phi(\mathbf{z})$, which maps a parameterised distribution into a standardised distribution such as the standard normal distribution $\mathcal{N}(\mathbf{0}, \mathbf{I})$ and the uniform distribution $\mathcal{U}[\mathbf{0}, \mathbf{1}]$. We show the examples below.

Reparameterisation for Gaussian. First let us suppose that $q(\mathbf{z}|x, \phi)$ is a diagonal Gaussian, $q(\mathbf{z}|x, \phi) \sim \mathcal{N}(\boldsymbol{\mu}, \text{diag}(\boldsymbol{\sigma}^2))$. For a Gaussian distribution $\mathcal{N}(\boldsymbol{\mu}, \text{diag}(\boldsymbol{\sigma}^2))$, the standardisation function is $s_\phi(\mathbf{z}) = \frac{\mathbf{z} - \boldsymbol{\mu}}{\boldsymbol{\sigma}}$, which is distributed as $\mathcal{N}(\mathbf{0}, \mathbf{I})$. Therefore, the reparameterisation method for a Gaussian random sample $\mathbf{z}$ is given by

$$
\begin{aligned}
\epsilon &\sim \mathcal{N}(\mathbf{0}, \mathbf{I}) \\
\mathbf{z} &= f_\phi(\epsilon) = s_\phi^{-1}(\epsilon) = \boldsymbol{\mu} + \boldsymbol{\sigma} \otimes \epsilon,
\end{aligned}
\tag{18.42}
$$

where $\boldsymbol{\mu}$ and $\boldsymbol{\sigma}^2$ are produced by the encoder using Eq 18.34.

Now consider the gradient of ϕ in Eq 18.33. We have

$$
\frac{\partial ELBO(x|\phi, \Theta)}{\partial \phi} = \frac{\partial E_{q(\mathbf{z}|x,\phi)}\left[\log P(x|\mathbf{z}, \Theta)\right]}{\partial \phi} - \frac{\partial KL\left(q(\mathbf{z}|x, \phi), p(\mathbf{z})\right)}{\partial \phi}.
$$

To estimate the first term, we need to generate samples from $q(\mathbf{z}|x, \phi)$. Using reparameterisation, the expectation can be rewritten as

$$
E_{q(\mathbf{z}|x,\phi)}\left[\log P(x|\mathbf{z}, \Theta)\right] = E_{q(\epsilon)}\left[\log P(x|f_\phi(\epsilon), \Theta)\right],
\tag{18.43}
$$

which says that we can estimate the expectation of a function of $\mathbf{z}$ over $q(\mathbf{z}|x, \phi)$ without knowing the explicit form of $q(\mathbf{z}|x, \phi)$, by using the independent base distribution $q(\epsilon)$ and the transformation function f_ϕ. Therefore, the gradient $\nabla_\phi E_{q(\mathbf{z}|x,\phi)}$ now can be estimated by

$$
\begin{aligned}
\frac{\partial E_{q(\mathbf{z}|x,\phi)}[\log P(x|\mathbf{z}, \Theta)]}{\partial \phi} &= \frac{\partial E_{\epsilon \sim \mathcal{N}(\mathbf{0},\mathbf{I})}[\log P(x|\boldsymbol{\mu} + \boldsymbol{\sigma} \otimes \epsilon, \Theta)]}{\partial \phi} \\
&= E_{\epsilon \sim \mathcal{N}(\mathbf{0},\mathbf{I})}\Big[\frac{\partial \log P(x|\boldsymbol{\mu} + \boldsymbol{\sigma} \otimes \epsilon, \Theta)}{\partial \phi}\Big].
\end{aligned}
\tag{18.44}
$$

Based on Eq 18.44, we can generate samples from $\mathcal{N}(\mathbf{0}, \mathbf{I})$, which does not involve $\boldsymbol{\mu}$ and $\boldsymbol{\sigma}$. Similarly, we can also apply the reparameterisation trick for the gradient of the KL divergence term. Sometimes, the KL divergence for two distributions has an analytical solution, which can be exploited to give accurate gradients for parameters. For example, given $q(\mathbf{z}|x, \phi) \sim \mathcal{N}(\boldsymbol{\mu}, \text{diag}(\boldsymbol{\sigma}^2))$ and $P(\mathbf{z}) \sim \mathcal{N}(\mathbf{0}, \mathbf{I})$, the KL divergence between $q(\mathbf{z}|x, \phi)$ and $p(\mathbf{z})$ is given by

$$
KL(q(\mathbf{z}|x, \phi), P(\mathbf{z})) = -\frac{1}{2} \sum_{j=1}^{d} (\log \sigma_j^2 - \sigma_j^2 - \mu_j^2 + 1),
\tag{18.45}
$$

where d is the feature dimension of $\mathbf{z}$.

The gradient can be directly back-propagated through the decoder to the inference network through $\boldsymbol{\mu}$ and $\boldsymbol{\sigma}$, without considering the ϵ or $\mathbf{z}$ samples.

Gumbel softmax. Gumbel softmax is a method to reparameterise categorical distributions. Suppose that z is a random sample of the categorical probability distribution π, where $z \in \{1, 2, \dots, K\}$ and $\pi = (\pi_1, \pi_2, \dots, \pi_K)$ $(\pi_k = P(z = i))$. We want to reparameterise π out of a sampling process by drawing samples from a uniform distribution. Formally, assume that the random vector $\mathbf{z}$ represents the one-hot vector of z. $\mathbf{z}$ can be represented by a **Gumbel distribution** $G = -\log(-\log(\mathbf{u}))$, where $\mathbf{u} \in \mathcal{U}[\mathbf{0}, \mathbf{1}]$ is a sample from the uniform distribution (Chapter 2):

$$
\begin{aligned}
\mathbf{u} &\sim \mathcal{U}[\mathbf{0}, \mathbf{1}] \\
\mathbf{g} &= -\log(-\log(\mathbf{u})) \\
\mathbf{z} &= \text{OneHot}\Big(\arg\max_k (\log \pi_k + g_k)\Big).
\end{aligned}
\tag{18.46}
$$

$\mathbf{g}$ above is also called the gumbel noise. $\text{OneHot}(k)$ returns a one-hot vector with the kth element being one and the other elements being zeros. Equation 18.46 is called **Gumbel-max trick**, which is a simple and effective way to draw random samples from categorial distributions. However, the arg max operation is non-differentiable, which makes back-propagation difficult. Instead, **Gumbel softmax** uses a *softmax* function to approximate the *max* function, where

$$
\begin{aligned}
\mathbf{z} &= \langle z_1, z_2, \dots, z_K \rangle \\
z_i &= \frac{\exp(\frac{\log \pi_k + g_k}{\tau})}{\sum_{k=1}^{K} \exp(\frac{\log \pi_k + g_k}{\tau})}.
\end{aligned}
\tag{18.47}
$$

Equation 18.47 is fully differentiable by using small numbers to replace 0s, and values close to 1 to approximate 1. τ is a temperature hyper-parameter to sharpen the *softmax* function, making only one element in $\mathbf{z}$ close to 1, and the other close to 0. In practice, when $\tau \to 0$, $\mathbf{z}$ moves towards the one-hot vector of the class. In contrast, when $\tau \to \infty$, $\mathbf{z}$ tends to a uniform random vector, which we do not prefer.

18.5 Neural Topic Models

In correspondence to the topic model discussed in Section 6.2.3, let us discuss neural variational topic models for document modelling by replacing the categorical latent variable with a dense latent vector. Suppose that the document representation is $\mathbf{d}$ and the latent vector is $\mathbf{z}$, we use ELBO as our learning objective according to Eq 18.33,

$$ELBO(\mathbf{d}|\phi, \Theta) = E_{q(\mathbf{z}|\mathbf{d}, \phi)}\Big(\log P(\mathbf{d}|\mathbf{z}, \Theta)\Big) - KL\Big(q(\mathbf{z}|\mathbf{d}, \phi), P(\mathbf{z})\Big), \tag{18.48}$$

where $\mathbf{z}$ represents topic-related features, $q(\mathbf{z}|\mathbf{d}, \phi)$ is the variational posterior distribution and $P(\mathbf{z})$ is the prior distribution. Different representations of $\mathbf{d}$, $\mathbf{z}$, $q(\mathbf{z}|\mathbf{d}, \phi)$ and $P(\mathbf{z})$ lead to different topic models. Below we give two increasingly complex models.

18.5.1 Neural Variational Document Model

Neural variational document model (NVDM) is a simple application of VAE for document modelling, which turns out to be an effective topic model. For NVDM, the document representation $\mathbf{d}$ is based on bag-of-words assumptions. Let the set of words in $\mathbf{d}$ be $\{w_i\}|_{i=1}^{n}$. Further let the prior $P(\mathbf{z})$ be $\mathcal{N}(\mathbf{0}, \mathbf{I})$ and the posterior be $\mathcal{N}(\boldsymbol{\mu}, \mathrm{diag}(\boldsymbol{\sigma}^2))$, which allows the gradients for the KL term of Eq 18.48 to be computed in a convenient way using Eq 18.45.

Given $\mathbf{d}, \boldsymbol{\mu}$ and $\mathrm{diag}(\boldsymbol{\sigma}^2)$ are predicted by the following inference network

$$\begin{aligned} \mathbf{h} &= f(MLP(\mathbf{d})) \\ \boldsymbol{\mu} &= l_1(\mathbf{h}) \\ \boldsymbol{\sigma}^2 &= \exp(l_2(\mathbf{h})), \end{aligned} \tag{18.49}$$

where f is a non-linear activation function. l_1 and l_2 denote two linear mapping functions.

For calculating gradients for the expectation term, we can use the reparameterisation trick to generate samples of $\mathbf{z}$ by indirectly generating samples of ϵ from uniform distributions. In particular, $\mathbf{z} = \boldsymbol{\mu} + \boldsymbol{\sigma} \otimes \epsilon$ and $\epsilon \in \mathcal{U}[\mathbf{0}, \mathbf{1}]$.

Given a sample $\mathbf{z}$, the reconstruction log-likelihood for the decoder can be rewritten as

$$\log P(\mathbf{d}|\mathbf{z}, \Theta) = \sum_{i=1}^{n} \log P(w_i|\mathbf{z}, \Theta),$$

where $P(w_i|\mathbf{z}, \Theta)$ is calculated using a *softmax* output layer

$$f(w_i, \mathbf{z}, \Theta) = \mathbf{z}^T \mathbf{E}(\mathrm{ONEHOT}(w_i)) + \mathbf{b}$$

$$P(w_i|\mathbf{z}, \Theta) = \frac{\exp\big(f(w_i, \mathbf{z}, \Theta)\big)}{\sum_{w' \in V}^{|V|} \exp\big(f(w', \mathbf{z}, \Theta)\big)}.$$

The ELBO is thus

$$ELBO(\mathbf{d}|\phi, \Theta) \approx \sum_{i=1}^{n} \log P(w_i|\mathbf{z}, \Theta) - KL\Big(q(\mathbf{z}|\mathbf{d}, \phi), P(\mathbf{z})\Big). \qquad (18.50)$$

Here $\textsc{OneHot}(w)$ gives a one-hot representation vector of the word w, and $\mathbf{E}\big(\textsc{OneHot}(w)\big)$ gives the embedding $emb(w)$. The matrix $\mathbf{E}$ is an embedding lookup table and $\mathbf{b}$ is a bias vector, which are model parameters shared across documents. In NVDM, each dimension in $\mathbf{z}$ can be implicitly considered as a latent topic. After the model is trained, the mean vector $\boldsymbol{\mu}$ produced by the inference network can be used for the topic representation.

18.5.2 Neural Topic Models

NVDM does not explicitly model topics since it does not consider discrete topics. **Neural topic models** (NTM) consider categorical document topic distributions by the following generative process:

$$\epsilon \sim \mathcal{N}(\mathbf{0}, \mathbf{I}), \ \mathbf{z} = f(\epsilon), \ t_i \sim \mathbf{z}, w_i \sim \Theta_{t_i}, \qquad (18.51)$$

where a Gaussian random vector ϵ is first generated, and then passed through a network function f to produce the document–topic distribution $\mathbf{z}$. A topic sample t_i for the ith word is selected according to $\mathbf{z}$ and finally a word w_i is sampled from the topic–word distribution Θ_{t_i}. $\Theta = \{\Theta_k\}|_{k=1}^{K}$ is a set of trainable model parameters and K is the number of topics.

In particular, we can have $f(\epsilon) = softmax(\mathbf{W}_1 \epsilon)$, where $\mathbf{W}_1$ is a model parameter. $\Theta_k = softmax((\mathbf{E})^T emb^t(t_k))$, where $\mathbf{E} \in \mathbb{R}^{d \times |V|}$ is the word embedding lookup table and $emb^t(t_k) \in \mathbb{R}^d$ is the topic embedding of t_k. $(\mathbf{E})^T emb^t(t_k) \in \mathbb{R}^{|V|}$ is a vector that stores the probability of each vocabulary word conditioned on the topic t_k.

Given a sampled $\mathbf{z}$, the latent variable t_i can be marginalised out to obtain $P(w_i|\mathbf{z}, \Theta)$ as:

$$\log P(w_i|\mathbf{z}, \Theta) = \log \sum_{t_i} \Big(P(w_i|\Theta_{t_i})P(t_i|\mathbf{z})\Big). \qquad (18.52)$$

With Eq 18.52, the rest of the model can be similar to NVDM.

18.6 VAEs for Language Modelling

Now let us consider variational inference for language modelling, including variational autoencoders for both single sequence and seq2seq modelling. For the former, we discuss a TextVAE model that can learn to generate a sentence from a random continuous vector. For seq2seq modelling, we extend the seq2seq models discussed in Chapter 16 with a continuous latent hidden vector.

18.6.1 TextVAE

TextVAE is a VAE model for sentences. Given an input sentence representation $\mathbf{X} = \mathbf{x}_1 \mathbf{x}_2 \ldots \mathbf{x}_n$, TextVAE encodes $\mathbf{X}$ into a latent variable $\mathbf{z}$ and learns to autoregressively reconstruct the input sentence from $\mathbf{z}$. Different from the discrete categorical latent RNN language model introduced in Section 18.2.3, we use a continuous latent variable here and put a Gaussian prior over $\mathbf{z}$ to regularise the vector space of $\mathbf{z}$. By introducing such latent vectors, we can allow more flexible text generation by conditioning on the random samples of $\mathbf{z}$.

The training objective is to maximise the generative likelihood of $P(\mathbf{X})$. Considering the latent variable $\mathbf{z}$, $P(\mathbf{X})$ can be written as

$$P(\mathbf{X}) = \int_{\mathbf{z}} P(\mathbf{X}, \mathbf{z})d\mathbf{z} = \int_{\mathbf{z}} P(\mathbf{z})P(\mathbf{X}|\mathbf{z})d\mathbf{z}. \tag{18.53}$$

As we discussed earlier, since this training objective is intractable, we turn to the ELBO of the log-likelihood function, using amortised variational inference for optimisation, where

$$\begin{aligned} ELBO(\mathbf{X}|\phi, \boldsymbol{\theta}) &= E_{q(\mathbf{z}|\mathbf{X},\phi)} \log P(\mathbf{X}|\mathbf{z}, \Theta) - KL\Big(q(\mathbf{z}|\mathbf{X},\phi), P(\mathbf{z}|\Theta)\Big) \\ &= E_{q(\mathbf{z}|\mathbf{X},\phi)} \sum_{i=1}^{n} \log P(\mathbf{x}_i|\mathbf{z}, \mathbf{x}_0, \dots, \mathbf{x}_{i-1}, \Theta) - KL\Big(q(\mathbf{z}|\mathbf{X},\phi), P(\mathbf{z}|\Theta)\Big). \end{aligned} \tag{18.54}$$

$q(\mathbf{z}|\mathbf{X}, \phi)$ is parameterised by an inference network based on an LSTM encoder over the input sequence $\mathbf{X}$, $P(\mathbf{x}_i|\mathbf{z}, \mathbf{x}_0, \dots, \mathbf{x}_{i-1}, \Theta)$ is the probability to decode the ith word depending on the previously generated words and the latent random vector $\mathbf{z}$ and $\mathbf{x}_0$ is the representation vector of the sentence starting symbol $\langle s \rangle$. Both $P(\mathbf{z}|\Theta)$ and $q(\mathbf{z}|\mathbf{X}, \phi)$ are assumed to be a multivariate diagonal Gaussian distribution. Particularly, $P(\mathbf{z}|\Theta) = \mathcal{N}(\mathbf{z}|\mathbf{0}, \mathbf{I})$ and $q(\mathbf{z}|\mathbf{X}, \phi) = \mathcal{N}(\mathbf{z}|\boldsymbol{\mu}, \text{diag}(\boldsymbol{\sigma}^2))$.

Parameterisation. Figure 18.3 shows the structure of a typical TextVAE model. We now discuss the parameterisation details of the variational encoder and the decoder. For the encoder, an LSTM is used to generate a sequence of hidden vectors based on the input word representation sequence $\mathbf{X}_{1:n}$,

$$\mathbf{H}_{1:n} = \mathbf{h}_1 \mathbf{h}_2 \dots \mathbf{h}_n = LSTM(\mathbf{X}_{1:n}, \phi^{\text{LSTM}}),$$

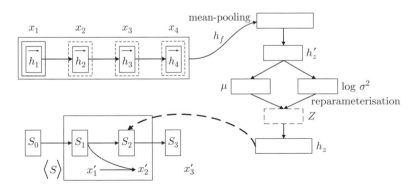

Figure 18.3 Variational recurrent language model.

where ϕ^{LSTM} denotes the parameters of the encoding LSTM. Then we take $\mathbf{h}_n$ or use a mean pooling function over $\mathbf{H}_{1:n}$ to obtain a feature vector to generate the variational parameters for the latent variable. Here we use a mean pooling function to generate the representation vector $\mathbf{h}_f$,

$$\mathbf{h}_f = avg(\mathbf{H}_{1:n})$$

$\mathbf{h}_f$ is fed to an MLP layer to derive the distribution parameters of $q(\mathbf{z}|\mathbf{X}, \phi)$, similar to Eq 18.49. Specifically,

$$\begin{aligned} \mathbf{h}'_z &= f(\mathbf{W}^s \mathbf{h}_s + \mathbf{b}^s) \\ \boldsymbol{\mu} &= \mathbf{W}^\mu \mathbf{h}'_z + \mathbf{b}^\mu \\ \boldsymbol{\sigma}^2 &= \exp(\mathbf{W}^\sigma \mathbf{h}'_z + \mathbf{b}^\sigma), \end{aligned} \tag{18.55}$$

where f is a non-linear activation function. $\mathbf{W}^s$, $\mathbf{W}^\mu$, $\mathbf{W}^\sigma$, $\mathbf{b}^s$, $\mathbf{b}^\mu$ and $\mathbf{b}^\sigma$ are the model parameters.

We can use the reparameterisation trick for Gaussian distributions to sample $\mathbf{z}'$ with a random noise vector ϵ from uniform distribution:

$$\mathbf{z}' = \boldsymbol{\mu} + \boldsymbol{\sigma} \otimes \epsilon. \tag{18.56}$$

Given $\mathbf{z}'$, the LSTM decoder reproduces the input sentence. For example, suppose that now we generate the third token given the first two reconstructed tokens $\mathbf{x}'_1$ and $\mathbf{x}'_2$. The LSTM decoder concatenates the latent vector $\mathbf{z}'$ with the current input $\mathbf{x}'_2$ as inputs to the LSTM decoder

$$\begin{aligned} \mathbf{s}_2 &= \text{LSTM\_STEP}(\mathbf{x}'_2 \oplus \mathbf{z}', \mathbf{s}_1, \Theta^{LSTM}) \\ P(x'_3|\langle s \rangle, \mathbf{x}'_1, \mathbf{x}'_2, \mathbf{z}, \Theta) &= softmax(\mathbf{W}^o \mathbf{s}_2 + \mathbf{b}^o), \end{aligned} \tag{18.57}$$

where Θ^{LSTM}, $\mathbf{W}^o$ and $\mathbf{b}^o$ are the model parameters of the decoder.

Based on the parameterisation above, the TextVAE model can be trained in end-to-end. During training, we sample $\mathbf{z}$ from the posterior $q(\mathbf{z}|X, \phi)$. At testing time, we can directly sample $\mathbf{z}$ from the prior distribution $P(\mathbf{z}|\Theta)$ to generate the sentence without consulting the posterior distribution.

Posterior collapse. One important issue for VAEs is the posterior collapse problem, where the decoder completely ignores the latent variable and degrades to a naïve RNN language model, which means $P(\mathbf{X}|\mathbf{z}, \Theta) \approx P(\mathbf{X}|\Theta)$. When this situation happens, maximising ELBO in Eq 18.33 leads to $KL(q(\mathbf{z}|\mathbf{X}, \phi), P(\mathbf{z})) \approx 0$, which means that the posterior $q(\mathbf{z}|\mathbf{X}, \phi)$ collapses to the prior distribution $P(\mathbf{z})$. This implies that $\mathbf{X}$ and $\mathbf{z}$ become conditionally independent. Take TextVAE for example, if the generation of a sentence is independent of the latent vector under posterior collapse situations, the model becomes a vanilla language model, which generates the same sentences, regardless of the input latent vector.

To alleviate the posterior collapse issue, there are three common solutions. The first idea is to force the decoder to depend on the latent variable by weakening the conditional dependence within the decoder. For example, for text VAE, we can apply dropout to the decoder steps when training the model, or apply conditional independence assumptions such as Markov assumptions to the decoder. The second idea is to inject semantic content into $\mathbf{z}$ by using additional regularisers so that the latent random vector $\mathbf{z}$ can capture global properties of the input sentence. One way is to include an additional bag-of-words loss into ELBO to enforce that $\mathbf{z}$ can directly predict the output contents

$$L_{bow} = ELBO(\mathbf{X}|\phi, \Theta) + \lambda_{bow} E_{q(\mathbf{z}|\mathbf{X},\phi)} \left[\frac{1}{N} \sum_{i=1}^{N} P(\mathbf{x}_i|\mathbf{z}, \Theta) \right], \qquad (18.58)$$

where λ_{bow} is a hyper-parameter for controlling the contributions of the bag-of-words loss. The third idea is KL annealing, where the KL divergence term is not used during the initial training iterations but is gradually enlarged after a few iterations. In this way, the matching constraint between the posterior distribution and the prior distribution is relaxed in the early stage. The model can therefore be forced to optimise the reconstruction loss by depending on $\mathbf{z}$ in the early stage, avoiding the posterior distribution moving close to the prior distribution too soon. In particular, the training objective becomes

$$E_{q(\mathbf{z}|x,\phi)} \log P(\mathbf{X}|\mathbf{z}, \Theta) - \beta KL\Big(q(\mathbf{z}|\mathbf{X}, \phi), P(\mathbf{z}) \Big), \qquad (18.59)$$

where β is an annealing hyper-parameter gradually increasing from 0 to 1.

18.6.2 Variational seq2seq Model

Recall that a seq2seq model in Chapter 16 achieves text-to-text tasks by representing a source sequence into hidden vectors, and then generating a target sequence from the source representation. A variational seq2seq model can introduce a latent hidden vector into the source representation to capture its latent semantic features. The latent vector serves to guide target generation together with the other source representation vectors. By introducing such latent vectors, we can allow more diverse target text generation by varying its sample value after the source is encoded.

Figure 18.4 shows the variational seq2seq model. Formally, a seq2seq model calculates a **conditional** probability distribution $P(\mathbf{Y}|\mathbf{X})$ for mapping a source sequence $\mathbf{X} = \mathbf{x}_1, \ldots, \mathbf{x}_n$ to a target sequence $\mathbf{Y} = \mathbf{y}_1, \ldots, \mathbf{y}_m$. Using a latent hidden vector $\mathbf{z}$, we can rewrite the generative probability distribution $P(\mathbf{Y}|\mathbf{X})$ as

$$P(\mathbf{Y}|\mathbf{X}) = \int_{\mathbf{z}} P(\mathbf{Y}, \mathbf{z}|\mathbf{X}) d\mathbf{z} = \int_{\mathbf{z}} P(\mathbf{z}|\mathbf{X}) P(\mathbf{Y}|\mathbf{z}, \mathbf{X}) d\mathbf{z}. \qquad (18.60)$$

A salient difference between Eq 18.60 and Eq 18.53 is that a conditional probability $P(\mathbf{Y}|\mathbf{X})$ is modelled instead of $P(\mathbf{X})$. Consequently, the condition on $\mathbf{X}$ is part of our parameterisation. In this model, we first generate a random vector $\mathbf{z}$ from the prior distribution $P(\mathbf{z}|\mathbf{X})$ and then generate the target sequence $\mathbf{Y}$ based on the sampled vector $\mathbf{z}$ and the source sequence $\mathbf{X}$. Different from Eq 18.53, we have the source sentence $\mathbf{X}$ as an additional condition to $\mathbf{z}$ here. Two probabilities should be calculated, namely the prior distribution $P(\mathbf{z}|\mathbf{X})$ and the target sequence generation probability distribution $P(\mathbf{Y}|\mathbf{z}, \mathbf{X})$. The former is modelled by a prior encoding network, and the latter is modelled by a seq2seq decoder network.

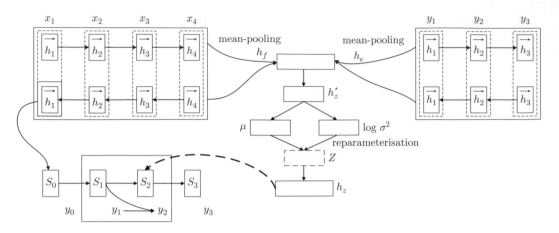

Figure 18.4 Variational seq2seq model.

Training. To optimise this model, we can use the amortised variational inference method by introducing a variational posterior distribution $q(\mathbf{z}|\mathbf{X}, \mathbf{Y}, \phi)$ to approximate the true posterior distribution $P(\mathbf{z}|\mathbf{X}, \mathbf{Y}, \Theta)$, where ϕ and Θ are parameters of the inference network and the decoder model, respectively. The ELBO of the likelihood $L(\mathbf{Y}|\mathbf{X}, \Theta)$ is

$$
\begin{aligned}
L(\mathbf{Y}|\mathbf{X}, \Theta) &\geq L_{ELBO}(\mathbf{Y}|\mathbf{X}, \Theta, \phi) \\
&= E_{q(\mathbf{z}|\mathbf{X}, \mathbf{Y}, \phi)} \log P(\mathbf{Y}|\mathbf{z}, \mathbf{X}, \Theta) - KL(q(z|\mathbf{X}, \mathbf{Y}, \phi), P(\mathbf{z}|\mathbf{X}, \Theta)).
\end{aligned}
\tag{18.61}
$$

Different from $P(\mathbf{X})$ alone, $P(\mathbf{Y}|\mathbf{X})$ is a conditional probability distribution. Therefore, we include $\mathbf{X}$ into the conditions of all the probability distribution compared to Eq 18.54. Without considering the condition on source sentence $\mathbf{X}$, this model becomes a TextVAE model for $\mathbf{Y}$ alone.

Similar to VAE, both the variational posterior distribution $q(\mathbf{z}|\mathbf{X}, \mathbf{Y}, \phi)$ and the prior distribution $P(\mathbf{z}|\mathbf{X}, \Theta)$ can be assumed to be multivariate diagonal Gaussian distributions:

$$
\begin{aligned}
q(\mathbf{z}|\mathbf{X}, \mathbf{Y}, \phi) &= \mathcal{N}(\mathbf{z}|\boldsymbol{\mu}_q, \mathrm{diag}(\boldsymbol{\sigma}_q^2)) \\
P(\mathbf{z}|\mathbf{X}, \Theta) &= \mathcal{N}(\mathbf{z}|\boldsymbol{\mu}_p, \mathrm{diag}(\boldsymbol{\sigma}_p^2)),
\end{aligned}
\tag{18.62}
$$

where $\boldsymbol{\mu}_q$ and $\boldsymbol{\sigma}_q^2$ denote the mean and variance of the posterior distribution, and $\boldsymbol{\mu}_p$ and σ_p^2 denote the mean and variance of the prior distribution, which will be discussed in detail later.

Different from VAE, the prior distribution $P(\mathbf{z}|\mathbf{X}, \Theta)$ is also parameterised according to the source sentence $\mathbf{X}$ instead of being a standard multivariate Gaussian distribution $\mathcal{N}(0, \mathbf{I})$. In this way, the prior contains global semantic information of $\mathbf{X}$.

Parameterisation. The above two Gaussian distributions can be parameterised by neural networks. Suppose that we use a bi-directional LSTM encoder network for the source sequence to compute hidden representations $\mathbf{H}^s = \mathbf{h}_1^s, \mathbf{h}_2^s, \ldots, \mathbf{h}_n^s$, and another bi-directional LSTM encoder for the target sequence to obtain $\mathbf{H}^t = \mathbf{h}_1^t, \mathbf{h}_2^t, \ldots, \mathbf{h}_m^t$. Mean pooling can be used to create global semantic vectors $\mathbf{h}_s$ and $\mathbf{h}_t$ of the source sentence and the target sequence, respectively:

$$\mathbf{h}_f = avg(\mathbf{H}^s), \quad \mathbf{h}_e = avg(\mathbf{H}^t). \tag{18.63}$$

For the prior distribution $P(\mathbf{z}|\mathbf{X}, \Theta)$, since $\mathbf{X}$ is inside the condition, we can use $\mathbf{h}_f$ to calculate $\boldsymbol{\mu}_p$ and σ_p^2,

$$\begin{aligned}
\mathbf{h}'_f &= f(\mathbf{W}^f \mathbf{h}_f + \mathbf{b}^f) \\
\boldsymbol{\mu}_p &= \mathbf{W}^{\mu p} \mathbf{h}'_f + \mathbf{b}^{\mu p}, \\
\sigma_p^2 &= \exp(\mathbf{W}^{\sigma p} \mathbf{h}'_f + \mathbf{b}^{\sigma p}),
\end{aligned} \tag{18.64}$$

where f is a non-linear activation function, $\mathbf{W}^f$, $\mathbf{W}^{\mu p}$, $\mathbf{W}^{\sigma p}$, $\mathbf{b}^f$, $\mathbf{b}^{\mu p}$ and $\mathbf{b}^{\sigma p}$ are model parameters.

Similarly, the parameters of the posterior distribution $q(\mathbf{z}|\mathbf{X}, \mathbf{Y}, \phi)$ conditioned on both $\mathbf{X}$ and $\mathbf{Y}$ can be obtained by

$$\begin{aligned}
\mathbf{h}'_{st} &= f(\mathbf{W}^{st}(\mathbf{h}_s \oplus \mathbf{h}_t) + \mathbf{b}^{st}) \\
\boldsymbol{\mu}_q &= \mathbf{W}^{\mu q} \mathbf{h}'_{st} + \mathbf{b}^{\mu q} \\
\sigma_q^2 &= \exp(\mathbf{W}^{\sigma q} \mathbf{h}'_{st} + \mathbf{b}^{\sigma q}),
\end{aligned} \tag{18.65}$$

where $\mathbf{W}^{st}$, $\mathbf{W}^{\mu q}$, $\mathbf{W}^{\sigma q}$, $\mathbf{b}^{st}$, $\mathbf{b}^{\mu q}$ and $\mathbf{b}^{\sigma q}$ are model parameters.

Since both the prior distribution $P(\mathbf{z}|\mathbf{X}, \Theta)$ and the posterior distribution $q(\mathbf{z}|\mathbf{X}, \mathbf{Y}, \phi)$ are multivariate Gaussians, $KL(q(\mathbf{z}|\mathbf{X}, \mathbf{Y}, \phi), P(\mathbf{z}|\mathbf{X}, \Theta))$ has a closed-form solution:

$$\begin{aligned}
KL(q(\mathbf{z}|\mathbf{X}, \mathbf{Y}, \phi), P(\mathbf{z}|\mathbf{X}, \Theta)) &= KL(\mathcal{N}(\boldsymbol{\mu}_q, \sigma_q^2), \mathcal{N}(\boldsymbol{\mu}_p, \sigma_p^2)) \\
&= \sum_{i=1}^{d} \left(\log \frac{\sigma_{p,i}}{\sigma_{q,i}} + \frac{\sigma_{q,i}^2 + (\mu_{q,i} - \mu_{p,i})^2}{2\sigma_{p,i}^2} - \frac{1}{2} \right),
\end{aligned} \tag{18.66}$$

where d is the feature dimension of the latent vector.

For the first term $E_{q(\mathbf{z}|\mathbf{X},\mathbf{Y},\phi)} \log P(\mathbf{Y}|\mathbf{z}, \mathbf{X}, \Theta)$ in Eq 18.61, we can sample one random vector $\mathbf{z}'$ from $q(\mathbf{z}|\mathbf{X}, \mathbf{Y}, \phi)$ during training to approximate the expectation. Specifically, we can use the reparameterisation trick for Gaussian distributions to sample $\mathbf{z}'$:

$$\mathbf{z}' = \boldsymbol{\mu}_q + \sigma_q \otimes \boldsymbol{\epsilon}, \tag{18.67}$$

where $\boldsymbol{\epsilon} \sim \mathcal{U}(\mathbf{0}, \mathbf{1})$ is a random uniform noise. $\mathbf{z}'$ can be further passed through an MLP layer g

$$\mathbf{h}_z = g(\mathbf{W}^z \mathbf{z}' + \mathbf{b}^z) \tag{18.68}$$

$\mathbf{W}^z$ and $\mathbf{b}^z$ are model parameters.

The log-likelihood $\log P(\mathbf{Y}|\mathbf{z}', \mathbf{X}, \Theta)$ can be rewritten as:

$$\log P(\mathbf{Y}|\mathbf{z}', \mathbf{X}, \Theta) = \log P(\mathbf{Y}|\mathbf{h}_z, \mathbf{X}, \Theta) = \sum_{j=1}^{m} \log P(\mathbf{y}_j|\mathbf{y}_{<j}, \mathbf{h}_z, \mathbf{X}, \Theta). \tag{18.69}$$

$\mathbf{y}_{<j}$ denotes $\mathbf{y}_1, \ldots, \mathbf{y}_{j-1}$. $\mathbf{h}_z$ is used at each decoding step. It can be regarded as an extended representation of the input token $\mathbf{y}_{j-1}$.

During training, $\mathbf{z}'$ is sampled from the posterior distribution $q(z|\mathbf{X}, \mathbf{Y}, \phi)$. For testing, in order to generate a flexible $\mathbf{Y}$ given an $\mathbf{X}$, we can sample a $\mathbf{z}'$ from the prior distribution $P(\mathbf{z}|\mathbf{X}, \Theta)$, which is then used to guide the generation of the target output.

Summary

In this chapter we have introduced:

- generalised EM and variational EM;
- structured latent variable;
- variational inference and variational autoencoders;
- reparameterisation trick and Gumbel *softmax*;
- neural variational document models and neural topic models;
- Text VAE and variational sequence-to-sequence model.

Chapter Notes

Kim et al. (2018) gave a tutorial on deep latent variable models for natural language. Dempster et al. (1977) discussed generalised EM (Neal and Hinton, 1998). Kim et al. (2017) proposed structured attention networks for including structured latent variables into neural networks. Kingma and Welling (2014) presented the variational autoencoding Bayes method and discussed the reparameterisation method (Rezende and Mohamed, 2015). Bowman et al. (2015) investigated VAEs in language modelling and studied the posterior collapse issue for text VAEs. Zhang et al. (2016) investigated variational seq2seq models for neural machine translation. Jang et al. (2017) proposed the Gumbel softmax distribution. Miao et al. (2016) proposed a neural variational document model. Miao et al. (2017) further presented neural topic models. Srivastava and Sutton (2017) proposed logistical normal LDA, which is a frequently used neural variational topic model. Deep latent variable models using variational inference have been used in various NLP tasks, such as morphological inflection (Zhou and Neubig, 2017), grammar induction (Kim et al., 2019), semantic parsing (Yin et al., 2018), text generation (Hu et al., 2017; Serban et al., 2017) and event extraction (Liu et al., 2019a).

Exercises

18.1 Discriminative latent variable models. In this chapter, we mainly discussed latent variables for generative models. In fact, latent variables can also be used for discriminative models. In Chapter 8, we have used CRF models to capture label dependencies of sequences. Latent variables can be used to refine the labels, leading to a latent CRF model. For example, considering the POS tagging task, suppose that each label can be split into two subcategories, such as "NN_1",

"NN_2","VV_1" and "VV_2". These subcategories are not annotated in the training data, which can be regarded as latent variables. They can help to learn the underlying interactions between the words and the implicit tag patterns, such as "$x_i NN_1 x_{i+1} VV_2$". Formally, given a training pair (X, Y), where X and Y are the corresponding input sequence and the output label sequence, latent CRFs are defined by

$$P(Y|X) = \frac{\sum_Z \exp(\mathbf{W}^T f(X, Y, Z; \Theta))}{\sum_{Y'} \sum_{Z'} \exp(\mathbf{W}^T f(X, Y', Z'; \Theta))}, \qquad (18.70)$$

where $\mathbf{W}^T$ and Θ are model parameters, Z denotes the sequence of refined labels, $f(X, Y, Z; \Theta)$ denotes the scores of the triplets X, Y and Z.

(a) Calculate the gradient of $\log P(Y|X)$ with respect to Θ and $\mathbf{W}$.
(b) Compare the forward–backward algorithm and the Viterbi algorithm for CRFs without latent variables and latent CRFs.
(c) Apart from CRFs, latent variables can also be applied to structured perceptrons discussed in Chapter 3. Think about how to define a latent structured perceptron. How can you optimise the structured perceptron with latent variables?

18.2 Recall Eq 18.15 for sequence labelling, where two potential functions $\psi_E(z_i, \mathbf{X}|\Theta)$ and $\psi_T(z_{i-1} z_i, \mathbf{X}|\Theta)$ are computed. Discuss neural network structures to parameterise the computation.

18.3 Recall the use of the forward–backward algorithm for computing the clique probability $P(z_{i-1} z_i | \mathbf{X}_{1:n}, \Theta)$. Show that the forward–backward algorithm is fully differentiable by showing that any loss from the marginal probability can be safely turned into back-propagation gradients on $\mathbf{x}_i, i \in [1, \ldots, n]$. Specify the gradients if you can.

18.4 In Eq 18.18 the start of subsequences are used to represent each subsequence. Can you think of alternative ways to represent subsequences for deriving $\mathbf{c}$? What are their advantages?

18.5 Recall in Section 18.3.3, we defined a 0th-order semi-Markov model for sequence segmentation by defining cliques C in Eq 18.18 over local segments. If the clique C is defined over two consecutive segments, we arrive at a first-order semi-CRF model, as discussed in Chapter 9. Rewrite Eq 18.19 and define a probability function to calculate $P(Z_{1:n}|\mathbf{X}_{1:n}, \Theta)$. Now with the new clique function, the expectation over each clique in Eq 18.18 requires the computation of marginal clique probabilities $P(z_C|\mathbf{X}_{1:n}, \Theta)$. The forward–backward algorithm discussed in Chapter 9 can be used. Discuss such algorithms.

18.6 Discuss different ways to define $\mathbf{v}_{ij}$ in Eq 18.21.

18.7 The constituent attention layer introduced in Section 18.1.2 uses a binary latent variable z_{ij} to represent whether the span $\mathbf{X}_{i:j}$ is a constituent or not. Consider an alternative way which uses a binary latent variable z_{ikj} to denote whether the span $\mathbf{X}_{i:j}$ composed by two children spans $\mathbf{X}_{i:k}$ and $\mathbf{X}_{k+1:j}$ is a unlabelled span production rule or not.

(a) Define a score function for the unlabelled span production rules.
(b) Define the inside score and the outside score for the span $\mathbf{X}_{i:j}$.
(c) Calculate the marginal probability distribution of the span $\mathbf{X}_{i:j}$ being a constituent using the inside and outside algorithm.

18.8 Consider extending the 0th-order constituent parser in Section 18.3.4 into a first-order parser by modelling the score of grammar rules.

18.9 Consider the problem of learning latent task-specific syntax trees for sentiment classification tasks using score-based gradient estimators. First, define a syntactic parser $q(\mathbf{t}|\mathbf{X}, \phi)$ discussed in previous chapters which assigns a probability for a latent tree $\mathbf{t}$ for an input sentence $\mathbf{X}$. Then, we can generate M random samples from $q(\mathbf{t}|\mathbf{X}, \phi)$ and use these samples to jointly train the classifier and the parser.

(a) What is your choice for the parser, constituent or dependency parser? How would you sample trees from your defined parser?
(b) What is your training objective function?
(c) Compute the gradients given the objective functions.

18.10 Consider text VAE in Section 18.6.1. We have only discussed how to deal with one random vector $\mathbf{z}$ in this chapter. In fact, we can introduce multiple latent random vectors $\mathbf{z}_1\mathbf{z}_2 \dots \mathbf{z}_K$ into the modelling process, requiring each latent vector $\mathbf{z}_i$ to focus on only one semantic aspect of the original input sentence $\mathbf{X}$. In this way, we can move towards *disentangled representations* of the latent space by decomposing one coupled latent vector into separate semantic spaces. For example, we can use $\mathbf{z}_1$ and $\mathbf{z}_2$ to model the *sentiment* and *tense* information of $\mathbf{X}$, respectively. We can flexibly manipulate the latent vectors to control the output sequence. Fixing $\mathbf{z}_1$ and varying $\mathbf{z}_2$ allow us to generate sentences with different tenses and the same sentiment. However, the modelling challenge also increases because the joint posterior distribution $P(\mathbf{z}_1, \mathbf{z}_2|\mathbf{X}, \Theta)$ is more complex than $P(\mathbf{z}|\mathbf{X}, \Theta, \phi)$ for only one random vector.

(a) The **mean field** method approximates the joint posterior distribution for multiple latent variables with a product of the marginal posterior distribution of each individual latent variables. For the sentiment and tense example above, we can approximate $P(\mathbf{z}_1, \mathbf{z}_2|\mathbf{X}, \Theta)$ with $\prod_{i=1}^{2} q(\mathbf{z}_i|\mathbf{X}, \phi)$. Derive ELBO for this example using the mean field assumption.
(b) Instead of using the mean field theory, we can let the latent vector $\mathbf{z}_1$ depend on $\mathbf{z}_2$. In this case, the true posterior distribution is approximated by $q(\mathbf{z}_2|\mathbf{X}, \phi)q(\mathbf{z}_1|\mathbf{X}, \mathbf{z}_2, \phi)$. Derive ELBO by using the new assumption and compare the difference between the ELBO results in (a) and (b).

Bibliography

Abney, S. 1997. Part-of-speech tagging and partial parsing. In *Corpus-Based methods in Language and Speech Processing*, pages 118–136. Springer.

Abney, S. 2002. Bootstrapping. In *Proceedings of the 40th Annual Meeting of the Association for Computational Linguistics*, pages 360–367.

Aggarwal, Charu C. and Chengxiang Zhai. 2012. An introduction to text mining. In *Mining Text Data*, pages 1–10. Springer.

Aho, Alfred V. and Jeffrey D. Ullman. 1973. *The Theory of Parsing, Translation, and Compiling*. Prentice Hall.

Andor, Daniel, Chris Alberti, David Weiss, Aliaksei Severyn, Alessandro Presta, Kuzman Ganchev, Slav Petrov, and Michael Collins. 2016. Globally normalized transition-based neural networks. In *Proceedings of the 54th Annual Meeting of the Association for Computational Linguistics (Volume 1: Long Papers)*, pages 2442–2452.

Ba, Jimmy Lei, Jamie Ryan Kiros, and Geoffrey E. Hinton. 2016. Layer normalization. In *Advances in Neural Information Processing Systems 2016 Deep Learning Symposium*.

Bahdanau, Dzmitry, Kyunghyun Cho, and Yoshua Bengio. 2015. Neural machine translation by jointly learning to align and translate. In *3rd International Conference on Learning Representations, 2015, San Diego, CA, USA, May 7-9, 2015, Conference Track Proceedings*.

Baker, James. 1975. The dragon system: an overview. *IEEE Transactions on Acoustics, Speech, and Signal Processing*, 23(1):24–29.

Bastings, Joost, Ivan Titov, Wilker Aziz, Diego Marcheggiani, and Khalil Sima'an. 2017. Graph convolutional encoders for syntax-aware neural machine translation. In *Proceedings of the 2017 Conference on Empirical Methods in Natural Language Processing*, pages 1957–1967.

Bates, Madeleine. 1995. Models of natural language understanding. *Proceedings of the National Academy of Sciences*, 92(22): 9977–9982.

Baum, Leonard E. 1972. An inequality and associated maximaization technique in statistical estimation for probablistic functions of Markov process. *Inequalities*, 3:1–8.

Baum, Leonard E. and Ted Petrie. 1966. Statistical inference for probabilistic functions of finite state Markov chains. *The Annals of Mathematical Statistics*, 37(6):1554–1563.

Beck, Daniel, Gholamreza Haffari, and Trevor Cohn. 2018. Graph-to-sequence learning using gated graph neural networks. In *Proceedings of the 56th Annual Meeting of the Association for Computational Linguistics (Volume 1: Long Papers)*, pages 273–283.

Bender, Emily M. 2013. Linguistic fundamentals for natural language processing: 100 essentials from morphology and syntax. *Synthesis Lectures on Human Language Technologies*, 6(3):1–184.

Bender, Emily M. and Alex Lascarides. 2019. Linguistic fundamentals for natural language processing II: 100 essentials from semantics and pragmatics. *Synthesis Lectures on Human Language Technologies*, 12(3):1–268.

Bengio, Yoshua, Réjean Ducharme, Pascal Vincent, and Christian Jauvin. 2003. A neural probabilistic language model. *Journal of Machine Learning Research*, 3(Feb):1137–1155.

Berger, Adam L., Vincent J. Della Pietra, and Stephen A. Della Pietra. 1996. A maximum entropy approach to natural language processing. *Computational Linguistics*, 22(1): 39–71.

Bilmes, Jeff A. 1998. A gentle tutorial of the EM algorithm and its application to parameter estimation for Gaussian mixture and hidden Markov models. *International Computer Science Institute*, 4(510):126.

Bird, Steven, Ewan Klein, and Edward Loper. 2009. *Natural Language Processing with Python: Analyzing Text with the Natural Language Toolkit*. O'Reilly Media, Inc.

Blei, David M. Andrew Y. Ng, and Michael I. Jordan. 2003. Latent Dirichlet allocation. *Journal of Machine Learning Research*, 3(Jan):993–1022.

Blum, Avrim and Tom Mitchell. 1998. Combining labeled and unlabeled data with co-training. In *Proceedings of the Eleventh Annual Conference on Computational Learning Theory*, pages 92–100.

Bohnet, Bernd and Joakim Nivre. 2012. A transition-based system for joint part-of-speech tagging and labeled non-projective dependency parsing. In *Proceedings of the 2012 Joint Conference on Empirical Methods in Natural Language Processing and Computational Natural Language Learning*, pages 1455–1465.

Booth, Taylor L. and Richard A. Thompson. 1973. Applying probability measures to abstract languages. *IEEE Transactions on Computers*, 100(5):442–450.

Borensztajn, Gideon and Willem Zuidema. 2007. Bayesian model merging for unsupervised constituent labeling and grammar induction. *Inst. for Logic, Language and Computation*.

Bottou, Léon. 1998. Online learning and stochastic approximations. *On-line Learning in Neural Networks*, 17(9):142.

Bottou, Léon. 2010. Large-scale machine learning with stochastic gradient descent. In *Proceedings of International Conference on Computational Statistics*, pages 177–186. Springer.

Bowman, Samuel R., Luke Vilnis, Oriol Vinyals, Andrew M. Dai, Rafal Jozefowicz, and Samy Bengio. 2015. Generating sentences from a continuous space. In *Proceedings of The 20th SIGNLL Conference on Computational Natural Language Learning*, pages 10–21.

Brants, Thorsten. 2000. TNT: a statistical part-of-speech tagger. In *Proceedings of the Sixth Conference on Applied Natural Language Processing*, pages 224–231.

Bromley, Jane, Isabelle Guyon, Yann Lecun, Eduard Sackinger, and Roopak Shah. 1993. Signature verification using a "Siamese" time delay neural network. In *Proceedings of the 6th International Conference on Neural Information Processing Systems*, pages 737–744.

Brown, Peter F., Vincent J. Della Pietra, Robert L. Mercer, Stephen A. Della Pietra, and Jennifer C. Lai. 1992. An estimate of an upper bound for the entropy of English. *Computational Linguistics*, 18(1):31–40.

Brown, Peter F., Vincent J. Della Pietra, Stephen A. Della Pietra, and Robert L. Mercer. 1993. The mathematics of statistical machine translation: Parameter estimation. *Computational Linguistics*, 19(2):263–311.

Caruana, Rich. 1997. Multitask learning. *Machine Learning*, 28(1):41–75.

Charniak, Eugene. 1997. Statistical techniques for natural language parsing. *AI magazine*, 18(4):33–33.

Charniak, Eugene. 2000. A maximum-entropy-inspired parser. In *Proceedings of the 1st North American Chapter of the Association for Computational Linguistics Conference*, pages 132–139.

Chen, Danqi, Jason Bolton and Christopher D. Manning. 2016. A thorough examination of the CNN/daily mail reading comprehension task. In *Proceedings of the 54th Annual Meeting of the Association for Computational Linguistics (Volume 1: Long Papers)*, pages 2358–2367, Berlin, Germany.

Chen, Danqi and Christopher D. Manning. 2014. A fast and accurate dependency parser using neural networks. In *Proceedings of the 2014 Conference on Empirical Methods in Natural Language Processing*, pages 740–750.

Chen, Stanley F. and Joshua Goodman. 1996. An empirical study of smoothing techniques for language modeling. In *Proceedings of 34th Annual Meeting of the Association for Computational Linguistics*, pages 310–318, Santa Cruz, California, USA.

Chen, Xinchi, Xipeng Qiu, Chenxi Zhu and Xuanjing Huang. 2015. Gated recursive neural network for Chinese word segmentation. In *Proceedings of the 53rd Annual Meeting of the Association for Computational Linguistics and the 7th International Joint Conference on Natural Language Processing (Volume 1: Long Papers)*, pages 1744–1753.

Cheng, Jianpeng, Li Dong and Mirella Lapata. 2016. Long short-term memory-networks for machine reading. In *Proceedings of the 2016 Conference on Empirical Methods in Natural Language Processing*, pages 551–561.

Cho, Kyunghyun, Bart Van Merriënboer, Caglar Gulcehre, Dzmitry Bahdanau, Fethi Bougares, Holger Schwenk and Yoshua Bengio. 2014. Learning phrase representations using rnn encoder-decoder for statistical machine translation. In *Proceedings of the 2014 Conference on Empirical Methods in Natural Language Processing*, pages 1724–1734.

Choi, Jinho D. Choi and Andrew McCallum. 2013. Transition-based dependency parsing with selectional branching. In *Proceedings of the 51st Annual Meeting of the Association for Computational Linguistics (Volume 1: Long Papers)*, pages 1052–1062.

Chomsky, Noam. 1957. Syntactic Structures Review of Verbal Behavior by BF Skinner, *Language*, 35:26–58.

Chung, Junyoung, Caglar Gulcehre, Kyunghyun Cho and Yoshua Bengio. 2014. Empirical evaluation of gated recurrent neural networks on sequence modeling. In *Neural Information Processing Systems 2014 Workshop on Deep Learning*.

Church, Kenneth W. 1989. A stochastic parts program and noun phrase parser for unrestricted text. In *International Conference on Acoustics, Speech, and Signal Processing*, pages 695–698. IEEE.

Church, Kenneth W. and William A. Gale. 1991. A comparison of the enhanced Good-Turing and deleted estimation methods for estimating probabilities of English bigrams. *Computer Speech & Language*, 5(1):19–54.

Church, Kenneth W. and Patrick Hanks. 1990. Word association norms, mutual information, and lexicography. *Computational Linguistics*, 16(1):22–29.

Clark, Stephen and James R. Curran. 2003. Log-linear models for wide-coverage CCG parsing. In *Proceedings of the 2003 Conference on Empirical Methods in Natural Language Processing*, pages 97–104.

Cocke, John. 1969. *Programming languages and their compilers: Preliminary notes.* New York University Press.

Collins, Michael. 1996. A new statistical parser based on bigram lexical dependencies. In *Proceedings of the 34th Annual Meeting of the Association for Computational Linguistics*, pages 184–191.

Collins, Michael. 1997. Three generative, lexicalised models for statistical parsing. In *35th Annual Meeting of the Association for Computational Linguistics and 8th Conference of the European Chapter of the Association for Computational Linguistics*, pages 16–23.

Collins, Michael. 2002. Discriminative training methods for hidden Markov models: Theory and experiments with perceptron algorithms. In *Proceedings of the 2002 Conference on Empirical Methods in Natural Language Processing. Volume 10*, pages 1–8.

Collins, Michael and Terry Koo. 2005. Discriminative reranking for natural language parsing. *Computational Linguistics*, 31(1):25–70.

Collins, Michael and Brian Roark. 2004. Incremental parsing with the perceptron algorithm. In *Proceedings of the 42nd Annual Meeting on Association for Computational Linguistics*, page 111.

Collobert, Ronan and Jason Weston. 2008. A unified architecture for natural language processing: Deep neural networks with multitask learning. In *Proceedings of the 25th International Conference on Machine learning*, pages 160–167. ACM.

Collobert, Ronan Jason Weston, Léon Bottou, Michael Karlen, Koray Kavukcuoglu and Pavel Kuksa. 2011. Natural language processing (almost) from scratch. *Journal of Machine Learning Research*, 12(Aug):2493–2537.

Cortes, Corinna and Vladimir Vapnik. 1995. Support-vector networks. *Machine Learning*, 20(3):273–297.

Cotter, Andrew, Ohad Shamir, Nati Srebro and Karthik Sridharan. 2011. Better mini-batch algorithms via accelerated gradient methods. In *Advances in Neural Information Processing Systems*, pages 1647–1655.

Crammer, Koby and Yoram Singer. 2001. On the algorithmic implementation of multiclass kernel-based vector machines. *Journal of Machine Learning Research*, 2(Dec):265–292.

Cui, Yiming, Zhipeng Chen, Si Wei, Shijin Wang, Ting Liu and Guoping Hu. 2016. Attention-over-attention neural networks for reading comprehension. In *Proceedings of the 55th Annual Meeting of the Association for Computational Linguistics (Volume 1: Long Papers)*, pages 593–602.

Della Pietra, Stephen, Vincent Della Pietra and John Lafferty. 1997. Inducing features of random fields. *IEEE Transactions on Pattern Analysis and Machine Intelligence*, 19(4):380–393.

Dempster, Arthur P. 1968. A generalization of bayesian inference. *Journal of the Royal Statistical Society: Series B (Methodological)*, 30(2):205–232.

Dempster, Arthur P., Nan M. Laird and Donald B. Rubin. 1977. Maximum likelihood from incomplete data via the em algorithm. *Journal of the Royal Statistical Society: Series B (Methodological)*, 39(1):1–22.

Devlin, Jacob, Ming-Wei Chang, Kenton Lee and Kristina Toutanova. 2018. BERT: Pre-training of deep bidirectional transformers for language understanding. In *Proceedings of the 2019 Conference of the North American Chapter of the Association for Computational Linguistics: Human Language Technologies, Volume 1 (Long and Short Papers)*, pages 4171–4186.

Domingos, Pedro and Michael Pazzani. 1997. On the optimality of the simple Bayesian classifier under zero-one loss. *Machine Learning*, 29(2-3):103–130.

Dozat, Timothy and Christopher D. Manning. 2017. Deep biaffine attention for neural dependency parsing. In *Proceedings of the 5th International Conference on Learning Representations*.

Duchi, John, Elad Hazan and Yoram Singer. 2011. Adaptive subgradient methods for online learning and stochastic optimization. *Journal of Machine Learning Research*, 12(Jul):2121–2159.

Durrett, Greg and Dan Klein. 2015. Neural CRF parsing. In *Proceedings of the 53rd Annual Meeting of the Association for Computational Linguistics and the 7th International Joint Conference on Natural Language Processing (Volume 1: Long Papers)*, pages 302–312.

Dyer, Chris, Adhiguna Kuncoro, Miguel Ballesteros and Noah A. Smith. 2016. Recurrent neural network grammars. In *Proceedings of the 2016 Conference of the North American Chapter of the Association for Computational Linguistics: Human Language Technologies*, pages 199–209.

Eddy, Sean R. 1998. Profile hidden Markov models. *Bioinformatics*, 14(9):755–763.

Eisenstein, Jacob. 2019. *Introduction to Natural Language Processing*. Adaptive Computation and Machine Learning series. MIT Press.

Elkan, Charles. 2001. The foundations of cost-sensitive learning. In *International Joint Conference on Artificial Intelligence*, volume 17, pages 973–978. Lawrence Erlbaum Associates Ltd.

Elman, Jeffrey L. 1990. Finding structure in time. *Cognitive Science*, 14(2):179–211.

Fillmore, Charles J. and Collin F. Baker. 2001. Frame semantics for text understanding. In *Proceedings of WordNet and Other Lexical Resources Workshop, North American Chapter of the Association for Computational Linguistics*, volume 6.

Freund, Yoav, Raj Iyer, Robert E Schapire and Yoram Singer. 2003. An efficient boosting algorithm for combining preferences. *Journal of Machine Learning Research*, 4(Nov):933–969.

Fukisaki, T., F. Jelinek, J. Cocke, E. Black and T. Nishino. 1989. Probabilistic parsing method for sentence disambiguation. In *Proceedings of the First International Workshop on Parsing Technologies*, pages 85–94, Pittsburgh, Pennsylvania, USA. Carnegy Mellon University.

Gale, William A. and Kenneth W. Church. 1994. What's wrong with adding one. *Corpus-Based Research into Language: In honour of Jan Aarts*, pages 189–200.

Garrette, Dan, Chris Dyer, Jason Baldridge and Noah A. Smith. 2015. Weakly-supervised grammar-informed Bayesian CCG parser learning. In *Twenty-Ninth AAAI Conference on Artificial Intelligence*.

Gelfand, Alan E., Susan E. Hills, Amy Racine-Poon and Adrian F. M. Smith. 1990. Illustration of Bayesian inference in normal data models using Gibbs sampling. *Journal of the American Statistical Association*, 85(412):972–985.

Ghahramani, Zoubin. 2001. An introduction to hidden Markov models and Bayesian networks. In *Hidden Markov Models: Applications in Computer Vision*, pages 9–41. World Scientific.

Gildea, Daniel and Daniel Jurafsky. 2002. Automatic labeling of semantic roles. *Computational Linguistics*, 28(3):245–288.

Goldberg, Yoav and Omer Levy. 2014. word2vec explained: deriving Mikolov et al.'s negative-sampling word-embedding method. *arXiv preprint arXiv:1402.3722.*

Goldwater, Sharon, Thomas L Griffiths and Mark Johnson. 2009. A Bayesian framework for word segmentation: Exploring the effects of context. *Cognition*, 112(1):21–54.

Goldwater, Sharon and Tom Griffiths. 2007. A fully Bayesian approach to unsupervised part-of-speech tagging. In *Proceedings of the 45th Annual Meeting of the Association of Computational Linguistics*, pages 744–751.

Gori, M. G. Monfardini and F. Scarselli. 2005. A new model for learning in graph domains. In *Proceedings. 2005 IEEE International Joint Conference on Neural Networks, 2005*, volume 2.

Grenander, Ulf. 1976. Lectures in pattern theory-volume 1: Pattern synthesis. *Applied Mathematical Sciences*, Springer.

Griffiths, Thomas L. and Mark Steyvers. 2004. Finding scientific topics. *Proceedings of the National Academy of Sciences*, 101(suppl 1):5228–5235.

Gu, Jiatao, Zhengdong Lu, Hang Li and Victor OK Li. 2016. Incorporating copying mechanism in sequence-to-sequence learning. In *Proceedings of the 54th Annual Meeting of the Association for Computational Linguistics (Volume 1: Long Papers)*, pages 1631–1640.

Gujarati, D. N. and D. C. Porter. 2009. How to measure elasticity: The log-linear model. *Basic Econometrics, McGraw-Hill/Irwin,* pages 159–162.

Harris, Zellig S. 1954. Distributional structure. *Word*, 10(2-3):146–162.

Hartley, Herman O. 1958. Maximum likelihood estimation from incomplete data. *Biometrics*, 14(2):174–194.

Hatori, Jun, Takuya Matsuzaki, Yusuke Miyao and Jun'ichi Tsujii. 2012. Incremental joint approach to word segmentation, pos tagging, and dependency parsing in chinese. In *Proceedings of the 50th Annual Meeting of the Association for Computational Linguistics (Long Papers: Volume 1)*, pages 1045–1053.

He, Kaiming, Xiangyu Zhang, Shaoqing Ren and Jian Sun. 2016. Deep residual learning for image recognition. In *Proceedings of the IEEE Conference on Computer Vision and Pattern Recognition*, pages 770–778.

Heinrich, Gregor. 2005. Parameter estimation for text analysis. Technical Report.

Hermann, Karl Moritz, Tomáš Kočiský, Edward Grefenstette, Lasse Espeholt, Will Kay, Mustafa Suleyman and Phil Blunsom. 2015. Teaching machines to read and comprehend. In *Proceedings of the 28th International Conference on Neural Information Processing Systems, Volume 1*, page 1693–1701, MIT Press.

Hochreiter, Sepp and Jürgen Schmidhuber. 1997. Long short-term memory. *Neural Computation*, 9(8):1735–1780.

Hofmann, Thomas. 1999. Probabilistic latent semantic analysis. In *Proceedings of the Fifteenth Conference on Uncertainty in Artificial Intelligence*, pages 289–296. Morgan Kaufmann Publishers Inc.

Hornik, Kurt, Maxwell Stinchcombe, Halbert White, et al. 1989. Multilayer feedforward networks are universal approximators. *Neural Networks*, 2(5):359–366.

Hu, Baotian, Zhengdong Lu, Hang Li and Qingcai Chen. 2014. Convolutional neural network architectures for matching natural language sentences. *Neural Information Processing Systems*, pages 2042–2050.

Hu, Zhiting, Zichao Yang, Xiaodan Liang, Ruslan Salakhutdinov and Eric P. Xing. 2017. Toward controlled generation of text. In *Proceedings of the 34th International Conference on Machine Learning, Volume 70*, pages 1587–1596.

Huang, Zhiheng, Wei Xu, and Kai Yu. 2015. Bidirectional LSTM-CRF models for sequence tagging. *ArXiv*, abs/1508.01991.

Iacobacci, Ignacio, Mohammad Taher Pilehvar and Roberto Navigli. 2015. Sensembed: Learning sense embeddings for word and relational similarity. In *Proceedings of the 53rd Annual Meeting of the Association for Computational Linguistics and the 7th International Joint Conference on Natural Language Processing (Volume 1: Long Papers)*, pages 95–105.

Ioffe, Sergey and Christian Szegedy. 2015. Batch normalization: Accelerating deep network training by reducing internal covariate shift. In *Proceedings of the 32nd International Conference on International Conference on Machine Learning – Volume 37*, pages 448–456.

Jang, Eric, Shixiang Gu and Ben Poole. 2017. Categorical reparameterization with gumbel-softmax. In *Proceedings of the 5th International Conference on Learning Representations*.

Jaynes, Edwin T. 1957. Information theory and statistical mechanics. *Physical Review*, 106(4): 620.

Jebara, Tony. 2004. Multi-task feature and kernel selection for svms. In *Proceedings of the Twenty-First International Conference on Machine learning*, page 55.

Jelinek, E., John Lafferty, David Magerman, Robert Mercer, Adwait Ratnaparkhi and Salim Roukos. 1994. Decision tree parsing using a hidden derivation model. In *Human Language Technology: Proceedings of a Workshop held at Plainsboro, New Jersey, March 8–11, 1994*.

Jelinek, Frederick. 1997. *Statistical Methods for Speech Recognition*. Language, Speech, and Communication series. MIT Press.

Jelinek, Frederick, Lalit Bahl and Robert Mercer. 1975. Design of a linguistic statistical decoder for the recognition of continuous speech. *IEEE Transactions on Information Theory*, 21(3):250–256.

Jensen, Finn V. et al. 1996. *An Introduction to Bayesian Networks*. UCL Press.

Johnson, Mark, Stuart Geman, Stephen Canon, Zhiyi Chi and Stefan Riezler. 1999. Estimators for stochastic unification-based grammars. In *Proceedings of the 37th Annual Meeting of the Association for Computational Linguistics on Computational Linguistics*, pages 535–541.

Johnson, Mark, Thomas L Griffiths and Sharon Goldwater. 2007. Adaptor grammars: A framework for specifying compositional nonparametric Bayesian models. In *Advances in Neural Information Processing Systems*, pages 641–648.

Jones, Karen S. 1972. A statistical interpretation of term specificity and its application in retrieval. *Journal of Documentation*, 28:11–21.

Jurafsky, Daniel and James H. Martin. 2008. *Speech and Language Processing: An Introduction to Speech Recognition, Computational Linguistics and Natural Language Processing*. Pearson Prentice Hall.

Kalchbrenner, Nal, Edward Grefenstette, and Phil Blunsom. 2014. A convolutional neural network for modelling sentences. In *Proceedings of the 52nd Annual Meeting of the Association for Computational Linguistics (Volume 1: Long Papers)*, pages 655–665.

Kasami, Tadao. 1966. An efficient recognition and syntax-analysis algorithm for context-free languages. *Coordinated Science Laboratory Report no. R-257*.

Klatz, Slava. 1987. Estimation of probabilities from sparse data for the language model component of a speech recognizer. *IEEE Transactions on Acoustics, Speech, and Signal Processing*, 35(3):400–401.

Kay, Martin. 1967. Experiments with a powerful parser. In *Proceedings of International Conference on Computational Linguistics 1967 Volume 1: Conference Internationale Sur Le Traitement Automatique Des Langues*.

Kim, Yoon. 2014. Convolutional neural networks for sentence classification. In *Proceedings of the*

2014 Conference on Empirical Methods in Natural Language Processing, pages 1746–1751.

Kim, Yoon, Carl Denton, Luong Hoang and Alexander M. Rush. 2017. Structured attention networks. In *Proceedings of the 5th International Conference on Learning Representations*.

Kim, Yoon, Chris Dyer and Alexander M. Rush. 2019. Compound probabilistic context-free grammars for grammar induction. *arXiv preprint arXiv:1906.10225*.

Kim, Yoon, Sam Wiseman and Alexander M. Rush. 2018. A tutorial on deep latent variable models of natural language. In *Proceedings of the 57th Annual Meeting of the Association for Computational Linguistics*, pages 2369–2385.

Kingma, Diederik P. and Jimmy Ba. 2014. Adam: A method for stochastic optimization. In *Proceedings of the 3rd International Conference on Learning Representations*.

Kingma, Diederik P. and Max Welling. 2014. Auto-encoding variational bayes. *stat*, 1050:1.

Kiperwasser, Eliyahu and Yoav Goldberg. 2016. Simple and accurate dependency parsing using bidirectional lstm feature representations. *Transactions of the Association for Computational Linguistics*, 4:313–327.

Kipf, Thomas N. and Max Welling. 2016. Semi-supervised classification with graph convolutional networks. In *Proceedings of the 5th International Conference on Learning Representations*.

Kitaev, Nikita and Dan Klein. 2018. Constituency parsing with a self-attentive encoder. In *Proceedings of the 56th Annual Meeting of the Association for Computational Linguistics (Volume 1: Long Papers)*, pages 2676–2686.

Klein, Dan and Christopher D Manning. 2003. Accurate unlexicalized parsing. In *Proceedings of the 41st Annual Meeting on Association for Computational Linguistics, Volume 1*, pages 423–430.

Koehn, Philipp. 2009. *Statistical Machine Translation*. Cambridge University Press.

Koehn, Phillip. 2020. *Neural Machine Translation*. Cambridge University Press.

Kübler, Sandra, Ryan McDonald and Joakim Nivre. 2009. Dependency parsing. *Synthesis Lectures on Human Language Technologies*, 1(1):1–127.

Kullback, Solomon and Richard A. Leibler. 1951. On information and sufficiency. *Annals of Mathematical Statistics*, 22(1):79–86.

Kupiec, Julian. 1992. Robust part-of-speech tagging using a hidden Markov model. *Computer Speech & Language*, 6(3):225–242.

Lafferty, John, Andrew McCallum and Fernando C. N. Pereira. 2001. Conditional random fields: Probabilistic models for segmenting and labeling sequence data. In *Proceedings of the Eighteenth International Conference on Machine Learning*, pages 282–289.

Lample, Guillaume, Miguel Ballesteros, Sandeep Subramanian, Kazuya Kawakami and Chris Dyer. 2016. Neural architectures for named entity recognition. In *Proceedings of the 2016 Conference of the North American Chapter of the Association for Computational Linguistics: Human Language Technologies*, pages 260–270.

Lample, Guillaume and Alexis Conneau. 2019. Cross-lingual language model pretraining. In *Proceedings of Advances in Neural Information Processing Systems*, pages 7057–7067.

LeCun, Yann, Léon Bottou, Yoshua Bengio and Patrick Haffner. 1998. Gradient-based learning applied to document recognition. *Proceedings of the IEEE*, 86(11):2278–2324.

Li, Mu, Tong Zhang, Yuqiang Chen and Alexander J. Smola. 2014. Efficient mini-batch training for stochastic optimization. In *Proceedings of the 20th ACM International Conference on Knowledge Discovery and Data Mining*, pages 661–670.

Ling, Wang, Yulia Tsvetkov, Silvio Amir, Ramon Fermandez, Chris Dyer, Alan W. Black, Isabel Trancoso, and Chu-Cheng Lin. 2015. Not all contexts are created equal: Better word representations with variable attention. In *Proceedings of the 2015 Conference on Empirical Methods in Natural Language Processing*, pages 1367–1372.

Liu, Bing. 2012. *Sentiment Analysis and Opinion Mining*. Morgan & Claypool Publishers.

Liu, Jiangming and Yue Zhang. 2017. In-order transition-based constituent parsing. *Transactions of the Association for Computational Linguistics*, 5:413–424.

Liu, Xiao, Heyan Huang, and Yue Zhang. 2019a. Open domain event extraction using neural latent variable models. In *Proceedings of the 57th Annual Meeting of the Association for Computational Linguistics*, pages 2860–2871.

Liu, Yinhan, Myle Ott, Naman Goyal, Jingfei Du, Mandar Joshi, Danqi Chen, Omer Levy, Mike Lewis, Luke Zettlemoyer and Veselin Stoyanov. 2019b. Roberta: A robustly optimized Bert pretraining approach. *arXiv preprint arXiv:1907.11692*.

Luhn, Hans Peter. 1957. A statistical approach to mechanized encoding and searching of literary information. *IBM Journal of Research and Development*, 1(4):309–317.

Ma, Xuezhe and Eduard Hovy. 2016. End-to-end sequence labeling via bi-directional LSTM-CNNs-CRF. In *Proceedings of the 54th Annual Meeting of the Association for Computational Linguistics (Volume 1: Long Papers)*, pages 1064–1074.

MacQueen, James et al. 1967. Some methods for classification and analysis of multivariate observations. In *Proceedings of the Fifth Berkeley Symposium on Mathematical Statistics and Probability*, volume 1, pages 281–297. Oakland, CA, USA.

Magerman, David M. 1995. Statistical decision-tree models for parsing. In *Proceedings of the 33rd Annual Meeting on Association for Computational Linguistics*, pages 276–283. Association for Computational Linguistics.

Manning, Christopher D., Prabhakar Raghavan and Hinrich Schütze. 2008. *Introduction to Information Retrieval*. Cambridge University Press.

Manning, Christopher D. and Hinrich Schütze. 1999. *Foundations of Statistical Natural Language Processing*. MIT Press.

Marcheggiani, Diego and Ivan Titov. 2017. Encoding sentences with graph convolutional networks for semantic role labeling. In *Proceedings of the 2017 Conference on Empirical Methods in Natural Language Processing*, pages 1506–1515, Copenhagen, Denmark.

Markov, Andrey A. 1913. Essai d'une recherche statistique sur le texte du roman "Eugene Onegin" illustrant la liaison des epreuve en chain ('Example of a statistical investigation of the text of "Eugene Onegin" illustrating the dependence between samples in chain'). *Izvistia Imperatorskoi Akademii Nauk (Bulletin de l'Académie Impériale des Sciences de St.-Pétersbourg)*, 7:153–162. English translation by Morris Halle, 1956.

Maron, Melvin E. and John L. Kuhns. 1960. On relevance, probabilistic indexing and information retrieval. *Journal of the ACM*, 7(3):216–244.

McCallum, Andrew, Dayne Freitag and Fernando C. N. Pereira. 2000. Maximum entropy Markov models for information extraction and segmentation. In *Proceedings of International Conference on Machine Learning*, volume 17, pages 591–598.

McCallum, Andrew and Wei Li. 2003. Early results for named entity recognition with conditional random fields, feature induction and web-enhanced lexicons. In *Proceedings of the Seventh Conference on Natural Language Learning at HLT-NAACL 2003, Volume 4*, pages 188–191.

McKeown, Kathleen. 1992. *Text Generation*. Studies in Natural Language Processing. Cambridge University Press.

McLachlan, Geoffrey J. and Thriyambakam Krishnan. 2007. *The EM Algorithm and Extensions*. John Wiley & Sons.

Medin, Douglas L. and Paula J. Schwanenflugel. 1981. Linear separability in classification learning. *Journal of Experimental Psychology: Human Learning and Memory*, 7(5):355.

Miao, Yishu, Edward Grefenstette and Phil Blunsom. 2017. Discovering discrete latent topics with neural variational inference. In *Proceedings of the 34th International Conference on Machine Learning, Volume 70*, pages 2410–2419.

Miao, Yishu, Lei Yu and Phil Blunsom. 2016. Neural variational inference for text processing. In

Proceedings of the 33th International Conference on Machine Learning, pages 1727–1736.

Mihalcea, Rada. 2004. Co-training and self-training for word sense disambiguation. In *Proceedings of the Eighth Conference on Computational Natural Language Learning*, pages 33–40.

Mikolov, Tomáš, Martin Karafiát, Lukáš Burget, Jan Černocký and Sanjeev Khudanpur. 2010. Recurrent neural network based language model. In *Eleventh Annual Conference of the International Speech Communication Association*.

Mikolov, Tomáš, Ilya Sutskever, Kai Chen, Greg S. Corrado and Jeff Dean. 2013. Distributed representations of words and phrases and their compositionality. In *Advances in Neural Information Processing Systems*, pages 3111–3119.

Miller, Alexander Holden, Adam Joshua Fisch, Jesse Dean Dodge, Amir-Hossein Karimi, Antoine Bordes and Jason E. Weston. 2018. Key-value memory networks. US Patent App. 16/002,463.

Minka, Thomas. 1998. Expectation-maximization as lower bound maximization. *Tutorial published on the web at www-white. media. mit .edu/tpminka/papers/em. html*, 7:2.

Minsky, Marvin and Seymour Papert. 1969. *An Introduction to Computational Geometry*. MIT Press.

Mintz, Mike, Steven Bills, Rion Snow and Dan Jurafsky. 2009. Distant supervision for relation extraction without labeled data. In *Proceedings of the Joint Conference of the 47th Annual Meeting of the ACL and the 4th International Joint Conference on Natural Language Processing of the AFNLP: Volume 2, pages 1003–1011*.

Miwa, Makoto and Mohit Bansal. 2016. End-to-end relation extraction using LSTMs on sequences and tree structures. In *Proceedings of the 54th Annual Meeting of the Association for Computational Linguistics (Volume 1: Long Papers)*, pages 1105–1116.

Mnih, Andriy and Geoffrey Hinton. 2007. Three new graphical models for statistical language modelling. In *Proceedings of the 24th International Conference on Machine Learning*, pages 641–648.

Moens, M. F. 2006. *Information Extraction: Algorithms and Prospects in a Retrieval Context*. Springer.

Morin, Frederic and Yoshua Bengio. 2005. Hierarchical probabilistic neural network language model. In *Proceedings of International Conference on Artifical Intelligence and Statistics*, volume 5, pages 246–252.

Nadeau, David and Satoshi Sekine. 2007. A survey of named entity recognition and classification. *Lingvisticae Investigationes*, 30(1):3–26.

Nakagawa, Tetsuji. 2004. Chinese and Japanese word segmentation using word-level and character-level information. In *Proceedings of the 20th International Conference on Computational Linguistics*, page 466.

Neal, Radford M. and Geoffrey E. Hinton. 1998. A view of the EM algorithm that justifies incremental, sparse, and other variants. In *Learning in Graphical Models*, pages 355–368. Springer.

Neapolitan, Richard E. 2004. *Learning Bayesian Networks*. Pearson Prentice Hall.

Neculoiu, Paul, Maarten Versteegh and Mihai Rotaru. 2016. Learning text similarity with Siamese recurrent networks. In *Proceedings of the 1st Workshop on Representation Learning for NLP*, pages 148–157.

Neubig, Graham, Masato Mimura, Shinsuke Mori, and Tatsuya Kawahara. 2012. Bayesian learning of a language model from continuous speech. *IEICE Transactions on Information and Systems*, 95(2):614–625.

Ng, Andrew Y. and Michael I. Jordan. 2002. On discriminative vs. generative classifiers: A comparison of logistic regression and Naive Bayes. In *Advances in Neural Information Processing Systems*, pages 841–848.

Niepert, Mathias, Mohamed Ahmed and Konstantin Kutzkov. 2016. Learning convolutional neural networks for graphs. In *International Conference on Machine Learning*, pages 2014–2023.

Nigam, Kamal, John Lafferty and Andrew McCallum. 1999. Using maximum entropy for text classification. In *IJCAI-99 Workshop on Machine Learning for Information Filtering*, volume 1, pages 61–67. Stockholom, Sweden.

Nivre, Joakim. 2003. An efficient algorithm for projective dependency parsing. In *Proceedings of the Eighth International Conference on Parsing Technologies*, pages 149–160, Nancy, France.

Nivre, Joakim. 2008. Algorithms for deterministic incremental dependency parsing. *Computational Linguistics*, 34(4):513–553.

Nivre, Joakim. 2009. Non-projective dependency parsing in expected linear time. In *Proceedings of the Joint Conference of the 47th Annual Meeting of the ACL and the 4th International Joint Conference on Natural Language Processing of the AFNLP: Volume 1*, pages 351–359.

Novikoff, A. B. J. 1962. Integral geometry as a tool in pattern perception. In *Principles of Self-Organization*, pages 347–368. Pergamon.

Pang, Bo and Lillian Lee. 2008. *Opinion Mining and Sentiment Analysis*. Foundations and Trends in Information Retrieval. Now Publishers.

Parikh, Ankur P., Oscar Tackstrom, Dipanjan Das and Jakob Uszkoreit. 2016. A decomposable attention model for natural language inference. In *Proceedings of the 2016 Conference on Empirical Methods in Natural Language Processing*, pages 2249–2255.

Pearl, Judea. 1985. Bayesian networks: A model of self-activated memory for evidential reasoning. In *Proceedings of the 7th Conference of the Cognitive Science Society*, pages 329–334.

Peng, Fuchun, Fangfang Feng and Andrew McCallum. 2004. Chinese segmentation and new word detection using conditional random fields. In *Proceedings of the 20th International Conference on Computational Linguistics*, page 562.

Peng, Hanchan, Fuhui Long and Chris Ding. 2005. Feature selection based on mutual information criteria of max-dependency, max-relevance, and min-redundancy. *IEEE Transactions on Pattern Analysis and Machine Intelligence*, 27(8):1226–1238.

Peng, Nanyun, Hoifung Poon, Chris Quirk, Kristina Toutanova and Wen-tau Yih. 2017. Cross-sentence n-ary relation extraction with graph LSTMs. *Transactions of the Association for Computational Linguistics*, 5:101–115.

Pennington, Jeffrey, Richard Socher and Christopher Manning. 2014. Glove: Global vectors for word representation. In *Proceedings of the 2014 Conference on Empirical Methods in Natural Language Processing*, pages 1532–1543.

Peters, Matthew E., Mark Neumann, Mohit Iyyer, Matt Gardner, Christopher Clark, Kenton Lee and Luke Zettlemoyer. 2018. Deep contextualized word representations. In *Proceedings of the 2018 Conference of the North American Chapter of the Association for Computational Linguistics: Human Language Technologies, Volume 1 (Long Papers)*, pages 2227–2237.

Petrov, Slav and Dan Klein. 2007. Improved inference for unlexicalized parsing. In *Human Language Technologies 2007: The Conference of the North American Chapter of the Association for Computational Linguistics;*, pages 404–411.

Pinto, David, Andrew McCallum, Xing Wei and W Bruce Croft. 2003. Table extraction using conditional random fields. In *Proceedings of the 26th Annual International ACM SIGIR Conference on Research and Development in Information retrieval*, pages 235–242.

Poggio, Tomaso, Vincent Torre, and Christof Koch. 1985. Computational vision and regularization theory. *Nature*, 317(6035):314–319.

Porteous, Ian, David Newman, Alexander Ihler, Arthur Asuncion, Padhraic Smyth and Max Welling. 2008. Fast collapsed Gibbs sampling for latent Dirichlet allocation. In *Proceedings of the 14th ACM International Conference on Knowledge Discovery and Data Mining*, pages 569–577. ACM.

Post, Matt and Daniel Gildea. 2009. Bayesian learning of a tree substitution grammar. In *Proceedings of the Joint Conference of the 47th Annual Meeting of the ACL and the 4th International Joint Conference on Natural Language Processing of the AFNLP Short Papers*, pages 45–48.

Qian, Xian and Yang Liu. 2012. Joint Chinese word segmentation, POS tagging and parsing. In *Proceedings of the 2012 Joint Conference on Empirical Methods in Natural Language Processing and Computational Natural Language Learning*, pages 501–511, Jeju Island, Korea.

Rabiner, Lawrence R. and Biing-Hwang Juang. 1986. An introduction to hidden Markov models. *IEEE ASSP Magazine*, 3(1):4–16.

Radford, Alec, Karthik Narasimhan, Tim Salimans and Ilya Sutskever. 2018. Improving language understanding by generative pre-training.

Ratinov, Lev and Dan Roth. 2009. Design challenges and misconceptions in named entity recognition. In *Proceedings of the Thirteenth Conference on Computational Natural Language Learning*, pages 147–155.

Ratnaparkhi, Adwait. 1996. A maximum entropy model for part-of-speech tagging. In *Conference on Empirical Methods in Natural Language Processing*.

Rei, Marek. 2017. Semi-supervised multitask learning for sequence labeling. In *Proceedings of the 55th Annual Meeting of the Association for Computational Linguistics (Volume 1: Long Papers)*, pages 2121–2130.

Rezende, Danilo and Shakir Mohamed. 2015. Variational inference with normalizing flows. In *International Conference on Machine Learning*, pages 1530–1538.

Riley, Darcey and Daniel Gildea. 2012. Improving the IBM alignment models using variational Bayes. In *Proceedings of the 50th Annual Meeting of the Association for Computational Linguistics (Short Papers: Volume 2)*, pages 306–310.

Robbins, Herbert and Sutton Monro. 1951. A stochastic approximation method. *Annals of Mathematical Statistics*, 22:400–407.

Rosenblatt, Frank. 1958. The perceptron: a probabilistic model for information storage and organization in the brain. *Psychological Review*, 65(6):386.

Roxbee Cox, D. and E. Joyce Snell. 1989. *Analysis of Binary Data*, volume 32. CRC Press.

Rumelhart, D. E., G. E. Hinton and R. J. Williams. 1986. Learning internal representations by error propagation. In *Parallel Distributed Processing*, Vol. 1.

Rush, Alexander M., Sumit Chopra and Jason Weston. 2015. A neural attention model for abstractive sentence summarization. In *Proceedings of the 2015 Conference on Empirical Methods in Natural Language Processing*, pages 379–389.

Sagae, Kenji and Alon Lavie. 2005. A classifier-based parser with linear run-time complexity. In *Proceedings of the Ninth International Workshop on Parsing Technology*, pages 125–132.

Sahami, Mehran. 1996. Learning limited dependence Bayesian classifiers. In *Proceedings of the Second International Conference on Knowledge Discovery and Data Mining*, pages 335–338.

Salton, Gerard and Michael McGill. 1983. Retrieval evaluation. *Introduction to Modern Information Retrieval*, pages 157–197.

Salton, Gerard, Anita Wong and Chung-Shu Yang. 1975. A vector space model for automatic indexing. *Communications of the Association for Computing Machinery*, 18(11):613–620.

Sarawagi, Sunita and William W. Cohen. 2005. Semi-Markov conditional random fields for information extraction. In *Advances in Neural Information Processing Systems*, pages 1185–1192.

Scarselli, Franco, Marco Gori, Ah Chung Tsoi, Markus Hagenbuchner and Gabriele Monfardini. 2008. The graph neural network model. *IEEE Transactions on Neural Networks*, 20(1):61–80.

Schabes, Yves, Michal Roth and Randy Osborne. 1993. Parsing the Wall Street Journal with the inside-outside algorithm. In *Sixth Conference of the European Chapter of the Association for Computational Linguistics*, Utrecht, The Netherlands.

Schafer, Joseph L. 1997. *Analysis of Incomplete Multivariate Data*. Chapman and Hall/CRC.

See, Abigail, Peter J. Liu and Christopher D. Manning. 2017. Get to the point: Summarization with pointer-generator networks. In *Proceedings of the 55th Annual Meeting of the Association for Computational Linguistics (Volume*

1: Long Papers), pages 1073–1083, Vancouver, Canada.

Sennrich, Rico, Barry Haddow and Alexandra Birch. 2015. Neural machine translation of rare words with subword units. In *Proceedings of the 54th Annual Meeting of the Association for Computational Linguistics (Volume 1: Long Papers)*, pages 1715–1725.

Seo, Min Joon, Aniruddha Kembhavi, Ali Farhadi and Hannaneh Hajishirzi. 2017. Bidirectional attention flow for machine comprehension. In *Proceedings of 5th International Conference on Learning Representations*.

Serban, Iulian Vlad, Alessandro Sordoni, Ryan Lowe, Laurent Charlin, Joelle Pineau, Aaron Courville and Yoshua Bengio. 2017. A hierarchical latent variable encoder-decoder model for generating dialogues. In *Thirty-First AAAI Conference on Artificial Intelligence*.

Sha Fei and Fernando Pereira. 2003. Shallow parsing with conditional random fields. In *Proceedings of the 2003 Conference of the North American Chapter of the Association for Computational Linguistics on Human Language Technology, Volume 1*, pages 134–141.

Shalev-Shwartz, Shai, Yoram Singer, Nathan Srebro and Andrew Cotter. 2011. Pegasos: Primal estimated sub-gradient solver for SVM. *Mathematical Programming*, 127(1):3–30.

Shannon, Claude E. 1948. A mathematical theory of communication. *Bell System Technical Journal*, 27(3):379–423.

Shibata, Yusuxke, Takuya Kida, Shuichi Fukamachi, Masayuki Takeda, Ayumi Shinohara, Takeshi Shinohara and Setsuo Arikawa. 1999. Byte pair encoding: A text compression scheme that accelerates pattern matching. Technical Report DOI-TR-161, Department of Informatics, Kyushu University.

Søgaard Anders and Yoav Goldberg. 2016. Deep multi-task learning with low level tasks supervised at lower layers. In *Proceedings of the 54th Annual Meeting of the Association for Computational Linguistics (Volume 2: Short Papers)*, pages 231–235.

Song, Linfeng, Yue Zhang, Zhiguo Wang and Daniel Gildea. 2018. A graph-to-sequence model for amr-to-text generation. In *Proceedings of the 56th Annual Meeting of the Association for Computational Linguistics (Volume 1: Long Papers)*, pages 1616–1626.

Sperduti, A. and A. Starita. 1997. Supervised neural networks for the classification of structures. *Transactions on Neural Networks*, 8(3):714–735.

Srivastava, Akash and Charles Sutton. 2017. Autoencoding variational inference for topic models. In *Proceedings of 5th International Conference on Learning Representations*.

Srivastava, Nitish, Geoffrey Hinton, Alex Krizhevsky, Ilya Sutskever and Ruslan Salakhutdinov. 2014. Dropout: a simple way to prevent neural networks from overfitting. *Journal of Machine Learning Research*, 15(1):1929–1958.

Srivastava, Rupesh Kumar, Klaus Greff and Jürgen Schmidhuber. 2015. Highway networks. *arXiv preprint arXiv:1505.00387*.

Steedman, Mark. 2000. *The Syntactic Process*. MIT Press.

Steedman, Mark, Miles Osborne, Anoop Sarkar, Stephen Clark, Rebecca Hwa, Julia Hockenmaier, Paul Ruhlen, Steven Baker and Jeremiah Crim. 2003. Bootstrapping statistical parsers from small datasets. In *Proceedings of the Tenth Conference of the European Chapter of the Association for Computational Linguistics, Volume 1*, pages 331–338.

Stratonovich, Ruslan Leont'evich 1965. Conditional Markov processes. In *Non-linear Transformations of Stochastic Processes*, pages 427–453. Elsevier.

Strubell, Emma, Patrick Verga, Daniel Andor, David Weiss, and Andrew McCallum. 2018. Linguistically-informed self-attention for semantic role labeling. In *Proceedings of the 2018 Conference on Empirical Methods in Natural Language Processing*, pages 5027–5038.

Sutskever, Ilya, Oriol Vinyals, and Quoc V Le. 2014. Sequence to sequence learning with neural networks. In *Advances in Neural Information Processing Systems 27*, pages 3104–3112. Curran Associates, Inc.

Sutton, Charles, Andrew McCallum, et al. 2012. An introduction to conditional random fields. *Foundations and Trends® in Machine Learning*, 4(4):267–373.

Tai, Kai Sheng, Richard Socher, and Christopher D. Manning. 2015. Improved semantic representations from tree-structured long short-term memory networks. In *Proceedings of the 53rd Annual Meeting of the Association for Computational Linguistics and the 7th International Joint Conference on Natural Language Processing (Volume 1: Long Papers)*, pages 1556–1566.

Tang, Buzhou, Hongxin Cao, Xiaolong Wang, Qingcai Chen, and Hua Xu. 2014. Evaluating word representation features in biomedical named entity recognition tasks. *BioMed Research International*, 2014.

Teng, Zhiyang and Yue Zhang. 2018. Two local models for neural constituent parsing. In *Proceedings of the 27th International Conference on Computational Linguistics*, pages 119–132.

Tesnière Lucien. 1959. Eléments de syntaxe structurale. Klincksieck.

Thede, Scott M. and Mary P Harper. 1999. A second-order hidden Markov model for part-of-speech tagging. In *Proceedings of the 37th Annual Meeting of the Association for Computational Linguistics*, pages 175–182.

Tieleman, Tijmen and Geoffrey Hinton. 2012. Lecture 6.5-rmsprop: Divide the gradient by a running average of its recent magnitude. *COURSERA: Neural Networks for Machine Learning*, 4(2):26–31.

Tkachenko, Maksim and Andrey Simanovsky. 2012. Named entity recognition: Exploring features. In *Proceedings of the 8th Conference on Natural Language Processing*, pages 118–127.

Toutanova, Kristina, Dan Klein, Christopher D Manning and Yoram Singer. 2003. Feature-rich part-of-speech tagging with a cyclic dependency network. In *Proceedings of the 2003 Conference of the North American Chapter of the Association for Computational Linguistics on Human Language Technology, volume 1*, pages 173–180.

Tsochantaridis, Ioannis, Thomas Hofmann, Thorsten Joachims and Yasemin Altun. 2004. Support vector machine learning for interdependent and structured output spaces. In *Proceedings of the Twenty-First International Conference on Machine Learning*, page 104. ACM.

Tsuruoka, Yoshimasa, Jun'ichi Tsujii and Sophia Ananiadou. 2009. Stochastic gradient descent training for L1-regularized log-linear models with cumulative penalty. In *Proceedings of the Joint Conference of the 47th Annual Meeting of the ACL and the 4th International Joint Conference on Natural Language Processing of the AFNLP: Volume 1*, pages 477–485.

Turian, Joseph, Lev Ratinov and Yoshua Bengio. 2010. Word representations: a simple and general method for semi-supervised learning. In *Proceedings of the 48th Annual Meeting of the Association for Computational Linguistics*, pages 384–394.

Turney, Peter D. 2002. Thumbs up or thumbs down?: semantic orientation applied to unsupervised classification of reviews. In *Proceedings of the 40th Annual Meeting of the Association for Computational Linguistics*, pages 417–424.

Vaswani, Ashish, Noam Shazeer, Niki Parmar, Jakob Uszkoreit, Llion Jones, Aidan N. Gomez, Łukasz Kaiser and Illia Polosukhin. 2017. Attention is all you need. In *Advances in Neural Information Processing Systems*, pages 5998–6008.

Veličković, Petar, Guillem Cucurull, Arantxa Casanova, Adriana Romero, Pietro Lio and Yoshua Bengio. 2017. Graph attention networks. In *Proceedings of 5th International Conference on Learning Representations*

Vintsyuk, Taras K. 1968. Speech discrimination by dynamic programming. *Cybernetics*, 4(1):52–57.

Vinyals, Oriol, Meire Fortunato and Navdeep Jaitly. 2015. Pointer networks. In *Advances in Neural Information Processing Systems*, pages 2692–2700.

Viterbi, Andrew. 1967. Error bounds for convolutional codes and an asymptotically optimum decoding algorithm. *IEEE Transactions on Information Theory*, 13(2):260–269.

Wald, Abraham. 1950. *Statistical Decision Functions*.

Wang, Shaolei, Yue Zhang, Wanxiang Che and Ting Liu. 2018. Joint extraction of entities and relations based on a novel graph scheme. In *Proceedings of the Twenty-Seventh International Joint Conference on Artificial Intelligence*, pages 4461–4467.

Wang, Mengqiu and Christopher D. Manning. 2013. Effect of non-linear deep architecture in sequence labeling. In *Proceedings of the Sixth International Joint Conference on Natural Language Processing*, pages 1285–1291.

Watanabe, Taro and Eiichiro Sumita. 2015. Transition-based neural constituent parsing. In *Proceedings of the 53rd Annual Meeting of the Association for Computational Linguistics and the 7th International Joint Conference on Natural Language Processing (Volume 1: Long Papers)*, pages 1169–1179.

Weischedel, Ralph, Richard Schwartz, Jeff Palmucci, Marie Meteer and Lance Ramshaw. 1993. Coping with ambiguity and unknown words through probabilistic models. *Computational Linguistics*, 19(2):361–382.

Weston, Jason, Chris Watkins, et al. 1999. Support vector machines for multi-class pattern recognition. In *Proceedings of the European Symposium on Artificial Neural Networks Bruge*, volume 99, pages 219–224.

Wu, C. F. Jeff 1983. On the convergence properties of the EM algorithm. *Annals of Statistics*, 11(1):95–103.

Xu, Kun, Lingfei Wu, Zhiguo Wang, Yansong Feng, Michael Witbrock and Vadim Sheinin. 2018. Graph2seq: Graph to sequence learning with attention-based neural networks. *arXiv preprint arXiv:1804.00823*.

Xue, Nianwen and Libin Shen. 2003. Chinese word segmentation as lmr tagging. In *Proceedings of the Second SIGHAN workshop on Chinese Language Processing, Volume 17*, pages 176–179.

Yamada, Hiroyasu and Yuji Matsumoto. 2003. Statistical dependency analysis with support vector machines. In *Proceedings of the Eighth International Conference on Parsing Technologies*.

Yang, Yiming and Xin Liu. 1999. A re-examination of text categorization methods. In *Proceedings of the 22nd Annual International ACM SIGIR Conference on Research and Development in Information Retrieval*, pages 42–49.

Yang, Zhilin, Zihang Dai, Yiming Yang, Jaime Carbonell, Russ R. Salakhutdinov and Quoc V. Le. 2019. XLNET: Generalized autoregressive pretraining for language understanding. In *Advances in Neural Information Processing Systems*, pages 5754–5764.

Yang, Zhilin, Ruslan Salakhutdinov and William W. Cohen. 2017. Transfer learning for sequence tagging with hierarchical recurrent networks. In *Proceedings of 5th International Conference on Learning Representations*

Yang, Zichao, Diyi Yang, Chris Dyer, Xiaodong He, Alex Smola and Eduard Hovy. 2016. Hierarchical attention networks for document classification. In *Proceedings of the 2016 Conference of the North American Chapter of the Association for Computational Linguistics: Human Language Technologies*, pages 1480–1489.

Yarowsky, David. 1995. Unsupervised word sense disambiguation rivaling supervised methods. In *33rd Annual Meeting of the Association for Computational Linguistics*, pages 189–196.

Yin, Pengcheng, Chunting Zhou, Junxian He and Graham Neubig. 2018. Structvae: Tree-structured latent variable models for semi-supervised semantic parsing. In *Proceedings of the 56th Annual Meeting of the Association for Computational Linguistics (Volume 1: Long Papers)*, pages 754–765.

Yin, Wenpeng, Katharina Kann, Mo Yu and Hinrich Schütze. 2017. Comparative study of CNN and RNN for natural language processing. *arXiv preprint arXiv:1702.01923*.

Yin, Wenpeng, Hinrich Schütze, Bing Xiang and Bowen Zhou. 2016. ABCNN: Attention-based convolutional neural network for modeling sentence pairs. *Transactions of the Association for Computational Linguistics*, 4:259–272.

Younger, Daniel H. 1967. Recognition and parsing of context-free languages in time n3. *Information and Control*, 10(2):189–208.

Zeiler, Matthew D. 2012. Adadelta: an adaptive learning rate method. *arXiv preprint arXiv:1212.5701*.

Zhang, Biao, Deyi Xiong, Jinsong Su, Hong Duan and Min Zhang. 2016. Variational neural machine translation. In *Proceedings of the 2016 Conference on Empirical Methods in Natural Language Processing*, pages 521–530, Austin, Texas.

Zhang, Junchi, Yanxia Qin, Yue Zhang, Mengchi Liu and Donghong Ji. 2018a. Extracting entities and events as a single task using a transition-based neural model. In *Proceedings of the Twenty-Eighth International Joint Conference on Artificial Intelligence*, pages 5422–5428.

Zhang, Meishan, Yue Zhang, Wanxiang Che and Ting Liu. 2014. Character-level Chinese dependency parsing. In *Proceedings of the 52nd Annual Meeting of the Association for Computational Linguistics (Volume 1: Long Papers)*, pages 1326–1336.

Zhang, Yue, and Stephen Clark. 2007. Chinese segmentation with a word-based perceptron algorithm. In *Proceedings of the 45th Annual Meeting of the Association of Computational Linguistics*, pages 840–847.

Zhang, Yue, and Stephen Clark. 2011. Syntactic processing using the generalized perceptron and beam search. *Computational Linguistics*, 37(1):105–151.

Zhang, Yue, and Jie Yang. 2018. Chinese NER using lattice LSTM. In *Proceedings of the 56th Annual Meeting of the Association for Computational Linguistics (Volume 1: Long Papers)*, pages 1554–1564.

Zhang, Yuhao, Peng Qi and Christopher D. Manning. 2018b. Graph convolution over pruned dependency trees improves relation extraction. In *Proceedings of the 2018 Conference on Empirical Methods in Natural Language Processing*, pages 2205–2215.

Zhou, Chunting and Graham Neubig. 2017. Morphological inflection generation with multi-space variational encoder-decoders. In *Proceedings of the CoNLL Special Interest Group on Computational Morphology and Phonology 2017 Shared Task: Universal Morphological Reinflection*, pages 58–65.

Zhou, Hao, Yue Zhang, Shujian Huang, and Jiajun Chen. 2015. A neural probabilistic structured-prediction model for transition-based dependency parsing. In *Proceedings of the 53rd Annual Meeting of the Association for Computational Linguistics and the 7th International Joint Conference on Natural Language Processing (Volume 1: Long Papers)*, pages 1213–1222.

Zhu, Muhua, Yue Zhang, Wenliang Chen, Min Zhang and Jingbo Zhu. 2013. Fast and accurate shift-reduce constituent parsing. In *Proceedings of the 51st Annual Meeting of the Association for Computational Linguistics (Volume 1: Long Papers)*, pages 434–443.

Zhu, Xiaodan, Parinaz Sobhani and Hongyu Guo. 2016. Dag-structured long short-term memory for semantic compositionality. In *Proceedings of the 2016 Conference of the North American Chapter of the Association for Computational Linguistics: Human Language Technologies*, pages 917–926.

Zhu, Xiaodan, Parinaz Sobihani and Hongyu Guo. 2015. Long short-term memory over recursive structures. In *International Conference on Machine Learning*, pages 1604–1612.

Index